THE DISTINCTION AND RELATIONSHIP BETWEEN
JUS AD BELLUM AND *JUS IN BELLO*

This book explores the distinction and relationship between two principal branches of international law regulating the use of force: *jus ad bellum* (international law regulating the resort to force) and *jus in bello* (international humanitarian law). Two princ ples traditionally govern the relationship between the two: 1) separation of *jus ad bellum* and *jus in bello* and 2) equal application of *jus in bello* to the conflicting parties. These principles emerged in response to the claim that a conflicting party using force illegally under *jus ad bellum* should not benefit from the protection for victims of armed conflict under *jus in bello*, which would completely defeat the humanitarian purpose of *jus in bello* to protect all victims of armed conflict impartially. There is, however, a third principle: concurrent application of *jus ad bellum* and *jus in bello*. Unlike in the past, *jus ad bellum* now regulates the use of force during a conflict alongside *jus in bello* and hence, the two are now considered as one set of rules applying during a conflict. The book explores in detail the interaction between *jus ad bellum* and *jus in bello* in the light of these three principles.

The relationship between the two has been principally discussed in the context of the use of force in self-defence and international armed conflict. However, this book examines the relationship in other contexts of a very different nature, namely the use of force under Chapter VII of the United Nations Charter, non-international armed conflict, and armed conflict of a mixed character. The book concludes that the three principles governing the relationship are equally valid, with certain variations, in these different contexts.

Volume 33 in the series Studies in International Law

Studies in International Law

Recent titles in this series

Human Dignity and the Foundations of International Law
Patrick Capps

Sovereignty and the Stateless Nation: Gibraltar in the Modern Legal Context
Keith Azopardi

The International Court of Justice and Self-Defence in International Law
James A Green

State Liability in Investment Treaty Arbitration: Global Constitutional and Administrative Law in the BIT Generation
Santiago Montt

Reappraising the Resort to Force: International Law, Jus ad Bellum and the War on Terror
Lindsay Moir

International Law and Dispute Settlement: New Problems and Techniques
Edited by Duncan French, Matthew Saul and Nigel White

The Democratic Legitimacy of International Law
Steven Wheatley

Reflections on the UN Declaration on the Rights of Indigenous Peoples
Edited by Stephen Allen and Alexandra Xanthaki

Contracting with Sovereignty: State Contracts and International Arbitration
Ivar Alvik

Multi-Sourced Equivalent Norms in International Law
Edited by Yuval Shany and Tomer Broude

The Distinction and Relationship between *Jus ad Bellum* and *Jus in Bello*
Keiichiro Okimoto

International Humanitarian Law and Terrorism
Andrea Bianchi and Yasmin Naqvi

For the complete list of titles in this series, see 'Studies in International Law' link at www.hartpub.co.uk/books/series.asp

The Distinction and Relationship between *Jus ad Bellum* and *Jus in Bello*

Keiichiro Okimoto

·HART·
PUBLISHING

OXFORD AND PORTLAND, OREGON
2011

Published in the United Kingdom by Hart Publishing Ltd
16C Worcester Place, Oxford, OX1 2JW
Telephone: +44 (0)1865 517530
Fax: +44 (0)1865 510710
E-mail: mail@hartpub.co.uk
Website: http://www.hartpub.co.uk

Published in North America (US and Canada) by
Hart Publishing
c/o International Specialized Book Services
920 NE 58th Avenue, Suite 300
Portland, OR 97213-3786
USA
Tel: +1 503 287 3093 or toll-free: (1) 800 944 6190
Fax: +1 503 280 8832
E-mail: orders@isbs.com
Website: http://www.isbs.com

British Library Cataloguing in Publication Data

Data Available

ISBN: 978-1-84946-055-2

Typeset by Hope Services, Abingdon
Printed and bound in Great Britain by
Lightning Source UK Ltd

Preface

This book is based on the doctoral thesis I completed at the University of Cambridge. My initial interest in the topic of the relationship between *jus ad bellum* and *jus in bello* developed when I was studying at the London School of Economics, which was also when the invasion of Iraq took place in March 2003. Since then, I have tried to observe various conflicts from the perspective of the relationship between *jus ad bellum* and *jus in bello* and also conducted research on past conflicts from the same perspective, in order to grasp the evolution of the issue and compare the past and the present. Since I left the University of Cambridge, I was posted to various conflict and post-conflict situations as a delegate and a legal adviser of the International Committee of the Red Cross (ICRC), namely to Iraq, Israel and the Occupied Territories, Philippines, and Rwanda. The time spent in these countries enlightened me in many ways, which I would have never experienced otherwise. Apart from what I saw, heard and felt about the impact of armed conflicts on each and every individual who survived or who was trying to survive, the important role that *jus ad bellum* and *jus in bello* played in a specific conflict was particularly striking. At the same time, the risk of divergent interpretations on particular rules of *jus ad bellum* and *jus in bello*, or on the relationship between *jus ad bellum* and *jus in bello*, was felt particularly when such divergence had the possibility of affecting the lives of people. This book was prepared against such a background.

This book takes into account a vast amount of material pertaining to the relationship between *jus ad bellum* and *jus in bello*, including official documents and statements of states; official documents and statements of the ICRC; resolutions, reports, verbatim records, official statements, and other documents of the United Nations organs; proceedings and judgments of international courts, tribunals, and arbitrations as well as national courts; and opinions of experts. I have tried to consult materials as much as my language ability permitted, namely in English, French, and Japanese, and tried to select case studies from different regions with a view to achieving an appropriate level of representativeness. Owing to the sheer extent of the topic, this book only covers the main aspects of the relationship between *jus ad bellum* and *jus in bello*, but it is hoped that it would be a basis for further research and discussion.

I am indebted to distinguished experts for their valuable comments, namely Professor Marc Weller, Judge Christopher Greenwood, and Professor Christine Gray. I am grateful to Dr Jean-Marie Henckaerts, who drew my attention to many important materials. I would also like to thank Professor Tatsuro Kunugi for strongly encouraging me to publish my doctoral thesis.

Finally, I would like to express my deepest gratitude to my wife, Tomoko, for her warm encouragement and technical support to many parts of the book, and to my parents for their constant support throughout the preparation of this book.

The views expressed in this book are personal and do not necessarily reflect the views of the ICRC, and any errors or omissions are solely my responsibility.

Table of Contents

List of Abbreviations

ADF	Allied Democratic Forces (Democratic Republic of the Congo)
APs	Additional Protocols to the Geneva Conventions, 1977
API	Protocol Additional to the Geneva Conventions of 12 August 1949, and Relating to the Protection of Victims of International Armed Conflicts (Protocol I), 1977
APMC	Convention on the Prohibition of the Use, Stockpiling, Production and Transfer of Anti-Personnel Mines and on Their Destruction, 1997
Art	Article
BWC	Convention on the Prohibition of the Development, Production and Stockpiling of Bacteriological (Biological) and Toxin Weapons and on Their Destruction, 1972
Chapter VII	Chapter VII of the Charter of the United Nations
CCW PII	Convention on Prohibitions and Restrictions on the Use of Certain Conventional Weapons Which May Be Deemed to Be Excessively Injurious or to Have Indiscriminate Effects, Protocol on Prohibitions or Restrictions on the Use of Mines, Booby-Traps and Other Devices (Protocol II), 1980
CICR	Comité international de la Croix-Rouge
CIHL	customary international humanitarian law
CPA	Coalition Provisional Authority (Iraq)
CPC	Convention for the Protection of Cultural Property in the Event of Armed Conflict, 1954
CPN-M	Communist Party of Nepal-Maoist
CPP	Communist Party of the Philippines
CRC	Convention on the Rights of the Child, 1989
CRC OPI	Optional Protocol to the Convention on the Rights of the Child on the Involvement of Children in Armed Conflict, 2001
CTS	Consolidated Treaty Series
CWC	Convention on the Prohibition of the Development, Production, Stockpiling and Use of Chemical Weapons and on Their Destruction, 1993
DOMREP	Mission of the Representative of the United Nations Secretary-General in the Dominican Republic
DRC	Democratic Republic of the Congo

ECOWAS	Economic Community of West African States
ERW	explosive remnants of war
EWCA	England and Wales Court of Appeal
GAOR	General Assembly Official Records
GCs	Geneva Conventions, 1949
GCIII	Geneva Convention Relative to the Treatment of Prisoners of War, 1949
GCIV	Geneva Convention Relative to the Protection of Civilian Persons in Time of War, 1949
GP	Protocol for the Prohibition of the Use of Asphyxiating, Poisonous or Other Gases, and of Bacteriological Methods of Warfare, 1925
ICC	International Criminal Court
ICCPR	International Covenant on Civil and Political Rights
ICJ	International Court of Justice
ICRC	International Committee of the Red Cross
ICTY	International Criminal Tribunal for the former Yugoslavia
IHL	international humanitarian law
ILC	International Law Commission (United Nations)
ILM	International Legal Materials
ILR	International Law Reports
ISAF	International Security Assistance Force (Afghanistan)
KFOR	Kosovo Forces (NATO)
LNTS	League of Nations Treaty Series
MINOPUH	United Nations Civilian Police Mission in Haiti
MINUGUA	United Nations Verification Mission in Guatemala
MINURCA	United Nations Mission in the Central African Republic
MINURSO	United Nations Mission for the Referendum in Western Sahara
MINUSTAH	United Nations Stabilization Mission in Haiti
MONUA	United Nations Observer Mission in Angola
MONUC	Mission de l'Organisation des Nations Unies en République démocratique du Congo
MONUSCO	Mission de l'Organisation des Nations Unies pour la stabilisation en République démocratique du Congo
NATO	North Atlantic Treaty Organization
NPA	New People's Army (Philippines)
Official Records	*Diplomatic Conference on the Reaffirmation and Development of International Humanitarian Law Applicable in Armed Conflicts, Geneva (1974–1977)*
ONU	Organisation des Nations Unies
ONUB	Opération des Nations Unies au Burundi
ONUC	Opération des Nations Unies au Congo
ONUCA	United Nations Observer Group in Central America

ONUMOZ	United Nations Operation in Mozambique
ONUSAL	United Nations Observer Mission in El Salvador
PLO	Palestine Liberation Organization
POW	prisoner of war
RPF	Rwandan Patriotic Front
SOFA	status of forces agreement
UK	United Kingdom of Great Britain and Northern Ireland
UN	United Nations
UNAMIC	United Nations Advance Mission in Cambodia
UNAMIR	United Nations Assistance Mission for Rwanda
UNAMSIL	United Nations Mission in Sierra Leone
UNASOG	United Nations Aouzou Strip Observer Group (Chad/Libya)
UNAVEM I, II, and III	United Nations Angola Verification Mission I, II, and III
UNCHR	United Nations Commission on Human Rights
UNCRO	United Nations Confidence Restoration Operation in Croatia
UNDOF	United Nations Disengagement Force (Middle East)
UNEF I and II	United Nations Emergency Force I and II
UNESCO	United Nations Educational, Scientific and Cultural Organization
UNFICYP	United Nations Peacekeeping Force in Cyprus
UNGA	United Nations General Assembly
UNGOMAP	United Nations Good Offices Mission in Afghanistan and Pakistan
UNHRC	United Nations Human Rights Council
UNIFIL	United Nations Interim Force in Lebanon
UNIIMOG	United Nations Iran–Iraq Military Observer Group
UNIKOM	United Nations Iraq–Kuwait Observation Mission
UNIPOM	United Nations India–Pakistan Observation Mission
UNITA	National Union for the Total Independence of Angola
UNITAF	Unified Task Force (Somalia)
UNMEE	United Nations Mission in Ethiopia and Eritrea
UNMIBH	United Nations Mission in Bosnia and Herzegovina
UNMIH	United Nations Mission in Haiti
UNMIK	United Nations Interim Administration Mission in Kosovo
UNMIL	United Nations Mission in Liberia
UNMIS	United Nations Mission in the Sudan
UNMISET	United Nations Mission of Support in East Timor
UNMIT	United Nations Integrated Mission in Timor-Leste
UNMOGIP	United Nations Military Observer Group in India and Pakistan
UNMOP	United Nations Mission of Observers in Prevlaka

UNMOT	United Nations Mission of Observers in Tajikistan
UNOCI	United Nations Operation in Côte d'Ivoire
UNOGIL	United Nations Observation Group in Lebanon
UNOMIG	United Nations Observer Mission in Georgia
UNOMIL	United Nations Observer Mission in Liberia
UNOMSIL	United Nations Observer Mission in Sierra Leone
UNOMUR	United Nations Observer Mission Uganda–Rwanda
UNOSOM I	United Nations Operation in Somalia I and II and II
UNPREDEP	United Nations Preventive Deployment Force (Former Yugoslav Republic of Macedonia)
UNPROFOR	United Nations Protection Force (former Yugoslavia)
UNSC	United Nations Security Council
UNSF	United Nations Security Force in West New Guinea
UNSMIH	United Nations Support Mission in Haiti
UNTAC	United Nations Transitional Authority in Cambodia
UNTAES	United Nations Transitional Administration for Eastern Slavonia, Baranja and Western Sirmium (Croatia)
UNTAET	United Nations Transitional Administration in East Timor
UNTAG	United Nations Transition Assistance Group (Namibia)
UNTMIH	United Nations Transition Mission in Haiti
UNTS	United Nations Treaty Series
UNTSO	United Nations Truce Supervision Organization (Middle East)
UNYB	Yearbook of the United Nations
UNYOM	United Nations Yemen Observation Mission
UPDF	Uganda Peoples' Defence Forces
US	United States of America
USSR	Union of Soviet Socialist Republics
WHO	World Health Organization
1899 HRs	Convention (II) with Respect to the Laws and Customs of War on Land and Its Annex: Regulations concerning the Laws and Customs of War on Land, 1899
1907 HRs	Convention (IV) Respecting the Laws and Customs of War on Land and Its Annex: Regulations concerning the Laws and Customs of War on Land, 1907

Table of Cases

Table of Treaties and Other Instruments

INTERNATIONAL

UN General Assembly

Resolutions

UN Security Council

Resolutions

NATIONAL

1

Introduction

INTRODUCTION

THIS BOOK IS about the distinction and relationship between the two areas of public international law regulating the use of force, *jus ad bellum* (international law regulating the resort to force) and *jus in bello* (international humanitarian law).[1]

Jus ad bellum provides when a state may or may not use force under international law and *jus in bello* provides rules dealing with various aspects of the conduct during armed conflict, in particular on how to protect persons placed outside the combat (wounded, sick, shipwrecked

[1] For an overview of the relationship between *jus ad bellum* and *jus in bello*, see H Lauterpacht, 'The Limits of the Operation of the Laws of War' (1953) 30 *British Year Book of International Law* 206; H Meyrowitz, *Le principe de l'égalité de belligérants devant le droit de la guerre* (Paris, Éditions Pedone, 1970); C Greenwood, 'The Relationship between *Jus ad Bellum* and *Jus in Bello*' (1983) 9 *Review of International Studies* 221; K Ipsen, 'International Law Preventing Armed Conflicts and International Law of Armed Conflict – A Combined Functional Approach' in C Swinarski (ed), *Studies and Essays on International Humanitarian Law and Red Cross Principles in Honour of Jean Pictet* (The Hague, Martinus Nijhoff, 1984); H Fujita, 'Kokusaijindōhō no kinōtenkai: Kokurenhō to no sōgoshintō' in H Fujita et al (eds), *Jinkenhō to jindōhō no shinseiki* (Tokyo, Tōshindō, 2001); F Bugnion, 'Just Wars, Wars of Aggression and International Humanitarian Law' (2002) 847 *International Review of the Red Cross* 523; J Gardam, *Necessity, Proportionality and the Use of Force* (Cambridge, Cambridge University Press, 2004); P Kooijmans, 'Is There a Change in the *Ius ad Bellum* and, if so, What Does It Mean for the *Ius in Bello*?' in L Lijnzaad et al (eds), *Making the Voice of Humanity Heard* (Dordrecht, Martinus Nijhoff, 2004); J Pastor-Ridruejo, 'On the Relationship between *Ius in Bello* and *Ius ad Bellum*: Can a Notion of International Humanitarian Law Influence in the Determination of the Legality of the Use of Force?' in PA Fernández-Sánchez (ed), *The New Challenges of Humanitarian Law in Armed Conflicts* (Leiden, Martinus Nijhoff, 2005); American Society of International Law, 'The Relationship between *Jus ad Bellum* and *Jus in Bello*: Past, Present, Future' (2006) *American Society of International Law Proceedings* 109; A Bouvier, 'Assessing the Relationship between *Jus in Bello* and *Jus ad Bellum*: An "Orthodox View"' (2006) *American Society of International Law Proceedings* 109; M Sassòli, '*Ius ad Bellum* and *Ius in Bello* – The Separation between the Legality of the Use of Force and Humanitarian Rules to Be Respected in Warfare: Crucial or Outdated?' in M Schmitt and J Pejic (eds), *International Law and Armed Conflict: Exploring the Faultlines* (The Netherlands, Koninklijke Brill BV, 2007); J Moussa, 'Can *Jus ad Bellum* Override *Jus in Bello*? Reaffirming the Separation of the Two Bodies of Law' (2008) 872 *International Review of the Red Cross* 963; A Roberts, 'The Equal Application of the Laws of War: A Principle under Pressure' (2008) 872 *International Review of the Red Cross* 931; I Österdahl, 'Dangerous Liaison? The Disappearing Dichotomy between *Jus ad Bellum* and *in Bello*' (2009) *Nordic Journal of International Law* 553.

combatants and fighters; captured combatants and fighters; and civilians), what means and methods of warfare may or may not be used, and the rights and obligations of neutral states. At present, it is established that the use of force is regulated in international law by *jus ad bellum* and *jus in bello*. Since both *jus ad bellum* and *jus in bello* deal with the same subject – use of force – it seems logical to think that there must be some relationship between the two. This was not the case until recently.

The regulation of the use of force in international law never developed coherently. *Jus in bello* emerged earlier than *jus ad bellum* when the Geneva Convention for the Amelioration of the Condition of the Wounded in Armies in the Field was adopted in 1864.[2] At that time, *jus ad bellum* was still nascent and the use of force per se was almost unregulated in international law with the exception of the still rudimentary principles of necessity and proportionality in customary international law. In the meantime, *jus in bello* developed rapidly, particularly at the 1899 and 1907 Peace Conferences.

With the adoption of the Covenant of the League of Nations in 1919[3] and the Pact of Paris on the Renunciation of War as an Instrument of National Policy in 1928,[4] waging 'war' itself was prohibited in international law for the first time. International law, for the first time, distinguished a legal war and an illegal war as opposed to the moral criterion of justness or unjustness of a war. As a result, one fundamental question emerged: when a state wages an illegal war, do the victims of war of the same state still benefit from the protection provided by *jus in bello*?

The subsequent developments in *jus ad bellum* and *jus in bello* had not settled this question. To the contrary, the more they developed, the more the relationship between the two became complicated. The adoption of the UN Charter in 1945[5] established a coherent system of *jus ad bellum* which is still in effect today. Article 2(4) aimed at improving the defects of the concept of 'war' by prohibiting 'use of force' between states. The only situations in which states could use force were now in self-defence or under Chapter VII of the UN Charter. Meanwhile, *jus in bello* continued to develop rapidly, the most notable achievement being the adoption

[2] Convention for the Amelioration of the Condition of the Wounded in Armies in the Field (adopted 22 August 1864, entered into force 22 June 1865) 129 CTS 361.

[3] Covenant of the League of Nations (adopted 28 April 1919, entered into force 10 January 1920) 225 CTS 188.

[4] Pact of Paris on the Renunciation of War as an Instrument of National Policy (adopted 27 August 1928, entered into force 25 July 1929) 94 LNTS 57.

[5] Charter of the United Nations (adopted 26 June 1945, entered into force 24 October 1945) 59 Statutes at Large 1031.

of the 1949 Geneva Conventions[6] and 1977 Additional Protocols[7] which deal with the protection of wounded, sick, and shipwrecked combatants, protection of prisoners of war, protection of civilians, and regulation of means and methods of warfare in international armed conflict (armed conflict between states) and a similar but more limited protection in non-international armed conflict (armed conflict within a state). By this time, *jus ad bellum* and *jus in bello* even regulated the use of force within a state[8] and not only between states.

Despite these developments, new issues, mostly negative, emerged concerning the relationship between *jus ad bellum* and *jus in bello*. The claim that the victims of armed conflict of the aggressor side do not benefit from *jus in bello* protection persisted. The question whether UN forces authorised under Chapter VII are bound to respect *jus in bello* obligations emerged. The involvement of non-state actors in armed conflicts in foreign countries complicated the relationship between *jus ad bellum* and *jus in bello*, since the two legal regimes regulate either an inter-state situation or an intra-state situation rather than an intra-state situation involving non-state actors from outside the country. A fierce doctrinal debate also took place where one side defended that the protection of the victims of armed conflict by *jus in bello* should not depend on whether they belong to the aggressor or the victim state, while others were sceptical about offering such a benefit to the aggressor.

Gradually, a consensus emerged on two principles which developed through state practice and opinions of experts: *jus ad bellum* and *jus in bello* should be kept separate and *jus in bello* applies equally to the conflicting parties, regardless of who started the conflict and whether it was lawful or not. These emerged from the conviction that all victims of armed conflict should be protected equally solely on the basis of humanitarian consideration and not the legal status of the conflicting parties under *jus ad bellum*.

[6] Geneva Convention for the Amelioration of the Condition of the Wounded and Sick in Armed Forces in the Field, as revised from 1929 (adopted 12 August 1949, entered into force 21 October 1950) 75 UNTS 31; Geneva Convention for the Amelioration of the Condition of Wounded, Sick and Shipwrecked Members of Armed Forces at Sea, as revised from 1929 (adopted 12 August 1949, entered into force 21 October 1950) 75 UNTS 85; Geneva Convention Relative to the Treatment of Prisoners of War, as revised from 1929 (adopted 12 August 1949, entered into force 21 October 1950) 75 UNTS 135; Geneva Convention Relative to the Protection of Civilian Persons in Time of War (adopted 12 August 1949, entered into force 21 October 1950) 75 UNTS 287.

[7] Protocol Additional to the Geneva Conventions of 12 August 1949, and Relating to the Protection of Victims of International Armed Conflicts (Protocol I) (adopted 8 June 1977, entered into force 7 December 1978) 1125 UNTS 3; Protocol Additional to the Geneva Conventions of 12 August 1949, and Relating to the Protection of Victims of Non-International Armed Conflicts (Protocol II) (adopted 8 June 1977, entered into force 7 December 1978) 1125 UNTS 609.

[8] See Chapter VII of the UN Charter, common Art 3 of the 1949 Geneva Conventions, and the 1977 Second Additional Protocol.

However, these principles alone are not enough to fully understand the relationship between *jus ad bellum* and *jus in bello*. This traditional understanding of the relationship between *jus ad bellum* and *jus in bello* is largely based on a passive approach, in other words, it concentrated on keeping the two apart and any interaction between the two was often seen as a revival of the danger of subjecting *jus in bello* to *jus ad bellum* and hence, depriving the victims of armed conflict of the aggressor side of *jus in bello* protection. Moreover, the two traditional principles were based on the premise that *jus in bello* succeeded *jus ad bellum* once a state resorted to force, and that there was no place for *jus ad bellum* thereafter. Generally speaking, this understanding is not mistaken since *jus ad bellum* judges whether the resort to force was legal or illegal, whereas *jus in bello* only concerns whether the conduct during the use of force was legal or not. Hence, once the question of whether the resort to force was legal or not is over (*jus ad bellum*), it is logical that *jus in bello* takes over from *jus ad bellum*. However, *jus ad bellum* now also regulates the use of force during a conflict and hence, *jus ad bellum* and *jus in bello* should now be considered as concurrently applicable even after a state resorted to force.

A prime example of *jus ad bellum* application after the resort to force is the principle of proportionality in the law of self-defence. The principle of proportionality requires that the use of force in self-defence must be proportionate to the armed attack inflicted by the aggressor. However, such use of force in self-defence must also comply with the rules of *jus in bello*, for example the rules on which weapons can be used and how. In this sense, *jus ad bellum* and *jus in bello* are applicable simultaneously even after a state resorts to force, and not in a neat chronological order from *jus ad bellum* to *jus in bello*. This indicates that both *jus ad bellum* and *jus in bello* impose limits on the use of force at the same time and this combination of limits imposed by the two legal regimes could be effective in preventing the excessive use of force if it is strictly applied. In this sense, *jus ad bellum* and *jus in bello* are not necessarily in conflict, as was thought before, but rather complementary.

It is worth noting that the three principles (separation between *jus ad bellum* and *jus in bello*, equal application of *jus in bello*, and concurrent application of *jus ad bellum* and *jus in bello*) emerged mainly in the context of self-defence and international armed conflict (armed conflict between states). This book examines whether these principles are equally valid in other contexts of a very different nature, namely the use of force under Chapter VII of the UN Charter, non-international armed conflict, and armed conflict of a mixture of international and non-international armed conflict.

For the sake of simplicity, the substantive part of the book is divided into four: 1) background to the issue of the relationship between *jus ad bellum* and *jus in bello*; 2) relationship between the law of self-defence and international humanitarian law; 3) relationship between Chapter VII of the UN Charter and international humanitarian law; and 4) particular problems in non-international armed conflict.

The present book does not deal with all possible situations where the relationship between *jus ad bellum* and *jus in bello* might arise.[9] It is hoped that this book will provide a framework to solve problems arising from the relationship between *jus ad bellum* and *jus in bello* in specific cases of use of force or armed conflict.

[9] Eg, the relationship between *jus ad bellum* and the law of neutrality has already been discussed extensively in H Lauterpacht (ed), L Oppenheim, *International Law: A Treaties* Vol II: Disputes, War and Neutrality, 7th edn (London, Longmans, Green and Co, 1952) 643 *ff*; E Castren, *The Present Law of War and Neutrality* (Helsinki, Suomalaisen Tiedeakatemian Toimituksia, 1954); Meyrowitz, *Le principe*, 311 *ff*; C Greenwood, 'The Concept of War in Modern International Law' (1987) 36 *International and Comparative Law Quarterly* 283; D Schindler, 'Transformations in the Law of Neutrality since 1945' in A Delissen and G Tanja (eds), *Humanitarian Law of Armed Conflict: Challenges Ahead, Essays in Honour of Frits Kalshoven* (Dordrecht, Martinus Nijhoff, 1991).

2

Background and Principles Governing the Relationship between Jus ad Bellum *and* Jus in Bello

IT MAY BE convenient to first set out a brief background on what *jus ad bellum* and *jus in bello* are and what distinguishes *jus ad bellum* from *jus in bello*. This chapter then sets out three widely accepted principles governing the relationship between *jus ad bellum* and *jus in bello*: the separation between *jus ad bellum* and *jus in bello*, equal application of *jus in bello* to the conflicting parties, and concurrent application of *jus ad bellum* and *jus in bello*. It will highlight that the past discussions mostly centred on self-defence and international armed conflict, and other contexts such as the use of force under Chapter VII of the UN Charter and non-international armed conflict were not given the same level of attention. The problems of these contexts other than self-defence and international armed conflict will be outlined in this chapter to highlight that the relationship between *jus ad bellum* and *jus in bello* should be discussed in relation to different contexts of a very different nature, and not only in relation to self-defence and international armed conflict.

The purpose of this chapter is to lay the foundation for the subsequent chapters which deal with detailed rules of *jus ad bellum* and *jus in bello*. Thus, this chapter is intended to be general in character and where necessary, cross-references will be made to other chapters where in-depth discussions can be found.

I. INTRODUCTION TO *JUS AD BELLUM* AND *JUS IN BELLO*

A. What are *Jus ad Bellum* and *Jus in Bello*?[1]

Jus ad bellum and *jus in bello* consist of a number of rules. Without knowing these detailed rules, one will not know what is being distinguished and what the relationship is between *jus ad bellum* and *jus in bello*.

'*Jus ad bellum*' is the Latin term for international law regulating the resort to force and '*jus in bello*' is the Latin term for international humanitarian law (IHL) or the law of armed conflict.[2] They are two branches of international law that are specifically directed at regulating the use of force by states and other actors.

Jus ad bellum[3] provides when a state may or may not use force under international law. The primary source of modern *jus ad bellum* is the UN Charter.[4] The cornerstone of modern *jus ad bellum* is Article 2(4) of the UN Charter, which prohibits the use of force by states in international relations. The two exceptions are: 1) the right of self-defence in Article 51; and 2) military enforcement action under Chapter VII.[5] In other words, states can use force in these two situations, but only in these two situations. The prohibition on the use of force by states in international relations is considered as both a rule of customary international law and *jus cogens*[6] and the right of self-defence as a rule of customary international law.[7] Moreover, the

[1] Writings on both *jus ad bellum* and *jus in bello* in general are voluminous. However, for *jus ad bellum*, see generally R Kolb, *Ius contra bellum: Le droit international relatif au maintien de la paix* (Bâle, Helbing et Lichtenhahn, 2003); C Gray, *International Law and the Use of Force*, 2nd edn (Oxford, Oxford University Press, 2004); Y Dinstein, *War, Aggression and Self-Defence*, 4th edn (Cambridge, Cambridge University Press, 2005).

For *jus in bello*, see generally H-P Gasser, *International Humanitarian Law: An Introduction* (Bern, Haupt, 1993); R Kolb, *Ius in bello: Le droit international des conflits armés* (Bâle, Helbing et Lichtenhahn, 2003).

[2] See generally R Kolb, 'Origin of the Twin Terms *Jus ad Bellum*/*Jus in Bello*' (1997) 320 *International Review of the Red Cross* 553.

[3] In this book, '*jus ad bellum*' is primarily used throughout the book but will be used interchangeably with 'Article 2(4) of the UN Charter', 'law of self-defence', and 'Chapter VII of the UN Charter'.

[4] Charter of the United Nations (hereafter UN Charter) (adopted 26 June 1945, entered into force 24 October 1945) 59 Statutes at Large 1031.

[5] Other alleged exceptions will not be dealt with here. The structure of modern *jus ad bellum* was clearly confirmed by the ICJ in the *Legality of the Threat or Use of Nuclear Weapons* (hereafter *Nuclear Weapons* case) (Advisory Opinion) [1996] ICJ Rep 226, para 38 and the *Armed Activities on the Territory of the Congo* (hereafter *Armed Activities* case) (*Democratic Republic of the Congo v Uganda*) (Merits) [2005] ICJ Rep 116, para 148.

The right of self-defence as an exception to the prohibition on the use of force was expressly confirmed in the *Military and Paramilitary Activities in and against Nicaragua* (hereafter *Nicaragua* case) (*Nicaragua v US*) (Merits) [1986] ICJ Rep 14, paras 188 and 193.

[6] *Nicaragua* case (Merits), paras 183–92.

[7] *Nicaragua* case (Merits), paras 192–200.

conduct of self-defence is regulated by the customary law principles of proportionality and necessity.[8]

Other previous treaties such as the 1919 Covenant of the League of Nations[9] and the 1928 Pact of Paris on the Renunciation of War as an Instrument of National Policy[10] also constitute *jus ad bellum* but they are now largely superseded by the UN Charter.

On the other hand, *jus in bello*[11] provides rules dealing with various aspects of the conduct during armed conflict, in particular on how to protect persons placed outside the combat (wounded, sick, shipwrecked combatants and fighters; captured combatants and fighters; and civilians), what means and methods of warfare may or may not be used, and the rights and obligations of neutral states. The applicable rules of IHL differ between international and non-international armed conflict but in any case, compared to *jus ad bellum*, *jus in bello* consists of a vast number of treaty provisions[12] and customary rules.[13] For example, the core IHL treaties applicable to international armed conflict, the 1949 Geneva

[8] *Nicaragua* case (Merits), para 186; *Nuclear Weapons* case (Advisory Opinion), para 41; *Case concerning Oil Platforms* (hereafter *Oil Platforms* case) (*Iran v US*) (Merits) [2003] ICJ Rep 161, para 43; *Armed Activities* case (Merits), para 147.

[9] See, eg, Art 10 of the Covenant of the League of Nations (adopted 28 April 1919, entered into force 10 January 1920) 225 CTS 188.

[10] Art I of the Pact of Paris on the Renunciation of War as an Instrument of National Policy (adopted 27 August 1928, entered into force 25 July 1929) 94 LNTS 57.

[11] In this book, '*jus in bello*', 'international humanitarian law' (or simply IHL), and 'law of international/non-international armed conflict' are used interchangeably.

[12] Refer to the following for a collection of IHL treaties in English and French: ICRC IHL Database, www.icrc.org/ihl; D Schindler and J Toman (eds), *Droit des conflits armés: Recueil des conventions, resolutions et autres documents* (Genève, Comité international de la Croix-Rouge and Institut Henry-Dunant, 1996); D Schindler and J Toman (eds), *The Laws of Armed Conflicts: A Collection of Conventions, Resolutions and Other Documents* (Leiden, Martinus Nijhoff, 2004). Main IHL treaties can also be found in Arabic, Chinese, Portuguese, Russian and Spanish on the ICRC website, www.icrc.org.

[13] For a suggestion of customary rules of IHL see, eg, J-M Henckaerts and L Doswald-Beck, *Customary International Humanitarian Law* Vol I: Rules (Geneva, International Committee of the Red Cross and Cambridge, Cambridge University Press, 2005). See also J-M Henckaerts and L Doswald-Beck (eds), *Customary International Humanitarian Law* Vol II: Practice (Geneva, International Committee of the Red Cross and Cambridge, Cambridge University Press, 2005). For a useful list of customary rules of IHL, see J Henckaerts, 'Study on Customary International Humanitarian Law: A Contribution to the Understanding and Respect for the Rule of Law in Armed Conflict' (2005) 857 *International Review of the Red Cross* 175, 198 *ff*.

For comments on this study, see, eg, E Wilmshurst and S Breau (eds), *Perspectives on the ICRC Study on Customary International Humanitarian Law* (Cambridge, Cambridge University Press, 2007).

Conventions[14] and the 1977 First Additional Protocol,[15] alone contain 531 articles.[16]

B. General Distinction between *Jus ad Bellum* and *Jus in Bello*

There are at least three fundamental aspects that distinguish *jus ad bellum* from *jus in bello*: the purpose of the law, how it applies, and the legal consequences for violations of the law. First, the purpose of the respective legal regime is different. *Jus ad bellum* focuses on regulating the resort to force by states in particular, as well as by international organisations and non-state actors, for the purpose of maintaining peace and security between states and within states.[17] On the other hand, *jus in bello* focuses on the individuals who were placed outside the combat as a result of the armed conflict and aims at protecting them and alleviating their suffering.[18]

Secondly, how the respective legal regime applies is different. *Jus ad bellum* creates an unequal status between the aggressor and the victim

[14] Geneva Convention for the Amelioration of the Condition of the Wounded and Sick in Armed Forces in the Field, as revised from 1929 (hereafter 1949 First Geneva Convention) (adopted 12 August 1949, entered into force 21 October 1950) 75 UNTS 31; Geneva Convention for the Amelioration of the Condition of Wounded, Sick and Shipwrecked Members of Armed Forces at Sea, as revised from 1929 (hereafter 1949 Second Geneva Convention) (adopted 12 August 1949, entered into force 21 October 1950) 75 UNTS 85; Geneva Convention Relative to the Treatment of Prisoners of War, as revised from 1929 (hereafter 1949 Third Geneva Convention) (adopted 12 August 1949, entered into force 21 October 1950) 75 UNTS 135; Geneva Convention Relative to the Protection of Civilian Persons in Time of War (hereafter 1949 Fourth Geneva Convention) (adopted 12 August 1949, entered into force 21 October 1950) 75 UNTS 287.

[15] Protocol Additional to the Geneva Conventions of 12 August 1949, and Relating to the Protection of Victims of International Armed Conflicts (Protocol I) (hereafter 1977 First Additional Protocol) (adopted 8 June 1977, entered into force 7 December 1978) 1125 UNTS 3.

[16] On the question of the extent of IHL rules having *jus cogens* status, see generally *Nuclear Weapons* case (Advisory Opinion), para 83; G Abi-Saab, 'The Specificities of Humanitarian Law' in C Swinarski (ed), *Studies and Essays on International Humanitarian Law and Red Cross Principles in Honour of Jean Pictet* (The Hague, Martinus Nijhoff, 1984) 270 *ff*; L Hannikainen, *Peremptory Norms (Jus Cogens) in International Law: Historical Development, Criteria, Present Status* (Helsinki, Lakimiesliiton Kustannus, 1988) 82–111, 139–45, and 596 *ff*; V Gowlland-Debbas, 'Security Council Enforcement Action and Issues of State Responsibility' (1994) 43 *International and Comparative Law Quarterly* 55, 93; C Bassiouni, 'International Crimes: *Jus Cogens* and *Obligatio Erga Omnes*' (1996) 59 *Law and Contemporary Problems* 63, 68; E David, *Principes de droit des conflits armés*, 3ème edn (Brussels, Bruylant, 2002) 94 *ff*; Kolb, *Ius in bello*, 223 *ff*; R Nieto-Navia, 'International Peremptory Norms (*Jus Cogens*) and International Humanitarian Law' in L Vohrah et al (eds), *Man's Inhumanity to Man: Essays on International Law in Honour of Antonio Cassese* (The Hague, Kluwer Law International, 2003); A Orakhelashvili, *Peremptory Norms in International Law* (Oxford, Oxford University Press, 2006) 61 *ff*.

[17] See Art 1(1) of the UN Charter.

[18] See, eg, Preamble to the 1868 Declaration Renouncing the Use, in Time of War, of Explosive Projectiles under 400 Grammes Weight (adopted and entered into force 11 December 1868) 138 CTS 297.

state. The aggressor can be subject to enforcement measures under Chapter VII of the UN Charter, including military action against it, whereas the victim state can lawfully take self-defence measures.[19] Moreover, Chapter VII even enables states and UN forces to intervene in non-international armed conflict and use force against states or armed groups.[20] On the other hand, *jus in bello* applies equally to the parties to an armed conflict whether they are an aggressor or a victim state, a state or a non-state actor, or UN forces.[21] This is linked to the exclusively humanitarian character of IHL, which is to protect all persons placed outside the combat, regardless of the legal status of the conflicting parties under *jus ad bellum*.

Thirdly, the legal consequences for violations of *jus ad bellum* and *jus in bello* mirror how the two legal regimes are applied, as outlined above. With regard to individual criminal responsibility for violations of *jus ad bellum*, namely the prohibition on the use of force, it is established that mainly high-level government and military officials belonging to the aggressor state bear such responsibility.[22] On the other hand, in the case of individual criminal responsibility for violations of *jus in bello* (both the law of international and non-international armed conflict), case law establishes that any person can bear such responsibility, ranging from combatants to civilians, and from heads of state to individual soldiers.[23]

[19] See especially Arts 41, 42, and 51 of the UN Charter. Furthermore, an aggressor state can be suspended from the exercise of the rights and privileges of UN membership (Art 5) or be expelled from the UN (Art 6).

[20] On this topic, see section 4.IV.

[21] See section 2.II.C for a discussion on the principle of the equal application of IHL to the conflicting parties. See section 3.II.B for a specific discussion on the equal application in self-defence; sections 4.IV.C and D for UN forces; and section 5.I for non-international armed conflict.

[22] See Article 8 *bis* (1) of the 'Amendments to the Rome Statute of the International Criminal Court on the Crime of Aggression', Review Conference of the Rome Statute of the International Criminal Court (Kampala 31 May to 11 June 2010) (11 June 2010) RC/Res.6, Annex I. See also Rome Statute of the International Criminal Court (adopted 17 July 1998, entered into force 1 July 2002) 2187 UNTS 3.

For the defendants who were found guilty of crimes against peace in the International Military Tribunal in Nürnberg, see International Military Tribunal in Nürnberg, *The Trial of German Major War Criminals: Proceedings of the International Military Tribunal Sitting at Nuremberg, Germany*, Part 22 (London, UK Stationary Office, 1946) 485 *ff*. For the defendants who were found guilty for crimes against peace in the International Military Tribunal in Tokyo, see B Röling and C Rüter (eds), *The Tokyo Judgment* Vol I (Amsterdam, APA-University Press Amsterdam BV, 1977) 443 ff.

An exception could be when the victim state used force in self-defence in violation of the principle of proportionality or necessity, where high-level officials of the victim state may be held responsible for violations of *jus ad bellum*. Such view is held by some states and experts: Statement of the USSR, UNGA Sixth Committee (1971) GAOR 26th Session, 144, para 9; Costa Rica, UNGA Sixth Committee (1971) GAOR 26th Session, 167, para 5; Zaire, UNGA Sixth Committee (1972) GAOR 27th Session, 233, para 27. See also UNGA Sixth Committee 'Report of L de Brouckère on Article 16 of the Covenant of the League of Nations' (3 October 1952) UN Doc A/2211, Annex, Agenda Item 54, 29, para 41; I Brownlie, *International Law and the Use of Force by States* (Oxford, Clarendon Press, 1963) 264.

[23] For an extensive list of practice, see Henckaerts and Doswald-Beck (eds), *Customary International Humanitarian Law* Vol II: Practice, Part II, 3611 *ff*.

Individuals belonging to the aggressor state and the victim state as well as to a state's armed forces and armed groups equally bear criminal responsibility for violations of IHL. Similarly, with regard to state responsibility, only the aggressor state is responsible for violations of *jus ad bellum*[24] whereas both the aggressor state and the victim state are responsible for violations of IHL.[25]

Despite the general distinction between *jus ad bellum* and *jus in bello*, it is also the case that they both share the ultimate goal of minimising human suffering through the regulation of the use of force. The UN Charter, which is the basis for modern *jus ad bellum*, provides in its Preamble as follows:

> We the peoples of the United Nations determined to save succeeding generations from the scourge of war, which twice in out lifetime has brought untold sorrow to mankind.

In addition, the Preamble to the 1907 Hague Convention (IV), of which its Annex still remains an important source of customary rules of IHL, provides as follows:

> [The High Contracting Parties] . . . Animated by the desire to serve, even in this extreme case [of armed conflict], the interests of humanity and the ever progressive needs of civilization; Thinking it important . . . to revise the general laws and customs of war, either with a view to defining them with greater precision or to confining them within such limits as would mitigate their severity as far as possible.

[24] See *Nicaragua* case (Merits), para 292 (13); *Legal Consequences of the Construction of a Wall in the Occupied Palestinian Territory* (hereafter *Wall* case) (Advisory Opinion) [2004] ICJ Rep 136, para 163 (C); *Armed Activities* case (Merits), para 245 (5); Eritrea–Ethiopia Claims Commission, *Jus ad Bellum, Ethiopia's Claim 1–8* (hereafter *Jus ad Bellum* case) (Partial Award) (2009) XXVI *Reports of International Arbitral Awards* 457, para IV (B) (3); Decision Number 7: Guidance regarding *Jus ad Bellum* Liability (2009) XXVI *Reports of International Arbitral Awards* 10 *ff*; *Ethiopia's Damages Claims* (Final Award) (2009) XXVI *Reports of International Arbitral Awards* 631, para XII (B).

As similar to the individual criminal responsibility, an exception could be when the victim state used force in self-defence in violation of the principles of necessity or proportionality, where the victim state may be held responsible for violations of *jus ad bellum*. See n 22 above.

[25] See Art 1 of ILC, 'Articles on Responsibility of States for Internationally Wrongful Acts' (hereafter ILC Articles on State Responsibility) (2001) UN Doc A/56/10 Supp No 10, paras 76 *ff*; Art 3 of Convention (IV) Respecting the Laws and Customs of War on Land and Its Annex: Regulations concerning the Laws and Customs of War on Land (hereafter 1907 Hague Regulations) (adopted 18 October 1907, entered into force 26 January 1910) 187 CTS 227; Art 91 of the 1977 First Additional Protocol. See also UNSC Res 1304 (16 June 2000) UN Doc S/RES/1304, para 14. See also Eritrea–Ethiopia Claims Commission, *Eritrea's Damages Claims* (Final Award) (2009) XXVI *Reports of International Arbitral Awards* 505, paras 48–50, 289, 310, 316, 342, and 366; *Ethiopia's Damages Claims* (Final Award), paras 48–50, 207, and 215.

On this topic in general see F Kalshoven, 'State Responsibility for Warlike Acts of the Armed Forces: From Article 3 of the Hague Convention IV of 1907 to Article 91 of the Additional Protocol I of 1977 and Beyond' (1991) 40 *International and Comparative Law Quarterly* 827; M Sassòli, 'State Responsibility for Violations of International Humanitarian Law' (2002) 846 *International Review of the Red Cross* 401; J Crawford et al (eds), *The Law of International Responsibility* (Oxford, Oxford University Press, 2010).

These still remain the underlying spirit of *jus ad bellum* and *jus in bello*, which should not be obscured by the technicalities inherent in the two legal regimes.

It should also be borne in mind that *jus ad bellum* and *jus in bello* are only two of the many branches of international law that are related to the regulation of the use of force. In order to achieve the most effective regulation of the use of force, and particularly to prevent excessive use of force, it is necessary to resort to other branches of international law such as international human rights law, disarmament law, and international environmental law.[26]

II. THREE PRINCIPLES GOVERNING THE RELATIONSHIP BETWEEN *JUS AD BELLUM* AND *JUS IN BELLO*

In this section, a brief history of how the issue of the relationship between *jus ad bellum* and *jus in bello* emerged will be explained. Then, it sets out three principles that were established over the years that govern the relationship between *jus ad bellum* and *jus in bello*: 1) separation between *jus ad bellum* and *jus in bello*; 2) equal application of *jus in bello* to the conflicting parties; and 3) concurrent application of *jus ad bellum* and *jus in bello*. Each of these principles has already been widely recognised in various practices but it is essential to set them out here clearly as one set of principles governing the relationship and to trace their foundations, which has rarely been done in most past writings.

It is worth noting at the outset that the issue of the relationship between *jus ad bellum* and *jus in bello* has mainly been discussed in the context of self-defence and international armed conflict (armed conflict between states). The principal issue was practically whether the protection for victims of armed conflict provided by *jus in bello* can be stripped from persons belonging to the conflicting party that used force illegally under *jus ad bellum*. However, this book examines whether the three principles set out here are equally valid in other contexts of a very different nature, namely the use of force under Chapter VII of the UN Charter, non-international armed conflict, and armed conflict of a mixed character.

A. Can the Application of *Jus in Bello* be Affected by *Jus ad Bellum*?

As briefly noted in the introductory chapter, with the codification of *jus ad bellum*, certain experts argued that the victims of armed conflict on the

[26] This was also the approach taken by the ICJ in the *Nuclear Weapons* case (Advisory Opinion).

aggressor side do not benefit from IHL protection,[27] particularly in the context of the relationship between the law of self-defence and the law of international armed conflict. This has been the core issue underlying the relationship between *jus ad bellum* and *jus in bello* for a long time. More recently, some experts viewed the conclusion of the International Court of Justice (ICJ) in the *Nuclear Weapons* Advisory Opinion as placing *jus in bello*, namely the law of international armed conflict, in subordination to *jus ad bellum* when a state is 'in an extreme circumstance of self-defence, in which the very survival of a State would be at stake'.[28] Moreover, self-defence against terrorist groups in the name of 'war on terror' was used as an excuse to categorically deny the protection provided in the law of international armed conflict for detainees, such as prisoners of war and civilian internees, even if, as a matter of law, they might have been entitled to such protection.[29] As can be seen, the issue of the subjection of *jus in bello* to *jus ad bellum* still remains a controversial one.

The practical consequences of the claim that *jus ad bellum* can override obligations under *jus in bello* can be serious. First, it is clear that such a claim can effectively terminate the protection provided for the victims of armed conflict. For example, in the case of the 'war on terror' as an ongoing self-defence measure, it was claimed that none of those who belonged to terrorist groups and who were captured in the course of the 'war on terror' were entitled to prisoner-of-war status and thus could be detained indefinitely.[30] However, there is a procedure in the law of international armed conflict which helps a state to determine the status of a person captured in an international armed conflict[31] and there are in fact various safeguards which do not permit detention for an indefinite period.[32]

[27] Q Wright, 'The Outlawry of War and the Law of War' (1953) 47 *American Journal of International Law* 365, 370 *ff*; G Scelle, 'Quelques réflexions sur l'abolition de la compétence de guerrer' (1954) 25 *Revue générale de droit international public* 5, 18–19; G Schwarzenberger, *International Law as Applied by International Courts and Tribunals* Vol II: The Law of Armed Conflict (London, Stevens and Sons, 1968) 105.

[28] *Nuclear Weapons* case (Advisory Opinion), para 105 (2) (E). See especially Dinstein, *War, Aggression and Self-Defence*, 161–62.

[29] See, eg, White House, 'White House Press Secretary Announcement of President Bush's Determination Re Legal Status of Taliban and Al Qaeda Detainees' (7 February 2002), US Department of State website, www.state.gov/s/l/38727.htm.

[30] See, eg, the letter of the US Department of Justice, 26 November 2002 in S Murphy (ed), 'U.S. Nationals Detained as Unlawful Combatants' (2003) 97 *American Journal of International Law* 196, 199–200.

[31] For the relevant provisions, see Arts 4, 5, 13, and 118 of the 1949 Third Geneva Convention; Arts 41, 42, 43, 49, 68, 78, 127, 128, and 147 of the 1949 Fourth Geneva Convention; Arts 43, 44, 45, 46, 47, 50, 51, and 75 of the 1977 First Additional Protocol. See generally K Okimoto, 'The Protection of Detainees in International Humanitarian Law' in S Perrigo and J Whitman (eds), *The Geneva Conventions under Assault* (London, Pluto Press, 2010).

[32] See Art 118 of the 1949 Third Geneva Convention; Arts 132 and 133 of the 1949 Fourth Geneva Convention. See also J Pejic, 'Procedural Principles and Safeguards for Internment/Administrative Detention in Armed Conflict and Other Situations of Violence' (2005) 858 *International Review of the Red Cross* 375.

However, some states attempted to curb these safeguards on the basis of the 'war on terror'. The consequences were grave: either the detainees were protected by the safeguards in the law of international armed conflict or they were in a 'legal black hole'[33] where a state was free to decide how to treat them.[34]

Moreover, the protection provided for the victims of armed conflict can come to a complete breakdown particularly through reprisals, where the aggressor state ceases to apply IHL because the victim state ceased to apply it. The danger was succinctly described by Hersch Lauterpacht:

> [I]t is impossible to visualize the conduct of hostilities in which one side would be bound by rules of warfare without benefiting from them and the other side would benefit from rules of warfare without being bound by them. Accordingly, any application to the actual conduct of war of the principle *ex injuria jus non oritur* would transform the contest into a struggle which may be subject to no regulation at all. The result would be the abandonment of most rules of warfare, including those which are of a humanitarian character.[35]

Gradually, a consensus emerged on two principles that developed through state practice and opinions of experts: *jus ad bellum* and *jus in bello* should be kept separate and *jus in bello* should be applied equally to the conflicting parties, regardless of their status under *jus ad bellum*. These emerged from the conviction that all victims of armed conflict should be protected equally solely on the basis of humanitarian consideration and not the legal status of the conflicting parties under *jus ad bellum*. The origins of the principle of the separation between *jus ad bellum* and *jus in bello* and the principle of the equal application of *jus in bello* to the conflicting parties will be traced back in turn.

B. Principle of the Separation between *Jus ad Bellum* and *Jus in Bello*

The principle of the separation between *jus ad bellum* and *jus in bello* is now universally accepted. It is interpreted in two ways: 1) the legal status of the conflicting parties under *jus ad bellum* does not affect the application of IHL; and 2) the application of IHL does not legitimise any illegal use of force under *jus ad bellum*. The rationale for the separation between *jus ad bellum* and *jus in bello* is precisely to protect the purely humanitarian pur-

[33] J Steyn, 'Guantanamo Bay: The Legal Black Hole' (2004) 53 *International and Comparative Law Quarterly* 1.

[34] Also refer to the case of the Vietnam War when the Democratic Republic of Vietnam refused to apply the 1949 Fourth Geneva Convention to US prisoners of war on the ground that the US carried out a war of aggression. See nn 49 and 50 below.

[35] H Lauterpacht, 'The Limits of the Operation of the Laws of War' (1953) 30 *British Year Book of International Law* 206, 212. See also F Bugnion, 'Just Wars, Wars of Aggression and International Humanitarian Law' (2002) 847 *International Review of the Red Cross* 523, 536–39; Dinstein, *War, Aggression and Self-Defence*, 158.

pose of IHL, which is to ensure that all victims of armed conflict should be protected impartially, and to avoid a situation where the victims of armed conflict of the aggressor are neglected while those of the victim state are protected.[36]

If one traces the origin of this principle, it is apparent that most practice relates to the first interpretation noted above. The first interpretation has long been accepted, even before *jus ad bellum* was codified in the UN Charter:

> Prior to the Covenant of the League of Nations, the General Treaty for the Renunciation of War, and the Charter of the United Nations, it was generally believed that whatever may be the cause of war, and whether or not the cause be a so-called just cause, the same rules of law applied between the belligerents *inter se* and the belligerents and neutrals.[37]

However, with the emergence of *jus ad bellum*, particularly since the 1928 Pact of Paris, war or the use of force became lawful or unlawful, not just or unjust. Thus, a new question arose whether the legality, as distinct from justness, of war or the use of force had any effect on the application of IHL. It is worth noting that the necessity to keep *jus ad bellum* and *jus in bello* separate became a more prominent issue with the emergence of modern *jus ad bellum* and particularly after the UN Charter was adopted.

The interest in the separation principle can already be seen in the period shortly after the adoption of the 1928 Pact of Paris. As long ago as 1934, experts of the International Law Association formulated the Articles of Interpretation of the 1928 Pact of Paris, in which Article 7 provides as follows:

> The Pact does not affect such humanitarian obligations as are contained in general treaties, such as The Hague Conventions of 1899 and 1907, the Geneva Conventions of 1864 and 1906, and the International Convention relating to the Treatment of Prisoners of War, 1929.[38]

The 1928 Pact of Paris was one of the core sources of *jus ad bellum* in the pre-UN Charter era and it is significant that the experts above anticipated the potential effects of the Pact on the existing IHL and formulated the principle of the separation in explicit terms.

Another interesting indication before the UN Charter era was the Draft Convention on Rights and Duties of States in Case of Aggression, drafted

[36] Lauterpacht, 'The Limits of the Operation', 212; Dinstein, *War, Aggression and Self-Defence*, 156–62.

[37] H Lauterpacht (ed), L Oppenheim, *International Law: A Treaties* Vol II: Disputes, War and Neutrality, 7th edn (London, Longmans, Green and Co, 1952) 217. Footnotes omitted.

[38] International Law Association, 'Report on the Effect of the Briand-Kellogg Pact of Paris on International Law: Articles of Interpretation Proposed by the Committee' in International Law Association Report of the Thirty-Eighth Conference (Budapest 1934) (International Law Association, Budapest 1934) 66, 68.

in 1939 by experts of the Harvard Research in International Law. Article 14 of the Draft Convention provides as follows:

> Nothing in this Convention shall be deemed to excuse any State for a violation of the humanitarian rules concerning the conduct of hostilities, prescribed by international law or by a treaty to which it is a party.[39]

These are important indications that the potential effects of *jus ad bellum* on *jus in bello* were already recognised in the early years of *jus ad bellum*, and that it was necessary to recognise in explicit terms that the legal status of the conflicting parties under *jus ad bellum* did not affect the application of IHL.

With the adoption of the UN Charter, *jus ad bellum* was codified clearer than ever, and its relation to *jus in bello* became a more prominent issue. The International Law Commission, in its consideration on whether to include the laws of war as a topic for codification, even opposed to the further codification of IHL for the following reason:

> It was considered that if the Commission, at the very beginning of its work, were to undertake this study, public opinion might interpret its action as showing lack of confidence in the efficiency of the means at the disposal of the United Nations for maintaining peace.[40]

While such concern quickly died out and the relevance of IHL was confirmed in the years following the end of the Second World War, the issue of whether the legal status of the conflicting parties under *jus ad bellum* affected the application of IHL persisted.

In the *Hostage* case at the US Military Tribunal at Nürnberg, prosecutors challenged the principle of the separation between the legal status of the conflicting parties under *jus ad bellum* and the application of IHL to the aggressor state, arguing, among others, that the law of occupation never became effective when Germany occupied Yugoslavia and Greece, since Germany's wars against these countries were 'aggressive wars' and that the occupation itself was unlawful.[41] However, the Tribunal rejected this argument in 1949 in the following terms:

[39] Advisory Committee of the Harvard Research in International Law, 'Draft Convention on Rights and Duties of States in Case of Aggression' (1939) 33 *American Journal of International Law Supplement* 827, 830.

[40] ILC, *Yearbook of the International Law Commission* (New York, United Nations, 1949) 281, para 18.

[41] US Military Tribunal in Nürnberg, *List and Others (Hostage Case)* (hereafter *Hostage* case) (Judgment) (1949) 8 *Law Reports of Trials of War Criminals* 34, 59. See also the arguments of the Chief Prosecutor of the UK and France respectively in the International Military Tribunal in Nürnberg. International Military Tribunal in Nürnberg, *The Trial of German Major War Criminals: Proceedings of the International Military Tribunal Sitting at Nuremberg, Germany*, Part 19 (London, UK Stationery Office, 1948) 423; International Military Tribunal in Nürnberg, *The Trial of German Major War Criminals: Proceedings of the International Military Tribunal Sitting at Nuremberg, Germany*, Part 4 (London, UK Stationery Office, 1946) 351.

> At the outset, we desire to point out that International Law makes no distinction between a lawful and an unlawful occupant in dealing with the respective duties of occupant and population in occupied territory. There is no reciprocal connection between the manner of the military occupation of territory and the rights and duties of the occupant and population to each other after the relationship has in fact been established. Whether the invasion was lawful or criminal is not an important factor in the consideration of this subject.[42]

Other judgments related to war crimes in the Second World War also followed the same approach.[43] These were important confirmations of the separation between the legal status of the conflicting parties under *jus ad bellum* and the application of IHL at a time when this principle was still nascent.

While these war crimes trials were ongoing, negotiations on the 1949 Geneva Conventions were ongoing in parallel. Incidentally, the four Geneva Conventions were adopted in 1949,[44] when the US Military Tribunal pronounced the position quoted above. Common Article 1 of the 1949 Geneva Conventions implicitly confirmed the position of the Tribunal:

> The High Contracting Parties undertake to respect and to ensure respect for the present Convention in all circumstances.

The phrase 'in all circumstances' signified that the 1949 Geneva Conventions applied independently from the legality of the use of force of the conflicting parties.[45]

On the other hand, in the 1950s, some experts argued that the application of *jus in bello* is limited by *jus ad bellum*.[46] However, the opinions of experts to date have been overwhelmingly in support of the position that the legal status of the conflicting parties under *jus ad bellum* does not affect the application of IHL.[47] For example, Hans Kelsen noted as follows in 1966:

[42] *Hostage* case (Judgment), 59.

[43] See, eg, Netherlands, Special Court (War Criminals), Arnhem, *Re Christiansen* (Judgment) (1948) *Annual Digest and Reports of Public International Law Cases* 412, 413; Netherlands, Special Court (War Criminals) of First Instance, Amsterdam, First Chamber, *In re Zühlke* (Judgment) (1948) *Annual Digest and Reports of Public International Law Cases* 415, 416.

[44] See n 14 above.

[45] J Pictet et al, *Commentary on the Geneva Conventions of 12 August 1949* Vol I (Geneva, International Committee of the Red Cross, 1952) 27.

[46] Wright, 'The Outlawry of War', 374; Scelle, 'Quelques réflexions sur l'abolition de la compétence de guerrer', 18–19; Schwarzenberger, *International Law*, 105.

[47] For references on the writings before 1970 supporting the separation principle, see generally the writings cited in I Brownlie, *International Law and the Use of Force by States* (Oxford, Clarendon Press, 1963) 406, note 3 and H Meyrowitz, *Le principe de l'égalité de belligérants devant le droit de la guerre* (Paris, Éditions Pedone, 1970) 78–80, note 1. For those after 1970, see C Rousseau, *Le droit des conflits armés* (Paris, Pedone, 1983) 24–26; M McDougal and F Feliciano, *The International Law of War* (New Haven, New Haven Press, 1994) 530–42; L Doswald-Beck (ed), *San Remo Manual on International Law Applicable to Armed Conflicts at Sea* (Cambridge, Cambridge University Press, 1995) 46; M Sassòli and A Bouvier (eds), *How Does Law Protect in War?* (Geneva, International Committee of the Red Cross, 1999)

> A clear distinction must be drawn . . . between the legality of resorting to war and the applicability of the rules regulating the conduct of war. The fact that the resort to war is, in principle, unlawful does not compel the conclusion that in a war illegally resorted to by one side the rules regulating interbelligerent relations are either inapplicable or substantially modified in their operation. The rights conferred and the duties imposed upon belligerents in the conduct of war are not dependent for their operation upon an equality of legal status as concerns the war itself.[48]

In the 1960s and 1970s, the Vietnam War was ongoing and during this war, the Democratic Republic of Vietnam refused to apply the 1949 Third Geneva Convention to the US prisoners of war on the basis that the US was waging a war of aggression.[49] The Democratic Republic of Vietnam confirmed this position during the negotiations on additional protocols to the 1949 Geneva Conventions:

> [T]he only types of war that could be covered by the legislation under discussion [1977 First Additional Protocol] should be legal wars. All the rest were crimes punishable under penal law . . . A general solution should therefore be found to the problem of the basic structure of draft Protocol I which made a sharp division between *jus ad bellum* and *jus in bello* with a view to placing both parties on an equal footing, even in illegal wars. Such equality was condemned not only by modern positive law but also by logic, intelligence and morality.[50]

Some other states also showed reservations to some provisions of the 1977 First Additional Protocol. For example, Afghanistan,[51] France[52] and

83–88; L Green, *The Contemporary Law of Armed Conflict*, 2nd edn (Manchester, Manchester University Press, 2000) 18–19; C Greenwood, 'International Humanitarian Law (Law of War)' in F Kalshoven (ed), *The Centennial of the First International Peace Conference: Reports and Conclusions* (Boston, Kluwer Law International, 2000) 173–92; A Roberts and R Guelff (eds), *Documents on the Laws of War*, 3rd edn (Oxford, Oxford University Press, 2000) 1–2; F Bugnion, 'Guerre juste, guerre d'agression et droit international humanitaire' (2002) 847 *Revue international de la Croix-Rouge* 523, 544–45; G Rona, 'Interesting Times for International Humanitarian Law: Challenges from the "War on Terror"' (2003) 27 *Fletcher Forum of World Affairs* 55, 67–68; J Pejic, 'Terrorist Acts and Groups: A Role for International Law?' (2004) 75 *British Year Book of International Law* 71, 98–99; Dinstein, *War, Aggression and Self-Defence*, 156–63.

[48] H Kelsen, *Principles of International Law*, 2nd edn (New York, Holt, Reinhart, and Wilson, 1966) 89.

[49] See ICRC, 'Réponse à l'appel du CICR pour le respect des règles humanitaires au Vietnam' (1965) 562 *Revue internationale de la Croix-Rouge* 485 (English translation in (1965) 5 *International Review of the Red Cross* 527); F Bugnion, '*Jus ad Bellum, Jus in Bello* and Non-International Armed Conflicts' (2003) 6 *Yearbook of International Humanitarian Law* 167, 174–75.

[50] *Official Records of the Diplomatic Conference on the Reaffirmation and Development of International Humanitarian Law Applicable in Armed Conflicts, Geneva (1974–1977)* (hereafter *Official Records*) (Bern, Federal Political Department, 1978) Vol XIV, CDDH/III/SR.16, para 21. See also *Official Records*, Vol IV, CDDH/41, 177–88.

[51] *Official Records* Vol VI, CDDH/SR.41, para 126.

[52] *Official Records* Vol VI, CDDH/SR.41, paras 111 and 114.

Romania[53] expressed concerns on Article 51 (which prohibits attacks on civilians and indiscriminate attacks) by stating that this provision cannot restrict the state's right of self-defence when it is faced with an aggression.

However, at the end, states confirmed the separation between the legality of the use of force under *jus ad bellum* and the application of IHL in the Preamble to the 1977 First Additional Protocol, which is now seen as an authoritative statement of the principle of the separation:

> The High Contracting Parties . . . Reaffirming further that the provisions of the Geneva Conventions of 12 August 1949 and of this Protocol must be fully applied in all circumstances to all persons who are protected by those instruments, without any adverse distinction based on the nature or origin of the armed conflict or on the causes espoused by or attributed to the Parties to the conflict.[54]

Hence, the state practice of the Democratic Republic of Vietnam and some other states was an exception.

In fact, besides the authoritative statement in the Preamble to the 1977 First Additional Protocol, state practice since 1945 has been almost unanimous in supporting the principle that the legal status of the conflicting parties under *jus ad bellum* does not affect the application of IHL. A brief survey of major international armed conflicts since 1945 shows that the application of *jus in bello* was not subject to *jus ad bellum*. In armed conflicts such as the 1950–53 Korean War,[55] 1967 Arab–Israeli Conflict,[56] 1971 India–Pakistan

[53] *Official Records* Vol VI, CDDH/SR.41, Annex.

[54] See also Y Sandoz et al (eds), *Commentary on the Additional Protocols of 8 June 1977 to the Geneva Conventions of 12 August 1949* (Geneva, International Committee of the Red Cross, 1987) paras 32 and 1928. The 1977 First Additional Protocol has 170 states parties as at September 2010. For the latest record of states parties, see the ICRC IHL Database website, www.icrc.org/ihl.

[55] UNSC, 'Letter Dated 5 July 1951 from the Representative of the United States of America to the Secretary-General' (6 July 1951) UN Doc S/2232. In addition, see the following for an extensive account relating to the treatment of prisoners of war, references to the 1949 Third Geneva Convention and violations of IHL: UNGA, 'The Question of Korea' (1951) UNYB 207, 245–48; UNGA, 'The Question of Korea' (1952) UNYB 155, 156–59, 171–73, 185 *ff*, and 204–07 in particular but see other relevant parts by referring to the index at 952, under the heading 'Prisoners of War'.

Note that the major conflicting parties, namely China, Democratic People's Republic of Korea, Republic of Korea, and the US were not parties to the 1949 Geneva Conventions at the time of the conflict but nevertheless accepted to apply them. However, other IHL treaties such as the 1907 Hague Regulations and 1929 Convention Relative to the Treatment of Prisoners of War (adopted 27 July 1929, entered into force 19 June 1931) 118 LNTS 343 were applicable, either as treaty law or customary international law.

[56] Statement in the Security Council of Israel, UNSC Verbatim Record (14 June 1967) UN Doc S/PV.1360, 12, para 127. See also the statement of Argentina, UNSC Verbatim Record (14 June 1967) UN Doc S/PV.1361, 2, para 7 and UNSC Res 237 (14 June 1967) UN Doc S/RES/237. See also ICRC, 'Le Comité international et le conflit au Proche-Orient' (1967) 583 *Revue internationale de la Croix-Rouge* 303.

Conflict,[57] 1973 Arab–Israeli Conflict,[58] 1979 China–Vietnam Conflict,[59] 1980–88 Iran–Iraq War,[60] 1991 Gulf War,[61] Eritrea–Ethiopia Conflict,[62] 1999

[57] Statements in the Security Council of India, UNSC Verbatim Record (12 December 1971) UN Doc S/PV.1611, 13, para 129 and Pakistan, UNSC Verbatim Record (13 December 1971) UN Doc S/PV.1613, 29, para 291.

[58] Statements in the Security Council of Syria, UNSC Verbatim Record (11 October 1973) UN Doc S/PV.1745, 11, paras 111 and 113; Israel, UNSC Verbatim Record (26 October 1973) UN Doc S/PV.1751, 16, para 156; Egypt, UNSC Verbatim Record (26 October 1973) UN Doc S/PV.1751, 17, para 167. See also the statement of Kenya, UNSC Verbatim Record (12 October 1973) UN Doc S/PV.1846, 2, para 7. See also ICRC, 'L'action du Comité international au Moyen-Orient' (1973) 660 *Revue internationale de la Croix-Rouge* 727.

[59] ICRC, 'Conflit sino-vietnamien' (1979) 716 *Revue internationale de la Croix-Rouge* 98. See also Bugnion, '*Jus ad Bellum*', 175.

[60] Statement of Iraq in the Security Council, UNSC Verbatim Record (17 October 1980) UN Doc S/PV.2251, 8, para 62. See also the following for UN Secretary-General's report on the responsibility of the initiation of Iran–Iraq War: UNSC, 'Further Report of the Secretary-General on the Implementation of Security Council Resolution 598 (1987)' (9 December 1991) UN Doc S/23273, 2, para 5. See further UN Secretary-General's reports on the use of chemical weapons by both sides: UNSC, 'Mission to Inspect Civilian Areas in Iran and Iraq Which Have Been Subject to Military Attack' (20 June 1983) UN Doc S/15834; UNSC, 'Report of the Specialists Appointed by the Secretary-General to Investigate Allegations by the Islamic Republic of Iran concerning the Use of Chemical Weapons' (26 March 1984) UN Doc S/16433; UNSC, 'Letter Dated 17 April 1985 from the Secretary-General Addressed to the President of the Security Council' (24 April 1985) UN Doc S/17127; UNSC, 'Report of the Mission Dispatched by the Secretary-General to Investigate Allegations of the Use of Chemical Weapons in the Conflict between the Islamic Republic of Iran and Iraq' (12 March 1986) UN Doc S/17911; UNSC, 'Report of the Mission Dispatched by the Secretary-General to Investigate Allegations of the Use of Chemical Weapons in the Conflict between the Islamic Republic of Iran and Iraq' (8 May 1987) UN Doc S/18852; UNSC, 'Report of the Mission Dispatched by the Secretary-General to Investigate Allegations of the Use of Chemical Weapons in the Conflict between the Islamic Republic of Iran and Iraq' (25 April 1988) UN Doc S/19823; UNSC, 'Report of the Mission Dispatched by the Secretary-General to Investigate Allegations of the Use of Chemical Weapons in the Conflict between the Islamic Republic of Iran and Iraq' (19 August 1988) UN Doc S/20134. See also UN Security Council resolutions on the conflict: UNSC Res 540 (31 October 1983) UN Doc S/RES/540, para 3; UNSC Res 582 (24 November 1986) UN Doc S/RES/582, Preamble, paras 2 and 4; UNSC Res 598 (20 July 1987) UN Doc S/RES/598, Preamble and para 3; UNSC Res 612 (9 May 1988) UN Doc S/RES/612; UNSC Res 620 (26 August 1988) UN Doc S/RES/620. See also ICRC, 'Conflit Irak–Iran' (1980) 720 *Revue internationale de la Croix-Rouge* 341.

[61] US Department of Defense, 'Final Report to Congress on the Conduct of Hostilities in the Persian Gulf' (1992), www.ndu.edu/library/epubs/cpgw.pdf. See also ICRC, 'Conflit au Moyen-Orient' (1991) 787 *Revue internationale de la Croix-Rouge* 23.

[62] See the following cases before the Eritrea–Ethiopia Claims Commission: *Prisoners of War, Eritrea's Claim 17* (hereafter *Prisoners of War, Eritrea* case) (Partial Award) (2009) XXVI *Reports of International Arbitral Awards* 23; *Prisoners of War, Ethiopia's Claim 4* (Partial Award) (2009) XXVI *Reports of International Arbitral Awards* 73; *Central Front, Eritrea's Claims 2, 4, 6, 7, 8 and 22* (hereafter *Central Front, Eritrea* case) (Partial Award) (2009) XXVI *Reports of International Arbitral Awards* 115; *Central Front, Ethiopia's Claim 2* (hereafter *Central Front, Ethiopia* case) (Partial Award) (2009) XXVI *Reports of International Arbitral Awards* 155; *Civilians Claims, Eritrea's Claims 15, 16, 23 and 27–32* (hereafter *Civilians, Eritrea* case) (Partial Award) (2009) XXVI *Reports of International Arbitral Awards* 195; *Civilians Claims, Ethiopia's Claim 5* (Partial Award) (2009) XXVI *Reports of International Arbitral Awards* 249; *Western Front, Aerial Bombardment and Related Claims, Eritrea's Claims 1, 3, 5, 9–13, 14, 21, 25 and 26* (hereafter *Western Front, Eritrea* case) (Partial Award) (2009) XXVI *Reports of International Arbitral Awards* 291; *Western and Eastern Fronts, Ethiopia's Claims 1 and 3* (hereafter *Western and Eastern Fronts, Ethiopia* case) (Partial Award) (2009) XXVI *Reports of International Arbitral Awards* 351; *Eritrea's Damages Claims* (Final Award), paras 48–50, 289, 310, 316, 342, and 366;

Kosovo Conflict,[63] 2001 US–Afghanistan Conflict,[64] 2003 Gulf War,[65] 2006 Lebanon Conflict,[66] 2008 Georgia Conflict,[67] and 2009 Gaza Conflict,[68] one of the parties or both parties to the conflict accepted the application of IHL and none of them expressly denied the application of IHL on grounds that the adversary was using force in violation of *jus ad bellum*. Note that the origins of most of these armed conflicts in terms of *jus ad bellum* were highly

Ethiopia's Damages Claims (Final Award), paras 48–50, 207, and 215. See also C Gray, 'The Eritrea/Ethiopia Claims Commission Oversteps Its Boundaries: A Partial Award?' (2006) 17 *European Journal of International Law* 699; A de Guttry et al (eds), *The 1998–2000 War between Eritrea and Ethiopia: An International Legal Perspective* (Hague, TMC Asser Press, 2009); R Kolb, 'Considération sur l'application du droit international humanitaire par la Commission arbitrale Erythrée/Ethiopie' in B Vukas and T Sosic (eds), *International Law: New Actors, New Concepts, Continuing Dilemmas: Liber Amicorum Bozidar Bakotic* (Leiden, Martinus Nijhoff, 2010).

[63] See ICTY, 'Final Report to the Prosecutor by the Committee Established to Review the NATO Bombing Campaign against the Federal Republic of Yugoslavia' (2000) 39 ILM 1257. See also ICRC, 'Statement by the International Committee of the Red Cross of 26 April 1999' (1999) 834 *International Review of the Red Cross* 408.

[64] UNSC, 'Letter Dated 7 October 2001 from the Permanent Representative of the United States of America to the United Nations Addressed to the President of the Security Council' (7 October 2001) UN Doc S/2001/946. See also ICRC, 'Afghanistan: ICRC Calls on All Parties to Conflict to Respect International Humanitarian Law' (2001) 844 *International Review of the Red Cross* 1181.

[65] UNSC Res 1472 (28 March 2003) UN Doc S/RES/1472, particularly para 1; UNSC Res 1483 (22 May 2003) UN Doc S/RES/1472, particularly para 5. See also ICRC, 'Conflict in Iraq: Memorandum to the Belligerents' (2003) 850 *International Review of the Red Cross* 423.

[66] Israel Ministry of Foreign Affairs, 'Responding to Hizbullah Attacks from Lebanon: Issues of Proportionality' (25 July 2006), Israel Ministry of Foreign Affairs website, www.mfa.gov.il/MFA/Government/Law/Legal+Issues+and+Rulings. See also the statement in the Security Council of Lebanon, UNSC Verbatim Record (14 July 2006) UN Doc S/PV.5489, 5. See also the statements in the Security Council of Peru in the Security Council, UNSC Verbatim Record (13 July 2006) UN Doc S/PV.5488, 4; Argentina, UNSC Verbatim Record (14 July 2006) UN Doc S/PV.5489, 9; UK, UNSC Verbatim Record (14 July 2006) UN Doc S/PV.5489, 12; Tanzania, UNSC Verbatim Record (14 July 2006) UN Doc S/PV.5489, 14; Denmark, UNSC Verbatim Record (14 July 2006) UN Doc S/PV.5489, 15; Greece, UNSC Verbatim Record (14 July 2006) UN Doc S/PV.5489, 17. See also ICRC, 'Israel and Lebanon: ICRC Gravely Concerned About the Plight of Civilians Caught Up in Hostilities' (13 July 2006) News Release 06/78; UNHRC, 'Report of the Commission of Inquiry on Lebanon Pursuant to Human Rights Council Resolution S-2/1' (23 November 2006) UN Doc A/HRC/3/2.

[67] Council of the European Union, Independent International Fact-Finding Mission on the Conflict in Georgia, 'Report' Vol II (September 2009) 300, Independent International Fact-Finding Mission on the Conflict in Georgia website, www.ceiig.ch.

[68] Israel Ministry of Foreign Affairs, 'Responding to Hamas Attacks from Gaza – Issues of Proportionality' (29 December 2008), Israel Ministry of Foreign Affairs website, www.mfa.gov.il/MFA/Government/Law/Legal+Issues+and+Rulings. See also the statements in the Security Council of Israel, UNSC Verbatim Record (6 January 2009) UN Doc S/PV.6061, 7; France, UNSC Verbatim Record (31 December 2008) UN Doc S/PV.6060, 9; Indonesia, UNSC Verbatim Record (31 December 2008) UN Doc S/PV.6060, 10; Burkina Faso, UNSC Verbatim Record (31 December 2008) UN Doc S/PV.6060, 15; Costa Rica, UNSC Verbatim Record (31 December 2008) UN Doc S/PV.6060, 16; Croatia, UNSC Verbatim Record (31 December 2008) UN Doc S/PV.6060, 17; Egypt, UNSC Verbatim Record (31 December 2008) UN Doc S/PV.6060, 18; League of Arab States, UNSC Verbatim Record (31 December 2008) UN Doc S/PV.6060, 19. See further UNHRC, 'Report of the United Nations Fact-Finding Mission on the Gaza Conflict' (25 September 2009) UN Doc A/HRC/12/48.

controversial, such as the 1950 Korean War, in which the use of force by the multinational forces was not clear whether it was collective self-defence or Chapter VII use of force, the 1967 Arab-Israel Conflict, which raised the question of anticipatory self-defence, and the 1999 Kosovo Conflict, which provoked the whole debate on the legality of humanitarian intervention. None of these controversies affected the application of IHL.

Besides the state practice, the Nürnberg trials, IHL treaties, and opinions of experts, the ICJ has also contributed to the confirmation of the principle that the legality of the use of force under *jus ad bellum* does not affect the application of IHL. Particularly since the *Nicaragua* case in 1986, the ICJ became increasingly involved in use of force questions and the practice in these cases supports this principle. First, the Court dealt with the issues of *jus ad bellum* and *jus in bello* separately in many cases relating to the use of force such as the *Nicaragua*,[69] *Nuclear Weapons*,[70] *Wall*,[71] and *Armed Activities* cases.[72] Moreover, in the *Nuclear Weapons* case, at least five states dealt with the issues of *jus ad bellum* and *jus in bello* separately.[73] These practices imply the distinction between *jus ad bellum* and *jus in bello*. Judge Kooijmans also noted as follows in the *Armed Activities* case in 2005:

> It [IHL] does not differentiate between belligerents. In particular, no distinction is made in the *ius in bello* between an occupation resulting from a lawful use of force and one which is the result of aggression. The latter issue is decided by application of the *ius ad bellum*, the law on the use of force, which attributes responsibility for the commission of the acts of which the occupation *is the result*.[74]

In the *Wall* case in 2003, many states explicitly confirmed that the legality of the use of force under *jus ad bellum* did not affect the application of IHL.[75] For example, the League of Arab States noted as follows:

[69] Judges Jennings and Schwebel also dealt with the issues of *jus ad bellum* and *jus in bello* separately in their respective opinions.

[70] Judges Fleischhauer, Higgins, Koroma, Schwebel, Shahabuddeen, and Weeramantry also dealt with the issues of *jus ad bellum* and *jus in bello* separately in their respective opinions.

[71] Judges Buergenthal, Higgins, and Kooijmans also dealt with the issues of *jus ad bellum* and *jus in bello* separately in their respective opinions.

[72] Judges Kateka, Kooijmans, Parra-Aranguren, Simma, Tomka, and Verhoeven also dealt with the issues of *jus ad bellum* and *jus in bello* separately in their respective opinions.

[73] *Nuclear Weapons* case, Written Statements of Egypt, Iran, Mexico, New Zealand, and UK. The written statements can be found at the ICJ website, www.icj-cij.org.

[74] *Armed Activities* case (Merits), Separate Opinion of Judge Kooijmans, 12, para 58. See also Declaration of Judge Verhoeven, para 4.

[75] *Wall* case, Written Statements of Indonesia, para 11; Jordan, para 5.79; League of Arab States, para 9.6; Saudi Arabia, para 31; Organisation of the Islamic Conference, para 29; Palestine, para 396. Other states simply dealt with the issue of *jus ad bellum* and *jus in bello* separately in their written statements which implies the separation between the two: Cuba, Lebanon, Malaysia, and South Africa. The written statements can be found at the ICJ website, www.icj-cij.org.

> Israel also argues that the construction of the wall is justified as a measure of self-defence within the meaning of art. 51 of the Charter [of the UN] . . . It erroneously blurs the dividing line between *ius in bello* and *ius ad bellum* . . . the argument of self-defence cannot be used to justify any deviation from the applicable rules of international humanitarian law. Thus, where a violation of international humanitarian law is at stake, the argument of self-defence has no place, it is irrelevant.[76]

However, the ICJ not only confirmed the principle of the separation between *jus ad bellum* and *jus in bello* but also revived the debate on whether *jus ad bellum* could override *jus in bello*. The most controversial paragraph in the ICJ's *Nuclear Weapons* Advisory Opinion reads as follows:

> It follows from the above-mentioned requirements that the threat or use of nuclear weapons would generally be contrary to the rules of international law applicable in armed conflict, and in particular the principles and rules of humanitarian law . . . However, in view of the current state of international law, and of the elements of fact at its disposal, the Court cannot conclude definitively whether the threat or use of nuclear weapons would be lawful or unlawful in an extreme circumstance of self-defence, in which the very survival of a State would be at stake.[77]

Many of the judges admitted that this paragraph was unclear as to its meaning. Some judges and experts put their own interpretation on this paragraph, but for the purpose of this book it is not suggested to read too much between the lines. At least what the paragraph seems to imply is that the Court could not say for sure, at the time of delivering the Advisory Opinion, that there is a circumstance where the threat or use of nuclear weapons is permitted under either *jus ad bellum* or *jus in bello*,[78] or that the threat or use of nuclear weapons is prohibited categorically by *jus ad bellum* or *jus in bello*, or both.

As can be seen from the wealth of materials, the principle that the legal status of the conflicting parties under *jus ad bellum* does not affect the appli-

[76] *Wall* case, Written Statement of the League of Arab States, para 9.6. The written statements can be found at the ICJ website, www.icj-cij.org.

[77] *Nuclear Weapons* case (Advisory Opinion), para 105(2)(E). See especially Dinstein, *War, Aggression and Self-Defence*, 162. See generally M Matheson, 'The Opinions of the International Court of Justice on the Threat or Use of Nuclear Weapons' (1997) 91 *American Journal of International Law* 417; Y Sandoz et al, 'Special Issue: The Advisory Opinion on the International Court of Justice on the Legality of Nuclear Weapons and International Humanitarian Law' (1997) 316 *International Review of the Red Cross* 1; T Gill, 'The Nuclear Weapons Advisory Opinion of the International Court of Justice and the Fundamental Distinction between the *Jus ad Bellum* and *Jus in Bello*' (1999) 12 *Leiden Journal of International Law* 613; L Boisson de Chazournes and P Sands (eds), *International Law, the International Court of Justice and Nuclear Weapons* (Cambridge, Cambridge University Press, 1999).

[78] Refer to the original question put to the Court: 'Is the threat or use of nuclear weapons in any circumstance permitted under international law?' See UNGA, 'Request for an Advisory Opinion from the International Court of Justice on the Legality of the Threat or Use of Nuclear Weapons' UNGA Res (15 December 1994) UN Doc A/RES/49/75 K.

cation of *jus in bello* is firmly established in IHL and customary international law. Hence, whether the conflicting parties in an armed conflict are using force in self-defence, or under the authorisation of Chapter VII of the UN Charter, or in violation of Article 2(4) of the UN Charter, has nothing to do with the application of IHL.

However, as noted at the beginning of this section, there is yet another interpretation of the principle of the separation between *jus ad bellum* and *jus in bello*: application of IHL does not legitimise any illegal use of force under *jus ad bellum*. This principle is also solidly established in IHL. The Preamble to the 1977 First Additional Protocol, again, is an authoritative source of this principle:

> The High Contracting Parties . . . Expressing their conviction that nothing in this Protocol or in the Geneva Conventions of 12 August 1949 can be construed as legitimizing or authorizing any act of aggression or any other use of force inconsistent with the Charter of the United Nations.[79]

A further expression of this principle can be found in Article 4 of the 1977 First Additional Protocol entitled 'Legal status of the Parties to the conflict', which provides as follows:

> The application of the Conventions [1949 Geneva Conventions] and of this Protocol, as well as the conclusion of the agreements provided for therein, shall not affect the legal status of the Parties to the conflict.[80]

Thus, for example, the application of IHL to the aggressor (in terms of *jus ad bellum*) does not excuse the aggressor from that status and thus, it continues to be subject to Chapter VII enforcement measures or self-defence by the victim state, as well as state and individual criminal responsibility for violating *jus ad bellum*.

These practices of states and international courts and tribunals, and expert opinions, show that the two interpretations of the principle of the separation between *jus ad bellum* and *jus in bello* have been consistently upheld and developed into legal principles in treaties (namely the 1977 First Additional Protocol) and customary international law.

The practice on the separation between *jus ad bellum* and *jus in bello* has mostly been related to the separation between the law of self-defence and the law of international armed conflict, and it is striking that the separation between Chapter VII and IHL and the role of this principle in non-international armed conflict have not been given the same level of attention. While it may be logical to extend the principle to these situations, its applicability will be discussed in later sections.[81]

[79] See also Y Sandoz et al (eds), *Commentary*, para 30.

[80] For non-international armed conflict, see common Art 3 (2) of the 1949 Geneva Conventions.

[81] For the discussion on the application of the separation principle to Chapter VII and IHL, see ch 4 and to non-international armed conflict, see ch 5.

C. Principle of the Equal Application of *Jus in Bello* to the Conflicting Parties

The second principle governing the relationship between *jus ad bellum* and *jus in bello* is the equal application of *jus in bello* between the conflicting parties, which is a corollary to the separation between *jus ad bellum* and *jus in bello*. The principle of the separation between *jus ad bellum* and *jus in bello* already implies the principle of equal application since the aim of the first principle is to exclude the possibility of depriving the protection in *jus in bello* for persons belonging to the conflicting party that resorted to force illegally under *jus ad bellum*, which, in effect, excludes the possibility of unequal application of *jus in bello*. *Jus in bello* focuses on persons (and not states or international security) and hence aims at protecting all victims of armed conflict, and not only some.

However, the principle of the equal application is only implicit in the principle of the separation between *jus ad bellum* and *jus in bello*. The principle of the equal application is an important principle that takes the principle of the separation one step further, and ensures the proper application of *jus in bello*. Hence, the principle of the equal application must be set out clearly as a separate principle.

As similar to the principle of the separation, the principle of the equal application is well-established and thus, this section primarily serves to trace the foundation of the principle.

In the past, there were claims that IHL applied unequally between the conflicting parties depending on the legality of the use of force. For example, during the negotiations on additional protocols to the 1949 Geneva Conventions, in the context of international armed conflict, China said that 'Wars were divided into two kinds, just and unjust . . . a distinction between just and unjust wars, should be made in the new Protocols.'[82] Some have elaborated this view, which can be divided into two types: 1) combatants belonging to an aggressor state do not benefit from the protection under IHL at all; and 2) combatants belonging to an aggressor state only benefit from a portion of IHL protection.

The first view was not held by many. An argument was made by the prosecution in the International Military Tribunal at Nürnberg[83] but as noted above, it was later rejected by other military tribunals on war crimes committed during the Second World War and did not gain any wide support in the subsequent years.[84]

The other view that combatants belonging to an aggressor state only benefit from a portion of IHL protection was held by some experts but has

[82] *Official Records* Vol V, CDDH/SR.12, para 15.
[83] See n 41 above.
[84] See nn 42 and 43 above.

now died out. For example, Quincy Wright argued in 1959 that 'some of the law of war is applicable to all states engaged in hostilities, whether their action has a legal character of defense, enforcement, or aggression, but that some of the advantages of this law are denied to aggressors'.[85] Wright went on to argue that an aggressor did not have the power to destroy foreign armed forces whereas the state engaged in 'legitimate hostilities' was entitled to destroy enemy forces.[86] This implied that the aggressor cannot even attack military objectives permitted under IHL[87] whereas the state using force could lawfully do so. However, in a later section, Wright qualified his statement in the following terms: 'insofar as the international law of war confers rights upon soldiers and civilians as individuals, they continue to enjoy these rights even though acting in behalf of a State engaged in illegal hostilities.'[88] A similar claim was made by Georg Schwarzenberger in 1968 in the context of reprisals,[89] but he also qualified that reprisals against combatants and the civilian population could '*rarely, if ever, be advisable* . . . in view of the chain reaction of negative reciprocity'.[90] Thus, even those who suggested unequal application of IHL qualified it by discouraging such position. In addition, considering that the comments were made a long time ago and that such views did not receive wide support is sufficient evidence that the claim of unequal application of IHL to the conflicting parties, as a matter of legal doctrine, died out.

In fact, the equal application principle has been confirmed by various practices. The Preamble to the 1977 First Additional Protocol and common Article 1 of the 1949 Geneva Conventions, as similar to the principle of the separation between *jus ad bellum* and *jus in bello*, are by far the clearest expression of the equal application principle. In particular, the Preamble to the First Additional Protocol states as follows:

> [T]he provisions of the Geneva Conventions of 12 August 1949 and of this Protocol must be fully applied in all circumstances . . . without any adverse distinction based on the nature or origin of the armed conflict.[91]

The state practice in major armed conflicts since 1945 examined in the previous section confirmed that IHL has not been applied unequally to the conflicting parties depending on the legality of the use of force.[92]

[85] Wright, 'The Outlawry of War', 374.
[86] Q Wright, 'The Strengthening of International Law' (1959) 98 *Recueil des Cours de l'Académie de Droit International* 5, 154.
[87] Art 52(2) of the 1977 First Additional Protocol and Rule 8 in Henckaerts and Doswald-Beck, *Customary International Humanitarian Law* Vol I, 29.
[88] Wright, 'The Strengthening of International Law', 155.
[89] Schwarzenberger, *International Law*, 105. Reprisals against the civilian population is prohibited in Art 33 of the 1949 Fourth Geneva Convention, Art 51 (6) of the 1977 First Additional Protocol and Rule 146 in Henckaerts and Doswald-Beck, *Customary International Humanitarian Law* Vol I, 519.
[90] Schwarzenberger, *International Law*, 106.
[91] See also Sandoz et al (eds), *Commentary*, para 1928.
[92] See nn 55–68 above.

International tribunals such as the military tribunals related to the Second World War[93] also confirmed the equal application principle. More recently, the ICJ also confirmed this principle in the *Wall* and *Armed Activities* cases. In the *Wall* Advisory Opinion, the Court noted that 'the drafters of the Fourth Geneva Convention sought to guarantee the protection of civilians in time of war, regardless of the status of the occupied territories'.[94] The Court then stated that the 1949 Fourth Geneva Convention applied between Israel and Jordan in and after 1967 since they were both parties to it.[95] This meant that IHL (namely the Fourth Geneva Convention) applied equally to Israel and Jordan regardless of how the territories were occupied in terms of *jus ad bellum*.[96]

Further in the *Armed Activities* case in 2005, the ICJ only considered the violations of IHL by Uganda and thus, whether IHL applied equally between the Democratic Republic of the Congo (DRC) and Uganda was not explicitly recognised. However, Judge Simma argued that IHL also applied when the DRC troops maltreated Ugandan nationals and diplomats at the airport in Kinshasa.[97] The Court did not consider the violations of IHL by the DRC simply because Uganda did not make such a claim before the Court. However, Judge Simma's observation indicated that IHL applied equally between the DRC and Uganda.

In recent years, the equal application principle has also been recognised in other international fora. For example, the Eritrea–Ethiopia Claims Commission dealt with *jus ad bellum* and *jus in bello* issues arising from the Eritrea–Ethiopia Conflict. In the *Jus ad Bellum* Award, the Claims Commission concluded that Eritrea violated Article 2(4) of the UN Charter[98] but also found violations of IHL by both Eritrea and Ethiopia in many other awards.[99] This clearly indicates that whatever the legal status of the conflicting parties under *jus ad bellum*, IHL applies equally between them.

Besides the state practice and case law, the International Committee of the Red Cross (ICRC), as the guardian of IHL,[100] has most consistently

[93] See nn 42 and 43 above.

[94] *Wall* case (Advisory Opinion), para 95.

[95] *Wall* case (Advisory Opinion), para 101.

[96] See also *Wall* case (Advisory Opinion), Written Statements of Jordan, paras 5.56 and 5.80; League of Arab States, para 9.6; Palestine, para 396. The written statements can be found at the ICJ website, www.icj-cij.org.

[97] *Armed Activities* case (Merits), Separate Opinion of Judge Simma, para 17.

[98] *Jus ad Bellum* case (Partial Award), para 16; *Ethiopia's Damages Claims* (Final Award), para 271.

[99] Eritrea–Ethiopia Claims Commission, *Prisoners of War, Eritrea* case (Partial Award); *Central Front, Eritrea* case (Partial Award); *Civilians, Eritrea* case (Partial Award); *Western Front, Eritrea* case (Partial Award); *Western and Eastern Fronts, Ethiopia* case (Partial Award); *Eritrea's Damages Claims* (Final Award), paras 48–50, 289, 310, 316, 342, and 366; *Ethiopia's Damages Claims* (Final Award), paras 48–50, 207, and 215.

[100] See Art 5(2)(c) of the Statutes of the International Red Cross and Red Crescent Movement reads, in part, as follows: 'The role of the International Committee [of the Red Cross], in

been applying the equal application principle. For example, it noted that 'The principle of equality of belligerents underlies the law of armed conflict; in other words, as a matter of law, there can be no wars in which one side has all the rights and the other has none'.[101]

Likewise, an overwhelming majority of experts confirm the equal application principle.[102] For example, Henri Meyrowitz, who devoted a whole book on the equal application principle, begins his concluding chapter as follows:

> L'égalité des belligérants devant le *jus in bello* est un principe qui sous-tend le droit moderne de la guerre, principe qui allait tellement de soi qu'il n'avait pas besoin d'être formulé. Il est certain que ce principe est toujours solidement établi en droit positif.[103]

It is thus clear that the principle of the equal application of IHL to the conflicting parties is widely accepted. The rationale for upholding the principle was well formulated by François Bugnion:

> It is impossible to demand that an adversary respect the laws and customs of war while at the same time declaring that every one of its acts will be treated as a war crime because of the mere fact that the act was carried out in the context of a war of aggression . . . Hence, the principle of the equality of the belligerents before the laws and customs of war must be upheld.[104]

accordance with its Statutes, is in particular . . . to work for the faithful application of international humanitarian law applicable in armed conflicts'. See ICRC and the International Federation of Red Cross and Red Crescent Societies, *Handbook of the International Red Cross and Red Crescent* (Geneva, International Committee of the Red Cross and International Federation of Red Cross and Red Crescent Societies, 2009). The Statutes were adopted by the International Conference of the Red Cross in 1986 which consists of states parties to the 1949 Geneva Conventions, National Red Cross and Red Crescent Societies, International Federation of Red Cross and Red Crescent Societies, and ICRC.

[101] ICRC, 'International Humanitarian Law and the Challenges of Contemporary Armed Conflicts' Report prepared for the 28th International Conference of the Red Cross and Red Crescent, Geneva, 2–3 December 2003, 19.

[102] See n 47 above. See also F Seyersted, 'United Nations Forces: Some Legal Problems' (1961) 37 *British Year Book of International Law* 351, 474; International Law Association, 'Committee on the Charter of the United Nations' in International Law Association Report of the Fiftieth Conference (International Law Association, Brussels 1962) 157, 160; M Bothe, 'Le droit de la guerre et les Nations Unies' (1967) 5 *Études et travaux de l'Institut Universitaire de Hautes Études Internationales* 135; Doswald-Beck (ed), *San Remo Manual*, Art 6; T Franck, *Fairness in International Law and Institutions* (Oxford, Clarendon Press, 1995) 275; C Greenwood, 'Historical Development and Legal Basis' in D Fleck (ed), *The Handbook of Humanitarian Law in Armed Conflicts* (Oxford, Oxford University Press, 1995) 7; Y Dinstein, *The Conduct of Hostilities under the Law of International Armed Conflict* (Cambridge, Cambridge University Press, 2004) 4.

[103] Meyrowitz, *Le principe*, 400. 'The equality of the belligerents before *jus in bello* is a principle that underlies the modern law of war, principle that had been so self-evident that it did not need to be formulated. It is certain that the principle has always been firmly established in positive law.' Translated by the author.

[104] Bugnion, 'Just Wars', 538.

In practice, the equal application principle means that the aggressor and the victim state have the same rights and obligations in the course of their conduct of hostilities against each other, and combatants of both sides will not be tried for their lawful conduct of hostilities within the meaning of IHL. However, at the same time, all combatants of both sides can be tried for violations of IHL. Similarly, both the aggressor and the victim state incur state responsibility for violations of IHL.[105]

More specifically, combatants of the aggressor state can, for example, directly participate in hostilities lawfully and can lawfully attack military objectives.[106] In terms of IHL, lawful conduct of hostilities of the aggressor state does not become unlawful just because it has violated *jus ad bellum*. At the same time, the aggressor state should implement the obligations under IHL, for example by treating prisoners of war of the victim state humanely according to the 1949 Third Geneva Convention and accepting visits of the ICRC to prisoners of war.[107] In terms of IHL, it is not as if the aggressor state can disregard all the obligations under IHL simply because it has violated *jus ad bellum*. Thus if, for example, the combatants of the aggressor state attack civilians or mistreat prisoners of war, they can be tried for war crimes.

With regard to the combatants of the victim state, it also has, for example, the same rights to directly participate in hostilities and lawfully attack military objectives. The victim state cannot deny such rights of the aggressor state to directly participate in hostilities and to attack military objectives. The victim state should also, for example, treat prisoners of war of the aggressor state humanely and accept visits of the ICRC in accordance with the 1949 Third Geneva Convention. Combatants of the victim state can be tried for war crimes if they commit violations of IHL. It is not as if they are absolved from any war crimes prosecution simply because they belong to the victim state. Moreover, the victim state cannot try combatants from the aggressor state for their lawful conduct of hostilities consistent with IHL. This is an obvious consequence of the equal application of IHL where even the combatants of the aggressor state have the right to directly participate in hostilities.

It is worth noting at this point that the principle of the equal application has been discussed almost exclusively in the context of whether combatants of the illegal party would benefit from the protection of *jus in bello* when they are wounded, sick, shipwrecked, or held as prisoners of war. The widely accepted response, as seen above, is that the combatants of the illegal party would benefit from the protection of *jus in bello*, or otherwise it would degenerate into a brutal and unregulated warfare. However, IHL in fact consists of a variety of other rules covering civilians, medi-

[105] See section 2.I.B above.
[106] Arts 43 and 52(2) of the 1977 First Additional Protocol.
[107] The 1949 Third Geneva Convention and Arts 13 and 126 therein in particular.

cal and religious personnel, and methods and means of warfare. Hence, questions could be asked by analogy: Are civilians belonging to the illegal party protected by *jus in bello*? Are medical and religious personnel of the illegal party protected? Are prohibition on methods and means of warfare equally applicable to the illegal party? If indeed the principle of the equal application is to preserve the purpose of IHL, which is to protect or alleviate the suffering of the individuals not participating in hostilities during an armed conflict, then the response to these questions must all be positive. A negative response will be directly contrary to the purpose of IHL, since civilians of the illegal party could be massacred with impunity whereas the civilians of the lawful party must be protected. Likewise, medical and religious personnel of the illegal party could be targeted and prohibited methods and means of warfare could be used against the illegal party, all with impunity. Hence, the principle of the equal application is valid in relation to all IHL rules.

However, it is also true that some flexibility is necessary in applying the principle of the equal application. For example, the obligations relating to occupying power are clearly applicable only to the occupying power and not to the occupied state. This, nevertheless, must not be construed as compromising the equal application principle. Occupation is a situation in an armed conflict that necessitates the occupying power to succeed obligations normally undertaken by the occupied state (as opposed to a combat between two states in the battlefield) and hence, specific regulations concerning the occupying power are necessary. Moreover, both conflicting parties could find themselves as an occupying power in the same armed conflict, in which case the parties must comply with the law of occupation in the respective territories they have occupied (a case in point is the Eritrea–Ethiopia Conflict).[108]

Similarly, in non-international armed conflict, the rules relating to judicial guarantees are normally applicable only to courts officially constituted by the parliament or the government.[109] A question can also be asked whether a party using force under Chapter VII of the UN Charter and the aggressor are equally bound by IHL.[110] While it may be logical to extend the principles to these situations, this book will examine these issues in detail throughout the book.

[108] Eritrea–Ethiopia Claims Commission, *Central Front, Ethiopia* case (Partial Award), paras 52, 70, and 73(4); *Central Front, Eritrea* case (Partial Award), paras 78, 93–105, 113, and 114; *Western Front, Eritrea* case (Partial Award), para 141.

[109] See section 5.I.B below.

[110] See section 4.IV below.

D. Principle of the Concurrent Application of *Jus ad Bellum* and *Jus in Bello*

The third principle governing the relationship between *jus ad bellum* and *jus in bello* is the concurrent application of *jus ad bellum* and *jus in bello*. This has two legal implications: 1) *jus ad bellum* and *jus in bello* are applicable at the same time, and not one after the other; and 2) the two can be complementary, and not simply mutually exclusive, self-contained legal regimes that never have an intersection.

The first principle discussed above confirmed the separation between *jus ad bellum* and *jus in bello* but this does not mean that they are applied one after the other in a sequence. To the contrary, *jus ad bellum* and *jus in bello* can be kept separate but be applied side by side at the same time, provided that the thresholds of the application of *jus ad bellum* and *jus in bello* are met.[111]

The concurrent application of *jus ad bellum* and *jus in bello* has been recognised in a majority of practice and the contrary position that *jus in bello* completely supersedes *jus ad bellum* is not held by many.[112] The latter position was particularly relevant in the pre-UN Charter era when 'war' was the common threshold of application for *jus ad bellum* and *jus in bello*.[113] Thus, violation of *jus ad bellum* was determined by establishing whether a state had resorted to 'war' or made a declaration of war, and that was also the end of the application of *jus ad bellum*. From there on, the situation was exclusively regulated by IHL.

However, even in the pre-UN Charter era, *jus ad bellum* was not only confined to the prohibition of war but also regulated the conduct of hostilities thereafter, particularly by the customary international law principles of proportionality and necessity, when the use of force was in self-defence.[114]

[111] See section 3.I and section 4.II.C.

[112] See, eg, I Scobbie, 'Words My Mother Never Taught Me: "In Defense of the International Court"' (2005) 99 *American Journal of International Law* 76, 84. See generally W Meng, 'War' in R Bernhardt (ed), *Encyclopaedia of Public International Law* Vol IV (Amsterdam, Elsevier Science BV, 2000) 1334.

[113] For an indication that 'war' was the threshold of application of *jus ad bellum*, see Art 16 of the Covenant of the League of Nations (adopted 28 April 1919, entered into force 10 January 1920) 225 CTS 188; Art I of the Pact of Paris on the Renunciation of War as an Instrument of National Policy (adopted 27 August 1928, entered into force 24 July 1929) 94 LNTS 57; Art 1 of the Convention (III) Relative to the Opening of Hostilities (adopted 18 October 1907, entered into force 26 January 1910) 205 CTS 264.

For *jus in bello*, see the Declaration Renouncing the Use, in Time of War, of Explosive Projectiles under 400 Grammes Weight (adopted and entered into force 11 December 1868) 138 CTS 297; Art 2 of the Convention (II) with Respect to the Laws and Customs of War on Land and Its Annex: Regulations concerning the Laws and Customs of War on Land (adopted 29 July 1899, entered into force 4 September 1900) 187 CTS 429.

[114] There is little practice on the principles of proportionality and necessity in self-defence in the pre-UN Charter era but certain evidence can be identified such as the Caroline incident in 1837. See generally 'Destruction of the "Caroline"' (1906) 2 *Digest of International Law* 409

Thus, the position that the conduct of hostilities is exclusively regulated by IHL after the commencement of 'war' was not sustainable even before the pre-UN Charter era. As will be seen below, this has not changed even after the threshold of application of *jus ad bellum* shifted to 'armed attack' and 'threat to the peace, breach of the peace, or act of aggression', and that of *jus in bello* to 'armed conflict'.

The concurrent application of *jus ad bellum* and *jus in bello*, particularly the regulation of the use of force by both IHL and the principles of proportionality and necessity in the law of self-defence has been widely supported in various practices since 1945. It has already been seen that the state practice in major international armed conflicts, case law of the war crimes trials on the Second World War, and case law of other international courts and arbitrations after 1945 applied both *jus ad bellum* and *jus in bello* simultaneously.[115] These in themselves confirm the concurrent application of the two legal regimes.

However, in ICJ cases in particular, the concurrent application was recognised explicitly and repeatedly. First, the Court made an important statement in the *Nuclear Weapons* Advisory Opinion, recognising the concurrent application of IHL and the principle of proportionality in the law of self-defence:

> A use of force that is proportionate under the law of self-defence, must, in order to be lawful, also meet the requirements of the law applicable in armed conflict which comprise in particular the principles and rules of humanitarian law.[116]

This position was shared by Iran[117] and Judge Koroma in the same case.[118]

The ICJ's approach in the *Nuclear Weapons* Advisory Opinion was followed in subsequent cases. In the *Oil Platforms* case in 2003, the US justified its use of force in self-defence as proportionate and in compliance

and R Jennings, 'The Caroline and McLeod Cases' (1938) 32 *American Journal of International Law* 82. See also statements recognising the Caroline incident as the source of the customary principles: Iraq, UNSC Verbatim Record (15 October 1980) UN Doc S/PV.2250, para 40; *Armed Activities* case (Merits), Reply of the DRC, para 3.159. The written proceedings can be found at the ICJ website, www.icj-cij.org.

For cautions on the over-reliance on the Caroline incident as a source of the principles of proportionality and necessity, see I Brownlie, 'The Use of Force in Self-Defence' (1961) 37 *British Year Book of International Law* 183, 265–66; C Gray, *International Law and the Use of Force*, 120–21; Dinstein, *War, Aggression and Self-Defence*, 249; J Green, *The International Court of Justice and Self-Defence in International Law* (Oxford, Hart Publishing, 2009) 64 *ff*. Schachter notes as follows: 'It cannot be said that the formulation [by the US Secretary of State in the Caroline incident on self-defence] reflects State practice'. See O Schachter, *International Law in Theory and Practice* (Dordrecht, Martinus Nijhoff, 1991) 151.

[115] See sections 2.II.B and C above.

[116] *Nuclear Weapons* case (Advisory Opinion), para 42.

[117] *Nuclear Weapons* case (Advisory Opinion), Oral Statement of Iran, 6 November 1995, para 28. The oral statements can be found at the ICJ website, www.icj-cij.org.

[118] *Nuclear Weapons* case (Advisory Opinion), Dissenting Opinion of Judge Koroma.

with IHL.[119] The following year in the *Wall* case in 2004, Malaysia stated as follows:

> Even if assuming that Israel can justifiably call on an international right of self-defence, any use of force in alleged self-defence has to meet the criteria of necessity and proportionality . . . Furthermore, it is widely acknowledged that a lawful exercise of the right to self-defence requires observance of the principles and rules of international humanitarian law.[120]

In the *Armed Activities* case in 2005, Uganda and the DRC heavily argued on the proportionality of the use of force by Uganda and violations of IHL by Uganda, both in relation to the same period of concern.[121] The ICJ also ruled that the use of force by Uganda was not proportionate and found numerous violations of IHL, both in relation to the same period of concern.[122] These practices in the ICJ clearly gave prominence to the concurrent application of *jus ad bellum* and *jus in bello* and the complementary role between *jus ad bellum* and *jus in bello*.

A small number of experts have also explicitly recognised the concurrent application of *jus ad bellum* and *jus in bello*. For example, Christopher Greenwood explained in the following terms:

> The fact that a particular action might be considered a necessary and proportionate act of self-defence cannot justify it if it is contrary to the laws of war but the fact that a particular use of force does not contravene the laws of war no longer suffices to make it lawful if it fails to meet the criteria of being necessary and proportionate for the achievement of the goals of self-defence, the discharge of a Security Council mandate, the exercise of an authority granted by the Security Council or, perhaps, some other goal for which the use of force may be permitted by international law.[123]

The potential strength of the dual constraints of *jus ad bellum* and *jus in bello* was emphasised by this expert.[124]

As shown above, the concurrent application of *jus ad bellum* and *jus in bello* is widely supported. This is understandable since the principles of proportionality and necessity in *jus ad bellum* are aimed at regulating the conduct of hostilities even after the victim state has commenced its action

[119] *Oil Platforms* case (Merits), Counter-Memorial of the US, para 4.01. The written proceedings can be found at the ICJ website, www.icj-cij.org.

[120] *Wall* case, Written Statement of Malaysia, para 150. See also Written Statements of Saudi Arabia, para 31; League of Arab States, para 9.6; Switzerland, para 27. The written statements can be found at the ICJ website, www.icj-cij.org.

[121] *Armed Activities* case (Merits), Rejoinder of Uganda, 119–26 and 245 *ff*; Reply of the DRC, 237–46 and 313 *ff*; Memorial of the DRC, 187 *ff*. The written statements can be found at the ICJ website, www.icj-cij.org.

[122] *Armed Activities* case (Merits), paras 147 and 205 *ff*.

[123] Greenwood, 'International Humanitarian Law', 184. See also Sandoz et al (eds), *Commentary*, para 3598; J Gardam, *Necessity, Proportionality and the Use of Force* (Cambridge, Cambridge University Press, 2004) 168–69.

[124] Greenwood, 'International Humanitarian Law', 184–86; Gardam, *Necessity*, 169 *ff*.

in self-defence. If such a case of self-defence amounts to an armed conflict, IHL also applies alongside the principles of proportionality and necessity in *jus ad bellum*.

If one accepts that *jus ad bellum* and *jus in bello* are concurrently applicable, it can pave the way to a more positive understanding of the relationship, namely to a relationship which is mutually complementary where *jus ad bellum* covers the gap in *jus in bello* and vice versa. It can be said that the concentration of discussion on the separation of the two has obscured the potentially positive aspect of the relationship. An example is the principle of proportionality in the law of self-defence and IHL. The scope of the principle of proportionality in the law of self-defence is broad and could be a constraint on the selection of targets and the amount of civilian casualties that can be tolerated as well as temporal and geographical extent of self-defence measures. On the other hand, the law of means and methods of warfare in IHL is more detailed and imposes substantial constraints on the conduct of self-defence by regulating which weapons can be used and how lawful weapons can be used. The complementary nature of the law of self-defence and IHL[125] and that of Chapter VII and IHL[126] will be discussed later.

At the same time, the concurrent application of *jus ad bellum* and *jus in bello* could lead to a confusion of similar concepts in the two legal regimes. The practical consequences of such confusions are that they unnecessarily blur the distinction between *jus ad bellum* and *jus in bello* and can be used as a pretext to choose the legal regime which best suits one's interest. For example, in the arguments relating to the wall in the Occupied Palestinian Territory, the principle of necessity in *jus ad bellum* and military necessity in IHL were often confused. As will be seen more in detail later,[127] the principle of necessity in *jus ad bellum* permits a wider scope of action in self-defence than military necessity in IHL. Thus, a state might resort to the principle of necessity in *jus ad bellum* to set aside IHL obligations and allow it to take a wider military action.[128]

Finally, it is worth noting that the concurrent application of *jus ad bellum* and *jus in bello* has the most bearing on the conduct of hostilities of the state using force lawfully under *jus ad bellum*, namely the state using force in self-defence. In practice, this means that the victim state is bound by the principles of proportionality and necessity on top of IHL, while the aggressor is only bound by IHL. At first glance, it seems that the victim state is constrained by too many obligations when it is attempting to remove the unlawful use of force by the aggressor, but as the state practice

[125] See ch 3.
[126] See sections 4.IV and 4.V.
[127] See section 3.III.
[128] For the potential danger of this approach, see *Wall* case, Written Statement of Palestine, para 534. The written statements can be found at the ICJ website, www.icj-cij.org.

shows, states have accepted the obligations under IHL regardless of their status under *jus ad bellum*.[129] Lassa Oppenheim noted that 'it is these rules [IHL] which, on the whole, have been generally observed in the past – for the reason perhaps that they do not seriously interfere with the achievement of the major purpose of the war'.[130] The aim of the additional constraints in *jus ad bellum*, on top of IHL, is not to obstruct the states using force lawfully to fulfil its objectives to defend their states or to maintain international peace and security, but to avoid giving a blanket title to use force, which may then degenerate into an endless total war.[131]

Moreover, it must not be forgotten that the aggressors are subject to various measures under public international law, such as the suspension of the rights and privileges under the UN Charter,[132] expulsion from UN membership,[133] military enforcement measures (such as the use of force under Chapter VII),[134] non-military enforcement measures (such as economic sanctions and arms embargoes),[135] and state responsibility (such as reparation).[136] Hence, while it may be true that the victim state appears to be bound by more rules than the aggressor if one takes only the conduct of hostilities during self-defence, in fact the aggressor state is, at the same time, subject to various sanctions if one looks from a wider perspective of public international law, which counter-balance the constraints faced by the victim state.

E. Relationship among the Three Principles

These three principles are not independent but interrelated. The three principles, when applied together, would ensure the proper application of *jus ad bellum* and *jus in bello*.

First, the separation between *jus ad bellum* and *jus in bello* underlies the equal application of IHL to the conflicting parties. If it is not recognised that IHL operates independently from *jus ad bellum*, it leaves the possibility that *jus ad bellum* can override *jus in bello* by claiming that an illegal party under *jus ad bellum* does not benefit from the protection for victims of armed conflict under *jus in bello*. By separating *jus ad bellum* and *jus in bello*, and by recognising the independence of each legal regime, it excludes such claims.

129 See nn 55–68 above.
130 Lauterpacht (ed), *International Law*, 218.
131 See sections 3.II and 3.III for the scope of the principles of proportionality and necessity in the law of self-defence and section 4.IV.B for the scope of *jus ad bellum* constraints on Chapter VII use of force.
132 Art 5 of the UN Charter.
133 Art 6 of the UN Charter.
134 Art 42 of the UN Charter.
135 Art 41 of the UN Charter.
136 Arts 38–41 of the ILC Articles on State Responsibility.

Excluding the claim that *jus ad bellum* can override *jus in bello* is necessary but not sufficient to ensure the proper application of *jus ad bellum* and *jus in bello*. While the principle of the separation ensures the independence of each legal regime, it does not ensure how the law is applied. In fact, what is of concern here is not the proper application of *jus ad bellum* but rather that of *jus in bello*. *Jus ad bellum* inevitably creates an unequal relationship between an illegal party (violator of *jus ad bellum*) and a party using force lawfully (self-defence or under Chapter VII). *Jus in bello* operates in totally the opposite way. In other words, it does not create illegal and legal parties to the conflict, but only concerns the protection of all individuals who no longer take part in hostilities during an armed conflict. The risk is hence on *jus in bello* since it might be applied unequally between illegal and legal parties to the conflict. This is why the principle of the equal application of *jus in bello* to the conflicting parties requires explicit recognition to prevent such a claim. However, for *jus in bello* to be applied equally to the conflicting parties, it is first and foremost necessary to separate *jus ad bellum* and *jus in bello*, and exclude any influence of *jus ad bellum* on *jus in bello*. Only then can *jus in bello* be applied equally to the conflicting parties.

At the same time, the separation between *jus ad bellum* and *jus in bello* does not mean that they cannot be applied at the same time. The two legal regimes can be separate but applied concurrently. However, when *jus ad bellum* and *jus in bello* are applied concurrently, the separation principle prevents the two from being confused and preserves the proper application of the respective legal regime, and especially the proper application of *jus in bello*. The concurrent application hence does not mean 'mixing' of *jus ad bellum* and *jus in bello* rules, but rather means application of the two side by side. Certain issues (such as the use of force in self-defence) can be regulated by *jus ad bellum* and *jus in bello* at the same time, but the issues are always dealt with separately from the perspective of *jus ad bellum* and *jus in bello*.

III. THREE PRINCIPLES IN CONTEXTS OTHER THAN THE USE OF FORCE IN SELF-DEFENCE

As noted in the previous sections, the relationship between *jus ad bellum* and *jus in bello* has been discussed mostly in the context of the application of the law of international armed conflict (IHL applicable in international armed conflict) during the use of force in self-defence. The main question here was whether the illegal party to the conflict, in terms of *jus ad bellum*, still benefited from the protection of IHL. More precisely, the question was whether the combatants of the illegal party to the conflict benefited from the protection for victims of armed conflict in IHL, when they were wounded, sick, shipwrecked, or held as prisoners of war. Admittedly, even with regard to the relationship between the law of self-defence and the law of international armed conflict, there are still unclear areas such as the relationship between the principle of proportionality in *jus ad bellum* and IHL. This book therefore discusses the remaining issues on the relationship between the law of self-defence and IHL.

However, *jus ad bellum* and *jus in bello* are not only about self-defence and international armed conflict. *Jus ad bellum* also consists of the prohibition on the use of force and the other exception to it besides the right of self-defence, the use of force under Chapter VII of the UN Charter. *Jus in bello* also regulates non-international armed conflict, and not only international armed conflict. In order to fully understand the relationship between *jus ad bellum* and *jus in bello*, these areas should also be examined. They pose issues of a very different nature compared to the relationship between the law of self-defence and the law of international armed conflict. Therefore, in this section, a brief problem analysis will be presented on four particular subjects that merit attention: threshold of application of *jus ad bellum* and *jus in bello*, IHL and the use of force under Chapter VII of the UN Charter, non-international armed conflict, and armed conflict of a mixed character. Detailed discussions on these topics will be presented in the subsequent chapters of this book.

A. Threshold of Application of *Jus ad Bellum* and *Jus in Bello*

By 'threshold of application', it means the act that triggers the application of *jus ad bellum* or *jus in bello*. In *jus ad bellum*, there are three thresholds of application:

1) use of force (*jus ad bellum* prohibits the 'use of force' between states);[137]
2) armed attack (*jus ad bellum* permits the use of force in self-defence if an 'armed attack' occurs);[138]
3) threat to the peace, breach of the peace, or act of aggression (*jus ad bellum* permits the use of force under Chapter VII of the UN Charter when the UN Security Council determines the existence of a 'threat to the peace, breach of the peace, or act of aggression').[139]

On the other hand, *jus in bello* has two thresholds of application:

1) international armed conflict (IHL applies to an armed conflict between two or more states, including cases of occupation);[140]

[137] Art 2(4) of the UN Charter. For its status as a rule of customary international law, see n 6 above.

[138] Art 51 of the UN Charter. For its status as a rule of customary international law, see n 7 above.

[139] Art 39 of the UN Charter.

[140] Common Art 2 of the 1949 Geneva Conventions.

2) non-international armed conflict (IHL applies to an armed conflict between a state's armed forces and armed groups, or between different armed groups).[141]

The relationship between the thresholds of application needs to be understood in order to understand when *jus ad bellum* and *jus in bello* apply concurrently. Only then can the interaction between the two legal regimes in a particular use of force be discussed.

Understanding the thresholds of application in the two legal regimes has also a subsidiary purpose: to clarify the distinction between the thresholds of application in *jus ad bellum* and *jus in bello*. The thresholds of application of the two legal regimes are often confused since the terms are sometimes similar (such as 'armed attack' and 'armed conflict') but since they are legal concepts with special meaning, they need to be clearly distinguished in order to ensure proper application of *jus ad bellum* and *jus in bello*.

B. Use of Force under Chapter VII of the UN Charter

The Security Council, as the main actor applying Chapter VII of the UN Charter and entrusted to maintain international peace and security, has been applying IHL in different contexts, but the relationship between Chapter VII and IHL has not been clarified to the fullest extent. In order to fully understand this relationship, the discussions need to be separated into four: 1) whether Chapter VII decisions can derogate from IHL pursuant to Article 103 of the UN Charter; 2) how IHL has been invoked by the Security Council in its resolutions; 3) how the use of force under Chapter VII is regulated by *jus ad bellum* and *jus in bello*; and 4) how Chapter VII decisions and IHL can be in conflict or be complementary.

Among these topics, 1) and 3) pose particular problems in relation to the three principles governing the relationship between *jus ad bellum* and *jus in bello*. For example, the principle of the separation between *jus ad bellum* and *jus in bello* faces problems of a different nature from self-defence and IHL. In the case of Chapter VII decisions, they qualify under Article 103 of the UN Charter as obligations under the UN Charter that prevail over obligations under international agreements other than the UN Charter, when there is a conflict between the two kinds of obligations. This leaves room for Chapter VII decisions to override IHL. The nature of the issue is different from the relationship between the law of self-defence and IHL since in the case of self-defence, there is no hierarchy between the law of self-defence and IHL. However, in the case of Chapter VII decisions,

[141] See common Art 3 of the 1949 Geneva Conventions and Art 1(1) of the 1977 Second Additional Protocol.

Article 103 of the UN Charter comes into play, which clearly puts hierarchy between UN Charter obligations and IHL obligations in the event of a conflict between the two. A recent case was whether Security Council resolution 1483, which dealt with the aftermath of the 2003 US/UK–Iraq Conflict, superseded parts of the law of occupation in IHL.[142]

The principle of the equal application of *jus in bello* also faces particular problems in the context of the use of force under Chapter VII. For example, the issue of whether IHL applies equally to UN peacekeeping forces or states authorised to use force under Chapter VII on one hand, and their adversaries on the other, has been an issue for a long time. In the past, the Institute of International Law adopted a resolution in 1963 which included the following paragraph:

> [T]here cannot be complete equality in the application of the rules of the law of war when the competent organ of the United Nations has determined that one of the belligerents has resorted to armed force in violation of the rules of the law of nation consecrated by the Charter of the United Nations.[143]

If, for example, IHL applies more advantageously to UN forces in relation to a state's armed forces or armed groups, it would be difficult to expect the latter to comply with the full spectrum of applicable IHL rules. As it will be seen in a later chapter, it is now accepted that in principle, IHL applies equally to Security Council authorised forces and their adversaries. However, during the application of IHL to the conduct of Security Council authorised forces, practical problems arise. For example, do the obligations on an occupying power in IHL apply to Security Council authorised forces when they are only given limited mandates and means by the Security Council? Could members of UN peacekeeping forces be considered prisoners of war when they are captured by a state's armed forces? These are some of the practical questions that arise in relation to an armed conflict involving Security Council authorised forces.

The principle of the concurrent application of *jus ad bellum* and *jus in bello* also plays a different role in the relationship between Chapter VII and IHL. In the case of the law of self-defence and IHL, the concurrent application would mean that the principles of proportionality and necessity in *jus ad bellum* as well as IHL rules on means and methods of warfare in particular regulate the use of force in self-defence. In the case of Chapter VII and IHL, the concurrent application would mean that Chapter VII resolutions authorising the use of force and IHL regulate the use of force under

[142] See, eg, K Dörmann and L Colassis, 'International Humanitarian Law in the Iraq Conflict' (2004) 47 *German Yearbook of International Law* 293; M Zwanenburg, 'Existentialism in Iraq: Security Council Resolution 1483 and the Law of Occupation' (2004) 856 *International Review of the Red Cross* 745; A Roberts, 'Transformative Military Occupation: Applying the Law of War and Human Rights' (2006) 100 *American Journal of International Law* 580.

[143] Institute of International Law, 'Equality of Application of the Rules of the Law of War to Parties to an Armed Conflict' (1963) 50–II *Annuaire de l'Institut de Droit International* 376.

Chapter VII. Moreover, Chapter VII enforcement actions could enforce parts of IHL, for example by protecting civilians in a non-international armed conflict. It is worth noting that Chapter VII can deal with both international and non-international armed conflict by authorising the use of force against states or armed groups. Hence, while the law of self-defence is most of the time concurrently applicable with the law of international armed conflict, Chapter VII can be applied concurrently with both the law of international and non-international armed conflict.

At the same time, the concurrent application of Chapter VII decisions and IHL can also lead to a confusion of similar concepts in the two legal regimes. The confusion between 'safe areas' under Chapter VII decisions and localities and zones under special protection in IHL was said to be partly the reason for the failure of the UN in Srebrenica that led to genocide during the 1992–95 conflict in Bosnia-Herzegovina.[144]

C. Non-international Armed Conflict

As noted above, the relationship between *jus ad bellum* and *jus in bello* has been discussed mostly in the context of the use of force in self-defence and international armed conflict. The relevance of the three principles governing the relationship between *jus ad bellum* and *jus in bello* in the context of non-international armed conflict has scarcely been discussed.

Non-international armed conflict is a term used in the context of IHL to signify an armed conflict between a state's armed forces and armed groups, or between different armed groups. However, in recent years, foreign forces have become involved in non-international armed conflict, which adds an international character to non-international armed conflict. This type of armed conflict is sometimes termed as 'internationalised non-international armed conflict',[145] which raises a number of issues with regard to the applicability of *jus ad bellum* and *jus in bello*.

The use of force in self-defence most often takes place between two states and in terms of IHL, this would most likely amount to an international armed conflict. However, if one accepts the position that an 'armed attack', the trigger to exercise the right of self-defence, can come from a

[144] See section 4.IV.D. The ICTY concluded that the events in Srebrenica were genocide. See *Krstic Case* (Judgment, Trial) ICTY-98-33-T (2 August 2001), para 599; *Krstic Case* (Judgment, Appeals) ICTY-IT-98-33-A (19 April 2004), para 38. The ICJ concluded that the events in Srebrenica were a violation by Serbia of the obligation to prevent genocide under the 1948 Genocide Convention. See *Application of the Convention on the Prevention and Punishment of the Crime of Genocide* (*Bosnia-Herzegovina v Serbia and Montenegro*) (Merits), para 471(5). The judgment is currently available at the ICJ website, www.icj-cij.org. Convention on the Prevention and Punishment of the Crime of Genocide (adopted 9 December 1948, entered into force 12 January 1951) 78 UNTS 277.

[145] See section 5.II.A.

non-state actor in one state against another state, then the conflict will be between a state and a non-state actor, which resembles a non-international armed conflict. If the non-state actor is supported by a state, self-defence may be employed against it since an armed attack from such a non-state actor will be considered as an attack from a state. However, self-defence against an armed attack from a non-state actor without any support from a state is still controversial. In either case, the level of support to the non-state actors is the crucial factor in determining whether self-defence could be employed or not. However, since the determination of the level of support heavily depends on facts, one can expect great difficulties in determining whether a state was entitled to employ self-defence against the non-state actor.

Non-international armed conflict involving foreign intervention can also raise problems regarding the applicability of IHL. As noted earlier, Chapter VII can deal with situations that are essentially within the domain of one state, including non-international armed conflict. There are countless cases in which the Security Council adopted resolutions under Chapter VII in relation to non-international armed conflicts, and in some cases, authorised the use of force. Such use of force normally took the form of peacekeeping forces that would be deployed in an already existing non-international armed conflict to keep the conflicting parties apart. However, in some cases, UN peacekeeping forces were dragged into the non-international armed conflict, to which they were originally not a party but became a party as they repeated combat with the original parties to the non-international armed conflict. This has raised questions as to the character of the armed conflict. Since IHL does not envisage the involvement of international organisations in an armed conflict, it is difficult to categorise a conflict between UN peacekeeping forces and armed groups as either international or non-international armed conflict. Hence, the applicable rules of IHL are also unclear in such types of armed conflict.

Non-international armed conflict also poses another particular problem regarding the principle of the equal application of *jus in bello*. In a non-international armed conflict, there is an inherent inequality between the government and armed groups opposing the established government, not in terms of *jus ad bellum*, but in terms of national law. Members of armed groups are normally considered as criminals under the criminal code of the country, whereas the government is lawfully enforcing the national law to maintain the security of the country. IHL applies alongside national law that creates such inequality between the conflicting parties. The question here is not whether the inequality created by *jus ad bellum* can also oblige IHL to be applied unequally, but whether national law could be the basis for the unequal application of IHL. The nature of the problem is nevertheless the same: whether the legality of the use of force can render the application of IHL in a discriminatory manner towards the illegal party.

D. Armed Conflict of a Mixed Character

Perhaps the most concerning trend in recent years that *jus ad bellum* and *jus in bello* face is the mixture of different types of armed conflict in one context. As mentioned earlier, IHL recognises two types of armed conflict: international and non-international armed conflict. To this, one may add so-called 'internationalised non-international armed conflict', which is a non-international armed conflict involving foreign intervention (by states or armed groups). As a matter of law, they can be distinguished neatly. However, in practice, several or all of these types of armed conflict could exist at the same time in one context (mixed armed conflict). A prime example is the eastern DRC where international, non-international, and internationalised non-international armed conflict all existed at the same time among numerous armed groups, states' armed forces, and UN peacekeeping forces. The applicable rules of IHL are different depending on the type of armed conflict and hence, when different types of armed conflict exist at the same time in one context, it is first difficult to distinguish which parties are involved in which type of armed conflict, and then to determine which rules of IHL are applicable to which conflicting parties. The legal complexity of a mixed armed conflict was well demonstrated in the *Tadic* case in the International Criminal Tribunal for the former Yugoslavia (ICTY).[146]

The same can be said for *jus ad bellum*. When different types of armed conflict with different types of actor are ongoing in a single context, it is difficult to establish the existence of the use of force and an armed attack, and to identify who is taking self-defence measures against whom and who should be complying with the principles of necessity and proportionality.

In practical terms, the compliance with the law by the conflicting parties becomes extremely difficult since the application of *jus ad bellum* and *jus in bello* is overly complicated.

IV. CONCLUSIONS

The discussions above clarified that the separation between *jus ad bellum* and *jus in bello* and the equal application of *jus in bello* to the conflicting parties are two principles that are universally accepted and deeply rooted in the practice of *jus ad bellum* and *jus in bello*, principally to preserve the

[146] *Tadic Case* (Jurisdiction, Appeals Chamber) ICTY-IT-94-1 (2 October 1995), para 77. For a contrasting view on this subject see T Meron, 'International Criminalization of Internal Atrocities' (1995) 89 *American Journal of International Law* 554 and C Greenwood, 'International Humanitarian Law and the *Tadic* Case' (1996) 7 *European Journal of International Law* 265.

purpose of IHL, which is to protect and assist all victims of armed conflict equally solely on the basis of humanitarian consideration. To these two principles, one can now add the principle that *jus ad bellum* and *jus in bello* apply concurrently, and not one after the other, which could potentially strengthen the regulation of the use of force by combining the two legal regimes.

The above discussions also clarified that the past discussions on the relationship between *jus ad bellum* and *jus in bello* centred on self-defence and international armed conflict. However, *jus ad bellum* consists also of the prohibition on the use of force and use of force under Chapter VII of the UN Charter. Likewise, *jus in bello* consists not only of rules applicable to international armed conflict but also those applicable to non-international armed conflict. Without discussing whether the three principles are equally valid in these contexts of a very different nature, the relationship between *jus ad bellum* and *jus in bello* cannot be fully understood. Therefore, the following chapters will discuss the relationship between *jus ad bellum* and *jus in bello* in three different contexts: 1) distinction and relationship between the law of self-defence and IHL; 2) distinction and relationship bextween Chapter VII and IHL; and 3) *jus ad bellum* and *jus in bello* in non-international armed conflict and mixed armed conflict.

3

Distinction and Relationship between the Law of Self-defence and IHL

THE PAST DISCUSSIONS on the relationship between *jus ad bellum* and *jus in bello* were mostly in the context of self-defence and international armed conflict. In tracing back the origins of the three principles governing the relationship between *jus ad bellum* and *jus in bello*, the previous chapter discussed to some extent the distinction and relationship between the law of self-defence and the law of international armed conflict. However, there were issues that were not discussed in the previous chapter, namely the distinction and relationship between the thresholds of application of 'armed attack' and 'armed conflict', the role of the principle of proportionality and IHL in the conduct of self-defence, the principle of necessity in *jus ad bellum* and *jus in bello*, and reprisals in *jus ad bellum* and *jus in bello*. The question on reprisals is located in this chapter since it naturally has a close relation to self-defence.

I. 'ARMED ATTACK' AND 'ARMED CONFLICT'[1]

A. Distinction and Relationship between 'Armed Attack' and 'Armed Conflict'

Before discussing the role of the law of self-defence and IHL during the use of force in self-defence, it is crucial to understand when the law of self-defence and IHL apply at the same time. For this purpose, it is essential to be clear with what triggers the application of the law of self-defence and IHL.

As noted briefly in the previous chapter, an 'armed attack' against a state triggers the right of self-defence of the attacked state and the principles of proportionality and necessity, which will be discussed more in

[1] See generally I Brownlie, *International Law and the Use of Force by States* (Oxford, Clarendon Press, 1963) 384 *ff*; D Schindler, 'State of War, Belligerency, Armed Conflict' in A Cassese (ed), *The New Humanitarian Law of Armed Conflict* (Napoli, Editoriale Scientifica, 1979); C Greenwood, 'The Concept of War in Modern International Law' (1987) 36 *International and Comparative Law Quarterly* 283.

the later sections, regulate the conduct of self-defence. On the other hand, the existence of an 'armed conflict' triggers the application of IHL. The relationship between the law of self-defence and IHL only arises when an 'armed attack' and an 'armed conflict' exist at the same time. The distinction between the two is essential since they are often invoked loosely as if they are interchangeable concepts.[2]

In this section, three factors that are common to the thresholds of armed attack and armed conflict will be set out in order to clarify the overlap and differences between the two thresholds: 1) parties; 2) location; and 3) intensity. This would give an idea of when the law of self-defence and IHL apply concurrently, and when they do not.

First, 'armed attack' is the threshold of application for the law of self-defence. Article 51 of the UN Charter provides as follows:

> Nothing in the present Charter shall impair the inherent right of individual or collective self-defence if an armed attack occurs against a Member of the United Nations.[3]

There is no universally accepted definition of 'armed attack' but indications of its scope can be found in the 1974 Definition of Aggression,[4] Amendments to the 1998 Statute of the International Criminal Court (hereafter ICC Statute),[5] international courts and arbitration cases,[6] and various state practices and examples given by experts.[7] It suffices to note

[2] See, eg, *Hamdan v Rumsfeld*, 548 U.S. 521, Brief for Respondents, 24.

[3] Charter of the United Nations (hereafter UN Charter) (adopted 26 June 1945, entered into force 24 October 1945) 59 Statutes at Large 1031. The ICJ confirmed this point in the following four cases: *Military and Paramilitary Activities in and against Nicaragua* (hereafter *Nicaragua* case) (*Nicaragua v US*) (Merits) [1986] ICJ Rep 14, para 195; *Legality of the Threat or Use of Nuclear Weapons* (hereafter *Nuclear Weapons* case) (Advisory Opinion) [1996] ICJ Rep 226, para 38; *Case concerning Oil Platforms* (hereafter *Oil Platforms* case) (*Iran v US*) (Merits) [2003] ICJ Rep 161, para 51; *Armed Activities on the Territory of the Congo* (hereafter *Armed Activities* case) (*Democratic Republic of the Congo v Uganda*) (Merits) [2005] ICJ Rep 116, para 146.

[4] UNGA, 'Definition of Aggression' UNGA Res 3314 (XXIX) (14 December 1974) (hereafter 1974 Definition of Aggression).

[5] Article 8 *bis* (2) of the 'Amendments to the Rome Statute of the International Criminal Court on the Crime of Aggression' Review Conference of the Rome Statute of the International Criminal Court (Kampala 31 May – 11 June 2010) (11 June 2010) RC/Res.6, Annex I. See also Rome Statute of the International Criminal Court (adopted 17 July 1998, entered into force 1 July 2002) 2187 UNTS 3.

[6] See *Nicaragua* case (Merits), *Nuclear Weapons* case (Advisory Opinion), *Oil Platforms* case (Merits), *Legal Consequences of the Construction of a Wall in the Occupied Palestinian Territory* (hereafter *Wall* case) (Advisory Opinion) [2004] ICJ Rep 136; *Armed Activities* case (Merits). See also Eritrea–Ethiopia Claims Commission, *Jus ad Bellum, Ethiopia's Claim 1–8* (hereafter *Jus ad Bellum* case) (Partial Award) (2009) XXVI *Reports of International Arbitral Awards* 457.

[7] Brownlie, *International Law and the Use of Force by States*, 361 *ff*; O Schachter, *International Law in Theory and Practice* (Dordrecht, Martinus Nijhoff, 1991) 110 *ff*; A Randelzhofer, 'Article 2 (4)' in B Simma et al (eds), *The Charter of the United Nations: A Commentary* 2nd edn Vol I (Oxford, Oxford University Press, 2002) 117 *ff*; R Kolb, *Ius contra bellum: Le droit international relatif au maintien de la paix* (Bâle, Helbing et Lichtenhahn, 2003) 172; C Gray, *International Law and the Use of Force*, 2nd edn (Oxford, Oxford University Press, 2004) 29 *ff*; Y Dinstein, *War, Aggression and Self-Defence*, 4th edn (Cambridge, Cambridge University Press, 2005)

the following for the purpose of this book, without proposing a comprehensive definition:

1) Parties: an armed attack is often carried out by a state against a state,[8] including by an armed group sponsored by a state.[9]
2) Location: an armed attack is normally launched across the international border.
3) Intensity: the threshold of 'armed attack' is generally higher than 'use of force' in Article 2(4) of the UN Charter but there is no agreement on the minimum intensity of an armed attack.[10] Nevertheless, the 1974 Definition of Aggression is most often cited as guidance.[11] Some take the position that an armed attack includes an imminent threat of attack.[12]

'Use of force', a term referred to above, is the threshold of application for *jus ad bellum*. Article 2(4) of the UN Charter provides as follows:

> All Members shall refrain in their international relations from the threat or use of force against the territorial integrity or political independence of any state, or in any other manner inconsistent with the Purposes of the United Nations.

There is no universally accepted definition of the term 'use of force',[13] but indications of its scope can generally be found in the 1970 Friendly Relations Declaration,[14] international courts and arbitration cases,[15] and various state practices and examples given by experts.[16] However, in the

85 *ff* and 193 *ff*. See also J Green, 'Fluctuating Evidentiary Standards for Self-Defence in the International Court of Justice' (2009) 58 *International and Comparative Law Quarterly* 163.

[8] *Wall* case (Advisory Opinion), para 139.

[9] *Nicaragua* case (Merits), para 195.

[10] See a summary of opposing positions in Kolb, *Ius contra bellum*, 201–02.

[11] See, eg, *Nicaragua* case (Merits), para 195; *Armed Activities* case (Merits), para 146.

[12] See contrasting views in, on one hand, Brownlie, *International Law and the Use of Force by States*, 257–61; Kolb, *Ius contra bellum*, 195, and on the other, H Waldock, 'The Regulation of the Use of Force by Individual States in International Law' (1952) 81 *Recueil des Cours de l'Académie de Droit International* 455, 496–98; D Bowett, *Self-Defence in International Law* (Manchester, Manchester University Press, 1958) 187–92; S Schwebel, 'Aggression, Intervention and Self-Defence in Modern International Law' (1972) 136 *Recueil des Cours de l'Académie de Droit International* 411, 478–83; R Jennings and A Watts (eds), *Oppenheim's International Law*, 9th edn Vol 1: Peace, Introduction and Part 1 (London, Longman, 1992) 421; Dinstein, *War, Aggression and Self-Defence*, 4th edn, 189–92.

[13] On this topic, see generally Brownlie, *International Law and the Use of Force by States*, 361–64; Gray, *International Law and the Use of Force*, 29 *ff*; Dinstein, *War, Aggression and Self-Defence*, 4th edn, 85 *ff*.

[14] UNGA, 'Declaration on Principles of International Law concerning Friendly Relations and Co-operation among States in Accordance with the Charter of the United Nations' UNGA Res 2625 (XXV) (24 October 1970) (hereafter 1970 Friendly Relations Declaration).

[15] *Corfu Channel Case* (*United Kingdom v Albania*) (Merits) [1949] ICJ Rep 4; *Nicaragua* case (Merits); *Wall* case (Advisory Opinion); *Armed Activities* case (Merits). See also Eritrea–Ethiopia Claims Commission, *Jus ad Bellum* case (Partial Award).

[16] Brownlie, *International Law and the Use of Force by States*, 361 *ff*; *International Law in Theory and Practice*, 110 *ff*; Jennings and Watts (eds), *Oppenheim's International Law*, 417 *ff*; Randelzhofer, 'Article 2(4)', 117 *ff*; Kolb, *Ius contra bellum*, 172; Gray, *International Law and the Use of Force*, 29 *ff*; Dinstein, *War, Aggression and Self-Defence*, 4th edn, 85 *ff* and 193 *ff*.

end, the determination of the existence of the use of force depends heavily on the facts of each case. It suffices to point out that the threshold of 'use of force' is generally lower than 'armed attack'.[17] In the *Nicaragua* case, the International Court of Justice (ICJ) indicated the dividing line between the two by stating that the training, arming, and logistical support for armed groups attacking another state amount to a 'threat or use of force' but not to an 'armed attack'.[18]

On the other hand, the existence of an 'armed conflict' is the requirement for the application of both the law of international and non-international armed conflict. First, common Article 2 of the 1949 Geneva Conventions is the threshold of application for international armed conflict, and provides as follows:

> [T]he present Convention shall apply to all cases of declared war or of any other armed conflict which may arise between two or more of the High Contracting Parties . . . [and] to all cases of partial or total occupation of the territory of a High Contracting Party.[19]

While there is no universally agreed definition of international armed conflict, it suffices to point out the following:

1) Parties: an international armed conflict takes place between states, including between states and armed groups sponsored by states.[20]
2) Location: an international armed conflict takes place across the international border.
3) Intensity: a widely employed threshold is set out in a commentary:

[17] See *Nicaragua* case (Merits), paras 191 and 195. See also Brownlie, *International Law and the Use of Force by States*, 365; Randelzhofer, 'Article 2(4)', 790; Kolb, *Ius contra bellum*, 188–90; Dinstein, *War, Aggression and Self-Defence*, 4th edn, 193 *ff*.

[18] *Nicaragua* case (Merits), paras 191, 195, and 228.

[19] The threshold of 'armed conflict' is used in many later IHL treaties: Art 18 of the Convention for the Protection of Cultural Property in the Event of Armed Conflict (hereafter 1954 Cultural Property Convention) (adopted 14 May 1954, entered into force 7 August 1956) 249 UNTS 240; Art I(2) of the Convention on the Prohibition of the Development, Production and Stockpiling of Bacteriological (Biological) and Toxin Weapons and on Their Destruction (hereafter 1972 Biological Weapons Convention) (adopted 10 April 1972, entered into force 26 March 1975) 1015 UNTS 163; Art 1(3) of the Protocol Additional to the Geneva Conventions of 12 August 1949, and Relating to the Protection of Victims of International Armed Conflicts (Protocol I) (hereafter 1977 First Additional Protocol) (adopted 8 June 1977, entered into force 7 December 1978) 1125 UNTS 3; Art 1(1) of Protocol Additional to the Geneva Conventions of 12 August 1949, and Relating to the Protection of Victims of Non-International Armed Conflicts (Protocol II) (hereafter 1977 Second Additional Protocol) (adopted 8 June 1977, entered into force 7 December 1978) 1125 UNTS 609; Art 1 of the Convention on Prohibitions and Restrictions on the Use of Certain Conventional Weapons Which May Be Deemed to Be Excessively Injurious or to Have Indiscriminate Effects (hereafter 1980 Convention on Conventional Weapons) (adopted 10 October 1980, entered into force 2 December 1983) 1342 UNTS 137 and its Amendment Art 1 (adopted 21 December 2001, entered into force 18 May 2004) 2260 UNTS 82; Art 3 of the Second Protocol to the 1954 Convention for the Protection of Cultural Property in the Event of Armed Conflict (hereafter 1954 Cultural Property Convention, Second Protocol) (adopted 26 March 1999, entered into force 9 March 2004) 2253 UNTS 172.

[20] *Tadic Case* (Judgment, Appeals), para 84.

> Any difference arising between two States and leading to the intervention of members of the armed forces is an armed conflict . . . it makes no difference how long the conflict lasts, how much slaughter takes place, or how numerous are the participating forces.[21]

The required intensity to constitute an international armed conflict is significantly low and the capture of a single army troop can bring the law of international armed conflict into play.[22]

It is worth noting that non-international armed conflict has its own threshold in common Article 3 of the 1949 Geneva Conventions and Article 1(1) of the 1977 Second Additional Protocol. It suffices to note at this point that both types of non-international armed conflict assume that it takes place within a single state and that there is no foreign intervention.[23] For this reason, as will be seen later, non-international armed conflict and armed attack has no relation, since an armed attack invariably involves an inter-state relation.

As can be seen from the above, armed attack and international armed conflict have their similarities and differences. The remaining part of this section will discuss situations where an armed attack and an international armed conflict co-exist, and where the two are at variance.

First, with regard to the conflicting parties, both armed attack and international armed conflict require state-to-state relation: an armed attack is carried out by a state against another state and international armed conflict takes place between states. A classic case is the invasion of Kuwait by Iraq in 1990. The same can be said when an armed group, sponsored by a state, launches an armed attack against another state (or vice versa). An armed conflict between a state-sponsored armed group and a state is an international armed conflict. The situations considered by the ICJ in the *Nicaragua* case and by the International Criminal Tribunal for the former Yugoslavia (ICTY) in the *Tadic* case are representative cases.[24] Likewise, when an armed attack is launched by a state-sponsored armed group against another state-sponsored armed group, an armed conflict between such armed groups is an international armed conflict. A classic case is the Vietnam War and a modern version is the eastern Democratic Republic of the Congo (DRC), where numerous state-sponsored armed groups fought against each other. However, when an armed group acting independently from any state attacks a particular state (or vice versa), there are still debates as to whether it qualifies as an armed attack, and as

[21] J de Preux, *Commentary on the Geneva Conventions of 12 August 1949* Vol III (Geneva, International Committee of the Red Cross, 1960) 23.

[22] Art 5 of the Geneva Convention Relative to the Treatment of Prisoners of War, as revised from 1929 (hereafter 1949 Third Geneva Convention) (adopted 12 August 1949, entered into force 21 October 1950) 75 UNTS 135. De Preux, *Commentary*, 23.

[23] For a detailed discussion on the threshold of application for non-international armed conflict, see section 5.II.A below.

[24] *Nicaragua* case (Merits), para 195; *Tadic Case* (Judgment, Appeals), para 84.

to the character of the armed conflict in terms of IHL. Three cases can be envisaged:

1) attack by state A against an armed group in state B not sponsored by any state (such as the attacks by Uganda on the armed groups in the DRC);
2) attack by an armed group in state A, without any state support, against state B (such as the armed groups in the DRC against Uganda);
3) attack by an armed group in state A against an armed group in state B, both without state support (such as the armed groups in the DRC against the armed groups in Uganda).

The problems of these cases will be dealt collectively in a later chapter.[25]

Secondly, with regard to the geographical element, an armed attack normally requires an attack which crosses an international border,[26] which is also a requirement for an international armed conflict (such as the invasion of Kuwait by Iraq in 1990).

It is equally clear that when an armed conflict is confined within a single state, that is, non-international armed conflict within the meaning of IHL (between a state's armed forces and armed groups, or between different armed groups), and when there is no foreign intervention, an armed attack does not exist and the law of self-defence remains irrelevant.[27] Non-international armed conflict has a closer relation to 'threat to the peace' in Article 39 of the UN Charter and is regulated through Chapter VII of the UN Charter and the law of non-international armed conflict.[28] The application of Chapter VII is possible since Article 2(7) of the UN Charter explicitly permits intervention in domestic matters, including non-international armed conflict, through enforcement measures. This is a power generally not authorised under the law of self-defence which is restricted by Article 2(4) of the UN Charter and the principle of non-intervention in internal affairs.[29] Thus, even though the law of self-defence is irrelevant to non-international armed conflict, Chapter VII replaces the task of regulating the use of force in non-international armed conflict.

[25] See section 5.II.A below.

[26] See *Wall* case (Advisory Opinion), para 139.

[27] See Kolb, *Ius contra bellum*, 173; Dinstein, *War, Aggression and Self-Defence*, 4th edn, 204–05.

[28] See section 4.II.C.

[29] However, for the particular problems of intervention by invitation of a government, see generally L Doswald-Beck, 'The Legal Validity of Military Intervention by Invitation of the Government' (1985) 56 *British Year Book of International Law* 189; Jennings and Watts (eds), *Oppenheim's International Law*, 427 *ff*; A Tanca, *Foreign Armed Intervention in Internal Conflict* (Dordrecht, Martinus Nijhoff, 1993); Gray, *International Law and the Use of Force*. See further the recent *Armed Activities* case (Merits), paras 42–54. Moreover, a use of force in pursuit of self-determination is a peculiar case since it is: 1) no longer a non-international armed conflict but classified as an international armed conflict pursuant to Art 1(4) of the 1977 First Additional Protocol; and 2) states' assistance to those using force in self-determination is generally accepted under the terms of the 1970 Friendly Relations Declaration.

Finally, intensity of an armed attack or an international armed conflict is probably a factor that most depends on the context. On one hand, there are clear-cut cases where an armed attack and an international armed conflict exist at the same time, such as acts of aggression enumerated in the 1974 Definition of Aggression.[30] For example, crossing of an international border by a state's armed forces and the occupation of another state's territory easily reach the intensity of armed attack and international armed conflict and thus, the law of self-defence and the law of international armed conflict become applicable concurrently. In this sense, there are common grounds between the two thresholds where the requirement of intensity overlaps.

On the other hand, there are situations where the threshold of intensity between armed attack and international armed conflict is at variance. For example, for those who view that an armed attack exists when there is an imminent threat of attack,[31] such as the situation prior to the attack of Israel against Egypt in the 1967 Arab–Israel Conflict,[32] there is no international armed conflict yet in the sense of IHL but it is a situation where the law of self-defence is applicable and where states can exercise the right of self-defence. On the contrary, there may be cases where an international armed conflict exists but an armed attack does not. For example, if one soldier infiltrates into another state's territory and is captured by the enemy forces, this may not amount to an armed attack but may amount to an international armed conflict. Such a capture of a member of armed forces brings the 1949 Third Geneva Convention on the treatment of prisoners of war into play.[33] A commentary on the Third Geneva Convention notes that 'Even if there has been no fighting, the fact that persons covered by the Convention [1949 Third Geneva Convention] are detained is sufficient for its application'.[34]

In short, an armed attack often amounts to an international armed conflict, particularly because the two are often between two states, which take place across the international border, and with certain intensity of the use of force. However, the two thresholds can be at variance, particularly with regard to the level of intensity required to qualify as an armed attack or an international armed conflict. Moreover, particular legal questions arise when armed groups without any ties with states are involved in a conflict. For this reason, it is best not to expect a quick and simple answer that an

[30] As will be seen later, all instances where the Security Council recognised the existence of an act of aggression were international armed conflict. See section 4.II.C.

[31] See, eg, Waldock, 'The Regulation of the Use of Force', 496–98; Bowett, *Self-Defence in International Law*, 187–92; Schwebel, 'Aggression, Intervention and Self-Defence', 478–83; Jennings and Watts (eds), *Oppenheim's International Law*, 421; Dinstein, *War, Aggression and Self-Defence*, 4th edn, 189–92.

[32] See, eg, Dinstein, *War, Aggression and Self-Defence*, 4th edn, 192.

[33] Art 5 of the 1949 Third Geneva Convention.

[34] De Preux, *Commentary*, 23.

armed attack always amounts to an international armed conflict and vice versa. To establish the simultaneous application of *jus ad bellum* and *jus in bello*, each threshold should be applied separately and according to the particular requirements therein.

B. Simultaneous Existence of an Armed Attack and an International Armed Conflict and the Equal Application of IHL

This section discusses one example, namely a cross-border invasion followed by occupation, in order to illustrate the simultaneous beginning and continuation of an armed attack and an international armed conflict. At the same time, it emphasises that the subsequent operation of the law of self-defence and the law of international armed conflict is completely different in the sense that the former applies unequally between the aggressor and the victim state whereas the latter applies equally to the conflicting parties throughout the conflict.[35]

In most cases of a cross-border invasion followed by occupation, an armed attack and an international armed conflict exist simultaneously and continue to exist until the end of the occupation. First, the 1974 Definition of Aggression and the Amendments to the ICC Statute list the following as an act of aggression:

> The invasion or attack by the armed forces of a State of the territory of another State, or any military occupation, however temporary, resulting from such invasion or attack, or any annexation by the use of the territory of another State or part thereof.[36]

This will be seen as an armed attack within the meaning of Article 51 of the UN Charter.[37] In terms of IHL, common Article 2 of the 1949 Geneva Conventions provides, in part, as follows:

> The Convention shall also apply to all cases of partial or total occupation of the territory of a High Contracting Party, even if the said occupation meets with no armed resistance.

[35] The following discussion does not deal with the law of non-international armed conflict since as noted above, the notion of 'armed attack' in principle has no relevance to non-international armed conflict. For further discussion, see section 5.II.A.

[36] Art 3(a) of the 1974 Definition of Aggression; Art 8 *bis* (2)(a) of the Amendments to the ICC Statute.

[37] See, eg, UNSC Res 82 (25 June 1950) UN Doc S/RES/82, UNSC Res 83 (27 June 1950) UN Doc S/RES/83, UNSC Res 84 (7 July 1950) UN Doc S/RES/84 on the invasion of the Democratic People's Republic of Korea (DPRK) of the Republic of Korea and UNSC Res 661 (6 August 1990) UN Doc S/RES/661 on the Iraq's invasion of Kuwait. The nexus between 'act of aggression' and 'armed attack' was discussed extensively during the drafting of the 1974 Definition of Aggression. See generally B Broms, 'The Definition of Aggression' (1977) 154 *Recueil des Cours de l'Académie de Droit International* 297; B Röling, 'The 1974 U.N. Definition of Aggression' in A Cassese (ed), *The Current Legal Regulation of the Use of Force* (Dordrecht, Martinus Nijhoff, 1986).

Once there is an armed attack in the form of occupation, it will continue so long as the occupation continues.[38] Four particular legal consequences follow: 1) the aggressor can be subject to various sanctions under the UN Charter, including military enforcement action under Chapter VII;[39] 2) the victim state is entitled to exercise the right of self-defence until the end of the occupation, either individually or collectively; but 3) the customary principles of proportionality and necessity will guide the self-defence measures taken by the victims state until the end of the occupation; and 4) the unequal status between the aggressor and the victim state continues until the end of the occupation.

Similarly, once there is an international armed conflict in the form of occupation, it will continue so long as the occupation continues. Three particular legal consequences follow: 1) the law of international armed conflict applies; 2) it applies so long as the occupation continues or until the release, repatriation, and re-establishment of protected persons;[40] and 3) it applies equally to the conflicting parties regardless of their legal status under *jus ad bellum*.

Thus, the beginning of occupation normally constitutes the beginning of an armed attack and an international armed conflict, which will continue so long as the occupation continues and where the law of self-defence, particularly the principles of proportionality and necessity, and the law of international armed conflict continue to apply simultaneously. The significant difference is, even with the continuation of the unequal status between the aggressor and the victim state under *jus ad bellum* throughout the occupation, the law of international armed conflict applies equally to the conflicting parties throughout the same occupation.

In practice, the Eritrea–Ethiopia Claims Commission recognised in its awards that an armed attack and an international armed conflict commenced simultaneously when Eritrea initiated a cross-border invasion against Ethiopia followed by occupation of parts of the Ethiopian territory, and continued until the end of the occupation. With regard to the

[38] See, eg, the repeated recognition of the Security Council that Angola was entitled to exercise the right of self-defence during the occupation of its territory by South Africa, which indicates that an armed attack can continue during the occupation: UNSC Res 546 (6 January 1984) UN Doc S/RES/546, para 5 and UNSC Res 574 (7 October 1985) UN Doc S/RES/574, para 4. See also *Oil Platforms* case (Merits), Reply of Iran, para 7.22. The written proceedings can be found at the ICJ website, www.icj-cij.org. Art 3(a) of the 1974 Definition of Aggression and Art 8 *bis* (2) (a) of the Amendments to the ICC Statute also provide that the following is an act of aggression: 'Any military occupation, however temporary, resulting from such invasion or attack [by the armed forces of a State].'

[39] See especially Arts 41 and 42 of the UN Charter. Furthermore, an aggressor state can be suspended from the exercise of the rights and privileges of UN membership (Art 5) or be expelled from the UN (Art 6).

[40] Art 6 of the Geneva Convention Relative to the Protection of Civilian Persons in Time of War (hereafter 1949 Fourth Geneva Convention) (adopted 12 August 1949, entered into force 21 October 1950) 75 UNTS 287.

existence of an armed attack, the Commission noted as follows in the *Jus ad Bellum* Award:

> As the text of Article 51 of the [UN] Charter makes clear, the predicate for a valid claim of self-defense under the Charter is that the party resorting to force has been subjected to an armed attack . . . the Commission holds that Eritrea violated Article 2, paragraph 4, of the Charter of the United Nations by resorting to armed force to attack and occupy Badame, then under peaceful administration by Ethiopia . . . in an attack that began on May 12, 1998 . . . once the armed attack in the Badame area occurred . . . Ethiopia decided to act in self-defense.[41]

It is worth noting that the Commission recognised that the armed attack took place in the form of occupation.

With regard to the existence of an international armed conflict, the Commission noted in the *Ports* Award that 'As described in the Commission's Partial Award relating to alleged violations of the *jus ad bellum*, an international armed conflict between the Parties began on May 12, 1998'.[42] The Commission did not clearly state that the international armed conflict was brought about by the occupation by Eritrea. However, since the Commission used the same date for the beginning of the armed attack and the international armed conflict, and since it stated clearly that the date was the beginning of the armed attack in the form of occupation, it can be easily inferred that the international armed conflict was also started with the occupation.

The continuation of the situation of an armed attack, in particular, and an international armed conflict during the continuing occupation is evidenced by the repeated recognition of this fact by the Commission in other cases that dealt with the conduct of Eritrea and Ethiopia subsequent to the initial armed attack and the commencement of the international armed conflict.[43] In terms of *jus ad bellum*, Eritrea was the aggressor state and Ethiopia was the victim state throughout the conflict.

However, even when it was found that Eritrea was the aggressor state and Ethiopia was the victim state under *jus ad bellum*, the Commission applied the law of international armed conflict, particularly the law of occupation,[44]

[41] Eritrea–Ethiopia Claims Commission, *Jus ad Bellum* case (Partial Award), paras 11, 16, and 19.

[42] Eritrea–Ethiopia Claims Commission, *Western and Eastern Fronts, Ethiopia's Claims 1 and 3* (hereafter *Western and Eastern Fronts, Ethiopia* case) (Partial Award) (2009) XXVI *Reports of International Arbitral Awards* 351, para 25. See also *Ports, Ethiopia's Claim 6* (hereafter *Ports, Ethiopia* case) (Final Award) (2009) XXVI *Reports of International Arbitral Awards* 489, para 11.

[43] See Eritrea–Ethiopia Claims Commissions, *Western and Eastern Fronts, Ethiopia* case (Partial Award), para 25. See also *Ports, Ethiopia* case (Final Award), para 11.

[44] 'Law of occupation' here refers particularly to Arts 42–56 of the Convention (IV) Respecting the Laws and Customs of War on Land and its Annex: Regulations concerning the Laws and Customs of War on Land (hereafter 1907 Hague Regulations) (adopted 18 October 1907, entered into force 26 January 1910) 187 CTS 227; 1949 Fourth Geneva Convention; and customary international law.

equally to Eritrea and Ethiopia, with regard to all the periods subsequent to the initial armed attack and the commencement of the international armed conflict. For example, the Commission found violations of Article 53 of the 1949 Fourth Geneva Convention, which prohibits destruction of private and public property in occupied territories, by both Eritrea and Ethiopia.[45] This indicates that even when the occupation had been initiated by the aggressor, the victim state can also find itself occupying parts of the adversary's territory during the course of the international armed conflict, in which case it is not violating *jus ad bellum* since it is acting in self-defence, but is responsible for violations of IHL, particularly the law of occupation.

Another case is the invasion by the Democratic People's Republic of Korea (DPRK) of the Republic of Korea in 1950. With regard to the existence of an armed attack, Security Council noted in resolution 82 'with grave concern the armed attack on the Republic of Korea by forces from North Korea'.[46] This was repeated in resolutions 83 and 84, which indicated the continuity of the initial armed attack by way of occupation. The applicability of IHL was also confirmed by the International Committee of the Red Cross (ICRC) on the following day of the invasion[47] and subsequently by the conflicting parties.[48]

In terms of *jus ad bellum*, the DPRK was the aggressor and the Republic of Korea was the victim state throughout the conflict. The entitlement to exercise the right of self-defence also extended to the allies that were acting in support of the Republic of Korea.[49]

However, even when the unequal status was created between the DPRK and the Republic of Korea (and its allies) under *jus ad bellum*, the law of international armed conflict applied equally between the two sides, with regard to all the periods subsequent to the initial armed attack and the

[45] Eritrea–Ethiopia Claims Commission, *Central Front, Ethiopia's Claim* 2 (Partial Award) (2009) XXVI *Reports of International Arbitral Awards* 155, paras 52, 70, and 73(4); *Central Front, Eritrea's Claims 2, 4, 6, 7, 8, and 22* (hereafter *Central Front, Eritrea* case) (Partial Award) (2009) XXVI *Reports of International Arbitral Awards* 195, paras 78, 93–105, and 113–14.

[46] UNSC Res 82 (25 June 1950) UN Doc S/RES/82, Preamble.

[47] F Bugnion, *The International Committee of the Red Cross and the Protection of War Victims* (Geneva, International Committee of the Red Cross, 2003), 476.

[48] See UNSC, 'Letter Dated 5 July 1951 from the Representative of the United States of America to the Secretary-General' (6 July 1951) UN Doc S/2232. In addition, see the following for an extensive account relating to the treatment of prisoners of war, references to the 1949 Third Geneva Convention, and violations of IHL: UNGA, 'The Question of Korea' (1951) 207, 245–48; UNGA, 'The Question of Korea' (1952) UNYB 155, 156–59, 171–73, 185 *ff*, and 204–07 in particular but see other relevant parts by referring to the index at 952.

Note that the major conflicting parties, namely China, DPRK, Republic of Korea and the US were not parties to the 1949 Geneva Conventions at the time of the conflict but nevertheless accepted to apply them. However, other IHL treaties such as the 1907 Hague Regulations and 1929 Convention Relative to the Treatment of Prisoners of War (adopted 27 July 1929, entered into force 19 June 1931) 118 LNTS 343 were applicable, either as treaty law or customary international law.

[49] Whether the multinational forces were acting in collective self-defence or authorised under Chapter VII to use force will not be discussed here. See generally n 55 below.

commencement of the international armed conflict.[50] The law of occupation also applied during the course of the conflict when the multinational forces gained control of the DPRK territory.

Another case is the invasion of Kuwait by Iraq in 1990. The Security Council effectively determined the existence of both an armed attack and an international armed conflict in resolution 661:

> *The Security Council . . . Determined* to bring the invasion and occupation of Kuwait by Iraq to an end . . . *Affirming* the inherent right of individual or collective self-defence, in response to the armed attack by Iraq against Kuwait, in accordance with Article 51 of the Charter.[51]

From this, it is clear that the invasion and the subsequent occupation of Kuwait by Iraq was an armed attack.[52] It is also clear from the words 'occupation of Kuwait by Iraq' that there was an international armed conflict.[53] The existence of an international armed conflict was later recognised by way of an explicit recognition of the applicability of the law of international armed conflict in resolution 666.[54]

In terms of *jus ad bellum*, Iraq was the aggressor and Kuwait was the victim state throughout the conflict. The entitlement to exercise the right of self-defence also extended to the allies of Kuwait that were acting in collective self-defence.[55]

However, the unequal status between Iraq and Kuwait (and its allies) under *jus ad bellum* did not affect the equal application of IHL to the two sides with regard to all the periods subsequent to the initial armed attack and the commencement of the international armed conflict.[56] The law of occupation may have even applied to the multinational forces when they occupied parts of the Iraqi territory shortly after the Iraqi armed forces were evicted from Kuwait.[57]

[50] See the references in n 48 above.

[51] UNSC Res 661 (6 August 1990) UN Doc S/RES/661, Preamble.

[52] See *Oil Platforms* case (Merits), Reply of Iran, para 7.22.

[53] See also ICRC, 'Middle East: Gulf Crisis' (1990) 278 *International Review of the Red Cross* 444; ICRC, 'Outline of Legal Aspects of the Conflict in the Middle East' (1991) 280 *International Review of the Red Cross* 28.

[54] UNSC Res 666 (13 September 1990) UN Doc S/RES/666, Preamble and para 2.

[55] There are different views on whether the actions of the multinational forces after 15 January 1991 were: 1) collective self-defence; 2) Chapter VII measure; or 3) a mixture of both. Among others see, for 1) Dinstein, *War, Aggression and Self-Defence*, 4th edn, 274; for 2) C Greenwood, 'New World Order or Old? The Invasion of Kuwait and the Rule of Law' (1992) 55 *Modern Law Review* 153, 165; and for 3) see the suggestion in O Schachter, 'United Nations Law in the Gulf Conflict' (1991) 85 *American Journal of International Law* 452, 462. For an overview of different positions see M Weller, 'The United Nations and the *Jus ad Bellum*' in P Rowe (ed), *The Gulf War 1990–91 in International and English Law* (London, Routledge, 1993) 40–41.

[56] See ICRC, 'Memorandum on the Applicability of International Humanitarian Law' (1991) 280 *International Review of the Red Cross* 24; ICRC, 'Outline of Legal Aspects of the Conflict', 28–30; US Department of Defense, 'Final Report to Congress on the Conduct of Hostilities in the Persian Gulf' (1992) www.ndu.edu/library/epubs/cpgw.pdf.

[57] For an indication, see US Department of Defense, 'Final Report', 339.

A further case is the 1980–88 Iran–Iraq War. The UN Secretary-General's report impliedly recognised the simultaneous occurrence and continuation of an armed attack and an international armed conflict when Iraq initiated a cross-border attack against Iran followed by occupation:

> The outstanding event under the violations referred to in paragraph 5 above [illegal use of force] is the attack of 22 September 1980 against Iran, which cannot be justified under the Charter of the United Nations . . . Even if before the outbreak of the conflict there had been some encroachment by Iran on Iraqi territory, such encroachment did not justify Iraq's aggression against Iran – which was followed by Iraq's continuous occupation of Iranian territory during the conflict – in violation of the prohibition of the use of force, which is regarded as one of the rules of *jus cogens*.[58]

This implies that the invasion and the subsequent occupation of Iran by Iraq was a use of force and an armed attack and it is also clear from the words 'Iraq's continuous occupation of Iranian territory during the conflict' that an international armed conflict continued throughout the conflict.

In terms of *jus ad bellum*, Iraq was the aggressor and Iran was the victim state throughout the conflict.

However, as similar to the previous three cases, the unequal status between Iraq and Iran did not affect the equal application of IHL to the two states with regard to all the periods subsequent to the initial armed attack and the commencement of an international armed conflict.[59] Thus, when Iran began occupying parts of the Iraqi territory during the course of the international armed conflict, it became responsible for violations of the law of occupation, but was not violating *jus ad bellum* since it was acting in self-defence.[60]

[58] UNSC, 'Further Report of the Secretary-General on the Implementation of Security Council Resolution 598 (1987)' (9 December 1991) UN Doc S/23273, paras 5 and 6. The formal recognition by the Security Council of the applicability of the law of international armed conflict only came two years later in UNSC Res 540 (31 October 1983) UN Doc S/RES/540, para 2. However, for an earlier recognition, see ICRC, 'Conflit Irak–Iran' (1980) 720 *Revue internationale de la Croix-Rouge* 341.

[59] See ICRC, 'Conflit Irak–Iran'.

[60] For an indication of Iran's occupation of Iraq, see UNSC, 'Iran–Iraq Armed Conflict' (1986) 40 UNYB 217, 218 *ff*. For other violations of IHL by Iran, see the UN reports on the use of chemical weapons: UNSC, 'Mission to Inspect Civilian Areas in Iran and Iraq Which Have Been Subject to Military Attack' (20 June 1983) UN Doc S/15834; UNSC, 'Report of the Specialists Appointed by the Secretary-General to Investigate Allegations by the Islamic Republic of Iran concerning the Use of Chemical Weapons' (26 March 1984) UN Doc S/16433; UNSC, 'Letter Dated 17 April 1985 from the Secretary-General Addressed to the President of the Security Council' (24 April 1985) UN Doc S/17127; UNSC, 'Report of the Mission Dispatched by the Secretary-General to Investigate Allegations of the Use of Chemical Weapons in the Conflict between the Islamic Republic of Iran and Iraq' (12 March 1986) UN Doc S/17911; UNSC, 'Report of the Mission Dispatched by the Secretary-General to Investigate Allegations of the Use of Chemical Weapons in the Conflict between the Islamic Republic of Iran and Iraq' (8 May 1987) UN Doc S/18852; UNSC, 'Report of the Mission Dispatched by the Secretary-General to Investigate Allegations of the Use of Chemical Weapons in the Conflict between the Islamic Republic of Iran and Iraq: Note by the Secretary-

The above cases all indicate that even when the occupation had been initiated by the aggressor, thereby initiating and continuing the situation of an armed attack and an international armed conflict, during the course of the conflict, the victim state can find itself occupying the adversary's territory, in which case it is not violating *jus ad bellum* but is responsible for violations of the law of occupation.

The peculiarity with the Iran–Iraq War was that during the eight years of conflict between 1980 and 1988, Iran's self-defence measures most likely developed into a disproportionate one, thereby becoming an aggressor state.[61] Such a legal consequence of disproportionate self-defence was recognised by Louis de Brouckère as long ago as 1926 in his report on Article 16 of the Covenant of the League of Nations:[62]

> Legitimate self-defence implies the adoption of measures proportionate to the seriousness of the attack and justified by the imminence of the danger. If a country flagrantly exceeded these limits, even if it were affronted by some incident of little intrinsic importance, it would become in actual fact the real aggressor and it would be only fair that that country should be made the object of the sanctions provided for in Article 16.[63]

Thus, in a long-term conflict, mostly involving occupation, a situation of armed attack and international armed conflict may exist concurrently until the end of the occupation, but the significance of the armed attack may gradually be lost once the victim state engages in disproportionate self-defence. With the disproportionate self-defence, both sides become the aggressor state and thus, whether or not the armed attack is continuing loses its relevance. However, even if the status of the victim state under *jus ad bellum* changes during the course of the conflict, the existence of an international armed conflict clearly remains intact so far as the occupation continues and thus, the equal application of the law of international armed conflict to the conflicting parties also remains intact.

General' (25 April 1988) UN Doc S/19823; UNSC, 'Report of the Mission Dispatched by the Secretary-General to Investigate Allegations of the Use of Chemical Weapons in the Conflict between the Islamic Republic of Iran and Iraq: Note by the Secretary-General' (19 August 1988) UN Doc S/20134. See further UN Security Council resolutions on the conflict: UNSC Res 540 (31 October 1983) UN Doc S/RES/540, para 3; UNSC Res 582 (24 November 1986) UN Doc S/RES/582, Preamble, paras 2 and 4; UNSC Res 598 (20 July 1987) UN Doc S/RES/598, Preamble and para 3; UNSC Res 612 (9 May 1988) UN Doc S/RES/612; UNSC Res 620 (26 August 1988) UN Doc S/RES/620.

[61] For an indication, see K Kaikobad, 'Self-Defence, Enforcement Action and the Gulf Wars, 1980–88 and 1990–91' (1992) 63 *British Year Book of International Law* 299, 332–33.

[62] Covenant of the League of Nations (adopted 28 April 1919, entered into force 10 January 1920) 225 CTS 188.

[63] UNGA Sixth Committee 'Report of L de Brouckère on Article 16 of the Covenant of the League of Nations' (3 October 1952) UN Doc A/2211, Annex, Agenda Item 54, para 41. See also statements of the USSR, UNGA Sixth Committee (1971) GAOR 26th Session, 144, para 9; Costa Rica, UNGA Sixth Committee (1971) GAOR 26th Session, 167, para 5; Zaire, UNGA Sixth Committee (1972) GAOR 27th Session, 233, para 27 See also Brownlie, *International Law and the Use of Force by States*, 264.

Thus, at least the beginning and the continuation of occupation are in most cases the simultaneous beginning and continuation of an armed attack and an international armed conflict. However, the operation of *jus ad bellum* and *jus in bello* takes the opposite course during the occupation. In terms of *jus ad bellum*, the aggressor state is occupying the adversary's territory unlawfully but the victim state can occupy the adversary's territory lawfully since it is acting in self-defence. However, the law of international armed conflict applies equally to both sides regardless of the status of the conflicting parties under *jus ad bellum*. This difference of the operation of the respective legal regime continues throughout the conflict. The equal application of the law of international armed conflict remains intact even when the victim state becomes an aggressor by carrying out disproportionate self-defence, thereby rendering its occupation of the adversary's territory unlawful.

This section clarified that 'armed attack' and 'armed conflict' are distinct thresholds. While an armed attack most often amounts to an international armed conflict, the two thresholds can be at variance and thus, to establish the concurrent application of *jus ad bellum* and *jus in bello*, the thresholds in the respective legal regime should be met separately. The involvement of armed groups operating independently from any state particularly complicates the establishment of the existence of an armed attack and an armed conflict. The simultaneous beginning of an armed attack and international armed conflict has no bearing on the subsequent application of *jus ad bellum* and IHL: *jus ad bellum* creates an unequal status between the aggressor and the victim state, whereas IHL continues to apply equally to the conflicting parties throughout the conflict.

II. ROLE OF THE PRINCIPLE OF PROPORTIONALITY AND IHL IN THE CONDUCT OF SELF-DEFENCE[64]

This section discusses the principle of proportionality in the law of self-defence and its relation to IHL. It will first clarify the distinction between the principle of proportionality in self-defence and the principle of proportionality in IHL, and then discuss the relationship between the two principles of proportionality. It will also discuss how the other rules of IHL, such as those on methods and means of warfare and occupation, play a role in self-defence. The applicable IHL is the law of international armed conflict since, as noted earlier,[65] the law of non-international armed conflict is in principle irrelevant to the law of self-defence.

[64] See generally C Greenwood, 'Self-Defence and the Conduct of International Armed Conflict' in Y Dinstein (ed), *International Law at a Time of Perplexity: Essays in Honour of Shabtai Rosenne* (Dordrecht, Martinus Nijhoff, 1989).

[65] See section 3.I.A.

A. Distinction and Relationship between the Principle of Proportionality in the Law of Self-defence and IHL

The principle of proportionality in the law of self-defence and that in IHL are separate legal concepts and each has its own meaning and scope. This section discusses the contents of each principle of proportionality in turn and then the relationship between the two.

Principle of Proportionality in the Law of Self-defence

It is worth noting at the outset that the principle of proportionality is now a universally recognised customary rule in the law of self-defence that regulates the conduct of self-defence[66] but there is no universal consensus on the content of it.[67] Moreover, the application of the principle heavily depends on the facts of each case.[68] However, from various practices, the following indications may be helpful in applying it.

It is widely accepted that the principle of proportionality entails a balancing test between 1) an armed attack and the military response taken against it or 2) an armed attack and the aim to halt and repel it. Furthermore, four elements are frequently used to assess the proportionality: 1) target selection; 2) effects on civilians; 3) geographical scope; and 4) temporal scope. The examination of the contents of the principle of proportionality is particularly important since it is often seen as the only indicator to assess the legality of the use of force.[69]

First, the balancing test between an armed attack and the military response taken against it is a widely accepted interpretation of the principle of proportionality. The ICJ in the *Nicaragua* case authoritatively stated that 'self-defence would warrant only measures which are proportional to the armed attack and necessary to respond to it'.[70] The ICJ concluded

[66] *Nicaragua* case (Merits), para 186; *Nuclear Weapons* case (Advisory Opinion), para 41; *Oil Platforms* case (Merits), para 43; *Armed Activities* case (Merits), para 147.

[67] For suggestions on the contents of the principles of proportionality and necessity, see Brownlie, *International Law and the Use of Force by States*, 261–64; Greenwood, 'Self-Defence'; Schachter, *International Law*, 153–55; A Arend and R Beck, *International Law and the Use of Force* (London, Routledge, 1993) 162–70; R Higgins, *Problems and Process: International Law and How We Use It* (Oxford, Clarendon Press, 1994) 230–32; Gardam, *Necessity*, 155 *ff*; Gray, *International Law and the Use of Force*, 120–26; Dinstein, *War, Aggression and Self-Defence*, 4th edn, 207–13; T Gazzini, *The Changing Rules on the Use of Force in International Law* (Manchester, Manchester University Press, 2005) 147 *ff*; T Franck, 'On Proportionality of Countermeasures in International Law' (2008) 102 *American Journal of International Law* 715, 719 *ff*.

[68] Gray, *International Law and the Use of Force*, 121.

[69] In most cases involving the question on self-defence, the ICJ rejected the claim that an armed attack existed and hence there was no need to proceed to the assessment of proportionality and necessity. However, the Court proceeded to such examination to show that the use of force was, in any case, unlawful because of the lack of necessity or proportionality. See, eg, *Nicaragua* case (Merits), para 237; *Oil Platforms* case (Merits), para 77; *Armed Activities* case (Merits), para 147. See also Gray, *International Law and the Use of Force*, 124.

[70] *Nicaragua* case (Merits), para 176.

in the same case that the US use of force against Nicaragua was not proportionate, by balancing the US use of force and alleged armed attacks by Nicaragua.[71] This approach was followed in the *Oil Platforms*[72] and *Armed Activities*[73] cases.

This interpretation of the principle of proportionality is supported by state practice and experts.[74] However, it is also widely understood among experts that the principle of proportionality does not require the same means and methods to be used in response to an armed attack. Thus, Judge Higgins noted in the *Nuclear Weapons* case that 'the concept of proportionality referred to was that which was proportionate to repelling the attack, and not a requirement of symmetry between the mode of the initial attack and the mode of response'.[75]

On the other hand, the balancing test between an armed attack and the aim to halt and repel is also a widely accepted interpretation of the principle of proportionality. The influential report of the UN International Law Commission on state responsibility stated that 'The requirement of the proportionality of the action taken in self-defence . . . concerns the relationship between that action and its purpose, namely . . . that of halting and repelling the attack'.[76] This interpretation has been constantly supported in various practices such as during the negotiations on the Definition of Aggression,[77] 1950–53 Korean War,[78] *Oil Platforms*

[71] *Nicaragua* case (Merits), para 237.

[72] *Oil Platforms* case (Merits), para 77; Reply of Iran, para 7.62; Counter-Memorial of the US, para 4.35.

[73] *Armed Activities* case (Merits), para 147.

[74] See, eg, UNGA Sixth Committee 'Report of L de Brouckère on Article 16 of the Covenant of the League of Nations' (3 October 1952) UN Doc A/2211, Annex, Agenda Item 54, 29, para 41; China, UNSC Verbatim Record (30 October 1956) UN Doc S/PV.749, para 133; Guatemala, UNGA Sixth Committee (1957) GAOR 12th Session, 49, para 5; Syria, UNGA (1957) GAOR 12th Session Supp 16, 15, para 121; Czechoslovakia, UNSC Verbatim Record (7 August 1964) UN Doc S/PV.1141, para 25; *Nuclear Weapons* case, Written Statement of Mexico, para 58; *Wall* case, Written Statement of Malaysia, 53, para 151. The written statements can be found at the ICJ website, www.icj-cij.org. See also O Schachter, 'General Course in Public International Law' (1982) 178 *Recueil des Cours de l'Académie de Droit International* 1, 155; Higgins, *Problems and Process*, 231; A Randelzhofer, 'Article 51' in B Simma et al (eds), *The Charter of the United Nations: A Commentary*, 2nd edn, Vol I (Oxford, Oxford University Press, 2002) 805; Kolb, *Ius contra bellum*, 205; Dinstein, *War, Aggression and Self-Defence*, 4th edn, 237.

[75] *Nuclear Weapons* case, Dissenting Opinion of Judge Higgins, para 5. See also ILC, *Yearbook of the International Law Commission* Vol II, Part One (New York, United Nations, 1980) para 121; L Doswald-Beck (ed), *San Remo Manual on International Law Applicable to Armed Conflicts at Sea* (Cambridge, Cambridge University Press, 1995) 76; Kolb, *Ius contra bellum*, 205.

[76] ILC, *Yearbook of the International Law Commission* Vol II, Part One (New York, United Nations, 1980) para 121.

[77] UNGA (1969) GAOR 24th Session Supp 20, 29, para 73.

[78] UNSC Res 83 (27 June 1950) UN Doc S/RES/83. Whether the use of force against the Democratic People's Republic of Korea was collective self-defence or use of force authorised under Chapter VII will not be discussed here. See, eg, UN Secretariat, 'Note to the Director of Asia and the Pacific Division, Office of the Assistant Secretary-General, Department of Political Affairs, United Nations' (2003) *United Nations Juridical Yearbook* 553, paras 3 and 4.

case,[79] *Wall* case,[80] and *Armed Activities* case.[81] For example, the ICJ noted in the *Armed Activities* case that 'In view of the finding that Uganda engaged in an illegal military operation against the DRC, the Court considers that the DRC was entitled to use force in order to repel Uganda's attacks.'[82] Experts such as Christine Gray also note that 'necessity and proportionality mean that self-defence must not be retaliatory or punitive; the aim should be to halt and repel an attack'.[83] Many other experts support this interpretation.[84]

However, some go even further, claiming that the principle of proportionality allows the victim state to take self-defence measures, not merely to halt and repel but also to deter a future armed attack.[85] This interpretation may become relevant, particularly when self-defence requires the destruction of the source of the armed attack to halt any further armed attack, for example when responding to cross-border attacks by clandestine armed groups. The US noted as follows in justifying its military action against Afghanistan in response to the terrorist attacks on the US on 11 September 2001:[86]

> In response to these attacks [terrorist attacks on 11 September 2001], and in accordance with the inherent right of individual and collective self-defence, United States armed forces have initiated actions designed to prevent and deter future attacks on the United States.[87]

[79] *Oil Platforms* case (Merits), Memorial of Iran, para 4.21.

[80] *Wall* case, Written Statement of Indonesia, para 5 and South Africa, para 36.

[81] *Armed Activities* case (Merits), para 304.

[82] *Armed Activities* case (Merits), para 304.

[83] Gray, *International Law and the Use of Force*, 121.

[84] See Art 4 of the San Remo Manual on International Law Applicable to Armed Conflicts at Sea in Doswald-Beck (ed), *San Remo Manual*. See also Waldock, 'The Regulation of the Use of Force', 464; G Schwarzenberger, 'The Fundamental Principles of International Law' (1955) 87 *Recueil des Cours de l'Académie de Droit International* 195, 335; Schachter, *International Law*, 152; Jennings and Watts (eds), *Oppenheim's International Law*, 421; Higgins, *Problems and Process*, 231; J Delbrück, 'Proportionality' in R Bernhardt (ed), *Encyclopaedia of Public International Law* Vol III (Amsterdam, Elsevier Science BV, 1997) 1141; Randelzhofer, 'Article 51', 805; J Verhoeven, 'Les "étirements" de la légitime défense' (2002) 48 *Annuaire français de droit international* 47, 66; Kolb, *Ius contra bellum*, 205.

[85] H Kelsen, *Principles of International Law*, 2nd edn (New York, Holt, Reinhart, and Wilson, 1966) 82–83; M McDougal and F Feliciano, *The International Law of War* (New Haven, New Haven Press, 1994) 222–23; T Parker, 'Proportionality Principle in the War on Terror' (2002) 15 *Hague Yearbook of International Law* 3, 5; Dinstein, *War, Aggression and Self-Defence*, 4th edn, 237–38. See also C Gray, 'A Crisis of Legitimacy for the UN Collective Security System?' (2007) 56 *International and Comparative Law Quarterly* 157, 161 *ff*.

[86] For the accounts on the events, see UNGA, 'International Terrorism' (2001) 55 UNYB 60, 60 *ff*.

[87] See UNSC, 'Letter Dated 7 October 2001 from the Permanent Representative of the United States of America to the United Nations Addressed to the President of the Security Council' (7 October 2001) UN Doc S/2001/946. See also UNSC, 'Letter Dated 7 October 2001 from the Chargé d'Affaires a.i. of the Permanent Mission of the United Kingdom of Great Britain and Northern Ireland to the United Nations Addressed to the President of the Security Council' (7 October 2001) UN Doc S/2001/947. See further *Armed Activities* case (Merits), para 143. In this case, Uganda argued that its use of force was 'to secure Uganda's

Whether the aim to deter future attacks is accommodated by the principle of proportionality is not yet clear. However, attacking the members and bases of armed groups endlessly in order to deter future armed attacks seems to defeat the purpose of the principle of proportionality and self-defence per se, which was meant to be a temporary right.[88] Thus, for example, it is questionable whether the attacks on suspected Al-Qaeda members in Yemen in 2002 could have been proportionate self-defence in response to the terrorist attacks on the US on 11 September 2001.[89] The limits should be drawn somewhere.[90]

In addition to these interpretations of the principle of proportionality, there are at least four elements to assess the proportionality of the conduct of self-defence that are frequently referred to: 1) target selection; 2) effects on civilians; 3) geographical scope; and 4) temporal scope.

First, on target selection, there is certain practice that the targets which the victim state is attacking should be objects that are relevant to the initial armed attack. For example, the ICJ noted in the *Oil Platforms* case that 'The United States must also show that its actions were necessary and proportional to the armed attack made on it, and that the platforms were a legitimate military target open to attack in the exercise of self-defence'.[91] The Court later found that the oil platform attacked was not 'an appropriate military target'.[92] The Court also took a similar approach in the *Nicaragua* case when it implied that the US use of force was out of context in relation to the alleged armed attacks by Nicaragua.[93] The same can be

legitimate security interests' and the ICJ characterised it as follows: 'The specified security needs are essentially preventative . . . to prevent attacks from "genocidal elements"'. The Court later found that Uganda's use of force could not have been proportionate in any case. See *Armed Activities* case (Merits), para 147.

[88] Art 51 of the UN Charter provides that the entitlement to the right of self-defence continues 'until the Security Council has taken the measures necessary to maintain international peace and security.' See also Gray, *International Law and the Use of Force*, 104–05.

[89] Whether the terrorist attacks on the US on 11 September 2001 would qualify as an 'armed attack' within the meaning of Art 51 is a different question which will not be dealt with here. For contrasting views, see Y Dinstein, *War, Aggression and Self-Defence*, 3rd edn (Cambridge, Cambridge University Press, 2001) 213–15 and G Guillaume, 'Terrorism and International Law' (2004) 53 *International and Comparative Law Quarterly* 537, 546. See also the discussions in section 5.II.A below.

[90] See, eg, A Cassese, 'Terrorism Is Also Disrupting Some Crucial Legal Categories of International Law' (2001) 12 *European Journal of International Law* 993, 997; M Byers, 'Terrorism, the Use of Force and International Law after 11 September' (2002) 51 *International and Comparative Law Quarterly* 400, 408; Verhoeven, 'Les "étirements" de la légitime défense', 67–68; V Lowe, 'Clear and Present Danger: Responses to Terrorism' (2005) 54 *International and Comparative Law Quarterly* 185, 191 *ff*.

[91] *Oil Platforms* case (Merits), para 51. See also para 74: 'One aspect of these criteria [of necessity and proportionality of the measures taken in self-defence] is the nature of the target of the force used avowedly in self-defence. In its communications to the Security Council, in particular in that of 19 October 1987 . . . the United States indicated the grounds on which it regarded the Iranian platforms as legitimate targets for an armed action in self-defence.'

[92] *Oil Platforms* case (Merits), para 77.

[93] *Nicaragua* case (Merits), para 237.

said when self-defence measures are in response to an armed attack by an armed group.[94] The self-defence measures should be directed against the objects and members of armed groups directly relevant to the initial armed attack.[95] The role of IHL in targeting in the conduct of self-defence will be discussed later but it suffices to note at this point that the contribution of the ICJ was to indicate that the targets of attacks in self-defence should be objects relevant to the original armed attack, which is an aspect IHL does not deal with.[96]

The limits on target selection also face challenges in relation to cross-border attacks by armed groups. First, if, for example, an armed group has a base at a frontier and its attacks are carried out against a neighbouring state, it may be possible for the attacked state to take self-defence measures against the objects or members of the armed group relevant to the initial armed attack. Thus, when the armed groups in the eastern DRC attacked Uganda across the border, it may have been realistic for Uganda to attack the objects and persons relevant to the initial armed attack.[97] A more difficult case is when an armed group has several bases in different countries and carries out attacks in several countries. In this case, can a state take self-defence measures against all the bases of the armed group in several countries or are the targets limited to the bases where the members of the armed group who carried out the actual attacks are present?[98] This

[94] On the question of whether an attack from an armed group can be qualified as an 'armed attack', see section 5.II.A below.

[95] C Greenwood, 'International Law and the United States' Air Operation against Libya' (1986–87) 89 *West Virginia Law Review* 933, 947.

[96] For further discussions on this topic, see Schachter, *International Law*, 154–55; Arend and Beck, *International Law and the Use of Force*, 166–69; Greenwood, 'International Law and the United States' Air Operation against Libya', 278–79; Higgins, *Problems and Process*, 232; Byers, 'Terrorism', 408.

[97] However, it is worth noting that Uganda carried out a disproportionate military action against the attacks from the DRC armed groups. The ICJ in the *Armed Activities* case noted as follows: 'The taking of airports and towns many hundreds of kilometres from Uganda's border would not seem proportionate to the series of transborder attacks it claimed had given rise to the right of self-defence, nor to be necessary to that end.' See *Armed Activities* case (Merits), para 143.

[98] For discussions on this topic, see Kelsen, *Principles of International Law*, 63; Brownlie, *International Law and the Use of Force by States*, 279; Greenwood, 'International Law and the United States' Air Operation against Libya', 947; S Alexandrov, *Self-Defense against the Use of Force in International Law* (The Hague, Kluwer Law International, 1996) 183; I Brownlie, 'General Course on Public International Law' (1995) 255 *Recueil des Cours de l'Académie de Droit International* 1, 204; Cassese, 'Terrorism', 997–98; J Delbrück, 'The Fight against Global Terrorism: Self-Defense or Collective Security as International Police Action? Some Comments on the International Legal Implications of the "War against Terrorism"' (2001) 44 *German Yearbook of International Law* 9, 17–18; Byers, 'Terrorism', 406–10; R Wolfrum and C Philipp, 'The Status of the Taliban: Their Obligations and Rights under International Law' (2002) 6 *Max Planck Yearbook of United Nations Law* 559, 586–96; R Wolfrum, 'The Attack of September 11, 2001, the Wars against the Taliban and Iraq: Is There a Need to Reconsider International Law on the Recourse to Force and the Rules in Armed Conflict?' (2003) 7 *Max Planck Yearbook of United Nations Law* 1, 35–39; M Schmitt, 'Targeting and Humanitarian Law: Current Issues' (2004) 34 *Israel Yearbook on Human Rights* 59, 81–89.

question arose when the US attacked the Sudan and Afghanistan following the terrorist attacks on the US embassies in Kenya and Tanzania[99] and when it attacked Libya following a number of terrorist attacks against US nationals, embassies, and bases around the world.[100] Similar cases were the Israeli attacks on the bases of the Palestine Liberation Organisation (PLO) in Lebanon and Tunisia.[101] More recently, the US attacks on Al-Qaeda bases in Afghanistan and Al-Qaeda members in Yemen raised the same question. If the attacks on the US on 11 September 2001 were considered as an armed attack, could the US attack the Al-Qaeda bases and members regardless of whether they were directly relevant to the initial armed attack? US Congress seemed to have answered these questions positively:

> The President is authorized to use all necessary and appropriate force against those nations, organizations, or persons he determines planned, authorized, committed, or aided the terrorist attack that occurred on September 11, 2001, or harboured such organizations or persons, in order to prevent any future acts of international terrorism against the United States by such nations, organizations or persons.[102]

However, if the victim state can attack the bases and members of armed groups regardless of their direct relevance to the initial armed attack, this may be overstretching the threshold of armed attack and defeat the purpose of the principle of proportionality which is aimed at regulating the conduct of self-defence.[103]

The second element is related to the first. The ICJ noted in the *Oil Platforms* case that proportionate self-defence should normally be directed

[99] For the accounts of these events, see UNGA, 'Measures to Eliminate Terrorism' (1998) 52 UNYB 1216, 1218–20; UNGA, 'Sudan' (1998) 52 UNYB 184, 184 *ff*; UNGA, 'Situation in Afghanistan' (1998) 52 UNYB 288, 291. See also UNSC, 'Letter Dated 20 August 1998 from the Permanent Representative of the United States of America to the United Nations Addressed to the President of the Security Council' (20 August 1998) UN Doc S/1998/780; Non-aligned Movement, XII Summit (Durban, 2–3 September 1998), 'Basic Documents of the XII Summit of the Non-Aligned Movement' (1998), para 179, Non-Aligned Movement website, www.nam.gov.za/xiisummit.

[100] See generally Greenwood, 'International Law and the United States' Air Operation against Libya'.

[101] For the accounts on Lebanon, see UNGA, 'Situation between Individual Arab States and Israel' (1982) 36 UNYB 425, 428 *ff* and for Tunisia, see UNGA, 'Related Questions' (1985) 39 UNYB 285, 285 *ff*. See also UNSC Res 520 (17 September 1982) UN Doc S/RES/520 condemning the Israeli incursion into Beirut, Lebanon in 1982 and UNSC Res 573 (4 October 1985) UN Doc S/RES/573 condemning the 'armed aggression' of Israel against Tunisia in 1985.

[102] US, Joint Resolution to Authorize the Use of United States Armed Forces against Those Responsible for the Recent Attacks Launched against the United States, Public Law No 107–40, 115 Stat. 224 (2001), Section 2(a). See also UNSC, 'Letter Dated 7 October 2001 from the Chargé d'Affaires a.i. of the Permanent Mission of the United Kingdom of Great Britain and Northern Ireland to the United Nations Addressed to the President of the Security Council' (7 October 2001) UN Doc S/2001/947.

[103] Cassese, 'Terrorism', 997–98; Byers, 'Terrorism', 408; Wolfrum and Philipp, 'The Status of the Taliban', 589–90.

against military objectives relevant to the initial armed attack which also implies that it excludes attacks on civilians or at least minimises effects on civilians. As will be seen later, target selection, including attacks on civilians, is an aspect which IHL regulates in great detail. However, the principle of proportionality in the law of self-defence, although not codified as clearly as IHL, also contains limits on the effects on civilians. Civilian casualties and damage to civilian objects have been employed as a reason to prove proportionate or disproportionate self-defence measures in many state practices, such as in the 1964 Harib Fort incident,[104]1971 India–Pakistan Conflict,[105] 1980–88 Iran–Iraq War,[106] 1982 Israeli attacks on Iraqi nuclear installations,[107] *Nuclear Weapons* case,[108] 2001 US attacks on Afghanistan,[109] *Oil Platforms* case,[110] *Wall* case,[111] 2006 Lebanon Conflict,[112] 2008 Georgia Conflict,[113] and the 2009 Gaza Conflict.[114] In particular, some

[104] Czechoslovakia, UNSC Verbatim Record (8 April 1964) UN Doc S/PV.1110, para 25; UK, UNSC Verbatim Record (2 April 1964) UN Doc S/PV.1106, para 54.

[105] India, UNSC Verbatim Record (12 December 1971) UN Doc S/PV.1613, para 202; Pakistan, UNSC Verbatim Record (21 December 1971) UN Doc S/PV.1621, para 108.

[106] Iraq, UNSC Verbatim Record (15 October 1980) UN Doc S/PV.2250, para 400; UNSC Verbatim Record (17 October 1980) UN Doc S/PV.2251, para 63.

[107] Israel, UNSC Verbatim Record (12 June 1981) UN Doc S/PV.2280, para 102.

[108] *Nuclear Weapons* case, Written Statement of the UK, 38.

[109] UNSC, 'Letter Dated 7 October 2001 from the Permanent Representative of the United States of America to the United Nations Addressed to the President of the Security Council' (7 October 2001) UN Doc S/2001/946.

[110] *Oil Platforms* case (Merits), Memorial of Iran, para 4.39; Counter-Memorial of the US, paras 4.34, 4.35, 4.47, and 4.50; Rejoinder of the US, paras 5.37, 5.40, and 5.51.

[111] *Wall* case, Written Statements of Indonesia, para 6; Malaysia, para 151; Saudi Arabia, paras 32 and 34; South Africa, para 36. See also Written Statement of Palestine, para 534.

[112] Many states in the Security Council pointed out the disproportionate measures of Israel based on the extent of civilian casualties and damage to civilian objects. See China, UNSC Verbatim Record (14 July 2006) UN Doc S/PV.5489, 11; Republic of the Congo, UNSC Verbatim Record (14 July 2006) UN Doc S/PV.5489, 13; France, UNSC Verbatim Record (14 July 2006) UN Doc S/PV.5489, 17; Greece, UNSC Verbatim Record (14 July 2006) UN Doc S/PV.5489, 17; Japan, UNSC Verbatim Record (14 July 2006) UN Doc S/PV.5489, 12; Russia, UNSC Verbatim Record (14 July 2006) UN Doc S/PV.5489, 7; Tanzania, UNSC Verbatim Record (14 July 2006) UN Doc S/PV.5489, 13. Other states stated that self-defence should be proportionate. See Denmark, UNSC Verbatim Record (14 July 2006) UN Doc S/PV.5489, 15; Peru, UNSC Verbatim Record (14 July 2006) UN Doc S/PV.5489, 14; UK, UNSC Verbatim Record (13 July 2006) UN Doc S/PV.5488, 5.

[113] Council of the European Union, Independent International Fact-Finding Mission on the Conflict in Georgia, 'Report' Vol II (September 2009) 272, Independent International Fact-Finding Mission on the Conflict in Georgia website, www.ceiig.ch. See also France, UNSC Verbatim Record (19 August 2008) UN Doc S/PV.5961, 6; Panama, UNSC Verbatim Record (10 August 2008) UN Doc S/PV.5953, 16.

[114] Many states in the Security Council pointed out the disproportionate measures of Israel based on the extent of civilian casualties and damage to civilian objects. See Burkina Faso, UNSC Verbatim Record (31 December 2008) UN Doc S/PV.6060, 15; Costa Rica, UNSC Verbatim Record (31 December 2008) UN Doc S/PV.6060, 16; France, UNSC Verbatim Record (31 December 2008) UN Doc S/PV.6060, 9; Indonesia, UNSC Verbatim Record (31 December 2008) UN Doc S/PV.6060, 10; Libya, UNSC Verbatim Record (31 December 2008) UN Doc S/PV.6060, 8; South Africa, UNSC Verbatim Record (31 December 2008) UN Doc S/PV.6060, 9; Vietnam, UNSC Verbatim Record (31 December 2008) UN Doc S/PV.6060, 13. Other states stated that self-defence should be proportionate. See Belgium, UNSC Verbatim Record

of the statements of states were strikingly similar to the principle of proportionality in IHL, which will be discussed later in this section. For example, the US, shortly after it commenced attacks on Afghanistan in 2001, noted that 'In carrying out these actions [in self-defence], the United States is committed to minimizing civilian casualties and damage to civilian property'.[115] It must, however, be stressed that the limits on attacking civilians imposed by the law of self-defence and IHL should not be considered as identical. The rules on targeting in IHL have their own scope and meaning, codified in detail in treaty law. Thus, violations of the IHL rules on targeting will not automatically amount to disproportionate self-defence. Violations of the IHL rules on targeting can be considered disproportionate self-defence only if those violations overstep the principle of proportionality in the law of self-defence. Mere IHL violations do not automatically constitute disproportionate self-defence. This distinction is crucial because the scope of the effects on civilians tolerated by the law of self-defence and IHL may be at variance. For example, if one civilian is directly targeted in a particular military operation during the course of self-defence, this is clearly a violation of IHL, namely Article 51(2) of the 1977 First Additional Protocol or Article 13(2) of the 1977 Second Additional Protocol,[116] or common Article 3(1)(a) of the 1949 Geneva Conventions, but it may not be disproportionate self-defence. To see the regulations on targeting in the law of self-defence and IHL as identical can lead to an unacceptable consequence where the argument in *jus ad bellum*, that the civilian casualties were within the bounds of the principle of proportionality, overrides the strict rules laid down in IHL, which prohibits targeting against even a single civilian. Thus, even when the effects on civilians seem to be within the bounds of proportionate self-defence, they should still be assessed against IHL.

Thirdly, on geographical scope, state practice has not led to any consensus yet. On one hand, some argue that self-defence measures should take place in the vicinity of where the armed attack occurred.[117] On the

(31 December 2008) UN Doc S/PV.6060, 17; Italy, UNSC Verbatim Record (31 December 2008) UN Doc S/PV.6060, 13.

[115] UNSC, 'Letter Dated 7 October 2001 from the Permanent Representative of the United States of America to the United Nations Addressed to the President of the Security Council' (7 October 2001) UN Doc S/2001/946. See also UNSC, 'Letter Dated 7 October 2001 from the Chargé d'Affaires a.i. of the Permanent Mission of the United Kingdom of Great Britain and Northern Ireland to the United Nations Addressed to the President of the Security Council' (7 October 2001) UN Doc S/2001/947.

[116] For their customary law status, see Rule 1 in J-M Henckaerts and L Doswald-Beck, *Customary International Humanitarian Law* Vol I: Rules (Geneva, International Committee of the Red Cross and Cambridge, Cambridge University Press, 2005) 3.

[117] See, eg, *Armed Activities* case (Merits), Reply of the DRC, para 3.168. The written proceedings can be found at the ICJ website, www.icj-cij.org. See also the following state practice: Czechoslovakia, UNSC Verbatim Record (7 August 1964) UN Doc S/PV.1141, paras 25 and 32; Pakistan, UNSC Verbatim Record (18 September 1965) UN Doc S/PV.1240, para 34; Israel–Lebanon Conflict, UNSC Res 270 (26 August 1969) UN Doc S/RES/270; Israel, UNSC

other hand, some argue that self-defence measures can be taken against the source of the armed attack, wherever that may be.

In many major uses of force in the past such as the 1964 Gulf of Tonkin incident,[118] 1965 India–Pakistan Conflict,[119] 1973 Arab–Israel Conflict,[120] 1980–88 Iran–Iraq War,[121] 1986 US attacks on Libya,[122] *Oil Platforms* case,[123] *Wall* case,[124] and the *Armed Activities* case,[125] many states implied that self-defence measures should be confined to a certain area that would be proportionate to the original armed attack.

The geographical limits imposed by the principle of proportionality may be more flexibly applied in the case of an on-the-spot armed attack. In such a case, the aggressor could often be far from the area of the armed attack and hence, self-defence measures against the aggressor might have to take place outside the area of the armed attack. For example, in the *Oil Platforms* case, the ICJ considered the missile attacks on a US tanker, *Sea Isle City*, and the subsequent US attacks against two Iranian oil fields in Reshadat and Resalat. The attack on the *Sea Isle City* took place near a harbour in Kuwait whereas the US attacks took place further south, near Qatar. The Court in this case concluded that the necessity to attack the Iranian oil fields was lacking and hence, the question of proportionality did not have to be answered. However, the Court mentioned that 'the attack of 19 October 1987 [by the US on the Iranian oil platforms] might, had the Court found that it was necessary in response to the Sea Isle City incident as an armed attack committed by Iran, have been considered proportionate'.[126] The Court, hence, did not seem to consider that the distance between the area of the armed attack (near Kuwait) and the area of the purported self-defence (near Qatar) as a factor in assessing the

Verbatim Record (9 October 1973) UN Doc S/PV.1744, para 89; India, UNSC Verbatim Record (9 October 1973) UN Doc S/PV.1744, para 180; Iraq, UNSC Verbatim Record (15 October 1980) UN Doc S/PV.2250, para 40; Libya, UNSC Verbatim Record (31 March 1986) UN Doc S/PV.2671, 38; *Oil Platforms* case (Merits), Memorial of Iran, para 4.24; *Wall* case, Written Statement of Jordan, paras 5.275–5.277; *Armed Activities* case (Merits), Rejoinder of Uganda, para 289. See also O Bring, 'The Falklands Crisis and International Law' (1982) 51 *Nordic Journal of International Law* 129, 143; C Greenwood, 'Self-Defence', 276–78; Higgins, *Problems and Process*, 232; E David, *Principes de droit des conflits armés*, 3rd edn (Brussels, Bruylant, 2002) 152–53; Gardam, *Necessity*, 162–67.

[118] Czechoslovakia, UNSC Verbatim Record (7 August 1994) UN Doc S/PV.1141, paras 25 and 32.

[119] Pakistan, UNSC Verbatim Record (18 September 1965) UN Doc S/PV.1240, para 34.

[120] India, UNSC Verbatim Record (9 October 1973) UN Doc S/PV.1744, para 180.

[121] Iraq, UNSC Verbatim Record (15 October 1980) UN Doc S/PV.2250, para 40; UNSC, 'Further Report of the Secretary-General on the Implementation of Security Council Resolution 598 (1987)' (9 December 1991) UN Doc S/23273, para 7.

[122] Libya, UNSC Verbatim Record (31 March 1986) UN Doc S/PV.2671, 38.

[123] *Oil Platforms* case (Merits), Memorial of Iran, para 4.24.

[124] *Wall* case, Written Statement of Jordan, paras 5.275–5.277.

[125] *Armed Activities* case (Merits), Reply of the DRC, paras 3.168 and 3.172; Rejoinder of Uganda, para 289.

[126] *Oil Platforms* case (Merits), para 77.

proportionality.[127] The Court seemed to put more emphasis on whether the targets were relevant to the initial armed attack.[128]

On the other hand, when there is a series of on-the-spot armed attacks, the self-defence measures are likely to last for a longer period than a response against a single armed attack. In such a case, the geographical expansion of the self-defence measures could be limited by the principle of proportionality. For example, in the *Armed Activities* case, the ICJ considered the alleged self-defence of Uganda against attacks from armed groups in the eastern DRC, at the border with Uganda. The Court recognised that the Ugandan armed forces were present in most major towns in the north east (Province Orientale) and north west (Equateur) of the DRC[129] and concluded that 'the Court cannot fail to observe . . . that the taking of airports and towns many hundreds of kilometres from Uganda's border would not seem proportionate to the series of transborder attacks it claimed had given rise to the right of self-defence'.[130] This case clearly demonstrated that the principle of proportionality imposes limits on the geographical extent of self-defence.

Another example is the 2006 Lebanon Conflict. This conflict began with attacks from an armed group in south Lebanon, Hizbullah, on Israel.[131] As the conflict progressed, Israel also attacked south Beirut and the Bekaa Valley, which were far from south Lebanon.[132] This could well be beyond proportionate self-defence.[133]

The 2008 Georgia Conflict also provides an indication. The Independent International Fact-Finding Commission on the Conflict in Georgia stated that if the Russian allegation that the Russian military base was attacked by Georgia was true, Russia could exercise the right of self-defence. However, the Commission also found that the attacks by Russia on the north-west of Georgia (upper Kodori Valley), deployment of armoured units to reach extensive parts of Georgia, setting up of military positions in and nearby major Georgian towns, control of major highways, and posting of military vessels in the Black Sea were not proportionate self-defence. This shows that there are certain limits to the geographical extent of self-defence measures.

The geographical limits also have significant impact when self-defence involves occupation of the aggressor's territory. As noted earlier, self-

[127] For the US position, see *Oil Platforms* case (Merits), Counter-Memorial of the US, para 4.32.

[128] For an indication, see *Oil Platforms* case (Merits), para 76.

[129] *Oil Platforms* case (Merits), paras 79–91.

[130] *Oil Platforms* case (Merits), para 147.

[131] UNHRC, 'Report of the Commission of Inquiry on Lebanon Pursuant to Human Rights Council Resolution S-2/1' (23 November 2006) UN Doc A/HRC/3/2, para 93.

[132] UNHRC, 'Report of the Commission of Inquiry on Lebanon Pursuant to Human Rights Council Resolution S-2/1' (23 November 2006) UN Doc A/HRC/3/2, paras 116 and 123.

[133] A Zimmermann, 'The Second Lebanon War: *Jus ad Bellum*, *Jus in Bello* and the Issue of Proportionality' (2007) 11 *Max Planck Yearbook of United Nations Law* 99.

defence is proportionate when it is to halt and repel the armed attack. Hence, in principle, the occupation of the aggressor's territory can rarely be justified under the principle of proportionality since if a state was invaded and occupied by the aggressor, it suffices to drive the aggressor out of the occupied state. At most, temporary and partial occupation of the aggressor's territory can be justified.

For example, in the 1982 Falklands/Malvinas Conflict, it was widely seen that Argentina invaded and occupied the Falklands/Malvinas Islands, which belonged to the UK.[134] The UK considered the invasion and occupation as an armed attack and exercised the right of self-defence. The UK subsequently drove out the Argentine forces from the Falklands/Malvinas Islands but did not pursue them to the Argentine mainland. It has been said that these self-defence measures of the UK were proportionate because the UK action was confined to regaining control over the Falklands/Malvinas Islands and did not extend to the Argentine mainland.[135]

Another example is the 1991 Gulf War. In this conflict, Iraq invaded Kuwait but was driven out from Kuwait by the multinational forces. The multinational forces subsequently pursued the Iraqi forces into the Iraqi territory and presumably temporarily occupied some towns during their military operations around Basra in the south of Iraq.[136] In contrast with the US/UK invasion of Iraq in 2003, which extended to the whole territory of Iraq, the multinational forces in the 1991 Gulf War did not go beyond southern Iraq and withdrew. The bulk of the multinational forces subsequently withdrew from Iraq within a few months. There are debates as to whether the actions of the multinational forces were collective self-defence or enforcement measures under Chapter VII of the UN Charter.[137] Supposing that they were collective self-defence, the multinational forces probably could not have gone beyond expelling the Iraqi forces from Kuwait and carrying out limited military operations in the Iraqi territory to pursue the remnants of the Iraqi forces.

The Eritrea–Ethiopia Conflict also provides an example of the geographical extent of occupation in self-defence. In the *Jus ad Bellum* Award, the Eritrea–Ethiopia Claims Commission concluded that Eritrea invaded and occupied, in violation of *jus ad bellum*, a town in western Ethiopia at the border with Eritrea. The town was clearly situated in the Ethiopian territory. The Eritrean offensive continued in the central part of the border between Eritrea and Ethiopia (what is called the 'Central Front' by the Commission) and occupied several towns in Ethiopia. Ethiopia for its part launched its counter-attacks in self-defence and drove out the Eritrean

[134] See generally UNGA, 'Status of the Falkland Islands (Malvinas)' (1982) UNYB 1320, 1320 *ff*.

[135] Bring, 'The Falklands Crisis', 143. See also Greenwood, 'Self-Defence', 277.

[136] See US Department of Defense, 'Final Report', 339.

[137] See n 55 above.

forces in the Central Front. It then occupied towns on the Eritrean side of the Central Front that were close to the Eritrea–Ethiopia border. While the Commission did not conclude on the proportionality of the occupation in self-defence by Ethiopia, it would not have been proportionate to pursue the Eritrean forces to the capital, Asmara, and occupy it. The most it could have done was probably to occupy several towns on the Eritrean side of the Central Front that were situated at the Eritrea–Ethiopia border, and only temporarily. Expanding the front beyond the Central Front (for example to the eastern part of the Eritrea–Ethiopia border), at the initiative of Ethiopia, would also not have been proportionate self-defence.[138] However, the Commission did recognise that once an armed attack occurred in the eastern part of the Eritrea–Ethiopia border, the conflict escalated and spread to the central and western parts of the border and hence implied that the self-defence of Ethiopia could not be confined to the area of the initial armed attack.[139] Even so, Ethiopia's occupation in self-defence inside Eritrea probably could not have gone beyond the border region.

In contrast, in the 1967 Arab–Israel Conflict, Israel claimed self-defence against an alleged armed attack from Egypt, which allegedly carried out bombardment from the air and land on villages along the border with Egypt and Israel.[140] However, at the end of the conflict, Israel had occupied the Gaza Strip, the Sinai Peninsula, the Golan Heights and the West Bank, which could hardly be argued as proportionate self-defence in terms of geographical extent.

The geographical limitation inherent in the principle of proportionality is a difficult question particularly in the context of transnational terrorism since the members of terrorist groups are often no longer in the vicinity of the original armed attack, as in the case of the terrorist attacks on the US on 11 September 2001.[141] In practice, the US has carried out attacks on alleged terrorist bases in the Sudan and Afghanistan in response to attacks from armed groups,[142] and Israel against the PLO bases in Lebanon[143] and Tunisia.[144] In these cases, the original armed attack (assuming that they qualify as 'armed attack' within the meaning of Article 51) did not take place where self-defence measures were directed against.

[138] See, however, the position of India during the 1971 India–Pakistan Conflict, UNSC Verbatim Record (12 December 1971) UN Doc S/PV.1611, para 95.

[139] Eritrea–Ethiopia Claims Commission, *Jus ad Bellum* case (Partial Award), para 19.

[140] UNSC, 'Outbreak of Hostilities on 5 June 1967 and Consideration by the Security Council' (1967) UNYB 174, 175.

[141] For discussions, see, eg, Schachter, *International Law*, 154; Delbrück, 'The Fight against Global Terrorism', 16–17.

[142] UNSC, 'Condemnation of Terrorist Attacks in Nairobi and Dar es Salaam' (1998) UNYB 1281, 1281 *ff*.

[143] UNSC, 'Israel and Lebanon' (1981) UNYB 283, 287 *ff*.

[144] UNSC, 'Related Questions' (1985) UNYB 285, 285 *ff*.

However, it is also questionable whether attacks from a terrorist group would entitle the victim state to carry out self-defence measures against the members of the terrorist group wherever they may be found. US Congress took the approach that there is no geographical limits to attack transnational terrorist groups.[145] While the US carried out major attacks only against Afghanistan, the above authorisation was not limited to the territory of Afghanistan. The US justification of its self-defence measures against Afghanistan in 2001 reflects this point when it said that 'We may find that our self-defence requires further actions with respect to other organizations and other States'.[146] A real case of the extended use of this authorisation seemed to be the US attacks on suspected Al-Qaeda members in Yemen in 2002. If one follows down this line of approach, it will give the victim state an unlimited right to attack members of terrorist groups anywhere on the globe. As noted earlier, this approach would render the principle of proportionality irrelevant.

Finally, on the temporal scope, there is a wide consensus that the principle of proportionality can be assessed in relation to: 1) instant self-defence; and 2) continuous self-defence.[147]

In discussing the principle of proportionality, the conclusion of the Chatham House International Law Programme provides that 'The force used must take into account the self-defence operation "as a whole". It does not relate to specific incidents of targeting (which is a matter for international humanitarian law).'[148] However, the ICJ in the *Nicaragua* and

[145] See text to n 102 above.

[146] UNSC, 'Letter Dated 7 October 2001 from the Permanent Representative of the United States of America to the United Nations Addressed to the President of the Security Council' (7 October 2001) UN Doc S/2001/946.

[147] The temporal element of the principle of proportionality may also include the duration between an armed attack and the beginning of self-defence measures (which is sometimes referred to as the principle of immediacy), but this relates more to when self-defence measures should be taken and not to the actual conduct of self-defence. See generally T Gill, 'The Temporal Dimension of Self-Defense: Anticipation, Pre-emption, Prevention and Immediacy' in M Schmitt and J Pejic (eds), *International Law and Armed Conflict: Exploring the Faultlines* (The Netherlands, Koninklijke Brill BV, 2007). This section is concerned more with the latter and thus, the discussion on the temporal element is limited to the duration of self-defence measures. See the following state practice: Iraq, UNSC Verbatim Record (3 April 1964) UN Doc S/PV.1107, para 17; Czechoslovakia, UNSC Verbatim Record (7 August 1964) UN Doc S/PV.1141, para 30; UNGA Special Committee for Defining Aggression (1970) GAOR 25th Session Supp 19, para 131; *Nicaragua* case (Merits), para 237; UNSC, 'Further Report of the Secretary-General on the Implementation of Security Council Resolution 598 (1987)' (9 December 1991) UN Doc S/23273, para 7; *Oil Platforms* case (Merits), Reply of Iran, paras 7.20, 7.47, and 7.57; Counter-Memorial of the US, para 4.35; *Wall* case, Written Statement of South Africa, para 38; *Armed Activities* case (Merits), Reply of the Democratic Republic of the Congo, para 3.175; Rejoinder of Uganda, para 290.

See also Greenwood, 'Self-Defence', 275–76; Jennings and Watts (eds), *Oppenheim's International Law*, n 5 in 418; Higgins, *Problems and Process*, 231; Gardam, *Necessity*, 167–68. Compare: Dinstein, *War, Aggression and Self-Defence*, 4th edn, 237.

[148] E Wilmshurst, 'The Chatham House Principles of International Law on the Use of Force in Self-Defence' (2006) 55 *International and Comparative Law Quarterly* 963, 969. See also

Oil Platforms cases took the approach that the principle of proportionality of self-defence covers both instant and continuous self-defence.[149] In the *Nicaragua* case, the Court assessed the proportionality of a specific US use of force by stating that 'the Court cannot regard the United States activities . . . those relating to the mining of the Nicaraguan ports and the attacks on ports, oil installations, etc., as satisfying that criterion [of proportionality].'[150] Similarly, in the *Oil Platforms* case, the Court dealt with two specific US attacks on Iranian oil platforms and the principle of proportionality was applied to these two cases.[151] Thus, the principle of proportionality covers instant self-defence.

At the same time, the principle of proportionality also covers continuous self-defence. In the *Oil Platforms* case, when the Court considered the proportionality of a US attack allegedly in self-defence against an Iranian oil platform, it noted that 'it cannot close its eyes to the scale of the whole operation' called 'Operation Praying Mantis', 'which involved . . . the destruction of two Iranian frigates and a number of other naval vessels and aircraft'.[152] The Court concluded that the whole operation as well as the specific attack allegedly in self-defence, which was part of the operation, could not have been a proportionate use of force in self-defence.[153] Another case is the ICJ in the *Armed Activities* case when the Court concluded that the DRC was acting in self-defence during the period after Uganda began capturing or occupying towns in the DRC. A further example is the 1982 Falklands/Malvinas Conflict when it was considered that the UK's self-defence continued until the occupation of the Falklands/Malvinas Islands by Argentina ended.

It is clear from the above that the proportionality of self-defence is measured not only against each individual self-defence measure but also the totality of self-defence measures. However, the difficult part in any use of force in self-defence is to determine until when a state can resort to force in self-defence. The answer to this question may be easier when a state is carrying out instant self-defence against an on-the-spot armed attack (such as the 1964 Gulf of Tonkin incident).[154] In this case, the use of force (armed attack and the self-defence measure taken against it) in question is of a limited nature which allows a simpler assessment of proportionality.

D Kritsiotis, 'On the *Jus ad Bellum* and *Jus in Bello* of Operation Enduring Freedom' (2003) *American Society of International Law Proceedings* 35, 38.

[149] On this topic, see, eg, Doswald-Beck (ed), *San Remo Manual*, 77. See also Council of the European Union, Independent International Fact-Finding Mission on the Conflict in Georgia, 'Report' Vol II (September 2009) 249–51.

[150] *Nicaragua* case (Merits), para 237. See also Bring, 'The Falklands Crisis', 143.

[151] *Oil Platforms* case (Merits), para 77.

[152] *Oil Platforms* case (Merits), para 77.

[153] *Oil Platforms* case (Merits), para 77.

[154] See UNGA, 'Complaint by United States concerning the Diplomatic Republic of Viet-Nam' (1964) UNYB 147, 147 *ff*.

A more difficult case is when there is no symmetry in duration between an armed attack and the self-defence measures, or when both are continuous. Different situations could be envisaged:

- instant self-defence against a continuous armed attack (such as Israel's frequent use of force against armed groups in neighbouring states);
- continuous self-defence against an on-the-spot armed attack (such as the US use of force against Al-Qaeda since 2001, if the Al-Qaeda attacks were to be considered as 'armed attacks');
- continuous self-defence against a continuous armed attack (such as the UK use of force against Argentina's occupation of the Falklands/Malvinas Islands in 1982);
- continuous self-defence against an accumulation of on-the-spot armed attacks (such as Israel's use of force against Hizbullah in Lebanon in 2006, if the attacks from Hizbullah were to be considered as 'armed attacks').

The principle of proportionality can be applied to all these cases but assessing the proportionality is not straightforward in all cases. The simple answer is that the use of force in self-defence can continue until the armed attack is halted and repelled. The problem with this answer is obviously to determine when the armed attack is considered halted and repelled. Such determination depends heavily on the facts of each case. However, a critical factor may be that the situation after self-defence measures must at least be the one before the armed attack by the aggressor. This, in practice, could mean that the aggressor is driven out from the territory that was invaded or occupied (as in the case of the Falklands/Malvinas Conflict), or military targets of the armed forces that carried out the armed attack are destroyed (as in the case of *Sea Isle City* incident considered in the *Oil Platforms* case).[155]

This is, in fact, where other factors of proportionality come into play. At the most fundamental level, the scale of the armed attack and the aim to halt and repel the armed attack impose limits on the duration of self-defence. In a more specific sense, when a state is invaded and part of its territory is occupied, the geographical factor would limit the self-defence measures to driving out the occupying forces, which would also be the time when the self-defence measures should end. Even if a state occupies parts of the aggressor's territory during self-defence in order to complete

[155] In this case, a US tanker *Sea Isle City* was allegedly attacked by missiles launched from oil platforms in Iran. The US attacked two oil platforms suspected of launching the missiles. The ICJ noted as follows in relation to this incident: 'As to the requirement of proportionality, the attack of 19 October 1987 might, had the Court found that it was necessary in response to the *Sea Isle City* incident as an armed attack committed by Iran, have been considered proportionate.' See *Oil Platforms* case (Merits), para 77. However, since the Court could not conclude that it was necessary to attack the oil platforms, it effectively rejected the US claim that it was acting in self-defence.

repelling the armed attack, a long-term occupation can rarely be justified. Self-defence measures can be taken until the armed attack is repelled and therefore, self-defence measures to ensure future security, including the long-term occupation of the aggressor's territory, cannot be justified under the principle of proportionality. The ICJ noted as follows on this point in the *Armed Activities* case:

> Article 51 of the Charter may justify a use of force in self-defence only within the strict confines there laid down. It does not allow the use of force by a State to protect perceived security interests beyond these parameters.[156]

Similarly, the requirement to attack a military target that is relevant to the initial armed attack would limit the self-defence measures to attacking the relevant military target that carried out the armed attack. The time when the relevant military target is destroyed is also the time when the self-defence measures should end. In this sense, the duration of self-defence is largely determined by other factors taken into account to assess the proportionality of self-defence.

In all the examples given above, the claim of self-defence was controversial but the strength of the principle of proportionality is that it can circumvent the question of whether the use of force was lawful self-defence. For example, Israel's attacks on civilians against an accumulation of on-the-spot armed attacks are controversial as to whether they were lawful self-defence but by resorting to the principle of proportionality, the scale of civilian casualties might be evidence of disproportionate self-defence and hence can render Israel's use of force unlawful without necessarily determining the use of force as self-defence. Thus, the principle of proportionality can be applied to instant and continuous use of force by a state claiming self-defence, even when the lawfulness of self-defence is not proven.

A particular difficulty is, again, transnational terrorism. For example, the terrorist attacks on the US on 11 September 2001 were on-the-spot type of attacks but there are difficulties in responding to those attacks since terrorist groups like Al-Qaeda are dispersed and act clandestinely, and are therefore difficult to eliminate in a short period of time, as can be seen from the long US campaign in Afghanistan.[157] However, it is also questionable whether the 'war on terror' would justify attacks against members of terrorist groups on the basis of self-defence until the 'war on terror' is over, which may be years ahead. Use of force against attacks which took place in the past could be seen as evidence of armed reprisals which are

[156] *Armed Activities* case (Merits), para 148. See also *Armed Activities* case (Merits), Reply of the DRC, para 3.175.

[157] As at September 2010, the US forces are still fighting Al-Qaeda in Afghanistan, a conflict which began in October 2001. For discussions, see, eg, Cassese, 'Terrorism', 997–98; Delbrück, 'The Fight against Global Terrorism', 16–17.

prohibited under *jus ad bellum*.[158] This question will be dealt with later in the section on reprisals.[159]

Principle of Proportionality in IHL and the Differences and Similarities with the Principle of Proportionality in the Law of Self-defence

The scope of the principle of proportionality in IHL is narrower than the principle of proportionality in the law of self-defence. It aims at limiting 'incidental loss of civilian life, injury to civilians, damage to civilian objects' in relation to 'concrete and direct military advantage anticipated'.[160] Article 51(5)(b) of the 1977 First Additional Protocol provides as follows:

> Among others, the following types of attack are to be considered as indiscriminate . . . an attack which may be expected to cause incidental loss of civilian life, injury to civilians, damage to civilian objects, or a combination thereof, which would be excessive in relation to the concrete and direct military advantage anticipated.[161]

[158] 1970 Friendly Relations Declaration.

[159] See section 3.IV.

[160] Writings on this topic are voluminous. See generally B Brown, 'The Proportionality Principle in the Humanitarian Law of Warfare: Recent Efforts at Codification' (1976–77) 10 *Cornell International Law Journal* 134; Y Sandoz et al (eds), *Commentary on the Additional Protocols of 8 June 1977 to the Geneva Conventions of 12 August 1949* (Geneva, International Committee of the Red Cross, 1987) para 625 *ff*; F Kalshoven, 'Implementing Limitations on the Use of Force: The Doctrine of Proportionality and Necessity, Remarks' (1992) 86 *American Society of International Law Proceedings* 40; W Fenrick, 'Attacking the Enemy Civilian as a Punishable Offense' (1997) 7 *Duke Journal of Comparative and International Law* 539; ICTY, 'Final Report to the Prosecutor by the Committee Established to Review the NATO Bombing Campaign against the Federal Republic of Yugoslavia' (2000) 39 ILM 1257, 1271 *ff*; Y Dinstein, *The Conduct of Hostilities under the Law of International Armed Conflict* (Cambridge, Cambridge University Press, 2004) 119 *ff*; Gardam, *Necessity*, 85 *ff*; J Holland, 'Military Objective and Collateral Damage: Their Relationship and Dynamics' (2004) 7 *Yearbook of International Humanitarian Law* 35; K Watkin, 'Assessing Proportionality: Moral Complexity and Legal Rules' (2005) 8 *Yearbook of International Humanitarian Law* 3; Franck, 'On Proportionality', 723 *ff*.

[161] See also Art 57(2)(a)(iii) of the 1977 First Additional Protocol. The principle of proportionality in IHL is applicable as a customary rule in both international and non-international armed conflict. See Rule 14 in Henckaerts and Doswald-Beck, *Customary International Humanitarian Law* Vol I, 46. Note that the term 'principle of proportionality' does not appear anywhere in IHL treaties. Moreover, the principle of proportionality is inherent in many other provisions of IHL treaties. However, as can be seen from the practice of states in the 1974–77 Diplomatic Conference, the term 'principle of proportionality' is almost exclusively used to refer to the rule set out in Art 51(5)(b) of the 1977 First Additional Protocol. See Australia, *Official Records of the Diplomatic Conference on the Reaffirmation and Development of International Humanitarian Law Applicable in Armed Conflicts, Geneva (1974–1977)* (hereafter *Official Records*) (Bern, Federal Political Department, 1978) Vol XIV, CDDH/SR.8, para 30; Canada, *Official Records* Vol XIV, CDDH/SR.7, para 36; Czechoslovakia, *Official Records* Vol XIV, CDDH/SR.8, para 82; Democratic People's Republic of Korea, *Official Records* Vol XIV, CDDH/SR.8, para 17; Democratic Republic of Vietnam, *Official Records* Vol XIV, CDDH/SR.21, para 81; Egypt, *Official Records* Vol XIV, CDDH/SR.7, para 49; Finland, *Official Records* Vol XIV, CDDH/SR.7, para 28; France, *Official Records* Vol XIV, CDDH/SR.8, para 55; German Democratic Republic, *Official Records* Vol XIV, CDDH/SR.7, para 48; Hungary, *Official Records* Vol XIV, CDDH/SR.8, para 79; Iraq, *Official Records* Vol XIV, CDDH/SR.7, para 25; Norway, *Official Records*

Thus, it must first be clarified that the principles of proportionality in the law of self-defence and IHL are distinct, with different scope, and require consideration of different elements. Moreover, the principle of proportionality in IHL applies equally to the conflicting parties whereas the principle of proportionality in the law of self-defence applies only to the victim state. The following section will highlight the differences and similarities between the two kinds of principle of proportionality.

The principle of proportionality in IHL aims at limiting civilian deaths, civilian injuries, and damage to civilian objects, which are also factors taken into account when applying the principle of proportionality in the law of self-defence. In this sense, the principle of proportionality in self-defence and that in IHL are similar.

However, the principle of proportionality in IHL is exclusively aimed at limiting civilian deaths, civilian injuries, and damage to civilian objects, whereas these are only a few of the factors taken into account when applying the principle of proportionality in the law of self-defence. The principle of proportionality in the law of self-defence also aims at limiting the military target that can be attacked in self-defence and the geographical and temporal extent of self-defence. These are aspects that the principle of proportionality in IHL does not aim at limiting.

The situations where the principle of proportionality applies are also different between the law of self-defence and IHL. As noted above, the proportionality of self-defence measures can be assessed in relation to both on-the-spot armed attack and continuous armed attack. In other words, the law of self-defence can assess the proportionality of specific and limited scope of military operation in self-defence as well as the proportionality of the whole conflict in self-defence. However, the principle of proportionality in IHL can only be applied to limited scope of military operation. This is clear from the phrase 'concrete and direct military advantage anticipated' in Article 51(5)(b) of the 1977 First Additional Protocol. The civilian deaths and injuries and damage to civilian objects are assessed against an advantage of a military nature, and not against a long-term political advantage. Hence, it is markedly different from the principle of proportionality in the law of self-defence, which can take into account the long-term aim of self-defence: to halt and repel the armed attack. Moreover, the principle of proportionality in IHL requires that the military advantage anticipated be 'concrete and direct'. Hence, military advantage must be a detailed and clear one that can be achieved with

Vol XIV, CDDH/SR.8, paras 4 and 6; Philippines, *Official Records* Vol XIV, CDDH/SR.8, para 2; Romania, *Official Records* Vol XIV, CDDH/SR.7, para 55; Sweden, *Official Records* Vol XIV, CDDH/SR.8, para 9; Syria, *Official Records* Vol XIV, CDDH/III/SR.6, para 38; UK, *Official Records* Vol XIV, CDDH/SR.8, paras 48 and 52; US, *Official Records* Vol XIV, CDDH/SR.8, para 69; Uruguay, *Official Records* Vol XIV, CDDH/SR.8, para 12; Yugoslavia, *Official Records* Vol XIV, CDDH/SR.7, para 7.

some certainty in the short term (and not some unforeseeable future).[162] This is also different from the principle of proportionality in the law of self-defence which normally accommodates a broader aim, to halt and repel the armed attack, when assessing the proportionality of self-defence measures.

Some states have made reservations on the term 'military advantage' in Article 51(5)(b) of the 1977 First Additional Protocol so that it covers not only each and every military operation but a wider military operation. For example, the reservation of the UK on this provision provides that 'the military advantage anticipated from an attack is intended to refer to the advantage anticipated from the attack considered as a whole and not only from isolated or particular parts of the attack'.[163] In the words of the reservation, it distinguishes 'attack as a whole' from 'isolated or particular parts of the attack'. However, even if the 'military advantage' is considered within the context of 'attack as a whole', it is clear that it does not mean 'armed conflict as a whole'. Thus, Knut Dörmann notes as follows:

> To the knowledge of the author, no official explanation is given by these States as to the meaning of 'attack as a whole'. It certainly cannot mean in the sense of the whole conflict. Such an interpretation could hardly be reconciled with the meaning of the words 'concrete and direct', and it would confuse 'proportionality' as required by the *ius ad bellum* rules of self-defence with the rules of proportionality in attack in the *ius in bello*.[164]

Hence, the principles of proportionality in the law of self-defence and IHL take into account different scopes of military operation. In this sense, Israel's analysis on the principle of proportionality during the 2006 Lebanon Conflict dangerously conflates the principle of proportionality in the law of self-defence and that in IHL.[165] In presenting its analysis on the principle of proportionality, Israel began by discussing the principle of proportionality in IHL.[166] However, towards the end of the analysis, it states as follows:

[162] Doswald-Beck (ed), *San Remo Manual*, 124.

[163] For reservations and declarations to the 1977 First Additional Protocol, see the website of the Switzerland Federal Department of Foreign Affairs, which acts as depositary of the Protocol, www.eda.admin.ch. Other states which made a similar reservation as the UK are Australia, Belgium, Canada, France, Germany, Italy, the Netherlands, New Zealand, and Spain.

[164] K Dörmann, *Elements of War Crimes under the Rome Statute of the International Criminal Court: Sources and Commentary* (Geneva, International Committee of the Red Cross, 2003) 171. See also Greenwood, 'Self-Defence', 278.

[165] See E Cannizario, 'Contexualizing Proportionality: *Jus ad Bellum* and *Jus in Bello* in the Lebanese War' (2006) 864 *International Review of the Red Cross* 779; Y Ronen, 'Israel, Hizbollah, and the Second Lebanon War' (2006) 9 *Yearbook of International Humanitarian Law* (2006) 362; Zimmermann, 'The Second Lebanon War'.

[166] Israel Ministry of Foreign Affairs, 'Responding to Hizbullah Attacks from Lebanon: Issues of Proportionality' (25 July 2006), Israel Ministry of Foreign Affairs website, www.mfa.gov.il/MFA/Government/Law/Legal+Issues+and+Rulings.

> The proportionality of a response to an attack is to be measured not in regard to the specific attack suffered by a state but in regard to what is necessary to remove the overall threat . . . Accordingly, the right of self-defence includes not only acts taken to prevent the immediate threat, but also to prevent subsequent attacks.[167]

In a similar memorandum during the 2009 Gaza Conflict, the reference to the proportionality in self-defence was removed.[168] It must be understood that the principle of proportionality in IHL and that in the law of self-defence apply to different scopes of military operations. The principle of proportionality in IHL applies to a more limited scope of military operations than the principle of proportionality in self-defence.

Admittedly, when the self-defence is limited to a response against an on-the-spot armed attack, the scope of military operation against which the proportionality is assessed could be similar between the law of self-defence and IHL. Even so, the equation is still different. In terms of *jus ad bellum*, the question to be asked is the following: were the side effects of self-defence measures (civilian casualties and damage to civilian objects) proportionate in order to halt and repel the armed attack? In terms of IHL, the question to be asked is, will the civilian deaths and injuries and damage to civilian objects be proportionate to achieve the anticipated military advantage that is concrete and direct? For example, in response to an on-the-spot armed attack causing massive civilian casualties, a victim state might choose to carry out self-defence measures that can cause a similar level of civilian casualties by arguing that they were proportionate to halt and repel the armed attack. However, the principle of proportionality in IHL does not allow massive civilian deaths and injuries as 'concrete and direct military advantage' cannot be anticipated from such a level of civilian deaths and injuries. Hence, it must be made clear at this point that the principle of proportionality in the law of self-defence and that in IHL apply to different scopes of situation.

It is also worth clarifying that the principle of proportionality in IHL requires an assessment before each military operation, and not after. In other words, expected civilian deaths and injuries and damage to civilian objects of a military operation, and whether such deaths, injuries and damage are justified in relation to the concrete and direct military advantage anticipated, must be assessed before each military operation is carried out. This is clear from Article 57(2)(a)(iii) of the 1977 First Additional Protocol. The same can be said for the principle of proportionality in the law of self-defence. The proportionality of self-defence measures must be assessed

[167] Israel Ministry of Foreign Affairs, 'Responding to Hizbullah Attacks from Lebanon: Issues of Proportionality'.

[168] Israel Ministry of Foreign Affairs, 'Responding to Hamas Attacks from Gaza – Issues of Proportionality' (29 December 2008), Israel Ministry of Foreign Affairs website, www.mfa.gov.il/MFA/Government/Law/Legal+Issues+and+Rulings.

before such measures are actually carried out. This includes an assessment on the overall aspect of self-defence, namely whether the planned self-defence measures are proportionate to halt and repel the initial armed attack, as well as other specific aspects such as whether the military targets selected are relevant to the initial armed attack, expected civilian casualties and damage to civilian objects, and the temporal and geographical extent of the self-defence measures. When it is necessary to continue self-defence measures over a certain period of time, the proportionality of such measures should be assessed constantly, both in terms of the overall self-defence measures and the specific aspects of such measures.

In applying the principle of proportionality in IHL, one must not forget that IHL prohibits targeting against civilians and civilian objects as such.[169] For example, the principle of proportionality in the law of self-defence might accommodate civilian casualties and damage to civilian objects as a result of direct attacks against them, in response to a prior armed attack that caused civilian casualties and damage to civilian objects. Arguably, this might be disproportionate self-defence or even an armed reprisal but whatever the debate in terms of *jus ad bellum,* IHL prohibits any direct attacks against civilians and civilian objects. IHL makes a clear distinction between direct attacks against civilians and civilian objects on one hand, and side effects of attacks on civilians and civilian objects on the other.[170] This nuance is normally not present in the principle of proportionality in the law of self-defence. States often refer to civilian casualties and damage to civilian objects as some of the factors in assessing the proportionality of self-defence, but they do not make it clear whether the casualties and damage were the result of direct attacks or side effects of attacks. Even if the principle of proportionality in the law of self-defence accommodates direct attacks on civilians and civilian objects, this is prohibited by IHL. In this sense, IHL imposes limits on certain conduct of self-defence, which might otherwise be lawful under the principle of proportionality in the law of self-defence.

From the above discussions, it can be said that the principle of proportionality in IHL puts limits on the conduct of self-defence in a different way from the principle of proportionality in the law of self-defence. First, the principle of proportionality in IHL obliges commanders to consider civilian deaths and injuries and damage to civilian objects in relation to limited scope of military operation that is anticipated to bring concrete and direct military advantage. It is a separate consideration from the assessment of whether self-defence measures would be proportionate to the armed attack,

[169] Arts 51(2) and 52(1) of the 1977 First Additional Protocol and Art 13(1) and (2) of the 1977 Second Additional Protocol. For customary law status, see Rules 1 and 7 in Henckaerts and Doswald-Beck, *Customary International Humanitarian Law* Vol I, 3 and 25; *Nuclear Weapons* case (Advisory Opinion), para 78.

[170] Art 51(5)(b) of the 1977 First Additional Protocol.

which requires consideration on not only civilian casualties and damage to civilian objects that would be caused by the self-defence measures, but also whether the military target is relevant to the initial armed attack and the geographical and temporal extent of self-defence. Secondly, IHL not only aims at limiting the side effects of a military operation on civilians and civilian objects but also prohibits direct attacks on civilians and civilian objects. The law of self-defence does not make such nuanced distinction and as a result, direct attacks on civilians and civilian objects might be accommodated. However, IHL puts limits on any self-defence measure that would involve direct attacks against civilians and civilian objects. Finally, it must be noted that the principle of proportionality in IHL not only applies to the state acting in self-defence, but also to the aggressor.

B. *Jus ad Bellum* and *Jus in Bello* Constraints on the Conduct of Self-defence

The ICJ in the *Nuclear Weapons* Advisory Opinion recognised the simultaneous application of IHL and the principle of proportionality in the law of self-defence:

> A use of force that is proportionate under the law of self-defence, must, in order to be lawful, also meet the requirements of the law applicable in armed conflict which comprise in particular the principles and rules of humanitarian law.[171]

The Court did not explain in detail what this meant and hence, this section takes this statement as a starting point and examines what it means. This subject was partly discussed in the previous section: it discussed how the principles of proportionality in the law of self-defence and IHL impose limits on the conduct of self-defence. This section goes one step further and examines how the law of international armed conflict as a whole imposes limits on the conduct of self-defence, alongside the principle of proportionality in the law of self-defence.

It is worth noting at the outset that *jus ad bellum* itself contains a built-in safeguard to control the exercise of the right of self-defence. Article 51 of the UN Charter only permits self-defence 'until the Security Council has taken measures necessary to maintain international peace and security' and self-defence measures 'shall be immediately reported to the Security Council'. Moreover, the self-defence measures do not 'in any way affect the authority and responsibility of the Security Council under the present Charter to take at any time such action as it deems necessary in order to maintain or restore international peace and security'. Thus, it makes it clear that the Security Council has primacy over individual UN Member States so far as the use of force is concerned.

171 *Nuclear Weapons* case (Advisory Opinion), para 42.

However, the dual constraints of IHL and the principle of proportionality in the law of self-defence can impose further limits on the conduct of self-defence. The principle of proportionality in the law of self-defence and the IHL rules on means and methods of warfare and on occupation in particular, impose constraints on almost all aspects of the conduct of self-defence. Hence, this section will set out the legal framework of the complementary nature of IHL and the principle of proportionality in the law of self-defence by referring to two examples which are particularly relevant: 1) means and methods of warfare; and 2) occupation. The applicable IHL is the law of international armed conflict.

Methods and Means of Warfare

As discussed earlier, the principle of proportionality in the law of self-defence requires a balancing act between an armed attack and the military response taken against it as well as between an armed attack and the aim to halt and repel the armed attack. In addition, four elements are frequently used to assess the proportionality: 1) target selection; 2) civilian casualties; 3) geographical scope; and 4) temporal scope.[172]

First, on means and methods of warfare in the conduct of self-defence, IHL has a particular bearing on the aspects of target selection and civilian casualties. IHL provides detailed rules on which objectives can be attacked, how they can be attacked, and which weapons can be used in attacks. For example, the ICJ in the *Nuclear Weapons* Advisory Opinion indicated that IHL rules on means and methods of warfare can impose limits on the conduct of self-defence. It first noted that 'Respect for the environment is one of the elements that go to assessing whether an action is in conformity with the principles of necessity and proportionality'.[173] It further stated that:

> Articles 35, paragraph 3, and 55 of Additional Protocol I provide additional protection for the environment. Taken together, those provisions embody a general obligation to protect the natural environment against widespread, long-term and severe environmental damage; the prohibition of methods and means of warfare which are intended, or may be expected, to cause such damage; and the prohibition of attacks against the natural environment by way of reprisals. These are powerful constraints for all the States having subscribed to these provisions.[174]

The same can be said with regard to the substantial constraints imposed by other rules on methods of warfare (how weapons can be used) as well

[172] See section 3.II.A.

[173] *Nuclear Weapons* case (Advisory Opinion), para 30.

[174] *Nuclear Weapons* case (Advisory Opinion), para 31. On the effects of armed conflict on the environment, see generally, A Westing (ed), *Environmental Warfare: Technical, Legal and Policy Appraisal* (London, Taylor and Francis, 1984); J Austin and C Bruch (eds), *The Environmental Consequences of War: Legal, Economic, and Scientific Perspectives* (Cambridge, Cambridge University Press, 2000).

as the rules on means of warfare (weapons per se), which are aspects that *jus ad bellum*, in particular the principle of proportionality in the law of self-defence, does not specify.

With regard to methods of warfare, the ICJ noted in the *Oil Platforms* case that the targets which the victim state is attacking should be objects that are relevant to the initial armed attack.[175] However, there are further requirements in IHL with regard to targeting.[176] Any starting point for targeting is the distinction between civilians and combatants (or civilians directly participating in hostilities) and between civilian objects and military objectives.[177] Only combatants / civilians directly participating in hostilities and military objectives can be attacked.[178] Thus, even if the targets are relevant to the initial armed attack, they cannot be attacked if they are civilians or civilian objects.[179]

Combatants / civilians directly participating in hostilities can be attacked wherever they are in the territory where IHL is applicable by the mere fact of their status.[180] Nevertheless, the important condition is that means and methods of warfare 'of a nature to cause superfluous injury or unnecessary suffering' should not be employed to attack them.[181]

Moreover, there is a specific definition of 'military objectives':

> Attacks shall be limited strictly to military objectives. In so far as objects are concerned, military objectives are limited to those objects which by their nature, location, purpose or use make an effective contribution to military action and whose total or partial destruction, capture or neutralization, in the circumstances ruling at the time, offers a definite military advantage.[182]

[175] *Oil Platforms* case (Merits), paras 51, 74, and 77.

[176] The customary rules referred to hereafter are mostly applicable to both international and non-international armed conflict.

[177] Arts 48, 51(2), and 52(1) of the 1977 First Additional Protocol and Art 13(1) and (2) of the 1977 Second Additional Protocol. For customary law status, see Rules 1 and 7 in Henckaerts and Doswald-Beck, *Customary International Humanitarian Law* Vol I, 3 and 25; *Nuclear Weapons* case (Advisory Opinion), para 78. Civilians lose their protection if they 'take a direct part in hostilities' pursuant to Art 51(3) of the 1977 First Additional Protocol and Art 13(3) of the 1977 Second Additional Protocol. See also Rule 6 in Henckaerts and Doswald-Beck, *Customary International Humanitarian Law* Vol I, 19. See generally ICRC, *Direct Participation in Hostilities under International Humanitarian Law* (Geneva, International Committee of the Red Cross, 2009).

[178] Arts 43, 51(3), and 52(2) of the 1977 First Additional Protocol and Rules 1, 6, and 7 in Henckaerts and Doswald-Beck, *Customary International Humanitarian Law* Vol I, 3, 19, and 25.

[179] Civilians and civilian objects include medical and religious personnel and objects, relief personnel and objects, and journalists who are specifically protected in the 1949 Geneva Conventions and 1977 Additional Protocols.

[180] Art 43(2) of the 1977 First Additional Protocol and Rule 3 in Henckaerts and Doswald-Beck, *Customary International Humanitarian Law* Vol I, 11. See also Sandoz et al (eds), *Commentary*, para 2017.

[181] Art 35(2) of the 1977 First Additional Protocol and Rule 70 in Henckaerts and Doswald-Beck, *Customary International Humanitarian Law* Vol I, 237. See also Art 23(g) of the 1907 Hague Regulations.

[182] Art 52(2) of the 1977 First Additional Protocol and Rule 8 in Henckaerts and Doswald-Beck, *Customary International Humanitarian Law* Vol I, 29.

Thus, even if the target is relevant to the initial armed attack, the target should additionally meet the definition of military objectives in IHL.

There are further requirements in IHL before military objectives can be attacked. First, there are specifically protected objects that cannot be attacked, namely cultural objects and places of worship,[183] objects indispensable to the survival of the civilian population,[184] natural environment,[185] and works and installations containing dangerous forces.[186] Secondly, certain methods of attack are prohibited, particularly indiscriminate attacks[187] (including the principle of proportionality in IHL[188]) and belligerent reprisals.[189] Thirdly, precautions in attacks and against the effects of attacks add further requirements such as the cancellation of attack if a planned attack can violate the rules on targeting,[190] provision of advance warning in case attacks may affect the civilian population,[191] selection of military objectives which may be expected to cause the least danger to civilians and civilian objects,[192] removal of civilian population from the vicinity of military objectives,[193] and avoidance of the establishment of military objectives in densely populated areas.[194] All these requirements

[183] Art 56 of the 1907 Hague Regulations, 1954 Cultural Property Convention, Art 53 of the 1977 First Additional Protocol, and Rules 38 and 39 in Henckaerts and Doswald-Beck, *Customary International Humanitarian Law* Vol I, 127 and 131.

[184] Art 54(2) of the 1977 First Additional Protocol and Rule 54 in Henckaerts and Doswald-Beck, *Customary International Humanitarian Law* Vol I, 189.

[185] Arts 35(3) and 55(1) of the 1977 First Additional Protocol and Rules 43–45 in Henckaerts and Doswald-Beck, *Customary International Humanitarian Law* Vol I, 143, 147, and 151.

[186] Art 56(1) of the 1977 First Additional Protocol and Rule 42 in Henckaerts and Doswald-Beck, *Customary International Humanitarian Law* Vol I, 139.

[187] Art 51(4) and (5) of the 1977 First Additional Protocol and Rule 11 in Henckaerts and Doswald-Beck, *Customary International Humanitarian Law* Vol I, 37.

[188] Art 51(5)(b) of the 1977 First Additional Protocol and Rule 14 in Henckaerts and Doswald-Beck, *Customary International Humanitarian Law* Vol I, 46.

[189] Art 45 of the Geneva Convention for the Amelioration of the Condition of the Wounded and Sick in Armed Forces in the Field, as revised from 1929 (hereafter 1949 First Geneva Convention) (adopted 12 August 1949, entered into force 21 October 1950) 75 UNTS 31; Art 47 of the Geneva Convention for the Amelioration of the Condition of Wounded, Sick and Shipwrecked Members of Armed Forces at Sea, as revised from 1929 (hereafter 1949 Second Geneva Convention) (adopted 12 August 1949, entered into force 21 October 1950) 75 UNTS 85; Art 13 of the 1949 Third Geneva Convention, Art 33 of the 1949 Fourth Geneva Convention; Art 4(4) of the 1954 the Cultural Property Convention; Rules 146 and 147 in Henckaerts and Doswald-Beck, *Customary International Humanitarian Law* Vol I, 519 and 523. See also Arts 20, 51(6), 52(1), 53(c), 54(4), 55(2), and 56(4) of the 1977 First Additional Protocol. See also the discussions in section 3.IV.B.

[190] Art 57(2)(b) of the 1977 First Additional Protocol and Rule 19 in Henckaerts and Doswald-Beck, *Customary International Humanitarian Law* Vol I, 60.

[191] Art 57(2)(c) of the 1977 First Additional Protocol and Rule 20 in Henckaerts and Doswald-Beck, *Customary International Humanitarian Law* Vol I, 62.

[192] Art 57(3) of the 1977 First Additional Protocol and Rule 21 in Henckaerts and Doswald-Beck, *Customary International Humanitarian Law* Vol I, 65.

[193] Art 58(a) of the 1977 First Additional Protocol and Rule 24 in Henckaerts and Doswald-Beck, *Customary International Humanitarian Law* Vol I, 74.

[194] Art 58(b) of the 1977 First Additional Protocol and Rule 23 in Henckaerts and Doswald-Beck, *Customary International Humanitarian Law* Vol I, 71.

should be met before an attack on a target that is relevant to the initial armed attack can be carried out.

An example is the award of the Eritrea–Ethiopia Claims Commission. In the *Jus ad Bellum* Award, the Commission concluded that Eritrea launched an armed attack against Ethiopia[195] and hence it made it clear that Ethiopia was entitled to take self-defence measures in accordance with the principles of proportionality and necessity. However, there were further requirements in IHL which Ethiopia had to meet before it could launch attacks in self-defence. In the *Western Front, Aerial Bombardment and Related Claims* Award, the Commission found that Ethiopia violated, among others, the customary rule prohibiting attacks on objects indispensable to the survival of the civilian population which can also be found in Article 54 of the 1977 First Additional Protocol.[196] Moreover, in the *Central Front* Award (Eritrea's Claims), the Commission found that Ethiopia violated, among others, Article 56 of the 1907 Hague Regulations prohibiting attacks on cultural property.[197] These indicate that even if certain self-defence measures may be permitted under the law of self-defence, the law of methods of warfare can prohibit such measures.

The constraints of the law of methods of warfare on the conduct of self-defence were already recognised in the 1974–77 Diplomatic Conference. For example, France noted as follows with reference to the prohibition on indiscriminate attacks:

> It [France] wished to point out, however, that the provisions of paragraphs 4, 5 and 7 of Article 46 [now Article 51 of the 1977 First Additional Protocol] were of a type which by their very complexity would seriously hamper the conduct of defensive military operations against an invader and prejudice the exercise of the inherent right of legitimate defence recognized in Article 51 of the Charter of the United Nations . . . because it considered that provisions concerning indiscriminate attacks could not prohibit a State from defending its territory against an invader, even if such defence might result in losses in its own civilian population, the French delegation considered that Article 46 went beyond the scope of its humanitarian aim and that it was likely seriously to impair the inherent right of legitimate defence.[198]

Afghanistan and Romania expressed a similar concern on the same provision.[199] This demonstrates that IHL, with its detailed rules on targeting, can significantly limit the conduct of self-defence.

[195] Eritrea–Ethiopia Claims Commission, *Jus ad Bellum* case (Partial Award), para 14.

[196] Eritrea–Ethiopia Claims Commission, *Western Front, Aerial Bombardment and Related Claims, Eritrea's Claims 1, 3, 5, 9–13, 14, 21, 25 and 26* (hereafter *Western Front, Eritrea* case) (Partial Award) (2009) XXVI *Reports of International Arbitral Awards* 291, para 105.

[197] Eritrea–Ethiopia Claims Commission, *Central Front, Eritrea* case (Partial Award), paras 113 and 114.

[198] *Official Records* Vol VI, CDDH/SR.41, paras 111 and 114.

[199] Afghanistan, *Official Records* Vol VI, CDDH/SR.41, para 126; Romania, *Official Records* Vol VI, CDDH/SR.41, Annex.

IHL imposes further constraints on targeting in the form of prohibitions or restrictions on means of warfare.[200] There is first a general prohibition on the use of weapons which is the prohibition to use means and methods of warfare 'of a nature to cause superfluous injury or unnecessary suffering'.[201] Then IHL imposes prohibitions and restrictions on specific weapons and the use of such weapons such as explosive projectiles;[202] expanding bullets;[203] poison or poisoned weapons;[204] weapons containing non-detectable fragments;[205] certain mines, booby-traps, and other devices;[206] incendiary weapons;[207] blinding laser weapons;[208] explosive remnants of war;[209] cluster munitions;[210] anti-personnel mines;[211] biological weapons;[212] and chemical weapons.[213] These rules on means of warfare

[200] See generally W Boothby, *Weapons and the Law of Armed Conflict* (Oxford, Oxford University Press, 2009).

[201] Art 35(2) of the 1977 First Additional Protocol and Rule 70 in Henckaerts and Doswald-Beck, *Customary International Humanitarian Law* Vol I, 237. See also Art 23(g) of the 1907 Hague Regulations.

[202] Declaration Renouncing the Use, in Time of War, of Explosive Projectiles under 400 Grammes Weight (adopted and entered into force 11 December 1868) 138 CTS 297 and Rule 78 in Henckaerts and Doswald-Beck, *Customary International Humanitarian Law* Vol I, 272.

[203] Declaration (IV.3) concerning Expanding Bullets (adopted 29 July 1899, entered into force 4 September 1900) 187 CTS 459 and Rule 77 in Henckaerts and Doswald-Beck, *Customary International Humanitarian Law* Vol I, 268.

[204] Art 23(a) of the 1907 Hague Regulations and Rule 72 in Henckaerts and Doswald-Beck, *Customary International Humanitarian Law* Vol I, 251.

[205] 1980 Convention on Conventional Weapons, Protocol on Non-Detectable Fragments (Protocol I) (adopted 10 October 1980, entered into force 2 December 1983) 1342 UNTS 168 and Rule 79 in Henckaerts and Doswald-Beck, *Customary International Humanitarian Law* Vol I, 275.

[206] 1980 Convention on Conventional Weapons, Protocol on Prohibitions or Restrictions on the Use of Mines, Booby-Traps and Other Devices (Protocol II) (hereafter 1980 Convention on Conventional Weapons, Protocol II) (adopted 10 October 1980, entered into force 2 December 1983) 1342 UNTS 168 and Rules 80–83 in Henckaerts and Doswald-Beck, *Customary International Humanitarian Law* Vol I, 278, 280, 283, and 285.

[207] 1980 Convention on Conventional Weapons, Protocol on Prohibitions or Restrictions on the Use of Incendiary Weapons (Protocol III) (adopted 10 October 1980, entered into force 2 December 1983) 1342 UNTS 171 and Rules 84–85 in Henckaerts and Doswald-Beck, *Customary International Humanitarian Law* Vol I, 287 and 289.

[208] 1980 Convention on Conventional Weapons, Protocol on Blinding Laser Weapons (Protocol IV) (adopted 13 October 1995, entered into force 30 July 1998) 2024 UNTS 167 and Rule 86 in Henckaerts and Doswald-Beck, *Customary International Humanitarian Law* Vol I, 292.

[209] 1980 Convention on Conventional Weapons, Protocol on Explosive Remnants of War (Protocol V) (adopted 28 November 2003, entered into force 12 November 2006) 2399 UNTS 100.

[210] Convention on Cluster Munitions (adopted 30 May 2008, entered into force 1 August 2010) (2009) 48 ILM 354.

[211] Convention on the Prohibition of the Use, Stockpiling, Production and Transfer of Anti-Personnel Mines and on their Destruction (hereafter 1997 Convention on Anti-Personnel Mines) (adopted 18 September 1997, entered into force 1 March 1999) 2056 UNTS 211.

[212] Protocol for the Prohibition of the Use of Asphyxiating, Poisonous or Other Gases, and of Bacteriological Methods of Warfare (hereafter 1925 Gas Protocol) (adopted 17 June 1925, entered into force 9 May 1926) 94 LNTS 65; 1972 Biological Weapons Convention; Rule 73 in Henckaerts and Doswald-Beck, *Customary International Humanitarian Law* Vol I, 256.

[213] Convention on the Prohibition of the Development, Production, Stockpiling and Use of Chemical Weapons and on Their Destruction (hereafter 1993 Chemical Weapons Convention) (adopted 3 September 1992, entered into force 29 April 1997) 1974 UNTS 45 and

limit the conduct of self-defence by limiting the weapons that can be used, and limiting how certain weapons can be used. Thus, the ICJ indicated as follows in the *Nuclear Weapons* Advisory Opinion:

> These provisions [Articles 2 (4), 51, and 42 of the UN Charter] do not refer to specific weapons. They apply to any use of force, regardless of the weapons employed. The Charter neither expressly prohibits, nor permits, the use of any specific weapon, including nuclear weapons. A weapon that is already unlawful *per se*, whether by treaty or custom, does not become lawful by reason of its being used for a legitimate purpose under the Charter.[214]

An example is the 1980–88 Iran–Iraq War in which both sides used chemical weapons. The UN Secretary-General found that Iraq violated *jus ad bellum* and hence made it clear that Iran was entitled to take self-defence measures in accordance with the principles of proportionality and necessity.[215] However, the Security Council's fact-finding mission to investigate the use of chemical weapons in the war found that both Iran and Iraq used chemical weapons, which were prohibited by the 1925 Gas Protocol and to which both Iran and Iraq were states parties.[216] Thus, although Iran was entitled to exercise the right of self-defence, it could not have used chemical weapons.[217] This indicates that the law of means of warfare can prohibit the use of certain weapons which might otherwise be lawful under the law of self-defence.

Thus, IHL can limit the conduct of self-defence by setting out rules on which objectives can be attacked, how they can be attacked, and which weapons can be used in attacks. However, the principle of proportionality in the law of self-defence can be complementary in the sense that it requires that the target for self-defence should be relevant to the initial armed attack and that the whole measures in self-defence should be weighed against the armed attack. The ICJ also noted in the *Oil Platforms* case in the course of assessing the proportionality of the US military action that 'it cannot close its eyes to the scale of the whole operation'.[218] These are aspects which IHL does not regulate. Thus, although IHL can limit the conduct of self-defence in most cases, the principle of proportionality in self-defence also regulates the targeting in self-defence from a wider perspective.

Rules 74–76 in Henckaerts and Doswald-Beck, *Customary International Humanitarian Law* Vol I, 259, 263, and 265.

214 *Nuclear Weapons* case (Advisory Opinion), para 39.

215 UNSC, 'Further Report of the Secretary-General on the Implementation of Security Council Resolution 598 (1987)' (9 December 1991) UN Doc S/23273, para 6.

216 Dates of accession: Iran on 15 August 1929 and Iraq on 8 September 1931. See the website of the France Ministry of Foreign Affairs, which acts as depositary of the 1925 Gas Protocol, www.doc.diplomatie.fr/pacte.

217 See F Kalshoven, 'Prohibitions or Restrictions on the Use of Methods and Means of Warfare' in H Post and I Dekker (eds), *The Gulf War of 1980–1988* (Dordrecht, Martinus Nijhoff, 1992) 101–02.

218 *Oil Platforms* case (Merits), para 77.

Occupation

Another example of the complementary nature between IHL and the principle of proportionality in the law of self-defence is occupation. In an earlier section, it was noted that a situation of occupation is where an armed attack and an international armed conflict exist at the same time.[219] Thus, it is clear that the law of self-defence and IHL apply concurrently, and particularly the principle of proportionality and the law of occupation.

It was observed in this chapter that the principle of proportionality in the law of self-defence could impose certain limits on the geographical and temporal extent of self-defence measures, which has a particular bearing on occupation in self-defence.[220] It has been noted that occupation in self-defence can rarely be justified under the principle of proportionality since the principle requires a state to limit its self-defence to halt and repel the armed attack. If a state was invaded and occupied, a proportionate response would be to expel the aggressor from the territory of the occupied state. At most, the victim state may occupy a limited area of the aggressor's territory in order to complete repelling the armed attack, but the geographical extent and the duration of the occupation cannot be extensive.

At the same time, once the occupation commences, IHL applies in accordance with Article 42 of the 1907 Hague Regulations[221] and common Article 2 of the 1949 Geneva Conventions[222] and imposes a number of obligations on the occupying power, ranging from the provision of humanitarian assistance to the humane treatment of civilian internees.[223] Other rules of IHL also apply and the law on methods and means of warfare imposes certain limits on the conduct of self-defence as discussed earlier. Even during the occupation, there are cases where conduct of hostilities is regulated by the law on methods and means of warfare, and not only by the law of occupation.[224]

The law of occupation, however, also imposes important limits on the conduct of self-defence in the form of occupation. This question was

[219] See section 3.I.B above.

[220] Note that occupation through the use of force per se is prohibited in *jus ad bellum*. See section 3.I.B above. Occupation by force is, however, lawful if it is in self-defence (provided that it is carried out in conformity with the principles of necessity and proportionality) or authorised under Chapter VII of the UN Charter.

[221] Art 42 of the 1907 Hague Regulations reads as follows: 'Territory is considered occupied when it is actually placed under the authority of the hostile army. The occupation extends only to the territory where such authority has been established and can be exercised.'

[222] Common Art 2 of the 1949 Geneva Conventions reads, in part, as follows: 'The Convention shall also apply to all cases of partial or total occupation of the territory of a High Contracting Party, even if the said occupation meets with no armed resistance.'

[223] See generally Y Dinstein, *The International Law of Belligerent Occupation* (Cambridge, Cambridge University Press, 2009).

[224] 'Law of occupation' here refers particularly to Arts 42–56 of the 1907 Hague Regulations, 1949 Fourth Geneva Convention, and customary international law.

partly considered in the *Wall* case by the ICJ. In this case, the Court considered the legality of the wall constructed in the Occupied Palestinian Territory. Israel argued that the wall was lawful on the basis of its right of self-defence under Article 51 of the UN Charter which, in this case, was exercised against attacks from the West Bank.[225] The Court, however, rejected the application of Article 51 of the UN Charter and hence rejected any argument on the basis of self-defence.[226] Hence, there was no consideration on the proportionality of self-defence. However, the Court applied IHL, in particular the law of occupation, and concluded whether the wall violated it or not. This illustrated how the law of occupation could impose limits on occupation in self-defence.

It is worth noting at the outset that the application of the law of occupation does not render the occupation lawful. This follows the principle of the separation between *jus ad bellum* and *jus in bello*: the application of IHL does not legitimise the use of force under *jus ad bellum*. Whether the occupation itself is a lawful self-defence measure or not is a question of *jus ad bellum* that must be considered in the light of Article 2(4) and Article 51 of the UN Charter and the customary principles of proportionality and necessity.

The law of occupation is composed of a number of obligations of a very different nature. They are such as the general obligation to treat persons in the hands of the occupying power humanely, to respect medical personnel and hospitals, and to treat civilian internees humanely (including their material conditions, correspondence with the exterior, judicial guarantees, and release and repatriation). The ICJ therefore applied various provisions in relation to the wall constructed in the Occupied Palestinian Territory. However, it is useful to focus on Article 53 of the 1949 Fourth Geneva Convention, which prohibits destruction of private or public property in occupied territories, in order to better understand the limits imposed by the law of occupation on occupation in self-defence.

In the *Wall* Advisory Opinion, the ICJ concluded that Israel violated Article 53 of the 1949 Fourth Geneva Convention on the basis that it destroyed approximately 10,000 hectares of fertile agricultural land, olive trees, wells, citrus groves, and hothouses that belonged to the Palestinians in the course of building the wall.[227] Many states and organisations concurred with this conclusion.[228]

On the other hand, Israel's position was, as mentioned earlier, that the wall was lawful on the basis of its right of self-defence under Article 51 of the UN Charter. It did not recognise the applicability of the 1949 Fourth

[225] UNGA, 'Summary Legal Position of the Government of Israel' (24 November 2003) UN Doc A/ES-10/248, Annex I.

[226] *Wall* case (Advisory Opinion), para 139.

[227] *Wall* case (Advisory Opinion), paras 132 and 133.

[228] *Wall* case, Written Statements of Egypt, 34; Indonesia, para 7; Malaysia, para 137; South Africa, para 48; League of Arab States, para 9.13; Palestine, para 524.

Geneva Convention and hence, Israel relied exclusively on *jus ad bellum* to justify the legality of the wall. It is essential here to recognise that Israel was not arguing that the applicability of IHL should not be considered at all. What it was asserting was that the Fourth Geneva Convention was not applicable to the present case. The fact that it rejected the applicability of the Fourth Geneva Convention actually reflected Israel's recognition that IHL can be applicable alongside the law of self-defence.

The Court nevertheless concluded to the contrary, that the 1949 Fourth Geneva Convention was applicable to the present case, and the law of self-defence was not applicable to the case. This is not the place to discuss which position was correct but supposing that both the law of self-defence and the Fourth Geneva Convention were applicable to the present case, the wall would be illegal in any case since it was already concluded on one count that it failed to comply with the Fourth Geneva Convention. Israel could circumvent the obligations under Article 53 of the Fourth Geneva Convention and argue solely on the basis of the right of self-defence to justify the wall. However, since the Court found that the wall was illegal partly on the basis of Article 53 of the Fourth Geneva Convention, even if the wall was a proportionate response in terms of *jus ad bellum* and therefore legal, the wall remained illegal under *jus in bello*. This is an obvious consequence of the principle of the concurrent application of *jus ad bellum* and *jus in bello* discussed in Chapter 2. The League of Arab States in the *Wall* case thus noted that 'the argument of self-defence cannot be used to justify any deviation from the applicable rules of international humanitarian law'.[229]

The same can be said for the *Armed Activities* case. In this case, the ICJ considered whether Uganda was acting in self-defence but it rejected such a claim.[230] At the same time, the Court recognised that Uganda was the occupying power in Ituri (north-east of the DRC, at the border with Uganda).[231] After citing various UN reports that illustrated the destruction of houses, schools, and public buildings by the Ugandan forces, the Court found that Uganda violated Article 53 of the 1949 Fourth Geneva Convention.[232] Supposing that Uganda was acting in self-defence, even if such destruction of private and public property could have been justified as proportionate under *jus ad bellum*, the destruction remained illegal under *jus in bello*.

A further example is the Eritrea–Ethiopia Conflict. The Eritrea–Ethiopia Claims Commission concluded that Eritrea was the aggressor and Ethiopia was acting in self-defence.[233] It also found that Ethiopia was

[229] *Wall* case, Written Statement of League of Arab States, para 9.6.
[230] *Armed Activities* case (Merits), para 147.
[231] *Armed Activities* case (Merits), para 178.
[232] *Armed Activities* case (Merits), para 219.
[233] Eritrea–Ethiopia Claims Commission, *Jus ad Bellum* case (Partial Award), paras 16 and 19.

the occupying power in several parts of Eritrea.[234] The Commission further found that Ethiopia violated Article 53 of the 1949 Fourth Geneva Convention for the destruction of residential buildings, a cemetery, government buildings, the electrical authority, a telecommunications building, a health centre and a hospital, hotels, a school, and an ancient monument located in three towns in western Eritrea.[235] There were no arguments made on the proportionality of self-defence by Ethiopia but even if it had argued that these destructions were proportionate in terms of *jus ad bellum*, they remained illegal under *jus in bello*.

The above examples demonstrate that the principle of proportionality in the law of self-defence and the law of occupation regulate different aspects of the occupation in self-defence. The principle of proportionality in the law of self-defence has a particular bearing on the geographical extent and the duration of the occupation. The law of occupation, on the other hand, imposes detailed obligations on the occupying power of its conduct during occupation. Among others, the prohibition on destruction of private or public property in occupied territories puts significant limits on the conduct of self-defence during the occupation. Even if the destructions of private and public property can be considered proportionate in terms of *jus ad bellum*, the same destructions would violate the prohibition in *jus in bello*. Therefore, such destructions remain illegal and must not be carried out. This is a logical consequence of the principle of the concurrent application of *jus ad bellum* and *jus in bello*. The principle of proportionality in the law of self-defence and the law of occupation regulate different aspects of occupation but the two are complementary and impose important limits to the occupation in self-defence.

Clearly, the separation of *jus ad bellum* and *jus in bello* should be maintained in order to preserve the integrity of IHL and to protect the victims of armed conflict in an impartial manner. However, the positive aspects of the relationship between *jus ad bellum* and *jus in bello* should also be recognised. The principle of proportionality in the law of self-defence can provide a broader restriction on the conduct of self-defence and can also be applied without necessarily determining which side had launched an armed attack. Even if both sides claim that they are entitled to exercise the right of self-defence, they should still prove that they are using force in accordance with the principle of proportionality. If either or both of the conflicting parties overstep what is required by the principle of proportionality, they are using force unlawfully under *jus ad bellum* and there is no longer the need to prove which side had launched an armed attack. At the same time, it should be recognised that the limits imposed on the conduct of self-defence

[234] Eritrea–Ethiopia Claims Commission, *Central Front, Eritrea* case (Partial Award), paras 78, 93–105, 113, and 114; *Western Front, Eritrea* case (Partial Award), para 141.

[235] Eritrea–Ethiopia Claims Commission, *Central Front, Eritrea* case (Partial Award), paras 78, 93–105, 113, and 114.

by IHL are substantial. Even if the planned attack in self-defence meets the tests of the principle of proportionality in the law of self-defence, there are further detailed requirements prescribed by IHL, in particular in the law of means and methods of warfare and the law of occupation. In this sense, IHL can limit the conduct of self-defence. Moreover, the IHL constraints are particularly important because they apply equally to the conflicting parties and thus, even if both conflicting parties claim the right of self-defence, the substantial constraints in IHL apply to both of them in any case.

III. PRINCIPLE OF NECESSITY IN *JUS AD BELLUM* AND *JUS IN BELLO*

This section clarifies the distinction and relationship between the principle of necessity in the law of self-defence and IHL. The principle of necessity in IHL is often referred to as 'military necessity', which has a special meaning distinct from the principle of necessity in the law of self-defence. This section clarifies the two kinds of the principle of necessity and then examines how they were invoked in connection with the wall in the Occupied Palestinian Territory.

A. Principle of Necessity in the Law of Self-defence

First, the principle of necessity in the law of self-defence is generally interpreted in two ways: 1) whether the measures in self-defence per se are necessary, that is, whether there are still alternatives other than the use of force; and 2) whether the measures taken in self-defence were only to the extent necessary to halt and repel an armed attack.

The first interpretation was employed by the ICJ in the *Nicaragua* case.[236] In this case, the US argued that it was acting in collective self-defence to help El Salvador to fight against the armed groups supported by Nicaragua. The Court eventually concluded as follows on the necessity of the US use of force:

> These measures [the US uses of force] were only taken, and began to produce their effects, several months after the major offensive of the armed opposition against the Government of El Salvador had been completely repulsed . . . and the actions of the opposition considerably reduced in consequence. Thus, it was possible to eliminate the main danger to the Salvadorian Government without the United States embarking on activities in and against Nicaragua. Accordingly, it cannot be held that these activities were undertaken in the light of necessity.[237]

[236] See also Art 25 of ILC, 'Articles on Responsibility of States for Internationally Wrongful Acts' (2001) UN Doc A/56/10 Supp No 10, which provides as follows: 'Necessity may not be invoked by a State as a ground for precluding the wrongfulness of an act not in conformity with an international obligation of that State unless the act . . . is the only way for the State to safeguard an essential interest against a grave and imminent peril.'

[237] *Nicaragua* case (Merits), para 237.

Thus, since the attacks from armed groups supported by Nicaragua were not present, the necessity to attack Nicaragua was also not present.

This approach was followed in the *Oil Platforms* case. Iran stated that 'there should be an immediate necessity to act, leaving the State invoking self-defence with no alternative means of protection'[238] and argued that such necessity was not present in the case of the US's claim of self-defence. In response, the US also argued that 'In the absence of peaceful means to restore security, military action in self-defense became necessary'.[239] The ICJ concluded as follows on the question of necessity:

> In the case both of the attack on the Sea Isle City and the mining of the USS Samuel B Roberts, the Court is not satisfied that the attacks on the [oil] platforms [of Iran] were necessary to respond to these incidents . . . the Court notes that there is no evidence that the United States complained to Iran of the military activities of the platforms, in the same way as it complained repeatedly of minelaying and attacks on neutral shipping, which does not suggest that the targeting of the platforms was seen as a necessary act.[240]

The conclusion of the Chatham House International Law Programme also notes as follows:

> Force may be used in self-defence only when this is necessary to bring an attack to an end, or to avert an imminent attack. There must be no practical alternative to the proposed use of force that is likely to be effective in ending or averting the attack.[241]

Occasionally, the principle of necessity is interpreted as requiring an assessment of whether measures taken in self-defence were only to the extent necessary to halt and repel an armed attack. For example, the ICJ stated in the *Nicaragua* case that 'self-defence would warrant only measures which are . . . necessary to respond to it [armed attack]'.[242] This interpretation is synonymous to the principle of proportionality.[243] The contents of the principle of proportionality have been already seen above[244] and thus will not be discussed further.

As similar to the principle of proportionality in the law of self-defence, the principle of necessity only applies to the victim state.

[238] *Oil Platforms* case (Merits), Memorial of Iran, 98.

[239] *Oil Platforms* case (Merits), Counter-Memorial of the US, para 4.26.

[240] *Oil Platforms* case (Merits), para 76.

[241] E Wilmshurst, 'The Chatham House Principles', 966. See also Jennings and Watts (eds), *Oppenheim's International Law*, 421.

[242] *Nicaragua* case (Merits), para 115. See also *Armed Activities* case (Merits), para 147.

[243] Kolb, Ius contra bellum, 205. See also Council of the European Union, Independent International Fact-Finding Mission on the Conflict in Georgia, 'Report' Vol II (September 2009) 248; Wilmshurst, 'The Chatham House Principles', 969.

[244] See section 3.II.A.

B. Military Necessity in IHL and the Differences with the Principle of Necessity in the Law of Self-defence

In contrast, the concept of 'military necessity' in IHL has a separate meaning and operates in a manner significantly different from the principle of necessity in the law of self-defence.[245] Military necessity can only be invoked when a treaty provision specifically permits to do so. Thus, as opposed to the principle of necessity in the law of self-defence, military necessity is not primarily a general principle. It is primarily a justification that can be invoked only when treaty provisions specifically permit to do so. The ICRC notes that 'an IHL rule cannot be derogated from by invoking military necessity unless that possibility is explicitly provided for in the rule in question. Military necessity cannot justify deviating from an IHL rule to seek a military advantage.'[246] Many other practices also support this interpretation.[247] Gerald Draper's statement is an accurate reflection of state practice:

> If military requirements have already been taken into account before the Regulations [1907 Hague Regulations] were framed then none of those Regulations is subject to the eroding effect of the claims of military necessity unless and until those same Regulations, or any later and new tules [*sic*] of war, make express allowance for such military necessity.[248]

There are two types of military necessity found in treaty provisions: 1) the provision permits the invocation of military necessity only in a specific situation; and 2) the provision permits the invocation of military necessity only in a specific situation, and then only if the conditions set out in the

[245] See generally G Draper, 'Military Necessity and Humanitarian Imperatives' (1973) 12 *Revue de droit pénal militaire et de droit de la guerre* 129; Sandoz et al (eds), *Commentary*, para 1389 *ff*; B Carnahan, 'Lincoln, Lieber and the Laws of War: The Origins and Limits of the Principle of Military Necessity' (1998) 92 *American Journal of International Law* 213; Dinstein, *The Conduct of Hostilities*, 16–20; N Hayashi, 'Requirements of Military Necessity in International Humanitarian Law and International Criminal Law' (2010) 28 *Boston University International Law Journal* 39; M Schmitt, 'Military Necessity and Humanity in International Humanitarian Law: Preserving the Delicate Balance' (2010) 50 *Virginia Journal of International Law* 795.

[246] ICRC, 'Existing Principles and Rules of International Humanitarian Law Applicable to Munitions that May Become Explosive Remnants of War' (28 July 2005) CCW/GGE/XI/WG.1/WP.7, para 6. See also Sandoz et al (eds), *Commentary*, para 1389.

[247] Group of Governmental Experts of the 1980 Convention on Conventional Weapons, Eleventh Session (Geneva 2–12 August 2005), Response of Argentina, CCW/GGE/XI/WG.1/WP.10 (2 August 2005); Canada, CCW/GGE/XI/WG.1/WP.2 (29 June 2005), para 7; France, CCW/GGE/XI/WG.1/WP.17 (11 August 2005), para 4; New Zealand, CCW/GGE/XI/WG.1/WP.16 (5 August 2005), para 3; Norway, CCW/GGE/XI/WG.1/WP.5 (29 July 2005), para 6; Switzerland, CCW/GGE/XI/WG.1/WP.13 (3 August 2005), para 4; UK, CCW/GGE/XI/WG.1/WP.1 (24 June 2005), para 1 (i); US, CCW/GGE/XI/WG.1/WP.4 (25 July 2005), para 2; *Wall* case (Advisory Opinion), para 135 and Written Statements of Egypt, 39; League of Arab Nations, para 9.5; Palestine, paras 442, 446, and 447.

[248] Draper, 'Military Necessity', 133. See also Switzerland, CCW/GGE/XI/WG.1/WP.13 (3 August 2005), para 3; 'Declaration' Conference of High Contracting Parties to the Fourth Geneva Convention (Geneva 5 December 2001) in (2001) 847 *International Review of the Red Cross* 661, para 5.

provision are met. An example of the first type is Article 71(3) of the 1977 First Additional Protocol, which requires the conflicting parties to assist the relief personnel in carrying out their mission. It then qualifies as follows:

> Only in case of imperative military necessity may the activities of the relief personnel be limited or their movements temporarily restricted.[249]

Hence, if a conflicting party could prove the 'imperative military necessity', the activities and movements of the relief personnel could be limited.

On the other hand, an example of the second type is Article 33 of the 1949 First Geneva Convention, which provides that the medical establishments of the armed forces may not be diverted from their purpose as long as they are required for the care of wounded and sick. It then qualifies as follows:

> [T]he commanders of forces in the field may make use of them, in case of urgent military necessity, provided that they make previous arrangements for the welfare of the wounded and sick who are nursed in them.[250]

[249] See also Art 1 of the Additional Articles to the 1864 Convention for the Amelioration of the Condition of the Wounded in Armies in the Field (adopted 20 October 1868, not entered into force); Art 13(g) of the Project of an International Declaration concerning the Laws and Customs of War (adopted 27 August 1874, not entered into force); Arts 15, 22, 32 (b), and 53 of the Institute of International Law, 'The Laws of War on Land, Oxford, 9 September 1880' (hereafter 1880 Oxford Manual on the Laws of War on Land) in D Schindler and J Toman (eds), *The Laws of Armed Conflicts: A Collection of Conventions, Resolutions and Other Documents* (Leiden, Martinus Nijhoff, 2004); Arts 23(g) and 49 of the Convention (II) with Respect to the Laws and Customs of War on Land and Its Annex: Regulations concerning the Laws and Customs of War on Land (hereafter 1899 Hague Regulations) (adopted 29 July 1899, entered into force 4 September 1900) 187 CTS 429; Art 12 of the Convention for the Amelioration of the Condition of the Wounded in Armies in the Field, as revised from 1864 (hereafter 1906 Geneva Convention) (adopted 6 July 1906, entered into force 9 August 1907) 11 LNTS 440; Arts 15 and 23(g) of the 1907 Hague Regulations; Arts 18, 54, and 71 of the 'Manual of the Law of Naval War, Oxford, 9 August 1913' (1913 Oxford Manual) in D Schindler and J Toman (eds), *The Laws of Armed Conflicts: A Collection of Conventions, Resolutions and Other Documents* (Leiden, Martinus Nijhoff, 2004); Art 8 of the 'Draft International Convention on the Condition and Protection of Civilians of Enemy Nationality Who Are on Territory Belonging to or Occupied by a Belligerent' XVth International Conference of the Red Cross (Tokyo 1934), ICRC IHL Database, www.icrc.org/ihl; Art 50 of the 1949 First Geneva Convention; Art 51 of the 1949 Second Geneva Convention; Art 8 of the 1949 Third Geneva Convention; Arts 5, 9, 53, 63, and 147 of the 1949 Fourth Geneva Convention; Art 4(2) of the 1954 Cultural Property Convention; Arts 14(3)(b), 54 (5), 62(1), and 71(3) of the 1977 First Additional Protocol; and Art 44 of the 1994 San Remo Manual on International Law Applicable to Armed Conflicts at Sea in Doswald-Beck (ed), *San Remo Manual*.

[250] See also Arts 22 and 51 of the 1880 Oxford Manual on the Laws of War on Land; Art 52 of the 1899 Hague Regulations; Arts 15 and 17(1) of the 1906 Geneva Convention; Arts 52 and 54 of the 1907 Hague Regulations; Art 29(1) of the Declaration concerning the Laws of Naval War (adopted 26 February 1909, not entered into force) 208 CTS 338; Arts 54, 58, 71, 104, and 114 of the 1913 Oxford Manual of the Law of Naval War; Arts 15 and 16 of the Convention for the Amelioration of the Condition of the Wounded in Armies in the Field, as revised from 1906 (adopted 27 July 1929, entered into force 19 June 1931) 118 LNTS 303; Arts 8 and 34 of the 1949 First Geneva Convention; Arts 8 and 28 of the 1949 Second Geneva Convention; Art 126 of the 1949 Third Geneva Convention; Arts 49, 55, 57, 60, 63, 108, and 143 of the 1949 Fourth Geneva Convention; Arts 4(2) and 11(2) of the 1954 Cultural Property Convention; Art 6 of the 1954 Cultural Property Convention, Second Protocol; Arts 54(5), 62(1), 67(4), 70(3)(c), and 71(3) of the 1977 First Additional Protocol; Art 17(1) of the 1977 Second Additional Protocol.

In this case, it imposes a stricter obligation than the first type since military necessity can be invoked only if additional conditions in the provisions are met.[251]

Thus, for example, a statement in the *Wall* case should be read with caution:

> The concepts of military necessity and proportionality have always been intimately linked in international humanitarian law . . . even if the construction of the wall and its associated régime could be justified as measures necessary to protect the legitimate rights of Israeli citizens, these measures would not pass the proportionality test.[252]

Military necessity is used as a possible justification to 'protect the legitimate rights of Israeli citizens' but nowhere in IHL permits such justification by military necessity; it can be invoked only if the relevant treaty provision expressly permits to invoke military necessity.

As similar to any rules of IHL, military necessity can be invoked by both the aggressor state and the victim state whereas the principle of necessity in the law of self-defence is only applicable to the victim state.

Hence, it is clear from the above that military necessity in IHL is distinct from the principle of necessity in the law of self-defence, which requires an assessment of whether self-defence measures per se are necessary to halt and repel the armed attack. Military necessity can only be invoked once an armed conflict commences and if the specific provisions in IHL permit it.

The distinction between the two kinds of principle of necessity has two consequences: 1) military necessity in IHL does not justify the use of force in self-defence; and 2) the principle of necessity in the law of self-defence cannot be invoked to derogate from IHL obligations.[253]

First, it is clear from the fundamental distinction between *jus ad bellum* and *jus in bello* that military necessity within the meaning of IHL cannot be invoked to justify the use of force under *jus ad bellum*. Thus, the US Military Tribunal in Nürnberg concluded in the *Ministries Trial* case that military necessity could not be invoked by Germany to justify the invasion of the neighbouring states carried out in violation of *jus ad bellum*:

[251] For further references to military necessity, see UNGA, 'Guidelines for Military Manuals and Instructions on the Protection of Environment in Times of Armed Conflict' (19 August 1994) UN Doc A/49/323, Annex, paras 8 and 9; Art 44 of the 1994 San Remo Manual on International Law Applicable to Armed Conflicts at Sea in Doswald-Beck (ed), *San Remo Manual*; Art 20(g) of ILC 'Draft Code of Crimes against the Peace and Security of Mankind' (1996) UN Doc A/CN.4/SER.A/1996/Add.1 (Part 2); Drafts of the Second Protocol to the 1954 Cultural Property Convention in J Hladík, 'The 1954 Hague Convention for the Protection of Cultural Property in the Event of Armed Conflict and the Notion of Military Necessity' (1999) 835 *International Review of the Red Cross* 621; Rules 38, 39, 43, 50, 51, and 56 in Henckaerts and Doswald-Beck, *Customary International Humanitarian Law* Vol I, 127, 131, 143, 175, 178, and 200.

[252] *Wall* case (Advisory Opinion), Separate Opinion of Judge Kooijmans, para 34.

[253] On the separation between *jus ad bellum* and *jus in bello*, see section 2.II.B.

> By resorting to armed force, Germany violated the Kellogg-Briand Pact. It thereby became an international outlaw . . . The doctrine of self-defence and military necessity was never available to Germany as a matter of international law, in view of its prior violation of that law.[254]

However, the Tribunal's categorical rejection of Germany's right to invoke military necessity is not consistent with IHL, since IHL applies equally to the conflicting parties and thus, military necessity as permitted in treaty provisions could have been equally invoked by Germany as well as its adversaries.

At the same time, it is also clear that the principle of necessity in the law of self-defence cannot be invoked to violate or disregard IHL. The contrary proposition was reflected in the concept of *Kriegraison geht vor Kriegsmanier*,[255] the meaning of which was described by Dunbar as follows: 'When the observance of rules of warfare endangers the safety of armed forces the limitations which they impose on hostile licence may be disregarded.'[256] This resembles the *Nuclear Weapons* Advisory Opinion in which the ICJ concluded that the threat or use of nuclear weapons would generally be contrary to IHL but 'cannot conclude definitively whether the threat or use of nuclear weapons would be lawful or unlawful in an extreme circumstance of self-defence, in which the very survival of a State would be at stake'.[257] However, the principle of the separation between *jus ad bellum* and *jus in bello* and the equal application of IHL to the conflicting parties in all circumstances[258] would reject the proposition that the necessity of self-defence can override the obligations under IHL.[259]

Nevertheless, this does not mean that the principle of necessity in the law of self-defence ceases to apply once an armed conflict commences. As noted earlier,[260] the law of self-defence and IHL can apply concurrently and thus, the principle of necessity in the law of self-defence and military necessity

[254] US Military Tribunal at Nürnberg, *In re Weizsaecker and Others (Ministries Trial)* (Judgment) (1949) *Annual Digest and Reports of Public International Law Cases* 344, 349.

[255] 'Necessity in war overrules the manner of warfare'. See H Lauterpacht (ed), L Oppenheim, *International Law: A Treaties* Vol II: Disputes, War and Neutrality, 7th edn (London, Longmans, Green and Co, 1952) 231 *ff*.

[256] N Dunbar, 'Military Necessity in War Crimes Trials' (1952) 29 *British Year Book of International Law* 442, 446.

[257] *Nuclear Weapons* case (Advisory Opinion), para 105(2)(E) and discussions on it in Y Sandoz et al, 'Special Issue: The Advisory Opinion on the International Court of Justice on the Legality of Nuclear Weapons and International Humanitarian Law' (1997) 316 *International Review of the Red Cross* 1, and L Boisson de Chazournes and P Sands (eds), *International Law, the International Court of Justice and Nuclear Weapons* (Cambridge, Cambridge University Press, 1999).

[258] See section 2.II.B and C.

[259] US Military Tribunal in Nürnberg, *List and Others (Hostage Case)* (Judgment) (1949) 8 *Law Reports of Trials of War Criminals* 34, 66; Switzerland, CCW/GGE/XI/WG.1/WP.13 (3 August 2005), para 3; Canada, CCW/GGE/XI/WG.1/WP.2 (29 June 2005), para 5; New Zealand, CCW/GGE/XI/WG.1/WP.16 (5 August 2005), para 2; Norway, CCW/GGE/XI/WG.1/WP.5 (29 July 2005), para 6; UK, CCW/GGE/XI/WG.1/WP.1 (24 June 2005), para 1 (i).

[260] See section 2.II.D.

in IHL are also concurrently applicable. It follows that a state is obliged to follow two principles of necessity during the conduct of self-defence: 1) the principle of necessity in the law of self-defence; and 2) military necessity in IHL. Thus, for example, when a victim state plans self-defence measures, it should first ask whether such measures per se are necessary and if there are any alternatives other than the use of force. During the course of the armed conflict, the victim state should constantly assess whether its self-defence measures per se are necessary to counter on-the-spot armed attack, continuous armed attack, or accumulation of on-the-spot armed attacks, as the case may be. If alternative measures can be found, such as sanctions under Chapter VII, self-defence measures should be halted. This is consistent with the temporary character of the right of self-defence as reflected in Article 51 of the UN Charter, which permits self-defence 'until the Security Council has taken measures necessary to maintain international peace and security'. At the same time, during the course of the armed conflict, if the victim state is planning to invoke military necessity in IHL, it should not be confused with the principle of necessity in the law of self-defence. The victim state should examine whether the planned invocation of military necessity is permitted by treaty provisions. If not, military necessity cannot be invoked.

A case in point is the *Wall* case in the ICJ. In this case, Israel primarily justified the construction of the wall on both *jus ad bellum* and *jus in bello* grounds. It first argued that 'The fence is a measure wholly consistent with the right of States to self-defence enshrined in Article 51 of the Charter'.[261] By relying on the right of self-defence, Israel became bound by the principle of necessity in the law of self-defence. Israel rejected the application of the 1949 Fourth Geneva Convention, which contains the bulk of the law of occupation. Nevertheless, it recognised the applicability of Article 23(g) of the 1907 Hague Regulations, which prohibits the destruction and seizure of enemy's property, 'unless such destruction or seizure be imperatively demanded by the necessities of war'.[262] By relying on this provision, it implicitly accepted that the destruction or seizure of enemy property, in order to build the wall, can only be justified by military necessity. These, taken together, indicate that Israel accepted the concurrent application of the principle of necessity in the law of self-defence and military necessity in IHL. In such a case, the limitation imposed on the conduct of self-defence is stricter than simply invoking the principle of necessity in the law of self-defence.

In this case, Israel had to prove that the self-defence measures per se were necessary and that there were no alternatives. In addition, Israel had

[261] UNGA (2003) GAOR 10th Emergency Special Session, UN Doc A/ES-10/PV.21, 6. The reliance on these resolutions was later rejected by the ICJ. See *Wall* case (Advisory Opinion), para 139.

[262] UNGA, 'Summary Legal Position of the Government of Israel' (24 November 2003) UN Doc A/ES-10/248, Annex I, para 2.

to comply with the principle of proportionality in the law of self-defence. Moreover, military necessity in IHL is so narrowly defined that the scope of self-defence measures permitted under the principles of necessity and proportionality was further reduced.

With regard to Article 23(g) of the 1907 Hague Regulations, which Israel relied on, it permits the destruction or seizure of the enemy's property only when 'imperatively demanded by the necessities of war'. The ICJ in the *Wall* case applied Article 53 of the 1949 Fourth Geneva Convention,[263] which resembles Article 23(g), to the destruction accompanying the construction of the wall and eventually rejected Israel's claim by stating that 'the Court is not convinced that the destructions carried out contrary to the prohibition in Article 53 of the Fourth Geneva Convention were rendered absolutely necessary by military operations'.[264]

The Court did not comment on the necessity and proportionality of Israel's alleged self-defence measures since it categorically dismissed the applicability of the law of self-defence.[265] Even if the principles of necessity and proportionality were applicable, any conclusion would have been controversial.[266] However, in the case of Article 53 of the 1949 Fourth Geneva Convention, the destruction of enemy property is permitted only if it is 'absolutely necessary by military operations', which is significantly narrower than the principles of necessity and proportionality in the law of self-defence.[267] In the case of the destruction of property caused by the construction of the wall, the Court saw it was clearly not possible to justify on the basis of military necessity and thus, the building of the wall was considered as unlawful.[268] Therefore, if it was already found that the construction was unlawful under IHL, there was no longer the need to assess whether it was necessary or proportionate self-defence. In this sense, military necessity, narrowly defined in IHL, could significantly limit the scope of the conduct of self-defence which might otherwise be permitted if only the principles of necessity and proportionality in the law of self-defence were applied. This is particularly the case with Article 23(g) of the 1907 Hague Regulations and Article 53 of the Fourth Geneva

[263] Art 53 of the 1949 Fourth Geneva Convention provides as follows: 'Any destruction by the Occupying Power of real or personal property belonging individually or collectively to private persons, or to the State, or to other public authorities, or to social or cooperative organizations, is prohibited, except where such destruction is rendered absolutely necessary by military operations.'

[264] *Wall* case (Advisory Opinion), para 135.

[265] *Wall* case (Advisory Opinion), para 139.

[266] This can be inferred from the disagreements of some judges with the Court, which concluded that the wall is contrary to international law and that it should be dismantled. See *Wall* case (Advisory Opinion), paras 163(3)(A) and (B). See also Declaration of Judge Buergenthal, para 5 and Separate Opinion of Judge Higgins, paras 33 and 34.

[267] O Uhler and H Coursier et al, *Commentary on the Geneva Conventions of 12 August 1949* Vol IV (Geneva, International Committee of the Red Cross, 1958) 302.

[268] *Wall* case (Advisory Opinion), para 163 (3) (A).

Convention, which first and foremost impose prohibition on the destruction of the enemy's property and then, in addition, the destruction on the basis of military necessity is permitted only in exceptional circumstances.

The concurrent application of the two kinds of principle of necessity does not allow a state to choose either one which best meets its needs in a particular circumstance. If, for example, the destruction of an enemy property cannot be justified by military necessity as defined in Article 23(g) of the 1907 Hague Regulations and Article 53 of the 1949 Fourth Geneva Convention, then the self-defence measures should not be carried out. A state cannot resort, as a second step, to the principle of necessity in the law of self-defence which may provide an adequate justification for the destruction of the same enemy property.[269]

As can be seen from the above, the principles of necessity in the law of self-defence and IHL are distinct. The principle of necessity in the law of self-defence covers a broader situation, particularly to assess whether self-defence measures per se are necessary and whether self-defence measures were only to the extent necessary to halt and repel the initial armed attack. On the other hand, military necessity in IHL has a narrower scope whose invocation is permitted only if the concerned treaty provision permits to invoke military necessity. Military necessity in IHL does not justify self-defence and the principle of necessity in the law of self-defence does not justify violations of IHL. However, the two can be applied concurrently and in some cases, military necessity in IHL imposes stricter limitation than the principle of necessity in the law of self-defence, thereby restricting the self-defence measures significantly.

IV. REPRISALS IN *JUS AD BELLUM* AND *JUS IN BELLO*[270]

This section clarifies the distinction and relationship between reprisals in *jus ad bellum* and *jus in bello*. It first makes it clear that reprisals in the sense of *jus ad bellum* and *jus in bello* are distinct. It also clarifies the scope of the prohibition on reprisals in *jus ad bellum* and *jus in bello* and the differences

[269] *Wall* case (Advisory Opinion), Written Statement of Palestine, para 534.

[270] For armed reprisals, see generally D Bowett, 'Reprisals Including Recourse to Armed Force' (1972) 66 *American Journal of International Law* 1; R Barsotti, 'Armed Reprisals' in Cassese (ed), *The Current Legal Regulation*; Dinstein, *War, Aggression and Self-Defence*, 4th edn, 221–24. For belligerent reprisals, see generally International Law Association, 'Committee on the Charter of the United Nations' in International Law Association Report of the Fiftieth Conference (Brussels 1962) (International Law Association, Brussels 1962) 157; H Meyrowitz, *Le Principe de l'égalité de belligérants devant le droit de la guerre* (Paris, Éditions Pedone, 1970) 121–27; F Hampson, 'Belligerent Reprisals and the 1977 Protocols to the Geneva Conventions of 1949' (1988) 37 *International and Comparative Law Quarterly* 818, 835–38; C Greenwood, 'Twilight of the Law of Belligerent Reprisals' (1989) 20 *Netherlands Yearbook of International Law* 35; F Kalshoven, 'Belligerent Reprisals Revisited' (1990) 21 *Netherlands Yearbook of International Law* 43; F Kalshoven, *Belligerent Reprisals* (Leiden, Martinus Nijhoff, 2005).

and similarities between the two. Finally, it will present a framework of how the prohibitions on reprisals in *jus ad bellum* and *jus in bello* can be complementary.

At the outset, it is worth noting that reprisals in *jus ad bellum* (commonly referred to as armed reprisals) and reprisals in *jus in bello* (commonly referred to as belligerent reprisals) are distinct concepts. This distinction should be made clear since in the past, there have been claims that a prior violation of *jus ad bellum* can render both armed reprisals and belligerent reprisals lawful.[271] As will be seen below, a prior violation of *jus ad bellum* no longer permits armed reprisals and with regard to belligerent reprisals, they are permitted not on the basis of a prior violation of *jus ad bellum* but a prior violation of IHL, and only if the concerned belligerent reprisals are not prohibited by IHL and conforms with certain conditions in customary international law. Neither armed reprisals nor belligerent reprisals are a term of art and thus are open to different interpretations but they are widely understood as follows.

A. Reprisals in *Jus ad Bellum*

On one hand, armed reprisals used to be a use of force which was normally unlawful under *jus ad bellum* but became lawful because it was directed against a prior use of force in violation of *jus ad bellum*.[272] Armed reprisals are, however, now widely viewed as being categorically prohibited under Article 2(4) of the UN Charter. The 1970 Friendly Relations Declaration, which elaborates Article 2(4), provides that 'States have a duty to refrain from acts of reprisal involving the use of force'.[273] The Security Council has, in numerous resolutions, condemned armed reprisals. An example is resolution 188 on the UK attack on Yemen in 1964 when the Security Council condemned 'reprisals as incompatible with the purposes and principles of the United Nations'.[274] Similar condemnations have been made in the resolutions relating to attacks by Israel and Portugal on neighbouring territories.[275] Most recently, the ICJ in the *Nuclear Weapons*

[271] G Schwarzenberger, 'Report on Self-Defence under the Charter of the United Nations and the Use of Prohibited Weapons' in International Law Association Report of the Fiftieth Conference (Brussels 1962) (International Law Association, Brussels 1962) 192, 221.

[272] For a classic case, see *Responsabilité de l'Allemagne à raison des dommages causés dans les colonies portugaises du Sud de l'Afrique* (*Portugal v Germany*) (1949) 2 *Reports of International Arbitral Awards* 1011, 1027. See alternatively, *Portugal v Germany* (The Naulilaa Case) (1927–28) *Annual Digest and Reports of Public International Law Cases* 526. See also Schachter, *International Law*, 185; Dinstein, *War, Aggression and Self-Defence*, 4th edn, 221.

[273] 1970 Friendly Relations Declaration.

[274] UNSC Res 188 (9 April 1964) UN Doc S/RES/188, para 1.

[275] UNSC Res 101 (24 November 1953) UN Doc S/RES/101, UNSC Res 111 (19 January 1956) UN Doc S/RES/111, UNSC Res 188 (9 April 1964) UN Doc S/RES/188, UNSC Res 228 (25 November 1966) UN Doc S/RES/228, UNSC Res 248 (24 March 1968) UN Doc S/

Advisory Opinion stated that 'The Court does not have to examine, in this context, the question of armed reprisals in time of peace, which are considered to be unlawful'.[276] Many experts also concur with the above practice.[277] Thus, the prohibition on armed reprisals is almost universally accepted.

The single but most difficult question is the distinction between armed reprisals and self-defence.[278] The distinction is particularly difficult because both armed reprisals and self-defence are use of force against a prior unlawful use of force, but armed reprisals are unlawful whereas self-defence is lawful under *jus ad bellum*. However, two criteria help to distinguish armed reprisals from self-defence: 1) the principle of proportionality; and 2) the punitive nature. For example, in the 1964 Harib Fort incident, UK noted as follows in the Security Council:

> There is, in existing law, a clear distinction to be drawn between two forms of self-help. One, which is of a retributive or punitive nature, is termed 'retaliation' or 'reprisals'; the other, which is expressly contemplated and authorized by the Charter, is self-defence against armed attack.[279]

As noted earlier, the UK attacks on Yemen in this incident were condemned as reprisals in Security Council resolution 188.

A similar position was taken by many states during the drafting of the 1974 Definition of Aggression. For example, Guatemala succinctly noted in the UN General Assembly's Sixth Committee that 'The concept of proportionality was an excellent criterion for determining whether an action was defensive or aggressive'.[280] This position was further confirmed by many states in ICJ cases. In the *Nuclear Weapons* case, Sweden noted that 'Reprisals which are disproportionate in comparison with the provocation which preceded them are prohibited'.[281] In the *Oil Platforms* case, Iran noted as follows:

> The distinction between lawful self-defence and unlawful reprisals is not, however, free from difficulty. The core of the distinction is believed to lie in the aim or purpose of the action taken. Essentially, self-defence has a protective aim:

RES/248, UNSC Res 256 (16 August 1968) UN Doc S/RES/256, UNSC Res 262 (31 December 1968) UN Doc S/RES/262, UNSC Res 265 (1 April 1969) UN Doc S/RES/265.

[276] *Nuclear Weapons* case (Advisory Opinion), para 46.

[277] Brownlie, *International Law and the Use of Force by States*, 281 and n 4 therein; Gardam, *Necessity*, 140; Gray, *International Law and the Use of Force*, 121; Dinstein, *War, Aggression and Self-Defence*, 4th edn, 226.

[278] See, eg, J Combacau, 'The Exception of Self-Defence in U.N. Practice' in Cassese (ed), *The Current Legal Regulation*, 27–29; J Green, 'Self-Defence: A State of Mind for States?' (2008) 55 *Netherlands International Law Review* 181.

[279] UNSC Verbatim Record (7 April 1965) UN Doc S/PV.1109, para 26. See also UNSC Verbatim Record (3 April 1964) UN Doc S/PV.1107, para 16.

[280] UNGA Sixth Committee (1971) GAOR 26th Session, 133, para 21. See also UNGA Special Committee for Defining Aggression (1970) GAOR 25th Session Supp No 19, 47, para 131; Jordan, UNGA Sixth Committee (1971) GAOR 26th Session, 138, para 12.

[281] *Nuclear Weapons* case, Written Statement of Sweden, 3.

> in contrast, reprisals aim at retribution or punishment, operating as a sanction against wrong committed.[282]

Iran further provided four criteria, which were the timing of self-defence,[283] disproportionate force,[284] premeditated nature of the action,[285] and selection of the 'wrong' target.[286]

In the *Wall* case, Indonesia noted that 'The requirement of necessity and proportionality means that self defence must not be retaliatory or punitive, the aim should be to halt and repel attacks'.[287] This position has been confirmed in other subsequent practice, such as during the 2006 Lebanon Conflict,[288] 2008 Georgia Conflict,[289] and 2009 Gaza Conflict.[290]

Thus, armed reprisals can be distinguished from self-defence by assessing whether the use of force was punitive, reflected in the form of disproportionate use of force. The principle of proportionality in the law of self-defence plays a central role in distinguishing armed reprisals and self-defence, and when the use of force is disproportionate, it can most likely be seen as an armed reprisal. The criteria to assess the proportionality of the use of force were discussed earlier.[291]

B. Reprisals in IHL and the Complementary Nature of the Prohibitions on the Two Kinds of Reprisals

On the other hand, belligerent reprisals are acts which are normally unlawful under IHL but become lawful because it is in response to a prior IHL violation. However, belligerent reprisals are not yet prohibited in a categorical manner like armed reprisals but rather take the form of prohibition on specific types of belligerent reprisals, and hence there may still be room for lawful belligerent reprisals. The following section only deals with belligerent reprisals in the law of international armed conflict since it is most relevant to armed reprisals.[292]

[282] *Oil Platforms* case (Merits), Memorial of Iran, para 4.30. See also Counter-Memorial of the US, paras 5.51.

[283] *Oil Platforms* case (Merits), Memorial of Iran, para 4.32.

[284] *Oil Platforms* case (Merits), Memorial of Iran, para 4.34.

[285] *Oil Platforms* case (Merits), Memorial of Iran, para 4.36.

[286] *Oil Platforms* case (Merits), Memorial of Iran, paras 4.38–4.41.

[287] *Wall* case, Written Statement of Indonesia, para 5. See also the Written Statement of South Africa, para 36.

[288] See Republic of the Congo, UNSC Verbatim Record (14 July 2006) UN Doc S/PV.5489, 13.

[289] Council of the European Union, Independent International Fact-Finding Mission on the Conflict in Georgia, 'Report' Vol II (September 2009) 271.

[290] See Costa Rica, UNSC Verbatim Record (31 December 2008) UN Doc S/PV.6060, 16.

[291] See section 3.II.A.

[292] Note that belligerent reprisals in non-international armed conflict are categorically prohibited by customary law. See Rule 148 in Henckaerts and Doswald-Beck, *Customary International Humanitarian Law* Vol I, 526.

Prohibitions on belligerent reprisals having customary law status and those which remain only as treaty law can be distinguished since the customary law status of some of the prohibitions in treaty law is still controversial.[293] First, the prohibitions on belligerent reprisals having customary law status are as follows: belligerent reprisals against wounded/sick/shipwrecked persons, medical personnel/buildings/vessels/equipment, religious personnel,[294] prisoners of war,[295] civilians in occupied territory,[296] other categories of civilians in the power of an adverse conflicting party,[297] civilian properties in the hands of the enemy,[298] and cultural objects.[299] The prohibitions on belligerent reprisals which still remain only as treaty law are as follows: belligerent reprisals against civilian population or civilians,[300] civilian objects,[301] cultural property,[302] objects indispensable to the survival of the civilian population,[303] natural environment,[304] and works and installations containing dangerous forces.[305] These are the only types of belligerent reprisals that are specifically prohibited in customary and treaty law. It follows that no state can carry out belligerent reprisals against those persons and objects protected by customary law, and states parties to the 1977 First Additional Protocol in particular cannot carry out belligerent reprisals that are prohibited therein.

Besides the specific prohibitions on belligerent reprisals, there are belligerent reprisals that are implicitly prohibited. First, there are IHL treaties that require states parties to comply with their obligations in 'all circumstances'

[293] For the customary law status of the prohibition on belligerent reprisals, see generally Hampson, 'Belligerent Reprisals', 835–38; Greenwood, 'Twilight of the Law of Belligerent Reprisals'; Kalshoven, 'Belligerent Reprisals Revisited'; Rules 145–48 in Henckaerts and Doswald-Beck, *Customary International Humanitarian Law* Vol I, 513, 519, 523, and 526. For the reservations on the provisions in the 1977 First Additional Protocol, see the website of the Switzerland Federal Department of Foreign Affairs, which acts as depositary of the Protocol, www.eda.admin.ch.

[294] See Art 46 of the 1949 First Geneva Convention, Art 47 of the 1949 Second Geneva Convention, Art 20 of the 1977 First Additional Protocol; Rule 146 in Henckaerts and Doswald-Beck, *Customary International Humanitarian Law* Vol I, 519.

[295] Art 13 of the 1949 Third Geneva Convention; Rule 146 in Henckaerts and Doswald-Beck, *Customary International Humanitarian Law* Vol I, 519.

[296] Art 33 of Fourth 1949 Geneva Convention; Rule 146 in Henckaerts and Doswald-Beck, *Customary International Humanitarian Law* Vol I, 519.

[297] Art 33 of Fourth 1949 Geneva Convention; Rule 146 in Henckaerts and Doswald-Beck, *Customary International Humanitarian Law* Vol I, 519.

[298] Art 33 of Fourth 1949 Geneva Convention; Rule 146 in Henckaerts and Doswald-Beck, *Customary International Humanitarian Law* Vol I, 519.

[299] Art 4(4) of the 1954 Cultural Property Convention; Rule 147 in Henckaerts and Doswald-Beck, *Customary International Humanitarian Law* Vol I, 523.

[300] Art 51(6) of the 1977 First Additional Protocol. This includes prohibition on the use of mines, booby-traps, and other devices against civilian population and civilians in belligerent reprisals, as provided in Art 3(2) of 1980 Convention on Conventional Weapons, Protocol II.

[301] Art 52(1) of the 1977 First Additional Protocol.

[302] Art 53(c) of the 1977 First Additional Protocol.

[303] Art 54(4) of the 1977 First Additional Protocol.

[304] Art 55(2) of the 1977 First Additional Protocol.

[305] Art 56(4) of the 1977 First Additional Protocol.

or 'any circumstances', which are the 1949 Geneva Conventions,[306] 1977 First Additional Protocol,[307] 1993 Chemical Weapons Convention,[308] and 1997 Convention on Anti-Personnel Mines.[309] Belligerent reprisals cannot be taken in response to prior violations of the provisions in these IHL treaties. A commentary on the term 'in all circumstances' in Article 1(1) of the 1977 First Additional Protocol also notes as follows:

> The prohibition against invoking reciprocity in order to shirk the obligations of humanitarian law is absolute . . . It does not allow the suspension of the application of the law either in part or as a whole, even if this is aimed at . . . a return to a respect for the law from him [the adversary].[310]

Belligerent reprisals involving the use of biological weapons have been a controversial question, but they seem to be prohibited now. Many of the states parties to the 1925 Gas Protocol made reservations to the effect that the use of biological weapons in response to a prior use of them is not prohibited[311] but subsequently, the states parties to the 1972 Biological Weapons Convention agreed to interpret Article I of the Convention, which prohibits the development, production, stockpile, acquisition, and retention of biological weapons (and not the use of biological weapons), as follows:

> The Conference [Fourth Review Conference of the states parties to the 1972 Biological Weapons Convention] reaffirms that the use by States Parties, in any way and under any circumstances, of microbial or other biological agents or toxins, that is not consistent with prophylactic, protective or other peaceful purposes, is effectively a violation of Article I of the convention.[312]

The phrase 'in any way and under any circumstances' would preclude belligerent reprisals. Such clarification was significant given that the 1925 Gas Protocol was inconclusive on this question.

As for the remaining weapons subject to IHL (explosive projectiles, expanding bullets, weapons with non-detectable fragments, blinding laser weapons, incendiary weapons, as well as the hostile use of environment) as means of belligerent reprisals, it is not clear whether their use is prohibited.[313]

306 Common Art 1 of the 1949 Geneva Conventions.

307 Art 1(1) of the 1977 First Additional Protocol.

308 Art I of the 1993 Chemical Weapons Convention.

309 Art 1 of the 1997 Convention on Anti-Personnel Mines.

310 Sandoz et al (eds), *Commentary*, para 51.

311 See, eg, the reservation of Iraq on the 1925 Gas Protocol. See the website of the France Ministry of Foreign Affairs, which acts as depositary of the 1925 Gas Protocol, www.doc.diplomatie.fr/pacte.

312 Fourth Review Conference of the Parties to the Convention on the Prohibition of the Development, Production and Stockpiling of Bacteriological (Biological) and Toxin Weapons and on Their Destruction (Geneva 25 November – 6 December 1996) 'Final Declaration' (1996) BWC/CONF.IV/9 Part II, 14, para 3.

313 Art 3(2) of the 1980 Convention on Conventional Weapons, Protocol II prohibits the use of mines, booby-traps, and other devices against civilian population and civilians in belliger-

Belligerent reprisals that are not explicitly or implicitly prohibited may be justified in limited circumstances, and only if they meet the requirements for lawful belligerent reprisals found in customary law. An example is the belligerent reprisals conducted against military objectives and combatants who can be attacked lawfully under IHL.[314] For example, if one of the conflicting parties uses an expanding bullet against a combatant, this would be a violation of the 1899 Hague Declaration (IV.3) but since there is no prohibition on belligerent reprisals in the Declaration, the other conflicting party may be able to use the expanding bullet against the combatants of the adversary. However, even if there may be cases of permissible belligerent reprisals, they are subject to at least five conditions found in customary international law:

1) they can only be conducted against a prior violation of IHL and only for the purpose of inducing the adversary to comply with IHL;
2) they can only be carried out as a measure of last resort;
3) they must be proportionate to the prior violation of IHL;
4) the decision to resort to them should be taken at the highest level of the government; and
5) they must cease as soon as the adversary complies with the law.[315]

Thus, belligerent reprisals might be justified in limited circumstances, but only if they meet the requirements for lawful belligerent reprisals found in customary international law.

In short, the differences between armed reprisals and belligerent reprisals are threefold. First, armed reprisals are regulated by *jus ad bellum* and belligerent reprisals are regulated by *jus in bello*. Secondly, armed reprisals are categorically prohibited in *jus ad bellum* whereas there is no general prohibition on belligerent reprisals and thus, they can be permissible in limited circumstances. Thirdly, the prohibition on armed reprisals is usually applicable to one of the conflicting parties, particularly the state which is a victim of an armed attack, but the prohibitions on belligerent reprisals are equally applicable to the conflicting parties. Thus, for example, a victim state that suffered an armed attack is obliged to refrain from carrying out armed reprisals but in terms of IHL, the victim state and the aggressor alike are obliged to refrain from carrying out belligerent reprisals prohibited by customary and treaty law. Conversely, both the victim state and the aggressor are entitled to carry out belligerent reprisals if they meet the requirements in customary international law.

However, even though the prohibition on armed reprisals and belligerent reprisals are distinct, they can also be complementary. With regard

ent reprisals, but it does not cover other persons hors de combat such as prisoners of war and civilian internees.

314 See, eg, Hampson, 'Belligerent Reprisals', 826.

315 Henckaerts and Doswald-Beck, *Customary International Humanitarian Law* Vol I, 515–18.

to the prohibition on armed reprisals, it supplements the prohibition on belligerent reprisals in at least three ways. First, the prohibition on armed reprisals is well established in customary international law and thus, there is no need to consider in detail about the customary law status like some of the treaty prohibitions on belligerent reprisals, and no need to consider whether the concerned conflicting party is a party to the IHL treaties containing prohibitions on belligerent reprisals.

Secondly, unlike belligerent reprisals, the prohibition on armed reprisals is categorical and thus, there is no need to consider whether a particular person or object, or the use of a particular weapon in armed reprisals, are prohibited. For example, with regard to reprisals against the civilian population and civilians, there has been much debate as to whether the prohibition on belligerent reprisals against them, as prohibited in Article 51(6) of the 1977 First Additional Protocol, has developed into a rule of customary international law.[316] Much of this debate can be circumvented by referring to the prohibition on armed reprisals since this does not specify which persons or objects cannot be attacked in reprisals and in past practice, attacks on the civilian population and civilians have been condemned by the Security Council as armed reprisals.[317] For example, in March 1968, Israel alleged that Jordan had attacked villages and refugee camps in Israel and thus, attacked villages in Jordan, which caused civilian deaths.[318] The Security Council subsequently condemned Israel's military action as 'military reprisals'.[319] Another example is the Iran–Iraq War. Prior to the armed conflict, Iran and Iraq were both states parties to the 1925 Gas Protocol but only Iraq made a reservation to the effect that the use of chemical and biological weapons in response to a prior use of them was not prohibited.[320] During the armed conflict, there was evidence that Iraq first used chemical weapons against Iran[321] but it was not clear

[316] For a discussion on this issue, see Greenwood, 'Twilight of the Law of Belligerent Reprisals', 62 *ff*.

[317] Bowett, 'Reprisals', 12–13.

[318] For the accounts of the events, see UNGA, 'The Status of the Cease-Fire' (1968) 22 UNYB 191, 191 *ff*.

[319] UNSC Res 248 (24 March 1968) UN Doc S/RES/248, para 3.

[320] See n 311 above.

[321] For certain evidence, see the UN Secretary-General's reports: UNSC, 'Mission to Inspect Civilian Areas in Iran and Iraq Which Have Been Subject to Military Attack' (20 June 1983) UN Doc S/15834; UNSC, 'Report of the Specialists Appointed by the Secretary-General to Investigate Allegations by the Islamic Republic of Iran concerning the Use of Chemical Weapons' (26 March 1984) UN Doc S/16433; UNSC, 'Letter Dated 17 April 1985 from the Secretary-General Addressed to the President of the Security Council' (24 April 1985) UN Doc S/17127; UNSC, 'Report of the Mission Dispatched by the Secretary-General to Investigate Allegations of the Use of Chemical Weapons in the Conflict between the Islamic Republic of Iran and Iraq' (12 March 1986) UN Doc S/17911; UNSC, 'Report of the Mission Dispatched by the Secretary-General to Investigate Allegations of the Use of Chemical Weapons in the Conflict between the Islamic Republic of Iran and Iraq' (8 May 1987) UN Doc S/18852; UNSC, 'Report of the Mission Dispatched by the Secretary-General to Investigate Allegations of the Use of Chemical Weapons in the Conflict between the Islamic Republic of

whether Iran was entitled to use chemical weapons in belligerent reprisals on the basis of the reservation of Iraq since it was not clear whether the reservation was still valid in the light of the subsequent state practice.[322] However, regardless of such uncertainty in IHL, the prohibition on armed reprisals would have applied when Iran subsequently used chemical weapons against Iraq, which would have significantly limited the use of chemical weapons by Iran.

Thirdly, the prohibition on armed reprisals also covers military objectives and combatants, who can otherwise be the objects of belligerent reprisals under IHL. For example, in the Iran–Iraq War, there were indications that Iran used chemical weapons against Iraqi combatants[323] but, as noted above, it was not clear whether the use of chemical weapons in belligerent reprisals was prohibited in the 1925 Gas Protocol. However, the prohibition on armed reprisals was categorical and thus, Iran's use of chemical weapons would have been prohibited, not only against civilians but also against combatants, if it was disproportionate and of a punitive nature.

On the other hand, with regard to the prohibitions on belligerent reprisals, they supplement the prohibition on armed reprisals in at least two ways. First, as noted above, armed reprisals are most often carried out by the victim state that suffered a prior armed attack and thus, the prohibition on armed reprisals is most often imposed on the victim state. However, the prohibitions on belligerent reprisals apply equally to the conflicting parties. Thus, the victim state and the aggressor alike should refrain from carrying out prohibited forms of belligerent reprisals. At the same time, the victim state and the aggressor can both carry out belligerent reprisals not prohibited in IHL, provided that they comply with the customary law requirements to carry out lawful belligerent reprisals.

Secondly, the prohibitions on belligerent reprisals, although not as categorical as the prohibition on armed reprisals, already impose substantial limitations on the conduct of self-defence, particularly those states which are parties to the 1977 First Additional Protocol. As noted above, the prohibitions on belligerent reprisals in the First Additional Protocol are extensive, which include the civilian population and civilians, civilian objects, cultural property, objects indispensable to the survival of the civilian population, natural environment, and works and installations containing dangerous forces. None of these can be attacked during the course

Iran and Iraq' (25 April 1988) UN Doc S/19823; UNSC, 'Report of the Mission Dispatched by the Secretary-General to Investigate Allegations of the Use of Chemical Weapons in the Conflict between the Islamic Republic of Iran and Iraq' (19 August 1988) UN Doc S/20134.

[322] See Kalshoven, 'Prohibitions or Restrictions', 101.

[323] UNSC, 'Report of the Mission Dispatched by the Secretary-General to Investigate Allegations of the Use of Chemical Weapons in the Conflict between the Islamic Republic of Iran and Iraq: Note by the Secretary-General' (25 April 1988) UN Doc S/19823, para 54 (c).

of carrying out self-defence measures, either as a first strike or in response to a prior violation. These are powerful constraints on the conduct of self-defence since in certain circumstances, the victim state may feel necessary to attack, for example, dams, dykes, and nuclear electrical generating stations (examples of works and installations containing dangerous forces listed in Article 56 of the First Additional Protocol) to respond to an armed attack and halt and repel the armed attack.[324] Prohibitions on belligerent reprisals even include those not covered by the prohibition on armed reprisals such as the prohibition on reprisals against prisoners of war.

The significance of the prohibitions on belligerent reprisals can be seen from the concerns expressed by states on such extensive prohibitions. With regard to the prohibition on belligerent reprisals against objects indispensable to the survival of the civilian population, states felt it necessary to add a condition because of the extensive constraint imposed by Article 54(2) of the 1977 First Additional Protocol.[325] Thus, Article 54(5) provides as follows:

> In recognition of the vital requirements of any Party to the conflict in the defence of its national territory against invasion, derogation from the prohibitions contained in paragraph 2 may be made by a Party to the conflict within such territory under its own control where required by imperative military necessity.

Such concern was already raised during the 1974–77 Diplomatic Conference. For example, Cyprus stated during the discussion on draft Article 54 that 'it would be unacceptable to place greater restriction on those fighting for the freedom of their country than on an army of occupation, for which such derogation was provided by Article 53 of the fourth Geneva Convention of 1949'.[326] The UK also noted as follows on the same provision:

> If a ban on reprisals was introduced, it should not . . . be absolute but qualified, so that the right should be retained, subject to strict legal restraint on its exercise, in the circumstances where a Party to the conflict was subjected to persistent attacks on its own civilians and civilian objects which did not cease despite repeated protests. In such circumstances a Party to the conflict would undoubtedly take reprisal measures.[327]

[324] See, eg, UNHRC, 'Report of the Commission of Inquiry on Lebanon Pursuant to Human Rights Council Resolution S-2/1' (23 November 2006) UN Doc A/HRC/3/2, para 76.

[325] Art 54(2) of the 1977 First Additional Protocol provides as follows: 'It is prohibited to attack, destroy, remove or render useless objects indispensable to the survival of the civilian population, such as foodstuffs, agricultural areas for the production of foodstuffs, crops, livestock, drinking water installations and supplies and irrigation works, for the specific purpose of denying them for their sustenance value to the civilian population or to the adverse Party, whatever the motive, whether in order to starve out civilians, to cause them to move away, or for any other motive'.

[326] *Official Records* Vol XV, CDDH/III/SR.58, para 6.

[327] *Official Records* Vol XIV, CDDH/III/SR.16, para 58.

The concern was also raised with regard to the other prohibitions on attacks on certain objects. Thus, the USSR noted as follows during the discussion on Article 52 of the 1977 First Additional Protocol, which prohibits attacks on civilian objects:

> [I]t was necessary to bear in mind that a party to an armed conflict which had been attacked and which was obliged to defend itself, must be enabled to carry out all the military operations required, making maximum use of any military advantages it might gain. It must not be deprived of the means of self-defence.[328]

France expressed a similar view on this provision.[329]

With regard to Article 56 of the 1977 First Additional Protocol which prohibits attacks on works and installations containing dangerous forces, the US noted as follows:

> The rule permitting reprisals encouraged Parties to the conflict to comply with the law. Reprisals were used against adversaries who violated the international rules of war. Accordingly, those who claimed to have had reprisals inflicted upon them must be admitting that they were guilty of illegal acts . . . The victims of illegal acts could take action against objects of the adversary. In his view such reprisals should be carefully considered as an important deterrent to illegal acts.[330]

A further example is the cases in the Ethiopia–Eritrea Claims Commission in which the Commission found several violations of the prohibition on attacks against certain objects. For example, in the *Western Front, Aerial Bombardment and Related Claims* Award, the Commission found that Ethiopia violated, among others, the customary rule prohibiting attacks on objects indispensable to the survival of the civilian population which can also be found in Article 54 of the 1977 First Additional Protocol.[331] In the *Central Front* Award (Eritrea's Claims), the Commission further found that Ethiopia violated, among others, Article 56 of the 1907 Hague Regulations prohibiting attacks on cultural property and customary law prohibiting attacks on civilian objects which can also be found in Article 52 of the First Additional Protocol.[332] These cases reflect the fact that states will attack prohibited objects even without any prior violation of the prohibition on attacking certain objects. They also imply that states would attack prohibited objects more readily if there are prior violations of similar IHL rules. What the prohibitions on belligerent reprisals do is to prohibit states to attack prohibited persons and objects even if there are

[328] *Official Records* Vol XIV, CDDH/III/SR.15, para 21.

[329] *Official Records* Vol VI, CDDH/SR.41, paras 111–13. See also *Official Records* Vol VI, CDDH/SR.41, Annex.

[330] *Official Records* Vol XIV, CDDH/III/SR.19, para 19.

[331] Eritrea–Ethiopia Claims Commission, *Western Front, Eritrea* case (Partial Award), para 105.

[332] Eritrea–Ethiopia Claims Commission, *Central Front, Eritrea* case (Partial Award), paras 113–14.

prior violations of IHL rules. Thus, the prohibitions on belligerent reprisals, although not as categorical as the prohibition on armed reprisals, already impose substantial limits on the conduct of self-defence, particularly those states which are parties to the 1977 First Additional Protocol.

The dual constraints on reprisals are also relevant when it is not clear whether the use of force is self-defence or armed reprisals. A particularly relevant case is self-defence in response to an 'accumulation of events'. It has long been controversial whether a series of on-the-spot armed attacks can be seen as one single armed attack and hence, would allow the victim state to use force in self-defence, not only against each armed attack but also against the whole series of armed attacks.[333] In practice, this question acutely highlights the grey zone between self-defence and armed reprisals: an on-the-spot armed attack clearly permits a state to carry out self-defence measures, but it may need some time to trace the aggressor or the armed group and prepare its response. Meanwhile, the aggressor or the armed group launches another on-the-spot armed attack and so, the response of the victim state against the first armed attack is perceived as being delayed, which can be evidence for armed reprisals. The determination of whether such series of armed attacks is a single armed attack or not is crucial since if it is considered as a single armed attack, the victim state's use of force will be a lawful self-defence whereas if they are not considered as such, it could be an armed reprisal. However, shifting the focus from armed attack to proportionality might be a more practical approach. The principle of proportionality can be applied to both patterns of armed attack, that is, each on-the-spot armed attack as well as a series of on-the-spot armed attacks. In other words, the proportionality can be assessed between an on-the-spot armed attack and the military response taken against it as well as a series of on-the-spot armed attacks and the military response taken against it. If, in either case, the victim state's military response is disproportionate, it is unlawful or can even amount to armed reprisals. Thus, by employing the principle of proportionality, the controversial question of whether a series of on-the-spot armed attacks can be considered as a single armed attack can be circumvented and yet, prevent the use of force by the victim state from developing into armed reprisals.[334]

All such controversies in *jus ad bellum* are irrelevant to *jus in bello*. *Jus in bello* itself does not judge whether the use of force taken against a series of on-the-spot armed attacks is self-defence or armed reprisals. Whatever the character of the use of force under *jus ad bellum*, IHL applies whenever there is an armed conflict and, as discussed above, the prohibitions on

[333] See generally Bowett, 'Reprisals', 5 *ff*; Dinstein, *War, Aggression and Self-Defence*, 4th edn, 230 *ff*.

[334] See Kolb, *Ius contra bellum*, 225; Dinstein, *War, Aggression and Self-Defence*, 4th edn, 230. For the content of the principle of proportionality in the law of self-defence, see section 3.II.A.

belligerent reprisals and IHL rules on targeting, in particular, impose a substantial limit on the conduct of the use of force.[335] Moreover, since IHL applies equally to the conflicting parties, even when it is not clear which side is the victim state, IHL can still ensure the regulation of excessive use of force by the possible victim state. Thus, since both the principle of proportionality in the law of self-defence and IHL are not dependent on the legality of the use of force per se, they have the potential to act as a safeguard to prevent self-defence measures against a series of on-the-spot armed attacks from developing into armed reprisals.

One aspect which is common to the principles of proportionality and necessity discussed in the previous sections is that the state which is claiming self-defence in particular cannot choose either *jus ad bellum* or *jus in bello* to meet its needs. Both the prohibitions on armed reprisals and belligerent reprisals apply concurrently. In particular, if a state uses force which amounts to an armed reprisal in the sense of *jus ad bellum*, it cannot then decide to turn to the argument that it was a permissible belligerent reprisal, knowing that some belligerent reprisals are permissible. If it is an armed reprisal, the use of force is prima facie unlawful under international law and should not be carried out in the first place, or it should be halted immediately. If the use of force further violates the prohibitions on belligerent reprisals, it is a double violation of *jus ad bellum* and *jus in bello* thereby incurring individual and state responsibility for violations of *jus ad bellum* and *jus in bello*. Thus, the prohibitions on armed reprisals and belligerent reprisals should be seen as one set, and a use of force by the state claiming self-defence in particular should always be assessed against two layers, the prohibition on armed reprisals and the prohibitions on belligerent reprisals. The use of force can be assessed against whichever prohibition in the first instance but if a violation of either of the prohibition is found, that suffices to conclude that the use of force is unlawful under international law. If, in the first instance, a violation of either of the prohibition on reprisals is not found, then a further assessment of whether there is a violation on the other prohibition should be carried out.

An example is the Eritrea–Ethiopia conflict. In the *Jus ad Bellum* Award, the Eritrea–Ethiopia Claims Commission concluded that Eritrea launched an armed attack against Ethiopia[336] and hence, it made it clear that Ethiopia was entitled to take self-defence measures. It was also an exceptional case where many of the provisions in the 1977 First Additional Protocol were applied as rules of customary international law, even though the Protocol did not apply as a treaty law.[337] At this point, Ethiopia was bound by both

[335] See section 3.II.B.

[336] Eritrea–Ethiopia Claims Commission, *Jus ad Bellum* case (Partial Award), para 14.

[337] Ethiopia was a party to the 1977 First Additional Protocol but Eritrea was not. For the dates of consent to be bound, see the website of the Switzerland Federal Department of Foreign Affairs, which acts as depositary of the Protocol, www.eda.admin.ch.

the prohibitions on armed reprisals and belligerent reprisals.[338] Thus, for example, if Ethiopia had carried out an armed reprisal, it could not have then turned to the argument that it was a permissible belligerent reprisal, knowing that some belligerent reprisals were permissible. Similarly, if Ethiopia had further violated the prohibitions on belligerent reprisals, it would have been a double violation of *jus ad bellum* and *jus in bello*. The Claims Commission did not find any of these violations but some of its awards implicitly illustrated how the prohibitions on armed reprisals and belligerent reprisals can be double-layered constraints on the conduct of self-defence.

In short, reprisals in *jus ad bellum* (armed reprisals) and reprisals in *jus in bello* (belligerent reprisals) are distinct concepts and are regulated by the respective legal regime. Armed reprisals are categorically prohibited under *jus ad bellum* and belligerent reprisals are prohibited only by specific treaty provisions or the corresponding customary law and there is no general prohibition like on armed reprisals. Some belligerent reprisals can therefore be permissible but only when they meet the requirements in customary international law. The prohibition on armed reprisals complements the prohibitions on belligerent reprisals since its customary law status is established, it is categorical, and it also covers military objectives and combatants who can normally be attacked lawfully in belligerent reprisals. On the other hand, the prohibitions on belligerent reprisals complement the prohibition on armed reprisals because they apply equally to the conflicting parties and impose significant constraints on the conduct of self-defence, particularly for the states parties to the 1977 First Additional Protocol. A state cannot claim that its use of force was a lawful belligerent reprisal in order to circumvent the prohibition on armed reprisals. If a particular use of force violated either the prohibition on armed reprisals or belligerent reprisals, it should not have been carried out in the first place or should be halted immediately, and state responsibility or individual criminal responsibility should be borne by the concerned state and individuals.

V. CONCLUSIONS

The discussions above demonstrate that there is a high risk of confusion between the rules in the law of self-defence and IHL. For this reason, a clear distinction between the similar rules in the law of self-defence and IHL is all the more important. However, while the similar rules must be clearly distinguished, they can apply to a particular use of force in self-defence simultaneously, and impose strict limits to the excessive use of force.

338 Prohibitions on belligerent reprisals also apply to Eritrea since these prohibitions apply equally to the conflicting parties, as explained earlier.

This chapter first distinguished the thresholds that trigger the application of the law of self-defence and IHL. 'Armed attack' is the threshold that triggers the application of the law of self-defence and 'armed conflict' is the threshold that triggers the application of IHL. So far as international armed conflict is concerned, the threshold of armed attack overlaps with it since they involve an attack between two or more states across the international border. However, the two thresholds differ particularly in terms of the requirement of intensity, since some argue that an armed attack can exist in case of an imminent threat of armed attack whereas such a situation does not qualify as an international armed conflict. Hence, the two thresholds need to be distinguished and the assessment of the existence of an armed attack and international armed conflict should be conducted separately. If an armed attack and an international armed conflict exist at the same time, then the law of self-defence and IHL apply simultaneously.

The principle of proportionality in the law of self-defence and IHL should not be confused. The former entails a balancing test between an armed attack and the military response taken against it or an armed attack and the aim to halt and repel it. Furthermore, four elements are frequently used to assess the proportionality: 1) target selection; 2) effects on civilians; 3) geographical scope; and 4) temporal scope. On the other hand, the principle of proportionality in IHL only aims at limiting incidental effects on civilians and civilian objects in relation to 'concrete and direct military advantage anticipated'. Unlike the principle of proportionality in self-defence, it only applies to a military operation of a limited scope and it does not impose limits on geographical or temporal scope. However, the two kinds of principle of proportionality might have overlap since they both impose limits on the effects on civilians. IHL complements the principle of proportionality in self-defence since it prohibits attacks on civilians per se and the extent of civilian casualties tolerated is very narrow, that is, only if they are not 'excessive in relation to the concrete and direct military advantage anticipated'.

IHL rules on means and methods of warfare and on occupation impose limits on almost all aspects of the conduct of self-defence. Together with the principles of proportionality in the law of self-defence, they impose limits on the conduct of self-defence at the macro and micro level.

The principle of necessity in the law of self-defence and IHL should also not be confused. The former requires an assessment of: 1) whether the measures in self-defence per se are necessary, that is, whether there are still alternatives other than the use of force; and 2) whether measures taken in self-defence were only to the extent necessary to halt and repel an armed attack. The latter, military necessity, can only be invoked if the provisions in IHL treaties expressly permit to do so. The two are concurrently applicable. If a use of force fails to meet the principle of necessity in self-defence, it cannot then turn to military necessity in IHL for justification (the same applies vice versa). The use of force is already unlawful and should be halted immediately.

Reprisals in *jus ad bellum* and *jus in bello* should also not be confused. The former, armed reprisals, are categorically prohibited while the latter, belligerent reprisals, may be permitted in limited circumstances. The categorical nature of the prohibition on armed reprisals can complement the gaps in the prohibitions on belligerent reprisals. At the same time, the prohibitions on belligerent reprisals are detailed and extensive, which could impose limits on the conduct of self-defence.

4

Distinction and Relationship between Chapter VII Measures and IHL[1]

AS MENTIONED IN the Introduction, one of the aims of this book is to examine the role of the three principles governing the relationship between *jus ad bellum* and *jus in bello* in contexts other than self-defence and international armed conflict. This Chapter therefore focuses on the other type of use of force permitted in international law, the use of force under Chapter VII of the UN Charter, and its relation to IHL.

A brief problem analysis on the relationship between Chapter VII use of force and IHL was presented in Chapter 2. It pointed out that the issues pertaining to this relationship were of a very different nature compared to those between the law of self-defence and the law of international armed conflict. This Chapter begins by elaborating on the difference in nature between self-defence/IHL relation and Chapter VII/IHL relation.

Then, two sections dealing with preliminary issues follow: one section on the principal legal issues of the relationship between Chapter VII and IHL, and the other section on the overview of the Security Council resolutions concerning IHL. The rest of the two sections deal with *jus ad bellum* and *jus in bello* constraints on military and non-military enforcement measures under Chapter VII.

I. DIFFERENT NATURE OF CHAPTER VII USE OF FORCE COMPARED TO SELF-DEFENCE

As noted earlier, use of force under international law is only possible if it is in self-defence (in other words, use of force by a state in response to an armed attack) or when the UN Security Council authorises the use of force under Chapter VII of the UN Charter. As regards these two types of lawful use of force, experts have discussed extensively on how the right of self-defence is related to IHL, and the previous chapter of this book has also elaborated on these earlier discussions. On the other hand, the use of

[1] As an introduction to this topic, see L Condorelli et al (eds), *Nations Unies et le droit international humanitaire: Actes du Colloque international à l'occasion du cinquantième anniversaire de l'ONU* (Paris, Éditions Pedone, 1996).

force in Chapter VII, and its relation to IHL, has not been given the same level of attention and the past writings have not clarified the relationship adequately.[2] The nature of the use of force in Chapter VII is significantly different from the use of force in self-defence, and this needs to be understood first since the differences also have an impact on the relationship between *jus ad bellum* and *jus in bello*.

First, it is worth noting that the use of force under Chapter VII of the UN Charter is a newly created type of lawful use of force with the adoption of the UN Charter which is different from the right of self-defence in many respects. The power to authorise the use of force is conferred on the Security Council, which is one of the organs of the UN, whose power is determined by the UN Charter. The decision of the Security Council is considered as a collective decision of the UN as a whole, and is aimed at maintaining and, at times, enforcing peace and security among states and within states. This is in marked contrast to the right of self-defence, which is an 'inherent right'[3] of each state under customary international law dating from the pre-UN Charter period, and now confirmed in Article 51 of the UN Charter. The decision to exercise the right of self-defence is entirely left up to the state and is not a collective decision on behalf of all states. The primary aim is to fend off the armed attack and preserve the sovereignty of the attacked state, rather than a broader aim to maintain international peace and security. The right of collective self-defence can also be exercised to help other states to defend themselves, but this is fundamentally different from Chapter VII use of force since UN Member States are obliged to accept and co-operate with the Security Council decision to use force, whereas states are free to participate or not in collective self-defence.

The Security Council, as an organ of the UN, is regulated by a number of provisions in the UN Charter. Among others, Article 24(1) of the UN Charter states that the UN Member States confer on the Security Council primary responsibility for the maintenance of international peace and security and agree that the Security Council acts on their behalf. Moreover, the UN Member States agree to accept and carry out the decisions of the Security Council pursuant to Article 25 of the UN Charter. The decisions clearly include Chapter VII authorisation to use force. The UN Charter here creates a hierarchy between the obligations under the UN Charter and other obligations 'under any other international agreement', pursuant to Article 103 of the UN Charter. This article puts UN Charter obligations over other obligations 'under any other international agreement' when the two are in conflict. The decisions of the Security Council

[2] See, eg, Condorelli et al (eds), *Nations Unies et le droit international humanitaire*.

[3] Art 51 of the Charter of the United Nations reads as follows: 'Nothing in the present Charter shall impair the inherent right of individual or collective self-defence.' Charter of the United Nations (hereafter UN Charter) (adopted 26 June 1945, entered into force 24 October 1945) 59 Statutes at Large 1031.

clearly qualify as obligations under the UN Charter and hence, Chapter VII authorisation to use force can prevail over other obligations 'under any other international agreement', including IHL treaties, when the former and the latter are in conflict. This is markedly in contrast with the right of self-defence, which has no hierarchical relation with IHL.

The Security Council, in order to decide any measures to maintain international peace and security, shall determine the existence of 'threat to the peace', 'breach of the peace', or 'act of aggression'. These are the thresholds that trigger the power of the Security Council to authorise the use of force under Chapter VII. These thresholds are entirely different from the threshold of 'armed attack', which triggers the right of self-defence. Hence, the situations where Chapter VII and IHL are applicable simultaneously are determined by the overlap between threat to the peace, breach of the peace, and act of aggression on one hand, and armed conflict on the other. A later section shows that Chapter VII use of force is not only limited to intervening in armed conflicts between states but can also intervene in armed conflicts within a state (non-international armed conflict). This is in contrast with the right of self-defence, which is traditionally limited to inter-state relations, in other words a response against an armed attack from a state or from an armed group supported by a state.[4]

The threshold of 'threat to the peace' in particular not only covers situations of armed conflict but also other situations such as racial discrimination[5] and violations of democratic principles.[6] As such, the means and methods used to address threats to the peace are also diverse. They are not limited to Chapter VII use of force but also non-military measures. Even armed conflicts are dealt with not only by Chapter VII use of force but also by non-military measures such as arms embargoes and economic sanctions. Even when the Security Council decides to resort to Chapter VII use of force, the actual use of force can be entrusted to UN forces established as the Security Council's subsidiary organ or to the Member States forming a coalition themselves. All these measures taken by the Security Council under Chapter VII have an impact on IHL in different ways. For example, how can UN forces be bound by IHL when the UN is not a party to any IHL treaty? What impact do economic sanctions have on the delivery of humanitarian assistance, as ensured by IHL, in the sanctioned state? This, again, is in marked contrast with the right of self-defence which primarily takes the form of military response by a state or states rather than non-military measures. Hence, the question was essentially about how the law of self-defence and IHL regulated the military response.

[4] Whether armed groups without any state support can launch an 'armed attack' within the meaning of Art 51 of the UN Charter will be discussed later in section 5.II.A.

[5] See, eg, UNSC Res 232 (16 December 1966) UN Doc S/RES/232 on Southern Rhodesia.

[6] See, eg, UNSC Res 841 (16 June 1993) UN Doc S/RES/841, UNSC Res 917 (6 May 1994) UN Doc S/RES/917, and UNSC Res 940 (31 July 1994) UN Doc S/RES/940 on Haiti.

Therefore, it is first critical to understand the different nature of the issues when discussing the relationship between Chapter VII of the UN Charter and IHL. Chapter VII measures pose different challenges to the three principles governing *jus ad bellum* and *jus in bello*: separation between *jus ad bellum* and *jus in bello*, equal application of *jus in bello* to the conflicting parties, and concurrent application of *jus ad bellum* and *jus in bello*. The issues that pose challenges to these principles, as explained briefly above, will be discussed in greater detail throughout this chapter.

II. CHAPTER VII OF THE UN CHARTER AND IHL

A. Legal Basis for the Security Council to Deal with Issues Related to IHL

Before going into the substantive discussions, it is first necessary to set out the legal basis for the Security Council to deal with issues related to IHL.

It should be made clear at the outset that in the UN Charter, there is no provision which specifically authorises the Security Council to deal with IHL issues. Its competence rather derives from more general provisions of Articles 24(1) and 39 of the UN Charter, coupled with Security Council practice.

Article 24(1) of the UN Charter provides that the Security Council has the primary responsibility for the maintenance of international peace and security and to fulfil this function, it can determine the situation as either a threat to the peace, breach of the peace, or act of aggression pursuant to Article 39 of the UN Charter, which then enables it to make recommendations or to take military or non-military enforcement measures under Chapter VII. In practice, it is widely accepted that the Security Council has a very wide discretion to decide certain situations as coming under Article 39,[7] except that it should observe Article 24(2), which obliges it to act in accordance with the Purposes and Principles of the UN as provided

[7] The ICTY Appeals Chamber noted as follows in the *Tadic* case: 'the Security Council plays a pivotal role and exercises a very wide discretion under this Article [Article 39]'. See *Tadic Case* (Jurisdiction, Appeals) ICTY-IT-94-1 (2 October 1995), paras 28 and 29.

For general discussions on the limitations on the powers of the Security Council, see V Gowlland-Debbas, 'Security Council Enforcement Action and Issues of State Responsibility' (1994) 43 *International and Comparative Law Quarterly* 55, 90 *ff*; T Gill, 'Legal and Some Political Limitations on the Power of the Security Council to Exercise Its Enforcement Powers under Chapter VII of the Charter' (1995) 26 *Netherlands Yearbook of International Law* 33; D Akande, 'The International Court of Justice and the Security Council: Is There Room for Judicial Control of Decisions of the Political Organs of the United Nations?' (1997) 46 *International and Comparative Law Quarterly* 309; S Lamb, 'Legal Limits to United Nations Security Council Powers' in G Goodwin-Gill and S Talmon (eds), *The Reality of International Law: Essays in Honour of Ian Brownlie* (Oxford, Oxford University Press, 1999); R Kolb, *Ius contra bellum: Le droit international relatif au maintien de la paix* (Bâle, Helbing et Lichtenhahn, 2003) 122 *ff*.

in Articles 1 and 2 of the UN Charter.[8] On this basis, the Security Council has recognised the applicability of IHL in many of its resolutions adopted under the terms of Article 39.[9]

However, in the majority of cases, the Security Council has invoked IHL without a determination of a situation under Article 39 of the UN Charter.[10] In such cases, the Security Council can still invoke IHL on the basis of Article 24(1) of the UN Charter alone, if the Security Council considers that the situation concerns its responsibility to maintain international peace and security. Article 39 is certainly a precondition to make recommendations or to take enforcement actions under Chapter VII, but it is not necessarily a precondition to invoke IHL. This can be done independently on the basis of Article 24(1).

As a part of its efforts to deal with IHL issues, the Security Council has authorised various forms of military and non-military enforcement measures. These enforcement measures may, intentionally or unintentionally, implement and complement IHL. The competence of the Security Council to implement IHL can generally be found in Article 24(2) of the UN Charter. As noted earlier, this article obliges the Security Council to act in accordance with the Purposes and Principles of the UN provided in Articles 1 and 2 of the UN Charter. Among others, Article 1(3) provides that one of the UN's purposes is to achieve international co-operation on humanitarian issues and promote the respect for human rights which, in a very general sense, might include the implementation of IHL.[11]

The implementation of IHL by the Security Council is, in fact, envisaged in IHL itself. In general, common Article 1 of the 1949 Geneva Conventions obliges the states parties to 'ensure respect' for the Conventions, which could also mean that the members of the Security Council are obliged to take decisions that would ensure respect for the Conventions in case a state party is not complying with them. Article 89 of the 1977 First Additional Protocol further provides as follows:

[8] The limitations imposed by Article 24(2) of the UN Charter was confirmed in *Legal Consequences for States of the Continued Presence of South Africa in Namibia (South-West Africa) Notwithstanding Security Council Resolution 276 (1970)* (hereafter *Namibia* case) (Advisory Opinion) [1971] ICJ Rep 16, para 110; *Tadic Case* (Jurisdiction, Appeals), para 28; *Application of the Convention on the Prevention and Punishment of the Crime of Genocide Case* (*Bosnia and Herzegovina v Serbia and Montenegro*) (hereafter *Bosnia Genocide* case) (Order of 13 September 1993) [1993] ICJ Rep 325, Separate Opinion of Judge Lauterpacht, paras 102–04.

[9] For further discussions, see section 4.III.A. For a useful list of Security Council resolutions related to IHL, see J-M Henckaerts and L Doswald-Beck (eds), *Customary International Humanitarian Law* Vol II: Practice (Geneva, International Committee of the Red Cross and Cambridge, Cambridge University Press, 2005) 4335 *ff*. See also Annex 1.

[10] See Annex 1. For example, UNSC Res 452 (20 July 1979) UN Doc S/RES/452, Preamble provides as follows: '*The Security Council* . . . *Considering* that the policy of Israel in establishing settlements in the occupied Arab territories has no legal validity and constitutes a violation of the Geneva Convention relative to the Protection of Civilian Persons in Time of War, of 12 August 1949.' This resolution was not adopted under the terms of Art 39 of the UN Charter.

[11] See n 8 above.

> In situations of serious violations of the Conventions [1949 Geneva Conventions] or of this Protocol, the High Contracting Parties undertake to act, jointly or individually, in co-operation with the United Nations and in conformity with the United Nations Charter.

A commentary on this provision envisages the following possible actions as examples:

- —Issuing an appeal to respect humanitarian law;
- —Setting up enquiries on compliance with the 1949 Geneva Conventions and the 1977 First Additional Protocol;
- —Coercive actions which may include the use of armed force;
- —Assistance in terms of material or personnel, given to Protecting Powers, their substitutes or to humanitarian organizations.[12]

In practice, and as will be seen throughout this chapter, all the actions listed above have been taken by the UN, particularly by the Security Council under Chapter VII. It is also noteworthy that the use of force under the UN Charter is envisaged as a means to address serious violations of IHL.

The 1972 Biological Weapons Convention,[13] the 1976 Environmental Modification Convention,[14] the 1993 Chemical Weapons Convention,[15] the 1996 Amended Protocol II to the 1980 Convention on Conventional Weapons,[16] and the 1997 Convention on Anti-Personnel Mines[17] also contain provisions on the co-operation between states and the Security Council.

The details of Security Council practice on IHL in its resolutions will be discussed more throughout this section. It suffices to note at this point

[12] Y Sandoz et al (eds), *Commentary on the Additional Protocols of 8 June 1977 to the Geneva Conventions of 12 August 1949* (Geneva, International Committee of the Red Cross, 1987) para 3597.

[13] Arts VI, VII, and XIII of the Convention on the Prohibition of the Development, Production and Stockpiling of Bacteriological (Biological) and Toxin Weapons and on Their Destruction (adopted 10 April 1972, entered into force 26 March 1975) 1015 UNTS 163.

[14] Art V(3)–(5) of the Convention on the Prohibition of Military or Any Hostile Use of Environmental Modification Techniques (adopted 10 December 1976, entered into force 5 October 1976) 1108 UNTS 151.

[15] Arts VIII(36), XII(4), and XVI(2) of the Convention on the Prohibition of the Development, Production, Stockpiling and Use of Chemical Weapons and on Their Destruction (adopted 3 September 1992, entered into force 29 April 1997) 1974 UNTS 45.

[16] Art 12(1)(c) of the Convention on Prohibitions and Restrictions on the Use of Certain Conventional Weapons Which May Be Deemed to Be Excessively Injurious or to Have Indiscriminate Effects, Amended Protocol on Prohibitions or Restrictions on the Use of Mines, Booby-Traps and Other Devices (Amended Protocol II) (hereafter 1980 Convention on Conventional Weapons, Amended Protocol II) (adopted 3 May 1996, entered into force 3 December 1998) 2048 UNTS 93.

[17] Art 20(2) of the Convention on the Prohibition of the Use, Stockpiling, Production and Transfer of Anti-Personnel Mines and on Their Destruction (adopted 18 September 1997, entered into force 1 March 1999) 2056 UNTS 211.

that the competence of the Security Council to deal with matters relating to IHL is undisputed.[18] The Security Council itself recognised 'its primary responsibility for the maintenance of international peace and security and, in this context, the need to promote and ensure respect for the principles and rules of international humanitarian law'.[19]

However, the whole range of practical and legal consequences of such Security Council actions have only become prominent recently with the rapid accumulation of practice. While the details of Security Council practice on IHL will be discussed more throughout this section, the *ad hoc* international and hybrid criminal tribunals established under Chapter VII to try violations of IHL will not be discussed as they go well beyond the scope of this book.[20]

It is worth mentioning that, in reading Security Council resolutions invoking IHL, two points are worth keeping in mind: *ad hoc* nature of Security Council practice on IHL and Security Council resolutions as one of many sources invoking IHL.

As noted earlier, the primary work of the Security Council is to make political decisions to maintain international peace and security.[21] It is not an organ that applies international law, including IHL, purely as a matter of law like the International Court of Justice (ICJ). Nor is the Security Council entrusted to enforce IHL as its primary work. Hence, its application of IHL cannot be expected to be precise and comprehensive. Clearly, the Security Council should act within the limits of the UN Charter but because of its primary function to maintain international peace and security, its application of IHL is not systematic.

For example, on the relationship between 'threat to the peace', 'breach of the peace', and 'act of aggression' on one hand, and 'armed conflict' on the other, the International Criminal Tribunal for the former Yugoslavia (ICTY) noted that the notion of 'threat to the peace' is 'more of a political concept'[22] and thus, when the Security Council invokes IHL in the context

[18] H-P Gasser, 'The United Nations and International Humanitarian Law: The International Committee of the Red Cross and the United Nations' Involvement in the Implementation of International Humanitarian Law' in Condorelli et al (eds), *Nations Unies et le droit international humanitaire*, 259.

[19] UNSC Res 1502 (26 August 2003) UN Doc S/RES/1052, Preamble.

[20] See generally A Cassese, *International Criminal Law*, 2nd edn (Oxford, Oxford University Press, 2008) 324 *ff*.

[21] See *Military and Paramilitary Activities in and against Nicaragua* (*Nicaragua v US*) (Jurisdiction) [1984] ICJ Rep 392, para 95.

[22] *Tadic Case* (Jurisdiction, Appeals), para 29. For the interpretation of UN resolutions, see *Namibia* case (Advisory Opinion), para 114; *Tadic Case* (Jurisdiction, Appeals), para 30; M Wood, 'The Interpretation of Security Council Resolutions' (1998) 2 *Max Planck Yearbook of United Nations Law* 73; UN Secretariat, 'Note to the Under-Secretary-General of the Department of Peacekeeping Operations, United Nations' (2003) *United Nations Juridical Yearbook* 538, 539; E Papastavridis, 'Interpretation of Security Council Resolutions under Chapter VII in the Aftermath of the Iraqi Crisis' (2007) 56 *International and Comparative Law Quarterly* 83.

of threat to the peace, it can be less rigorous than what is required by IHL. On the beginning of the application of IHL, Security Council resolutions often do not specify whether the law of international or non-international armed conflict is applicable. On the end of the application of IHL, the Security Council has only indicated it in the Gulf Wars in 1991 and 2003 but not to other armed conflicts around the world. Finally on the equal application of IHL, the Security Council can demand compliance with IHL against one party to the conflict and not against the other. Such *ad hoc* nature and ambiguity of Security Council resolutions relating to IHL calls for a cautious approach, in particular, not to read too much between the lines.

In addition, Security Council resolutions should be seen as one of many entities invoking IHL. Certainly, Chapter VII decisions are legally binding under Article 25 of the UN Charter and thus, the UN Member States are obliged to follow the Security Council's determination on the applicability of IHL. However, in practice, other sources which invoke IHL carry certain weight and should also be taken into account. State practice is clearly an important source since sates are the primary actors required to apply IHL.[23] The practice of the International Committee of the Red Cross (ICRC) is also an important source since the ICRC is entrusted to ensure the proper application of IHL.[24] Others include the practice of international and 'hybrid' courts and tribunals, international and regional organisations, international conferences, and experts in IHL. Thus, there are many sources which need to be taken into account when the interpretation of IHL is at issue, and the Security Council is only one of them.

[23] A clear indication is common Art 1 of the 1949 Geneva Conventions, which provides as follows: 'The High Contracting Parties undertake to respect and to ensure respect for the present Convention in all circumstances.' Geneva Convention for the Amelioration of the Condition of the Wounded and Sick in Armed Forces in the Field, as revised from 1929 (hereafter 1949 First Geneva Convention) (adopted 12 August 1949, entered into force 21 October 1950) 75 UNTS 31; Geneva Convention for the Amelioration of the Condition of Wounded, Sick and Shipwrecked Members of Armed Forces at Sea, as revised from 1929 (hereafter 1949 Second Geneva Convention) (adopted 12 August 1949, entered into force 21 October 1950) 75 UNTS 85; Geneva Convention Relative to the Treatment of Prisoners of War, as revised from 1929 (hereafter 1949 Third Geneva Convention) (adopted 12 August 1949, entered into force 21 October 1950) 75 UNTS 135; Geneva Convention Relative to the Protection of Civilian Persons in Time of War (hereafter 1949 Fourth Geneva Convention) (adopted 12 August 1949, entered into force 21 October 1950) 75 UNTS 287.

[24] Art 5(2)(c) of the Statutes of the International Red Cross and Red Crescent Movement reads, in part, as follows: 'The role of the International Committee [of the Red Cross], in accordance with its Statutes, is in particular . . . to work for the faithful application of international humanitarian law applicable in armed conflicts.' See ICRC and the International Federation of Red Cross and Red Crescent Societies, *Handbook of the International Red Cross and Red Crescent* (Geneva, International Committee of the Red Cross and International Federation of Red Cross and Red Crescent Societies, 2009). The Statutes were adopted by the International Conference of the Red Cross in 1986 which consists of states parties to the 1949 Geneva Conventions, National Red Cross and Red Crescent Societies, International Federation of Red Cross and Red Crescent Societies, and ICRC.

B. Can Chapter VII Decisions Prevail over IHL Pursuant to Article 103 of the UN Charter?[25]

While it is now clear that the Security Council can deal with IHL issues, resolutions that are adopted under Chapter VII pose particular problems, especially in relation to the principle of the separation between *jus ad bellum* and *jus in bello*. The core issue is whether Article 103 of the UN Charter permits Chapter VII decisions to prevail over IHL. This section

[25] See generally *Military and Paramilitary Activities in and against Nicaragua* (hereafter *Nicaragua* case) (*Nicaragua v US*) (Merits) [1986] ICJ Rep 14, para 107; *Questions of Interpretation and Application of the 1971 Montreal Convention Arising from the Aerial Incident at Lockerbie* (*Libyan Arab Jamahiriya v United Kingdom*) (hereafter *Lockerbie* case) (Order of 14 April 1992) [1992] ICJ Rep 3, para 39 and the Separate Opinion of Judge Shahabuddeen and Dissenting Opinion of Judge Weeramantry; *Bosnia Genocide* case (Order of 13 September 1993), Separate Opinion of Judge Lauterpacht, paras 102–04.

See further R Lauwaars, 'The Interrelationship between United Nations Law and the Law of Other International Organizations' (1983–84) 82 *Michigan Law Review* 1604; L Condorelli, 'Le Droit Humanitaire dans la Crise et la "Guerre" du Golfe' in B Stern (ed), *Les aspects juridiques de la crise et de la guerre du Golfe: Aspects de droit international public et de droit international privé* (Paris, Montchresties, 1991) 195–96; C Dominicé, 'L'article 103 de la Charte des Nations Unies et le droit international humanitaire' in Condorelli et al (eds), *Nations Unies et le droit international humanitaire*; D Bowett, 'Judicial and Political Functions of the Security Council and the International Court of Justice' in H Fox (ed), *The Changing Constitution of the United Nations* (London, British Institute of International and Comparative Law, 1997) 81–82; R Bernhardt, 'Article 103' in B Simma et al (eds), *The Charter of the United Nations: A Commentary*, 2nd edn, Vol II (Munich, CH Beck, 2002); R Lee, 'The *Jus ad Bellum* in Outer Space: The Interrelation between Article 103 of the Charter of the United Nations and Article IV of the Outer Space Treaty' (2002) *Proceedings of the Forty-Fifth Colloquium on the Law of Outer Space (Houston 10–19 October 2002)* 139; R Kolb, 'Does Article 103 of the Charter of the United Nations Apply Only to Decisions or Also to Authorizations Adopted by the Security Council?' (2004) 64 *Zeitschrift für Ausländisches Öffentliches Recht und Völkerrecht* (*Heidelberg Journal of International Law*) 21; E Lagrange, 'Le Conseil de Sécurité des Nations Unies peut-il violer le droit international?' (2004) 37 *Revue belge de droit international* 568; A Toublanc, 'L'article 103 et la valeur juridique de la Charte des Nations Unies' (2004) 108 *Revue générale de droit international public* 439; J-M Thouvenin, 'Article 103' in J-P Cot et al, *La Charte des Nations Unies: Commentaire article par article* (Paris, Economica, 2005); UN Secretariat, 'The Effect of Armed Conflict on Treaties: An Examination of Practice and Doctrine (Memorandum by the Secretariat)' (1 February 2005) UN Doc A/CN.4/550, para 144; M Zwanenburg, *Accountability of Peace Support Operations* (Leiden, Martinus Nijhoff, 2005) 139 *ff*; ILC, 'Fragmentation of International Law: Difficulties Arising from the Diversification and Expansion of International Law, Report of the Study Group of the International Law Commission' (13 April 2006) UN Doc A/CN.4/L.682, 168 *ff*; M Wood, 'The UN Security Council and International Law, First Lecture: The Legal Framework of the Security Council' (7 November 2006) Sir Hersch Lauterpacht Memorial Lectures, Lauterpacht Research Centre for International Law website, www.lcil.cam.ac.uk; A Orakhelashvili, 'The Acts of the Security Council: Meaning and Standards of Review' (2007) 11 *Max Planck Yearbook of United Nations Law* 143, 149 *ff*; LMH Martínez, 'The Legislative Role of the Security Council in Its Fight Against Terrorism: Legal, Political and Practical Limits' (2008) 57 *International and Comparative Law Quarterly* 333, 344 *ff*; R Liivoja, 'The Scope of the Supremacy Clause of the United Nations Charter' (2008) 57 *International and Comparative Law Quarterly* 583.

This question also implies the conflict between the Security Council and the ICRC at the operational level. See M Bothe, 'The United Nations Actions for the Respect of International Humanitarian Law and the Coordination of Related International Operations' in Condorelli et al (eds), *Nations Unies et le droit international humanitaire*, 228.

sets out the role of Article 103 in the relationship between Chapter VII and IHL and possible ways of resolving conflicts between the two.

Article 103 of the UN Charter states as follows:

> In the event of a conflict between the obligations of the Members of the United Nations under the present Charter and their obligations under any other international agreement, their obligations under the present Charter shall prevail.

While there are many controversial questions inherent in this provision,[26] it suffices to note that Security Council decisions, particularly those adopted under Chapter VII, are widely considered as UN Charter obligations which prevail over other international obligations.[27]

Security Council decisions become binding on all the UN Member States by virtue of Article 25 of the UN Charter, which provides as follows:

> The Members of the United Nations agree to accept and carry out the decisions of the Security Council.

The specific decisions are spelled out in the resolutions adopted by the Security Council. It is worth highlighting that the UN Charter makes a distinction between 'recommendations' and 'decisions'. Whether Security Council 'recommendations' qualify as UN Charter obligations within the meaning of Article 103 is not clear.[28] However, Security Council

[26] For a summary of the issues and arguments, see Kolb, 'Does Article 103'.

[27] *Namibia* case (Advisory Opinion), para 116; *Lockerbie* case (Order of 14 April 1992), para 39 and the Separate Opinion of Judge Shahabuddeen and Dissenting Opinion of Judge Weeramantry; *The Queen (on the application of Hilal Abdul-Razzaq Ali Al-Jedda) v Secretary of State for Defence* [2006] EWCA Civ 327; Art 8 of the San Remo Manual on International Law Applicable to Armed conflicts at Sea in L Doswald-Beck (ed), *San Remo Manual on International Law Applicable to Armed Conflicts at Sea* (Cambridge, Cambridge University Press, 1995) 8 and 79–80 for a commentary.

See also Lauwaars, 'The Interrelationship', 1606; G Fitzmaurice, *The Law and Procedure of the International Court of Justice* Vol 2 (Cambridge, Grotius Publications, 1986) 431; UN Secretariat, 'Article 103' in UN Secretariat, *Repertory of Practice of United Nations Organs* Supp No 8 (1989–94) Vol 6, 2, www.un.org/law/repertory; K Zemanek, 'The Legal Foundations of the International System' (1997) 266 *Recueil des Cours de l'Académie de Droit International* 9, 229–30; Bernhardt, 'Article 103', 1296; Toublanc, 'L'article 103', 445–46; Thouvenin, 'Article 103', 2135 and 2142; ILC, 'Fragmentation of International Law', 168–69; UN Secretariat, 'The Effect of Armed Conflict on Treaties', para 145; Wood, 'The UN Security Council and International Law', 19.

[28] Art 39 of the UN Charter envisages both 'recommendations' and 'decisions': 'The Security Council . . . shall make recommendations, or decide what measures shall be taken in accordance with Articles 41 and 42, to maintain or restore international peace and security.' See J Frowein and N Krisch, 'Article 39' in Simma et al (eds), *The Charter of the United Nations*, 727 *ff*; Kolb, 'Does Article 103', 23.

However, some are unequivocal that only binding decisions of the UN, such as decisions of the Security Council, qualify as obligations under the UN Charter within the meaning of Art 103. See, eg, J Combacau, *Le pouvoir de sanction de l'ONU: Étude théorique de la coercion non militaire* (Paris, Éditions Pedone, 1974) 284; Lauwaars, 'The Interrelationship', 1607; UN Secretariat, 'Memorandum to the Special Adviser to the Secretary-General' (1994) *United Nations Juridical Yearbook* 502; Bernhardt, 'Article 103', 1296; Toublanc, 'L'article 103', 448; ILC, 'Fragmentation of International Law', 169.

On the interpretation of Security Council resolution, see generally n 22 above.

'decisions' are clearly considered as UN Charter obligations within the meaning of Article 103, regardless of whether the concerned resolutions were adopted under Chapter VII or not. Hence, the Security Council decisions clearly prevail over other international obligations when the two are in conflict.[29]

The term 'international agreement' in Article 103 is widely seen as indicating treaties and thus excludes other sources of international law, particularly *jus cogens*.[30] There is no consensus on whether customary international law is excluded but when similar or identical customary rules can be found in treaty provisions, it would seem absurd to say that the treaty provisions are subject to Article 103 while the similar or identical customary rules are not.[31] It follows that Security Council 'decisions', particularly those taken under Chapter VII, are obligations which clearly prevail over, at least, other treaty obligations and possibly obligations under customary international law, but do not prevail over *jus cogens*.[32]

However, Article 103 is unclear on at least three aspects: 1) the authority to decide when the UN Charter prevails over other international agreements; 2) when a 'conflict' exists between the two obligations; and 3) the legal consequences in the event of a 'conflict'.

First, Article 103 does not specify who decides that the UN Charter obligations prevail over other international agreements. The Security Council

[29] *Namibia* case (Advisory Opinion), para 113. See also Lauwaars, 'The Interrelationship', 1606; Fitzmaurice, *The Law and Procedure*, 430–31; Bernhardt, 'Article 103'; Toublanc, 'L'article 103', 445–46; ILC, 'Fragmentation of International Law', 168–69; Wood, 'The Interpretation', 19.

[30] See *Bosnia Genocide* case (Order of 13 September 1993), Separate Opinion of Judge Lauterpacht, para 100; *Ahmed Ali Yusuf and Al Barakaat International Foundation v Council of the European Union and Commission of the European Communities* [2005] ECR II–3533, para 281.

See also H Kelsen, *The Law of the United Nations: A Critical Analysis of Its Fundamental Problems* (London, Stevens and Sons, 1950) 111; C Cadoux, 'La supériorité du droit des Nations Unies sur le droit des États membres' (1959) 63 *Revue générale de droit international public* 649, 658-59; H-P Gasser, 'Collective Economic Sanctions and International Humanitarian Law' (1996) 56 *Zeitschrift für Ausländisches Öffentliches Recht und Völkerrecht (Heidelberg Journal of International Law)* 871; A Segall, 'Economic Sanctions: Legal and Policy Analysis' (1999) 836 *International Review of the Red Cross* 763; L Condorelli, 'La compatibilité des sanctions du Conseil de Sécurité avec le droit international humanitaire – Commentaire' in V Gowlland-Debbas (ed), *United Nations Sanctions and International Law* (The Hague, Kluwer Law International, 2001); D Momtaz, 'La compatibilité des sanctions du Conseil de Sécurité avec le droit international humanitaire' in Gowlland-Debbas (ed), *United Nations Sanctions;* M Sassòli, 'Sanctions and International Humanitarian Law – Commentary' in Gowlland-Debbas (ed), *United Nations Sanctions;* Kolb, *Ius contra bellum*, 149; Toublanc, 'L'article 103', 446–50; Wood, 'The Interpretation', 20. On the limitations on the Security Council powers in general, see n 7 above.

[31] On whether customary international law is subject to Art 103 of the UN Charter, see P-M Dupuy, 'The Constitutional Dimension of the Charter of the United Nations Revisited' (1997) 1 *Max Planck Yearbook of United Nations Law* 1, 13–14; Zemanek, 'The Legal Foundations', 232; Bernhardt, 'Article 103', 1298–99; ILC, 'Fragmentation of International Law', 176; N White and A Abass, 'Countermeasures and Sanctions' in M Evans (ed), *International Law*, 2nd edn (Oxford, Oxford University Press, 2006); Wood, 'The Interpretation', 19.

[32] On Chapter VII decisions and *jus cogens*, see section 4.II.A.

has adopted Chapter VII resolutions which explicitly implement Article 103,[33] but in many other cases, the question was left open on whether Chapter VII decisions prevail over other international agreements. Thus, the structural problem with Article 103 is that there is no authority to decide when the UN Charter obligations prevail over other international agreements and hence, the effects of Chapter VII decisions on other international agreements, including IHL, could often remain inconclusive.

Secondly, a 'conflict' between the UN Charter obligations and other international agreements is the trigger to invoke Article 103 but when exactly a 'conflict' exists remains an open question. Contrary to the general impression, Article 103 does not permit the UN Charter obligations to always prevail over other international agreements; they only prevail when there is a 'conflict' between the two. Thus, Article 103 does not come into play when there is no 'conflict' in the first place. However, since there is no definition of when a 'conflict' exists, establishing its existence is problematic. On one hand, there may be clear-cut cases such as a treaty permitting the exercise of the right of self-defence without an armed attack which would clearly be in 'conflict' with Article 51 of the UN Charter and where the latter prevails. Such was the case when the USSR invaded Czechoslovakia in 1968.[34] In this case, the USSR relied on Article 5 of the 1955 Warsaw Treaty, which reads as follows:

> The Parties shall likewise take such other concerted action as may be necessary to reinforce their defensive strength, in order to defend the peaceful labour of their peoples, guarantee the inviolability of their frontiers and territories and afford protection against possible aggression.[35]

It appears to enable self-defence beyond what is permitted in Article 51 of the UN Charter, which limits the situation to 'if an armed attack occurs'.

[33] See, eg, UNSC Res 660 (2 August 1990) UN Doc S/RES/660, Preamble; UNSC Res 670 (25 September 1990) UN Doc S/RES/670, para 3; UNSC Res 713 (25 September 1991) UN Doc S/RES/713, para 6; UNSC Res 724 (15 December 1991) UN Doc S/RES/724, para 5 (a); UNSC Res 727 (8 January 1992) UN Doc S/RES/727, para 6; UNSC Res 748 (31 March 1992) UN Doc S/RES/748, para 7; UNSC Res 757 (30 May 1992) UN Doc S/RES/757, para 11; UNSC Res 820 (17 April 1993) UN Doc S/RES/820, para 17; UNSC Res 841 (16 June 1993) UN Doc S/RES/841, para 9; UNSC Res 864 (15 September 1993) UN Doc S/RES/864, para 20; UNSC Res 883 (11 November 1993) UN Doc S/RES/883, para 2; UNSC Res 917 (6 May 1993) UN Doc S/RES/917, para 12; UNSC Res 918 (17 May 1994) UN Doc S/RES/918, para 15; UNSC Res 1127 (28 August 1997) UN Doc S/RES/1127, para 10; UNSC Res 1169 (27 May 1998) UN Doc S/RES/1169, para 10; UNSC Res 1173 (12 June 1998) UN Doc S/RES/1173, para 17; UNSC Res 1267 (15 October 1999) UN Doc S/RES/1267, para 7; UNSC Res 1298 (17 May 2000) UN Doc S/RES/1298, para 9. See also UN Secretariat, 'Article 103' in UN Secretariat, *Repertory of Practice of United Nations Organs* (1945–94), www.un.org/law/repertory.

[34] See the accounts in UN Secretariat, 'Article 103' in UN Secretariat, *Repertory of Practice of United Nations Organs*, Supp No 4 (1966–69) Vol 2, 366–67, paras 7–13, www.un.org/law/repertory.

[35] Treaty of Friendship, Co-operation and Mutual Assistance (adopted 14 May 1955, entered into force 6 June 1955) 219 UNTS 3. Authentic texts are in Russian, Polish, Czech, and German. English and French translations in 219 UNTS 24 *ff* and 25 *ff* respectively.

In this specific case, Article 103 would have enabled Article 51 of the UN Charter to prevail over Article 5 of the 1955 Warsaw Treaty.[36]

Similarly, it is also clear that the Security Council cannot adopt resolutions that would violate the Purposes and Principles of the UN in Articles 1 and 2 of the UN Charter. This is an obligation of the Security Council required in Article 24(2) of the UN Charter.[37] Particularly relevant for the purpose of this book is Article 1(3), which provides one of the Purposes of the UN:

> To achieve international co-operation in solving international problems of an economic, social, cultural, or humanitarian character, and in promoting and encouraging respect for human rights and for fundamental freedoms for all.[38]

Thus, for example, a Chapter VII resolution denying prisoners of war status to certain combatants, even though they are entitled to such status, would clearly fall short of meeting the obligation in Article 1(3) and thus, Chapter VII decisions cannot prevail over the 1949 Third Geneva Convention on the treatment of prisoners of war, despite the supremacy of Chapter VII decisions under Article 103. There are, however, many other cases where it is not clear whether there is a 'conflict'. It suffices to note at this point that the existence of a 'conflict' between the UN Charter and other international agreements is decisive to invoke Article 103 but since there is no definition of the term 'conflict', it is left to a case-by-case assessment. If the Security Council is assessing the existence of a 'conflict', it must take into account Article 1(3) of the UN Charter and exclude rules of a humanitarian character from being subjected to Security Council decisions. This may mean that most of the rules of IHL, whether as treaty law or customary international law, are excluded from being subjected to Security Council decisions due to their essentially humanitarian character. Rules of IHL that are considered as *jus cogens* are in any case excluded, since Security Council decisions do not prevail over *jus cogens* under Article 103 of the UN Charter.

Thirdly, Article 103 does not specify about the legal consequences of a 'conflict' between the UN Charter and other international agreements, and it only provides that 'their [UN Member States'] obligations under the present Charter shall prevail'.[39] This is in contrast with the 1969 Vienna Convention on the Law of Treaties, which provides detailed rules on the

[36] Bernhardt, 'Article 103', 1297. See also B Conforti, 'Cours général de droit international public' (1988) 212 *Recueil des Cours de l'Académie de Droit International* 9, 133.

[37] See n 8 above.

[38] The importance of the obligation imposed by Art 1(3) of the UN Charter pursuant to Art 24(2) was underlined by Lauterpacht. See *Bosnia Genocide* case (Order of 13 September 1993), Separate Opinion of Judge Lauterpacht, paras 102–04.

See also Gasser, 'Collective Economic Sanctions', 881 *ff*; Gasser, 'The United Nations and International Humanitarian Law', 259; Gill, 'Legal and Some Political Limitations', 79 *ff*.

[39] Bernhardt, 'Article 103', 1295.

legal consequences when a treaty is in conflict with *jus cogens*.[40] In the case of Article 103, an indication can be found in the resolution of the Institute of International Law on the effects of armed conflicts on treaties:

> A State complying with a resolution by the Security Council of the United Nations concerning action with respect to threats to the peace, breaches of the peace or acts of aggression shall either terminate or suspend the operation of a treaty which would be incompatible with such resolution.[41]

However, since Article 103 does not specify any legal consequences, they can be anything ranging from a termination or suspension of the concerned treaty obligation, to a mere recognition that the UN Charter obligations have priority over other international obligations without necessarily affecting the continuing applicability of those international obligations. Nevertheless, at least two rules on the legal consequences of a 'conflict' can be found in Article 103 itself.

First, the phrase 'obligations under any other international agreement' seems to indicate that the 'conflict' between the UN Charter and another international agreement occurs between specific provisions therein. Thus, for example, if some of the provisions in a treaty are in 'conflict' with a provision in the UN Charter but other provisions are not, only the former are subject to Article 103 and the latter continue to apply. Thus, it is not possible to do away with the whole treaty simply because one of the provisions is in 'conflict' with the UN Charter obligations.[42] If other provisions are not in 'conflict' with the UN Charter obligations, they continue to apply. Secondly, from the phrase 'In the event of a conflict', it seems that a 'conflict' between UN Charter and other international agreements continues only so long as the 'conflict' exists. Thus, for example, when a Chapter VII decision in a resolution expires, the 'conflict' also terminates at the same time.[43] In this sense, it is different from reservations to treaties, or termination and suspension of the operation of treaties within the meaning of the law of treaties since these effects can last indefinitely if states choose to do so, whereas the validity of Chapter VII decisions normally has time limits.

Beyond this point, the legal consequences of a 'conflict' between the two obligations are unclear but the ambiguity can potentially provide room for a practical interpretation to resolve the 'conflict' between Chapter VII decisions and IHL. In particular, even if there is a 'conflict' between Chapter VII decisions and other international agreements, they can still be applied side by side without necessarily terminating or suspending the latter. Chapter VII decisions are simply given the priority and not neces-

[40] See Art 71 of the Vienna Convention on the Law of Treaties (adopted 23 May 1969, entered into force 27 January 1980) 1155 UNTS 331.

[41] Institute of International Law, 'Resolution on the Effects of Armed Conflicts on Treaties' (1986) 61–II *Annuaire de l'Institut de Droit International* 278, 280.

[42] Bernhardt, 'Article 103', 1297.

[43] Bernhardt, 'Article 103', 1297–98.

sarily the superiority. The reconciliation between the two is then left to practical interpretation which would bring the Chapter VII decisions in line with the concerned international agreements.[44] Such an approach was envisaged by the Special Rapporteur of the UN International Law Commission on the law of treaties:

> The rationale of Article 103 clearly is that priority is to be given to the Charter, not that invalidity is to attach to a treaty which conflicts with it. The conflicting treaty may be unenforceable, if to enforce it involves a violation of the Charter; but it is not void.[45]

Such practical application of Article 103 may be possible because it does not specify the legal consequences of a 'conflict' and thus leaves the resolution of the 'conflict' to practical interpretation. This approach will be discussed throughout this chapter.[46]

Applying the former analyses specifically to Security Council decisions and IHL, as a matter of law, Security Council decisions can prevail over IHL treaties when there is a 'conflict' between the two. However, considering that the Security Council must take into account the Purposes of the UN pursuant to Article 24(2) of the UN Charter, the rules of IHL, which are essentially humanitarian in character, should not be subjected to Security Council decisions. Hence, the conflict of obligations should be avoided through practical measures such as bringing Chapter VII decisions in line with treaties and customary rules of IHL at the drafting stage of the resolutions. In the event of a conflict between the two, it can be reconciled by interpreting Chapter VII decisions in a way which would be in harmony with IHL treaties and customary rules of IHL. Such practical interpretation is possible because Article 103 of the UN Charter leaves the legal consequences of a 'conflict' of obligations unspecified. Such practical measure or interpretation is crucial because of the paramount importance of the separation between *jus ad bellum* and *jus in bello*.

C. Distinction and Relationship between 'Threat to the Peace'/'Breach of the Peace'/'Act of Aggression' and 'Armed Conflict'

As can be seen, Chapter VII decisions can override IHL in limited circumstances when they are in conflict. However, the conflict occurs only when both Chapter VII and IHL are applicable. Since the conditions of application

[44] Toublanc, 'L'article 103', 454.

[45] ILC, 'Second Report on the Law of Treaties, by Sir Humphrey Waldock, Special Rapporteur' (20 March, 10 April, 30 April, and 5 June 1963) UN Doc A/CN.4/156 and Add.1–3 in (1963 Vol II) *Yearbook of International Law Commission* 36, 55, para 10.

See also Lauwaars, 'The Interrelationship', 1605; ILC, 'Fragmentation of International Law', 170.

[46] See sections 4.IV and V.

of Chapter VII are different from self-defence, the situations where Chapter VII and IHL are both applicable are also different. As mentioned earlier, in self-defence, 'armed attack' triggers the right of self-defence and the existence of an 'armed conflict' triggers the application of IHL. When both exist at the same time, the law of self-defence and IHL apply at the same time.

On the other hand, 'threat to the peace', 'breach of the peace', or 'act of aggression' trigger enforcement measures under Chapter VII pursuant to Article 39 of the UN Charter. The trigger to apply IHL, however, remains the same, which is the existence of an 'armed conflict'. In the case of self-defence, it involves an inter-state relation (an armed attack by a state and self-defence by the attacked state) most of the time and hence, international armed conflict (armed conflict between states) was the most relevant threshold. However, in the case of Chapter VII, it also covers armed conflicts within a state (non-international armed conflict). In IHL, the threshold to bring IHL into operation is different between international and non-international armed conflict. Hence, this section will also discuss the threshold of non-international armed conflict and its relation to Article 39. This would clarify when Chapter VII decisions and IHL apply at the same time.[47]

It is worth noting at the outset that the purpose of meeting these thresholds is distinctly different between Article 39 of the UN Charter and IHL. Article 39 determination is the first step to implement the primary responsibility of the Security Council to 'do away with the conflict itself'[48] and not necessarily to deal with the specific conduct during an armed conflict. This is one of the reasons why Security Council practice on IHL is *ad hoc* in nature. IHL is invoked only if IHL matters need to be addressed in the course of halting or doing away with the armed conflict per se.

On the other hand, IHL focuses exclusively at regulating the conduct during armed conflict and does not touch upon a wider aim to remove the armed conflict itself. Moreover, the application of IHL does not depend on a decision of any entity. Once the facts show that there is an armed conflict, that is enough to apply IHL. This is based on the past lessons where the applicability of IHL was denied due to the absence of a declaration of war by the conflicting parties. On the other hand, enforcement measures to maintain international peace and security can only be taken when the Security Council decides that either a threat to the peace, breach of the peace, or act of aggression exists.

Neither 'threat to the peace', 'breach of the peace' and 'act of aggression' nor 'armed conflict' have a universally accepted definition but it

[47] Security Council resolutions invoking IHL but not adopted under the terms of Art 39 or Chapter VII of the UN Charter are excluded from this section. In fact, the majority of Security Council resolutions invoking IHL are not adopted under the terms of Art 39 or Chapter VII. See Annex 1.

[48] Gasser, 'The United Nations and International Humanitarian Law', 273.

is clear that 'armed conflict' is narrower. First, on 'threat to the peace', 'breach of the peace' and 'act of aggression', at best, 'act of aggression' is defined in the 1974 Definition of Aggression[49] and Article 8 *bis* (2) of the Amendments to the 1998 Statute of the International Criminal Court (ICC Statute),[50] but even this definition is not conclusive or universally accepted.[51] The scope of the thresholds of 'breach of the peace' and 'threat to the peace' has developed entirely through Security Council practice. The ICTY in the *Tadic* case even went so far as to state that threat to the peace is 'more of a political concept'.[52] Its wide scope can be evidenced from the Security Council resolutions which determined racial discrimination[53] and violations of democratic principles[54] as 'threats to the peace'.

On the other hand, the threshold of 'armed conflict' in IHL is flexible enough but defined more in detail than Article 39 thresholds. In the case of international armed conflict, common Article 2 of the 1949 Geneva Conventions requires that it should be between two or more of the states parties, which includes cases of partial or total occupation of the territory of a state party. Likewise, in the case of non-international armed conflict, common Article 3 of the 1949 Geneva Conventions requires that the armed conflict should take place in the territory of one of the states parties and Article 1(1) of the 1977 Second Additional Protocol further requires that the armed conflict should take place between a state's armed forces and dissident armed forces or other organised armed groups, which should be: 1) under responsible command; and 2) exercise control over a part of the state's territory as to enable them to carry out sustained and concerted military operation and to implement the Second Additional Protocol. Thus, it is clear that the thresholds of 'threat to the peace, breach of the peace, or act of aggression' cover wider situations than the concept of 'armed conflict'.

Nevertheless, practice shows that whenever the Security Council determined a situation as a breach of the peace or an act of aggression, the situation was always international armed conflict within the meaning of IHL.

[49] UNGA, 'Definition of Aggression' UNGA Res 3314 (XXIX) (14 December 1974). Note that, after listing the possible acts amounting to aggression in Art 3, Art 4 provides as follows: 'The acts enumerated above are not exhaustive and the Security Council may determine that other acts constitute aggression under the provisions of the Charter.' Thus, the threshold of 'act of aggression' can be wider than that defined in the General Assembly resolution.

[50] 'Amendments to the Rome Statute of the International Criminal Court on the Crime of Aggression' Review Conference of the Rome Statute of the International Criminal Court (Kampala 31 May–11 June 2010) (11 June 2010) RC/Res.6, Annex I. See also Rome Statute of the International Criminal Court (adopted 17 July 1998, entered into force 1 July 2002) 2187 UNTS 3.

[51] See generally B Broms, 'The Definition of Aggression' (1977) 154 *Recueil des Cours de l'Académie de Droit International* 297.

[52] *Tadic Case* (Jurisdiction, Appeals), para 29.

[53] See, eg, UNSC Res 232 (16 December 1966) UN Doc S/RES/232 on Southern Rhodesia.

[54] See, eg, UNSC Res 841 (16 June 1993) UN Doc S/RES/841, UNSC Res 917 (6 May 1994) UN Doc S/RES/917, and UNSC Res 940 (31 July 1994) UN Doc S/RES/940 on Haiti.

However, 'threat to the peace' covered wider situations than 'breach of the peace' or 'act of aggression', namely international armed conflict, non-international armed conflict, and a mixture of the two. It even covered situations short of armed conflict.

With regard to the threshold of 'act of aggression', the 28 resolutions that determined the concerned situation as an 'act of aggression' were all in the context of international armed conflict in the sense of IHL.[55] The resolutions related to the attacks by South Africa on the neighbouring states[56] including Angola,[57] Botswana,[58] Lesotho,[59] Namibia,[60] and Seychelles;[61] attacks by Southern Rhodesia (now Zimbabwe) on

[55] UNSC Res 387 (31 March 1976) UN Doc S/RES/387, UNSC Res 405 (14 April 1977) UN Doc S/RES/405, UNSC Res 411 (30 June 1977) UN Doc S/RES/411, UNSC Res 418 (4 November 1977) UN Doc S/RES/418, UNSC Res 419 (24 November 1977) UN Doc S/RES/419, UNSC Res 423 (14 March 1978) UN Doc S/RES/423, UNSC Res 424 (17 March 1978) UN Doc S/RES/424, UNSC Res 428 (6 May 1978) UN Doc S/RES/428, UNSC Res 445 (8 March 1979) UN Doc S/RES/445, UNSC Res 447 (28 March 1979) UN Doc S/RES/447, UNSC Res 454 (2 November 1979) UN Doc S/RES/454, UNSC Res 466 (11 April 1980) UN Doc S/RES/466, UNSC Res 475 (27 June 1980) UN Doc S/RES/475, UNSC Res 496 (15 December 1981) UN Doc S/RES/496, UNSC Res 507 (28 May 1982) UN Doc S/RES/507, UNSC Res 527 (15 December 1982) UN Doc S/RES/527, UNSC Res 546 (6 January 1984) UN Doc S/RES/546, UNSC Res 554 (17 August 1984) UN Doc S/RES/554, UNSC Res 567 (20 June 1985) UN Doc S/RES/567, UNSC Res 568 (21 June 1985) UN Doc S/RES/568, UNSC Res 572 (30 September 1985) UN Doc S/RES/572, UNSC Res 573 (4 October 1985) UN Doc S/RES/573, UNSC Res 574 (7 October 1985) UN Doc S/RES/574, UNSC Res 577 (6 December 1985) UN Doc S/RES/577, UNSC Res 580 (30 December 1985) UN Doc S/RES/580, UNSC Res 581 (13 February 1986) UN Doc S/RES/581, UNSC Res 602 (25 November 1987) UN Doc S/RES/602, and UNSC Res 611 (25 April 1988) UN Doc S/RES/611.

[56] UNSC Res 387 (31 March 1976) UN Doc S/RES/387, UNSC Res 418 (4 November 1977) UN Doc S/RES/418, UNSC Res 428 (6 May 1978) UN Doc S/RES/428, UNSC Res 447 (28 March 1979) UN Doc S/RES/447, UNSC Res 454 (2 November 1979) UN Doc S/RES/454, UNSC Res 466 (11 April 1980) UN Doc S/RES/466, UNSC Res 475 (27 June 1980) UN Doc S/RES/475, UNSC Res 496 (15 December 1981) UN Doc S/RES/496, UNSC Res 507 (28 May 1982) UN Doc S/RES/507, UNSC Res 527 (15 December 1982) UN Doc S/RES/527, UNSC Res 546 (6 January 1984) UN Doc S/RES/546, UNSC Res 554 (17 August 1984) UN Doc S/RES/554, UNSC Res 567 (20 June 1985) UN Doc S/RES/567, UNSC Res 568 (21 June 1985) UN Doc S/RES/568, UNSC Res 572 (30 September 1985) UN Doc S/RES/572, UNSC Res 574 (7 October 1985) UN Doc S/RES/574, UNSC Res 577 (6 December 1985) UN Doc S/RES/577, UNSC Res 580 (30 December 1985) UN Doc S/RES/580, UNSC Res 581 (13 February 1986) UN Doc S/RES/581, and UNSC Res 602 (25 November 1987) UN Doc S/RES/602.

[57] UNSC Res 387 (31 March 1976) UN Doc S/RES/387, UNSC Res 428 (6 May 1978) UN Doc S/RES/428, UNSC Res 447 (28 March 1979) UN Doc S/RES/447, UNSC Res 454 (2 November 1979) UN Doc S/RES/454, UNSC Res 475 (27 June 1980) UN Doc S/RES/475, UNSC Res 546 (6 January 1984) UN Doc S/RES/546, UNSC Res 567 (20 June 1985) UN Doc S/RES/567, UNSC Res 574 (7 October 1985) UN Doc S/RES/574, UNSC Res 577 (6 December 1985) UN Doc S/RES/577, and UNSC Res 602 (25 November 1987) UN Doc S/RES/602.

[58] UNSC Res 568 (21 June 1985) UN Doc S/RES/568 and UNSC Res 572 (30 September 1985) UN Doc S/RES/572.

[59] UNSC Res 572 (30 September 1985) UN Doc S/RES/572 and UNSC Res 580 (30 December 1985) UN Doc S/RES/580.

[60] UNSC Res 447 (28 March 1979) UN Doc S/RES/447 and UNSC Res 454 (2 November 1979) UN Doc S/RES/454.

[61] UNSC Res 496 (15 December 1981) UN Doc S/RES/496 and UNSC Res 507 (28 May 1982) UN Doc S/RES/507.

the neighbouring states[62] including Botswana,[63] Mozambique,[64] and Zambia;[65] attacks by Israel on Tunisia;[66] and attacks on Benin.[67] The close link between act of aggression and international armed conflict is also a logical consequence since the acts of aggression enumerated in the 1974 Definition of Aggression and Article 8 *bis* (2) of the Amendments to the ICC Statute clearly amount to an international armed conflict.

With regard to 'breach of the peace', the six resolutions that determined the concerned situation as a 'breach of the peace' were all in the context of international armed conflict in the sense of IHL.[68] The resolutions related to the 1950–53 Korean War,[69] 1982 Falklands/Malvinas Conflict,[70] 1980–88 Iran-Iraq War,[71] and 1990–91 Gulf War.[72] The ICTY also noted in the *Tadic* case that 'If it [the armed conflict in the former Yugoslavia] is considered an international armed conflict, there is no doubt that it falls within the literal sense of the words "breach of the peace" '.[73] Hence, the past practice of the Security Council shows that whenever it determined a situation as either an 'act of aggression' or a 'breach of the peace', it was always an international armed conflict in the IHL sense.

When the Security Council determined a situation as a 'threat to the peace' in the past, it was either international or non-international armed conflict, or a mixture of these armed conflicts, or even situations short of armed conflict. On international armed conflict as a threat to the peace, there were at least six situations (13 resolutions in total) that amounted to a threat to the peace and where the applicability of IHL was recognised.[74] These

[62] UNSC Res 411 (30 June 1977) UN Doc S/RES/411, UNSC Res 423 (14 March 1978) UN Doc S/RES/423, UNSC Res 424 (17 March 1978) UN Doc S/RES/424, and UNSC Res 445 (8 March 1979) UN Doc S/RES/445.

[63] UNSC Res 411 (30 June 1977) UN Doc S/RES/411 and UNSC Res 424 (17 March 1978) UN Doc S/RES/424.

[64] UNSC Res 411 (30 June 1977) UN Doc S/RES/411 and UNSC Res 424 (17 March 1978) UN Doc S/RES/424.

[65] UNSC Res 411 (30 June 1977) UN Doc S/RES/411, UNSC Res 424 (17 March 1978) UN Doc S/RES/424, and UNSC Res 466 (11 April 1980) UN Doc S/RES/466.

[66] UNSC Res 573 (4 October 1985) UN Doc S/RES/573 and UNSC Res 611 (25 April 1988) UN Doc S/RES/611.

[67] UNSC Res 405 (14 April 1977) UN Doc S/RES/405 and UNSC Res 419 (24 November 1977) UN Doc S/RES/419. These resolutions on Benin might be exceptions since the source of the attack could not be identified until the end and thus it was not clear whether it was an international armed conflict or not. See UNGA, 'Complaint by Benin' (1977) UNYB 207, 207–15.

[68] UNSC Res 82 (25 June 1952) UN Doc S/RES/82, UNSC Res 83 (27 June 1950) UN Doc S/RES/83, UNSC Res 84 (7 July 1950) UN Doc S/RES/84, UNSC Res 502 (3 April 1982) UN Doc S/RES/502, UNSC Res 598 (20 July 1987) UN Doc S/RES/598, and UNSC Res 660 (2 August 1990) UN Doc S/RES/660. See also a commentary in Frowein and Krisch, 'Article 39', 721.

[69] UNSC Res 82 (25 June 1952) UN Doc S/RES/82, UNSC Res 83 (27 June 1950) UN Doc S/RES/83, and UNSC Res 84 (7 July 1950) UN Doc S/RES/84.

[70] UNSC Res 502 (3 April 1982) UN Doc S/RES/502.

[71] UNSC Res 598 (20 July 1987) UN Doc S/RES/598.

[72] UNSC Res 660 (2 August 1990) UN Doc S/RES/660.

[73] *Tadic Case* (Jurisdiction, Appeals), para 30.

[74] UNSC Res 271 (15 September 1969) UN Doc S/RES/271, UNSC Res 787 (16 December 1992) UN Doc S/RES/787, UNSC Res 815 (30 March 1993) UN Doc S/RES/815, UNSC Res

situations were those in the Middle East (Occupied Palestinian Territories),[75] Bosnia-Herzegovina,[76] Croatia,[77] Eritrea-Ethiopia,[78] DRC,[79] Iraq,[80] and the Great Lakes region.[81] With regard to non-international armed conflict as a threat to the peace, the ICTY noted as follows in the *Tadic* case on this point:

> [E]ven if it were considered merely as an 'internal armed conflict', it would still constitute a 'threat to the peace' according to the settled practice of the Security Council and the common understanding of the United Nations membership in general . . . there is a common understanding, manifested by the 'subsequent practice' of the membership of the United Nations at large, that the 'threat to the peace' of Article 39 may include, as one of its species, internal armed conflicts.[82]

As the ICTY notes, Security Council practice clearly supports that non-international armed conflict can be a threat to the peace. There were at least 15 cases (49 resolutions in total) that amounted to a threat to the peace and where the applicability of IHL was recognised.[83] These

819 (16 April 1993) UN Doc S/RES/819, UNSC Res 820 (17 April 1993) UN Doc S/RES/820, UNSC Res 836 (4 June 1993) UN Doc S/RES/836, UNSC Res 941 (23 September 1994) UN Doc S/RES/941, UNSC Res 1009 (10 August 1995) UN Doc S/RES/1009, UNSC Res 1031 (15 December 1995) UN Doc S/RES/1031, UNSC Res 1227 (10 February 1999) UN Doc S/RES/1227, UNSC Res 1234 (9 April 1999) UN Doc S/RES/1234, UNSC Res 1297 (12 may 2000) UN Doc S/RES/1297, UNSC Res 1329 (5 December 2000) UN Doc S/RES/1329, UNSC Res 1546 (8 June 2004) UN Doc S/RES/1546, and UNSC Res 1653 (27 January 2006) UN Doc S/RES/1653.

75 UNSC Res 271 (15 September 1969) UN Doc S/RES/271.

76 UNSC Res 787 (16 December 1992) UN Doc S/RES/787, UNSC Res 819 (16 April 1993) UN Doc S/RES/819, UNSC Res 820 (17 April 1993) UN Doc S/RES/820, UNSC Res 836 (4 June 1993) UN Doc S/RES/836, UNSC Res 941 (23 September 1994) UN Doc S/RES/941, UNSC Res 1031 (15 December 1995) UN Doc S/RES/1031, and UNSC Res 1329 (5 December 2000) UN Doc S/RES/1329.

77 UNSC Res 815 (30 March 1993) UN Doc S/RES/815, UNSC Res 1009 (10 August 1995) UN Doc S/RES/1009, and UNSC Res 1329 (5 December 2000) UN Doc S/RES/1329.

78 UNSC Res 1227 (10 February 1999) UN Doc S/RES/1227 and UNSC Res 1297 (12 May 2000) UN Doc S/RES/1297.

79 UNSC Res 1234 (9 April 1999) UN Doc S/RES/1234.

80 UNSC Res 1546 (8 June 2004) UN Doc S/RES/1546.

81 UNSC Res 1653 (27 January 2006) UN Doc S/RES/1653.

82 *Tadic Case* (Jurisdiction, Appeals), para 30.

83 UNSC Res 787 (16 December 1992) UN Doc S/RES/787, UNSC Res 788 (19 November 1992) UN Doc S/RES/788, UNSC Res 794 (3 December 1992) UN Doc S/RES/794, UNSC Res 813 (26 March 1993) UN Doc S/RES/813, UNSC Res 814 (26 March 1993) UN Doc S/RES/814, UNSC Res 815 (30 March 1993) UN Doc S/RES/815, UNSC Res 819 (16 April 1993) UN Doc S/RES/819, UNSC Res 820 (17 April 1993) UN Doc S/RES/820, UNSC Res 836 (4 June 1993) UN Doc S/RES/836, UNSC Res 876 (19 October 1993) UN Doc S/RES/876, UNSC Res 881 (4 November 1993) UN Doc S/RES/881, UNSC Res 918 (17 May 1994) UN Doc S/RES/918, UNSC Res 941 (23 September 1994) UN Doc S/RES/941, UNSC Res 1009 (10 August 1995) UN Doc S/RES/1009, UNSC Res 1031 (15 December 1995) UN Doc S/RES/1031, UNSC Res 1080 (15 November 1996) UN Doc S/RES/1080, UNSC Res 1234 (9 April 1999) UN Doc S/RES/1234, UNSC Res 1264 (15 September 1999) UN Doc S/RES/1264, UNSC Res 1267 (15 October 1999) UN Doc S/RES/1267, UNSC Res 1270 (22 October 1999) UN Doc S/RES/1270, UNSC Res 1272 (25 October 1999) UN Doc S/RES/1272, UNSC Res 1329 (5 December 2000) UN Doc S/RES/1329, UNSC Res 1333 (19 December 2000) UN Doc S/RES/1333, UNSC Res 1355 (15 June 2001) UN Doc S/RES/1355, UNSC Res 1464 (4 February 2003) UN Doc S/RES/1464, UNSC Res 1479 (13 May 2003) UN Doc S/RES/1479, UNSC Res 1483 (22 May 2003) UN Doc

cases were in Bosnia-Herzegovina,[84] Croatia,[85] Liberia,[86] Somalia,[87]

S/RES/1483, UNSC Res 1484 (30 May 2003) UN Doc S/RES/1484, UNSC Res 1493 (28 July 2003) UN Doc S/RES/1493, UNSC Res 1509 (19 September 2003) UN Doc S/RES/1509, UNSC Res 1528 (27 February 2004) UN Doc S/RES/1528, UNSC Res 1545 (21 May 2004) UN Doc S/RES/1545, UNSC Res 1556 (30 July 2004) UN Doc S/RES/1556, UNSC Res 1564 (18 September 2004) UN Doc S/RES/1564, UNSC Res 1565 (1 October 2004) UN Doc S/RES/1565, UNSC Res 1572 (15 November 2004) UN Doc S/RES/1572, UNSC Res 1574 (19 November 2004) UN Doc S/RES/1574, UNSC Res 1577 (1 December 2004) UN Doc S/RES/1577, UNSC Res 1590 (24 March 2005) UN Doc S/RES/1590, UNSC Res 1591 (29 March 2005) UN Doc S/RES/1591, UNSC Res 1592 (30 March 2005) UN Doc S/RES/1592, UNSC Res 1602 (31 May 2005) UN Doc S/RES/1602, UNSC Res 1621 (6 September 2005) UN Doc S/RES/1621, UNSC Res 1633 (21 October 2005) UN Doc S/RES/1633, UNSC Res 1635 (28 October 2005) UN Doc S/RES/1635, UNSC Res 1637 (11 November 2005) UN Doc S/RES/1637, UNSC Res 1643 (15 December 2005) UN Doc S/RES/1643, UNSC Res 1649 (21 December 2005) UN Doc S/RES/1649, UNSC Res 1653 (27 January 2006) UN Doc S/RES/1653, UNSC Res 1711 (29 September 2006) UN Doc S/RES/1711, UNSC Res 1721 (1 November 2006) UN Doc S/RES/1721, UNSC Res 1723 (28 November 2006) UN Doc S/RES/1723, UNSC Res 1727 (15 December 2006) UN Doc S/RES/1727, UNSC Res 1736 (22 December 2006) UN Doc S/RES/1736, UNSC Res 1746 (23 March 2007) UN Doc S/RES/1746, UNSC Res 1756 (15 May 2007) UN Doc S/RES/1756, UNSC Res 1762 (29 June 2007) UN Doc S/RES/1762, UNSC Res 1765 (16 July 2007) UN Doc S/RES/1765, UNSC Res 1769 (31 July 2007) UN Doc S/RES/1769, UNSC Res 1770 (10 August 2007) UN Doc S/RES/1770, UNSC Res 1772 (20 August 2007) UN Doc S/RES/1772, UNSC Res 1776 (19 September 2007) UN Doc S/RES/1776, UNSC Res 1778 (25 September 2007) UN Doc S/RES/1778, UNSC Res 1782 (29 October 2007) UN Doc S/RES/1782, UNSC Res 1790 (18 December 2007) UN Doc S/RES/1790, UNSC Res 1794 (21 December 2007) UN Doc S/RES/1794, UNSC Res 1795 (15 January 2008) UN Doc S/RES/1795, UNSC Res 1801 (20 February 2000) UN Doc S/RES/1801, UNSC Res 1807 (31 March 2008) UN Doc S/RES/1807, UNSC Res 1812 (30 April 2008) UN Doc S/RES/1812, UNSC Res 1814 (15 May 2008) UN Doc S/RES/1814, UNSC Res 1822 (30 June 2008) UN Doc S/RES/1822, UNSC Res 1826 (29 July 1998) UN Doc S/RES/1826, UNSC Res 1828 (31 July 2008) UN Doc S/RES/1828, UNSC Res 1833 (22 September 2008) UN Doc S/RES/1833, UNSC Res 1834 (24 September 2008) UN Doc S/RES/1834, UNSC Res 1842 (29 October 2008) UN Doc S/RES/1842, UNSC Res 1843 (20 November 2008) UN Doc S/RES/1843, UNSC Res 1851 (16 December 2008) UN Doc S/RES/1851, UNSC Res 1856 (22 December 2008) UN Doc S/RES/1856, UNSC Res 1857 (22 December 2008) UN Doc S/RES/1857, UNSC Res 1861 (14 January 2009) UN Doc S/RES/1861, UNSC Res 1863 (16 January 2009) UN Doc S/RES/1863, UNSC Res 1865 (27 January 2009) UN Doc S/RES/1865, UNSC Res 1870 (20 May 2009) UN Doc S/RES/1870, UNSC Res 1880 (30 July 2009) UN Doc S/RES/1880, UNSC Res 1881 (6 August 2009) UN Doc S/RES/1881, UNSC Res 1890 (8 October 2009) UN Doc S/RES/1890, UNSC Res 1893 (29 October 2009) UN Doc S/RES/1893, UNSC Res 1896 (7 December 2009) UN Doc S/RES/1896, UNSC Res 1904 (17 December 2009) UN Doc S/RES/1904, UNSC Res 1906 (23 December 2009) UN Doc S/RES/1906, UNSC Res 1910 (28 January 2010) UN Doc S/RES/1910, UNSC Res 1911 (28 January 2010) UN Doc S/RES/1911, UNSC Res 1919 (29 April 2010) UN Doc S/RES/1919, UNSC Res 1923 (25 May 2010) UN Doc S/RES/1923, and UNSC Res 1925 (28 May 2010) UN Doc S/RES/1925.

[84] UNSC Res 787 (16 December 1992) UN Doc S/RES/787, UNSC Res 819 (16 April 1993) UN Doc S/RES/819, UNSC Res 820 (17 April 1993) UN Doc S/RES/820, UNSC Res 836 (4 June 1993) UN Doc S/RES/836, UNSC Res 941 (23 September 1994) UN Doc S/RES/941, UNSC Res 1031 (15 December 1995) UN Doc S/RES/1031, and UNSC Res 1329 (5 December 2000) UN Doc S/RES/1329.

[85] UNSC Res 815 (30 March 1993) UN Doc S/RES/815, UNSC Res 1009 (10 August 1995) UN Doc S/RES/1009, and UNSC Res 1329 (5 December 2000) UN Doc S/RES/1329.

[86] UNSC Res 788 (19 November 1992) UN Doc S/RES/788, UNSC Res 794 (3 December 1992) UN Doc S/RES/794, UNSC Res 813 (26 March 1993) UN Doc S/RES/813, and UNSC Res 1509 (19 September 2003) UN Doc S/RES/1509.

[87] UNSC Res 788 (19 November 1992) UN Doc S/RES/788, UNSC Res 814 (26 March 1993) UN Doc S/RES/814, UNSC Res 1772 (20 August 2007) UN Doc S/RES/1772, UNSC Res

Georgia,[88] Rwanda,[89] Zaire[90] DRC,[91] East Timor,[92] Afghanistan,[93] Sierra Leone,[94] Côte d'Ivoire,[95] Iraq,[96] Burundi,[97] Sudan,[98] Great Lakes

1801 (20 February 2000) UN Doc S/RES/1801, Res 1814 (15 May 2008) UN Doc S/RES/1814, UNSC Res 1851 (16 December 2008) UN Doc S/RES/1851, UNSC Res 1863 (16 January 2009) UN Doc S/RES/1863, and UNSC Res 1910 (28 January 2010) UN Doc S/RES/1910.

[88] UNSC Res 876 (19 October 1993) UN Doc S/RES/876 and UNSC Res 881 (4 November 1993) UN Doc S/RES/881.

[89] UNSC Res 918 (17 May 1994) UN Doc S/RES/918 and UNSC Res 1329 (5 December 2000) UN Doc S/RES/1329.

[90] UNSC Res 1080 (15 November 1996) UN Doc S/RES/1080.

[91] UNSC Res 1234 (9 April 1999) UN Doc S/RES/1234, UNSC Res 1355 (15 June 2001) UN Doc S/RES/1355, UNSC Res 1484 (30 May 2003) UN Doc S/RES/1484, UNSC Res 1493 (28 July 2003) UN Doc S/RES/1493, UNSC Res 1565 (1 October 2004) UN Doc S/RES/1565, UNSC Res 1592 (30 March 2005) UN Doc S/RES/1592, UNSC Res 1621 (6 September 2005) UN Doc S/RES/1621, UNSC Res 1635 (28 October 2005) UN Doc S/RES/1635, UNSC Res 1649 (21 December 2005) UN Doc S/RES/1649, UNSC Res 1711 (29 September 2006) UN Doc S/RES/1711, UNSC Res 1736 (22 December 2006) UN Doc S/RES/1736, UNSC Res 1756 (15 May 2007) UN Doc S/RES/1756, UNSC Res 1794 (21 December 2007) UN Doc S/RES/1794, UNSC Res 1807 (31 March 2008) UN Doc S/RES/1807, UNSC Res 1843 (20 November 2008) UN Doc S/RES/1843, UNSC Res 1856 (22 December 2008) UN Doc S/RES/1856, UNSC Res 1857 (22 December 2008) UN Doc S/RES/1857, UNSC Res 1896 (7 December 2009) UN Doc S/RES/1896, UNSC Res 1906 (23 December 2009) UN Doc S/RES/1906, and UNSC Res 1925 (28 May 2010) UN Doc S/RES/1925.

[92] UNSC Res 1264 (15 September 1999) UN Doc S/RES/1264 and UNSC Res 1272 (25 October 1999) UN Doc S/RES/1272.

[93] UNSC Res 1267 (15 October 1999) UN Doc S/RES/1267, UNSC Res 1333 (19 December 2000) UN Doc S/RES/1333, UNSC Res 1746 (23 March 2007) UN Doc S/RES/1746, UNSC Res 1776 (19 September 2007) UN Doc S/RES/1776, UNSC Res 1822 (30 June 2008) UN Doc S/RES/1822, UNSC Res 1833 (22 September 2008) UN Doc S/RES/1833, UNSC Res 1890 (8 October 2009) UN Doc S/RES/1890, and UNSC Res 1904 (17 December 2009) UN Doc S/RES/1904.

[94] UNSC Res 1270 (22 October 1999) UN Doc S/RES/1270 and UNSC Res 1464 (4 February 2003) UN Doc S/RES/1464.

[95] UNSC Res 1479 (13 May 2003) UN Doc S/RES/1479, UNSC Res 1528 (27 February 2004) UN Doc S/RES/1528, UNSC Res 1572 (15 November 2004) UN Doc S/RES/1572, UNSC Res 1633 (21 October 2005) UN Doc S/RES/1633, UNSC Res 1643 (15 December 2005) UN Doc S/RES/1643, UNSC Res 1721 (1 November 2006) UN Doc S/RES/1721, UNSC Res 1727 (15 December 2006) UN Doc S/RES/1727, UNSC Res 1765 (16 July 2007) UN Doc S/RES/1765, UNSC Res 1782 (29 October 2007) UN Doc S/RES/1782, UNSC Res 1795 (15 January 2008) UN Doc S/RES/1795, UNSC Res 1826 (29 July 1998) UN Doc S/RES/1826, UNSC Res 1842 (29 October 2008) UN Doc S/RES/1842, UNSC Res 1865 (27 January 2009) UN Doc S/RES/1865, UNSC Res 1880 (30 July 2009) UN Doc S/RES/1880, UNSC Res 1893 (29 October 2009) UN Doc S/RES/1893, and UNSC Res 1911 (28 January 2010) UN Doc S/RES/1911.

[96] UNSC Res 1483 (22 May 2003) UN Doc S/RES/1483, UNSC Res 1637 (11 November 2005) UN Doc S/RES/1637, UNSC Res 1723 (28 November 2006) UN Doc S/RES/1723, UNSC Res 1762 (29 June 2007) UN Doc S/RES/1762, UNSC Res 1770 (10 August 2007) UN Doc S/RES/1770, and UNSC Res 1790 (18 December 2007) UN Doc S/RES/1790.

[97] UNSC Res 1545 (21 May 2004) UN Doc S/RES/1545, UNSC Res 1577 (1 December 2004) UN Doc S/RES/1577, and UNSC Res 1602 (31 May 2005) UN Doc S/RES/1602.

[98] UNSC Res 1556 (30 July 2004) UN Doc S/RES/1556, UNSC Res 1564 (18 September 2004) UN Doc S/RES/1564, UNSC Res 1574 (19 November 2004) UN Doc S/RES/1574, UNSC Res 1590 (24 March 2005) UN Doc S/RES/1590, UNSC Res 1591 (29 March 2005) UN Doc S/RES/1591, UNSC Res 1769 (31 July 2007) UN Doc S/RES/1769, UNSC Res 1812 (30 April 2008) UN Doc S/RES/1812, UNSC Res 1828 (31 July 2008) UN Doc S/RES/1828, UNSC Res 1870 (20 May 2009) UN Doc S/RES/1870, UNSC Res 1881 (6 August 2009) UN Doc S/RES/1881, and UNSC Res 1919 (29 April 2010) UN Doc S/RES/1919.

region,[99] and at the borders of the Sudan, Chad and the Central African Republic.[100]

In fact, in most of these cases, the situation was a mixture of international and non-international armed conflict. This is one of the advantages of the threshold of 'threat to the peace' since it can deal with a complex situation simply by labelling it as 'threat to the peace', without having to determine whether it is an armed conflict in the first place, then whether it is international or non-international, or a mixture of the two. The complexity of 'mixed' armed conflict will be seen later,[101] which will amply show the advantages of the threshold of 'threat to the peace'.

However, it is worth noting that 'threat to the peace' covers situations outside an armed conflict, such as racial discrimination and violations of democratic principles, as noted above. In this regard, a threat to the peace is not automatically a situation of armed conflict and thus, the best way is to determine 'threat to the peace' and 'armed conflict' separately.

In short, the overlap between 'threat to the peace', 'breach of the peace', and 'act of aggression' on one hand and 'armed conflict' on the other is less complex than in the context of 'use of force' or 'armed attack'. 'Breach of the peace' and 'act of aggression' most likely amount to international armed conflict, but 'threat to the peace' can amount to either international or non-international armed conflict, a mixture of the two, or situations short of armed conflict. Since 'threat to the peace' can cover situations outside armed conflict, it is best to determine 'threat to the peace' and 'armed conflict' separately. Nevertheless, the advantages of 'threat to the peace' should be underlined, namely because it can deal with different types of armed conflict under one category, rather than dividing one situation into several categories of armed conflict.

D. Role of Security Council Resolutions in the Beginning and the End of the Application of IHL

The close relationship between Article 39 of the UN Charter and 'armed conflict' is clear, but this still does not answer the question whether Security Council resolutions have any role to play in determining the applicability of IHL. Thus, this section discusses the role of Security Council resolutions in the beginning and end of the application of IHL. It first discusses whether Security Council resolutions play any significant role in determining the existence of an armed conflict and in what kind of

[99] UNSC Res 1653 (27 January 2006) UN Doc S/RES/1653.

[100] UNSC Res 1778 (25 September 2007) UN Doc S/RES/1778, UNSC Res 1834 (24 September 2008) UN Doc S/RES/1834, UNSC Res 1861 (14 January 2009) UN Doc S/RES/1861, and UNSC Res 1923 (25 May 2010) UN Doc S/RES/1923.

[101] See section 5.II.B.

situation the Council begins to apply IHL. It then discusses whether the Council plays any role in ending the application of IHL.

It is worth remembering at the outset that IHL begins to apply whenever an armed conflict commences in the factual sense.[102] A declaration of war or, for the purpose of this section, the determination of a situation as a threat to the peace, breach of the peace, or act of aggression under Article 39 of the UN Charter is not necessary to apply IHL in a given armed conflict. However, since determining the existence of an armed conflict within the meaning of IHL is often a complex process, whether it be an international or non-international armed conflict, Security Council resolutions can serve as a useful practice to determine the existence of an armed conflict and the ensuing applicability of IHL.

In practice, Security Council resolutions do not determine the existence of an armed conflict directly but they imply its existence by invoking the term 'international humanitarian law', IHL treaties, specific provisions in IHL treaties, or clauses which reflect IHL rules.[103] In a few cases, it has used the term 'armed conflict', but in a more common usage of the term rather than in the legal sense.[104]

Even when the Security Council invokes IHL, as mentioned above, references are often made simply to 'international humanitarian law' and thus it is not clear whether it is the law of international or non-international armed conflict that applies. Moreover, even when specific IHL treaties are invoked, the resolutions are not clear about whether the treaties apply to all kinds of armed conflict under consideration or whether different treaties apply to different kinds of armed conflict. An example is resolution 764 on Bosnia-Herzegovina, in which the Security Council reaffirmed that 'all parties are bound to comply with the obligations under international humanitarian law and in particular the Geneva Conventions of 12 August 1949'.[105] This resolution was adopted in July 1992 and by that time, according to the ICTY in the *Tadic* case, international and non-international armed conflicts were taking place simultaneously.[106] However, resolution 764 is not clear 1) whether the 1949 Geneva Conventions applied to all armed conflicts in Bosnia-Herzegovina regardless of international or non-

[102] Refer to common Art 2 of the 1949 Geneva Conventions for international armed conflict and common Art 3 of the 1949 Geneva Conventions and Art 1(1) of the 1977 Second Additional Protocol for non-international armed conflict. See also Sandoz et al (eds), *Commentary*, paras 61–63. Protocol Additional to the Geneva Conventions of 12 August 1949, and Relating to the Protection of Victims of Non-International Armed Conflicts (Protocol II) (hereafter 1977 Second Additional Protocol) (adopted 8 June 1977, entered into force 7 December 1978) 1125 UNTS 609.

[103] See section 4.II.A.

[104] A resolution on the Eritrea-Ethiopia situation provides as follows: '*The Security Council . . . Expressing* grave concern over the risk of armed conflict between Ethiopia and Eritrea'. UNSC Res 1226 (29 January 1999) UN Doc S/RES/1226, Preamble.

[105] UNSC Res 764 (13 July 1992) UN Doc S/RES/764, para 10.

[106] *Tadic Case* (Jurisdiction, Appeals), paras 72–77.

international; 2) whether they applied primarily to the international armed conflict in Bosnia-Herzegovina; or 3) whether only common Article 3 of the 1949 Geneva Conventions was invoked in relation to the non-international armed conflict in Bosnia-Herzegovina. The ambiguity can also lead to the conclusion that it could have meant both 2) and 3).[107]

However, a further issue is that even when the applicability of IHL treaties is recognised by Security Council resolutions, it does not list all the IHL treaties applicable. For example, in resolution 1234 on the Democratic Republic of the Congo (DRC), the 1949 Geneva Conventions and the 1977 Additional Protocols were specifically mentioned but there were many other IHL treaties and customary rules of IHL that were applicable to the international and non-international armed conflicts taking place in the DRC.[108] The advantage of this approach has already been pointed out in the previous section – that the Security Council can deal with a complex situation without having to determine whether it is an armed conflict in the first place, then whether it is an international or non-international armed conflict, and finally, whether it is a mixture of the two.

The practice of the Security Council amply shows that it invokes IHL, not because it determines the situation as an armed conflict, but because it considers that IHL contributes to the overall maintenance of international peace and security. Due to the paramount importance of the Security Council to maintain international peace and security, it has not taken any consistent approach on the recognition of the applicability of IHL. In a few cases, the recognition was swift whereas in many other cases, the recognition came far too late to serve as a useful indication of the beginning of the application of IHL. When the recognition was swift, it was not necessarily a certain type of armed conflict; it could be an international or non-international armed conflict. Moreover, even when the Security Council began invoking IHL, in some cases it was at the abstract level by simply invoking the term 'international humanitarian law' whereas in other cases, it invoked specific provisions in specific IHL treaties. Such *ad hoc* nature of the invocation of IHL by the Security Council is obviously due to its primary concern to do away with armed conflicts altogether rather than to deal with the various humanitarian issues arising from such armed conflicts. In this sense, the role of the Security Council in determining the beginning of the application of IHL is marginal.

[107] A rare case was resolution 1234 on the DRC, which provides as follows: 'The Security Council . . . Calls upon all parties to the conflict in the Democratic Republic of the Congo to protect human rights and to respect international humanitarian law, in particular, as applicable to them, the Geneva Conventions of 1949 and the Additional Protocols of 1977.' UNSC Res 1234 (9 April 1999) UN Doc S/RES/1234. The clause 'as applicable to them' would enable the application of IHL according to the different types of armed conflicts in the DRC. Nevertheless, the Security Council did not go so far as to determine which IHL rules applied between which conflicting parties in the DRC.

[108] See section 5.II.B.

However, it is still worth examining the situations where the Security Council begins to apply IHL. The following pattern can be observed: until the 1991 Gulf War, the recognition of the applicability of IHL came shortly after the armed conflict began and the invocation of IHL was in response to a specific humanitarian question requiring recourse to IHL whereas the period after that shows that the recognition was belated and the invocation tended to be in response to the overall situation of an armed conflict.

Until 1991, there were only five cases where the applicability of IHL was recognised: 1967 Arab–Israel Conflict,[109] 1971 India–Pakistan Conflict,[110] 1980–88 Iran–Iraq War,[111] 1982 Israel–Lebanon Conflict,[112] and 1991 Gulf War.[113] It only took three days to recognise the applicability of IHL to the 1971 India–Pakistan Conflict,[114] nine days for the 1967 Arab–Israel Conflict,[115] 15 days for the 1982 Israel–Lebanon Conflict,[116] and 1.5 months

[109] UNSC Res 237 (14 June 1967) UN Doc S/RES/237. See also UNSC Res 248 (24 March 1968) UN Doc S/RES/248, UNSC Res 271 (15 September 1969) UN Doc S/RES/271, UNSC Res 446 (22 March 1979) UN Doc S/RES/446, UNSC Res 452 (20 July 1979) UN Doc S/RES/452, UNSC Res 459 (19 December 1979) UN Doc S/RES/459, UNSC Res 465 (1 March 1980) UN Doc S/RES/465, UNSC Res 468 (8 May 1980) UN Doc S/RES/468, UNSC Res 471 (5 June 1980) UN Doc S/RES/471, UNSC Res 476 (30 June 1980) UN Doc S/RES/476, UNSC Res 478 (20 August 1980) UN Doc S/RES/478, UNSC Res 484 (19 December 1980) UN Doc S/RES/484, UNSC Res 497 (17 December 1981) UN Doc S/RES/497, UNSC Res 592 (8 December 1981) UN Doc S/RES/592, UNSC Res 605 (22 December 1987) UN Doc S/RES/605, UNSC Res 607 (5 January 1988) UN Doc S/RES/607, UNSC Res 636 (6 July 1989) UN Doc S/RES/636, UNSC Res 641 (30 August 1989) UN Doc S/RES/641, UNSC Res 672 (12 October 1990) UN Doc S/RES/672, UNSC Res 681 (20 December 1990) UN Doc S/RES/681, UNSC Res 694 (24 May 1991) UN Doc S/RES/694, UNSC Res 726 (6 January 1992) UN Doc S/RES/726, UNSC Res 799 (18 December 1992) UN Doc S/RES/799, UNSC Res 904 (18 March 1994) UN Doc S/RES/904, UNSC Res 1397 (12 March 2002) UN Doc S/RES/1397, UNSC Res 1405 (19 April 2002) UN Doc S/RES/1405, UNSC Res 1435 (24 September 2002) UN Doc S/RES/1435, and UNSC Res 1544 (19 May 2004) UN Doc S/RES/1544.

[110] UNSC Res 307 (21 December 1971) UN Doc S/RES/307.

[111] UNSC Res 540 (31 October 1983) UN Doc S/RES/540. See also UNSC Res 582 (24 November 1986) UN Doc S/RES/582, UNSC Res 598 (20 July 1987) UN Doc S/RES/598, UNSC Res 612 (9 May 1988) UN Doc S/RES/612, and UNSC Res 620 (26 August 1988) UN Doc S/RES/620.

[112] UNSC Res 512 (19 June 1982) UN Doc S/RES/512. See also UNSC Res 513 (4 July 1982) UN Doc S/RES/513, UNSC Res 515 (29 July 1982) UN Doc S/RES/515, and UNSC Res 1052 (18 April 1996) UN Doc S/RES/1052.

[113] UNSC Res 666 (13 September 1990) UN Doc S/RES/666. See also UNSC Res 670 (25 September 1990) UN Doc S/RES/670, UNSC Res 674 (29 October 1990) UN Doc S/RES/674, UNSC Res 686 (2 March 1991) UN Doc S/RES/686, and UNSC Res 687 (3 April 1991) UN Doc S/RES/687.

[114] The armed conflict began around December 1971. See UNGA, 'The Situation in the India-Pakistan Subcontinent' (1971) UNYB 137, 146 *ff*. The first Security Council resolution recognising the applicability of IHL was UNSC Res 307 (21 December 1971) UN Doc S/RES/307.

[115] The armed conflict began on 5 June 1967. See UNGA, 'Outbreak of Hostilities on 5 June 1967 and Consideration by the Security Council' (1967) UNYB 174. The first Security Council resolution recognising the applicability of IHL was UNSC Res 237 (14 June 1967) UN Doc S/RES/237.

[116] The armed conflict began on 4 June 1982. See UNGA, 'Situation between Individual Arab States and Israel' (1982) UNYB 425, 433. The first Security Council resolution recognising the applicability of IHL was UNSC Res 512 (19 June 1982) UN Doc S/RES/512.

for the 1991 Gulf War.[117] All of these were clearly international armed conflicts and thus, the applicability of IHL was uncontroversial. The 1980–88 Iran–Iraq War was a peculiar case since it took more than three years until the Security Council recognised the applicability of IHL[118] even though by that time, widespread violations of IHL had already taken place.[119] Clearly, the recognition should have come immediately after the outbreak of the armed conflict.

In almost all cases, Security Council resolutions invoking IHL played a major role in addressing specific humanitarian issues arising from the international armed conflicts. The 1967 Arab–Israel Conflict remains an outstanding case where the Security Council not only recognised the applicability of the 1949 Third and Fourth Geneva Conventions shortly after the outbreak of the international armed conflict but also continued to apply the 1949 Fourth Geneva Convention in great detail throughout the subsequent occupation. The specific situations include Israel's legislative and administrative measures taken to change the status of Jerusalem[120] and local law,[121] establishment of Israeli settlements in the occupied territories,[122] deportation of Palestinian civilians,[123] and attacks on civilians in the occupied territories.[124]

[117] The armed conflict began on 2 August 1990. See UNGA, 'Iraq–Kuwait' (1990) UNYB 189. The first Security Council resolution recognising the applicability of IHL was UNSC Res 666 (13 September 1991) UN Doc S/RES/666.

[118] The armed conflict began on 22 September 1980. See UNSC, 'Further Report of the Secretary-General on the Implementation of Security Resolution 598 (1987)' (9 December 1991) UN Doc S/23273, para 6. The first Security Council resolution recognising the applicability of IHL was UNSC Res 540 (31 October 1983) UN Doc S/RES/540.

[119] See ICRC, 'Memorandum from the International Committee of the Red Cross to the States Parties to the Geneva Conventions of August 12, 1949 concerning the Conflict between Islamic Republic of Iran and Republic of Iraq' in M Sassòli and A Bouvier (eds), *How Does Law Protect in War?*, 2nd edn, Vol II (Geneva, International Committee of the Red Cross, 2006) 1529.

[120] UNSC Res 271 (15 September 1969) UN Doc S/RES/271, UNSC Res 476 (30 June 1980) UN Doc S/RES/476, and UNSC Res 478 (20 August 1980) UN Doc S/RES/478.

[121] UNSC Res 497 (17 December 1981) S/RES/497.

[122] UNSC Res 446 (22 March 1979) UN Doc S/RES/446, UNSC Res 452 (20 July 1979) UN Doc S/RES/452, and UNSC Res 465 (1 March 1980) UN Doc S/RES/465.

[123] UNSC Res 468 (8 May 1980) UN Doc S/RES/468, UNSC Res 469 (20 May 1980) UN Doc S/RES/469 (reference to common Art 1 of the 1949 Geneva Conventions and Art 49 of the 1949 Fourth Geneva Convention), UNSC Res 484 (19 December 1980) UN Doc S/RES/484, UNSC Res 607 (5 January 1988) UN Doc S/RES/607 (reference to Arts 47 and 49 of the 1949 Fourth Geneva Convention), UNSC Res 636 (6 July 1989) UN Doc S/RES/636, UNSC Res 641 (30 August 1989) UN Doc S/RES/641 (reference to Arts 47 and 49 of the 1949 Fourth Geneva Convention), UNSC Res 694 (24 May 1991) UN Doc S/RES/694, UNSC Res 681 (20 December 1990) UN Doc S/RES/681 (reference to common Art 1 of the 1949 Geneva Conventions), UNSC Res 726 (6 January 1992) UN Doc S/RES/726, and UNSC Res 799 (18 December 1992) UN Doc S/RES/799.

[124] UNSC Res 471 (5 June 1980) UN Doc S/RES/471 (reference to Art 27 of the 1949 Fourth Geneva Convention), UNSC Res 592 (8 December 1986) UN Doc S/RES/592, UNSC Res 605 (22 December 1987) UN Doc S/RES/605, UNSC Res 672 (12 October 1990) UN Doc S/RES/672, UNSC Res 904 (18 March 1994) UN Doc S/RES/904, UNSC Res 1397 (12 March 2002) UN Doc S/RES/1397, UNSC Res 1405 (19 April 2002) UN Doc S/RES/1405, UNSC Res

In the 1971 India–Pakistan Conflict, the Security Council only recognised the applicability of the 1949 Geneva Conventions at the outset of the international armed conflict but in the 1980–88 Iran–Iraq War, the applicability of IHL was continually recognised. The 1949 Geneva Conventions were invoked when attacks against civilians and civilian objects took place[125] and later the 1949 Third Geneva Convention and the 1925 Gas Protocol[126] when the release of prisoners of war[127] and the use of chemical weapons became major issues.[128]

In the 1982 Israel–Lebanon Conflict, the Security Council invoked the 1907 Hague Regulations and the 1949 Geneva Conventions, particularly in relation to the civilians affected[129] and the blockade of Beirut.[130]

In the 1991 Gulf War, the applicability of IHL was recognised on a variety of occasions. First, the Security Council invoked the 1949 Fourth Geneva Convention when the treatment of third state nationals[131] and Kuwaiti nationals in Iraq became a concern.[132] Later, the 1949 Third Geneva Convention was invoked in relation to the release of prisoners of war[133] and the 1925 Gas Protocol and the 1972 Biological Weapons Conventions in relation to the use of chemical weapons in previous conflicts.[134]

Since 1991, the applicability of IHL has been recognised more frequently but the recognition came much later in the armed conflict.[135] Moreover, the Security Council has not applied IHL to specific issues. The situations where the Security Council recognised the applicability of IHL shifted to the following: 1) widespread violations of IHL and large-scale civilian

1435 (24 September 2002) UN Doc S/RES/1435, and UNSC Res 1544 (19 May 2004) UN Doc S/RES/1544.

125 UNSC Res 540 (31 Oct 1983) UN Doc S/RES/540 and UNSC Res 582 (24 Feb 1986) UN Doc S/RES/582.

126 Protocol for the Prohibition of the Use of Asphyxiating, Poisonous or Other Gases, and of Bacteriological Methods of Warfare (hereafter 1925 Gas Protocol) (adopted 17 June 1925, entered into force 9 May 1926) 94 LNTS 65.

127 UNSC Res 598 (20 July 1987) UN Doc S/RES/598.

128 UNSC Res 582 (24 February 1986) UN Doc S/RES/582, UNSC Res 612 (9 May 1988) UN Doc S/RES/612, and UNSC Res 620 (26 August 1988) UN Doc S/RES/620.

129 UNSC Res 512 (19 June 1982) UN Doc S/RES/512, UNSC Res 513 (4 July 1982) UN Doc S/RES/513, UNSC Res 515 (29 July 1982) UN Doc S/RES/515, and UNSC Res 1052 (18 April 1996) UN Doc S/RES/1052.

130 UNSC Res 515 (29 July 1982) UN Doc S/RES/515.

131 UNSC Res 666 (13 September 1990) UN Doc S/RES/666 and UNSC Res 674 (29 October 1990) UN Doc S/RES/674.

132 UNSC Res 670 (25 September 1990) UN Doc S/RES/670 and UNSC Res 674 (29 October 1990) UN Doc S/RES/674.

133 UNSC Res 686 (2 March 1991) UN Doc S/RES/686.

134 UNSC Res 687 (3 April 1991) UN Doc S/RES/687.

135 For example, in the case of the Sudan, it took around a year and a half for the Security Council to recognise the applicability of IHL in its resolution. The armed conflict began sometime in late 2002 or beginning of 2003. See UNSC, 'Report of the International Commission of Inquiry on Darfur to the United Nations Secretary-General' (25 January 2005) UN Doc S/2005/60, para 63. The first Security Council resolution recognising the applicability of IHL was UNSC Res 1547 (11 June 2004) UN Doc S/RES/1547.

victims; 2) continuation or resumption of hostilities; and 3) other isolated cases such as occupation and residual IHL issues after armed conflict. It is worth noting that in most cases, the armed conflicts had already been at their height by the time the Security Council invoked IHL. In this sense, the Security Council played a marginal role in determining the beginning of the application of IHL.

In most cases, when Security Council invoked IHL in its resolutions, widespread IHL violations and large-scale civilian victims were explicitly recognised in the same resolutions. The relevant situations were the former Yugoslavia,[136] Bosnia-Herzegovina,[137] Croatia,[138] Liberia,[139] Somalia,[140] Angola,[141] Rwanda,[142] Armenia-Azerbaijan,[143] Georgia,[144] Burundi,[145]

[136] UNSC Res 771 (13 August 1992) UN Doc S/RES/771, UNSC Res 780 (6 October 1992) UN Doc S/RES/780, UNSC Res 787 (16 November 1992) UN Doc S/RES/787, UNSC Res 808 (22 February 1993) UN Doc S/RES/808, UNSC Res 815 (30 March 1993) UN Doc S/RES/815, UNSC Res 819 (16 April 1993) UN Doc S/RES/819, UNSC Res 820 (17 April 1993) UN Doc S/RES/820, UNSC Res 836 (4 June 1993) UN Doc S/RES/836, UNSC Res 844 (18 June 1993) UN Doc S/RES/844, UNSC Res 941 (23 September 1994) UN Doc S/RES/941, UNSC Res 1031 (15 December 1995) UN Doc S/RES/1031, and UNSC Res 1034 (21 December 1995) UN Doc S/RES/1034.

[137] UNSC Res 771 (13 August 1992) UN Doc S/RES/771, UNSC Res 780 (6 October 1992) UN Doc S/RES/780, UNSC Res 787 (16 November 1992) UN Doc S/RES/787, UNSC Res 815 (30 March 1993) UN Doc S/RES/815, UNSC Res 819 (16 April 1993) UN Doc S/RES/819, UNSC Res 820 (17 April 1993) UN Doc S/RES/820, UNSC Res 836 (4 June 1993) UN Doc S/RES/836, UNSC Res 844 (18 June 1993) UN Doc S/RES/844, and UNSC Res 941 (23 September 1994) UN Doc S/RES/941.

[138] UNSC Res 815 (30 March 1993) UN Doc S/RES/815.

[139] UNSC Res 950 (21 October 1994) UN Doc S/RES/950. See also UNSC Res 788 (19 November 1992) UN Doc S/RES/788, UNSC Res 866 (22 September 1993) UN Doc S/RES/866, UNSC Res 911 (21 April 1994) UN Doc S/RES/911, UNSC Res 972 (13 January 1995) UN Doc S/RES/972, UNSC Res 985 (13 April 1995) UN Doc S/RES/985, UNSC Res 1001 (30 June 1995) UN Doc S/RES/1001, UNSC Res 1014 (15 September 1995) UN Doc S/RES/1014, UNSC Res 1020 (10 November 1995) UN Doc S/RES/1020, UNSC Res 1041 (29 January 1996) UN Doc S/RES/1041, UNSC Res 1059 (31 May 1996) UN Doc S/RES/1059 UNSC Res 1071 (30 August 1996) UN Doc S/RES/1071, UNSC Res 1083 (27 November 1996) UN Doc S/RES/1083, and UNSC Res 1509 (19 September 2003) UN Doc S/RES/1509.

[140] UNSC Res 794 (3 December 1992) UN Doc S/RES/794 and UNSC Res 814 (26 March 1993) UN Doc S/RES/814.

[141] UNSC Res 804 (29 January 1993) UN Doc S/RES/804, UNSC Res 811 (12 March 1993) UN Doc S/RES/811, UNSC Res 834 (1 June 1993) UN Doc S/RES/834, UNSC Res 851 (15 July 1993) UN Doc S/RES/851, UNSC Res 864 (15 September 1993) UN Doc S/RES/864, and UNSC Res 1213 (3 December 1998) UN Doc S/RES/1213.

[142] UNSC Res 912 (21 April 1994) UN Doc S/RES/912, UNSC Res 918 (17 May 1994) UN Doc S/RES/918, UNSC Res 935 (1 July 1994) UN Doc S/RES/935, and UNSC Res 955 (8 November 1994) UN Doc S/RES/955.

[143] UNSC Res 822 (30 April 1993) UN Doc S/RES/822, UNSC Res 853 (29 July 1993) UN Doc S/RES/853, and UNSC Res 874 (14 October 1993) UN Doc S/RES/874.

[144] UNSC Res 876 (19 October 1993) UN Doc S/RES/876, UNSC Res 881 (4 November 1993) UN Doc S/RES/881, UNSC Res 993 (12 May 1995) UN Doc S/RES/993, and UNSC Res 1036 (12 January 1996) UN Doc S/RES/1036.

[145] UNSC Res 1012 (28 August 1995) UN Doc S/RES/1012, UNSC Res 1545 (21 May 2004) UN Doc S/RES/1545, UNSC Res 1577 (1 December 2004) UN Doc S/RES/1577, and UNSC Res 1602 (31 May 2005) UN Doc S/RES/1602.

Afghanistan,[146] DRC,[147] Sierra Leone,[148] Kosovo,[149] Eritrea-Ethiopia,[150] East Timor,[151] Côte d'Ivoire,[152] and Sudan.[153] Widespread IHL violations and large-scale civilian victims were also recognised as a threat to international peace and security. The Security Council noted that 'the deliberate targeting of civilian populations or other protected persons and the committing of systematic, flagrant and widespread violations of international humanitarian and human rights law in situations of armed conflict may constitute a threat to international peace and security'.[154] This confirms that the Security Council perceives itself as competent to invoke IHL when IHL violations amount to a 'threat to the peace' under Article 39 of the UN Charter.

In certain cases when the Security Council invoked IHL, the continuation or resumption of hostilities was specifically referred to, namely on Armenia-Azerbaijan,[155] Georgia,[156] DRC,[157] Kosovo,[158] Eritrea-Ethiopia,[159]

[146] UNSC Res 1378 (14 November 2001) UN Doc S/RES/1378, UNSC Res 1589 (24 March 2005) UN Doc S/RES/1589, and UNSC Res 1662 (23 March 2006) UN Doc S/RES/1662.

[147] UNSC Res 1234 (9 April 1999) UN Doc S/RES/1234, UNSC Res 1258 (6 August 1999) UN Doc S/RES/1258, UNSC Res 1279 (30 November 1999) UN Doc S/RES/1279, UNSC Res 1355 (15 June 2001) UN Doc S/RES/1355, UNSC Res 1484 (30 May 2003) UN Doc S/RES/1484, UNSC Res 1493 (28 July 2003) UN Doc S/RES/1493, UNSC Res 1565 (1 October 2004) UN Doc S/RES/1565, UNSC Res 1592 (30 March 2005) UN Doc S/RES/1592, UNSC Res 1621 (6 September 2005) UN Doc S/RES/1621, UNSC Res 1635 (28 October 2005) UN Doc S/RES/1635, and UNSC Res 1649 (21 December 2005) UN Doc S/RES/1649.

[148] UNSC Res 1181 (13 July 1998) UN Doc S/RES/1181, UNSC Res 1231 (11 March 1999) UN Doc S/RES/1231, UNSC Res 1260 (20 August 1999) UN Doc S/RES/1260, UNSC Res 1270 (22 October 1999) UN Doc S/RES/1270, and UNSC Res 1400 (28 March 2002) UN Doc S/RES/1400.

[149] UNSC Res 1199 (23 September 1998) UN Doc S/RES/1199 and UNSC Res 1239 (14 May 1999) UN Doc S/RES/1239.

[150] UNSC Res 1227 (10 February 1999) UN Doc S/RES/1227 and UNSC Res 1297 (12 May 2000) UN Doc S/RES/1297.

[151] UNSC Res 1264 (15 September 1999) UN Doc S/RES/1264 and UNSC Res 1272 (25 October 1999) UN Doc S/RES/1272.

[152] UNSC Res 1572 (15 November 2004) UN Doc S/RES/1572, UNSC Res 1633 (21 October 2005) UN Doc S/RES/1633, and UNSC Res 1643 (15 December 2005) UN Doc S/RES/1643.

[153] UNSC Res 1547 (11 June 2004) UN Doc S/RES/1547, UNSC Res 1556 (30 July 2004) UN Doc S/RES/1556, UNSC Res 1564 (18 September 2004) UN Doc S/RES/1564, UNSC Res 1574 (19 November 2004) UN Doc S/RES/1574, UNSC Res 1590 (24 March 2005) UN Doc S/RES/1590, and UNSC Res 1591 (29 March 2005) UN Doc S/RES/1591.

[154] UNSC Res 1296 (19 April 2000) UN Doc S/RES/1296. See also UNSC Res 1314 (11 August 2000) UN Doc S/RES/1314, UNSC Res 1674 (28 April 2006) UN Doc S/RES/1674, and UNSC Res 1738 (23 December 2006) UN Doc S/RES/1738. All were thematic resolution on civilians in armed conflict.

[155] UNSC Res 822 (30 April 1993) UN Doc S/RES/822, UNSC Res 853 (29 July 1993) UN Doc S/RES/853, and UNSC Res 874 (14 October 1993) UN Doc S/RES/874.

[156] UNSC Res 881 (4 November 1993) UN Doc S/RES/881.

[157] UNSC Res 1234 (9 April 1999) UN Doc S/RES/1234, UNSC Res 1493 (28 July 2003) UN Doc S/RES/1493, UNSC Res 1565 (1 October 2004) UN Doc S/RES/1565, UNSC Res 1592 (30 March 2005) UN Doc S/RES/1592, UNSC Res 1621 (6 September 2005) UN Doc S/RES/1621, UNSC Res 1635 (28 October 2005) UN Doc S/RES/1635, and UNSC Res 1649 (21 December 2005) UN Doc S/RES/1649.

[158] UNSC Res 1199 (23 September 1998) UN Doc S/RES/1199.

[159] NSC Res 1227 (10 February 1999) UN Doc S/RES/1227 and UNSC Res 1297 (12 May 2000) UN Doc S/RES/1297.

and Côte d'Ivoire.[160]

The situation in Iraq in 2003 was an exceptional case since it resembled more of the classical cases prior to 1991. The situation of occupation was formally recognised and the applicability of the 1949 Geneva Conventions, particularly the Fourth Geneva Convention and the 1907 Hague Regulations, was recognised.[161] In the past, the applicability of the 1949 Fourth Geneva Convention was only recognised in relation to the occupied territories in the Middle East[162] and DRC[163] and the applicability of the 1907 Hague Regulations only in the 1982 Israel–Lebanon Conflict.[164] It also invoked Article 55 of the 1949 Fourth Geneva Convention to highlight the obligation of the occupying power to ensure food and medical supplies to the population in the occupied territories.[165] This resolution still remains the only one which invoked specific provision in an IHL treaty besides those relating to the occupied territories in the Middle East[166] and some thematic resolutions.[167]

The case of Iraq is also unique in the sense that the applicability of IHL after the end of the occupation was recognised explicitly.[168]

The applicability of IHL is also recognised in post-conflict situations to deal with residual issues of armed conflicts, such as the release of prisoners of war and the prosecution of war crimes. Eritrea-Ethiopia[169] and Western Sahara[170] remain the outstanding cases with regard to the release of prisoners of war and Iraq,[171] Sierra Leone,[172] and Côte d'Ivoire[173] with regard to the prosecution of war crimes.

On the other hand, the Security Council rarely determined the end of the application of IHL and it simply dropped the reference to IHL at some point without specifying the reason, which might have been a genuine

160 UNSC Res 1572 (15 November 2004) UN Doc S/RES/1572.

161 UNSC Res 1472 (28 March 2003) UN Doc S/RES/1472 and UNSC Res 1483 (22 May 2003) UN Doc S/RES/1483.

162 See n 109 above.

163 UNSC Res 1355 (15 June 2001) UN Doc S/RES/1355.

164 See nn 129 and 130 above.

165 UNSC Res 1472 (28 March 2003) UN Doc S/RES/1472.

166 See n 195 below.

167 See n 196 below.

168 UNSC Res 1546 (8 June 2004) UN Doc S/RES/1546. See also UNSC Res 1637 (11 November 2005) UN Doc S/RES/1637. For further discussions, see section 4.IV.D below.

169 UNSC Res 1369 (14 September 2001) UN Doc S/RES/1369, UNSC Res 1398 (15 March 2002) UN Doc S/RES/1398, UNSC Res 1430 (14 August 2002) UN Doc S/RES/1430, UNSC Res 1434 (6 September 2002) UN Doc S/RES/1434, and UNSC Res 1466 (14 March 2003) UN Doc S/RES/1466.

170 UNSC Res 1359 (29 June 2001) UN Doc S/RES/1359, UNSC Res 1429 (30 July 2002) UN Doc S/RES/1429, UNSC Res 1495 (31 July 2003) UN Doc S/RES/1495, and UNSC Res 1598 (28 April 2005) UN Doc S/RES/1598.

171 UNSC Res 687 (3 April 1991) UN Doc S/RES/687.

172 UNSC Res 1400 (28 March 2002) UN Doc S/RES/1400.

173 UNSC Res 1464 (4 February 2003) UN Doc S/RES/1464 and UNSC Res 1479 (13 May 2003) UN Doc S/RES/1479.

end of the application of IHL or simply an omission.[174] Reading too much between the lines is not suggested here, particularly because Security Council resolutions are often ambiguous and more so with the motives of their adoption. However, as will be seen below, the exceptions are resolutions 686 and 1546 on Iraq.

The application of IHL normally ends with the 'general close of military operations' or the end of occupation,[175] which can take place in a *de facto* sense, such as *debellatio*, or in the form of a permanent cessation of hostilities by a formal agreement, such as capitulation, armistice, or peace agreement.[176] However, the end of the application of IHL is not always identical with the end of an armed conflict since there can be a termination of an armed conflict by a formal agreement but in reality, there may still be prisoners of war to release and repatriate, in which case the 1949 Third Geneva Convention continues to apply. Thus, the end of the application of IHL should focus on whether there are no more residual issues arising from an armed conflict which require recourse to IHL. The IHL rules that apply after the 'general close of military operations' or the end of occupation are such as those concerning occupied territories,[177] persons hors de combat and prisoners of war,[178] and certain weapons.[179]

Resolution 686 on the 1991 Gulf War was a peculiar case which implied the 'general close of military operations'. The Security Council noted 'the suspension of offensive combat operations by the forces of Kuwait and the Member States cooperating with Kuwait pursuant to resolution 678 (1990)'.[180] The phrase 'suspension of offensive combat operations' appears to recognise the 'general close of military operations' and thus, the end of

[174] See, eg, UNSC Res 1036 (12 January 1996) UN Doc S/RES/1036 on Georgia which refers to IHL but the next resolution on Georgia, UNSC Res 1065 (12 July 1996) UN Doc S/RES/1065, does not refer to IHL, despite the fact that the non-international armed conflict there was on-going.

[175] Art 6 of the 1949 Geneva Conventions and Art 3 of the 1977 First Additional Protocol. Protocol Additional to the Geneva Conventions of 12 August 1949, and Relating to the Protection of Victims of International Armed Conflicts (Protocol I) (hereafter 1977 First Additional Protocol) (adopted 8 June 1977, entered into force 7 December 1978) 1125 UNTS 3.

[176] O Uhler and H Coursier et al, *Commentary on the Geneva Conventions of 12 August 1949* Vol IV (Geneva: International Committee of the Red Cross, 1958) 62.

[177] See Art 6 of the 1949 Fourth Geneva Convention and Art 3(b) of the 1977 First Additional Protocol.

[178] Art 5 of the 1949 First Geneva Convention, Art 5 of the 1949 Third Geneva Convention, Arts 3(b) and 75(6) of the 1977 First Additional Protocol.

[179] Art I of the 1972 Biological Weapons Convention, Art I(1) of the 1993 Chemical Weapons Convention, Art 1(1) of the 1997 Convention on Anti-Personnel Mines apply in any or all circumstances. See also Convention on Prohibitions or Restrictions on the Use of Certain Conventional Weapons Which May Be Deemed to be Excessively Injurious or to Have Indiscriminate Effects, Protocol on Explosive Remnants of War (Protocol V) (adopted 28 November 2003, entered into force 12 November 2006) 2399 UNTS 100.

[180] UNSC Res 686 (2 March 1991) UN Doc S/RES/686, Preamble.

the application of IHL. Despite this indication, the end of the application of IHL might have taken place independently when the cessation of hostilities took place in the battlefield on 28 February 1991, two days before the adoption of this resolution.[181] The fact that resolution 686 recognised a 'suspension of offensive combat operations' might have been irrelevant to the end of the application of IHL.

Resolution 686 also shows that the end of the application of IHL and the end of an armed conflict are different. The resolution, taken together with resolution 687, which set out the conditions of ceasefire, primarily recognised a ceasefire and not the end of an armed conflict. If the armed conflict in Iraq had been considered as a 'war', perhaps the state of war continued after the adoption of resolutions 686 and 687 since a ceasefire per se does not end a war. Nevertheless, the application of IHL might have ended when a 'general close of military operations' took place on 28 February 1991 or when residual issues requiring resort to IHL ceased to exist, such as the repatriation of prisoners of war.

Resolution 1546 on the occupation of Iraq after the 2003 Gulf War went slightly further than a mere ceasefire; it clearly recognised the end of the occupation in Iraq. In this resolution, the Security Council welcomed that 'by 30 June 2004, the occupation will end and the Coalition Provisional Authority will cease to exist, and that Iraq will reassert its full sovereignty'.[182] The question was whether it also terminated the application of the law of occupation. As a matter of law, the end of occupation should be assessed in the light of Article 42 of the 1907 Hague Regulations and not on the basis of Security Council resolution. This article provides as follows:

> The territory is considered occupied when it is actually placed under the authority of a hostile army.

The multinational forces in Iraq were in fact stationed there with the consent of the Iraqi government and thus they were no longer a 'hostile army' and hence no longer an occupying power.[183] Thus, the occupation had

[181] C Greenwood, 'Scope of Application of Humanitarian Law' in D Fleck (ed), *The Handbook of Humanitarian Law in Armed Conflicts* (Oxford, Oxford University Press, 1995) 63. The combat ceased on 28 February 1991, which was two days before the adoption of resolution 686, UNSC Res 686 (2 March 1991) UN Doc S/RES/686. See US Department of Defense, 'Final Report to Congress on the Conduct of Hostilities in the Persian Gulf' (1992) www.ndu.edu/library/epubs/cpgw.pdf.

[182] UNSC Res 1546 (8 June 2004) UN Doc S/RES/1546, para 2. For discussions on whether the law of occupation was applicable beyond 30 June 2004, see K Dörmann and L Colassis, 'International Humanitarian Law in the Iraq Conflict' (2004) 47 *German Yearbook of International Law* 293; A Roberts, 'The End of Occupation: Iraq 2004' (2005) 54 *International and Comparative Law Quarterly* 27.

[183] Resolution 1546 provides as follows: '*The Security Council* . . . *Notes* that the presence of the multination force in Iraq is at the request of the incoming Interim Government of Iraq'. See UNSC Res 1546 (8 June 2004) UN Doc S/RES/1546, para 2.

ended with the consent of the Iraqi government and hence the application of the law of occupation had also ended.[184] In this sense, resolution 1546 per se did not terminate the application of IHL; it was Article 42 of the 1907 Hague Regulations that was the legal basis for the termination of the law of occupation. However, so long as the residual issues requiring recourse to IHL remained, the relevant rules of the law of international armed conflict continued to apply. Moreover, since other types of armed conflict emerged, such as the non-international armed conflict between the Iraqi armed forces and armed groups or between the multinational forces and armed groups, different sets of rules applied to these armed conflicts in parallel with the law of international armed conflict.[185]

In other resolutions, the Security Council demanded that the conflicting parties cease hostilities[186] or that the occupying power end its occupation,[187] but none of them went so far as to recognise the end of hostilities or occupation, thereby implying the end of an armed conflict or the application of IHL. Thus, the Security Council has never terminated the application of IHL in explicit terms and only gave slight indications in the resolutions relating to the 1991 and 2003 Gulf Wars. However, these cases were exceptions and it can be said that Security Council resolutions have played a minor role in the end of the application of IHL.

As can be seen from the above, there is no consistent approach in the Security Council to recognise the beginning of the application of IHL. However, there are certain indications on when it is prepared to invoke IHL. In recent years, this has taken place when there were widespread violations of IHL and large-scale civilian victims, but this also meant that an armed conflict had already become full-blown and thus the recognition had a marginal role in determining the beginning of the application of IHL or an armed conflict. Moreover, Security Council resolutions were almost always irrelevant to the end of the application of IHL. The role of Security Council resolutions is more relevant during and after an armed conflict.[188]

[184] See Dörmann and Colassis, 'International Humanitarian Law in the Iraq Conflict', 313.

[185] See Dörmann and Colassis, 'International Humanitarian Law in the Iraq Conflict', 313.

[186] See, eg UNSC Res 514 (12 July 1982) UN Doc S/RES/514 on the Iran–Iraq War.

[187] See, eg, UNSC Res 242 (22 November 1967) UN Doc S/RES/242 on Israel's occupation of the West Bank.

[188] See sections 4.III.A, 4.IV.D, and 4.V below.

III. SECURITY COUNCIL RESOLUTIONS AND IHL

A. Overview of the Security Council Resolutions Relating to IHL[189]

This section provides a comprehensive overview of Security Council resolutions relating to IHL. This will not only help to understand how the Security Council has been invoking IHL in its resolutions, but also what issues the resolutions raise on the relationship between Chapter VII and IHL.

The Security Council resolutions invoking IHL can be largely divided into two categories: 1) those which invoke the term 'international humanitarian law', specific IHL treaties, or provisions in specific IHL treaties; and 2) those containing clauses which reflect certain IHL rules. An example of the first type is resolution 1193 on Afghanistan, in which the Security Council reaffirmed that 'all parties to the conflict are bound to comply with their obligations under international humanitarian law and in particular the Geneva Conventions of 12 August 1949'.[190] An example of the second type is resolution 540 on the Iran–Iraq War, which contains a clause reflecting Article 52(1) of the 1977 First Additional Protocol on the prohibition on attacks on civilian objects. In this resolution, the Security Council called 'for the immediate cessation of all military operations against civilian targets, including city and residential areas'.[191]

As at September 2010, the total number of the first and second type of Security Council resolutions was at least 622, of which 258 were adopted under either Chapter VII or Article 39 of the UN Charter, or both.[192] There were at least 254 Security Council resolutions belonging to the first type, of which 116 were adopted under either Chapter VII or Article 39, or both.[193] On the other hand, there were at least 593 Security Council resolutions belonging to the second type, of which 246 were adopted under either Chapter VII or Article 39, or both.[194] In practice, most resolutions contained both ways of invoking IHL.

[189] For earlier writings, see T van Boven, 'Reliance on Norms of Humanitarian Law by United Nations' Organs' in A Delissen and G Tanja (eds), *Humanitarian Law of Armed Conflict: Challenges Ahead, Essays in Honour of Frits Kalshoven* (Dordrecht, Martinus Nijhoff, 1991); E Suy, 'International Humanitarian Law and the Security Council Resolutions on the 1990–1991 Gulf Conflict' in Delissen and Tanja (eds), *Humanitarian Law of Armed Conflict*; C Bourloyannis, 'The Security Council of the United Nations and the Implementation of International Humanitarian Law' (1991–92) 20 *Denver Journal of International Law and Policy* 335; L Boisson de Chazournes, 'Les résolutions des organs des Nations Unies, et en particulier celles du Conseil de sécurité, en tant que source de droit international humanitaire' in Condorelli et al (eds), *Nations Unies et le droit international humanitaire*; Gasser, 'The United Nations and International Humanitarian Law'.

[190] UNSC Res 1193 (28 August 1998) UN Doc S/RES/1193, para 12.

[191] UNSC Res 540 (31 October 1983) UN Doc S/RES/540, para 2.

[192] See Annex 1.

[193] See Annex 1.

[194] See Annex 1.

The 254 Security Council resolutions studied here which invoked IHL (the first type) can be categorised into three: 1) those invoking specific provisions in IHL treaties; 2) those invoking IHL treaties but not the provisions therein; and 3) those simply invoking the term 'international humanitarian law'. There were only nine resolutions which invoked specific provisions in IHL treaties, of which six were in relation to the Occupied Palestinian Territories,[195] two to civilians in armed conflict[196] and the other to the 2003 Iraq–US/UK conflict.[197] There were 17 cases (74 resolutions in total) where specific IHL treaties were invoked which were in relation to the Occupied Palestinian Territories;[198] the 1971 India–Pakistan Conflict,[199] 1982 Israel–Lebanon War,[200] 1980–88 Iran–Iraq War,[201] 1990–91 Gulf War,[202] 1991–95 conflicts in the former Yugoslavia,[203] Afghanistan conflict,[204] conflicts in the DRC,[205] 1999 Kosovo Conflict,[206] children in armed conflict,[207]

[195] UNSC Res 469 (20 May 1980) UN Doc S/RES/469, UNSC Res 471 (5 June 1980) UN Doc S/RES/471, UNSC Res 607 (5 January 1988) UN Doc S/RES/607, UNSC Res 636 (6 July 1989) UN Doc S/RES/636, UNSC Res 641 (30 August 1989) UN Doc S/RES/641, and UNSC Res 681 (20 December 1990) UN Doc S/RES/681.

[196] UNSC Res 1265 (17 September 1999) UN Doc S/RES/1265 and UNSC Res 1738 (23 December 2006) UN Doc S/RES/1738.

[197] UNSC Res 1472 (28 March 2003) UN Doc S/RES/1472.

[198] UNSC Res 237 (14 June 1967) UN Doc S/RES/237, UNSC Res 248 (24 March 1968) UN Doc S/RES/248, UNSC Res 271 (15 September 1969) UN Doc S/RES/271, UNSC Res 446 (22 March 1979) UN Doc S/RES/446, UNSC Res 452 (20 July 1979) UN Doc S/RES/452, UNSC Res 459 (19 December 1979) UN Doc S/RES/459, UNSC Res 465 (1 March 1980) UN Doc S/RES/465, UNSC Res 468 (8 May 1980) UN Doc S/RES/468, UNSC Res 476 (30 June 1980) UN Doc S/RES/476, UNSC Res 478 (20 August 1980) UN Doc S/RES/478, UNSC Res 484 (19 December 1980) UN Doc S/RES/484, UNSC Res 497 (17 December 1981) UN Doc S/RES/497, UNSC Res 592 (8 December 1986) UN Doc S/RES/592, UNSC Res 605 (22 December 1987) UN Doc S/RES/605, UNSC Res 672 (12 October 1990) UN Doc S/RES/672, UNSC Res 694 (24 May 1991) UN Doc S/RES/694, UNSC Res 726 (6 January 1992) UN Doc S/RES/726, UNSC Res 799 (18 December 1992) UN Doc S/RES/799, UNSC Res 904 (18 March 1994) UN Doc S/RES/904, UNSC Res 1435 (24 September 2002) UN Doc S/RES/1435, and UNSC Res 1544 (19 May 2004) UN Doc S/RES/1544.

[199] UNSC Res 307 (21 December 1971) UN Doc S/RES/307.

[200] UNSC Res 512 (19 June 1982) UN Doc S/RES/512, UNSC Res 513 (4 July 1982) UN Doc S/RES/513, and UNSC Res 515 (29 July 1982) UN Doc S/RES/515.

[201] UNSC Res 540 (31 October 1983) UN Doc S/RES/540, UNSC Res 582 (24 February 1986) UN Doc S/RES/582, UNSC Res 598 (20 July 1987) UN Doc S/RES/598, UNSC Res 612 (9 May 1988) UN Doc S/RES/612, and UNSC Res 620 (26 August 1988) UN Doc S/RES/620.

[202] UNSC Res 666 (13 September 1990) UN Doc S/RES/666, UNSC Res 670 (25 September 1990) UN Doc S/RES/670, UNSC Res 674 (29 October 1990) UN Doc S/RES/674, UNSC Res 686 (2 March 1991) UN Doc S/RES/686, and UNSC Res 687 (3 April 1991) UN Doc S/RES/687.

[203] UNSC Res 764 (13 July 1992) UN Doc S/RES/764, UNSC Res 771 (13 August 1992) UN Doc S/RES/771, UNSC Res 780 (6 October 1992) UN Doc S/RES/780, UNSC Res 787 (16 November 1992) UN Doc S/RES/787, UNSC Res 808 (22 February 1993) UN Doc S/RES/808, UNSC Res 815 (30 March 1993) UN Doc S/RES/815, and UNSC Res 941 (23 September 1994) UN Doc S/RES/941.

[204] UNSC Res 1193 (28 August 1998) UN Doc S/RES/1193.

[205] UNSC Res 1234 (9 April 1999) UN Doc S/RES/1234 and UNSC Res 1355 (15 June 2001) UN Doc S/RES/1355.

[206] UNSC Res 1239 (14 May 1999) UN Doc S/RES/1239.

[207] UNSC Res 1261 (30 August 1999) UN Doc S/RES/1261, UNSC Res 1314 (11 August 2000) UN Doc S/RES/1314, UNSC Res 1379 (20 November 2001) UN Doc S/RES/1379,

civilians in armed conflict,[208] Ethiopia–Eritrea conflict,[209] 2003 Gulf War and its consequences,[210] safety of UN personnel,[211] weapons of mass destruction,[212] sexual violence,[213] and women in armed conflict.[214] The invoked IHL treaties were diverse.[215] Two hundred and twelve resolutions mentioned 'international humanitarian law', without specifying whether it is the law of international or non-international armed conflict. In many cases, the resolutions which referred to specific IHL treaties and specific provisions therein also mentioned 'international humanitarian law' at the same time. Thus, in general, the Security Council has invoked IHL in its resolutions mostly at the abstract level.

Leaving aside the general references to the term 'international humanitarian law',[216] the 254 resolutions studied here have invoked IHL mostly

UNSC Res 1460 (30 January 2003) UN Doc S/RES/1460, UNSC Res 1539 (22 April 2004) UN Doc S/RES/1539, UNSC Res 1612 (26 July 2005) UN Doc S/RES/1612, and UNSC Res 1882 (4 August 2009) UN Doc S/RES/1882.

208 UNSC Res 1265 (17 September 1999) UN Doc S/RES/1265, UNSC Res 1296 (19 April 2000) UN Doc S/RES/1296, UNSC Res 1674 (28 April 2006) UN Doc S/RES/1674, UNSC Res 1738 (23 December 2006) UN Doc S/RES/1738, and UNSC Res 1894 (11 November 2009) UN Doc S/RES/1894.

209 UNSC Res 1398 (15 March 2002) UN Doc S/RES/1398, UNSC Res 1430 (14 August 2002) UN Doc S/RES/1430, and UNSC Res 1434 (6 September 2002) UN Doc S/RES/1434.

210 UNSC Res 1472 (28 March 2003) UN Doc S/RES/1472, UNSC Res 1483 (22 May 2003) UN Doc S/RES/1483, UNSC Res 1762 (29 June 2007) UN Doc S/RES/1762, UNSC Res 1770 (10 August 2007) UN Doc S/RES/1770, UNSC Res 1830 (7 August 2008) UN Doc S/RES/1830, and UNSC Res 1936 (5 August 2010) UN Doc S/RES/1936.

211 UNSC Res 1502 (26 August 2003) UN Doc S/RES/1502.

212 UNSC Res 1540 (28 April 2004) UN Doc S/RES/1540 and UNSC Res 1810 (25 April 2008) UN Doc S/RES/1810.

213 UNSC Res 1888 (30 September 2009) UN Doc S/RES/1888.

214 UNSC Res 1889 (5 October 2009) UN Doc S/RES/1889.

215 Convention (II) with Respect to the Laws and Customs of War on Land and Its Annex: Regulations concerning the Laws and Customs of War on Land (adopted 29 July 1899, entered into force 4 September 1900) 187 CTS 429; Convention (IV) Respecting the Laws and Customs of War on Land and Its Annex: Regulations concerning the Laws and Customs of War on Land (hereafter 1907 Hague Regulations) (adopted 18 October 1907, entered into force 26 January 1910) 187 CTS 227; 1925 Gas Protocol; 1949 Geneva Conventions (particularly Third and Fourth); Convention for the Protection of Cultural Property in the Event of Armed Conflict (hereafter 1954 Cultural Property Convention) (adopted 14 May 1954, entered into force 7 August 1956) 249 UNTS 240; 1972 Biological Weapons Convention; 1977 Additional Protocols; Convention on the Rights of the Child (adopted 20 November 1989, entered into force 2 September 1990) 1577 UNTS 3; 1993 Chemical Weapons Convention; 1980 Convention on Conventional Weapons, Amended Protocol II; 1997 Convention on Anti-Personnel Mines; Optional Protocol to the Convention on the Rights of the Child on the Involvement of Children in Armed Conflict (adopted 25 May 2000, entered into force 12 February 2002) 2173 UNTS 222.

216 UNSC Res 468 (8 May 1980) UN Doc S/RES/468, UNSC Res 469 (20 May 1980) UN Doc S/RES/469, UNSC Res 471 (5 June 1980) UN Doc S/RES/471, UNSC Res 476 (30 June 1980) UN Doc S/RES/476, UNSC Res 512 (19 June 1982) UN Doc S/RES/512, UNSC Res 513 (4 July 1982) UN Doc S/RES/513, UNSC Res 515 (29 July 1982) UN Doc S/RES/515, UNSC Res 592 (8 December 1986) UN Doc S/RES/592, UNSC Res 605 (22 December 1987) UN Doc S/RES/605, UNSC Res 607 (5 January 1988) UN Doc S/RES/607, UNSC Res 636 (6 July 1989) UN Doc S/RES/636, UNSC Res 641 (30 August 1989) UN Doc S/RES/641, UNSC Res 687 (3 April 1991) UN Doc S/RES/687, UNSC Res 764 (13 July 1992) UN Doc S/RES/764,

in ways which resemble IHL rules relating to the applicability of IHL, compliance with and enforcement of IHL obligations, and the legal consequences of violations of IHL.

First, the applicability of IHL treaties has been explicitly recognised in relation to armed conflicts between Israel and the neighbouring states,[217] between Iraq and Kuwait,[218] and in the DRC.[219] In other cases, the applicability of IHL treaties has been recognised indirectly by, for example, condemning violations of IHL treaties. In a rare case of the thematic resolutions on children in armed conflict, the Security Council explicitly qualified that the resolution 'does not seek to make any legal determination as to whether situations . . . are or are not armed conflicts within the context of the Geneva Conventions and the Additional Protocols thereto'.[220]

By far the most frequent cases were on the compliance with IHL obligations. As a preliminary step, the Security Council urged states to become parties to certain IHL treaties.[221] However, the most extensive practice

UNSC Res 827 (25 May 1993) UN Doc S/RES/827, UNSC Res 941 (23 September 1994) UN Doc S/RES/941, UNSC Res 955 (8 November 1994) UN Doc S/RES/955, UNSC Res 1031 (15 December 1995) UN Doc S/RES/1031, UNSC Res 1170 (28 May 1998) UN Doc S/RES/1170, UNSC Res 1208 (19 November 1998) UN Doc S/RES/1208, UNSC Res 1239 (14 May 1999) UN Doc S/RES/1239, UNSC Res 1366 (30 August 2001) UN Doc S/RES/1366, UNSC Res 1472 (28 March 2003) UN Doc S/RES/1472, UNSC Res 1509 (19 September 2003) UN Doc S/RES/1509, UNSC Res 1540 (28 April 2004) UN Doc S/RES/1540, and UNSC Res 1674 (28 April 2006) UN Doc S/RES/1674. See also Annex 1.

217 UNSC Res 446 (22 March 1979) UN Doc S/RES/446, UNSC Res 465 (1 March 1980) UN Doc S/RES/465, UNSC Res 471 (5 June 1980) UN Doc S/RES/471, UNSC Res 478 (20 August 1980) UN Doc S/RES/478, UNSC Res 484 (19 December 1980) UN Doc S/RES/484, UNSC Res 497 (17 December 1981) UN Doc S/RES/497, UNSC Res 592 (8 December 1986) UN Doc S/RES/592, UNSC Res 605 (22 December 1987) UN Doc S/RES/605, UNSC Res 607 (5 January 1988) UN Doc S/RES/607, UNSC Res 636 (6 July 1989) UN Doc S/RES/636, UNSC Res 641 (30 August 1989) UN Doc S/RES/641, UNSC Res 670 (25 September 1990) UN Doc S/RES/670, UNSC Res 672 (12 October 1990) UN Doc S/RES/672, UNSC Res 674 (29 October 1990) UN Doc S/RES/674, UNSC Res 726 (6 January 1992) UN Doc S/RES/726, UNSC Res 799 (18 December 1992) UN Doc S/RES/799, and UNSC Res 904 (18 March 1994) UN Doc S/RES/904.

218 UNSC Res 670 (25 September 1990) UN Doc S/RES/670 and UNSC Res 674 (29 October 1990) UN Doc S/RES/674.

219 UNSC Res 1234 (9 April 1999) UN Doc S/RES/1234.

220 UNSC Res 1539 (22 April 2004) UN Doc S/RES/1539, UNSC Res 1612 (26 July 2005) UN Doc S/RES/1612, UNSC Res 1882 (4 August 2009) UN Doc S/RES/1882, UNSC Res 1888 (30 September 2009) UN Doc S/RES/1888, and UNSC Res 1889 (5 October 2009) UN Doc S/RES/1889.

221 UNSC Res 687 (3 April 1991) UN Doc S/RES/687, UNSC Res 1265 (17 September 1999) UN Doc S/RES/1265, UNSC Res 1674 (28 April 2006) UN Doc S/RES/1674, UNSC Res 1738 (23 December 2006) UN Doc S/RES/1738, UNSC Res 1762 (29 June 2007) UN Doc S/RES/1762, UNSC Res 1820 (19 June 2008) UN Doc S/RES/1820, UNSC Res 1888 (30 September 2009) UN Doc S/RES/1888, and UNSC Res 1894 (11 November 2009) UN Doc S/RES/1894. UNSC Res 1296 (19 April 2000) UN Doc S/RES/1296 took note of the entry into force of the 1997 Convention on Anti-Personnel Mines and the 1980 Convention on Conventional Weapons, Amended Protocol II.

is on the obligation to 'respect and to ensure respect' for IHL.[222] This is provided in common Article 1 of the 1949 Geneva Conventions but significantly, the Security Council did not make any distinction between international and non-international armed conflict when it implemented this rule.[223] More significantly, the Security Council itself has recognised its responsibility 'to promote and ensure respect for the principles and rules of international humanitarian law'.[224] In practice, it took the following actions:

- requesting states parties to ensure respect for IHL by conflicting parties;[225]
- reminding the conflicting parties of their IHL obligations;[226]

[222] See generally L Boisson de Chazournes and L Condorelli, 'Common Article 1 of the Geneva Conventions Revisited: Protecting Collective Interests' (2000) 837 *International Review of the Red Cross* 67.

[223] For the customary law status of common Art 1 of the 1949 Geneva Conventions, see Rule 139 in J-M Henckaerts and L Doswald-Beck, *Customary International Humanitarian Law* Vol I: Rules (Geneva, International Committee of the Red Cross and Cambridge, Cambridge University Press, 2005), 495.

[224] UNSC Res 1502 (26 August 2003) UN Doc S/RES/1502.

[225] UNSC Res 681 (20 December 1990) UN Doc S/RES/681 and UNSC Res 1674 (28 April 2006) UN Doc S/RES/1674.

[226] UNSC Res 237 (14 June 1967) UN Doc S/RES/237, UNSC Res 248 (24 March 1968) UN Doc S/RES/248, UNSC Res 271 (15 September 1969) UN Doc S/RES/271, UNSC Res 307 (21 December 1971) UN Doc S/RES/307, UNSC Res 471 (5 June 1980) UN Doc S/RES/471, UNSC Res 484 (19 December 1980) UN Doc S/RES/484, UNSC Res 582 (24 February 1986) UN Doc S/RES/582, UNSC Res 592 (8 December 1986) UN Doc S/RES/592, UNSC Res 605 (22 December 1987) UN Doc S/RES/605, UNSC Res 607 (5 January 1988) UN Doc S/RES/607, UNSC Res 612 (9 May 1988) UN Doc S/RES/612, UNSC Res 666 (13 September 1990) UN Doc S/RES/666, UNSC Res 670 (25 September 1990) UN Doc S/RES/670, UNSC Res 672 (12 October 1990) UN Doc S/RES/672, UNSC Res 674 (29 October 1990) UN Doc S/RES/674, UNSC Res 681 (20 December 1990) UN Doc S/RES/681, UNSC Res 687 (3 April 1991) UN Doc S/RES/687, UNSC Res 764 (13 July 1992) UN Doc S/RES/764, UNSC Res 771 (13 August 1992) UN Doc S/RES/771, UNSC Res 780 (6 October 1992) UN Doc S/RES/780, UNSC Res 787 (16 November 1992) UN Doc S/RES/787, UNSC Res 788 (19 November 1992) UN Doc S/RES/788, UNSC Res 794 (3 December 1992) UN Doc S/RES/794, UNSC Res 808 (22 February 1993) UN Doc S/RES/808, UNSC Res 811 (12 March 1993) UN Doc S/RES/811, UNSC Res 812 (12 March 1993) UN Doc S/RES/812, UNSC Res 813 (26 March 1993) UN Doc S/RES/813, UNSC Res 814 (26 March 1993) UN Doc S/RES/814, UNSC Res 815 (30 March 1993) UN Doc S/RES/815, UNSC Res 819 (16 April 1993) UN Doc S/RES/819, UNSC Res 820 (17 April 1993) UN Doc S/RES/820, UNSC Res 822 (30 April 1993) UN Doc S/RES/822, UNSC Res 834 (1 June 1993) UN Doc S/RES/834, UNSC Res 846 (22 June 1993) UN Doc S/RES/846, UNSC Res 851 (15 July 1993) UN Doc S/RES/851, UNSC Res 853 (29 July 1993) UN Doc S/RES/853, UNSC Res 864 (15 September 1993) UN Doc S/RES/864, UNSC Res 866 (22 September 1993) UN Doc S/RES/866, UNSC Res 911 (21 April 1994) UN Doc S/RES/911, UNSC Res 912 (21 April 1994) UN Doc S/RES/912, UNSC Res 935 (1 July 1994) UN Doc S/RES/935, UNSC Res 941 (23 September 1994) UN Doc S/RES/941, UNSC Res 950 (21 October 1994) UN Doc S/RES/950, UNSC Res 972 (13 January 1995) UN Doc S/RES/972, UNSC Res 985 (13 April 1995) UN Doc S/RES/985, UNSC Res 993 (12 May 1995) UN Doc S/RES/993, UNSC Res 1001 (30 June 1995) UN Doc S/RES/1001, UNSC Res 1009 (10 August 1995) UN Doc S/RES/1009, UNSC Res 1012 (28 August 1995) UN Doc S/RES/1012, UNSC Res 1014 (15 September 1995) UN Doc S/RES/1014, UNSC Res 1019 (9 November 1995) UN Doc S/RES/1019, UNSC Res 1020 (10 November 1995) UN Doc S/RES/1020, UNSC Res 1034 (21 December 1995) UN Doc S/RES/1034, UNSC Res 1036 (12 January 1996) UN Doc S/

- urging the implementation of IHL;[227]

RES/1036, UNSC Res 1041 (29 January 1996) UN Doc S/RES/1041, UNSC Res 1052 (18 April 1996) UN Doc S/RES/1052, UNSC Res 1059 (31 May 1996) UN Doc S/RES/1059, UNSC Res 1071 (30 August 1996) UN Doc S/RES/1071, UNSC Res 1072 (30 August 1996) UN Doc S/RES/1072, UNSC Res 1083 (27 November 1996) UN Doc S/RES/1083, UNSC Res 1097 (18 February 1997) UN Doc S/RES/1097, UNSC Res 1181 (13 July 1998) UN Doc S/RES/1181, UNSC Res 1193 (28 August 1998) UN Doc S/RES/1193, UNSC Res 1213 (3 December 1998) UN Doc S/RES/1213, UNSC Res 1214 (8 December 1998) UN Doc S/RES/1214, UNSC Res 1227 (10 February 1999) UN Doc S/RES/1227, UNSC Res 1231 (11 March 1999) UN Doc S/RES/1231, UNSC Res 1233 (6 April 1999) UN Doc S/RES/1233, UNSC Res 1234 (9 April 1999) UN Doc S/RES/1234, UNSC Res 1258 (6 August 1999) UN Doc S/RES/1258, UNSC Res 1260 (20 August 1999) UN Doc S/RES/1260, UNSC Res 1261 (30 August 1999) UN Doc S/RES/1261, UNSC Res 1265 (17 September 1999) UN Doc S/RES/1265, UNSC Res 1270 (22 October 1999) UN Doc S/RES/1270, UNSC Res 1296 (19 April 2000) UN Doc S/RES/1296, UNSC Res 1297 (12 May 2000) UN Doc S/RES/1297, UNSC Res 1314 (11 August 2000) UN Doc S/RES/1314, UNSC Res 1318 (7 September 2000) UN Doc S/RES/1318, UNSC Res 1344 (15 March 2001) UN Doc S/RES/1344, UNSC Res 1355 (15 June 2001) UN Doc S/RES/1355, UNSC Res 1369 (14 September 2001) UN Doc S/RES/1369, UNSC Res 1378 (14 November 2001) UN Doc S/RES/1378, UNSC Res 1379 (20 November 2001) UN Doc S/RES/1379, UNSC Res 1397 (12 March 2002) UN Doc S/RES/1397, UNSC Res 1398 (15 March 2002) UN Doc S/RES/1398, UNSC Res 1405 (19 April 2002) UN Doc S/RES/1405, UNSC Res 1430 (14 August 2002) UN Doc S/RES/1430, UNSC Res 1435 (24 September 2002) UN Doc S/RES/1435, UNSC Res 1460 (30 January 2003) UN Doc S/RES/1460, UNSC Res 1466 (14 March 2003) UN Doc S/RES/1466, UNSC Res 1472 (28 March 2003) UN Doc S/RES/1472, UNSC Res 1483 (22 May 2003) UN Doc S/RES/1483, UNSC Res 1484 (30 May 2003) UN Doc S/RES/1484, UNSC Res 1493 (28 July 2003) UN Doc S/RES/1493, UNSC Res 1502 (26 August 2003) UN Doc S/RES/1502, UNSC Res 1544 (19 May 2004) UN Doc S/RES/1544, UNSC Res 1545 (21 May 2004) UN Doc S/RES/1545, UNSC Res 1556 (30 July 2004) UN Doc S/RES/1556, UNSC Res 1564 (18 September 2004) UN Doc S/RES/1564, UNSC Res 1565 (1 October 2004) UN Doc S/RES/1565, UNSC Res 1574 (19 November 2004) UN Doc S/RES/1574, UNSC Res 1649 (21 December 2005) UN Doc S/RES/1649, UNSC Res 1662 (23 March 2006) UN Doc S/RES/1662, UNSC Res 1674 (28 April 2006) UN Doc S/RES/1674, UNSC Res 1721 (1 November 2006) UN Doc S/RES/1721, UNSC Res 1738 (23 December 2006) UN Doc S/RES/1738, UNSC Res 1746 (23 March 2007) UN Doc S/RES/1746, UNSC Res 1756 (15 May 2007) UN Doc S/RES/1756, UNSC Res 1762 (29 June 2007) UN Doc S/RES/1762, UNSC Res 1776 (19 September 2007) UN Doc S/RES/1776, UNSC Res 1820 (19 June 2008) UN Doc S/RES/1820, UNSC Res 1888 (30 September 2009) UN Doc S/RES/1888, and UNSC Res 1935 (30 July 2010) UN Doc S/RES/1935.

[227] UNSC Res 598 (20 July 1987) UN Doc S/RES/598, UNSC Res 612 (9 May 1988) UN Doc S/RES/612, UNSC Res 674 (29 October 1990) UN Doc S/RES/674, UNSC Res 681 (20 December 1990) UN Doc S/RES/681, UNSC Res 771 (13 August 1992) UN Doc S/RES/771, UNSC Res 1318 (7 September 2000) UN Doc S/RES/1318, UNSC Res 1359 (29 June 2001) UN Doc S/RES/1359, UNSC Res 1369 (14 September 2001) UN Doc S/RES/1369, UNSC Res 1398 (15 March 2002) UN Doc S/RES/1398, UNSC Res 1429 (30 July 2002) UN Doc S/RES/1429, UNSC Res 1430 (14 August 2002) UN Doc S/RES/1430, UNSC Res 1434 (6 September 2002) UN Doc S/RES/1434, UNSC Res 1479 (13 May 2003) UN Doc S/RES/1479, UNSC Res 1495 (31 July 2003) UN Doc S/RES/1495, UNSC Res 1502 (26 August 2003) UN Doc S/RES/1502, UNSC Res 1540 (28 April 2004) UN Doc S/RES/1540, UNSC Res 1556 (30 July 2004) UN Doc S/RES/1556, UNSC Res 1564 (18 September 2004) UN Doc S/RES/1564, UNSC Res 1565 (1 October 2004) UN Doc S/RES/1565, UNSC Res 1598 (28 April 2005) UN Doc S/RES/1598, UNSC Res 1649 (21 December 2005) UN Doc S/RES/1649, UNSC Res 1653 (27 January 2006) UN Doc S/RES/1653, UNSC Res 1756 (15 May 2007) UN Doc S/RES/1756, UNSC Res 1765 (16 July 2007) UN Doc S/RES/1765, UNSC Res 1770 (10 August 2007) UN Doc S/RES/1770, UNSC Res 1772 (20 August 2007) UN Doc S/RES/1772, UNSC Res 1778 (25 September 2007) UN Doc S/RES/1778, UNSC Res 1787 (10 December 2007) UN Doc S/RES/1787, UNSC Res 1790 (18 December 2007) UN Doc S/RES/1790, UNSC Res 1794 (21 December 2007) UN Doc S/RES/1794, UNSC Res 1795 (15 January 2008) UN Doc

- recognising the implementation of IHL by states;[228]
- establishing IHL violations;[229]
- condemning and deploring IHL violations;[230] and

S/RES/1795, UNSC Res 1801 (20 February 2008) UN Doc S/RES/1801, UNSC Res 1805 (20 March 2008) UN Doc S/RES/1805, UNSC Res 1806 (20 March 2008) UN Doc S/RES/1806, UNSC Res 1807 (31 March 2008) UN Doc S/RES/1807, UNSC Res 1812 (30 April 2008) UN Doc S/RES/1812, UNSC Res 1813 (30 April 2008) UN Doc S/RES/1813, UNSC Res 1820 (19 June 2008) UN Doc S/RES/1820, UNSC Res 1826 (29 July 2008) UN Doc S/RES/1826, UNSC Res 1830 (7 August 2008) UN Doc S/RES/1830, UNSC Res 1833 (22 September 2008) UN Doc S/RES/1833, UNSC Res 1843 (20 November 2008) UN Doc S/RES/1843, UNSC Res 1851 (16 December 2008) UN Doc S/RES/1851, UNSC Res 1856 (22 December 2008) UN Doc S/RES/1856, UNSC Res 1857 (22 December 2008) UN Doc S/RES/1857, UNSC Res 1861 (14 January 2009) UN Doc S/RES/1861, UNSC Res 1863 (16 January 2009) UN Doc S/RES/1863, UNSC Res 1865 (27 January 2009) UN Doc S/RES/1865, UNSC Res 1868 (23 March 2009) UN Doc S/RES/1868, UNSC Res 1870 (20 May 2009) UN Doc S/RES/1870, UNSC Res 1880 (30 July 2009) UN Doc S/RES/1880, UNSC Res 1881 (6 August 2009) UN Doc S/RES/1881, UNSC Res 1882 (4 August 2009) UN Doc S/RES/1882, UNSC Res 1883 (7 August 2009) UN Doc S/RES/1883, UNSC Res 1890 (8 October 2009) UN Doc S/RES/1890, UNSC Res 1896 (7 December 2009) UN Doc S/RES/1896, UNSC Res 1906 (23 December 2009) UN Doc S/RES/1906, UNSC Res 1917 (22 March 2010) UN Doc S/RES/1917, UNSC Res 1919 (29 April 2010) UN Doc S/RES/1919, UNSC Res 1923 (25 May 2010) UN Doc S/RES/1923, UNSC Res 1925 (28 May 2010) UN Doc S/RES/1925, and UNSC Res 1936 (5 August 2010) UN Doc S/RES/1936.

[228] UNSC Res 459 (19 December 1979) UN Doc S/RES/459, UNSC Res 686 (2 March 1991) UN Doc S/RES/686, UNSC Res 1434 (6 September 2002) UN Doc S/RES/1434, and UNSC Res 1756 (15 May 2007) UN Doc S/RES/1756.

[229] UNSC Res 465 (1 March 1980) UN Doc S/RES/465, UNSC Res 469 (20 May 1980) UN Doc S/RES/469, UNSC Res 471 (5 June 1980) UN Doc S/RES/471, UNSC Res 476 (30 June 1980) UN Doc S/RES/476, UNSC Res 582 (24 February 1986) UN Doc S/RES/582, UNSC Res 598 (20 July 1987) UN Doc S/RES/598, UNSC Res 612 (9 May 1988) UN Doc S/RES/612, UNSC Res 620 (26 August 1988) UN Doc S/RES/620, UNSC Res 670 (25 September 1990) UN Doc S/RES/670, UNSC Res 674 (29 October 1990) UN Doc S/RES/674, UNSC Res 681 (20 December 1990) UN Doc S/RES/681, UNSC Res 694 (24 May 1991) UN Doc S/RES/694, UNSC Res 799 (18 December 1992) UN Doc S/RES/799, UNSC Res 819 (16 April 1993) UN Doc S/RES/819, UNSC Res 851 (15 July 1993) UN Doc S/RES/851, UNSC Res 864 (15 September 1993) UN Doc S/RES/864, UNSC Res 941 (23 September 1994) UN Doc S/RES/941, and UNSC Res 1034 (21 December 1995) UN Doc S/RES/1034.

[230] UNSC Res 540 (31 October 1983) UN Doc S/RES/540, UNSC Res 582 (24 February 1986) UN Doc S/RES/582, UNSC Res 598 (20 July 1987) UN Doc S/RES/598, UNSC Res 612 (9 May 1988) UN Doc S/RES/612, UNSC Res 620 (26 August 1988) UN Doc S/RES/620, UNSC Res 674 (29 October 1990) UN Doc S/RES/674, UNSC Res 681 (20 December 1990) UN Doc S/RES/681, UNSC Res 694 (24 May 1991) UN Doc S/RES/694, UNSC Res 771 (13 August 1992) UN Doc S/RES/771, UNSC Res 780 (6 October 1992) UN Doc S/RES/780, UNSC Res 787 (16 November 1992) UN Doc S/RES/787, UNSC Res 794 (3 December 1992) UN Doc S/RES/794, UNSC Res 799 (18 December 1992) UN Doc S/RES/799, UNSC Res 804 (29 January 1993) UN Doc S/RES/804, UNSC Res 808 (22 February 1993) UN Doc S/RES/808, UNSC Res 814 (26 March 1993) UN Doc S/RES/814, UNSC Res 819 (16 April 1993) UN Doc S/RES/819, UNSC Res 820 (17 April 1993) UN Doc S/RES/820, UNSC Res 827 (25 May 1993) UN Doc S/RES/827, UNSC Res 836 (4 June 1993) UN Doc S/RES/836, UNSC Res 844 (18 June 1993) UN Doc S/RES/844, UNSC Res 876 (19 October 1993) UN Doc S/RES/876, UNSC Res 918 (17 May 1994) UN Doc S/RES/918, UNSC Res 935 (1 July 1994) UN Doc S/RES/935, UNSC Res 941 (23 September 1994) UN Doc S/RES/941, UNSC Res 950 (21 October 1994) UN Doc S/RES/950, UNSC Res 955 (8 November 1994) UN Doc S/RES/955, UNSC Res 1009 (10 August 1995) UN Doc S/RES/1009, UNSC Res 1010 (10 August 1995) UN Doc S/RES/1010, UNSC Res 1012 (28 August 1995) UN Doc S/RES/1012, UNSC Res 1019 (9 November 1995) UN Doc S/RES/1019, UNSC Res 1034 (21 December 1995) UN Doc S/RES/1034, UNSC Res 1076 (22 October 1996)

- demanding an end to IHL violations.[231]

UN Doc S/RES/1076, UNSC Res 1080 (15 November 1996) UN Doc S/RES/1080, UNSC Res 1193 (28 August 1998) UN Doc S/RES/1193, UNSC Res 1199 (23 September 1998) UN Doc S/RES/1199, UNSC Res 1214 (8 December 1998) UN Doc S/RES/1214, UNSC Res 1231 (11 March 1999) UN Doc S/RES/1231, UNSC Res 1234 (9 April 1999) UN Doc S/RES/1234, UNSC Res 1264 (15 September 1999) UN Doc S/RES/1264, UNSC Res 1265 (17 September 1999) UN Doc S/RES/1265, UNSC Res 1267 (15 October 1999) UN Doc S/RES/1267, UNSC Res 1272 (25 October 1999) UN Doc S/RES/1272, UNSC Res 1279 (30 November 1999) UN Doc S/RES/1279, UNSC Res 1333 (19 December 2000) UN Doc S/RES/1333, UNSC Res 1344 (15 March 2001) UN Doc S/RES/1344, UNSC Res 1378 (14 November 2001) UN Doc S/RES/1378, UNSC Res 1400 (28 March 2002) UN Doc S/RES/1400, UNSC Res 1464 (4 February 2003) UN Doc S/RES/1464, UNSC Res 1468 (20 March 2003) UN Doc S/RES/1468, UNSC Res 1493 (28 July 2003) UN Doc S/RES/1493, UNSC Res 1502 (26 August 2003) UN Doc S/RES/1502, UNSC Res 1545 (21 May 2004) UN Doc S/RES/1545, UNSC Res 1547 (11 June 2004) UN Doc S/RES/1547, UNSC Res 1556 (30 July 2004) UN Doc S/RES/1556, UNSC Res 1565 (1 October 2004) UN Doc S/RES/1565, UNSC Res 1574 (19 November 2004) UN Doc S/RES/1574, UNSC Res 1577 (1 December 2004) UN Doc S/RES/1577, UNSC Res 1590 (24 March 2005) UN Doc S/RES/1590, UNSC Res 1591 (29 March 2005) UN Doc S/RES/1591, UNSC Res 1592 (30 March 2005) UN Doc S/RES/1592, UNSC Res 1602 (31 May 2005) UN Doc S/RES/1602, UNSC Res 1621 (6 September 2005) UN Doc S/RES/1621, UNSC Res 1633 (21 October 2005) UN Doc S/RES/1633, UNSC Res 1635 (28 October 2005) UN Doc S/RES/1635, UNSC Res 1643 (15 December 2005) UN Doc S/RES/1643, UNSC Res 1649 (21 December 2005) UN Doc S/RES/1649, UNSC Res 1653 (27 January 2006) UN Doc S/RES/1653, UNSC Res 1711 (29 September 2006) UN Doc S/RES/1711, UNSC Res 1736 (22 December 2006) UN Doc S/RES/1736, UNSC Res 1756 (15 May 2007) UN Doc S/RES/1756, UNSC Res 1765 (16 July 2007) UN Doc S/RES/1765, UNSC Res 1769 (31 July 2007) UN Doc S/RES/1769, UNSC Res 1778 (25 September 2007) UN Doc S/RES/1778, UNSC Res 1782 (29 October 2007) UN Doc S/RES/1782, UNSC Res 1794 (21 December 2007) UN Doc S/RES/1794, UNSC Res 1795 (15 January 2008) UN Doc S/RES/1795, UNSC Res 1804 (13 March 2008) UN Doc S/RES/1804, UNSC Res 1813 (30 April 2008) UN Doc S/RES/1813, UNSC Res 1826 (29 July 2008) UN Doc S/RES/1826, UNSC Res 1828 (31 July 2008) UN Doc S/RES/1828, UNSC Res 1834 (24 September 2008) UN Doc S/RES/1834, UNSC Res 1842 (29 October 2008) UN Doc S/RES/1842, UNSC Res 1861 (14 January 2009) UN Doc S/RES/1861, UNSC Res 1865 (27 January 2009) UN Doc S/RES/1865, UNSC Res 1881 (6 August 2009) UN Doc S/RES/1881, UNSC Res 1893 (29 October 2009) UN Doc S/RES/1893, UNSC Res 1894 (11 November 2009) UN Doc S/RES/1894, UNSC Res 1896 (7 December 2009) UN Doc S/RES/1896, UNSC Res 1906 (23 December 2009) UN Doc S/RES/1906, UNSC Res 1910 (28 January 2010) UN Doc S/RES/1910, UNSC Res 1911 (28 January 2010) UN Doc S/RES/1911, UNSC Res 1923 (25 May 2010) UN Doc S/RES/1923, UNSC Res 1925 (28 May 2010) UN Doc S/RES/1925, UNSC Res 1933 (30 June 2010) UN Doc S/RES/1933, and UNSC Res 1935 (30 July 2010) UN Doc S/RES/1935.

[231] UNSC Res 612 (9 May 1988) UN Doc S/RES/612, UNSC Res 674 (29 October 1990) UN Doc S/RES/674, UNSC Res 771 (13 August 1992) UN Doc S/RES/771, UNSC Res 780 (6 October 1992) UN Doc S/RES/780, UNSC Res 794 (3 December 1992) UN Doc S/RES/794, UNSC Res 808 (22 February 1993) UN Doc S/RES/808, UNSC Res 814 (26 March 1993) UN Doc S/RES/814, UNSC Res 876 (19 October 1993) UN Doc S/RES/876, UNSC Res 874 (14 October 1993) UN Doc S/RES/874, UNSC Res 881 (4 November 1993) UN Doc S/RES/881, UNSC Res 1019 (9 November 1995) UN Doc S/RES/1019, UNSC Res 1034 (21 December 1995) UN Doc S/RES/1034, UNSC Res 1193 (28 August 1998) UN Doc S/RES/1193, UNSC Res 1344 (15 March 2001) UN Doc S/RES/1344, UNSC Res 1464 (4 February 2003) UN Doc S/RES/1464, UNSC Res 1479 (13 May 2003) UN Doc S/RES/1479, UNSC Res 1493 (28 July 2003) UN Doc S/RES/1493, UNSC Res 1528 (27 February 2004) UN Doc S/RES/1528, UNSC Res 1556 (30 July 2004) UN Doc S/RES/1556, UNSC Res 1564 (18 September 2004) UN Doc S/RES/1564, UNSC Res 1590 (24 March 2005) UN Doc S/RES/1590, UNSC Res 1591 (29 March 2005) UN Doc S/RES/1591, UNSC Res 1633 (21 October 2005) UN Doc S/RES/1633, UNSC Res 1828 (31 July 2008) UN Doc S/RES/1828, UNSC Res 1856 (22 December 2008) UN Doc S/RES/1856, UNSC Res 1894 (11 November 2009) UN Doc S/RES/1894, UNSC Res 1910 (28 January 2010) UN Doc S/RES/1910, and UNSC Res 1925 (28 May 2010) UN Doc S/RES/1925.

In certain specific cases, the Security Council provided more detailed guidance to implement common Article 1 of the 1949 Geneva Conventions according to each case.[232] As a part of implementing this rule, the dissemination of IHL has been highlighted in some cases.[233]

[232] See the following references:

- Requesting the UN Secretary-General to assist states and regional organisations to implement IHL: UNSC Res 1208 (19 November 1998) UN Doc S/RES/1208 (this was in relation to African states, OAU [now African Union], and other subregional organisations).
- Requesting the UN Secretary-General to convene a conference of state parties to IHL treaties: UNSC Res 681 (20 December 1990) UN Doc S/RES/681 (this was proposed in relation to the Occupied Palestinian Territories).
- Inviting the UN Secretary-General to report the Security Council on serious IHL violations: UNSC Res 1366 (30 August 2001) UN Doc S/RES/1366 (thematic resolution on prevention of armed conflict).
- Authorising UN forces to monitor respect for IHL: UNSC Res 866 (22 September 1993) UN Doc S/RES/866 (on UNOMIL in Liberia to report on any major violations of IHL to the Secretary-General), UNSC Res 1181 (13 July 1998) UN Doc S/RES/1181 (on UNOMSIL in Sierra Leone to assist in monitoring respect for IHL), UNSC Res 1542 (30 April 2004) UN Doc S/RES/1542 (on MINUSTAH in Haiti to assist the government in the investigation of IHL violations), and UNSC Res 1565 (1 October 2004) UN Doc S/RES/1565 (on MONUC in the DRC to assist the government to ensure that those responsible for IHL violations are brought to justice).
- Noting that multinational forces should comply with IHL: UNSC Res 1546 (8 June 2004) UN Doc S/RES/1546, UNSC Res 1637 (11 November 2005) UN Doc S/RES/1637, and UNSC Res 1723 (28 November 2006) UN Doc S/RES/1723 (all on the multinational forces in Iraq since 2003).
- Noting that counter-terrorism measures should be consistent with IHL: UNSC Res 1269 (19 October 1999) UN Doc S/RES/1269, UNSC Res 1535 (26 March 2004) UN Doc S/RES/1535, UNSC Res 1566 (8 October 2004) UN Doc S/RES/1566, UNSC Res 1624 (14 September 2005) UN Doc S/RES/1624, UNSC Res 1787 (10 December 2007) UN Doc S/RES/1787, UNSC Res 1805 (20 March 2008) UN Doc S/RES/1805, UNSC Res 1822 (30 June 2008) UN Doc S/RES/1822, and UNSC Res 1904 (17 December 2009) UN Doc S/RES/1904 (all were thematic resolutions on counter-terrorism).
- Noting the possibility to respond by UN field missions to incitement of IHL violation by media broadcast: UNSC Res 1296 (19 April 2000) UN Doc S/RES/1296 (thematic resolution on civilians in armed conflict).
- Urging parties to consult the UN in the future to include provisions on compliance with IHL in peace agreements: UNSC Res 1327 (13 November 2000) UN Doc S/RES/1327 (thematic resolution on peacekeeping operations).
- Requesting that IHL record should be taken into account when selecting new government officials: UNSC Res 1468 (20 March 2003) UN Doc S/RES/1468, UNSC Res 1592 (30 March 2005) UN Doc S/RES/1592 (on the DRC at the time when the transitional government was still in the course of formation), UNSC Res 1756 (15 May 2007) UN Doc S/RES/1756, UNSC Res 1794 (21 December 2007) UN Doc S/RES/1794, UNSC Res 1856 (22 December 2008) UN Doc S/RES/1856, and UNSC Res 1888 (30 September 2009) UN Doc S/RES/1888.

[233] For the customary law status of this obligation, see Rules 142 and 143 in Henckaerts and Doswald-Beck, *Customary International Humanitarian Law* Vol I, 501 and 505. See the following references:

- Underlining the importance of the dissemination of IHL: UNSC Res 1265 (17 September 1999) UN Doc S/RES/1265, UNSC Res 1296 (19 April 2000) UN Doc S/RES/1296, and UNSC Res 1894 (11 November 2009) UN Doc S/RES/1894 (both thematic resolution on civilians in armed conflict).
- Requesting the UN Secretary-General to train peacekeepers in IHL: UNSC Res 1265 (17 September 1999) UN Doc S/RES/1265 (thematic resolution on civilians in armed conflict),

In a few cases, the Security Council indicated that it would adopt measures directly by itself to enforce IHL rather than calling upon the UN Member States to do so. In the 1980–88 Iran–Iraq War, the Security Council decided to 'consider immediately . . . appropriate and effective measures . . . should there be any future use of chemical weapons in violation of international law'.[234] With regard to Côte d'Ivoire, the Security Council noted that 'it is fully prepared to impose targeted measures against persons . . . Responsible for serious violations of . . . international humanitarian law'.[235] This aspect will be discussed further in a later chapter.[236]

Legal consequences of violations of IHL, particularly war crimes, are another area where Security Council resolutions have played a major role. Above all, the establishment of *ad hoc* international and hybrid criminal courts and tribunals is well known.[237] It also developed the substantive and procedural aspects of international criminal law. In a few cases, it recognised that serious violations of IHL entail both state responsibility[238] and individual criminal responsibility.[239] Moreover, in a number of cases,

UNSC Res 1270 (22 October 1999) UN Doc S/RES/1270 (on UNAMSIL in Sierra Leone), UNSC Res 1272 (25 October 1999) UN Doc S/RES/1272 (on UNTAET in Timor-Leste), and UNSC Res 1379 (20 November 2001) UN Doc S/RES/1379 (thematic resolution on children in armed conflict).

- Noting that UN forces should include media component to disseminate IHL: UNSC Res 1296 (19 April 2000) UN Doc S/RES/1296 and UNSC Res 1674 (28 April 2006) UN Doc S/RES/1674 (both thematic resolution on civilians in armed conflict).
- Providing mandate to UN forces to train national armed forces: UNSC Res 1756 (15 May 2007) UN Doc S/RES/1756 and UNSC Res 1856 (22 December 2008) UN Doc S/RES/1856 (on DRC).
- Role of the ICRC and other components of the International Red Cross and Red Crescent Movement in the dissemination of IHL: UNSC Res 1894 (11 November 2009) UN Doc S/RES/1894.

[234] UNSC Res 620 (26 August 1988) UN Doc S/RES/620.

[235] UNSC Res 1727 (15 December 2006) UN Doc S/RES/1727 and UNSC Res 1782 (29 October 2007) UN Doc S/RES/1782.

[236] See section 4.IV.D.

[237] UNSC Res 808 (22 February 1993) UN Doc S/RES/808 (ICTY), UNSC Res 827 (25 May 1993) UN Doc S/RES/827 (ICTY), UNSC Res 955 (8 November 1994) UN Doc S/RES/955 (ICTR), and UNSC Res 1315 (14 August 2000) UN Doc S/RES/1315 (Special Court for Sierra Leone).

[238] UNSC Res 471 (5 June 1980) UN Doc S/RES/471, UNSC Res 674 (29 October 1990) UN Doc S/RES/674, UNSC Res 686 (2 March 1991) UN Doc S/RES/686, UNSC Res 687 (3 April 1991) UN Doc S/RES/687, and UNSC Res 827 (25 May 1993) UN Doc S/RES/827.

[239] UNSC Res 670 (25 September 1990) UN Doc S/RES/670, UNSC Res 674 (29 October 1990) UN Doc S/RES/674, UNSC Res 764 (13 July 1992) UN Doc S/RES/764, UNSC Res 771 (13 August 1992) UN Doc S/RES/771, UNSC Res 780 (6 October 1992) UN Doc S/RES/780, UNSC Res 794 (3 December 1992) UN Doc S/RES/794, UNSC Res 808 (22 February 1993) UN Doc S/RES/808, UNSC Res 814 (26 March 1993) UN Doc S/RES/814, UNSC Res 819 (16 April 1993) UN Doc S/RES/819, UNSC Res 820 (17 April 1993) UN Doc S/RES/820, UNSC Res 827 (25 May 1993) UN Doc S/RES/827, UNSC Res 859 (24 August 1993) UN Doc S/RES/859, UNSC Res 913 (22 April 1994) UN Doc S/RES/913, UNSC Res 935 (1 July 1994) UN Doc S/RES/935, UNSC Res 941 (23 September 1994) UN Doc S/RES/941, UNSC Res 955 (8 November 1994) UN Doc S/RES/955, UNSC Res 1009 (10 August 1995) UN Doc S/RES/1009, UNSC Res 1012 (28 August 1995) UN Doc S/RES/1012, UNSC Res 1034 (21 December 1995) UN Doc S/RES/1034, UNSC Res 1072 (30 August 1996) UN Doc S/RES/1072, UNSC Res

the Security Council urged the investigation and prosecution of IHL violations in general[240] or specifically by the UN Secretary-General,[241] UN forces,[242] or governments.[243] On international co-operation, it has requested the collection[244] and protection[245] of evidence of IHL violations and in a rare case on the Sudan, the Security Council demanded the Sudanese government to 'submit to the African Union Mission . . . the names of those arrested for . . . violations of international humanitarian law'.[246] In another case on the DRC, the Security Council decided that the prohibition on the movement of certain persons did not apply to persons who were 'participating in efforts to bring to justice perpetrators of grave violations of

1193 (28 August 1998) UN Doc S/RES/1193, UNSC Res 1214 (8 December 1998) UN Doc S/RES/1214, UNSC Res 1264 (15 September 1999) UN Doc S/RES/1264, UNSC Res 1272 (25 October 1999) UN Doc S/RES/1272, UNSC Res 1315 (14 August 2000) UN Doc S/RES/1315, UNSC Res 1355 (15 June 2001) UN Doc S/RES/1355, UNSC Res 1649 (21 December 2005) UN Doc S/RES/1649, and UNSC Res 1711 (29 September 2006) UN Doc S/RES/1711.

240 UNSC Res 1355 (15 June 2001) UN Doc S/RES/1355, UNSC Res 1464 (4 February 2003) UN Doc S/RES/1464, UNSC Res 1468 (20 March 2003) UN Doc S/RES/1468, UNSC Res 1479 (13 May 2003) UN Doc S/RES/1479, UNSC Res 1484 (30 May 2003) UN Doc S/RES/1484, UNSC Res 1493 (28 July 2003) UN Doc S/RES/1493, UNSC Res 1509 (19 September 2003) UN Doc S/RES/1509, UNSC Res 1574 (19 November 2004) UN Doc S/RES/1574, UNSC Res 1602 (31 May 2005) UN Doc S/RES/1602, UNSC Res 1635 (28 October 2005) UN Doc S/RES/1635, UNSC Res 1649 (21 December 2005) UN Doc S/RES/1649, UNSC Res 1711 (29 September 2006) UN Doc S/RES/1711, UNSC Res 1736 (22 December 2006) UN Doc S/RES/1736, UNSC Res 1738 (23 December 2006) UN Doc S/RES/1738, UNSC Res 1756 (15 May 2007) UN Doc S/RES/1756, UNSC Res 1794 (21 December 2007) UN Doc S/RES/1794, UNSC Res 1888 (30 September 2009) UN Doc S/RES/1888, and UNSC Res 1894 (11 November 2009) UN Doc S/RES/1894.

241 UNSC Res 620 (26 August 1988) UN Doc S/RES/620, UNSC Res 780 (6 October 1992) UN Doc S/RES/780, UNSC Res 787 (16 November 1992) UN Doc S/RES/787, UNSC Res 808 (22 February 1993) UN Doc S/RES/808, UNSC Res 814 (26 March 1993) UN Doc S/RES/814, UNSC Res 827 (25 May 1993) UN Doc S/RES/827, UNSC Res 918 (17 May 1994) UN Doc S/RES/918, UNSC Res 935 (1 July 1994) UN Doc S/RES/935, UNSC Res 1019 (9 November 1995) UN Doc S/RES/1019, UNSC Res 1034 (21 December 1995) UN Doc S/RES/1034, UNSC Res 1214 (8 December 1998) UN Doc S/RES/1214, UNSC Res 1355 (15 June 2001) UN Doc S/RES/1355, UNSC Res 1556 (30 July 2004) UN Doc S/RES/1556, and UNSC Res 1564 (18 September 2004) UN Doc S/RES/1564.

242 UNSC Res 1856 (22 December 2008) UN Doc S/RES/1856.

243 UNSC Res 1019 (9 November 1995) UN Doc S/RES/1019, UNSC Res 1231 (11 March 1999) UN Doc S/RES/1231, UNSC Res 1468 (20 March 2003) UN Doc S/RES/1468, UNSC Res 1528 (27 February 2004) UN Doc S/RES/1528, UNSC Res 1556 (30 July 2004) UN Doc S/RES/1556, UNSC Res 1565 (1 October 2004) UN Doc S/RES/1565, UNSC Res 1633 (21 October 2005) UN Doc S/RES/1633, UNSC Res 1649 (21 December 2005) UN Doc S/RES/1649, UNSC Res 1653 (27 January 2006) UN Doc S/RES/1653, UNSC Res 1738 (23 December 2006) UN Doc S/RES/1738, and UNSC Res 1756 (15 May 2007) UN Doc S/RES/1756.

244 UNSC Res 674 (29 October 1990) UN Doc S/RES/674, UNSC Res 771 (13 August 1992) UN Doc S/RES/771, UNSC Res 780 (6 October 1992) UN Doc S/RES/780, UNSC Res 935 (1 July 1994) UN Doc S/RES/935, UNSC Res 1010 (10 August 1995) UN Doc S/RES/1010, and UNSC Res 1906 (23 December 2009) UN Doc S/RES/1906.

245 UNSC Res 1019 (9 November 1995) UN Doc S/RES/1019.

246 UNSC Res 1564 (18 September 2004) UN Doc S/RES/1564.

. . . international humanitarian law'.[247] In one case, the Security Council encouraged the use of the International Fact-Finding Commission established by Article 90 of the 1977 First Additional Protocol.[248]

Besides these resolutions which relate to the obligation to implement IHL, there were two minor cases. First, IHL violations were invoked to impose non-military enforcement action. In several cases, the Security Council demanded states to prevent the entry or transit of those who violated IHL.[249] The 1980–88 Iran–Iraq War was a rare case since the Security Council called upon states to control exports of chemical-weapons-related products to the conflicting parties once the IHL violation for using chemical weapons was established.[250] Secondly, widespread IHL violations were considered as a threat to international peace and security.[251]

On the other hand, the 593 resolutions studied here contain clauses which reflect certain IHL rules (the second type). Unlike the first type of resolutions examined above, these resolutions reflected rules in almost all areas of IHL such as specifically protected persons and objects, treatment of civilians and persons hors de combat, methods of warfare, means of warfare, and implementation of IHL. For a more detailed categorisation of the Security Council resolution according to specific IHL rules, see Annex 2.

The IHL clauses vary from detailed and precise ones to abstract ones. An example of a relatively detailed and precise formulation is resolution 664 on the 1991 Gulf War:

> *The Security Council* . . . *Demands* that Iraq permit and facilitate the immediate departure from Kuwait and Iraq of third-state nationals and grant immediate and continuing access of consular officials to such nationals . . . *Also demands* that Iraq take no action to jeopardize the safety, security or health of such nationals.[252]

This reflects Articles 35 and 36 of the 1949 Fourth Geneva Convention, which provide the right of aliens to leave the territory of a party to the conflict and to ensure satisfactory conditions of safety, hygiene, sanitation and food during their departure. On the other hand, an example of a rela-

[247] UNSC Res 1807 (31 March 2008) UN Doc S/RES/1807.

[248] UNSC Res 1894 (11 November 2009) UN Doc S/RES/1894.

[249] UNSC Res 1572 (15 November 2004) UN Doc S/RES/1572, UNSC Res 1591 (29 March 2005) UN Doc S/RES/1591, UNSC Res 1633 (21 October 2005) UN Doc S/RES/1633, UNSC Res 1643 (15 December 2005) UN Doc S/RES/1643, UNSC Res 1649 (21 December 2005) UN Doc S/RES/1649, UNSC Res 1807 (31 March 2008) UN Doc S/RES/1807, UNSC Res 1842 (29 October 2008) UN Doc S/RES/1842, UNSC Res 1857 (22 December 2008) UN Doc S/RES/1857, and UNSC Res 1893 (29 October 2009) UN Doc S/RES/1893.

[250] UNSC Res 620 (26 August 1988) UN Doc S/RES/620.

[251] UNSC Res 1296 (19 April 2000) UN Doc S/RES/1296. See also UNSC Res 1314 (11 August 2000) UN Doc S/RES/1314, UNSC Res 1674 (28 April 2006) UN Doc S/RES/1674, UNSC Res 1738 (23 December 2006) UN Doc S/RES/1738, and UNSC Res 1894 (11 November 2009) UN Doc S/RES/1894. All were thematic resolutions on civilians in armed conflict.

[252] UNSC Res 664 (18 August 1990) UN Doc S/RES/664, paras 1 and 2.

tively abstract clause is resolution 403 on attacks by Southern Rhodesia on Botswana. In this resolution, the Security Council noted that it was '*Deeply* grieved and concerned at the loss of human life and damage to property caused by the acts of the illegal régime in Southern Rhodesia against Botswana'.[253] This paragraph is unclear on many points to ascertain whether it implements IHL in any way, for example, whether the preambular paragraph has any significance in implementing IHL; whether it imposes any obligation on a conflicting party; and whether 'human life' and 'property' refer only to civilians and civilian objects or to both civilians and combatants as well as to civilian objects and military objectives. Thus, many Security Council resolutions contain clauses which reflect certain IHL rules but the precision of these clauses varies greatly from detailed and precise ones to abstract ones.

In short, Security Council practice with regard to IHL has been diverse in its usage of IHL and large in the number of resolutions referring or reflecting IHL. There are two types of IHL-related resolutions: 1) those which refer to the term 'international humanitarian law'; IHL treaties or specific provisions in IHL treaties; and 2) those which contain clauses which reflect certain IHL rules. The references to IHL have been generally at the abstract level and in the majority of resolutions, references are only made to 'international humanitarian law'. References to IHL treaties and specific provisions in IHL treaties are exceptional. On the other hand, the clauses which reflect certain IHL rules can be detailed and precise, or abstract, depending on the resolution.

B. Specific Issues Arising from Security Council Resolutions Related to IHL

Both military and non-military enforcement measures authorised by the Security Council under Chapter VII can have an impact on the relationship between *jus ad bellum* and *jus in bello*.

With regard to military enforcement action, the Security Council has given various mandates to UN forces. Nowadays, the mandates are not only limited to keeping the conflicting parties apart but also protecting civilians and engaging in a full-scale armed conflict with the aggressors. The increasing involvement of UN forces into armed conflict (both international and non-international) has first raised the question of the applicability of IHL to UN forces. This question will be discussed in detail later. However, the essence of the question is whether the UN as an international organisation can be bound by IHL when the UN is not a party to any IHL treaty. This problem arises in the case of the so-called 'UN peacekeeping operations'.

[253] UNSC Res 403 (14 January 1977) UN Doc S/RES/403, Preamble.

It does not arise in the case of states authorised to use force by the Security Council, such as the multinational forces in the 1991 Gulf War, in which case IHL applies to each state participating in the use of force.

IHL rules on means and methods of warfare are obviously the most relevant rules to military enforcement actions under Chapter VII, in particular when they are undertaken by states authorised to use force. A clear-cut case is the 1991 Gulf War when a full-scale armed conflict took place between the multinational forces and Iraq where IHL rules regulating which weapons can be used, and how, applied. There has not been a Chapter VII use of force that paralleled that in the 1991 Gulf War, but the increasing involvement of UN peacekeeping operations in armed conflict in recent years proved that the IHL rules on means and methods of warfare are also applicable to UN peacekeeping operations. At the same time, *jus ad bellum*, including Security Council resolutions, imposes limits on the use of force by states and UN peacekeeping operations. The rules of *jus ad bellum* regulating the use of force under Chapter VII will also be examined to understand the whole range of rules imposing limits on the use of force under Chapter VII.

More specific aspects of the military enforcement action under Chapter VII will also be discussed. Protection of civilians has been one of the most frequent mandates of UN forces. IHL also provides a wide range of protection for civilians. A later section will point out the differences and similarities in the two types of protection of civilians. At the same time, the potential danger of having UN forces protecting civilians will be discussed, particularly when the UN forces themselves are parties to the armed conflict.

Protection of humanitarian personnel and humanitarian aid has also been a frequent mandate of UN forces. This again raises concerns as to the neutrality and impartiality expected from humanitarian personnel and humanitarian aid, particularly when UN forces are parties to the concerned armed conflict. It is also a dilemma for IHL and UN forces since they require the conflicting parties to respect and protect humanitarian personnel and aid. At a time when humanitarian personnel and aid are under attack in many armed conflict situations, states and UN forces and even humanitarian organisations themselves may be tempted to resort to force to protect humanitarian personnel and aid. However, there are still conflicting views as to whether force should be used to protect humanitarian personnel and aid at the expense of neutrality and impartiality, which are the cornerstones of the work of humanitarian organisations.

The status of captured UN force personnel is also another complicated area. While it is generally accepted that troops of the states authorised to use force under Chapter VII, and which are engaged in an international armed conflict, can be prisoners of war and benefit from the 1949 Third Geneva Convention, the status of captured personnel of UN peacekeeping forces is less clear. The fundamental problem is that they can be considered as either civilians or combatants depending on whether they are participating in a combat or not. Such a position would be untenable if UN peacekeeping forces are engaged in a continuous combat and could be considered as parties to the armed conflict. The 1994 Convention on the Safety of UN and Associated Personnel and the Statute of the International Criminal Court, which criminalised attack and detention of UN and associated personnel, also raised the question of whether UN force personnel are a special category of persons outside the bounds of IHL rules that regulate captured persons during armed conflict.

Occupation is also an area that raises issues on the separation of *jus ad bellum* and *jus in bello*. Particularly in relation to the occupation of Iraq by the US and UK between 2003 and 2004, many experts debated whether the measures taken by the US and UK derogated from their obligations under the law of occupation in IHL. An issue of a very different nature can also be identified in relation to UN peacekeeping forces. In the case of UN peacekeeping forces, they are only given limited means to achieve the mandates given by the Security Council, but in the course of executing the mandates, UN peacekeeping forces could find themselves administering a part of the territory where they are deployed to. Such a case raises the question of whether they must comply with the law of occupation with their limited means available.

On the other hand, some non-military enforcement measures also pose problems in relation to IHL. For example, arms embargoes have been imposed in many instances to contain the escalation of armed conflicts. This could complement the existing prohibitions on certain weapons in IHL. However, at the same time, some have argued that the limitation on the military power could encourage violations of IHL, particularly when civilians cannot be protected because of the reduced military power of a conflicting party.

Economic sanctions and restrictions on certain means of transportation have also been two of the most frequent types of non-military enforcement measures under Chapter VII. They have been imposed not only to contain the escalation of armed conflicts but also to other situations outside the armed conflict context such as the development of nuclear weapons for military purpose.[254] However, in cases where they were imposed in an armed conflict situation, they could have an impact on the delivery of humanitarian aid that is normally ensured by IHL.

The issues outlined here will be discussed in greater detail in the subsequent sections.

[254] For the Democratic People's Republic of Korea, see UNSC Res 1718 (14 October 2006) UN Doc S/RES/1718 and UNSC Res 1874 (12 June 2009) UN Doc S/RES/1874. For Iran, see UNSC Res 1737 (27 December 2006) UN Doc S/RES/1737, UNSC Res 1747 (24 March 2007) UN Doc S/RES/1747, UNSC Res 1803 (3 March 2008) UN Doc S/RES/1803, and UNSC Res 1929 (9 June 2010) UN Doc S/RES/1929.

IV. MILITARY ENFORCEMENT MEASURES UNDER CHAPTER VII OF THE UN CHARTER AND IHL

This section discusses the *jus ad bellum* and *jus in bello* constraints on the military enforcement measures under Chapter VII of the UN Charter, and how Chapter VII decisions and IHL can be in conflict or complementary.

A. Two Types of UN Forces Authorised under Chapter VII

Upon the determination of a situation as a threat to the peace, breach of the peace, or act of aggression pursuant to Article 39 of the UN Charter, military enforcement measures may be authorised by the Security Council under Chapter VII. Military enforcement measures are executed by two types of forces: by the individual armed forces of the UN Member States or by forces under the UN command.[255]

First, the Security Council can authorise UN Member States to use force in order to carry out certain mandates by their armed forces (hereafter state-led UN forces). The use of force can be by one state or by several states acting under the command of a lead state. At least in 21 instances, UN Member States were authorised to use force under the term 'use all necessary means'.[256] Examples are such as the multinational forces in the 1991 Gulf War and the Unified Task Force (UNITAF) in Somalia.

[255] On this topic, see generally D Sarooshi, *The United Nations and the Development of Collective Security: The Delegation by the UN Security Council of Its Chapter VII Powers* (Oxford, Clarendon Press, 1999). See also UN Secretariat, 'Interoffice memorandum to the Director of the Codification Division, Office of Legal Affairs and Secretary of the International Law Commission regarding the Topic of Responsibility of International Organizations' (2004) *United Nations Juridical Yearbook* 352, 355; L-A Sicilianos, 'Entre multilatéralism et unilatéralism: l'autorisation par le Conseil de sécurité de recourir à la force' (2008) 339 *Recueil des Cours de l'Académie de Droit International* 9. The distinction is crucial when applying IHL, as will be seen in section 4.IV.C.

[256] For the ongoing authorisation to use force as at September 2010, see:

- Bosnia and Herzegovina, UNSC Res 1031 (15 December 1995) UN Doc S/RES/1031, UNSC Res 1088 (12 December 1996) UN Doc S/RES/1088, UNSC Res 1174 (15 June 1998) UN Doc S/RES/1174, UNSC Res 1247 (18 June 1999) UN Doc S/RES/1247, UNSC Res 1305 (21 June 2000) UN Doc S/RES/1305, UNSC Res 1357 (21 June 2001) UN Doc S/RES/1357, UNSC Res 1423 (12 July 2002) UN Doc S/RES/1423, UNSC Res 1491 (11 July 2003) UN Doc S/RES/1491, UNSC Res 1551 (9 July 2004) UN Doc S/RES/1551, UNSC Res 1575 (22 November 2004) UN Doc S/RES/1575, UNSC Res 1639 (21 November 2005) UN Doc S/RES/1639, UNSC Res 1722 (21 November 2006) UN Doc S/RES/1722, UNSC Res 1785 (21 November 2007) UN Doc S/RES/1785, UNSC Res 1845 (20 November 2008) UN Doc S/RES/1845, and UNSC Res 1895 (18 November 2009) UN Doc S/RES/1895.
- Afghanistan, UNSC Res 1386 (20 December 2001) UN Doc S/RES/1386, UNSC Res 1413 (23 May 2002) UN Doc S/RES/1413, UNSC Res 1444 (27 November 2002) UN Doc S/RES/1444, UNSC Res 1510 (13 October 2003) UN Doc S/RES/1510, UNSC Res 1563 (17 September 2004) UN Doc S/RES/1563, UNSC Res 1623 (13 September 2005) UN Doc S/RES/1623, UNSC Res 1707 (12 September 2006) UN Doc S/RES/1707, UNSC Res 1776 (19 September 2007) UN Doc S/RES/1776, UNSC Res 1833 (22 September 2008) UN Doc S/RES/1833, and UNSC Res 1890 (8 October 2009) UN Doc S/RES/1890.

On the other hand, the Security Council can establish UN forces as a subsidiary organ of the Security Council pursuant to Article 29 of the UN Charter. [257] They are commanded and controlled by the UN and have the UN Secretary-General as the commander-in-chief (hereafter UN-commanded forces). They are also commonly referred to as 'UN peacekeeping operations'.

Article 29 of the UN Charter provides as follows:

- Côte d'Ivoire, UNSC Res 1464 (4 February 2003) UN Doc S/RES/1464, UNSC Res 1498 (4 August 2003) UN Doc S/RES/1498, UNSC Res 1527 (4 February 2004) UN Doc S/RES/1527, UNSC Res 1528 (27 February 2004) UN Doc S/RES/1528, UNSC Res 1594 (4 April 2005) UN Doc S/RES/1594, UNSC Res 1603 (3 June 2005) UN Doc S/RES/1603, UNSC Res 1609 (24 June 2005) UN Doc S/RES/1609, UNSC Res 1652 (24 January 2006) UN Doc S/RES/1652, UNSC Res 1726 (15 December 2006) UN Doc S/RES/1726, UNSC Res 1738 (23 December 2006) UN Doc S/RES/1738, UNSC Res 1765 (16 July 2007) UN Doc S/RES/1765, UNSC Res 1795 (15 January 2008) UN Doc S/RES/1795, UNSC Res 1826 (29 July 2008) UN Doc S/RES/1826, UNSC Res 1865 (27 January 2009) UN Doc S/RES/1865, UNSC Res 1880 (30 July 2009) UN Doc S/RES/1880, and UNSC Res 1911 (28 January 2010) UN Doc S/RES/1911.
- Somalia, UNSC Res 1744 (21 February 2007) UN Doc S/RES/1744, UNSC Res 1772 (20 August 2007) UN Doc S/RES/1772, UNSC Res 1831 (19 August 2008) UN Doc S/RES/1831, and UNSC Res 1910 (28 January 2010) UN Doc S/RES/1910.

For terminated authorisation to use force, see:

- Iraq, UNSC Res 678 (29 November 1990) UN Doc S/RES/678.
- Former Yugoslavia, UNSC Res 770 (13 August 1992) UN Doc S/RES/770, UNSC Res 787 (16 November 1992) UN Doc S/RES/787, UNSC Res 816 (31 March 1993) UN Doc S/RES/816, UNSC Res 836 (4 June 1993) UN Doc S/RES/836, UNSC Res 844 (18 June 1993) UN Doc S/RES/844, UNSC Res 908 (31 March 1994) UN Doc S/RES/908, and UNSC Res 958 (19 November 1994) UN Doc S/RES/958.
- Somalia, UNSC Res 794 (3 December 1992) UN Doc S/RES/794.
- Haiti 1993, UNSC Res 875 (16 October 1993) UN Doc S/RES/875 and UNSC Res 917 (6 May 1994) UN Doc S/RES/917.
- Rwanda, UNSC Res 929 (22 June 1994) UN Doc S/RES/929.
- Haiti 1994, UNSC Res 940 (31 July 1994) UN Doc S/RES/940.
- Croatia 1995, UNSC Res 981 (31 March 1995) UN Doc S/RES/981.
- Zaire, UNSC Res 1080 (15 November 1996) UN Doc S/RES/1080.
- Croatia 1996, UNSC Res 1037 (15 January 1996) UN Doc S/RES/1037 and UNSC Res 1120 (14 July 1997) UN Doc S/RES/1120.
- East Timor, UNSC Res 1264 (15 September 1999) UN Doc S/RES/1264.
- Côte d'Ivoire, UNSC Res 1464 (4 February 2003) UN Doc S/RES/1464.
- DRC 2003, UNSC Res 1484 (30 May 2003) UN Doc S/RES/1484.
- Liberia, UNSC Res 1497 (1 August 2003) UN Doc S/RES/1497.
- Haiti 2004, UNSC Res 1529 (29 February 2004) UN Doc S/RES/1529 and UNSC Res 1542 (30 April 2004) UN Doc S/RES/1542.
- Iraq, UNSC Res 1511 (16 October 2003) UN Doc S/RES/1511, UNSC Res 1546 (8 June 2004) UN Doc S/RES/1546, and UNSC Res 1790 (18 December 2007) UN Doc S/RES/1790.
- DRC 2006, UNSC Res 1671 (25 April 2006) UN Doc S/RES/1671.
- Chad/Central African Republic, UNSC Res 1778 (25 September 2007) UN Doc S/RES/1778, UNSC Res 1834 (24 September 2008) UN Doc S/RES/1834, and UNSC Res 1861 (14 January 2009) UN Doc S/RES/1861.

[257] See UN Secretariat, 'Interoffice memorandum to the Director of the Codification Division, Office of Legal Affairs and Secretary of the International Law Commission regarding the Topic of Responsibility of International Organizations' (2004) *United Nations Juridical Yearbook* 352, 354. The General Assembly can also establish UN-commanded forces but except for UNEF, all other UN-commanded forces have been established by the Security Council in practice.

> The Security Council may establish such subsidiary organs as it deems necessary for the performance of its functions.[258]

Many of the status-of-forces agreements for UN-commanded forces also confirm that they were established as subsidiary organs of the UN.[259] They are a collective entity operating under the UN authority and are not simply a collection of states like the state-led UN forces.

Not all UN-commanded forces are authorised to use force. The Security Council has established at least 62 UN-commanded forces, among which 13 were authorised to use force under Chapter VII under the term 'use all necessary means' or a similar term,[260] mostly in the context of non-international armed conflict.

[258] See also Art 7(2) of the UN Charter, which provides that 'Such subsidiary organs as may be found necessary may be established in accordance with the present Charter'.

[259] See n 339 below.

[260] For ongoing authorisation to use force by UN-commanded forces as at September 2010, see:

- UNIFIL (Lebanon), UNSC Res 1701 (11 August 2006) UN Doc S/RES/1701, UNSC Res 1773 (24 August 2007) UN Doc S/RES/1773, UNSC Res 1832 (27 August 2008) UN Doc S/RES/1832, and UNSC Res 1884 (27 August 2009) UN Doc S/RES/1884.
- MONUSCO (DRC), UNSC Res 1291 (24 February 2000) UN Doc S/RES/1291, UNSC Res 1316 (23 August 2000) UN Doc S/RES/1316, UNSC Res 1323 (13 October 2000) UN Doc S/RES/1323, UNSC Res 1332 (14 December 2000) UN Doc S/RES/1332, UNSC Res 1355 (15 June 2001) UN Doc S/RES/1355, UNSC Res 1417 (14 June 2002) UN Doc S/RES/1417, UNSC Res 1489 (26 June 2003) UN Doc S/RES/1489, UNSC Res 1493 (28 July 2003) UN Doc S/RES/1493, UNSC Res 1533 (12 March 2004) UN Doc S/RES/1533, UNSC Res 1555 (29 July 2004) UN Doc S/RES/1555, UNSC Res 1565 (1 October 2004) UN Doc S/RES/1565, UNSC Res 1592 (30 March 2005) UN Doc S/RES/1592, UNSC Res 1596 (3 May 2005) UN Doc S/RES/1596, UNSC Res 1621 (6 September 2005) UN Doc S/RES/1621, UNSC Res 1628 (30 September 2005) UN Doc S/RES/1628, UNSC Res 1635 (28 October 2005) UN Doc S/RES/1635, UNSC Res 1711 (29 September 2006) UN Doc S/RES/1711, UNSC Res 1736 (22 December 2006) UN Doc S/RES/1736, UNSC Res 1742 (15 February 2007) UN Doc S/RES/1742, UNSC Res 1751 (13 April 2007) UN Doc S/RES/1751, UNSC Res 1756 (15 May 2007) UN Doc S/RES/1756, UNSC Res 1794 (21 December 2007) UN Doc S/RES/1794, UNSC Res 1856 (22 December 2008) UN Doc S/RES/1856, UNSC Res 1906 (23 December 2009) UN Doc S/RES/1906, and UNSC Res 1925 (28 May 2010) UN Doc S/RES/1925.
- UNOCI (Côte d'Ivoire), UNSC Res 1528 (27 February 2004) UN Doc S/RES/1528, UNSC Res 1594 (4 April 2005) UN Doc S/RES/1594, UNSC Res 1600 (4 May 2005) UN Doc S/RES/1600, UNSC Res 1603 (3 June 2005) UN Doc S/RES/1603, UNSC Res 1609 (24 June 2005) UN Doc S/RES/1609, UNSC Res 1652 (24 January 2006) UN Doc S/RES/1652, UNSC Res 1726 (15 December 2006) UN Doc S/RES/1726, UNSC Res 1739 (10 January 2007) UN Doc S/RES/1739, UNSC Res 1763 (29 June 2007) UN Doc S/RES/1763, UNSC Res 1765 (16 July 2007) UN Doc S/RES/1765, UNSC Res 1795 (15 January 2008) UN Doc S/RES/1795, UNSC Res 1826 (29 July 2008) UN Doc S/RES/1826, UNSC Res 1865 (27 January 2009) UN Doc S/RES/1865, UNSC Res 1880 (30 July 2009) UN Doc S/RES/1880, UNSC Res 1911 (28 January 2010) UN Doc S/RES/1911, and UNSC Res 1924 (27 May 2010) UN Doc S/RES/1924.
- UNMIS (Sudan), UNSC Res 1590 (24 March 2005) UN Doc S/RES/1590, UNSC Res 1627 (23 September 2005) UN Doc S/RES/1627, UNSC Res 1663 (24 March 2006) UN Doc S/RES/1663, UNSC Res 1706 (31 August 2006) UN Doc S/RES/1706, UNSC Res 1709 (22 September 2006) UN Doc S/RES/1709, UNSC Res 1714 (6 October 2006) UN Doc S/RES/1714, UNSC Res 1755 (30 April 2007) UN Doc S/RES/1755, UNSC Res 1784 (31 October 2007) UN Doc S/RES/1784, UNSC Res 1812 (30 April 2008) UN Doc S/RES/1812,

The Security Council has authorised these UN forces to enforce various mandates through the use of force, including IHL-related mandates such as the following: 1) protection of civilians and civilian objects, including UN personnel and equipment, humanitarian workers, humanitarian assistance, and 'safe areas';[261] 2) facilitation of humanitarian

UNSC Res 1870 (20 May 2009) UN Doc S/RES/1870, and UNSC Res 1919 (29 April 2010) UN Doc S/RES/1919.
- UNAMID (Sudan), UNSC Res 1769 (31 July 2007) UN Doc S/RES/1769, UNSC Res 1828 (31 July 2008) UN Doc S/RES/1828, and UNSC Res 1881 (6 August 2009) UN Doc S/RES/1881.
- MINURCAT (Central African Republic and Chad), UNSC Res 1861 (14 January 2009) UN Doc S/RES/1861, UNSC Res 1913 (12 March 2010) UN Doc S/RES/1913, UNSC Res 1922 (12 May 2010) UN Doc S/RES/1922, and UNSC Res 1923 (25 May 2010) UN Doc S/RES/1923.

For terminated authorisation to use force by UN-commanded forces, see:
- UNPROFOR (former Yugoslavia), UNSC Res 836 (4 June 1993) UN Doc S/RES/836 and UNSC Res 871 (4 October 1993) UN Doc S/RES/871.
- UNOSOM I (Somalia), UNSC Res 794 (3 December 1992) UN Doc S/RES/794.
- UNOSOM II (Somalia), UNSC Res 837 (6 June 1993) UN Doc S/RES/837 and UNSC Res 954 (4 November 1994) UN Doc S/RES/954.
- UNAMSIL (Sierra Leone), UNSC Res 1270 (22 October 1999) UN Doc S/RES/1270, UNSC Res 1289 (7 February 2000) UN Doc S/RES/1289, and UNSC Res 1389 (16 January 2002) UN Doc S/RES/1389.
- UNTAET (East Timor), UNSC Res 1272 (25 October 1999) UN Doc S/RES/1272.
- UNMISET (East Timor), UNSC Res 1410 (17 May 2002) UN Doc S/RES/1410.
- ONUB (Burundi), UNSC Res 1545 (21 May 2004) UN Doc S/RES/1545.

UNMIL (Liberia), UNSC Res 1509 (19 September 2003) UN Doc S/RES/1509 and MINUSTAH (Haiti), UNSC Res 1529 (29 February 2004) UN Doc S/RES/1529 were only authorised under Chapter VII. For the purpose of this chapter, UN-commanded forces not authorised under Chapter VII are excluded.

[261] UN-commanded forces: UNPROFOR (former Yugoslavia), UNSC Res 836 (4 June 1993) UN Doc S/RES/836; UNOSOM II (Somalia), UNSC Res 814 (26 March 1993) UN Doc S/RES/814 and UNSC Res 954 (4 November 1994) UN Doc S/RES/954; UNAMSIL (Sierra Leone), UNSC Res 1270 (22 October 1999) UN Doc S/RES/1270; MONUC (DRC), UNSC Res 1291 (24 February 2000) UN Doc S/RES/1291, UNSC Res 1417 (14 June 2002) UN Doc S/RES/1417, UNSC Res 1493 (28 July 2003) UN Doc S/RES/1493, UNSC Res 1565 (1 October 2004) UN Doc S/RES/1565, UNSC Res 1592 (30 March 2005) UN Doc S/RES/1592, UNSC Res 1856 (22 December 2008) UN Doc S/RES/1856, UNSC Res 1906 (23 December 2009) UN Doc S/RES/1906, and UNSC Res 1925 (28 May 2010) UN Doc S/RES/1925; UNMIL (Liberia), UNSC Res 1509 (19 September 2003) UN Doc S/RES/1509; UNOCI (Côte d'Ivoire), UNSC Res 1528 (27 February 2004) UN Doc S/RES/1528, UNSC Res 1609 (24 June 2005) UN Doc S/RES/1609, and UNSC Res 1739 (10 January 2007) UN Doc S/RES/1739; ONUB (Burundi), UNSC Res 1545 (21 May 2004) UN Doc S/RES/1545; UNMIS (Sudan), UNSC Res 1590 (24 March 2005) UN Doc S/RES/1590 and UNSC Res 1706 (31 August 2006) UN Doc S/RES/1706; UNIFIL (Lebanon), UNSC Res 1701 (11 August 2006) UN Doc S/RES/1701; UNAMID (Sudan), UNSC Res 1769 (31 July 2007) UN Doc S/RES/1769; MIURCAT (Chad/Central African Republic), UNSC Res 1861 (14 January 2009) UN Doc S/RES/1861, and UNSC Res 1923 (25 May 2010) UN Doc S/RES/1923. State-led UN forces: Rwanda, UNSC Res 929 (22 June 1994) UN Doc S/RES/929; Kosovo, UNSC Res 1244 (10 June 1999) UN Doc S/RES/1244; East Timor, UNSC Res 1264 (15 September 1999) UN Doc S/RES/1264; Afghanistan, UNSC Res 1386 (20 December 2001) UN Doc S/RES/1386 and UNSC Res 1510 (13 October 2003) UN Doc S/RES/1510; DRC 2003, UNSC Res 1484 (30 May 2003) UN Doc S/RES/1484; Côte d'Ivoire, UNSC Res 1464 (4 February 2003) UN Doc S/RES/1464 and UNSC Res 1528 (27 February 2004) UN Doc S/RES/1528; Iraq, UNSC Res 1511 (16 October

assistance;[262] 3) administration of a state's territory;[263] and 4) certain rare mandates such as carrying out mine action.[264] While these are primarily IHL obligations of states and armed groups, UN forces have directly implemented or complemented parts of IHL. It must be noted, however,

2003) UN Doc S/RES/1511; Haiti, UNSC Res 1529 (29 February 2004) UN Doc S/RES/1529; DRC 2006, UNSC Res 1671 (25 April 2006) UN Doc S/RES/1671; Somalia, UNSC Res 1744 (21 February 2007) UN Doc S/RES/1744; Chad/Central African Republic, UNSC Res 1778 (25 September 2007) UN Doc S/RES/1778.

[262] UN-commanded forces: UNOSOM II (Somalia), UNSC Res 814 (26 March 1993) UN Doc S/RES/814; UNPROFOR (former Yugoslavia), UNSC Res 836 (4 June 1993) UN Doc S/RES/836; UNCRO (Croatia), UNSC Res 981 (31 March 1995) UN Doc S/RES/981; UNAMSIL (Sierra Leone), UNSC Res 1270 (22 October 1999) UN Doc S/RES/1270; UNTAET (East Timor), UNSC Res 1272 (25 October 1999) UN Doc S/RES/1272; MONUC (DRC), UNSC Res 1291 (24 February 2000) UN Doc S/RES/1291, UNSC Res 1417 (14 June 2002) UN Doc S/RES/1417, UNSC Res 1493 (28 July 2003) UN Doc S/RES/1493, UNSC Res 1565 (1 October 2004) UN Doc S/RES/1565, UNSC Res 1756 (15 May 2007) UN Doc S/RES/1756, and UNSC Res 1856 (22 December 2008) UN Doc S/RES/1856; UNMIL (Liberia), UNSC Res 1509 (19 September 2003) UN Doc S/RES/1509; UNOCI (Côte d'Ivoire), UNSC Res 1528 (27 February 2004) UN Doc S/RES/1528, UNSC Res 1609 (24 June 2005) UN Doc S/RES/1609, and UNSC Res 1739 (10 January 2007) UN Doc S/RES/1739; MINUSTAH (Haiti), UNSC Res 1542 (30 April 2004) UN Doc S/RES/1542; ONUB (Burundi), UNSC Res 1545 (21 May 2004) UN Doc S/RES/1545; UNMIS (Sudan), UNSC Res 1590 (24 March 2005) UN Doc S/RES/1590 and UNSC Res 1706 (31 August 2006) UN Doc S/RES/1706; UNIFIL (Lebanon), UNSC Res 1701 (11 August 2006) UN Doc S/RES/1701; UNAMID (Sudan), UNSC Res 1769 (31 July 2007) UN Doc S/RES/1769; MINURCAT (Chad/Central African Republic), UNSC Res 1861 (14 January 2009) UN Doc S/RES/1861.

State-led UN forces: former Yugoslavia, UNSC Res 770 (13 August 1992) UN Doc S/RES/770, UNSC Res 836 (4 June 1993) UN Doc S/RES/836, UNSC Res 844 (18 June 1993) UN Doc S/RES/844, and UNSC Res 958 (19 November 1994) UN Doc S/RES/958; Somalia, UNSC Res 794 (3 December 1992) UN Doc S/RES/794; Zaire, UNSC Res 1080 (15 November 1996) UN Doc S/RES/1080; Kosovo, UNSC Res 1244 (10 June 1999) UN Doc S/RES/1244; East Timor, UNSC Res 1264 (15 September 1999) UN Doc S/RES/1264; DRC, UNSC Res 1484 (30 May 2003) UN Doc S/RES/1484; Liberia, UNSC Res 1497 (1 August 2003) UN Doc S/RES/1497; Haiti, UNSC Res 1529 (29 February 2004) UN Doc S/RES/1529; Somalia, UNSC Res 1744 (21 February 2007) UN Doc S/RES/1744; Chad/Central African Republic, UNSC Res 1778 (25 September 2007) UN Doc S/RES/1778.

[263] UN-commanded forces: UNPROFOR (former Yugoslavia), UNSC Res 836 (4 June 1993) UN Doc S/RES/836, para 5; UNOSOM II (Somalia), UNSC Res 837 (6 June 1993) UN Doc S/RES/837, para 5; UNTAES (Croatia), UNSC Res 1037 (15 January 1996) UN Doc S/RES/1037, para 10(c) and 11(b) and (c); UNTAET (East Timor), UNSC Res 1272 (25 October 1999) UN Doc S/RES/1272, para 2; UNMISET (East Timor), UNSC Res 1410 (17 May 2002) UN Doc S/RES/1410, para 2; MINUSTAH (Haiti), UNSC Res 1702 (15 August 2006) UN Doc S/RES/1702, para 14.

State-led UN forces in Kosovo, UNSC Res 1244 (10 June 1999) UN Doc S/RES/1244, paras 9(c) and (d) and 11(b) and (i); East Timor, UNSC Res 1264 (15 September 1999) UN Doc S/RES/1264, para 3; DRC, UNSC Res 1484 (30 May 2003) UN Doc S/RES/1484, para 1; Liberia, UNSC Res 1497 (1 August 2003) UN Doc S/RES/1497, para 1; Côte d'Ivoire, UNSC Res 1528 (27 February 2004) UN Doc S/RES/1528, para 16; Iraq, UNSC Res 1511 (16 October 2003) UN Doc S/RES/1511, para 13 and UNSC Res 1546 (8 June 2004) UN Doc S/RES/1546, para 10; Haiti, UNSC Res 1529 (29 February 2004) UN Doc S/RES/1529, para 2.

[264] UNOSOM II (Somalia), UNSC Res 819 (16 April 1993) UN Doc S/RES/819, para 5; MONUC (DRC), UNSC Res 1291 (24 February 2000) UN Doc S/RES/1291, para 7(i); ONUB (Burundi), UNSC Res 1545 (21 May 2004) UN Doc S/RES/1545, para 5; UNMIS (Sudan), UNSC Res 1590 (24 March 2005) UN Doc S/RES/1590, para 4(c).

that none of these actions of UN forces absolve states and armed groups from complying with their IHL obligations.

The Security Council authorisation to 'use all necessary means' is in most cases limited to specific mandates such as those mentioned above but in some cases, the authorisation extends to all mandates, which may include other situations beyond the reach of IHL. These are such as to apprehend, detain and deport foreign military elements and mercenaries;[265] monitor ceasefire agreements; monitor the borders; guard weapons, ammunition and other military materiel; protect government ministers;[266] collect and secure weapons and military materiel; dismantle militias; disarm fighters; monitor illegal flow of arms across borders; and ensure secure environment for national borders.[267] These may have significant impact, particularly in non-international armed conflict, on limiting the use of force by a state's armed forces and armed groups and hence, on preventing violations of IHL.[268]

UN forces as an actor implementing IHL will be discussed in a later section. First, though, UN forces as an actor bound by *jus ad bellum* and *jus in bello* will be examined.

B. *Jus ad Bellum* Constraints on the Use of Force by UN Forces

This section considers UN forces as an actor bound by *jus ad bellum*. By '*jus ad bellum*' in this section, it means the UN Charter, Security Council resolutions, principles of necessity and proportionality, and the principle of self-defence. These rules and principles constitute *jus ad bellum* constraints on the use of force by UN forces.

Since the applicable constraints are different according to the type of UN forces, this section discusses the following two types in turn: 1) use of force by UN-commanded forces not authorised to use force; and 2) Chapter VII use of force authorised for the UN Member States and UN-commanded forces.

265 ONUC (Congo), UNSC Res 169 (24 November 1961) UN Doc S/RES/169, para 4.

266 For these mandates, see UNOCI (Côte d'Ivoire), UNSC Res 1528 (27 February 2004) UN Doc S/RES/1528, para 6.

267 For these mandates, see ONUB (Burundi), UNSC Res 1545 (21 May 2004) UN Doc S/RES/1545, para 5. MONUC (DRC), UNSC Res 1493 (28 July 2003) UN Doc S/RES/1493, UNSC Res 1533 (12 March 2004) UN Doc S/RES/1533 has also carried out major disarmament operation through the use of force in the eastern DRC.

268 For the nexus between arms availability and violations of IHL, see section 4.V.A. For discussions on internationalised non-international armed conflict and mixed armed conflict, see section 5.II.

UN Forces not Authorised to Use Force: Limitation by the Principle of Self-defence

As noted earlier, most of the UN-commanded forces are not authorised to use force. In other words, they cannot initiate the use of force, but are entitled to use force only in self-defence.[269] Out of the 62 UN-commanded forces that were established up to September 2010, 49 were not authorised to use force and thus most UN-commanded forces were only entitled to use force in self-defence.[270] The right of self-defence by UN-commanded forces is different from that in Article 51 of the UN Charter since the latter permits the defence of a state as such while the former is more limited, as will be seen below. The right of self-defence for UN-commanded forces has developed entirely through practice but it can now be considered as having attained customary law status.[271] The principle of proportionality in self-defence by UN-commanded forces is also well established. The UN Legal Counsel stated that 'United Nations forces have . . . always been

[269] For discussions on the right of self-defence of UN-commanded forces, see generally R Higgins, *The Development of International Law through the Political Organs of the United Nations* (London, Oxford University Press, 1963) 232–35; D Bowett, *Self-Defence in International Law* (Manchester, Manchester University Press, 1958) 108, 202–03, and 555–57; M Arsanjani, 'Defending the Blue Helmets: Protection of United Nations Personnel' in Condorelli et al (eds), *Nations Unies et le droit international humanitaire*, 134–41; H McCoubrey and N White, *The Blue Helmets: Legal Regulation of United Nations Military Operations* (Aldershot, Dartmouth, 1996) 84–88; M Bothe, 'Peace-keeping' in Simma et al (eds), *The Charter of the United Nations*, 682–83; T Findlay, *The Use of Force in UN Peace Operations* (Oxford, Oxford University Press, 2002); R Zacklin, 'The Use of Force in Peacekeeping Operations' in N Blokker and N Schrijver (eds), *The Security Council and the Use of Force: Theory and Reality – A Need for Change?* (Leiden, Martinus Nijhoff, 2005) 92–97.

[270] On-going UN-commanded forces not authorised to use force in the order of the year of establishment: UNTSO (Middle East), UNMOGIP (India–Pakistan), UNFICYP (Cyprus), UNDOF (Golan Heights), MINURSO (Western Sahara), UNMIK (Kosovo), UNMIL (Liberia), MINUSTAH (Haiti), and UNMIT (Timor-Leste).

Completed UN-commanded forces in the order of the year of establishment: UNEF I (Middle East), UNOGIL (Lebanon), ONUC (Congo), UNSF (West New Guinea), UNYOM (Yemen), DOMREP (Dominican Republic), UNIPOM (India–Pakistan), UNEF II (Middle East), UNIIMOG (Iran–Iraq), UNGOMAP (Afghanistan–Pakistan), UNAVEM I (Angola), UNTAG (Namibia), ONUCA (Central America), UNIKOM (Iraq–Kuwait), ONUSAL (El Salvador), UNAVEM II (Angola), UNAMIC (Cambodia), UNTAC (Cambodia), ONUMOZ (Mozambique), UNOMUR (Rwanda–Uganda), UNOMIG (Georgia), UNOMIL (Liberia), UNMIH (Haiti), UNAMIR (Rwanda), UNASOG (Chad–Libya), UNMOT (Tajikistan), UNAVEM III (Angola), UNCRO (Croatia), UNPREDEP (Macedonia), UNMIBH (Bosnia and Herzegovina), UNTAES (Croatia), UNMOP (Prevlaka Peninsula), UNSMIH (Haiti), MINUGUA (Guatemala), MONUA (Angola), UNTMIH (Haiti), MIPONUH (Haiti), MINURCA (Central African Republic), UNOMSIL (Sierra Leone), and UNMEE (Ethiopia–Eritrea).

[271] See Art 21 of the Convention on the Safety of United Nations and Associated Personnel (hereafter 1994 Safety Convention) (adopted 9 December 1994, entered into force 15 January 1999) 2051 UNTS 363: 'Nothing in this Convention shall be construed so as to derogate from the right to act in self-defence.' See also Higgins, *The Development of International Law*, 233; UN Secretariat, 'Memorandum to the Senior Political Adviser to the Secretary-General' (1993) *United Nations Juridical Yearbook* 371, para 1.

regarded as entitled to the right of self-defence . . . the use of force in self-defence is not limitless but must be proportional'.[272]

There is no universally accepted definition of the right of self-defence or the principle of proportionality for UN-commanded forces but its scope generally has two levels. First, at the minimum, the use of force in self-defence is only limited to the defence of personnel and objects of UN forces and should be proportionate to the initial attack, as established in the case of UNFICYP (Cyprus):

> Troops of UNFICYP shall not take the initiative in the use of armed force. The use of armed force is permissible only in self-defence.
>
> The expression 'self-defence' includes:
>
> (a) the defence of United Nations posts, premises and vehicles under armed attack;
> (b) the support of other personnel of UNFICYP under armed attack.[273]

The scope of self-defence is clearly narrower than Article 51 of the UN Charter. The 'armed attack' in this context is also different from 'armed attack' in Article 51. 'Armed attack' in the sense of Article 51 can only be directed against a state, and not against an international organisation. Hence, an armed attack against UN forces does not trigger the right of self-defence within the meaning of Article 51 but rather the right of self-defence as a customary rule applicable to UN-commanded forces. However, the balancing elements for proportionality are the same as self-defence in the sense of Article 51 since they are on one hand an armed attack and on the other hand, the use of force in self-defence.

Secondly, a slightly wider scope of self-defence has also been adopted by the UN which appears not to require an armed attack. In the case of UNIFIL (Lebanon), the UN Secretary-General noted that 'Self-defence would include resistance to attempts by forceful means to prevent it [UNIFIL] from discharging its duties under the mandate of the Security Council'.[274] The interpretation of this formulation is not easy. First, the

[272] UN Secretariat, 'Memorandum to the Senior Political Adviser to the Secretary-General' (1993) *United Nations Juridical Yearbook* 371, paras 1 and 2. The principle of necessity can also be identified in the case of UNFICYP: 'When acting in self-defence . . . armed force will be used only when all peaceful means of persuasion have failed.' See UNSC, 'Aide-Mémoire of the Secretary-General concerning Some Questions Relating to the Function and Operation of the United Nations Peace-keeping Force in Cyprus' (11 April 1964) UN Doc S/5653, para 18. See further ILC, 'Responsibility of International Organizations' (hereafter ILC Draft Articles on the Responsibility of International Organizations) (2009) UN Doc A/64/10 Supp No 10, 96–97.

[273] UNSC, 'Aide-Mémoire', para 16.

[274] UNSC, 'Report of the Secretary-General on the Implementation of Security Council Resolution 425 (1978)' (19 March 1978) UN Doc S/12611, para 4(d). This formulation was also employed for UNEF II (Middle East). See UNSC, 'Report of the Secretary-General on the Implementation of Security Council Resolutions 340 (1973)' (27 October 1973) UN Doc S/11052/Rev.1, para 4(d).

word 'attempts' raises the question whether UN forces can act in self-defence when they are actually subject to 'forceful means' or whether a mere threat of 'forceful means' would suffice. The former interpretation adds nothing new to the UNFICYP formulation, but the latter interpretation would clearly widen the scope of self-defence.[275] Secondly, the term 'forceful means' is not clear. Does it mean direct physical attacks on UN forces or does an obstruction of the movements of UN forces suffice, without any direct attacks on them? The former interpretation adds nothing new to the UNFICYP formulation; if UN forces are attacked directly, they can clearly act in self-defence. However, the latter interpretation widens the scope of self-defence which was actually employed in the Congo in 1962 when ONUC cleared road blocks obstructing its movement.[276] In any case, the most liberal interpretation of the above formulation would allow UN forces to act in self-defence whenever they see that 'forcible measures' are attempted and a mere threat of such 'forcible measures' would suffice. This may even be, for example, a threat to set up road blocks to prevent the movements of UN forces. Thus, the UNFICYP formulation of self-defence is limited and clear but if the UNIFIL formulation is employed, depending on the interpretation, the scope of self-defence can widen significantly.

Thus, the scope of self-defence and proportionality for UN-commanded forces are generally interpreted in two ways: 1) use of force in defence of personnel and objects of UN forces and which is in response to an initial attack; and 2) use of force against 'attempts by forceful means to prevent' UN-commanded forces from carrying out their mandate. Beyond this point, an authorisation to use force by the Security Council is required, which will be discussed now.[277]

[275] Note that Art 51 of the UN Charter does not permit self-defence against a mere threat of 'armed attack'. At most, 'imminent threat' of armed attack is suggested by some experts but this interpretation remains controversial. See contrasting views in, on one hand, I Brownlie, *International Law and the Use of Force by States* (Oxford, Clarendon Press, 1963) 257–61; Kolb, *Ius contra bellum*, 195, and on the other, H Waldock, 'The Regulation of the Use of Force by Individual States in International Law' (1952) 81 *Recueil des Cours de l'Académie de Droit International* 455, 496–98; D Bowett, *Self-Defence in International Law* (Manchester, Manchester University Press, 1958) 187–92; S Schwebel, 'Aggression, Intervention and Self-Defence in Modern International Law' (1972) 136 *Recueil des Cours de l'Académie de Droit International* 411, 478–83; R Jennings and A Watts (eds), *Oppenheim's International Law*, 9th edn, Vol 1: Peace, Introduction and Part 1 (London, Longman, 1992) 421; Y Dinstein, *War, Aggression and Self-Defence*, 4th edn (Cambridge, Cambridge University Press, 2005) 189–92.

[276] See Higgins, *The Development of International Law*, 233.

[277] The dividing line between 2) above and the use of force authorised by the Security Council can be a fine one. However, it is clear that non-authorised UN-commanded forces cannot initiate the use of force, for example, to disarm and demobilise armed groups, as carried out by MONUC in the DRC. See UNSC Res 1556 (30 July 2004) UN Doc S/RES/1556, paras 4(g) and 5(c).

UN Forces Authorised to Use Force: Limitation by Security Council Resolutions

A clear difference with UN-commanded forces not authorised to use force is that the UN forces authorised to use force under Chapter VII can initiate the use force in order to carry out their mandates given by the Security Council. However, the use of force by both state-led UN forces and UN-commanded forces is strictly regulated by Security Council resolutions.[278]

There have been at least 35 cases of such Chapter VII use of force among which 22 were authorised for the UN Member States[279] and 13 were for UN-commanded forces.[280] Among the 35 cases, only one case on UNPROFOR (former Yugoslavia) was explicitly authorised to use force under Chapter VII and others were authorised under the term 'use all necessary measures' or similar terms.[281] The limits on such Chapter VII use of force through Security Council resolutions are imposed in five ways: 1) mandates for which the use of force is authorised; 2) temporal limit; 3) geographical limit; 4) military capacity; and 5) only when the situation requires.

First, Chapter VII use of force is invariably authorised to carry out specific mandates and is never an open-ended authorisation. The mandates provided vary in scope. On one hand, there are mandates whose scope is significantly wide. For example, some of the mandates of UNTAET (Timor-Leste) were 'To provide security and maintain law and order throughout the territory of East Timor' and 'To establish an effective

[278] See generally N Blokker, 'Is the Authorization Authorized? Powers and Practice of the Security Council to Authorize the Use of Force by "Coalitions of the Able and Willing"' (2000) 1 *European Journal of International Law* 541.

[279] See n 256 above.

[280] See n 260 above.

[281] See UNSC Res 836 (4 June 1993) UN Doc S/RES/836, para 9; UNSC Res 871 (4 October 1993) UN Doc S/RES/871, para 9. See, however, UNSC Res 161 (21 February 1961) UN Doc S/RES/161, para 1 and UNSC Res 169 (24 November 1961) UN Doc S/RES/169, para 1 on ONUC, which was not authorised under Chapter VII.

In a recent memorandum, the UN Legal Counsel noted that UNMIL (Liberia) was not authorised to use force under the term 'all necessary means' but was nevertheless entitled to use force beyond self-defence. See UN Secretariat, 'Note to the Under-Secretary-General of the Department of Peacekeeping Operations, United Nations' (2003) *United Nations Juridical Yearbook* 538. However, such 'implied authorisation' is controversial as the Security Council practice after resolution 678 on Iraq is to authorise the use of force explicitly.

On the issue of 'implied authorisation', see generally R Falk, 'Kosovo, World Order, and the Future of International Law' (1999) 93 *American Journal of International Law* 847; J Lobel and M Ratner, 'Bypassing the Security Council: Ambiguous Authorizations to Use Force, Cease-Fires and the Iraqi Inspection Regime' (1999) 93 *American Journal of International Law* 124; N White, 'The Legality of Bombing in the Name of Humanity' (2000) 5 *Journal of Conflict and Security Law* 27, 32; T Gazzini, 'NATO Coercive Military Activities in the Yugoslav Crisis (1992–1999)' (2001) 12 *European Journal of International Law* 391; C Gray, 'From Unity to Polarization: International Law and the Use of Force against Iraq' (2002) 12 *European Journal of International Law* 1.

administration'.[282] On the other hand, there are mandates whose scope is narrower. In the case of UNOSOM II (Somalia), the Security Council provided the following authorisation:

> UNOSOM II military forces to take those actions necessary to protect UNOSOM II mission and the withdrawal of UNOSOM II personnel and assets, and, to the extent that the Force Commander deems it practicable and consistent, in the context of withdrawal, to protect personnel of relief organizations.[283]

These mandates themselves limit the scope of Chapter VII use of force. However, the Security Council has tightened its control in recent authorisations to use force by setting additional conditions.

Most of the recent authorisations to use force are limited in duration. Some earlier authorisations to use force by the Security Council did not contain a time limit, such as resolution 678, which authorised the use of force against the invasion of Kuwait by Iraq and thus, when the US and UK invaded Iraq in 2003, one of the principal questions was whether resolution 678, adopted in 1990, was still valid in 2003.[284] The Security Council practice has changed to set a time limit on the authorisation, such as on the French forces in Rwanda when the Council decided 'that the mission of Member States cooperating with the Secretary-General will be limited to a period of two months following the adoption of this resolution'.[285] In other cases, the time limit was set not on the authorisation to use of force but on the duration of deployment of the UN forces.[286]

[282] UNSC Res 1272 (25 October 1999) UN Doc S/RES/1272, paras 2(a) and (b).

[283] UNSC Res 954 (4 November 1994) UN Doc S/RES/954, para 6.

[284] See, eg, UNSC, 'Letter Dated 20 March 2003 from the Permanent Representative of the United States of America to the United Nations Addressed to the President of the Security Council' (21 March 2003) UN Doc S/2003/351; R Singh and C Kilroy, 'In the Matter of the Potential Use of Armed Force by the UK against Iraq and in the Matter of Reliance for That Use of Force on United Nations Security Council Resolution 1441' in G Farebrother and N Kollerstrom (eds), *The Case against War: The Essential Legal Inquiries, Opinions and Judgments concerning War in Iraq* (Hailsham, The Legal Inquiry Steering Group, 2003); UK Attorney-General, 'Iraq: Resolution 1441'. See also L Moir, *Reappraising the Resort to Force* (Oxford, Hart Publishing, 2010) 73 *ff*; M Weller, *Iraq and the Use of Force in International Law* (Oxford, Oxford University Press, 2010); R Zacklin, *The United Nations Secretariat and the Use of Force in a Unipolar World* (Cambridge, Cambridge University Press, 2010) 145 *ff*.

[285] UNSC Res 929 (22 June 1994) UN Doc S/RES/929, para 4.

[286] See, eg, on ONUB (Burundi) in UNSC Res 1545 (21 May 2004) UN Doc S/RES/1545, para 2. '*The Security Council . . . Decides*, for an initial period of six months as from 1 June 2004 . . . the deployment of a peacekeeping operation in Burundi'. For UN-commanded forces, see: UNOSOM II (Somalia), UNSC Res 814 (26 March 1993) UN Doc S/RES/814 and UNSC Res 954 (4 November 1994) UN Doc S/RES/954; UNPROFOR (former Yugoslavia), UNSC Res 871 (4 October 1993) UN Doc S/RES/871; UNAMSIL (Sierra Leone), UNSC Res 1270 (22 October 1999) UN Doc S/RES/1270; UNTAET (East Timor), UNSC Res 1272 (25 October 1999) UN Doc S/RES/1272; MONUC (DRC), UNSC Res 1291 (24 February 2000) UN Doc S/RES/1291, UNSC Res 1417 (14 June 2002) UN Doc S/RES/1417, UNSC Res 1493 (28 July 2003) UN Doc S/RES/1493, UNSC Res 1565 (1 October 2004) UN Doc S/RES/1565, UNSC Res 1592 (30 March 2005) UN Doc S/RES/1592, UNSC Res 1756 (15 May 2007) UN Doc S/RES/1756, UNSC Res 1856 (22 December 2008) UN Doc S/RES/1856, UNSC Res 1906 (23 December 2009) UN Doc S/RES/1906, and UNSC Res 1925 (28 May 2010) UN Doc S/

The geographical extent of the use of force is normally limited to a specific area in the concerned state and it does not cover the whole state or beyond. For example, the Security Council authorised UNOCI (Côte d'Ivoire) 'to use all necessary means to carry out its mandate, within . . . its areas of deployment'.[287] Clearly, the 'areas of deployment' would vary from one UN force to another; some might cover the whole territory of a state[288] while

RES/1925; UNMISET (East Timor), UNSC Res 1410 (17 May 2002) UN Doc S/RES/1410; UNMIL (Liberia), UNSC Res 1509 (19 September 2003) UN Doc S/RES/1509; UNOCI (Côte d'Ivoire), UNSC Res 1528 (27 February 2004) UN Doc S/RES/1528, UNSC Res 1609 (24 June 2005) UN Doc S/RES/1609, and UNSC Res 1739 (10 January 2007) UN Doc S/RES/1739; MINUSTAH (Haiti), UNSC Res 1542 (30 April 2004) UN Doc S/RES/1542; ONUB (Burundi), UNSC Res 1545 (21 May 2004) UN Doc S/RES/1545; UNMIS (Sudan), UNSC Res 1590 (24 March 2005) UN Doc S/RES/1590 and UNSC Res 1706 (31 August 2006) UN Doc S/RES/1706; UNIFIL (Lebanon), UNSC Res 1701 (11 August 2006) UN Doc S/RES/1701; UNAMID (Sudan), UNSC Res 1769 (31 July 2007) UN Doc S/RES/1769; MINURCAT (Chad/Central African Republic), UNSC Res 1861 (14 January 2009) UN Doc S/RES/1861 and UNSC Res 1923 (25 May 2010) UN Doc S/RES/1923.

For state-led UN forces, see: Rwanda, UNSC Res 929 (22 June 1994) UN Doc S/RES/929; DRC, UNSC Res 1080 (15 November 1996) UN Doc S/RES/1080, UNSC Res 1484 (30 May 2003) UN Doc S/RES/1484, and UNSC Res 1671 (25 April 2006) UN Doc S/RES/1671; Bosnia and Herzegovina, UNSC Res 1174 (15 June 1998) UN Doc S/RES/1174; Afghanistan, UNSC Res 1386 (20 December 2001) UN Doc S/RES/1386 and UNSC Res 1510 (13 October 2003) UN Doc S/RES/1510; Liberia, UNSC Res 1497 (1 August 2003) UN Doc S/RES/1497; Côte d'Ivoire, UNSC Res 1464 (4 February 2003) UN Doc S/RES/1464 and UNSC Res 1528 (27 February 2004) UN Doc S/RES/1528; Iraq, UNSC Res 1511 (16 October 2003) UN Doc S/RES/1511, UNSC Res 1546 (8 June 2004) UN Doc S/RES/1546, and UNSC Res 1790 (18 December 2007) UN Doc S/RES/1790; Haiti, UNSC Res 1529 (29 February 2004) UN Doc S/RES/1529; Somalia, UNSC Res 1744 (21 February 2007) UN Doc S/RES/1744; Chad/Central African Republic, UNSC Res 1778 (25 September 2007) UN Doc S/RES/1778.

[287] UNSC Res 1528 (27 February 2004) UN Doc S/RES/1528, para 8. For UN-commanded forces, see: UNAMSIL (Sierra Leone), UNSC Res 1270 (22 October 1999) UN Doc S/RES/1270; MONUC (DRC), UNSC Res 1291 (24 February 2000) UN Doc S/RES/1291, UNSC Res 1417 (14 June 2002) UN Doc S/RES/1417, UNSC Res 1493 (28 July 2003) UN Doc S/RES/1493, UNSC Res 1533 (12 March 2004) UN Doc S/RES/1533, UNSC Res 1565 (1 October 2004) UN Doc S/RES/1565, UNSC Res 1592 (30 March 2005) UN Doc S/RES/1592, UNSC Res 1756 (15 May 2007) UN Doc S/RES/1756, UNSC Res 1856 (22 December 2008) UN Doc S/RES/1856, UNSC Res 1906 (23 December 2009) UN Doc S/RES/1906, and UNSC Res 1925 (28 May 2010) UN Doc S/RES/1925; UNOCI (Côte d'Ivoire), UNSC Res 1528 (27 February 2004) UN Doc S/RES/1528, UNSC Res 1609 (24 June 2005) UN Doc S/RES/1609, and UNSC Res 1739 (10 January 2007) UN Doc S/RES/1739; ONUB (Burundi), UNSC Res 1545 (21 May 2004) UN Doc S/RES/1545; UNMIS (Sudan), UNSC Res 1590 (24 March 2005) UN Doc S/RES/1590 and UNSC Res 1706 (31 August 2006) UN Doc S/RES/1706; UNIFIL (Lebanon), UNSC Res 1701 (11 August 2006) UN Doc S/RES/1701; UNAMID (Sudan), UNSC Res 1769 (31 July 2007) UN Doc S/RES/1769; MINURCAT (Chad/Central African Republic), UNSC Res 1861 (14 January 2009) UN Doc S/RES/1861 and UNSC Res 1923 (25 May 2010) UN Doc S/RES/1923.

For state-led UN forces, see: former Yugoslavia, UNSC Res 836 (4 June 1993) UN Doc S/RES/836, UNSC Res 844 (18 June 1993) UN Doc S/RES/844; DRC, UNSC Res 1080 (15 November 1996) UN Doc S/RES/1080, UNSC Res 1484 (30 May 2003) UN Doc S/RES/1484, and UNSC Res 1671 (25 April 2006) UN Doc S/RES/1671; Côte d'Ivoire, UNSC Res 1464 (4 February 2003) UN Doc S/RES/1464 and UNSC Res 1528 (27 February 2004) UN Doc S/RES/1528; Haiti, UNSC Res 1529 (29 February 2004) UN Doc S/RES/1529; Chad/Central African Republic, UNSC Res 1778 (25 September 2007) UN Doc S/RES/1778.

[288] See the deployment maps of MONUSCO (DRC), UNAMSIL (Sierra Leone), and UNOCI (Côte d'Ivoire) at the UN Cartographic Section website, www.un.org/Depts/Cartographic/english/htmain.htm.

others only a portion of it.[289] The geographical limit of Chapter VII use of force was the subject of a recent memorandum of the UN Legal Counsel on MONUC (DRC). In this case, the Special Representative of the Secretary-General to the DRC expressed the concern that a unit of MONUC could be operating beyond its mandated area of operations and that 'members of MONUC's military component could potentially be using force . . . in an area where MONUC does not . . . have any authority or responsibility'.[290] The UN Legal Counsel concluded that 'any authorisation to use force within the boundaries of [State] in order to protect the activities of the Riverine Unit and secure its freedom of movement would have to be granted by the Security Council'.[291] This clearly shows the practical implications of the geographical limit in Chapter VII mandates: MONUC is not authorised to use force outside the DRC because the Security Council had not extended the authorisation to include a territory outside the DRC. The UN Legal Counsel's opinion also implies that, if MONUC uses force beyond the border of the DRC, it could be in violation of the relevant Security Council resolutions and Article 2(7) of the UN Charter which provides the principle of non-intervention except under Chapter VII.[292]

Moreover, in many recent cases, the use of force is authorised only within the limits of the military capability of the concerned UN forces. For example, such limit is provided for UNMIS (Sudan) when the Security Council decided that it 'is authorized to take the necessary action . . . as it deems within its capabilities'.[293]

[289] See the deployment maps of ONUB (Burundi), UNIFIL (Lebanon), and UNMIS (Sudan), at the UN Cartographic Section website, www.un.org/Depts/Cartographic/english/htmain.htm.

In some cases, the area is specified such as in resolution 1493 on MONUC (DRC): '*The Security Council . . . Authorizes* MONUC to use all necessary means to fulfil its mandate in the Ituri district and, as it deems it within its capabilities, in North and South Kivu'. See UNSC Res 1493 (28 July 2003) UN Doc S/RES/1493, para 26. However, in the same resolution, MONUC was authorised 'to take the necessary measures in the areas of deployment of its armed units' and thus the above paragraph should be seen as emphasising that MONUC is clearly entitled to use force in Ituri and North/South Kivu but does not necessarily prevent the use of force in other areas in the DRC.

[290] UN Secretariat, 'Note to the Director of the Africa Division, Department of Peacekeeping Operations, United Nations' (2003) *United Nations Juridical Yearbook* 534, 535.

[291] UN Secretariat, 'Note to the Director of the Africa Division, Department of Peacekeeping Operations, United Nations' (2003) *United Nations Juridical Yearbook* 534, 535. Note that the name of the concerned state is omitted from the published version and replaced by '[State]'.

[292] Art 2(7) of the UN Charter provides as follows: 'Nothing contained in the present Charter shall authorize the United Nations to intervene in matters which are essentially within the domestic jurisdiction of any state or shall require the Members to submit such matters to settlement under the present Charter; but this principle shall not prejudice the application of enforcement measures under Chapter VII.'

[293] UNSC Res 1590 (24 March 2005) UN Doc S/RES/1590, para 16(i). For UN-commanded forces, see: UNOSOM II (Somalia), UNSC Res 954 (4 November 1994) UN Doc S/RES/954; UNAMSIL (Sierra Leone), UNSC Res 1270 (22 October 1999) UN Doc S/RES/1270; MONUC (DRC), UNSC Res 1291 (24 February 2000) UN Doc S/RES/1291, 1417 (14 June 2002) UN Doc S/RES/1417, UNSC Res 1493 (28 July 2003) UN Doc S/RES/1493, UNSC Res 1533 (12

Finally, in three cases, the use of force was authorised only if the situation required it. For example on the multinational force in the DRC, the Security Council authorised the 'deployment of an Interim Emergency Multinational Force in Bunia . . . if the situation requires it, to contribute to the safety of civilian population, United Nations personnel and the humanitarian presence in the town'.[294]

A model case including most of these conditions is resolution 1464 on the multinational forces in Côte d'Ivoire:

> *The Security Council* . . . authorizes Member States participating in the ECOWAS forces . . . to take the necessary steps . . . to ensure . . . the protection of civilians immediately threatened with physical violence within their zones of operation, using the means available to them, for a period of six months after which the Council will . . . decide whether to renew this authorization.[295]

As can be seen from above, in recent years, the Security Council has tightened its control over the authorisation of use of force, particularly through five conditions: 1) mandates for which the use of force is authorised; 2) temporal limit; 3) geographical limit; 4) military capacity; and 5) only when the situation requires it.

In the case of Chapter VII use of force by UN-commanded forces in particular, it is regulated additionally by the principle of self-defence. In practice, the Chapter VII authorisation of use of force almost invariably covers the protection of UN personnel and thus the principle of self-defence is not necessary as a justification to use force. However, in some cases, Chapter VII authorisation does not cover the protection of UN personnel. In such cases, when the UN-commanded forces are attacked, they are entitled to use force but only in self-defence.[296]

March 2004) UN Doc S/RES/1533, UNSC Res 1565 (1 October 2004) UN Doc S/RES/1565, UNSC Res 1592 (30 March 2005) UN Doc S/RES/1592, UNSC Res 1756 (15 May 2007) UN Doc S/RES/1756, UNSC Res 1856 (22 December 2008) UN Doc S/RES/1856, UNSC Res 1906 (23 December 2009) UN Doc S/RES/1906, and UNSC Res 1925 (28 May 2010) UN Doc S/RES/1925; UNMISET (East Timor), UNSC Res 1410 (17 May 2002) UN Doc S/RES/1410; UNOCI (Côte d'Ivoire), UNSC Res 1528 (27 February 2004) UN Doc S/RES/1528, UNSC Res 1609 (24 June 2005) UN Doc S/RES/1609, and UNSC Res 1739 (10 January 2007) UN Doc S/RES/1739; ONUB (Burundi), UNSC Res 1545 (21 May 2004) UN Doc S/RES/1545; UNMIS (Sudan), UNSC Res 1590 (24 March 2005) UN Doc S/RES/1590 and UNSC Res 1706 (31 August 2006) UN Doc S/RES/1706; UNIFIL (Lebanon), UNSC Res 1701 (11 August 2006) UN Doc S/RES/1701; UNAMID (Sudan), UNSC Res 1769 (31 July 2007) UN Doc S/RES/1769; MINURCAT (Chad/Central African Republic), UNSC Res 1861 (14 January 2009) UN Doc S/RES/1861 and UNSC Res 1923 (25 May 2010) UN Doc S/RES/1923.

For state-led UN forces, see: East Timor, UNSC Res 1264 (15 September 1999) UN Doc S/RES/1264; Côte d'Ivoire, UNSC Res 1464 (4 February 2003) UN Doc S/RES/1464; DRC, UNSC Res 1671 (25 April 2006) UN Doc S/RES/1671; Chad/Central African Republic, UNSC Res 1778 (25 September 2007) UN Doc S/RES/1778.

[294] UNSC Res 1484 (30 May 2003) UN Doc S/RES/1484, para 1. See further, Côte d'Ivoire, UNSC Res 1528 (27 February 2004) UN Doc S/RES/1528, para 16; Haiti, UNSC Res 1529 (29 F[illegible] 2004) UN Doc S/RES/1529, para 2(a).

[illegible] Res 1464 (4 February 2003) UN Doc S/RES/1464, para 9.

[illegible] scope of self-defence by UN-commanded forces, see the earlier discussion in

UN Forces Authorised to Use Force: Limitation by the Principles of Necessity and Proportionality

The principles of proportionality and necessity also bind the conduct of Chapter VII use of force.[297] They are inherent in the Security Council resolutions themselves and are increasingly referred to in state practice and by experts. As similar to the principles of proportionality and necessity in the law of self-defence, the principles are not set out in the UN Charter in explicit terms. They have rather developed through the practice of states and the UN.

The principles of proportionality and necessity as rules regulating Chapter VII use of force have been discussed in the recent practice of states[298] and the UN,[299] but most experts have omitted the discussion on this topic. Some experts support the applicability of the principles, as Judith Gardam notes:

> The development of the law on the use of force indicates that the requirement of proportionality has long been a determinant of the legitimacy of the use of force . . . It is a principle of general international law that governs all use of force, whether individual or through collective security system.[300]

Such a view is supported by few other experts.[301] Despite such dearth of discussion on this topic, the principles of proportionality and necessity

[297] Whether the principles of proportionality and necessity, as rules regulating Chapter VII use of force, have become customary international law is not yet clear. For the formal requirements to form customary international law, see *Continental Shelf* (*Libyan Arab Jamahiriya/Malta*) [1985] ICJ Rep 13, para 27; *North Sea Continental Shelf* (*Federal Republic of Germany/Denmark; Federal Republic of Germany/Netherlands*) (Merits) [1969] ICJ Rep 3, para 74.

[298] The UK Attorney-General noted as follows in his legal advice on the legality of military action against Iraq in 2003: 'Finally, I must stress that the lawfulness of military action depends not only on the existence of a legal basis, but also on the question of proportionality. Any force used pursuant to the authorisation in resolution 678 (whether or not there is a second resolution): must have as its objective the enforcement [of] the terms of the cease-fire in resolution 687 (1990) and subsequent relevant resolutions; be limited to what is necessary to achieve the objective; and must be a proportionate response to that objective, ie securing compliance with Iraq's disarmament obligations.' See United Kingdom Attorney-General, 'Iraq: Resolution 1441' (7 March 2003) para 36, UK Attorney-General's Office website, www.attorneygeneral.gov.uk.

[299] The UN Secretary-General's High Level Panel on Threats, Challenges and Change noted as follows on the use of force authorised by the Security Council: 'In considering whether to authorize or endorse the use of military force, the Security Council should always address . . . at least the following five basic criteria of legitimacy . . . (c) *Last resort*. Has every non-military option for meeting the threat in question been explored, with reasonable grounds for believing that other measures will not succeed? (d) *Proportional means*. Are the scale, duration and intensity of the proposed military action the minimum necessary to meet the threat in question?' UNGA, 'A More Secure World: Our Shared Responsibility, Report of the High-level Panel on Threats, Challenges and Change' (2 December 2004) UN Doc A/59/565, para 207(d).

[300] J Gardam, *Necessity, Proportionality and the Use of Force* (Cambridge, Cambridge University Press, 2004) 212.

[301] Gasser, 'Collective Economic Sanctions', 882; C Greenwood, 'International Humanitarian Law (Law of War)' in F Kalshoven (ed), *The Centennial of the First International*

are inherent in the process of the Security Council authorisation to use force, although in a different form compared to the law of self-defence.

First, on the principle of necessity, the two interpretations in the context of self-defence[302] *mutatis mutandis* apply to Chapter VII use of force. With regard to the test of whether alternatives other than the use of force are available, the Security Council, in the first instance, has at its disposal a range of options for peaceful settlement of disputes under Chapter VI of the UN Charter. The Security Council can directly resort to Chapter VII without necessarily going through Chapter VI options, but Chapter VII itself incorporates the essence of the principle of necessity. First, the requirement to determine a situation as a threat to the peace, breach of the peace, or act of aggression under Article 39 of the UN Charter naturally requires a consideration on whether Chapter VII enforcement measures have become necessary. Secondly, a decision to undertake Chapter VII use of force is possible if non-military enforcement action does not prove to be an adequate measure to maintain international peace and security. Article 42 of the UN Charter provides that the Security Council may take military enforcement action should it consider that 'measures provided for in Article 41 would be inadequate or have proved to be inadequate'. Finally, Article 51 of the UN Charter assumes that the Security Council only takes measures only if they are necessary. It provides as follows:

> Measures taken by Members in the exercise of this right of self-defence . . . shall not in any way affect the authority and responsibility of the Security Council under the present Charter to take at any time such action as it deems necessary in order to maintain or restore international peace and security.

Thus, the principle of necessity, as interpreted as a requirement to consider non-military options, is inherent in the UN Charter, particularly in Chapters VI and VII.[303]

With regard to the test whether Chapter VII use of force was only to the extent necessary to achieve the mandates, this reflects the principle of proportionality and thus, the following section will consider the principle of proportionality as found in Security Council resolutions. As discussed earlier, Chapter VII use of force is invariably authorised to carry out specific mandates and the extent of the use of force cannot go beyond them. In this sense, the elements to be put on the two sides of the scale to assess the pro-

Peace Conference: Reports and Conclusions (Boston, Kluwer Law International, 2000) 183; B Oswald, 'The Creation and Control of Places of Protection during United Nations Peace Operations' (2001) 844 *International Review of the Red Cross* 1013, para 1034; Frowein and Krisch, 'Article 39', 711–12; Kolb, *Ius contra bellum*, 124 *ff*.

[302] 1) Whether the measures in self-defence per se are necessary, that is, whether there are still other alternatives than the use of force and 2) whether the measures taken in self-defence were only to the extent that they were necessary to halt and repel the armed attack. See section 3.III.A.

[303] This is consistent with the recommendation of the UN Secretary-General's High Level Panel on Threats, Challenges and Change quoted above. See n 299 above.

portionality are on one hand, the mandates and on the other, the use of force. In other words, the use of force should be proportionate to achieve the mandates. However, this also means that the scope of the use of force is commensurate to the scope of the mandates and as discussed earlier, the mandates can vary from wide to narrow ones. For example, the Security Council authorised the multinational forces in the 1991 Gulf War 'to use all necessary means to uphold and implement resolution 660 (1990) and all subsequent relevant resolutions and to restore international peace and security in the area'.[304] This enabled the multinational forces to wage a full-scale armed conflict against Iraq. However, an issue was whether the multinational forces were only permitted to repel the Iraqi armed forces from Kuwait and back into their territory, or could pursue a wider aim.[305]

On the other hand, there are mandates whose scope is narrower, such as that on UNOSOM II:

> *The Security Council . . . Authorizes* UNOSOM II military forces to take those actions necessary to protect UNOSOM II mission and the withdrawal of UNOSOM II personnel and assets, and, to the extent that the Force Commander deems it practicable and consistent, in the context of withdrawal, to protect personnel of relief organizations.[306]

Thus, even though Chapter VII use of force should be proportionate to achieve the concerned mandates, the scope of the mandates determines the permitted scope of the use of force, which can range from a full-scale armed conflict like in the 1991 Gulf War to a limited one such as the protection of UN and relief personnel.

[304] UNSC Res 678 (29 November 1990) UN Doc S/RES/678, para 2.

[305] C Greenwood, 'New World Order or Old? The Invasion of Kuwait and the Rule of Law' (1992) 55 *Modern Law Review* 153, 165 *ff*. See also J Gardam, 'Proportionality and Force in International Law' (1993) 87 *American Journal of International Law* 391, 405; Dinstein, *War, Aggression and Self-Defence*, 242.

[306] UNSC Res 954 (4 November 1994) UN Doc S/RES/954, para 6. The earlier mandate for UNOSOM II caused controversies: '*The Security Council . . . Reaffirms* that the Secretary-General is authorized . . . to take all necessary measures against all those responsible for the armed attacks . . . to establish the effective authority of UNOSOM II throughout Somalia, including to secure the investigation of their actions and their arrest and detention for prosecution, trial and punishment'. See UNSC Res 837 (6 June 1993) UN Doc S/RES/837, para 5.

In theory, the mandate to 'establish effective authority of UNOSOM throughout Somalia' could be interpreted so far as to enable UNOSOM II to use force as a national police or armed force maintaining security in Somalia, including Somaliland and Puntland, which are highly autonomous regions in Somalia, even though in practice UNOSOM II was only able to maintain presence in the capital, Mogadishu.

Even the interpretation of the narrower mandate to 'secure the investigation of their actions and their arrest and detention for prosecution, trial and punishment' was problematic. The UN Legal Counsel noted that 'the prosecution, trial and punishment do not fall within the existing mandate of UNOSOM II nor do we find that paragraph 5 [quoted above] creates such a mandate. Paragraph 5 clearly contemplates that prosecution, trial and punishment should take place, but its language is neutral as to how it should take place.' See UN Secretariat, 'Memorandum to the Under-Secretary-General for Peacekeeping Operations' (1993) *United Nations Juridical Yearbook* 447, para 7.

Three major differences between the principle of proportionality in the law of self-defence and Chapter VII use of force can be highlighted: 1) purpose of the use of force; 2) balancing elements in considering the proportionality; and 3) other elements found in the principle of proportionality in the law of self-defence. First, the fundamental difference between the use of force in self-defence and Chapter VII is that the former is primarily to defend a state by halting and repelling an armed attack but the latter has a broader objective to maintain international peace and security, which can range from establishing and maintaining security of a state by intervening in a non-international armed conflict, to directly confronting an aggressor state to help the victim state, such as in the 1991 Gulf War. Thus, the principle of proportionality also has a different role in the respective use of force. In self-defence, the principle of proportionality is aimed at avoiding the use of excessive force which goes beyond halting and repelling the armed attack. In Chapter VII use of force, the principle of proportionality is aimed at avoiding the use of force which goes beyond the extent necessary to achieve the mandates given by the Security Council. These mandates are not always to halt and repel the armed attack like in self-defence but consist of a range of mandates as discussed earlier. Thus, the proportionality of the use of force is assessed in more diverse situations compared to self-defence.

The second difference is related to the first one. As discussed earlier, the balancing elements in the principle of proportionality in the law of self-defence are: 1) an armed attack and self-defence measures; and 2) an armed attack and the aim to halt and repel the armed attack. However, with regard to Chapter VII use of force, the balancing elements are the mandates and the use of force. They are similar in the sense that the scope of the use of force is commensurate to the initial armed attack or Chapter VII mandates. However, the principle of proportionality in the law of self-defence has its limits: it can only be meaningful if the armed attack and self-defence measures do not develop into a full-scale armed conflict.[307] On the other hand, the principle of proportionality as found in Security Council resolutions remains relevant even when Chapter VII use of force develops into a full-scale armed conflict. For example, in the 1991 Gulf War, although the meaning of 'use all necessary means . . . to restore international peace and security in the area' gave rise to controversy, the use of force by the multinational forces should have been proportionate to this mandate. Thus, the principle of proportionality retains its utility in Chapter VII use of force since, whatever the scope of the mandates, the

[307] The report of the UN International Law Commission on state responsibility notes as follows: 'the limits inherent in the requirement of proportionality are clearly meaningless where the armed attack and the likewise armed resistance to it lead to a state of war between the two countries.' ILC, *Yearbook of the International Law Commission* Vol II, Part One (New York, United Nations, 1980) para 123.

proportionality will always be assessed against those mandates whereas in the use of force in self-defence, it loses its utility once the situation develops into a full-scale armed conflict.

Thirdly, other elements in the principle of proportionality in the law of self-defence, particularly the restrictions on target selection, temporal scope and geographical scope of self-defence, should always be considered in the conduct of self-defence but these elements are applicable to Chapter VII use of force only if they are included in the relevant Security Council resolutions. As noted earlier, the principle of proportionality in the law of self-defence can limit the choice of the targets to be attacked in self-defence, extent of effects on civilians, duration of the conduct of self-defence, and geographical extent of self-defence.[308] It has also been noted that the duration and geographical extent of Chapter VII use of force can also be limited by Security Council resolutions.[309] However, such limitations are applicable only when they are explicitly included in the relevant Security Council resolutions. Otherwise, there are no general restrictions as to the duration or the geographical extent of Chapter VII use of force. For example, in the 1991 Gulf War, resolution 678 set no limits on the duration of the authorisation to use force, which later caused controversies on whether it was still valid in 2003 when the US and UK invaded Iraq.[310] On the other hand, the elements inherent in the principle of proportionality are one set which apply to all self-defence measures. Nevertheless, as discussed earlier, the Security Council has increasingly imposed additional limits, including on the duration and geographical extent of Chapter VII use of force, in order to avoid the consequences of an open-ended authorisation like resolution 678.

The distinction between the use of force in self-defence and under Chapter VII is fundamental since in the former case, the scope of the use of force can be more limited by the principle of proportionality compared to the latter. For example, with regard to the 1991 Gulf War, one of the critical questions was whether the multinational forces could attack Iraq only so far as to halt and repel the invasion of Kuwait by Iraq, or beyond. The scope of the use of force depended on how it was characterised, in this case, either collective self-defence or Chapter VII use of force.[311] If it

[308] See section 3.II.A.

[309] See section 4.IV.B.

[310] See n 284 above.

[311] There are different views on whether the actions of the multinational forces after 15 January 1991 were: 1) collective self-defence; 2) Chapter VII measure; or 3) a mixture of both. Among others see, for 1) Dinstein, *War, Aggression and Self-Defence*, 274; for 2) Greenwood, 'New World Order or Old?', 165; and for 3) see the suggestion in O Schachter, 'United Nations Law in the Gulf Conflict' (1991) 85 *American Journal of International Law* 452, 462. For an overview of different positions see M Weller, 'The United Nations and the *Jus ad Bellum*' in P Rowe (ed), *The Gulf War 1990–91 in International and English Law* (London, Routledge, 1993) 40–41.

was collective self-defence, the use of force was regulated by the principle of proportionality and thus, the use of force was limited to halting and repelling the invasion by Iraq. However, if it was a Chapter VII use of force, the use of force could have continued until international peace and security was restored in the area, as authorised by resolution 678. The consequences were succinctly described by Christopher Greenwood:

> [T]he right of self-defence would have justified the coalition in doing only what was necessary to defend Kuwait. Only a further resolution from the Council [the Security Council] could have provided the legal justification for more extensive war aims, such as the re-establishment of stability in the region.[312]

Thus, the distinction between the use of force in self-defence and under Chapter VII is crucial to determine the permitted extent of the use of force. In practice, this consideration has been relevant only in the 1950–53 Korean War and the 1991 Gulf War since the majority of the use of force in self-defence was not authorised by the Security Council concurrently.

In short, the use of force by UN forces is regulated by *jus ad bellum* itself, namely the principle of self-defence, Security Council resolutions, and principles of necessity and proportionality. UN-commanded forces not authorised to use force are only permitted to use force in self-defence and only if it is proportionate, which is narrowly defined by UN practice. Chapter VII use of force, either by UN-commanded forces or state-led UN forces, is regulated by Security Council resolutions and the principles of necessity and proportionality. Chapter VII use of force by UN-commanded forces is additionally regulated by the principle of self-defence. The determination of whether the use of force is in self-defence under Article 51 of the UN Charter or customary international law, or under Chapter VII, is crucial since in the former case, the principle of proportionality only allows a limited use of force to halt and repel the armed attack whereas the latter might permit an extensive use of force, depending on the Security Council mandates.

[312] Greenwood, 'New World Order or Old?', 165.

C. *Jus in Bello* Constraints on the Use of Force by UN Forces[313]

Chapter VII use of force is not only regulated by *jus ad bellum* but also by *jus in bello*. These dual constraints form the principal basis for the regulation of Chapter VII use of force. This section first clarifies the applicability of IHL to UN forces and the next section discusses issues that arise when *jus ad bellum* and *jus in bello* regulating Chapter VII use of force apply simultaneously. As noted at the beginning, this section does not discuss all the questions relating to the applicability of IHL to UN forces since issues such as the legal consequences of IHL violations by UN forces[314] go beyond the scope of this book.

The applicability of IHL to UN forces is well established by state and UN practice but there are difficult questions particular to UN forces, which is a peculiar case compared to the application of IHL to typical international or non-international armed conflict. Therefore, careful considerations on a number of questions are necessary. For the purpose of examining the

[313] See generally D Bowett, *United Nations Forces* (London, Sweet & Maxwell, 1964); F Seyersted, *United Nations Forces in the Law of Peace and War* (Leyden, Sijthoff, 1966); D Schindler, 'United Nations Forces and International Humanitarian Law' in C Swinarski (ed), *Studies and Essays on International Humanitarian Law and Red Cross Principles in Honour of Jean Pictet* (The Hague, Martinus Nijhoff, 1984); G-J van Hegelsom, 'The Law of Armed Conflict and United Nations Peace-keeping and Peace-enforcing Operations' (1993) 6 *Hague Yearbook of International Law* 45; U Palwankar, 'Applicability of International Humanitarian Law to United Nations Peace-keeping Forces' (1993) 294 *International Review of the Red Cross* 227; ICRC, *Symposium on Humanitarian Action and Peace-keeping Operations* (Geneva, International Committee of the Red Cross, 1994); S Turley, 'Keeping the Peace: Do the Laws of War Apply?' (1994) 73 *Texas Law Review* 139; J Peck, 'The UN and the Law of War: How Can the World's Peacekeepers Be Held Accountable?' (1995) 21 *Syracuse Journal of International Law and Commerce* 283; McCoubrey and White, *The Blue Helmets*; Condorelli et al (eds), *Nations Unies et le droit international humanitaire*; C Greenwood, 'International Humanitarian Law and United Nations Military Operations' (1998) 1 *Yearbook of International Humanitarian Law* 3; D Shraga, 'The United Nations as an Actor Bound by International Humanitarian Law' (1998) 5 *International Peacekeeping* 64; M Zwanenburg, 'Compromise or Commitment: Human Rights and International Humanitarian Law Obligations for UN Peace Forces' (1998) 11 *Leiden Journal of International Law* 229; R Kolb, *Droit humanitaire et opérations de paix internationals* (Bâle, Helbing et Lichtenhahn, 2002); A Faite and J Grenier (eds), *Expert Meeting on Multinational Peace Operations: Applicability of International Humanitarian Law and International Human Rights Law to UN Mandated Forces* (Geneva, International Committee of the Red Cross, 2004); R Kolb et al, *L'application du droit international humanitaire et des droits de l'homme aux organisations internationales: Forces de paix et administrations civiles transitoires* (Bruxelles, Bruylant, 2005); K Okimoto, 'Violations of International Humanitarian Law by United Nations Forces and Their Legal Consequences' (2003) 6 *Yearbook of International Humanitarian Law* 199; M Zwanenburg, *Accountability of Peace Support Operations* (Leiden, Martinus Nijhoff, 2005), UN Secretariat, 'Note on the Protection of Peacekeeping Personnel under International Humanitarian Law' (2006) *United Nations Juridical Yearbook* 518; O Engdahl, 'Compliance with International Humanitarian Law in Multinational Peace Operations' (2009) *Nordic Journal of International Law* 513.

[314] See generally D Shraga, 'UN Peacekeeping Operations: Applicability of International Humanitarian Law and Responsibility for Operation-Related Damage' (2000) 94 *American Journal of International Law* 407; Okimoto, 'Violations of International Humanitarian Law', 220 *ff*; Zwanenburg, *Accountability*, 209 *ff*.

applicability of IHL to UN forces, it is necessary to distinguish state-led UN forces and UN-commanded forces.[315]

Applicability of IHL to State-led UN Forces

With regard to state-led UN forces, although more than one state normally act under the command of a lead state, IHL applies between each troop-contributing state and the adversary.[316] This is due to the manner in which the forces are composed. The Security Council authorises UN Member States to use force and some of these states contribute their armed forces on the basis of the authorisation given to each of those states. Although state-led UN forces may be acting under the command of a lead state, each contingent contributed from different states acts on behalf of its own state. Hence, state-led UN forces are not bound by IHL as a collective entity, but each troop contributing state is bound individually by IHL.

The adversary can be a state or an armed group. The nature of the armed conflict and the applicable rules of IHL are different depending on which one the state-led UN forces are fighting. When state-led UN forces are engaged in an armed conflict with State A (or an armed group supported by a state), it is a classic case of international armed conflict in the sense that it is an armed conflict between two or more states.[317] Customary rules applicable in international armed conflict apply in the same manner between all the troop-contributing states and State A since customary international law does not depend on the ratification by states. On the other hand, the application of IHL treaties applicable in international armed conflict is more complex.[318] A treaty is only applicable among states parties to it and thus, IHL treaties are only applicable if both the troop-contributing states and State A are parties to them. In other words, a particular IHL treaty might be applicable between State A and several troop-contributing states but the same IHL treaty might not be applicable between State A and other troop-contributing states because the latter are not parties to it. Thus, the treaty relation between State A and the troop-contributing states is highly complex and State A has to change the applicable IHL treaties according to the troop-contributing state it is confronting. While the universally ratified 1949 Geneva Conventions will not cause such a problem, other IHL treaties that are not universally ratified will cause such a problem.

[315] See section 4.IV.A for the distinction.

[316] See, eg, UNSC Res 1546 (8 June 2004) UN Doc S/RES/1546, UNSC Res 1637 (11 November 2005) UN Doc S/RES/1637, and UNSC Res 1723 (28 November 2006) UN Doc S/RES/1723, which confirmed the applicability of IHL to 'all forces promoting the maintenance of security and stability in Iraq'.

[317] See common Art 2 of the 1949 Geneva Conventions.

[318] Greenwood, 'International Humanitarian Law and United Nations Military Operations', 19.

An example is the airstrikes of the North Atlantic Treaty Organization (NATO) on the Bosnian Serb forces.[319] In this case, the ICTY concluded that the Bosnian Serb forces were acting under the overall control of and on behalf of the Federal Republic of Yugoslavia[320] and hence the armed conflict between NATO states and the Bosnian Serb forces was an international armed conflict. The 1977 First Additional Protocol was applicable between Germany/Italy/Netherlands/Spain on one hand and the Bosnian Serb forces on the other, but not between France/Turkey/UK/US and the Bosnian Serb forces. This is because Germany, Italy, the Netherlands, Spain, and the Federal Republic of Yugoslavia were all parties to the First Additional Protocol whereas France, Turkey, the UK and the US were not parties to it at the time of the conflict.[321]

The same problem occurs when state-led UN forces are fighting armed groups not supported by a state. State-led UN forces have increasingly been intervening in an existing non-international armed conflict and instances where state-led UN forces become engaged in an armed conflict with local armed groups have also increased.[322] As will be seen in the next chapter, an armed conflict between state-led UN forces and armed groups is not envisaged in IHL. Such an armed conflict is between armed forces of states and armed groups, which resembles non-international armed conflict. However, non-international armed conflict in the IHL sense is

[319] See UNSC Res 770 (13 August 1992) UN Doc S/RES/770, para 2; UNSC Res 787 (16 November 1992) UN Doc S/RES/787, para 14; UNSC Res 816 (31 March 1993) UN Doc S/RES/816, para 4; UNSC Res 836 (4 June 1993) UN Doc S/RES/836, para 10; UNSC Res 844 (18 June 1993) UN Doc S/RES/844, para 4; UNSC Res 908 (31 March 1994) UN Doc S/RES/908, para 8; UNSC Res 958 (19 November 1994) UN Doc S/RES/958. For UNPROFOR combat activities and NATO air strikes, see the UN Secretary-General's reports and letters: UNSC, 'Letter Dated 6 February 1994 from the Secretary-General Addressed to the President of the Security Council' (7 February 1994) UN Doc S/1994/131; UNSC, 'Report of the Secretary-General Pursuant to Resolution 871 (1993)' (16 March 1994) UN Doc S/1994/300; UNSC, 'Letter Dated 18 April 1994 from the Secretary-General Addressed to the President of the Security Council' (19 April 1994) UN Doc S/1994/466; UNSC, 'Report of the Secretary-General Pursuant to Resolution 913 (1994)' (19 May 1994) UN Doc S/1994/600; UNSC, 'Report of the Secretary-General Pursuant to Resolution 908 (1994)' (17 September 1994) UN Doc S/1994/1067; UNSC, 'Report of the Secretary-General Pursuant to Resolution 959 (1994)' (1 December 1994) UN Doc S/1994/1389; UNSC, 'Report of the Secretary-General Pursuant to Resolution 947 (1994)' (22 March 1995) UN Doc S/1995/222; UNSC, 'Report of the Secretary-General Pursuant to Security Council Resolutions 982 (1995) and 987 (1995)' (30 May 1995) UN Doc S/1995/444; UNSC, 'Report of the Secretary-General Pursuant to Resolution 844 (1993)' (9 May 1994) UN Doc S/1994/555; UNSC, 'Report of the Secretary-General Pursuant to Security Council Resolutions 981 (1995), 982 (1995) and 983 (1995)' (23 November 1995) UN Doc S/1995/987; UNGA, 'Report of the Secretary-General Pursuant to General Assembly Resolution 53/35: The Fall of Srebrenica' (15 November 1999) UN Doc A/54/549.

[320] See *Tadic Case* (Judgment, Appeals), para 162.

[321] For the latest record of states parties to IHL treaties, see the ICRC IHL Database, www.icrc.org/ihl. As at September 2010, the US has not become a party to the 1977 First Additional Protocol.

[322] See n 256 above for instances where the Security Council authorised the use of force under Chapter VII in non-international armed conflict situation.

confined to the territory of one state, whereas state-led UN forces come from outside the concerned state. Therefore, it is not a non-international armed conflict in the strict IHL sense. Neither is it an international armed conflict, since it is not an armed conflict between states.

Nevertheless, since the character of the armed conflict resembles non-international armed conflict, it is widely accepted that the IHL rules applicable in non-international armed conflict apply between foreign states, including state-led UN forces, and armed groups not supported by a state. These rules are common Article 3 of the 1949 Geneva Conventions, IHL treaties applicable in non-international armed conflict as well as in all circumstances,[323] and customary law of non-international armed conflict.[324]

Customary law of non-international armed conflict clearly applies between all states participating in state-led UN forces, and armed groups since it does not depend on the ratification status of either states participating in state-led UN forces or the state in which armed groups operate. Likewise, common Article 3 of the 1949 Geneva Conventions apply in any armed conflict between state-led UN forces and armed groups since the Geneva Conventions are universally ratified. Problems arise with the application of IHL treaties applicable in non-international armed conflict. The nature of the problem is the same as the applicability of IHL treaties to an armed conflict between state-led UN forces and a state. IHL treaties applicable in non-international armed conflict only apply if the troop-contributing states and the state in which armed groups operate are both parties to them. However, in practice, many states where state-led UN forces have been deployed are not yet parties to these IHL treaties and thus they are often not applicable between state-led UN forces and the armed

[323] They are, 1954 Cultural Property Convention; Protocol for the Protection of Cultural Property in the Event of Armed Conflict (adopted 13 May 1954, entered into force 7 August 1956) 249 UNTS 358; 1972 Biological Weapons Convention; Convention on Prohibitions and Restrictions on the Use of Certain Conventional Weapons Which May Be Deemed to Be Excessively Injurious or to Have Indiscriminate Effects (adopted 10 October 1980, entered into force 2 December 1983) 1342 UNTS 137; Protocol on Non-Detectable Fragments (Protocol I) (adopted 10 October 1980, entered into force 2 December 1983) 1342 UNTS 168; Protocol on Prohibitions or Restrictions on the Use of Mines, Booby-Traps and Other Devices (Protocol II) (adopted 10 October 1980, entered into force 2 December 1983) 1342 UNTS 168; Protocol on Prohibitions or Restrictions on the Use of Incendiary Weapons (Protocol III) (adopted 10 October 1980, entered into force 2 December 1983) 1342 UNTS 171; Protocol on Blinding Laser Weapons (Protocol IV) (adopted 13 October 1995, entered into force 30 July 1998) 2024 UNTS 167; Amended Protocol II; Protocol on Explosive Remnants of War (Protocol V) (adopted 28 November 2003, entered into force 12 November 2006) 2399 UNTS 100; 1993 Chemical Weapons Convention; 1997 Convention on Anti-Personnel Mines; Convention on Cluster Munitions (adopted 30 May 2008, entered into force 1 August 2010) (2009) 48 ILM 354.

[324] For a list of customary rules of IHL applicable in non-international armed conflict, see J Henckaerts, 'Study on Customary International Humanitarian Law: A Contribution to the Understanding and Respect for the Rule of Law in Armed Conflict' (2005) 857 *International Review of the Red Cross* 175, 198 *ff*.

groups.[325] An example is the International Security Assistance Force (ISAF) in Afghanistan. Since Afghanistan is not a party to, for example, the 1954 Cultural Property Convention, this IHL treaty does not apply between the states participating in ISAF and the armed groups in Afghanistan, even though many states of ISAF are parties to the Convention.[326] However, when more states become parties to these IHL treaties, the issue of which of these IHL treaties are applicable between states participating in state-led UN forces and armed groups will become more real.

Since state-led UN forces do not have a collective legal personality, it seems inevitable that different IHL treaties are applicable between the adversary and each troop-contributing state. However, it is equally clear that it creates a highly complex web of bilateral treaty application between the adversary and the troop contributing states, which is impractical for those who need to comply with the law.

Applicability of IHL to UN-commanded Forces

With regard to UN-commanded forces, the applicability of IHL is confirmed through state and UN practice but in reality, the applicability of IHL to UN-commanded forces is a far more difficult question than state-led UN forces.

Unlike state-led UN forces, UN-commanded forces are a collective entity and therefore it raises a more general question: is the UN bound by international law as an international organisation? On this point, the ICJ stated in the *Reparations* Advisory Opinion that the UN is an international person which 'is a subject of international law and capable of possessing international rights and duties'.[327] It further stated that 'the rights and duties of an entity such as the Organization [UN] must depend upon its purposes and functions as specified or implied in its constituent documents and developed practice'.[328] The Court also stated in the *WHO-Egypt Agreement* Advisory Opinion that 'international organizations are subjects of international law and as such, are bound by any obligations incumbent upon them under general rules of international law'.[329] More recently,

[325] For the states to which state-led UN forces were deployed, see n 256 above. For the latest record of states parties to the above IHL treaties, see the ICRC IHL Database, www.icrc.org/ihl.

[326] As at September 2010, out of the 47 states contributing to ISAF, 41 were parties to the 1954 Cultural Property Convention. Iceland, Ireland, Republic of Korea, Singapore, United Arab Emirates, and UK were the states that were not parties to it. For the troop-contributing states, see the ISAF website, www.isaf.nato.int.

[327] *Reparation for Injuries Suffered in the Service of the United Nations* (hereafter *Reparations* case) (Advisory Opinion) [1949] ICJ Rep 174, 179.

[328] *Reparations* case (Advisory Opinion), 180.

[329] *Interpretation of the Agreement of 25 March 1951 between the WHO and Egypt* (Advisory Opinion) [1980] ICJ Rep 73, para 37.

the UN International Law Commission provided as follows in the Draft Articles on the Responsibility of International Organizations:

> The conduct of an organ or agent of an international organization in the performance of functions of that organ or agent shall be considered as an act of that organization under international law.[330]

From these statements, the applicability of customary rules of IHL to UN-commanded forces seems clear. Customary international law does not require consent to be bound by states or in the case of international organisations, an act of formal confirmation.[331] By becoming a subject of international law, the UN is automatically bound by customary international law, including customary rules of IHL.

IHL treaties are a different issue since treaties require consent to be bound by states or an act of formal confirmation by international organisations in order for the treaties to become binding on them.[332] However, the UN is not a party to any IHL treaties.[333] The applicability of at least the 'principles and spirit' of IHL treaties has, however, been confirmed through, in the words of the ICJ, the 'developed practice' of states and the UN. In the early years of the UN, the Force Regulations of UNEF I (Middle East),[334] ONUC (Congo),[335] and UNFICYP (Cyprus) recognised that 'The Force shall observe the principles and spirit of the general international Conventions applicable to the conduct of military personnel',[336] and the UN Secretary-General interpreted this provision as including the 1949 Geneva Conventions and 1954 Cultural Property Convention.[337]

[330] Art 5(1) of ILC, 'Responsibility of International Organizations' (hereafter ILC Draft Articles on the Responsibility of International Organizations) (2009) UN Doc A/64/10 Supp No 10, paras 50 *ff*. See also UN Secretariat, 'Interoffice memorandum to the Director of the Codification Division, Office of Legal Affairs and Secretary of the International Law Commission regarding the Topic of Responsibility of International Organizations' (2004) *United Nations Juridical Yearbook* 352, 354.

[331] See Art 2 (b bis) of the Vienna Convention on the Law of Treaties between States and International Organizations or between International Organizations (hereafter 1986 Vienna Convention on the Law of Treaties) (adopted 21 March 1986, not yet entered into force) 25 ILM 543.

[332] Art 2 (b bis) of the 1986 Vienna Convention on the Law of Treaties.

[333] The UN Legal Counsel, in fact, concluded that the UN cannot become a party to the 1949 Geneva Conventions. See UN Secretariat, 'Question of the Possible Accession of Intergovernmental Organizations to the Geneva Conventions for the Protection of War Victims' (1972) *United Nations Juridical Yearbook* 153.

[334] UN Secretary-General, 'Regulations for the United Nations Emergency Force' 271 UNTS 168, para 44.

[335] See para 43 of UN Secretary-General, 'Regulations for the United Nations Force in Congo' (15 July 1963) UN Doc ST/SGB/ONUC/1 in R Siekmann, *Basic Documents on United Nations and Related Peace-keeping Forces* (The Hague, TMC Asser Instituut, 1985).

[336] UN Secretary-General, 'Regulations for the United Nations Force in Cyprus' 555 UNTS 132, para 40.

[337] Exchange of Letters Constituting an Agreement between the United Nations and Australia concerning the Service with the United Nations Peace-keeping Force in Cyprus of the National Contingent Provided by the Government of Australia (adopted 25 February 1966, entered into force 25 February 1966) 557 UNTS 86, para 11; Exchange of Letters

Status-of-forces agreements (SOFAs)[338] of a number of UN-commanded forces have also confirmed as follows:

> [T]he United Nations shall ensure that the UN forces and forces shall conduct their activities . . . with full respect for the principles and spirit of the general conventions applicable to the conduct of military personnel; these international conventions include the four Geneva Conventions of 12 August 1949 and their Additional Protocols of 8 June 1977 and the UNESCO Convention of 14 May 1954 on the Protection of Cultural Property in the event of armed conflict.[339]

Constituting an Agreement between the United Nations and Canada concerning the Service with the United Nations Peace-keeping Force in Cyprus of the National Contingent Provided by the Government of Canada (adopted 21 February 1966, entered into force 21 February 1966) 557 UNTS 120, para 11; Exchange of Letters Constituting an Agreement between the United Nations and Austria concerning the Service with the United Nations Peace-keeping Force in Cyprus of the National Contingent Provided by the Government of Austria (adopted 28 June 1966, entered into force 28 June 1966) 557 UNTS 130, para 11.

338 Status of forces agreements are concluded between the UN and the state to which the concerned UN forces will be deployed.

339 See the following SOFAs with slight variations for each UN forces.

- UNPROFOR (Croatia) / UNCRO (Croatia) / UNPREDEP (Macedonia)
  Agreement on the United Nations Forces and Operations in Croatia (adopted 15 May 1995, entered into force 15 May 1995) 1864 UNTS 287, paras 7(a) and (b).
- UNPROFOR (Macedonia)
  Exchange of Letters Constituting an Agreement on the Status of the United Nations Protection Force in the Former Yugoslav Republic of Macedonia (adopted 14 June 1994, entered into force 14 June 1994) 1788 UNTS 257, paras 7(a) and (b).
- UNAMIR (Rwanda)
  Agreement on the Status of the United Nations Assistance Mission for Rwanda (adopted 5 November 1993, entered into force 5 November 1993) 1748 UNTS 17, paras 7(a) and (b).
- UNAVEM III (Angola)
  Agreement on the Status of the United Nations Peace-keeping Operation in Angola (adopted 3 May 1995, entered into force 3 May 1995) 1864 UNTS 193, paras 6(a) and (b).
- UNMIH (Haiti)
  Agreement on the Status of the United Nations Mission in Haiti (adopted 15 March 1995, entered into force 15 March 1995) 1861 UNTS 269, paras 7(a) and (b).
- UNIFIL (Lebanon)
  Agreement on the Status of the United Nations Interim Force in Lebanon (adopted 15 December 1995, entered into force provisionally 15 December 1995, entered into force definitively 21 August 2008) 1901 UNTS 397, paras 7(a) and (b).
- UNSMIH (Haiti)
  Exchange of Letters Constituting an Agreement between the United Nations and Haiti on the Status of the United Nations Mission in Haiti (UNSMIH) (adopted 4 July 1996, entered into force 4 July 1996) 1929 UNTS 80;
- MINURCA (Central African Republic)
  Agreement concerning the Status of the United Nations Mission in the Central African Republic (adopted 8 May 1998, entered into force 8 May 1998) 2015 UNTS 727, paras 6(a) and (b).
- MONUC (DRC / Uganda)
  Memorandum of Understanding between the United Nations and the Government of the Republic of Uganda concerning the Activities of the United Nations Organization Mission in the Democratic Republic of the Congo in Uganda (adopted 8 August 2003, entered into force 8 August 2003) 2221 UNTS 298, Art IV.

The UN Model Agreement between the UN and Member States Contributing Personnel and Equipment to United Nations Peace-keeping Operations further confirmed as follows:

> [The United Nations peace-keeping operation] shall observe and respect the principles and spirit of the general international conventions applicable to the

- MONUC (DRC)
  Protocol Amending the Agreement between the United Nations and the Democratic Republic of the Congo on the Status of the United Nations Mission in the Democratic Republic of the Congo (hereafter 2006 MONUC SOFA Protocol) (adopted 6 June 2006, entered into force 6 June 2006) UNTS No 36644, para 1.
- UNMISET (East Timor)
  Agreement between the Democratic Republic of East Timor and the United Nations concerning the Status of the United Nations Mission of Support in East Timor (hereafter 2002 UNMISET SOFA) (adopted 20 May 2002, entered into force 20 May 2002) 2185 UNTS 368, paras 6(a) and (b).
- UNAMSIL (Sierra Leone)
  Agreement between the United Nations and Sierra Leone concerning the Status of the United Nations Mission in Sierra Leone (adopted 4 August 2000, entered into force 4 August 2000) 2118 UNTS 190, paras 6(a) and (b).
- UNMEE (Eritrea/Ethiopia)
  Agreement between Ethiopia and the United Nations concerning the Status of the United Nations Mission in Ethiopia and Eritrea (adopted 23 March 2001, entered into force 23 March 2001) 2141 UNTS 24, paras 6(a) and (b).
- UNOCI (Côte d'Ivoire)
  Agreement between the United Nations and the Government of the Republic of Côte d'Ivoire Regarding the Status of the United Nations Operation in Côte d'Ivoire (adopted 29 June 2004, entered into force 29 June 2004) 2268 UNTS 161, paras 6(a) and (b).
- MINUSTAH (Haiti)
  Agreement between the United Nations and the Government of Haiti concerning the Status of the United Nations Operation in Haiti (adopted 9 July 2004, entered into force 9 July 2004) 2271 UNTS 251, paras 6(a) and (b).
- UNMIL (Liberia)
  Agreement between Liberia and the United Nations concerning the Status of the United Nations Mission in Liberia (adopted 6 November 2003, entered into force 6 November 2003) 2300 UNTS 128, paras 6(a) and (b).
- ONUB (Burundi)
  Agreement between the United Nations and Burundi concerning the Status of the United Nations Operation in Burundi (adopted 17 June 2005, entered into force 17 June 2005) 2321 UNTS 95, paras 6(a) and (b).
- UNMIS (Sudan)
  Agreement between the Government of Sudan and the United Nations concerning Status of the United Nations Mission in Sudan (adopted 28 December 2005, entered into force 28 December 2005) 2351 UNTS 64, paras 6(a) and (b).
- UNMIT (East Timor)
  Agreement between the United Nations and the Democratic Republic of Timor-Leste on the Status of the United Nations Integrated Mission in Timor-Leste (UNMIT) (adopted 4 October 2006, entered into force 4 October 2006) 2387 UNTS 350.
- UNAMID (Sudan)
  Agreement between the United Nations and the African Union and the Government of Sudan concerning the Status of the African Union/United Nations Hybrid Operation in Darfur (adopted 9 February 2008, entered into force 9 February 2008) 2497 UNTS 1, paras 6(a) and (b).

conduct of military personnel. The international conventions referred to above include the four Geneva Conventions of 12 August 1949 and their Additional Protocols of 8 June 1977 and the UNESCO Convention of 14 May 1954 on the Protection of Cultural Property in the event of armed conflict.[340]

More recently, the UN Secretary-General issued a bulletin entitled 'Observance by United Nations Forces of International Humanitarian Law',[341] which, for the first time, specified the IHL rules applicable to UN-commanded forces. A number of other UN reports and documents also clearly recognise the applicability of IHL to UN-commanded forces.[342] Therefore, state and UN practice clearly confirms that at least the 'principles and spirit' of IHL treaties are applicable to UN-commanded forces.

Finally, recent developments in international law indicate that states are able to provide rights and obligations for international organisations which are not parties to a particular treaty. Indications can be found in the 1986 Vienna Convention on the Law of Treaties between States and International Organizations or between International Organizations.[343] Articles 35 and 36 reserve the opportunity for an international organisation to hold rights and obligations of a treaty even if it is not a party to that treaty, provided that the parties to that treaty intend to provide such rights and obligations and the concerned international organisation accepts those rights and obligations. If this approach is followed, it is possible for the UN to hold rights and obligations under IHL treaties which the UN is not a party to. As can be seen from the UN Model Agreement, which was adopted by states in the General Assembly, and the SOFAs, certain states seem to accept that IHL treaties apply to UN forces and the UN, in turn, also seems to accept that IHL conventions apply to UN forces, as can be seen from the SOFAs and the UN Secretary-General's Bulletin.

[340] UNGA, 'Model Agreement between the United Nations and Member States Contributing Personnel and Equipment to United Nations Peace-keeping Operations' (23 May 1991) UN Doc A/46/185, para 28. Apart from SOFAs, the UN normally concludes agreements with states which contribute troops to the concerned UN forces. The UN Model Agreement is a standard form for such agreements.

[341] UN Secretary-General, 'Secretary-General's Bulletin: Observance by United Nations Forces of International Humanitarian Law' (6 August 1999) UN Doc ST/SGB/1999/13.

[342] See in particular, Art 2(2) of the 1994 Safety Convention; UN Secretariat, 'The Comprehensive Report on Lessons Learned from the United Nations Operation in Somalia (UNOSOM)' (1995) para 58, UN Peacekeeping Resource Hub website, www.peacekeepingbestpractices.unlb.org; UNGA, 'Report of the Secretary-General on Financing of the United Nations Protection Force, the United Nations Confidence Restoration Operation in Croatia, the United Nations Preventive Deployment Force and the United Nations Peace Forces Headquarters' (20 September 1996) UN Doc A/51/389, para 16; UNSC, 'Report of the Secretary-General to the Security Council on the Protection of Civilians in Armed Conflict' (8 September 1999) UN Doc S/1999/957, para 61; UN Secretariat, *Handbook on United Nations Multidimensional Peacekeeping Operations* (New York, United Nations, 2003) 58.

[343] See n 331 above.

The 'principles and spirit' of all IHL treaties are applicable to UN-commanded forces, regardless of whether the UN or troop-contributing states have consented to be bound by them or not. SOFAs and the UN Model Agreement quoted above make explicit mention of the 1949 Geneva Conventions, 1977 Additional Protocols, and 1954 Cultural Property Convention but they do not exclude the applicability of other IHL treaties.

When UN-commanded forces are engaged in an armed conflict with a state's armed forces or armed groups supported by a state, it is an international armed conflict where the law of international armed conflict is fully applicable.[344] IHL treaties applicable to international armed conflict are applicable when the state fighting with UN-commanded forces is a party to the treaties.

As similar to state-led UN forces, when UN-commanded forces are engaged in an armed conflict with armed groups not supported by a state, it is neither an international armed conflict nor a non-international armed conflict, since it is not an armed conflict between states or an armed conflict in the territory of a state (either between a state's armed forces and armed groups, or between different armed groups). In this case, as similar to state-led UN forces, UN-commanded forces are foreign forces that intervene in a non-international armed conflict, which engage in an armed conflict with local armed groups. However, since the character of the armed conflict is similar to non-international armed conflict, in other words, between, on one hand, UN-commanded forces that are composed of armed forces of different states, and armed groups on the other, IHL rules applicable to non-international armed conflict apply.[345] This conclusion is the same as state-led UN forces that are engaged in an armed conflict with armed groups without any support from a state. Customary rules applicable to non-international armed conflict apply in any armed conflict between UN-commanded forces and armed groups without state support. This is because customary international law does not require consent to be bound or an act of formal confirmation by the UN or the state where armed groups are operating, in order for customary international law to become binding on them. Likewise, common Article 3 of the 1949 Geneva Conventions applies in any armed conflict between UN-commanded forces and armed groups since the Geneva Conventions are universally ratified and, as seen above, the Conventions clearly apply to the UN. Therefore, wherever the armed conflict is taking place, the

[344] See, eg, the fighting between the Bosnian Serb forces and UNPROFOR over Vrbanja bridge in Sarajevo, UNGA, 'Report of the Secretary-General Pursuant to General Assembly Resolution 53/35: The Fall of Srebrenica' (15 November 1999) UN Doc A/54/549, para 192.

[345] Common Art 3 of the 1949 Geneva Conventions, IHL treaties applicable in non-international armed conflict as well as in all circumstances, and customary law of non-international armed conflict.

state where armed groups are operating will be a party to the Geneva Conventions and common Article 3 becomes applicable whenever the armed groups engage in an armed conflict in that state, including an armed conflict with UN-commanded forces. With regard to IHL treaties applicable in non-international armed conflict, they are applicable only if the state in which armed groups are operating is a party to them. The question of intervention by states and armed groups into another state and its impact on the applicability of *jus ad bellum* and *jus in bello* will be discussed in more depth in the next chapter.

The above analyses show that UN forces are actors bound by *jus ad bellum* and *jus in bello*. *Jus ad bellum* constraints are composed of the principle of self-defence, Security Council resolutions, and the principles of necessity and proportionality. *Jus in bello* is applicable to both state-led UN forces and UN-commanded forces. The applicable rules, however, differ depending on whether they are engaged in an armed conflict with a state (including armed groups supported by a state) or armed groups not supported by a state. Any use of force under Chapter VII must comply with the requirements in both *jus ad bellum* and *jus in bello*. When UN forces are not authorised to use force under Chapter VII but become engaged in an armed conflict, they can use force only in self-defence and such use of force in self-defence must comply with IHL.

D. Specific Issues Pertaining to the Relationship between Chapter VII Use of Force and IHL

As noted earlier, the use of force under Chapter VII is authorised for various mandates, which is in marked contrast to the use of force in self-defence (within the meaning of Article 51 of the UN Charter), which is limited to halting and repelling an armed attack. Chapter VII use of force can of course resemble the use of force in self-defence such as in the case of the 1991 Gulf War when the multinational forces engaged in a direct military confrontation with the Iraqi forces and drove them out from Kuwait. However, UN forces could be authorised to use force in order to protect civilians and humanitarian personnel, which is a use of force of a very different nature from self-defence. This section discusses selected issues of Chapter VII use of force that may affect the relationship between *jus ad bellum* and *jus in bello*.

Means and Methods of Warfare

The use of force under Chapter VII has a direct relation with IHL rules on means and methods of warfare, which regulate which weapons can be used and how. Neither the UN Charter nor Security Council resolutions specify which weapons can be used and how and hence, IHL plays an exclusive role in the conduct of hostilities by UN forces.[346] However, Security Council resolutions determine when force can be used by UN forces and to what extent. These are areas that IHL does not deal with.

Security Council resolutions are the primary source that regulate when and to what extent UN forces can use force. This is the same for state-led UN forces and UN-commanded forces. The mandates are specified in the relevant Security Council resolutions, which determine when UN forces can use force. For example, in Côte d'Ivoire, the Economic Community of West African States (ECOWAS) and France were authorised to use force in order to 'guarantee the security and freedom of movement of their personnel' and to 'ensure . . . the protection of civilians immediately threatened with physical violence within their zone of operation, using the means available to them, for a period six months'.[347] This imposed limits on the purpose, geographical area, and the duration of Chapter VII use of force, which are aspects that IHL does not regulate.

At the same time, ECOWAS and French forces had to comply with IHL when they were using force to carry out their mandates. A question that must be answered before that is obviously whether ECOWAS and French forces were engaged in an armed conflict. Supposing that they were, the customary rules on means and methods of warfare applied. These include such fundamental rules as the distinction between civilians and persons directly participating in hostilities and prohibition on indiscriminate attacks. For example, when the French forces came to assist the Côte d'Ivoire armed forces when the latter was attacked by an armed group, the combat resulted in some 20 deaths, mainly of civilians.[348] While it was not indicated how they were killed, the relevant rules that applied between the French forces/Côte d'Ivoire armed forces and the armed group were customary rules on means and methods of warfare, in particular the prohibition on attacks on civilians and the principle of proportionality.

The same can be said for UN-commanded forces. For example, MONUC in the DRC was authorised to use force to 'seize or collect . . . the arms and any related materiel' of armed groups. MONUC, therefore, could not use force for other purposes, for example to destroy the bases of armed groups. Moreover, the area of operation was limited to North and South Kivu.[349]

[346] The rules on means and methods of warfare were already explained in the context of self-defence. See section 3.II.B.

[347] UNSC Res 1464 (4 February 2003) UN Doc S/RES/1464, para 9.

[348] UNSC, 'Second Report of the Secretary-General on the United Nations Operation in Côte d'Ivoire' (27 August 2004) S/2004/697, para 3.

[349] The mandate is provided in UNSC Res 1533 (12 March 2004) UN Doc S/RES/1533, para 4 and the authorisation to use force in UNSC Res 1493 (28 July 2003) UN Doc S/RES/1493, para 26. For the accounts on heavy fighting with the DRC armed groups, see UN Secretary-General's reports on MONUC: UNSC, 'Third Special Report of the Secretary-General on the

Thus, the extent of the use of force was limited to a specific mandate and within a specific geographical area. At the same time, MONUC had to comply with IHL whenever it used force to carry out the mandate, particularly the law on means and methods of warfare. For example, in North Kivu in December 2005, MONUC and the DRC armed forces carried out a major military operation against an armed group which resulted in an estimated 86 deaths on the armed group side and one death on the MONUC side.[350] In this case, the customary rules on means and methods of warfare applied, in particular the distinction between civilians and civilians participating directly in hostilities.

Thus, the use of force by UN forces can only be carried out lawfully by complying with the dual constraints of *jus ad bellum* and *jus in bello*, namely within the limits imposed by the relevant Security Council resolutions and the applicable IHL rules.

A particular difficulty with UN forces is the ratification status of the 1977 Additional Protocols, which contain the bulk of the rules on means and methods of warfare applicable in international and non-international armed conflict. As mentioned before, IHL treaties apply only among conflicting states that are parties to the treaties. Different problems arise for the First Additional Protocol and Second Additional Protocol.

With regard to the First Additional Protocol, some states participating in state-led UN forces might be parties to the Protocol but some might not. If state-led UN forces are fighting State A, which is a party to the Protocol, then the Protocol applies only between states participating in the state-led UN forces that are parties to the Protocol and State A. If State A is not a party to the Protocol, then it does not apply between any of the states participating in the state-led UN forces and State A. For example, when NATO carried out airstrikes against the Federal Republic of Yugoslavia

United Nations Organization Mission in the Democratic Republic of the Congo' (16 August 2004) UN Doc S/2004/650, para 45 (armed group v MONUC); UNSC, 'Sixteenth Report of the Secretary-General on the United Nations Organization Mission in the Democratic Republic of the Congo' (31 December 2004) UN Doc S/2004/1034, para 11 (armed group v MONUC); UNSC, 'Seventeenth Report of the Secretary-General on the United Nations Organization Mission in the Democratic Republic of the Congo' (15 March 2005) UN Doc S/2005/167, paras 16 and 19 (armed groups v MONUC); UNSC, 'Eighteenth Report of the Secretary-General on the United Nations Organization Mission in the Democratic Republic of the Congo' (2 August 2005) UN Doc S/2005/506, para 34 (armed group v MONUC); UNSC, 'Twentieth Report of the Secretary-General on the United Nations Organization Mission in the Democratic Republic of the Congo' (28 December 2005) UN Doc S/2005/832, paras 23 and 26 (armed groups v MONUC); UNSC, 'Report Pursuant to Paragraphs 10 and 14 of Security Council Resolution 1649 (2005)' (22 May 2006) UN Doc S/2006/310, para 29 (armed groups v MONUC); UNSC, 'Twenty-First Report of the Secretary-General on the United Nations Organization Mission in the Democratic Republic of the Congo' (13 June 2006) UN Doc S/2006/390, paras 33, 35, 36, 37, and 39 (armed groups v MONUC).

[350] UNSC, 'Report Pursuant to Paragraphs 10 and 14 of Security Council Resolution 1649 (2005)' (22 May 2006) UN Doc S/2006/310, para 29.

in 1995,[351] the 1977 First Additional Protocol applied between Germany/Italy/Netherlands/Spain and the Federal Republic of Yugoslavia because they were all parties to the Protocol, but not between France/Turkey/US/UK and the Federal Republic of Yugoslavia because the former four states were not parties to the Protocol. Hence, the rules on means and methods of warfare in the First Additional Protocol were binding among the first group of states whereas it was not among the second group of states. Nevertheless, customary rules of means and methods of warfare applied to all the conflicting parties, regardless of their ratification status of the First Additional Protocol.

This problem does not arise with UN-commanded forces since they are a collective entity established by the Security Council. For example, UNPROFOR used force against the Bosnian Serb forces, which were acting on behalf of the Federal Republic of Yugoslavia, to 'deter attacks against the safe areas'.[352] In this case, the 1977 First Additional Protocol applied between UNPROFOR as a collective entity and the Bosnian Serb forces.

With regard to the 1977 Second Additional Protocol, it does not apply to UN forces since Article 1(1) of the Protocol requires an armed conflict to 'take place in the territory of a High Contracting Party between its armed forces and dissident armed forces or other organized armed groups'. UN forces intervene in an armed conflict in the territory of a particular state and hence the armed conflict is not taking place in their territory (UN forces do not possess their own territory in any case) and they are not armed forces of the territorial state. Therefore, the Second Additional Protocol a priori does not apply to an armed conflict between UN forces and armed groups.

UN-commanded forces, whether or not authorised to use force under Chapter VII, are bound not only by Security Council resolutions and IHL, but also additionally by the principle of self-defence. As noted above, the principle of self-defence and the principle of proportionality which accompanies it require that UN-commanded forces can only use force to protect themselves and only against: 1) an 'armed attack'; or 2) 'attempts by forceful means to prevent' UN-commanded forces from carrying out their mandates.[353] However, even when UN-commanded forces are using force in self-defence, their conduct is fully regulated by IHL if they

[351] See UNGA, 'Report of the Secretary-General Pursuant to General Assembly Resolution 53/35: The Fall of Srebrenica' (15 November 1999) UN Doc A/54/549, paras 442–45.

[352] See, eg, the fighting between the Bosnian Serb forces and UNPROFOR over Vrbanja bridge in Sarajevo; UNGA, 'Report of the Secretary-General Pursuant to General Assembly Resolution 53/35: The Fall of Srebrenica' (15 November 1999) UN Doc A/54/549, 48, para 192.

[353] See section 4.IV.B.

become a party to an armed conflict. Therefore, Article 49(1) of the 1977 First Additional Protocol provides as follows:

> 'Attacks' means acts of violence against the adversary, whether in offence or in defence.[354]

This indicates that even when UN-commanded forces are using force in self-defence as a party to an armed conflict, IHL is applicable. The UN Secretary-General's Bulletin confirms the point that 'The fundamental principles and rules of international humanitarian law set out in the present bulletin are applicable . . . in enforcement actions, or in peacekeeping operations when the use of force is permitted in self-defence.'[355]

Thus, for example, if UNAMIR in Rwanda had used force against the attacks from the Rwanda armed forces and armed groups,[356] it was regulated by the principle of self-defence and the principle of proportionality which accompanies it, as well as IHL. UNAMIR was not authorised to use force and thus they could only use force in self-defence, but even then, IHL regulated the conduct of their use of force. Since UNAMIR was confronted by a mixture of the Rwanda armed forces and armed groups, the applicable IHL rules were either the law of international armed conflict or the law of non-international armed conflict depending on the adversary. These include such fundamental rules as the distinction between civilians and those directly participating in hostilities and prohibition on indiscriminate attacks.[357]

Protection of Civilians[358]

The relationship between Chapter VII use of force and IHL is not only about UN forces being an actor bound by *jus ad bellum* and *jus in bello* but also about UN forces implementing IHL. This can be observed when mandates given to UN forces resemble IHL obligations. The two most frequent mandates are the protection of civilians and the protection and facilitation of relief personnel and consignments. However, such mandates of UN forces are still different from IHL obligations. Hence, the differences and similarities between the two should be made clear. This section discusses the protection of civilians by UN forces and IHL and the next section the

[354] See also Art 49(2) of the 1977 First Additional Protocol: 'The provisions of this Protocol with respect to attacks apply to all attacks in whatever territory conducted.'

[355] UN Secretary-General, 'Secretary-General's Bulletin', Section 1.1.

[356] For attacks on UNAMIR, see UNSC, 'Report of the Independent Inquiry into the Actions of the United Nations during the 1994 Genocide in Rwanda' (16 December 1999) UN Doc S/1999/1257.

[357] See n 324 above.

[358] For an overview of the complementary nature of UN forces and IHL, see A Aeschlimann, 'Overview of Protection Issues in Contexts of Multinational Peace Operations' in Faite and Grenier (eds), *Expert Meeting on Multinational Peace Operations*.

protection and facilitation of relief personnel and consignments by UN forces and IHL.

The protection of civilians in IHL is, by now, extensive. With regard to civilians in general they are protected by the 1949 Fourth Geneva Convention and the 1977 First Additional Protocol in international armed conflict, and by a reduced form in common Article 3 of the 1949 Geneva Conventions and the 1977 Second Additional Protocol in non-international armed conflict. Among the many provisions for civilian protection, the basic rule is set out in Article 51(2) of the First Additional Protocol and Article 18(2) of the Second Additional Protocol, which provides as follows:

> The civilian population as such, as well as individual civilians, shall not be the object of attack.

This rule is well-established as a customary rule.[359]

The protection of civilians, however, does not seem to mean that states parties are obliged to physically protect each and every civilian. For example, Article 16 of the 1949 Fourth Geneva Convention, which applies to both civilians and combatants,[360] provides as follows:

> The wounded and sick, as well as the infirm, and expectant mothers, shall be the object of particular protection and respect.[361]

A commentary to this provision indicates the possible measures to implement it:

> [I]t will not always be possible to evacuate civilian wounded at once, and it will be necessary to protect them in the meantime against pillage and ill-treatment . . . The present paragraph requires belligerents to facilitate steps taken to prevent any act of pillage either by civilians or by members of the armed forces, whatever their nationality.[362]

Thus, at most, the prevention of certain acts against civilians is required and not the physical protection of each and every civilian.

On the other hand, one of the most frequent mandates of UN forces has been to physically protect civilians by the use of force, which appears to go beyond what IHL requires. There have been at least nine UN-commanded

[359] For its customary law status, see Rule 1 in Henckaerts and Doswald-Beck, *Customary International Humanitarian Law* Vol I, 3.

[360] See Uhler and Coursier et al, *Commentary*, 134.

[361] Other provisions explicitly requiring protection of civilians can be found in the 1949 Geneva Conventions and the 1977 First Additional Protocol.

[362] Uhler and Coursier et al, *Commentary*, 137.

forces[363] and five state-led UN forces[364] with such mandate and an example is Security Council resolution 1545 for ONUB (Burundi), which authorised it 'to use all necessary means . . . to protect civilians under imminent threat of physical violence'.[365] This is an important indication that UN forces can implement and complement IHL obligations through the use of force. However, there are at least four aspects that are critically different from the protection of civilians in IHL: 1) category of civilians; 2) geographical scope; 3) duration; and 4) other specific conditions in Security Council resolutions.

First, and perhaps the most critical difference, is that IHL rules on civilian protection cover all civilians in armed conflict. Admittedly, there is special protection for certain categories of persons such as women, children and journalists, but additional protection on top of the general protection for civilians and civilian population.[366] On the other hand, Chapter VII mandate on civilian protection is of more limited scope. Normally, only those civilians who are under 'imminent threat of physical violence' are protected as can be seen, for example, in resolution 1270 when UNAMSIL (Sierra Leone) was authorised to 'take the necessary action . . . to afford

[363] UNAMSIL (Sierra Leone), UNSC Res 1270 (22 October 1999) UN Doc S/RES/1270, para 14; MONUC (DRC), UNSC Res 1291 (24 February 2000) UN Doc S/RES/1291, para 8, UNSC Res 1417 (14 June 2002) UN Doc S/RES/1417, para 7, UNSC Res 1493 (28 July 2003) UN Doc S/RES/1493, para 25, UNSC Res 1565 (1 October 2004) UN Doc S/RES/1565, para 4(b), UNSC Res 1592 (30 March 2005) UN Doc S/RES/1592, para 7, UNSC Res 1756 (15 May 2007) UN Doc S/RES/1756, para 2(a), UNSC Res 1856 (22 December 2008) UN Doc S/RES/1856, para 3(a), UNSC Res 1906 (23 December 2009) UN Doc S/RES/1906, para 5(a), and UNSC Res 1925 (28 May 2010) UN Doc S/RES/1925, para 12(a); UNMIL (Liberia), UNSC Res 1509 (19 September 2003) UN Doc S/RES/1509, para 3(j); UNOCI (Côte d'Ivoire), UNSC Res 1528 (27 February 2004) UN Doc S/RES/1528, para 6(i), UNSC Res 1609 (24 June 2005) UN Doc S/RES/1609, para 2(a), and UNSC Res 1739 (10 January 2007) UN Doc S/RES/1739, para 2(f); ONUB (Burundi), UNSC Res 1545 (21 May 2004) UN Doc S/RES/1545, para 5; UNMIS (Sudan), UNSC Res 1590 (24 March 2005) UN Doc S/RES/1590, para 16(i) and UNSC Res 1706 (31 August 2006) UN Doc S/RES/1706, para 12(a); UNIFIL (Lebanon), UNSC Res 1701 (11 August 2006) UN Doc S/RES/1701, para 12; UNAMID (Sudan), UNSC Res 1769 (31 July 2007) UN Doc S/RES/1769, para 15(a)(ii); MINURCAT (Chad/Central African Republic), UNSC Res 1861 (14 January 2009) UN Doc S/RES/1861, para 7(a)(i) and 7(b)(ii) and UNSC Res 1923 (25 May 2010) UN Doc S/RES/1923, para 10.

[364] Rwanda, UNSC Res 929 (22 June 1994) UN Doc S/RES/929, para 2; DRC 2003, UNSC Res 1484 (30 May 2003) UN Doc S/RES/1484, para 1; Côte d'Ivoire, UNSC Res 1464 (4 February 2003) UN Doc S/RES/1464, para 9 and UNSC Res 1528 (27 February 2004) UN Doc S/RES/1528, paras 6(i) and 16; DRC 2006, UNSC Res 1671 (25 April 2006) UN Doc S/RES/1671, para 8; Chad/Central African Republic, UNSC Res 1778 (25 September 2007) UN Doc S/RES/1778, para 6(a)(1).

[365] UNSC Res 1545 (21 May 2004) UN Doc S/RES/1545, para 5.

[366] See Arts 76–79 of the 1977 First Additional Protocol. For their customary law status, see Rules 34, 119, 120, and 134–37 in Henckaerts and Doswald-Beck, *Customary International Humanitarian Law* Vol I, 115, 431, 433, 475, 479, 482, and 485.

protection to civilians under imminent threat of physical violence'.[367] If there is no 'imminent threat of physical violence', it is not clear whether UNAMSIL could protect civilians. Moreover, the term 'imminent threat' is unclear and could be interpreted arbitrarily.

Moreover, in some cases, only a specific category of civilians is protected as can be seen, for example, in resolution 1484 when the multinational force in the DRC was authorised 'to ensure the protection of . . . the internally displaced persons in the camps in Bunia'.[368] In this case, civilians who do not qualify as internally displaced persons could be excluded. Moreover, since there is no universally agreed definition of 'internally displaced persons', the determination of who qualifies under the term could be open to debate.[369]

Secondly, on the geographical scope, IHL rules on civilian protection apply to where IHL is applicable: to all states parties to IHL treaties or all states in the case of customary law and to the whole territory of the concerned states.[370] On the other hand, Chapter VII authorisation to protect civilians by the use of force is limited, not only to a specific state, but also to a specific area in the state. In most cases, this is the 'area of deployment' as can be seen from resolution 1545 when ONUB (Burundi) was authorised 'in the areas where its armed units are deployed . . . to protect

[367] UNSC Res 1270 (22 October 1999) UN Doc S/RES/1270, para 14. See further, MONUC (DRC), UNSC Res 1291 (24 February 2000) UN Doc S/RES/1291, para 8, UNSC Res 1417 (14 June 2002) UN Doc S/RES/1417, para 7, UNSC Res 1493 (28 July 2003) UN Doc S/RES/1493, para 25, UNSC Res 1565 (1 October 2004) UN Doc S/RES/1565, para 4(b), UNSC Res 1592 (30 March 2005) UN Doc S/RES/1592, para 7, UNSC Res 1756 (15 May 2007) UN Doc S/RES/1756, para 2(a), and UNSC Res 1856 (22 December 2008) UN Doc S/RES/1856, para 3(a); UNMIL (Liberia), UNSC Res 1509 (19 September 2003) UN Doc S/RES/1509, para 3(j); UNOCI (Côte d'Ivoire), UNSC Res 1528 (27 February 2004) UN Doc S/RES/1528, para 6(i), UNSC Res 1609 (24 June 2005) UN Doc S/RES/1609, para 2(a), and UNSC Res 1739 (10 January 2007) UN Doc S/RES/1739, para 2(f); ONUB (Burundi), UNSC Res 1545 (21 May 2004) UN Doc S/RES/1545, para 5; UNMIS (Sudan), UNSC Res 1590 (24 March 2005) UN Doc S/RES/1590, para 16(i) and UNSC Res 1706 (31 August 2006) UN Doc S/RES/1706, para 12(a); UNIFIL (Lebanon), 1701 (11 August 2006) UN Doc S/RES/1701, para 12; MINURCAT (Chad/Central African Republic), UNSC Res 1861 (14 January 2009) UN Doc S/RES/1861, para 7(a)(i) and 7(b)(ii) and UNSC Res 1923 (25 May 2010) UN Doc S/RES/1923, para 10; Côte d'Ivoire, UNSC Res 1464 (4 February 2003) UN Doc S/RES/1464, para 9 and UNSC Res 1528 (27 February 2004) UN Doc S/RES/1528, para 6(i); DRC 2006, UNSC Res 1671 (25 April 2006) UN Doc S/RES/1671, para 8; Chad/Central African Republic, UNSC Res 1778 (25 September 2007) UN Doc S/RES/1778, para 6(a)(i).

[368] UNSC Res 1484 (30 May 2003) UN Doc S/RES/1484, para 1.

[369] For a suggestion of a definition of internally displaced persons, see UNCHR, 'Guiding Principles on Internal Displacement' (11 February 1998) UN Doc E/CN.4/1998/53/Add.2, para 2 of the Introduction. For discussions on this document, see J-P Lavoyer, 'Guiding Principles on International Displacement: A Few Comments on the Contribution of International Humanitarian Law' (1998) 324 *International Review of the Red Cross* 467; W Kälin, 'Flight in Times of War' (2001) 843 *International Review of the Red Cross* 629.

[370] See *Tadic Case* (Jurisdiction, Appeals), para 70: 'International humanitarian law continues to apply in the whole territory of the warring States or, in the case of internal conflicts, the whole territory under the control of a party, whether or not actual combat takes place there.'

civilians'.[371] In this case, many of the civilians outside the areas were excluded from the protection of ONUB.

Thirdly, IHL rules on civilian protection are applicable whenever an armed conflict (international or non-international) occurs and for the whole duration of the armed conflict. In some cases such as occupation, they apply even beyond the duration of the armed conflict.[372] Chapter VII mandate, on the other hand, is normally authorised only for certain duration, as can be seen from resolution 1528 when the French forces in Côte d'Ivoire were authorised 'for a period of 12 months . . . the French forces . . . in particular to . . . Help to protect civilians'.[373]

[371] UNSC Res 1545 (21 May 2004) UN Doc S/RES/1545, para 5. See further, UNAMSIL (Sierra Leone), UNSC Res 1270 (22 October 1999) UN Doc S/RES/1270, para 14; MONUC (DRC), UNSC Res 1291 (24 February 2000) UN Doc S/RES/1291, para 8, UNSC Res 1417 (14 June 2002) UN Doc S/RES/1417, para 7, UNSC Res 1493 (28 July 2003) UN Doc S/RES/1493, para 25, UNSC Res 1565 (1 October 2004) UN Doc S/RES/1565, para 6, UNSC Res 1592 (30 March 2005) UN Doc S/RES/1592, para 7, UNSC Res 1756 (15 May 2007) UN Doc S/RES/1756, para 4, UNSC Res 1856 (22 December 2008) UN Doc S/RES/1856, para 5, and UNSC Res 1925 (28 May 2010) UN Doc S/RES/1925, para 11; UNOCI (Côte d'Ivoire), UNSC Res 1528 (27 February 2004) UN Doc S/RES/1528, para 8, UNSC Res 1609 (24 June 2005) UN Doc S/RES/1609, para 8, and UNSC Res 1739 (10 January 2007) UN Doc S/RES/1739, para 5; UNMIS (Sudan), UNSC Res 1590 (24 March 2005) UN Doc S/RES/1590, para 16(i) and UNSC Res 1706 (31 August 2006) UN Doc S/RES/1706, para 12(a); UNIFIL (Lebanon), UNSC Res 1701 (11 August 2006) UN Doc S/RES/1701, para 12; UNAMID (Sudan), UNSC Res 1769 (31 July 2007) UN Doc S/RES/1769, para 15(a); MINURCAT (Chad/Central African Republic), UNSC Res 1861 (14 January 2009) UN Doc S/RES/1861, paras 7(a) and (b) and UNSC Res 1923 (25 May 2010) UN Doc S/RES/1923, para 10; Côte d'Ivoire, UNSC Res 1464 (4 February 2003) UN Doc S/RES/1464, para 9 and UNSC Res 1528 (27 February 2004) UN Doc S/RES/1528, paras 6(i), 8, and 16; DRC 2006, UNSC Res 1671 (25 April 2006) UN Doc S/RES/1671, para 8(b); Chad/Central African Republic, UNSC Res 1778 (25 September 2007) UN Doc S/RES/1778, para 6(a).

In two resolutions related to the DRC, the area was specified by the name of the region. See UNSC Res 1484 (30 May 2003) UN Doc S/RES/1484, para 1 and UNSC Res 1493 (28 July 2003) UN Doc S/RES/1493, para 25. In two resolutions related to Chad/Central African Republic, the part of the region in the country was specified. See UNSC Res 1861 (14 January 2009) UN Doc S/RES/1861, paras 7(a) and (b) and UNSC Res 1923 (25 May 2010) UN Doc S/RES/1923, para 10. In one case, the area was specified as the 'zone of operation'. See Côte d'Ivoire, UNSC Res 1464 (4 February 2003) UN Doc S/RES/1464, para 9.

[372] See Art 6 of the 1949 Fourth Geneva Convention and Art 3(b) of the 1977 First Additional Protocol.

[373] UNSC Res 1528 (27 February 2004) UN Doc S/RES/1528, paras 1 and 16. See further UNAMSIL (Sierra Leone), UNSC Res 1270 (22 October 1999) UN Doc S/RES/1270, para 8; MONUC (DRC), UNSC Res 1291 (24 February 2000) UN Doc S/RES/1291, para 3, UNSC Res 1417 (14 June 2002) UN Doc S/RES/1417, para 1, UNSC Res 1493 (28 July 2003) UN Doc S/RES/1493, para 2, UNSC Res 1565 (1 October 2004) UN Doc S/RES/1565, para 1, UNSC Res 1592 (30 March 2005) UN Doc S/RES/1592, para 1, UNSC Res 1756 (15 May 2007) UN Doc S/RES/1756, para 1, UNSC Res 1856 (22 December 2008) UN Doc S/RES/1856, para 1, and UNSC Res 1925 (28 May 2010) UN Doc S/RES/1925, para 1; UNOCI (Côte d'Ivoire), UNSC Res 1528 (27 February 2004) UN Doc S/RES/1528, para 1, UNSC Res 1609 (24 June 2005) UN Doc S/RES/1609, para 1, and UNSC Res 1739 (10 January 2007) UN Doc S/RES/1739, para 1; ONUB (Burundi), UNSC Res 1545 (21 May 2004) UN Doc S/RES/1545, para 2; UNMIS (Sudan), UNSC Res 1590 (24 March 2005) UN Doc S/RES/1590, para 1; UNIFIL (Lebanon), UNSC Res 1701 (11 August 2006) UN Doc S/RES/1701, para 16; UNAMID (Sudan), UNSC Res 1769 (31 July 2007) UN Doc S/RES/1769, para 1; MINURCAT (Chad/Central African Republic), UNSC Res 1861 (14 January 2009) UN Doc S/RES/1861, para 1 and UNSC Res

Fourthly, the conflicting parties are obliged to 'respect and to ensure respect for' IHL in 'all circumstances', including the IHL rules on civilian protection.[374] Civilian protection by Chapter VII UN forces is often limited 'within its capabilities' as can be seen in resolution 1509 when UNMIL (Liberia) was authorised to use force 'to protect civilians . . . within its capabilities'.[375] In this case, if the military capability of UNMIL was not sufficient to protect civilians, it could not protect them. Moreover, the determination of when the military capability is sufficient to protect civilians is open to debate.

Thus, Chapter VII mandate of the UN forces to protect civilians can implement the IHL rules on civilian protection by physically protecting civilians but its scope is limited by a number of conditions.[376] In this sense, IHL remains the primary basis for the protection of civilians in armed conflict since it applies to all civilians in any kind of armed conflict, and

1923 (25 May 2010) UN Doc S/RES/1923, para 1; Rwanda, UNSC Res 929 (22 June 1994) UN Doc S/RES/929, para 4; Côte d'Ivoire, UNSC Res 1464 (4 February 2003) UN Doc S/RES/1464, para 9 and UNSC Res 1528 (27 February 2004) UN Doc S/RES/1528, para 1; DRC, UNSC Res 1484 (30 May 2003) UN Doc S/RES/1484, para 1 and UNSC Res 1671 (25 April 2006) UN Doc S/RES/1671, para 2; Chad/Central African Republic, UNSC Res 1778 (25 September 2007) UN Doc S/RES/1778, para 6(a).

[374] Common Art 1 of the 1949 Geneva Conventions. It is also a customary rule which applies in both international and non-international armed conflict. See Rule 139 in Henckaerts and Doswald-Beck, *Customary International Humanitarian Law* Vol I, 495.

[375] UNSC Res 1509 (19 September 2003) UN Doc S/RES/1509, para 3(j). See further UNAMISL (Sierra Leone), UNSC Res 1270 (22 October 1999) UN Doc S/RES/1270, para 14; MONUC (DRC), UNSC Res 1291 (24 February 2000) UN Doc S/RES/1291, para 8, UNSC Res 1417 (14 June 2002) UN Doc S/RES/1417, para 7, UNSC Res 1493 (28 July 2003) UN Doc S/RES/1493, para 25, UNSC Res 1565 (1 October 2004) UN Doc S/RES/1565, para 6, UNSC Res 1592 (30 March 2005) UN Doc S/RES/1592, para 7, UNSC Res 1756 (15 May 2007) UN Doc S/RES/1756, para 4, UNSC Res 1856 (22 December 2008) UN Doc S/RES/1856, para 5, and UNSC Res 1925 (28 May 2010) UN Doc S/RES/1925, para 11; UNOCI (Côte d'Ivoire), UNSC Res 1528 (27 February 2004) UN Doc S/RES/1528, para 8, UNSC Res 1609 (24 June 2005) UN Doc S/RES/1609, para 8, and UNSC Res 1739 (10 January 2007) UN Doc S/RES/1739, para 5; ONUB (Burundi), UNSC Res 1545 (21 May 2004) UN Doc S/RES/1545, para 5; UNMIS (Sudan), UNSC Res 1590 (24 March 2005) UN Doc S/RES/1590, para 16(i) and UNSC Res 1706 (31 August 2006) UN Doc S/RES/1706, para 12(a); UNIFIL (Lebanon), UNSC Res 1701 (11 August 2006) UN Doc S/RES/1701, para 12; UNAMID (Sudan), UNSC Res 1769 (31 July 2007) UN Doc S/RES/1769, para 15(a); MINURCAT (Chad/Central African Republic), UNSC Res 1861 (14 January 2009) UN Doc S/RES/1861, paras 7(a) and (b) and UNSC Res 1923 (25 May 2010) UN Doc S/RES/1923, para 10; Côte d'Ivoire, UNSC Res 1464 (4 February 2003) UN Doc S/RES/1464, para 9 and UNSC Res 1528 (27 February 2004) UN Doc S/RES/1528, paras 6(i) and 8; DRC, UNSC Res 1671 (25 April 2006) UN Doc S/RES/1671, para 8(b); Chad/Central African Republic, UNSC Res 1778 (25 September 2007) UN Doc S/RES/1778, para 6(a). In two cases, the protection of civilians was only authorised 'if the situation requires it' as in resolution 1484 authorising the UN Member States to protect civilians in the DRC: '*The Security Council . . . Authorizes* the deployment of . . . an Interim Emergency Multinational Force in Bunia . . . if the situation requires it, to contribute to the safety of the civilian population'. UNSC Res 1484 (30 May 2003) UN Doc S/RES/1484, para 1. See also on Côte d'Ivoire, UNSC Res 1528 (27 February 2004) UN Doc S/RES/1528, para 16.

[376] A rare case was Security Council resolution 929 on Rwanda, which authorised the protection of civilians by the UN Member States without adding any conditions. See UNSC Res 929 (22 June 1994) UN Doc S/RES/929, paras 2 and 3.

imposes obligations on all states and armed groups involved in an armed conflict.

Such contribution of Chapter VII decisions to enhance civilian protection in armed conflict is notable but they have also created problems, namely with regard to the 'safe areas' established under Chapter VII and protected by UN forces, which are similar but distinct from localities and zones under special protection in IHL.[377]

In IHL (both in the law of international and non-international armed conflict), there are at least four kinds of localities and zones under special protection:[378] 1) hospital and safety zones and localities;[379] 2) neutralised zones;[380] 3) non-defended localities;[381] and 4) demilitarised zones.[382] In practice, these localities and zones have been used in a flexible manner[383] but the conditions to establish such localities and zones are provided in treaty provisions in detail.

First, with regard to hospital and safety zones and localities, they are generally of a permanent character established outside the combat zone in order to shelter wounded and sick combatants[384] and certain categories of the civilian population.[385] As a practical matter, such zones and localities are often set up for both combatants and civilians, although they are dealt with separately in IHL.[386] A commentary notes that consent of the conflicting parties is required:

[377] See generally Y Sandoz, 'The Establishment of Safety Zones for Persons Displaced Within Their Country of Origin' in N Al-Nauimi and R Messe, *International Legal Issues Arising under the United Nations Decade of International Law: Proceedings of the Qatar International Law Conference 1994* (The Hague, Martinus Nijhoff, 1995) 916–25; Boisson de Chazournes, 'Les résolutions des organs des Nations Unies', 159–60; Gasser, 'The United Nations and International Humanitarian Law', 259.

[378] In addition to the provisions below, see Art 25 of the 1907 Hague Regulations on the protection of undefended towns, villages, dwellings, or buildings.

[379] Art 23 of the 1949 First Geneva Convention; Art 14 of the 1949 Fourth Geneva Convention. For its customary law status, see Rule 35 of Henckaerts and Doswald-Beck, *Customary International Humanitarian Law* Vol I, 119.

[380] Art 15 of the 1949 Fourth Geneva Convention. For its customary law status, see Rule 35 of Henckaerts and Doswald-Beck, *Customary International Humanitarian Law* Vol I, 119.

[381] Art 59 of the 1977 First Additional Protocol. For its customary law status, see Rule 37 of Henckaerts and Doswald-Beck, *Customary International Humanitarian Law* Vol I, 122.

[382] Art 60 of the 1977 First Additional Protocol. For its customary law status, see Rule 36 of Henckaerts and Doswald-Beck, *Customary International Humanitarian Law* Vol I, 120.

[383] See J Pictet et al, *Commentary on the Geneva Conventions of 12 August 1949* Vol I (Geneva, International Committee of the Red Cross, 1952) 207; Uhler and Coursier et al, *Commentary*, 121; F Bugnion, *The International Committee of the Red Cross and the Protection of War Victims* (Geneva, International Committee of the Red Cross, 2003) 484.

[384] Art 23 of the 1949 First Geneva Convention. For its customary law status, see Rule 35 of Henckaerts and Doswald-Beck, *Customary International Humanitarian Law* Vol I, 119.

[385] Art 14 of the 1949 Fourth Geneva Convention. For its customary law status, see Rule 35 of Henckaerts and Doswald-Beck, *Customary International Humanitarian Law* Vol I, 119. See Pictet et al, *Commentary* Vol I, 206–07; Uhler and Coursier et al, *Commentary*, 120. The categories of civilians recognised in Art 14 of the 1949 Fourth Geneva Convention are wounded, sick, aged persons, children under 15, expectant mothers, and mothers of children under seven.

[386] See n 383 above.

> The zones will not, strictly speaking, have any legal existence, or enjoy protection under the Convention, until such time as they have been recognized by the adverse Party. This will entail the conclusion of an agreement between the Power which has established zones in its territory and the Powers with which it is at war.[387]

Secondly, neutralised zones[388] are different from hospital and safety zones and localities since they are: 1) temporary in character; 2) intended for wounded and sick combatants and all civilians (as opposed to certain categories of civilians); 3) in the actual combat zone; and 4) to protect them from military operations in the neighbourhood.[389] Neutralised zones also require consent of the conflicting parties.[390]

Thirdly, non-defended localities[391] are an extension of neutralised zones but they are different from the other three concepts since they can be established by a unilateral declaration by an appropriate authority of the conflicting party, and an agreement of the conflicting parties is not required.[392] This allows a more rapid establishment of protected localities which cover wider scope of persons.[393]

Finally, demilitarised zones[394] are almost identical to non-defended localities but the crucial difference is that they require consent of the conflicting parties.[395]

Thus, as can be seen from the above, localities and zones under special protection in IHL are defined in detail. The so-called 'safe areas' established under Chapter VII can be confused with such localities and zones in IHL.

Security Council practice shows that 'safe areas' are most frequently imposed unilaterally on the conflicting parties under Chapter VII and do not require consent from them. The distinction is crucial since Chapter VII 'safe areas' once failed to prevent the genocide in Srebrenica,[396] which will be discussed below.

[387] Pictet et al, *Commentary* Vol I, 215. See also Uhler and Coursier et al, *Commentary*, 127.

[388] Art 15 of the 1949 Fourth Geneva Convention. For its customary law status, see Rule 35 of Henckaerts and Doswald-Beck, *Customary International Humanitarian Law* Vol I, 119.

[389] Pictet et al, *Commentary* Vol I, 207; Uhler and Coursier et al, *Commentary*, 120.

[390] Uhler and Coursier et al, *Commentary*, 133.

[391] Art 59 of the 1977 First Additional Protocol. For its customary law status, see Rule 37 of Henckaerts and Doswald-Beck, *Customary International Humanitarian Law* Vol I, 122.

[392] See Sandoz et al (eds), *Commentary*, paras 2260–62.

[393] See Sandoz et al (eds), *Commentary*, para 2262.

[394] Art 60 of the 1977 First Additional Protocol. For its customary law status, see Rule 36 of Henckaerts and Doswald-Beck, *Customary International Humanitarian Law* Vol I, 120.

[395] See Art 60(2) of the 1977 First Additional Protocol.

[396] The ICTY concluded that the events in Srebrenica were genocide. *Krstic Case* (Judgment, Trial) ICTY-98-33-T (2 August 2001), para 599; *Krstic* (Judgment, Appeals) ICTY-98-33-A (19 April 2004), para 38. The ICJ concluded that the events in Srebrenica were a violation by Serbia of the obligation to prevent genocide under the 1948 Genocide Convention. See *Bosnia Genocide* case (Merits), para 471 (5). The judgment is currently available at the ICJ website, www.icj-cij.org. Convention on the Prevention and Punishment of the Crime of Genocide (adopted 9 December 1948, entered into force 12 January 1951) 78 UNTS 277.

In the former Yugoslavia, the original plan for 'safe areas'[397] was similar to demilitarised zones envisaged in Article 60 of the 1977 First Additional Protocol but in practice, they were imposed on the conflicting parties under Chapter VII, thus rendering them different from demilitarised zones. On 16 April 1993, the Security Council in its resolution 819 (Chapter VII) designated Srebrenica as a 'safe area' in the following terms:

> *The Security Council . . . Demands* that all parties and others concerned treat Srebrenica and its surroundings as a safe area which should be free from any armed attack or any other hostile act; *Demands also* to that effect the immediate cessation of armed attacks by Bosnian Serb paramilitary units against Srebrenica and their immediate withdrawal from the areas surrounding Srebrenica.[398]

The word 'demands' clearly indicates that the 'safe area' was imposed on rather than agreed to by the conflicting parties. However, two days later, on 18 April 1993, a demilitarisation agreement for Srebrenica was concluded between the conflicting parties (Bosnian Serb forces and the Bosnia and Herzegovina armed forces) which resembled demilitarised zones in Article 60 of the 1977 First Additional Protocol.[399] Regardless of this development in the field, on 6 May 1993, the Security Council in its resolution 824 (Chapter VII) further extended the scope of the 'safe areas':

> *The Security Council . . . Declares* that the capital city of the Republic of Bosnia and Herzegovina, Sarajevo, and other such threatened areas, in particular the towns of Tuzla, Zepa, Gorazde, Bihac, as well as Srebrenica, and their surroundings should be treated as safe areas by all the parties concerned and should be free from armed attacks and from any other hostile act; *Demands* to that end that all parties and others concerned cooperate fully with UNPROFOR and take any necessary measures to respect these safe areas.[400]

As similar to resolution 819, the 'safe areas' were imposed on rather than agreed to by the conflicting parties. However, again, two days later, on 8 May 1993, another demilitarisation agreement was signed between the same conflicting parties which had the following character:

> [T]he agreement of 8 May stated specifically that Srebrenica was to be considered a 'demilitarized zone', as referred to in article 60 of the Protocol Additional to the Geneva Conventions of 12 August 1949, and relating to the Protection of Victims of International Armed Conflicts (Protocol I).[401]

[397] UNGA, 'Report of the Secretary-General Pursuant to General Assembly Resolution 53/35: The Fall of Srebrenica' (15 November 1999) UN Doc A/54/549, para 48. See also UNGA, 'An Agenda for Peace: Preventive Diplomacy, Peacemaking and Peace-keeping' (17 June 1992) UN Doc A/47/277-S/24111, para 33.

[398] UNSC Res 819 (16 April 1993) UN Doc S/RES/819, paras 1 and 2.

[399] Agreement for the Demilitarization of Srebrenica (30 April 1993) UN Doc S/25700, Annex II. The applicability of the law of international armed conflict between the Bosnia and Herzegovina and the Bosnian Serb forces after 19 May 1992 was confirmed by the ICTY. See *Tadic Case* (Judgment, Appeals) ICTY-94-1-A (15 July 1999), para 162.

[400] UNSC Res 824 (6 May 1993) UN Doc S/RES/824, paras 3 and 5.

[401] UNGA, 'Report of the Secretary-General Pursuant to General Assembly Resolution 53/35: The Fall of Srebrenica' (15 November 1999) UN Doc A/54/549, para 65.

Despite this development, on 4 June 1993, the Security Council in its resolution 836 (Chapter VII) further strengthened the protection of the 'safe areas':

> *The Security Council* . . . *Decides* to extend . . . the mandate of UNPROFOR in order to enable it . . . to deter attacks against the safe areas . . . *Authorizes* UNPROFOR . . . acting in self-defence, to take the necessary measures, including the use of force, in reply to bombardments against the safe areas by any of the parties or to armed incursion into them.[402]

Thus, there were two parallel measures taken: 1) demilitarisation agreements similar to that envisaged in Article 60 of the 1977 First Additional Protocol agreed to by the conflicting parties; and 2) Chapter VII resolutions which imposed the concept of 'safe areas' on the conflicting parties. The gap between the Chapter VII resolutions and the demilitarisation agreements had already been recognised by UNPROFOR and the UN Secretariat,[403] and a UN report later noted as follows:

> Protected zones and safe areas can have a role in protecting civilians in armed conflict, but it is clear that either they must be demilitarized and established by the agreement of the belligerents, as in the case of the 'protected zones' and 'safe havens' recognized by international humanitarian law, or they must be truly safe areas, fully defended by a credible military deterrent. The two concepts are absolutely distinct and must not be confused . . . The safe areas were established by the Security Council without the consent of the parties and without the provision of any credible military deterrent. They were neither protected areas nor safe havens in the sense of international humanitarian law, nor safe areas in any militarily meaningful sense.[404]

The danger of Chapter VII 'safe areas' was amply shown in Srebrenica, where genocide took place in the presence of UNPROFOR.[405] Thus, localities or zones under special protection in IHL and 'safe areas' established under Chapter VII should be distinguished since the former normally require consent of the conflicting parties whereas the latter are imposed on the conflicting parties.[406]

The discrepancy between localities and zones under special protection in IHL and Chapter VII 'safe areas' raises the question of whether the latter prevails pursuant to Article 103 of the UN Charter, but as the UN report on the fall of Srebrenica quoted above indicates, the two should be brought in line in practice.[407]

[402] UNSC Res 836 (4 June 1993) UN Doc S/RES/836, paras 5 and 9.

[403] UNGA, 'Report of the Secretary-General Pursuant to General Assembly Resolution 53/35: The Fall of Srebrenica' (15 November 1999) UN Doc A/54/549, para 69.

[404] UNGA, 'Report of the Secretary-General Pursuant to General Assembly Resolution 53/35: The Fall of Srebrenica' (15 November 1999) UN Doc A/54/549, para 499.

[405] See n 396 above.

[406] Rwanda was another case where 'humanitarian areas' were established under Chapter VII. See UNSC Res 925 (8 June 1994) UN Doc S/RES/925, paras 4(a) and (b) and UNSC Res 929 (22 June 1994) UN Doc S/RES/929, paras 2 and 3.

[407] See text to n 404 above.

Protection and Facilitation of Relief Personnel and Consignments

Alongside the protection of civilians, the protection and facilitation of relief personnel and consignments have become one of the most frequent mandates given to UN forces under Chapter VII but this may have certain consequences on the impartiality and neutrality of relief personnel and consignments, particularly with regard to the ICRC.

The protection and facilitation of relief personnel and consignments are extensive in IHL, in both the law of international and non-international armed conflict. There are at least two categories: 1) protection specifically related to medical activities; and 2) protection and facilitation of relief personnel and consignments in general. With regard to the protection specifically related to medical activities, besides some of the older IHL treaties,[408] many of the provisions in the 1949 Geneva Conventions, 1977 Additional Protocols, and customary international law provide protection for medical personnel,[409] medical units[410] and medical transportation,[411] mostly without distinction between military and civilian character.[412] In addition, the protection and facilitation of relief personnel[413] and the protection

[408] See the earlier Geneva Conventions of 1864, 1906, and 1929. Convention for the Amelioration of the Condition of the Wounded in Armies in the Field (adopted 22 August 1864, entered into force 22 June 1865) 129 CTS 361; Convention for the Amelioration of the Condition of the Wounded in Armies in the Field, as revised from 1864 (adopted 6 July 1906, entered into force 9 August 1907) 11 LNTS 440; Convention for the Amelioration of the Condition of the Wounded in Armies in the Field, as revised from 1906 (adopted 27 July 1929, entered into force 19 June 1931) 118 LNTS 303.

[409] For the definition see Art 8(c) of the 1977 First Additional Protocol. The relevant provisions can be found in Arts 24–32 of the 1949 First Geneva Convention; Arts 36 and 37 of the 1949 Second Geneva Convention; Art 33 of the 1949 Third Geneva Convention; Art 20 of the 1949 Fourth Geneva Convention; Arts 15–20 of the 1977 First Additional Protocol; Arts 9 and 10 of the 1977 Second Additional Protocol. For their customary law status, see Rules 25 and 26 in Henckaerts and Doswald-Beck, *Customary International Humanitarian Law* Vol I, 79 and 86.

[410] For the definition see Art 8(e) of the 1977 First Additional Protocol. The relevant provisions can be found in Arts 19–23, 33, and 34 of the 1949 First Geneva Convention; Arts 14, 15, 18, 19, 56, and 57 of the 1949 Fourth Geneva Convention; Arts 12–14 of the 1977 First Additional Protocol; Art 11 of the 1977 Second Additional Protocol. For their customary law status, see Rule 28 in Henckaerts and Doswald-Beck, *Customary International Humanitarian Law* Vol I, 91.

[411] For the definition see Art 8(f) of the 1977 First Additional Protocol. The relevant provisions can be found in Arts 35–37 of the 1949 First Geneva Convention; Arts 22–35 and 38–40 of the 1949 Second Geneva Convention; Arts 21 and 22 of the 1949 Fourth Geneva Convention; Arts 21–31 of the 1977 First Additional Protocol; Art of 11 of the 1977 Second Additional Protocol. For their customary law status, see Rule 29 in Henckaerts and Doswald-Beck, *Customary International Humanitarian Law* Vol I, 98.

[412] This is clear from the definitions in Arts 8(c), (e), and (g) of the 1977 First Additional Protocol. For example, the definition of 'medical transports' in Art 8(g) reads as follows: '"medical transports" means any means of transportation, whether military or civilian, permanent or temporary, assigned exclusively to medical transportation and under the control of a competent authority of a Party to the conflict'.

[413] Art 59 of the 1949 Fourth Geneva Convention; Art 71 of the 1977 First Additional Protocol. For their customary law status, see Rule 31 in Henckaerts and Doswald-Beck, *Customary International Humanitarian Law* Vol I, 105.

and facilitation of relief consignments[414] can be found in the 1949 Fourth Geneva Convention, 1977 Additional Protocols, and customary international law. Thus, even without the mandate of UN forces, IHL imposes substantial obligations on states and armed groups to protect and facilitate relief personnel and the distribution of relief consignments, both in international and non-international armed conflict.

Among the relief organisations, the components of the International Red Cross and Red Crescent Movement (hereafter Movement),[415] particularly the ICRC and the National Red Cross and Red Crescent Societies (hereafter National Societies), are specifically protected by the 1949 Geneva Conventions and 1977 Additional Protocols.[416] However, their special protection is based on the requirement that they are impartial and neutral. The principles of impartiality and neutrality are two of the most important principles of the Fundamental Principles of the Movement. This is provided for in the Statutes of the Movement,[417] which are not binding as a treaty but are binding on the components of the Movement, including the ICRC and National Societies.[418] The requirement to abide by the Fundamental Principles is formally recognised in Article 81(2) of the 1977 First Additional Protocol:

[414] See Arts 23, 55, 59–63, 108–09, and 142 of the 1949 Fourth Geneva Convention; Arts 69, 70, and 81 of the 1977 First Additional Protocol; Art 18 of the 1977 Second Additional Protocol. For their customary law status, see Rules 32 and 55 in Henckaerts and Doswald-Beck, *Customary International Humanitarian Law* Vol I, 109 and 193.

[415] The three components of the International Red Cross and Red Crescent Movement are the International Committee of the Red Cross, International Federation of Red Cross and Red Crescent Societies, and National Red Cross and Red Crescent Societies. Each of them is independent but they co-operate regularly between one another as a part of the International Red Cross and Red Crescent Movement. For their respective mandates, see the Statutes of the International Red Cross and Red Crescent Movement in ICRC and the International Federation of Red Cross and Red Crescent Societies, *Handbook*.

[416] For the ICRC, see common Art 3(2) of the 1949 Geneva Conventions; Arts 9 and 10 of the 1949 First Geneva Convention; Arts 9 and 10 of the 1949 Second Geneva Convention; Arts 9, 10, and 125 of the 1949 Third Geneva Convention; Arts 10, 11, and 142 of the 1949 Fourth Geneva Convention; Art 81(1) of the 1977 First Additional Protocol; Art 18 of the 1977 Second Additional Protocol. For the National Societies, see Art 26 of the 1949 First Geneva Convention; Art 63 of the 1949 Fourth Geneva Convention; Arts 81(2) and (3) of the 1977 First Additional Protocol; Art 18 of the 1977 Second Additional Protocol .

[417] The seven Fundamental Principles are humanity, impartiality, neutrality, independence, voluntary service, unity, and universality. See Preamble of the Statues of the International Red Cross and Red Crescent Movement in ICRC and the International Federation of Red Cross and Red Crescent Societies, *Handbook*. For discussions on the practical application of these principles, see generally M Harroff-Tavel, 'Neutralité et impartialité – De l'importance et de la difficulté, pour le Mouvement international de la Croix-Rouge et du Croissant-Rouge, d'être guidé par ces principes' (1989) 780 *Revue international de la Croix-Rouge* 563.

[418] F Bugnion, 'Red Cross Law' (1995) 308 *International Review of the Red Cross* 491.

> The Parties to the conflict shall grant to their respective Red Cross (Red Crescent, Red Lion and Sun) organizations the facilities necessary for carrying out their humanitarian activities in favour of the victims of the conflict, in accordance with the provisions of the Conventions and this Protocol and the fundamental principles of the Red Cross as formulated by the International Conferences of the Red Cross.[419]

Thus, it is clear from the above that the ICRC and National Societies are granted special protection under IHL on the assumption that they are impartial and neutral.

At the same time, the obligation of states to protect and facilitate relief personnel and consignments might prejudice the impartiality and neutrality in certain cases. Article 70(4) of the 1977 First Additional Protocol provides as follows:

> The Parties to the conflict shall protect relief consignments and facilitate their rapid distribution.

Article 71(2) further provides as follows:

> Such personnel [relief personnel] shall be respected and protected.[420]

A commentary identifies the potential effect this obligation might have on the impartiality and neutrality of the ICRC:

> Relief actions undertaken under the auspices of the ICRC, and consequently enjoying the protection of the red cross emblem, raise a special problem with regard to the obligations of the Parties to the conflict benefiting from the relief to ensure the protection of the relief consignments.
>
> The protective emblem should by itself ensure the protection of such consignments and the neutrality of the emblem should preclude them from being escorted by members of the armed forces.[421]

A similar concern arises when UN forces are mandated to protect and facilitate relief personnel and consignments. There have been at least

[419] See also Art 44 of the 1949 First Geneva Convention; Art 63 of the 1949 Fourth Geneva Convention; Art 70(1) of the 1977 First Additional Protocol. Although there is no reference to the ICRC to observe the Fundamental Principles, a commentary on Art 81(2) of the 1977 First Additional Protocol notes as follows: 'It is clear that the principles must be followed by the Red Cross as a whole, and although they are not mentioned in the first paragraph of Article 81 [on the special status of the ICRC], the ICRC, the traditional guardian of the Movement's principles, has also to observe them.' See Sandoz et al (eds), *Commentary*, para 3322.

[420] See also Art 70(2) of the 1977 First Additional Protocol.

[421] Sandoz et al (eds), *Commentary*, paras 2860–61. See also A Viotti, 'In Search of Symbiosis: The Security Council in the Humanitarian Domain' (2007) 865 *International Review of the Red Cross* 131.

14 UN-commanded forces[422] and 10 state-led UN forces[423] which were authorised under Chapter VII to protect and facilitate relief personnel and consignments. For example, the Security Council authorised in its resolution 836 UNPROFOR (former Yugoslavia) 'to take the necessary measures including the use of force . . . in the event of any deliberate obstruction in or around those areas to the freedom of movement of . . . protected humanitarian convoys'.[424] The same resolution further provided that 'Member States . . . may take . . . all necessary measures, through the use of air power . . . to support UNPROFOR in the performance of its mandate set out in paragraphs 5 and 9 above [paragraph 9 quoted above]'.[425] Thus, such Chapter VII mandate can complement the IHL obligations to protect and facilitate relief personnel and consignments but it also raises the concern whether it affects the impartiality and neutrality of the ICRC and National Societies.

The ICRC has consistently avoided protection, in particular, by UN forces. Jean de Courten, a former ICRC Director of Operations, notes as follows:

> Un autre critère d'intervention est que nous [le Comité international de la Croix-Rouge] n'utilisons pas la protection armée. En Bosnie, nous n'avons pas

[422] UNOSOM II (Somalia), UNSC Res 814 (26 March 1993) UN Doc S/RES/814, para 5 and UNSC Res 954 (4 November 1994) UN Doc S/RES/954, para 6; UNPROFOR (former Yugoslavia), UNSC Res 836 (4 June 1993) UN Doc S/RES/836, paras 5 and 9; UNCRO (Croatia), UNSC Res 981 (31 March 1995) UN Doc S/RES/981, para 3(e); UNAMSIL (Sierra Leone), UNSC Res 1270 (22 October 1999) UN Doc S/RES/1270, para 8(g); UNTAET (East Timor), UNSC Res 1272 (25 October 1999) UN Doc S/RES/1272, para 2(d); MONUC (DRC), UNSC Res 1291 (24 February 2000) UN Doc S/RES/1291, para 7(g), UNSC Res 1417 (14 June 2002) UN Doc S/RES/1417, para 7, UNSC Res 1493 (28 July 2003) UN Doc S/RES/1493, para 25, UNSC Res 1565 (1 October 2004) UN Doc S/RES/1565, para 4(d), UNSC Res 1756 (15 May 2007) UN Doc S/RES/1756, para 2(d), and UNSC Res 1856 (22 December 2008) UN Doc S/RES/1856, para 3(d); UNMIL (Liberia), UNSC Res 1509 (19 September 2003) UN Doc S/RES/1509, para 3(k); UNOCI (Côte d'Ivoire), UNSC Res 1528 (27 February 2004) UN Doc S/RES/1528, para 6(k), UNSC Res 1609 (24 June 2005) UN Doc S/RES/1609, para 2(o), and UNSC Res 1739 (10 January 2007) UN Doc S/RES/1739, para 2(h); MINUSTAH (Haiti), UNSC Res 1542 (30 April 2004) UN Doc S/RES/1542, para 2(b); ONUB (Burundi), UNSC Res 1545 (21 May 2004) UN Doc S/RES/1545, para 5; UNMIS (Sudan), UNSC Res 1590 (24 March 2005) UN Doc S/RES/1590, para 4(b) and UNSC Res 1706 (31 August 2006) UN Doc S/RES/1706, para 12(a); UNIFIL (Lebanon), UNSC Res 1701 (11 August 2006) UN Doc S/RES/1701, para 12; UNAMID (Sudan), UNSC Res 1769 (31 July 2007) UN Doc S/RES/1769, para 15(a)(i); MIURCAT (Chad/Central African Republic), UNSC Res 1861 (14 January 2009) UN Doc S/RES/1861, paras 7(a)(ii) and (iii) and 7(b)(iii).

[423] Former Yugoslavia, UNSC Res 770 (13 August 1992) UN Doc S/RES/770, UNSC Res 836 (4 June 1993) UN Doc S/RES/836, UNSC Res 844 (18 June 1993) UN Doc S/RES/844, and UNSC Res 958 (19 November 1994) UN Doc S/RES/958; Somalia, UNSC Res 794 (3 December 1992) UN Doc S/RES/794; Zaire, UNSC Res 1080 (15 November 1996) UN Doc S/RES/1080; Kosovo, UNSC Res 1244 (10 June 1999) UN Doc S/RES/1244; East Timor, UNSC Res 1264 (15 September 1999) UN Doc S/RES/1264; DRC, UNSC Res 1484 (30 May 2003) UN Doc S/RES/1484; Liberia, UNSC Res 1497 (1 August 2003) UN Doc S/RES/1497; Haiti, UNSC Res 1529 (29 February 2004) UN Doc S/RES/1529; Somalia, UNSC Res 1744 (21 February 2007) UN Doc S/RES/1744; Chad/Central African Republic, UNSC Res 1778 (25 September 2007) UN Doc S/RES/1778.

[424] UNSC Res 836 (4 June 1993) UN Doc S/RES/836, para 9.

[425] UNSC Res 836 (4 June 1993) UN Doc S/RES/836, para 10.

> utilisé la protection de la FORPRONU [French acronym for UNPROFOR] dans le cadre de notre action, à l'exception de la protection de certains convoys de prisonniers qui étaient libérés et qui rejoignaient leurs zones respectives.[426]

The UN also acknowledged that Chapter VII use of force could affect the impartiality of the UN forces themselves. Referring to the use of air power by NATO, the UN Secretary-General expressed concerns over the impartiality of UNPROFOR during the conflict in the former Yugoslavia, stating that 'by using air power against the Serbs we would be perceived as having entered the war against them, something not authorized by the Security Council and potentially fatal for a peacekeeping operation.'[427] Since the impartiality of UNPROFOR was in question, it was widely recognised that their protection and facilitation of relief personnel and consignments could also not be impartial or neutral. Resolution 776 reflects the concerns of the ICRC and the UN, which authorised 'the enlargements of UNPROFOR's mandate and strength in Bosnia and Herzegovina . . . including the protection of convoys of released detainees if requested by the International Committee of the Red Cross'.[428] The clause 'if requested' avoids unilateral protection by UNPROFOR. However, as a matter of law, the Security Council can authorise the use of force under Chapter VII to protect and facilitate relief personnel and consignments, even when such use of force is susceptible to be perceived as not impartial or neutral, since its priority is to maintain international peace and security. Thus, the UN has its own definition of impartiality and neutrality:

> Impartiality for such operations [UN peacekeeping operations] must therefore mean adherence to the principles of the Charter and to the objectives of a mandate that is rooted in those Charter principles. Such impartiality is not the same as neutrality or equal treatment of all parties in all cases for all time, which can amount to a policy of appeasement. In some cases, local parties consist not of moral equals but of obvious aggressors and victims, and peacekeepers may not only be operationally justified in using force but morally compelled to do so . . . If a United Nations peace operation is already on the ground, carrying out those actions may become its responsibility, and it should be prepared.[429]

[426] J de Courten, 'Le Comité international de la Croix-Rouge et l'action des Nations Unies dans les conflits armés' in Condorelli et al (eds), *Nations Unies et le droit international humanitaire*, 342. 'Another criterion of intervention is that we [the ICRC] do not use the armed protection. In Bosnia, we have not used the protection of UNPROFOR in the framework of our action, with the exception of the protection of certain convoys of prisoners who were released and who returned to their respective areas.' Translated by the author.

See also ICRC, 'Report on the Protection of War Victims' (1993) 296 *International Review of the Red Cross* 391, 427–8; Y Sandoz, 'Rapport général' in Condorelli et al (eds), *Nations Unies et le droit international humanitaire*, 73.

[427] UNGA, 'Report of the Secretary-General Pursuant to General Assembly Resolution 53/35: The Fall of Srebrenica' (15 November 1999) UN Doc A/54/549, para 482.

[428] UNSC Res 776 (14 September 1992) UN Doc S/RES/776, para 2.

[429] UNGA, 'Report of the Panel on United Nations Peace Operations' (21 August 2000) UN Doc A/55/305-S/2000/809, para 50.

This is in marked contrast with the definition of impartiality and neutrality of the International Red Cross and Red Crescent Movement:

> **Impartiality** It makes no discrimination as to nationality, race, religious beliefs, class or political opinions. It endeavours to relieve the suffering of individuals, being guided solely by their needs, and to give priority to the most urgent cases of distress.
>
> **Neutrality** In order to continue to enjoy the confidence of all, the Movement may not take sides in hostilities or engage at any time in controversies of a political, racial, religious or ideological nature.[430]

This raises the question of whether Article 103 of the UN Charter would permit Chapter VII mandate to protect and facilitate relief personnel and consignments to prevail over the requirements of impartiality and neutrality as provided in IHL. However, such potential conflict between Chapter VII decisions and IHL should be avoided by practical measures as the ICRC has always done. Michael Bothe's comment is relevant in this regard:

> A strict adherence to the principle of impartiality is a pre-requisite for ensuring the respect of the laws of war in all conflicts. The ICRC has gained reputation for taking the initiative to ensure the application of international humanitarian law in all armed conflict, regardless of political preferences, media attention or lack thereof . . . It should be a matter of political prudence, not of law, that the United Nations and the ICRC try not to create obstacles for each other's operations, but rather to assume complementary roles. For the United Nations, this means, *inter alia,* that it respects the particular working methods of the ICRC and refrains from trying to impose on the ICRC duties incompatible with these methods.[431]

Detention

The capture of personnel of UN forces and the capture of persons by UN forces raise problems of a different nature. They directly touch upon the principle of the equal application of IHL to the conflicting parties. This is particularly because the personnel of UN forces are specifically protected by the 1994 Convention on the Safety of United Nations and Associated Personnel (hereafter 1994 Safety Convention). Due to the increasingly hostile environment in which UN-commanded forces operate,[432] attacking and

[430] See Preamble of the Statutes of the International Red Cross and Red Crescent Movement in ICRC and the International Federation of Red Cross and Red Crescent Societies, *Handbook*.

[431] Bothe, 'The United Nations Actions', 228.

[432] UN-commanded forces such as ONUC (Congo), UNOSOM II (Somalia), UNPROFOR (Bosnia-Herzegovina), UNAMSIL (Sierra Leone), and MONUC (DRC) have particularly operated in a significantly hostile environment.

For the reports on the Congo, including accounts of the fighting between ONUC and armed groups, see UNSC, 'Report of the Officer-in-Charge of the United Nations Operation in the Congo to the Secretary-General Relating to the Implementation of Paragraph A-2 of the

detaining UN forces personnel are now criminalised in the 1994 Safety Convention and attacks against UN-commanded forces are criminalised in the 1998 Statute of the International Criminal Court (hereafter ICC Statute). This raises the question of whether UN forces personnel are not on an equal footing with the adversary, where the capture of UN forces personnel is always a crime whereas the capture of persons by UN forces is lawful.

The question of the status of captured UN forces personnel and persons captured by UN forces under IHL has immense practical importance since there are several legal regimes applicable to persons deprived of their liberty during armed conflict, and the scope of the protection differs depending on the category of the captured persons. This question is not theoretical but real since in the past, UN forces personnel were captured

Security Council Resolution of 21 February 1961' (14 September 1961 – 22 December 1961) UN Doc S/4940 and UN Doc S/4940/Add.1-19; UNGA, 'Report of the Officer-in-Charge of the United Nations Operation in the Congo to the Secretary-General on Developments Relating to the Application of the Security Council Resolutions of 21 February and 24 November 1961' (9 January 1962 – 30 January 1963) UN Doc S/5053 and UN Doc S/5053/Add.1-15.

See also G Abi-Saab, *The United Nations Operation in the Congo 1960–1964* (Oxford, Oxford University Press, 1978); A Burns and N Heathcote, *Peace-keeping by U.N. Forces* (London, Pall Mall Press, 1963); L Tondel (ed), *The Legal Aspects of the United Nations Action in the Congo* (New York, Oceana Publications, 1963); K Gordon, *The United Nations in the Congo: A Quest for Peace* (New York, Carnegie Endowment for International Peace, 1962); C Hoskyns, *The Congo Since Independence: January 1960 – December 1961* (London, Oxford University Press, 1965); E Lefever, *Crisis in the Congo: A United Nations Force in Action* (Washington DC, The Brookings Institution, 1965); G Martelli, *Experiment in World Government: An Account of the United Nations Operation in the Congo 1960–1964* (London, Johnson Publications, 1966).

For an overview of the situation in Somalia and the activities of UNOSOM II in 1993, see UNGA, 'Somalia' (1993) UNYB 288, 288–304. See the full report on the incident on 5 June 1993 in which 24 Pakistani UNOSOM II troops were killed: UNSC, 'Report of the Commission of Inquiry Established Pursuant to Security Council Resolution 885 (1993) to Investigate Armed Attacks on UNOSOM II Personnel Which Led to Casualties among Them' (1 June 1994) UN Doc S/1994/653.

For UNPROFOR combat activities and NATO air strikes, see the UN Secretary-General's reports and letters: UNSC, 'Letter Dated 6 February 1994 from the Secretary-General Addressed to the President of the Security Council' (7 February 1994) UN Doc S/1994/131; UNSC, 'Report of the Secretary-General Pursuant to Resolution 871 (1993)' (16 March 1994) UN Doc S/1994/300; UNSC, 'Letter Dated 18 April 1994 from the Secretary-General Addressed to the President of the Security Council' (19 April 1994) UN Doc S/1994/466; UNSC, 'Report of the Secretary-General Pursuant to Resolution 913 (1994)' (19 May 1994) UN Doc S/1994/600; UNSC, 'Report of the Secretary-General Pursuant to Resolution 908 (1994)' (17 September 1994) UN Doc S/1994/1067; 'Report of the Secretary-General Pursuant to Resolution 959 (1994)' (1 December 1994) UN Doc S/1994/1389; UNSC, 'Report of the Secretary-General Pursuant to Resolution 947 (1994)' (22 March 1995) UN Doc S/1995/222; UNSC, 'Report of the Secretary-General Pursuant to Security Council Resolutions 982 (1995) and 987 (1995)' (30 May 1995) UN Doc S/1995/444; UNSC, 'Report of the Secretary-General Pursuant to Resolution 844 (1993)' (9 May 1994) UN Doc S/1994/555.

For attacks on UNAMSIL and the capture of 461 troops by the armed groups, see the UN Secretary-General's reports: UNSC, 'Fourth Report of the Secretary-General on the United Nations Mission in Sierra Leone' (19 May 2000) UN Doc S/2000/455, paras 56–71 and 'Fifth Report of the Secretary-General on the United Nations Mission in Sierra Leone' (31 July 2000) UN Doc S/2000/751, para 24.

For MONUC's combat activity, see n 349 above.

during armed conflict[433] and UN forces were mandated to detain certain persons.[434]

Protection of Persons Deprived of their Liberty in IHL

At the outset, it is essential to outline the IHL rules applicable to persons deprived of their liberty during an armed conflict.[435] The rules differ between international and non-international armed conflict.

In an international armed conflict, there are two main categories, prisoners of war and civilians deprived of their liberty. Prisoners of war are principally members of armed forces and certain persons accompanying the armed forces.[436] They are protected by the 1949 Third Geneva Convention. In IHL, prisoner-of-war status implies combatant status, and combatant status implies that the person is a member of the armed forces,[437] who has the right to participate in hostilities[438] and is immune from prosecution for the mere participation in hostilities. For this reason, prisoner-of-war status does not exist in non-international armed conflict since most states are not willing to confer any legitimacy to the armed groups opposing the government by recognising that the members of armed groups have the right to participate in hostilities and are immune from prosecution for their participation in hostilities.

On the other hand, civilians deprived of liberty in an international armed conflict are principally protected by the 1949 Fourth Geneva Convention. They are persons who 'find themselves . . . in the hands of a Party to the conflict or Occupying Power of which they are not nationals' and are not protected by their diplomatic representation or by the 1949 First, Second, and Third Geneva Conventions.[439] The possibility of internment of civilians is envisaged in Articles 41, 42, 68, and 78 of the Fourth Geneva Convention. When a protected person is suspected of having engaged in hostile activities against the security of a conflicting party, the Fourth Geneva Convention still applies but the rights and privileges under the Convention are suspended.[440]

433 See, eg, UNSC, 'Report of the Secretary-General Pursuant to Security Council Resolutions 982 (1995) and 987 (1995)' (30 May 1995) UN Doc S/1995/444, para 63.

434 See UNSC Res 169 (24 November 1961) UN Doc S/RES/169 on ONUC and UNSC Res 837 (6 June 1993) UN Doc S/RES/837 on UNOSOM II.

435 See generally K Okimoto, 'The Protection of Detainees in International Humanitarian Law' in S Perrigo and J Whitman (eds), *The Geneva Conventions under Assault* (London, Pluto Press, 2010); E Crawford, *The Treatment of Combatants and Insurgents under the Law of Armed Conflict* (Oxford, Oxford University Press, 2010).

436 Art 4(A) of the 1949 Third Geneva Convention.

437 Art 43(2) of the 1977 First Additional Protocol; Rule 3 in Henckaerts and Doswald-Beck, *Customary International Humanitarian Law* Vol I, 11.

438 Art 43(2) of the 1977 First Additional Protocol.

439 Art 4 of the 1949 Fourth Geneva Convention.

440 Art 5 of the 1949 Fourth Geneva Convention.

In non-international armed conflict, detained persons are not categorised like in international armed conflict. All persons deprived of their liberty are protected uniformly by common Article 3 of the 1949 Geneva Conventions, 1977 Second Additional Protocol (where applicable), and customary rules of IHL.[441]

The question here is whether these IHL rules are applicable to captured UN forces personnel and persons captured by UN forces. At this point, it is necessary to distinguish between personnel in state-led UN forces and those in UN-commanded forces.

Status of Persons Deprived of Liberty in an Armed Conflict Involving UN Forces[442]

With regard to state-led UN forces, when they are engaged in an armed conflict with State A, this is an international armed conflict where IHL rules applicable in international armed conflict fully apply. As discussed earlier, this is a traditional type of international armed conflict where more than two states are engaged in an armed conflict. In such a case, when the personnel of state-led UN forces are captured by State A, they are prisoners of war and are protected by the 1949 Third Geneva Convention. The same applies when the troops of State A are captured by the state-led UN forces. Such was the case during the 1991 Gulf War when the troops of the multinational forces and Iraqi forces were captured by each other. Article 2(2) of the 1994 Safety Convention also confirms this point:

> United Nations operation authorized by the Security Council as an enforcement action under Chapter VII of the Charter of the United Nations in which any of the personnel are engaged as combatants against organized armed forces and to which the law of international armed conflict applies.

When state-led UN forces are engaged in an armed conflict with armed groups, it resembles a non-international armed conflict and hence the IHL rules applicable in non-international armed conflict apply. In this case, when the personnel of the state-led UN forces are captured by the armed groups, or when members of the armed groups are captured by the state-led UN forces, they are all protected uniformly by common Article 3 of the 1949 Geneva Conventions and customary rules of IHL.[443]

UN-commanded forces are slightly more complicated. Normally, when UN-commanded forces are deployed, it is not envisaged to become a

[441] M Bothe, 'The Status of Captured Fighters in Non-International Armed Conflict' in C Tomuschat et al (eds), *The Right to Life* (Leiden, Martinus Nijhoff, 2010).

[442] See generally O Engdahl, 'The Status of Peace Operation Personnel under International Humanitarian Law' (2008) 11 *Yearbook of International Humanitarian Law* 109; M Wood, 'Detention during International Military Operations: Article 103 of the UN Charter and the *Al-Jedda* Case' (2009) 47 *Revue de droit militaire et de droit de la guerre* 139.

[443] The 1977 Second Additional Protocol does not apply for reasons explained earlier. See section 4.IV.D.

party to an existing armed conflict. This was clearly the case with the UN-commanded forces in the early years, with the exception of ONUC in the Congo, when they were primarily deployed to keep the conflicting parties apart and to monitor the cease-fire. However, even if the mandates have diversified since then, and even if the use of force has been authorised under Chapter VII more often, the primary purpose of UN-commanded forces has never been the same as state-led UN forces. Some recent UN-commanded forces that were authorised to use force under Chapter VII such as UNPROFOR (former Yugoslavia), UNOSOM II (Somalia), and MONUC (DRC) had mandates that came close to state-led UN forces, but their primary purpose was to stabilise the situation rather than to engage in an armed conflict with the local forces. However, as is widely known, some of the UN-commanded forces were engaged in intense combat with local forces and in some cases became parties to the existing armed conflict. The difficulty with UN-commanded forces is that since they are not deployed primarily to become a party to an existing armed conflict, the personnel are primarily considered as civilians under IHL. In other words, the personnel are protected just as other civilians are protected under IHL.

When UN-commanded forces are deployed in the midst of an international armed conflict, and when the personnel are detained, the detention must be justified on grounds that allow internment of civilians set out in Articles 41, 42, 68, and 78 of the 1949 Fourth Geneva Convention. Once they are interned, the Fourth Geneva Convention provides protection.

When UN-commanded forces are deployed in the midst of a non-international armed conflict, and when the personnel are detained, common Article 3 of the 1949 Geneva Conventions and customary rules of IHL provide protection.

However, views are divided as to the status of personnel of UN-commanded forces once they become parties to an armed conflict. In particular, there is no clear consensus as to whether the personnel retain the status of civilians or become combatants.

In case where UN-commanded forces become engaged in an armed conflict with State A, if the personnel of the UN-commanded forces retain the status of civilians, then the armed conflict between the UN-commanded forces and State A will not be an international armed conflict but rather a non-international armed conflict. In this case, the UN-commanded forces resemble an organised armed group in a non-international armed conflict, which are normally composed of civilians. These civilians in an organised armed group are civilians who directly participate in hostilities and hence lose their protection as civilians.[444] However, they do not lose their civilian

[444] Common Art 3 of the 1949 Geneva Conventions; Rule 6 in Henckaerts and Doswald-Beck, *Customary International Humanitarian Law* Vol I, 19. See also Art 51(3) of the 1977 First Additional Protocol; Art 13(3) of the 1977 Second Additional Protocol; ICRC, 'Interpretive Guidance on the Notion of Direct Participation in Hostilities under International

status. They only lose their protection as civilians. The same can be said for the UN-commanded forces. If the personnel in the UN-commanded forces retain their status as civilians at all times, once they are engaged in an armed conflict, they are civilians directly participating in hostilities. In this case, the armed conflict between the UN-commanded forces and State A would be a non-international armed conflict and hence when the personnel of the UN-commanded forces are captured by State A, they are protected by common Article 3 of the 1949 Geneva Conventions and customary rules of IHL. The same protection is available for the troops of State A when they are captured by the UN-commanded forces.

The situation becomes different if the personnel of the UN-commanded forces change their status from civilians to combatants once they become engaged in an armed conflict with State A. It is worth remembering at this point that civilians normally do not change their status once they participate in hostilities. They retain their status as civilians but lose the protection for civilians. Hence, their civilian status continues at all times. The only moment civilians change their status is when they join a state's armed forces. They then become combatants in the sense of Article 43(2) of the 1977 First Additional Protocol and obtain the right to participate directly in hostilities and be treated as prisoners of war when they are captured.

In the case of the UN-commanded forces, if the personnel change their status from civilians to combatants once they are engaged in an armed conflict with State A, this is not a common practice in terms of IHL. However, there are certain practices that recognise the change in the status of UN forces personnel. For example, the UN Secretary-General's Bulletin on the Observance by United Nations of International Humanitarian Law (hereafter UN Secretary-General's Bulletin) of 1999 states as follows:

> The fundamental principles and rules of international humanitarian law set out in the present bulletin are applicable to United Nations forces when in situations of armed conflict they are actively engaged therein as combatants, to the extent and for the duration of their engagement. The promulgation of this bulletin does not affect the protected status of members of peacekeeping operations under the 1994 Convention on the Safety of United Nations and Associated Personnel or their status as non-combatants, as long as they are entitled to the protection given to civilians under the international law of armed conflict.[445]

This paragraph, read as a whole, implies that when the personnel of the UN-commanded forces are 'actively engaged' in an armed conflict, they are combatants. If not, they are protected as civilians under IHL. This effectively means that the status of the UN personnel alternates between

Humanitarian Law' (2008) 872 *International Review of the Red Cross* 991. See further N Melzer, *Targeted Killing in International Law* (Oxford, Oxford University Press, 2008).

[445] UN Secretary-General, 'Secretary-General's Bulletin', Section 1.

civilians and combatants, depending on whether they are actively engaged in an armed conflict or not. It also implies that even if the UN-commanded forces become a party to an armed conflict, the personnel therein are only combatants when they are 'actively engaged' in the armed conflict. In other words, the personnel are not combatants throughout the armed conflict, even if the UN-commanded forces they belong to are a party to the armed conflict.

A further indication is the ICC Statute. Articles 8(2)(b)(iii) and (e)(iii) provide the following as a war crime in international and non-international armed conflict:

> Intentionally directing attacks against personnel . . . involved in peacekeeping mission . . . as long as they are entitled to the protection given to civilians . . . under the international law of armed conflict.[446]

This provision is, however, different from the UN Secretary-General's Bulletin since it does not assume whether the personnel of UN-commanded forces retain the status of civilians or change their status to combatants once they are engaged in an armed conflict. The bottom line of this provision is that the UN forces personnel can be considered as civilians and attacks against them can be a war crime. However, this article begs the question about what happens to the status of the UN forces personnel once they are engaged in an armed conflict. The article implies that they lose the protection of civilians. This is clear from the phrase 'as long as they are entitled to the protection given to civilians . . . under the international law of armed conflict'. The question here is, do they lose the protection for civilians because the UN forces personnel are civilians directly participating hostilities, or because they change their status to combatants?

This question is particularly relevant in international armed conflict, since combatants and civilians are distinct categories of persons and are entitled to different protection once captured. In non-international armed conflict, there is no division between combatants and civilians. All captured persons in non-international armed conflict are entitled to the same protection under common Article 3 of the 1949 Geneva Conventions, 1977 Second Additional Protocol (where applicable), and customary rules of IHL. On the other hand, the scope of protection differs in international armed conflict depending on the status of the captured persons. If they are captured as combatants, in other words as members of armed forces, then they are prisoners of war and are entitled to protection under the 1949 Third Geneva Convention. They will not be prosecuted for their mere participation in hostilities, unless their conduct amounted to a war crime. If they are captured as civilians directly participating in hostilities, they can be interned and are

[446] Rome Statute of the International Criminal Court (hereafter ICC Statute) (adopted 17 July 1998, entered into force 1 July 2002) 2187 UNTS 3. See also Art 4(b) of the Statute of the Special Court for Sierra Leone.

then protected by the 1949 Fourth Geneva Convention. They can be prosecuted for their mere participation in hostilities. Hence, the determination of whether the UN forces personnel are civilians or combatants once they become engaged in an armed conflict is crucial.

The distinction between combatants and civilians in international armed conflict is not without a purpose. Its primary purpose is to minimise the risk of attacks against civilians by distinguishing them from combatants, and designate the latter as the only persons that can be attacked. If the status of the personnel in UN-commanded forces changes from civilians to combatants frequently during a particular armed conflict, it contradicts with the primary purpose of the distinction between civilians and combatants.

At the same time, it does not seem plausible to consider the personnel of UN-commanded forces as civilians directly participating in hostilities, mainly because they are originally members of armed forces. UN-commanded forces are composed of contingents from different states and hence the nature of the forces is markedly different from organised armed groups. Moreover, the UN concludes a status-of-forces agreement with the state receiving the UN-commanded forces. In that sense, the UN-commanded forces resemble a state's armed forces that were deployed with the invitation and consent of the receiving state.

From the above analysis, the position that the personnel of UN-commanded forces change their status from civilians to combatants when UN-commanded forces are engaged in an armed conflict with State A seems a compromise.[447] However, the interpretation in the UN Secretary-General's Bulletin seems too narrow and difficult to apply in practice since it considers that the personnel of UN-commanded forces are combatants only when they are 'actively engaged' in an armed conflict and 'to the extent and for the duration of their engagement'. The primary purpose of the distinction between civilians and combatants would be compromised if the status of these personnel changes frequently between civilians and combatants in a particular armed conflict. Hence, it may be acceptable to consider the personnel of UN-commanded forces as civilians until the forces become a party to the armed conflict. It may also be acceptable to conclude that these personnel change their status from civilians to combatants once the UN-commanded forces become a party to the armed conflict. However, it does not seem sound to conclude that the personnel return to the civilian status when they are not 'actively engaged' in the armed conflict. Once the UN-commanded forces become a party to the armed conflict, they remain as such until they withdraw or until the armed conflict is over. Hence, the personnel of the UN-commanded forces also remain as combatants so long as the forces remain a party to the armed conflict. This takes into account

[447] UN Secretariat, 'Note on the Protection of Peacekeeping Personnel under International Humanitarian Law' (2006) *United Nations Juridical Yearbook* 518, 520.

both the position in the UN Secretary-General's Bulletin and the purpose of the distinction between civilians and combatants.

It follows that when UN-commanded forces are engaged in an armed conflict with State A, this is an international armed conflict and the personnel of the UN-commanded forces are considered as combatants. Once they are captured, they are prisoners of war and are protected under the 1949 Third Geneva Convention. At the same time, when the troops of State A are captured by the UN-commanded forces, they are also prisoners of war and are protected by the Third Geneva Convention. This is largely in line with the UN Secretary-General's Bulletin and the 1994 Safety Convention. The UN Secretary-General's Bulletin provides as follows:

> [D]etained members of the armed forces and other persons who no longer take part in military operations by reason of detention . . . shall be treated in accordance with the relevant provisions of the Third Geneva Convention of 1949, as may be applicable to them *mutatis mutandis*.[448]

Moreover, Article 8 of the 1994 Safety Convention provides as follows:

> Pending their release such personnel [United Nations and associated personnel] shall be treated in accordance with . . . the principles and spirit of the Geneva Conventions of 1949.[449]

When UN-commanded forces are engaged in an armed conflict with organised armed groups, as mentioned earlier, it is essentially a non-international armed conflict. So far as detained persons are concerned, it is not necessary to determine the status of these persons before capture, since the protection for detainees is the same for all detainees in non-international armed conflict. As noted above, the protection is provided under common Article 3 of the 1949 Geneva Conventions and customary rules of IHL. This is largely in line with the UN Secretary-General's Bulletin and the 1994 Safety Convention as noted above.

In short, international law does not put UN forces personnel in a more advantageous position when UN-commanded forces are a party to an armed conflict.

Problems with the 1994 Safety Convention

The 1994 Safety Convention appeared several times in the previous section and it is convenient to discuss its problems here. As noted above, the Convention criminalises attacks and detention of UN and associated personnel, including the personnel of UN forces. However, it is worth noting that, in principle, the Convention did not intend to affect the application of IHL in any way, as can be seen from its saving clause:

448 UN Secretary-General, 'Secretary-General's Bulletin', Section 8.
449 See also 2006 MONUC SOFA Protocol, para 1. See n 339 above.

> Nothing in this Convention shall affect . . . the applicability of international humanitarian law . . . in relation to . . . the responsibility of such personnel [UN and associated personnel] to respect such law and standards.[450]

There is, however, one particular difficulty with the 1994 Safety Convention which is to determine which law (IHL or the Safety Convention) is applicable to which UN forces.[451] The problem stems from Article 2(2) of the Safety Convention:

> United Nations operation authorized by the Security Council as an enforcement action under Chapter VII of the Charter of the United Nations in which any of the personnel are engaged as combatants against organized armed forces and to which the law of international armed conflict applies.

This makes it clear that, when UN forces are a party to an armed conflict, only IHL applies instead of both the Safety Convention and IHL, to avoid compromising the equal application principle.

The problem with Article 2(2) is threefold. First, which UN forces qualify as 'United Nations operation authorized by the Security Council as an enforcement action under Chapter VII of the Charter of the United Nations' is not clear. The Convention assumes that all UN forces can be neatly categorised into Chapter VII enforcement action and non-Chapter VII action. However, there have been UN forces such as UNOSOM II and UNPROFOR which were authorised under Chapter VII but it was not clear whether they were enforcement actions like the multinational forces in the 1991 Gulf War. In the case of these UN-commanded forces, the UN Secretary-General was at pains to justify them as non-enforcement actions, but once they were drawn into the armed conflict, such justification was untenable.[452]

[450] Art 20(a) of the 1994 Safety Convention.

[451] See generally C Greenwood, 'Protection of Peacekeepers: The Legal Regime' (1996–97) 7 *Duke Journal of Comparative and International Law* 203. See also E Bloom, 'Protecting Peacekeepers: The Convention on the Safety of United Nations and Associated Personnel' (1995) 89 *American Journal of International Law* 621; C Bourloyannis, 'The Convention on the Safety of United Nations and Associated Personnel' (1995) 44 *International and Comparative Law Quarterly* 560; A Bouvier, 'Convention on the Safety of United Nations and Associated Personnel: Presentation and Analysis' (1995) 309 *International Review of the Red Cross* 638.

[452] For UN Secretary-General's concern over the character of UNPROFOR, see UNSC, 'Report of the Secretary-General Pursuant to Resolution 871 (1993)' (16 March 1994) UN Doc S/1994/300, para 34; UNSC, 'Report of the Secretary-General Pursuant to Resolution 908 (1994)' (17 September 1994) UN Doc S/1994/1067, para 43. For UN Secretary-General's concern over the impartiality of UNPROFOR, see: UNSC, 'Report of the Secretary-General Pursuant to Resolution 844 (1993)' (9 May 1994) UN Doc S/1994/555, para 10; UNSC, 'Report of the Secretary-General Pursuant to Security Council Resolutions 982 (1995) and 987 (1995)' (30 May 1995) UN Doc S/1995/444, paras 40 and 58. For hostage-taking of UNPROFOR troops, see: UNSC, 'Report of the Secretary-General Pursuant to Resolution 913 (1994)' (19 May 1994) UN Doc S/1994/600, para 17; UNSC, 'Report of the Secretary-General Pursuant to Security Council Resolutions 982 (1995) and 987 (1995)' (30 May 1995) UN Doc S/1995/444, paras 14 and 57.

Second, even if it is assumed that all UN forces can be categorised into enforcement or non-enforcement action, Article 2(2) does not answer whether IHL or the 1994 Safety Convention applies when UN forces deployed as a non-enforcement action are engaged in an armed conflict. What happens if UN forces not authorised to use force under Chapter VII forcibly respond in self-defence? In such a situation, common Articles 2 and 3 of the 1949 Geneva Conventions are the only relevant criteria to answer the question. They determine the existence of an international or non-international armed conflict based on the facts. It is worth remembering that self-defence cannot be an excuse to avoid IHL application.[453] Therefore, it must be assumed that the Safety Convention ceases to apply when UN forces are a party to an armed conflict, even if they are not enforcement action under Chapter VII. This position is consistent with that of the UN, ICRC, and ICC Statutes, which take the position that IHL applies only when UN forces are a party to an armed conflict.[454]

Third, Article 2(2) does not envisage an armed conflict between UN forces and armed groups where the IHL rules applicable to non-international armed conflict apply. It only deals with a situation where UN forces are engaged in an armed conflict with a state's armed forces where the law of international armed conflict applies (such as the multinational forces in the 1991 Gulf War), and hence does not answer the question. In such a situation, it can only be inferred that when there is an armed conflict between the UN forces and armed groups, IHL rules applicable in non-international armed conflict apply and not the 1994 Safety Convention.

In practice, the potential conflict between the 1994 Safety Convention and IHL is becoming more real as more states are becoming parties to the Safety Convention.[455] Since the implementation of the Safety Convention depends heavily on the co-operation of the host states,[456] whether they are states parties to the Safety Convention is the key. Out of the 15 host states of the ongoing UN-commanded forces, five have already become states parties to the Safety Convention.[457] In places like Côte d'Ivoire and

[453] See text to nn 354 and 355 above.

[454] UN Secretary-General, 'Secretary-General's Bulletin', Section 1; ICRC, *International Humanitarian Law: Answers to Your Questions* (Geneva, International Committee of the Red Cross, 2002) 38; Arts 8(2)(b)(iii) and 8(2)(e)(iii) of the ICC Statute.

[455] For the latest record of states parties, see the UN Treaty Collection website, treaties.un.org.

[456] See, eg, UNSC Res 868 (29 September 1993) UN Doc S/RES/868, para 6.

[457] Côte d'Ivoire, Cyprus, Lebanon, Liberia, and Serbia. The concerned UN-commanded forces are UNOCI, UNFICYP, UNIFIL, UNMIL, and UNMIK respectively. Note, however, that recent Security Council resolutions establishing UN-commanded forces frequently refer to the 1994 Safety Convention, either in the preamble or in the operative paragraphs. Those Security Council resolutions were all adopted after the Safety Convention entered into force on 15 January 1999. See UNSC Res 1291 (24 February 2000) UN Doc S/RES/1291 (MONUC in the DRC), UNSC Res 1410 (17 May 2002) UN Doc S/RES/1410 (UNMISET in Timor-Leste), and UNSC Res 1545 (21 May 2004) UN Doc S/RES/1545 (ONUB in Burundi).

Liberia, where UN-commanded forces were more likely to be drawn into the armed conflict, the uncertainty on whether IHL or the Safety Convention is applicable can have serious consequences on the lives of UN forces personnel.

However, the lack of ratification still prevents the 1994 Safety Convention from being fully operational. For example, not all troop-contributing states to UN-commanded forces are parties to the Safety Convention and thus it may be applicable between the host state and some of the troop-contributing states but not vis-à-vis other troop-contributing states.

The attack on UNIFIL during the armed conflict in Lebanon in 2006 raised various questions.[458] Since Lebanon is a party to the 1994 Safety Convention, it was applicable between Lebanon and certain troop-contributing states and thus Lebanon had the duty to ensure safety and security of UNIFIL personnel. As at September 2010, the Safety Convention is applicable between Lebanon and 21 troop-contributing states.[459] However, the Convention is not applicable between Lebanon and eight troop-contributing states.[460] Article 7 of the 1994 Safety Convention reads as follows:

> States Parties shall take all appropriate measures to ensure the safety and security of United Nations and associated personnel. In particular, States Parties shall take all appropriate steps to protect United Nations and associated personnel who are deployed in their territory from the crimes set out in article 9.

A relevant case is when an attack by the Israel forces killed four UNIFIL personnel from Austria, Canada, China, and Finland.[461] All four states were parties to the Safety Convention at the time of the attack and thus it was applicable vis-à-vis Lebanon. However, since Israel was not a party to the Convention, it was not applicable between Israel and the four states. Hence, the four UNIFIL personnel were not protected by the Safety Convention vis-à-vis Israel.

Nevertheless, as civilians in an international armed conflict, they were protected by the IHL rules on civilian protection. Thus, in some cases, IHL might be a more certain legal basis for the protection of UN forces personnel since the IHL rules on civilian protection are well established as

[458] See UNHRC, 'Report of the Commission of Inquiry on Lebanon Pursuant to Human Rights Council Resolution S-2/1' (23 November 2006) UN Doc A/HRC/3/2, para 233 *ff*.

[459] Bangladesh, Belgium, Brunei Darussalam, China, Croatia, Cyprus, Denmark, France, Former Yugoslav Republic of Macedonia, Germany, Greece, Guatemala, Hungary, Ireland, Italy, Nepal, Portugal, Republic of Korea, Slovenia, Spain, and Turkey. For the latest information on troop contributing states, see the UN Department of Peacekeeping Operations website, www.un.org/en/peacekeeping.

[460] El Salvador, Ghana, India, Indonesia, Malaysia, Nigeria, Qatar, and Tanzania.

[461] See UNSC, 'Statement by the President of the Security Council' (27 July 2006) UN Doc S/PRST/2006/34.

customary law and apply to all states and armed groups in any kind of armed conflict.[462]

Occupation[463]

Finally, the potential impact of UN forces and Chapter VII decisions concerning occupation regimes on the law of occupation will be discussed.[464]

Before going into details, it is worth noting that the law of occupation applies whenever there is *de facto* occupation pursuant to the following two provisions:

1) Common Article 2 of the 1949 Geneva Conventions:

> The Convention shall also apply to all cases of partial or total occupation of the territory of a High Contracting Party, even if the said occupation meets with no armed resistance.

2) Article 42 of the 1907 Hague Regulations:

> Territory is considered occupied when it is actually placed under the authority of the hostile army. The occupation extends only to the territory where such authority has been established and can be exercised.[465]

When UN forces, regardless of state-led UN forces or UN-commanded forces, are deployed into a particular state, they inevitably occupy parts of the territory of the concerned state. The extent of the territory occupied by UN forces varies from one UN forces to another. However, the occupation of parts of the territory by UN forces is not always occupation within the meaning of IHL. In particular, when the state which receives the UN forces gives consent, the presence of the UN forces is not seen as occupation since the UN forces are no longer a 'hostile army'

[462] See UNHRC, 'Report of the Commission of Inquiry on Lebanon Pursuant to Human Rights Council resolution S-2/1' (23 November 2006) UN Doc A/HRC/3/2, para 233 *ff*. For IHL rules on civilian protection, see section 4.IV.D.

[463] See generally A Faite, 'Applicability of the Law of Occupation to United Nations-Mandated Forces' in Faite and Grenier (eds), *Expert Meeting on Multinational Peace Operations;* M Sassòli, 'Outline of *de Jure* and *de Facto* Applicability of the Law of Occupation to United Nations-Mandated Forces' in Faite and Grenier (eds), *Expert Meeting on Multinational Peace Operations;* M Starita, 'L'occupation de l'Iraq: Le Conseil de Sécurité, le droit de la guerre et le droit des peuples à disposer d'eux-mêmes' (2004) 108 *Revue générale de droit international public* 883; R Kolb et al, *L'application du droit international humanitaire;* M Zwanenburg, 'Pieces of the Puzzle: Peace Operations, Occupation and the Use of Force' (2006) 45 *Revue de droit militaire et de droit de la guerre* 239; A Faite, 'Multinational Forces Acting Pursuant to a Mandate of the United Nations: Specific Issues on the Applicability of International Humanitarian Law' (2007) 11 *International Peacekeeping (The Yearbook of International Peace Operations)* 143.

[464] 'Law of occupation' here refers particularly to Arts 42–56 of the 1907 Hague Regulations, 1949 Fourth Geneva Convention, and customary international law.

[465] Note that the authentic text is French, not English. See also M Zwanenburg, 'The Law of Occupation Revisited: The Beginning of an Occupation' (2007) 10 *Yearbook of International Humanitarian Law* 75.

within the meaning of Article 42 of the 1907 Hague Regulations.[466] The law of occupation, therefore, does not come into operation. In fact, in most cases states provide consent for the presence of state-led UN forces and UN-commanded forces. These UN forces were given mandates that resembled the obligations of occupying powers, or even beyond them. For example, UNMISET (East Timor) was given the following mandates:

(a) To provide assistance to core administrative structures critical to the viability and political stability of East Timor;
(b) To provide interim law enforcement and public security and to assist in the development of a new law enforcement agency in East Timor, the East Timor Police Service (ETPS);
(c) To contribute to the maintenance of the external and internal security of East Timor.[467]

Despite the fact that UNMISET was authorised to use force under Chapter VII to carry out these mandates, since there was consent by East Timor to be present in the country,[468] their activities on behalf of the government was not seen as those of the occupying power.

On the other hand, there were cases where there was no consent or where it was doubtful whether the consent was valid in the whole territory of the receiving state. Such problems surfaced when UN forces were deployed to a state's territory where the central government had little or no control, or when there was no government to gain consent from in the first place. In such cases, it is possible that UN forces could have been subject to the law of occupation when they occupied parts of the territory of the concerned state.[469] Examples are such as the 1991 Gulf War when the multinational forces briefly occupied parts of southern Iraq towards the end of the international armed conflict.[470] In this case, there was no consent from Iraq to be stationed on the territory of Iraq and hence, the territory of Iraq that was placed under the authority of the multinational forces was occupied in the sense of IHL.[471] In contrast,

[466] This is the case so long as the UN forces act within the limits of the consent by the host state. See Art 3(e) of the 1974 Definition of Aggression: 'The use of armed forces of one State which are within the territory of another State with the agreement of the receiving State, in contravention of the conditions provided for in the agreement or any extension of their presence in such territory beyond the termination of the agreement.' This indicates that if the UN forces act beyond the limits of consent by the host state, they can be considered as a 'hostile army' within the meaning of Art 42 of the 1907 Hague Regulations.

[467] UNSC Res 1410 (17 May 2002) UN Doc S/RES/1410, para 2.

[468] 2002 UNMISET SOFA.

[469] For the applicability of IHL to UN forces, see section 4.IV.C. See also Greenwood, 'International Humanitarian Law and United Nations Military Operations', 28; Faite, 'Multinational Forces', 149–50.

[470] US Department of Defense, 'Final Report', 339.

[471] Other cases of state-led UN forces that occupied parts of a state's territory can be found in Haiti, UNSC Res 940 (31 July 1994) UN Doc S/RES/940 and UNSC Res 1529 (29 February 2004) UN Doc S/RES/1529; Rwanda, UNSC Res 929 (22 June 1994) UN Doc S/RES/929; East Timor, UNSC Res 1264 (15 September 1999) UN Doc S/RES/1264; Liberia, UNSC Res

the multinational forces in Iraq since July 2004 that was authorised by Security Council resolution 1546 was arguably not an occupying power since there was consent from the Iraqi government.[472] Not only state-led UN forces but also UN-commanded forces could find themselves occupying parts of the state's territory in the sense of IHL. Such was probably the case when UNOSOM II was mandated to 'establish the effective authority of UNOSOM II throughout Somalia, including to secure the investigation of their actions [the attacks against UNOSOM II] and their arrest and detention for prosecution, trial and punishment'.[473] At the time, there was no government in Somalia that could give consent to the presence of UNOSOM II. In cases where there is occupation by UN forces, they are bound by two sets of obligations: mandates provided by the Security Council and the law of occupation.

On this point, there are debates as to whether Security Council mandates under Chapter VII take precedence over the law of occupation. On one hand, there are those who suggest that the Security Council mandates under Chapter VII can supersede the law of occupation, once the Security Council adopts measures that are considered necessary for the restoration of peace and security.[474] On the other hand, some take the view that such an interpretation can blur the separation between *jus ad bellum* and *jus in bello*.[475] There are still others who suggest that Chapter VII decisions and the law of occupation are not always in conflict but can be complementary. According to this view, the law of occupation itself accommodates certain degree of flexibility which allows certain measures that go beyond the maintenance of the status quo, such as the development of infrastructure and economy.[476] It follows that the measures taken by the Security Council that address certain aspects of the occupation may not always be in conflict with the law of occupation but rather complement it.

It should be noted at the outset that the law of occupation prefers a status quo of the occupied state and the occupying power is merely considered as

1497 (1 August 2003) UN Doc S/RES/1497; Côte d'Ivoire, UNSC Res 1528 (27 February 2004) UN Doc S/RES/1528.

472 UNSC Res 1546 (8 June 2004) UN Doc S/RES/1546, Preamble.

473 UNSC Res 837 (6 June 1993) UN Doc S/RES/837, para 5.

474 Greenwood, 'International Humanitarian Law and United Nations Military Operations', 28. See also Kelsen, *The Law of the United Nations*, 116; P Reuter, *Introduction au droit des traits*, 3ème edn, revue et augmentée par Philippe Cahier (Paris, Presses Universitaires de France, 1995) 130–31; Bernhardt, 'Article 103', 1300; D Scheffer, 'Beyond Occupation Law' (2003) 97 *American Journal of International Law* 842, 853; Faite and Grenier (eds), *Expert Meeting on Multinational Peace Operations*, 15.

475 Sassòli, 'Outline of *de Jure* and *de Facto* Applicability', 33–34. See also ICRC, 'Report on the Protection of War Victims', 429; S Oeter, 'Civil War, Humanitarian Law and the United Nations' (1997) 1 *Max Planck Yearbook of United Nations Law* 195, 229.

476 Faite, 'Applicability of the Law of Occupation', 75. See also H Tigroudja, 'Le régime d'occupation en Iraq' (2004) 50 *Annuaire français de droit international* 77, 89–91; A Roberts, 'Transformative Military Occupation: Applying the Law of War and Human Rights' (2006) 100 *American Journal of International Law* 580, 622.

a 'de facto administrator'.[477] It does not have sovereignty over the occupied state.[478] Article 43 of the 1907 Hague Regulations clearly reflects the fundamental idea behind the law of occupation which prefers the status quo of the occupied state, including the laws (both domestic and international law) in force:[479]

> The authority of the legitimate power having in fact passed into the hand of the occupant, the latter shall take all the measures in his power to restore, and ensure, as far as possible, public order and safety, while respecting, unless absolutely prevented, the laws in force in the country.

This provision not only sets out what the occupying power should do, but also sets the limits on what the occupying power can do. The occupying power's main task is to restore and ensure public order and safety in accordance with the laws in force in the occupied state. This task is normally undertaken by the executive branch (government) of the occupied state and hence, during the occupation, the occupying power is only replacing the executive branch of the occupied state. Since the occupying power is not superseding the sovereignty of the occupied state but is merely a *de facto* administrator, it cannot be said that the occupying power replaces other state powers, namely the judicial and the legislative branch.

With regard to the judicial branch, Article 54 of the 1949 Fourth Geneva Convention provides as follows:

> The occupying power may not alter the status of public officials or judges in the occupied territories.

Article 64 further provides, in part, as follows:

> [T]he tribunals of the occupied territory shall continue to function in respect of all offences covered by the said laws [the penal laws of the occupied territory].

[477] Uhler and Coursier et al, *Commentary*, 273.

[478] The 1970 Friendly Relations Declaration provides that 'The territory of a State shall not be the object of acquisition by another State resulting from the threat or use of force. No territorial acquisition resulting from the threat or use of force shall be recognized as legal.' UNGA, 'Declaration on Principles of International Law concerning Friendly Relations and Co-operation among States in Accordance with the Charter of the United Nations' UNGA Res 2625 (XXV) (24 October 1970). Art 3(a) of the 1974 Definition of Aggression also provides that 'any annexation by the use of force of the territory of another State or part thereof' is an act of aggression.

[479] *Armed Activities on the Territory of the Congo* (hereafter *Armed Activities* case) (*Democratic Republic of the Congo v Uganda*) (Merits) [2005] ICJ Rep 116, para 178: 'The Court thus concludes that Uganda was the occupying Power in Ituri at the relevant time. As such it was under an obligation, according to Article 43 of the Hague Regulations of 1907, to take all the measures in its power to restore, and ensure, as far as possible, public order and safety in the occupied area, while respecting, unless absolutely prevented, the laws in force in the DRC. This obligation comprised the duty to secure respect for the applicable rules of international human rights law and international humanitarian law, to protect the inhabitants of the occupied territory against acts of violence, and not to tolerate such violence by any third party.'

These provisions clearly show that the judicial branch of the occupied state should be kept intact. However, the occupying power may exceptionally try certain criminal cases in military courts established by it. Article 66 of the Fourth Geneva Convention provides as follows:

> In case of a breach of the penal provisions promulgated by it by virtue of the second paragraph of Article 64 the Occupying Power may hand over the accused to its properly constituted, non-political military courts, on condition that the said courts sit in the occupied country.

This article permits the establishment of military courts, but they must be 'properly constituted, non-political military courts' which ensure all the judicial guarantees in domestic and international law.[480] The jurisdiction of these courts is only limited to breaches of the penal provisions promulgated by the occupying power in order for it to, among others, fulfil its obligations under the Fourth Geneva Convention and maintain the orderly government of the occupied territory. Therefore, the occupying power can supplement the judicial branch of the occupied state but only exceptionally in relation to breaches of penal provisions promulgated by the occupying power.

With regard to the legislative branch, the occupying power clearly cannot replace it since the occupying power is a replacement of the executive branch of the occupied state, and the executive branch cannot perform the powers of the legislative branch.

However, the occupying power may be equated to a government that is facing a state of emergency, in which case certain extraordinary measures can be taken to restore public order and safety in accordance with the law. While the occupying power cannot assume the legislative power of the occupied state, the law of occupation leaves room for the occupying power to address the security issues that arise as a consequence of displacing the existing authority. Article 43 of the 1907 Hague Regulations provides that the occupying power should restore and ensure public order and safety according to the laws in force in the occupied territory, 'unless absolutely prevented'. The saving clause 'unless absolutely prevented' leaves room for the occupying power to adopt additional rules to administer the territory. Article 43 was elaborated in Article 64 of the 1949 Fourth Geneva Convention, which provides as follows:

> The penal laws of the occupied territory shall remain in force, with the exception that they may be repealed or suspended by the Occupying Power in cases where they constitute a threat to its security or an obstacle to the application

[480] The judicial guarantees are detailed in the 1949 Fourth Geneva Convention itself. In addition, Arts 9 and 14 of the International Covenant on Civil and Political Rights as well as the domestic law governing the military courts set out the similar or additional judicial guarantees. International Covenants on Civil and Political Rights (adopted 16 December 1966, entered into force 23 March 1976) 999 UNTS 171.

> of the present Convention. The Occupying Power may, however, subject the population of the occupied territory to provisions which are essential to enable the Occupying Power to fulfil its obligations under the present Convention, to maintain the orderly government of the territory, and to ensure the security of the Occupying Power, of the members and property of the occupying forces or administration, and likewise of the establishments and lines of communication used by them.

This should be seen in the light of Article 43 above, which obliges the occupying power to respect the laws in force 'unless absolutely prevented'. If such a situation arises, Article 64 above specifies the situations in which the occupying power can repeal or suspend the penal laws, or promulgate provisions additional to the laws in force. The situations in which the penal laws can be repealed or suspended are limited to: 1) cases where the penal laws pose a threat to the security of the occupying power; or 2) the penal laws prevent the occupying power to implement the Fourth Geneva Convention. The situations in which the occupying power can adopt additional provisions are limited to three situations, namely when additional provisions are necessary: 1) to fulfil the obligations under the Fourth Geneva Convention; 2) to maintain the orderly government of the occupied territory; and 3) to ensure the security of the occupying power, including the members, property, establishments, and lines of communication of the occupying forces or administration. The list of situations is exhaustive.[481]

Finally, Article 7 of the 1949 Fourth Geneva Convention provides a further ground for the occupying power to adopt provisions additional to complement the law of occupation, which provides as follows:

> [T]he High Contracting Parties may conclude other special agreements for all matters concerning which they may deem it suitable to make separate provision.[482]

A commentary on this provision notes as follows on its value:

> [T]he position of civilians can be much improved by special agreements concluded between the belligerents in cases other than those provided for in the Convention itself. The Convention represents a minimum which many States will doubtless wish to exceed whenever they can.[483]

481 Uhler and Coursier et al, *Commentary*, 273, 336, and 337.

482 See also Art 83 of the Convention Relative to the Treatment of Prisoners of War (adopted 27 July 1929, entered into force 19 June 1931) 118 LNTS 343; common Art 3(2) of the 1949 Geneva Conventions; Art 6 of the 1949 First, Second, and Third Geneva Conventions. On this topic, see generally R Monaco, 'Les conventions entre belligérants' (1949) 75 *Recueil des Cours de l'Académie de Droit International* 18; Pictet et al, *Commentary* Vol I, 65 *ff*; Uhler and Coursier et al, *Commentary*, 64 *ff*; J Pictet et al, *Commentary on the Geneva Conventions of 12 August 1949* Vol II (Geneva, International Committee of the Red Cross, 1960) 45 *ff*; J de Preux, *Commentary on the Geneva Conventions of 12 August 1949* Vol III (Geneva, International Committee of the Red Cross, 1960) 78 *ff*.

483 Uhler and Coursier et al, *Commentary*, 67.

These agreements are normally concluded between the conflicting parties such as 'local arrangements of a purely temporary nature (evacuation), sometimes of actual regulations (distribution of relief consignments), sometimes of a quasi-political agreement (substitute for the Protecting Power, investigations)'.[484] However, the format of the agreement is not specified[485] and hence there may be a possibility for the UN Member States, which are all states parties to the 1949 Geneva Conventions,[486] to adopt such agreements in the form of Security Council resolutions. The states parties to the 1949 Geneva Conventions also have the general obligation to 'ensure respect' for the Conventions by other states parties in common Article 1, and thus creating a special agreement to deal effectively with the situation of occupation seems to come under this general obligation.[487] If the states parties consider the necessity to adopt additional rules for occupation, it seems possible that the Security Council can be entrusted to adopt Chapter VII mandates on behalf of all the UN Member States pursuant to Article 24(1) of the UN Charter. The condition for such a special agreement is provided in Article 7 of the Fourth Geneva Convention:

> No special agreement shall adversely affect the situation of protected persons, as defined by the present Convention, nor restrict the rights which it confers upon them.[488]

Thus, if additional rules for occupation are going to be adopted by the Security Council, the existing protection in the Fourth Geneva Convention must not be affected.[489] In this sense, Article 7 only permits the adoption of additional rules to the law of occupation and not the repeal or suspension.

As can be seen from the above, the occupying power, in principle, can only carry out the powers normally entrusted to the executive branch. The powers of the judicial and legislative branches can only be exercised in very limited circumstances prescribed in the 1949 Fourth Geneva Convention. The law of occupation does not rule out the possibility of complementing the law of occupation by Chapter VII decisions but this

[484] Uhler and Coursier et al, *Commentary*, 68.

[485] See Uhler and Coursier et al, *Commentary*, 67–68.

[486] For the latest record of states parties to IHL treaties, see the ICRC IHL Database, www.icrc.org/ihl. For the UN Charter, see the UN Treaty Collection website, treaties.un.org.

[487] *Legal Consequences of the Construction of a Wall in the Occupied Palestinian Territory* (Advisory Opinion) [2004] ICJ Rep 136, para 158.

[488] See also Art 47 of the 1949 Fourth Geneva Convention: 'Protected persons who are in occupied territory shall not be deprived, in any case or in any manner whatsoever, of the benefits of the present Convention by any change introduced, as a result of the occupation of a territory, into the institution or government of the said territory, nor by any agreement concluded between the authorities of the occupied territories and the Occupying Power, nor by any annexation by the latter of the whole or part of the occupied territory.'

[489] Such obligation can generally be derived from Art 24(2) of the UN Charter, which obliges the Security Council to act in accordance with the Purposes and Principles of the UN, including Art 1(3) on international co-operation on humanitarian issues and promotion of the respect for human rights. See n 8 and text to n 38 above.

should be done within the limits of the 1907 Hague Regulations and the Fourth Geneva Convention.

The occupation of Iraq by the US and UK from 2003 to 2004 put the question of whether Chapter VII decisions can override the law of occupation into focus. During the occupation, a number of official documents were issued by the Coalition Provisional Authority (or CPA, the name of the occupying powers): 12 Regulations, 100 Orders, and 17 Memoranda.[490] According to the CPA, Regulations are 'instruments that define the institutions and authorities of the Coalition Provisional Authority', Orders are 'binding instructions or directives to the Iraqi people that create the penal consequences or have a direct bearing on the way Iraqis are regulated, including changes to Iraqi law', and a Memorandum 'expands on Orders or Regulations by creating or adjusting procedures applicable to an Order or Regulation'.[491] Many experts have commented on the legality of these official documents under the law of occupation and whether some could have been lawful derogations from the law of occupation justified by Chapter VII decisions.[492]

Security Council resolution 1483 was adopted, under Chapter VII, on 22 May 2003 in the aftermath of the US and UK invasion of Iraq on 20 March 2003, which set out the framework for the reconstruction of Iraq. Paragraph 1 begins by setting out a general appeal to the UN Member States and concerned organisations 'to assist the people of Iraq in their efforts to reform their institutions and rebuild their country, and to contribute to conditions of stability and security in Iraq in accordance with this resolution'. Paragraph 4 then sets out the general mandate of the occupying powers:

> *The Security Council . . . Calls* upon the Authority [CPA], consistent with the Charter of the United Nations and other relevant international law, to promote the welfare of the Iraqi people through the effective administration of the territory, including in particular working towards the restoration of conditions of security and stability and the creation of conditions in which the Iraqi people can freely determine their own political future.

The 'restoration of conditions of security and stability' is clearly an obligation of the occupying power but 'to promote the welfare of the Iraqi people' and 'the creation of conditions in which the Iraqi people can freely determine their own political future' are unclear as to their scope in practice.

Experts have pointed out that some of the CPA Orders went too far and hence violated the law of occupation.[493] For example, Order 37 suspended

490 See the CPA website, www.iraqcoalition.org/regulations.

491 Ibid.

492 See, eg, Roberts, 'Transformative Military Occupation'; Tigroudja, 'Le régime d'occupation en Iraq'; M Zwanenburg, 'Existentialism in Iraq: Security Council Resolution 1483 and the Law of Occupation' (2004) 856 *International Review of the Red Cross* 745.

493 See n 492 above.

certain taxes, Order 39 opened up Iraq to foreign investments to an unprecedented degree, and Order 64 amended the existing company law. These changes to Iraqi laws did not seem consistent with the requirements in Article 64 of the 1949 Fourth Geneva Convention, which limits the repeal and suspension of law to penal laws, and limits the adoption of additional rules only when it is necessary to fulfil the obligations under the Fourth Geneva Convention, maintain the orderly government of the occupied territory, and ensure the security of the occupying power.

Many have questioned whether the extensive changes made to Iraqi law by CPA Orders could be justified by the mandates provided in paragraphs 1 and 4 in Security Council resolution 1483 (which was adopted under Chapter VII), even though the CPA Orders violated the law of occupation. However, resolution 1483 itself made it clear that the occupying power had to comply with the law of occupation since the Security Council called upon 'all concerned to comply fully with their obligations under international law including in particular the Geneva Conventions of 1949 and the Hague Regulations of 1907'.[494] It seems to be clear enough that whatever mandates were given to the occupying powers by resolution 1483, the actions of the occupying power must comply with the law of occupation.

Experts have also pointed out that the mandates of the occupying power set out in resolution 1483 in very broad terms cannot constitute a basis for derogating from the law of occupation.[495] As noted above, the occupying power was called upon 'to promote the welfare of the Iraqi people through the effective administration of the territory . . . and the creation of conditions in which the Iraqi people can freely determine their own political future'. Whether this instantly permitted the occupying power to change Iraqi laws concerning foreign investment, taxes, and companies was seriously doubtful. If these changes had to be introduced, this could have been effectuated through special agreements under Article 7 of the 1949 Fourth Geneva Convention, decisions of the Security Council specifically setting out the derogation from the law of occupation, or amendments by the Iraqi parliament.

The case of Iraq was unusual in the sense that the Security Council expressly recognised the US and UK as the occupying powers in Iraq and provided a general mandate for them under Chapter VII. Therefore, the potential conflict between the law of occupation and Chapter VII decisions was visible in the Security Council resolution. However, the potential conflict is more subtle in many cases. In particular, there were several UN forces that were not mandated to perform the function similar to occupying powers but found themselves in a situation where they had to

[494] See, eg, Roberts, 'Transformative Military Occupation', 609.

[495] See, eg, Roberts, 'Transformative Military Occupation', 615; Zwanenburg, 'Existentialism in Iraq', 757*ff*.

do so, in particular in a state's territory where the central government had little or no control. In such cases, were they required to apply the law of occupation or only follow the limited mandates provided by the Security Council? In such cases, UN forces were the only authority that the civilians could rely on and thus they might have been required to apply the law of occupation.

Examples can be found in the Congo and Somalia. In the Congo[496] during the 1960s, the tide towards the secession of Katanga province from the Congo was at its height. Against this background, ONUC was authorised, by Security Council resolution 161, to 'take immediately all appropriate measures to prevent the occurrence of civil war in the Congo, including arrangements for cease-fires, the halting of all military operations, the prevention of clashes, and the use of force, if necessary, in the last resort'.[497] In December 1962, ONUC launched a major offensive against Élisabethville (now Lubumbashi) and Jadotville (now Likasi) comprising airstrike and ground operations. ONUC eventually took control of the two towns and the surrounding areas by early January 1963.[498] The central government of the Congo did not have control over these parts of its territory, but since ONUC was present in the Congo with the consent of the central government,[499] the capture of Élisabethville and Jadotville could not be considered as occupation in the sense of IHL. As mentioned earlier, Article 42 of the 1907 Hague Regulations provides as follows:

> Territory is considered occupied when it is actually placed under the authority of the hostile army.

ONUC was not a 'hostile army' since the Congolese government consented to its presence. However, due to the complete lack of control by the central government over parts of Katanga province, and since ONUC was the sole authority that the civilians could rely on in the area, ONUC was put in a situation similar to an occupying power.

The case of Somalia in the 1990s was worse, where there was virtually no central government and thus virtually the whole territory of Somalia was not under government control.[500] The first UN force, UNOSOM I, which

[496] The official country name was the 'Republic of the Congo' at the time of independence, but as at September 2010 the name is the 'Democratic Republic of the Congo'.

[497] UNSC Res 161 (12 February 1961) UN Doc S/RES/161, para 1.

[498] UNSC, 'Report of the Officer-in-Charge of the United Nations Operation in the Congo to the Secretary-General on Developments Relating to the Application of the Security Council Resolutions of 21 February and 24 November 1961' (30 January 1963) UN Doc S/5053/Add.15, paras 23–37.

[499] Agreement relating to the Legal Status, Facilities, Privileges and Immunities of the United Nations Organization in the Congo (adopted 27 November 1961, entered into force 27 November 1961) 414 UNTS 231.

[500] UNSC, 'Report of the Commission of Inquiry Established Pursuant to Security Council Resolution 885 (1993) to Investigate Armed Attacks on UNOSOM II Personnel Which Led to Casualties among Them' (1 June 1994) UN Doc S/1994/653, paras 19–22.

was authorised under Security Council resolution 751 in April 1992, was deployed with the consent of the 'principal factions in Mogadishu',[501] but the consent was not in any way an equivalent to consent from the central government. By the time, the Unified Task Force (UNITAF) was deployed pursuant to Security Council resolution 794, adopted in December 1992, there was no 'government . . . in Somalia that could request and allow such use of force [by the UN or Member States authorised by the Security Council]'.[502] UNITAF, which was a state-led UN forces under US command, was therefore deployed to Somalia without any consent from a national authority. Therefore, a question arose whether the law of occupation applied in the areas where UNITAF was deployed.[503] On this point, the US nuanced its view by mentioning that the 'law of occupation (Fourth Geneva Convention) was used as a model in defining US relationships with the civilian population'.[504] Assuming that the law of occupation applied to the areas where UNITAF was deployed, the question then was whether there was a conflict with the mandates provided by the Security Council under a resolution adopted under Chapter VII. As noted earlier, Article 43 of the 1907 Hague Regulations establishes that the primary obligation of the occupying power is to 'restore, and ensure, as far as possible, public order and safety' in parts of the territory that are under occupation, and the detailed obligations are set out in the 1949 Fourth Geneva Convention. On the other hand, the mandate of UNITAF was more limited, which was to 'use all necessary means to establish as soon as possible a secure environment for humanitarian relief operations in Somalia'. This put into question whether the Chapter VII mandate, which was limited in scope, could have exempted UNITAF from the full spectrum of obligations under the law of occupation.

By the time UNOSOM II was established pursuant to Security Council resolution 814, adopted in March 1993, the absence of the central government still continued.[505] This was probably the first time that UN-commanded forces were deployed to a state without a central government that could give consent. Therefore, as similar to UNITAF, a question arose whether the law of occupation applied in parts of the territory where UNOSOM II was deployed.[506] A UN report on UNOSOM II concluded that 'in an environment of state collapse, the Fourth Geneva Convention

[501] UNGA, 'Somalia' (1992) UNYB 198, 204.

[502] UNSC, 'Letter Dated 29 November 1992 from the Secretary-General Addressed to the President of the Security Council' (30 November 1992) UN Doc S/24868, 3.

[503] It is reported that the area under UNITAF control comprised 40 per cent of Somalia's territory. See UNSC, 'Further Report of the Secretary-General Submitted in Pursuance of Paragraphs 18 and 19 of Resolution 794 (1992)' (3 March 1993) UN Doc S/25354, para 72.

[504] US Department of the Army, 'FM 100-23 Peace Operations' (December 1994), 48–49, www.dtic.mil/doctrine/jel/service_pubs/fm100_23.pdf.

[505] UNSC, 'Further Report of the Secretary-General Submitted in Pursuance of Paragraphs 18 and 19 of Resolution 794 (1992)' (3 March 1993) UN Doc S/25354, para 41.

[506] See Faite, 'Multinational Forces', 150.

could supply adequate guidelines for regulating relations between peacekeeping force personnel and the local populations'.[507] Assuming that the law of occupation applied in areas where UNOSOM II was deployed, as similar to UNITAF, this put into question whether there was a conflict with the mandates provided under Chapter VII. Although UNOSOM II's mandates were extensive, they did not encompass the obligations of the occupying power. The mandates that came closest to the general obligation of the occupying power were the following:

> To secure or maintain security at all ports, airports and lines of communications required for the delivery of humanitarian assistance;
>
> To protect, as required, the personnel, installations and equipments [*sic*] of United Nations and its agencies, ICRC as well as NGOs and to take such forceful action as may be required to neutralize armed elements that attack, or threaten to attack, such facilities.[508]

These mandates were still far from the general obligation of the occupying power to restore and ensure public order and safety. As similar to UNITAF, this puts into question whether Chapter VII mandates could have exempted UNOSOM II from certain obligations under the law of occupation.

The above cases of UNITAF and UNOSOM II have been explained in detail to illustrate the potential conflict between the law of occupation and Chapter VII mandates. However, before discussing the consequences of the conflict, one other question needs to be addressed. This is the requirement that the territory should be 'actually placed under the authority' in order for it to be considered as occupied. The ICJ noted as follows in the *Armed Activities* case in the context of the international armed conflict between the DRC and Uganda:

> In order to reach a conclusion as to whether a State . . . is an 'occupying Power' . . . the Court must examine whether there is sufficient evidence to demonstrate that the said authority [authority of the hostile army] was in fact established and exercised by the intervening State in the areas in question. In the present case the Court will need to satisfy itself that the Uganda armed forces in the DRC were not only stationed in particular locations but also that they had substituted their own authority for that of the Congolese Government.[509]

[507] UN Secretariat, 'The Comprehensive Report', para 58. Note, however, that no reference is made to the law of occupation in a memorandum of the UN Legal Counsel concerning the maintenance of law and order in Somalia by UNOSOM II. See UN Secretariat, 'Memorandum to the Under-Secretary-General for Peacekeeping Operations' (1993) *United Nations Juridical Yearbook* 447.

[508] UNSC, 'Further Report of the Secretary-General Submitted in Pursuance of Paragraphs 18 and 19 of Resolution 794 (1992)' (3 March 1993) UN Doc S/25354, paras 57(e) and (f). UNSC Res 814 (26 March 1993) UN Doc S/RES/814, para 5 refers to this report for the mandates of UNOSOM II.

[509] *Armed Activities* case (Merits), para 173.

The Court then concluded that Ituri was occupied by Uganda since a commander in the Ugandan armed forces declared the creation of a new province and appointed a governor for it. The Court, however, rejected that Kisangani Airport was occupied by the mere presence of Ugandan troops, which follows the Court's approach that the existing authority has to be substituted, and not merely stationed in particular locations.

If one follows this standard, it is questionable to what extent UNITAF and UNOSOM II actually placed the territory under its control and hence could be considered as an occupying power. A UN Secretary-General's report on Somalia reported that 'UNITAF had 37,000 troops distributed over approximately 40 per cent of the territory of Somalia'.[510] However, the mere deployment does not instantly mean occupation within the meaning of IHL. A US report to the Security Council provided a stronger indication that UNITAF could have been occupying parts of the territory of Somalia. The report mentioned that 'phase I began with the successful seizure of the airfield and port in Mogadishu . . . this was followed by the seizure of Baidoa [a city in southern Somalia].'[511] With regard to UNOSOM II, a UN Secretary-General's report indicated that it was deployed to many parts of the territory of Somalia,[512] but as similar to UNITAF, the mere deployment did not instantly mean occupation. On the other hand, the extensive operations of UNOSOM II in Mogadishu to restore security and law and order, namely the destruction of arms depots and radio stations inciting violence against UNOSOM II,[513] could have been seen as substituting the authority of Somalia that should have existed. In this sense, UNOSOM II might have played a role as an occupying power in Mogadishu. The total extent of the occupation by UNITAF and UNOSOM II depends heavily on the facts, and the interpretation of the facts, which is not the main aim of this section. The point here is rather to clarify that the mere deployment of UN forces does not instantly constitute occupation, but only when they substitute the existing authority.

Nevertheless, occupation can exist, however short in terms of duration and small in terms of geographical extent. From the point of view of IHL, there is either occupation or not, and the full spectrum of the obligations under the law of occupation applies to the occupying power whenever there is occupation. The occupying power cannot opt to be bound by a

[510] UNSC, 'Further Report of the Secretary-General Submitted in Pursuance of Paragraph 18 of Resolution 814 (1993)' (17 August 1993) UN Doc S/26317, para 6.

[511] UNSC, 'Letter Dated 19 January 1993 from the Permanent Representative of the United States of America to the United Nations Addressed to the President of the Security Council' (19 January 1993) UN Doc S/25126, Annex.

[512] UNSC, 'Further Report of the Secretary-General Submitted in Pursuance of Paragraph 19 of Resolution 814 (1993) and Paragraph A 5 of Resolution 865 (1993)' (12 November 1993) S/26738, paras 44 *ff*.

[513] UNSC, 'Report of the Commission of Inquiry Established Pursuant to Security Council Resolution 885 (1993) to Investigate Armed Attacks on UNOSOM II Personnel Which Led to Casualties among Them' (1 June 1994) UN Doc S/1994/653, para 137.

portion of the obligations under the law of occupation. If one follows this line of argument, then UN forces are bound by the full spectrum of the obligations under the law of occupation, when they are occupying parts of the territory.

On the other hand, it is often the case that the mandates of UN forces are limited to specific tasks, such as offering security for safe delivery of humanitarian assistance, and the fulfilment of the obligations under the law of occupation is not envisaged. The equipment provided is therefore commensurate to the mandate, and not to fulfil the obligations under the law of occupation. Here, there is clearly a conflict between Chapter VII mandates and the law of occupation.

In order to avoid unnecessary derogations from IHL by Chapter VII decisions, it is essential to obtain consent of the state where the UN forces will be deployed to. In most cases, UN forces have been deployed with the consent of the host state, except in cases such as the 1991 Gulf War when the multinational forces expelled Iraq from Kuwait and occupied parts of Iraq. Hence, in practice, UN forces do not have to face the dilemma of whether to follow the Chapter VII mandates or the law of occupation.

In cases where UN forces cannot obtain the consent of the concerned state, the Security Council may have to envisage a situation where UN forces may have to occupy parts of the territory of the concerned state, which would give rise to the application of the law of occupation. In such cases, necessary equipment for the UN forces needs to be reflected upon, and the choice between state-led UN forces or UN-commanded forces, or both, should be decided upon.

In cases where the consent of the concerned state cannot be obtained and the necessary equipment for the UN forces to be prepared for possible occupation cannot be secured, an express derogation should be made in the relevant Security Council resolutions. However, this must be the last resort as it risks the distinction between *jus ad bellum* and *jus in bello*, and eventually weakens the protection for the persons affected by armed conflict.

Finally, by way of completing the discussion, it is worth mentioning that UN forces not operating under Chapter VII mandates will not face the issue of whether the mandates provided by the Security Council or the law of occupation prevail. UN forces not operating under Chapter VII cannot enter a state's territory without the consent of the concerned state. Entering into a state's territory by force and without the consent of the concerned state is only permitted if the use of force is in self-defence or under Chapter VII. Otherwise, Articles 2(4) and 2(7) of the UN Charter serve as a bar to forcibly enter a state's territory without consent, not to mention the occupation of the state's territory. Article 2(4), as already cited elsewhere, prohibits the use of force against a state. Article 2(7) further prohibits the UN to intervene in matters which are essentially within the domestic jurisdiction of any state, except when the UN is undertaking enforcement measures under Chapter VII. It follows that non-Chapter VII UN forces must obtain consent from the concerned state before deployment. This also renders the law of occupation inapplicable since, pursuant to the consent, the UN forces can no longer be considered as a 'hostile army'. As seen earlier, there is occupation when a territory is 'actually placed under the authority of the hostile army'. Since the law of occupation does not apply to non-Chapter VII UN forces, the conflict between UN Charter obligations and the law of occupation does not arise in the first place.

V. NON-MILITARY ENFORCEMENT MEASURES UNDER CHAPTER VII AND IHL[514]

The previous section discussed the relationship between military enforcement measures under Chapter VII and IHL. However, as noted earlier in this chapter, the response of the Security Council to 'threat to the peace, breach of the peace, or act of aggression' does not necessarily have to be military enforcement measures. To the contrary, Article 42 of the UN Charter suggests that non-military enforcement measures under Article 41 should be tried out before resorting to military enforcement measures.[515] Article 41 of the UN Charter provides as follows:

> The Security Council may decide what measures not involving the use of armed force are to be employed to give effect to its decisions, and it may call upon the Members of the United Nations to apply such measures. These may include complete or partial interruption of economic relations and of rail, sea, air, postal, telegraphic, radio, and other means of communication, and the severance of diplomatic relations.[516]

Under this provision or under Chapter VII, all of the actions listed in Article 41 as well as those not listed, such as arms embargoes and the

[514] See generally N Schrijver, 'The Use of Economics Sanctions by the UN Security Council: An International Law Perspective' in H Post (ed), *International Economic Law and Armed Conflict* (Dordrecht, Martinus Nijhoff, 1994); Boisson de Chazournes, 'Les résolutions des organs des Nations Unies', 160–62; Dominicé, 'L'article 103', 189–90; Gasser, 'The United Nations and International Humanitarian Law', 275–78; Sandoz, 'Rapport général', 72–73; Gasser, 'Collective Economic Sanctions'; Segall, 'Economic Sanctions'; Momtaz, 'La compatibilité des sanctions'; Condorelli, 'La compatibilité des sanctions'; Sassòli, 'Sanctions and International Humanitarian Law'; M Craven, 'Humanitarianism and the Quest for Smarter Sanctions' (2002) 13 *European Journal of International Law* 43; M O'Connell, 'Debating the Law of Sanctions' (2002) 13 *European Journal of International Law* 63.

[515] Art 42 of the UN Charter provides that 'Should the Security Council consider that measures provided for in Article 41 [non-military enforcement measures] would be inadequate or have proved to be inadequate, it may take such action by air, sea, or land forces as may be necessary to restore international peace and security.'

[516] See also Art 16 of the Covenant of the League of Nations (adopted 28 April 1919, entered into force 10 January 1920) 225 CTS 188.

establishment of *ad hoc* international criminal tribunals, have been taken in the past.[517] The implementation of Article 41 most often takes the form of sanctions and there have been at least 26 cases of sanctions,[518] particularly arms embargoes,[519] economic sanctions,[520] restrictions on certain means of

[517] See generally J Frowein and N Krisch, 'Article 41' in B Simma et al (eds), *The Charter of the United Nations: A Commentary*, 2nd edn, Vol I (Oxford, Oxford University Press, 2002); *Tadic Case* (Jurisdiction, Appeals), para 36.

[518] In many cases, a particular resolution contained several types of sanctions. Ongoing sanctions are as follows: Somalia, UNSC Res 733 (23 January 1992) UN Doc S/RES/733; Al-Qaeda and Taliban, UNSC Res 1267 (15 October 1999) UN Doc S/RES/1267; Iraq, UNSC Res 1483 (22 May 2003) UN Doc S/RES/1483; DRC, UNSC Res 1493 (28 July 2003) UN Doc S/RES/1493; Liberia, UNSC Res 1521 (22 December 2003) UN Doc S/RES/1521; Sudan, UNSC Res 1556 (30 July 2004) UN Doc S/RES/1556; Côte d'Ivoire, UNSC Res 1572 (15 November 2004) UN Doc S/RES/1572; Lebanon-Syria, UNSC Res 1636 (31 October 2005) UN Doc S/RES/1636; Democratic People's Republic of Korea, UNSC Res 1718 (14 October 2006) UN Doc S/RES/1718; Iran, UNSC Res 1737 (27 December 2006) UN Doc S/RES/1737; Eritrea, UNSC Res 1907 (23 December 2009) UN Doc S/RES/1907.

Completed sanctions are as follows: Southern Rhodesia, UNSC Res 217 (20 Nov 1965) UN Doc S/RES/217 and UNSC Res 232 (16 December 1966) UN Doc S/RES/232; South Africa, UNSC Res 418 (4 Nov 1977) UN Doc S/RES/418; Iraq-Kuwait, UNSC Res 661 (6 August 1990) UN Doc S/RES/661; former Yugoslavia, UNSC Res 713 (25 September 1991) UN Doc S/RES/713; Bosnia and Herzegovina, UNSC Res 787 (16 November 1992) UN Doc S/RES/787; Libya, UNSC Res 748 (31 Mar 1992) UN Doc S/RES/748; Liberia, UNSC Res 788 (19 November 1992) UN Doc S/RES/788; Haiti, UNSC Res 841 (16 June 1993) UN Doc S/RES/841; Angola, UNSC Res 864 (15 September 1993) UN Doc S/RES/864; Rwanda, UNSC Res 918 (17 May 1994) UN Doc S/RES/918; Sudan, UNSC Res 1054 (26 April 1996) UN Doc S/RES/1054; Sierra Leone, UNSC Res 1132 (8 October 1997) UN Doc S/RES/1132; Serbia and Montenegro, UNSC Res 1160 (31 March 1998) UN Doc S/RES/1160; Eritrea-Ethiopia, UNSC Res 1298 (17 May 2000) UN Doc S/RES/1298; Liberia, UNSC Res 1343 (7 March 2001) UN Doc S/RES/1343.

[519] Southern Rhodesia, UNSC Res 232 (16 December 1966) UN Doc S/RES/232; South Africa, UNSC Res 418 (4 Nov 1977) UN Doc S/RES/418; former Yugoslavia, UNSC Res 757 (30 May 1992) UN Doc S/RES/757; Libya, UNSC Res 748 (31 Mar 1992) UN Doc S/RES/748; Liberia, UNSC Res 788 (19 November 1992) UN Doc S/RES/788; Angola, UNSC Res 864 (15 September 1993) UN Doc S/RES/864; Serbia and Montenegro, UNSC Res 1160 (31 March 1998) UN Doc S/RES/1160; Eritrea-Ethiopia, UNSC Res 1298 (17 May 2000) UN Doc S/RES/1298; Liberia, UNSC Res 1343 (7 March 2001) UN Doc S/RES/1343; Somalia, UNSC Res 733 (23 January 1992) UN Doc S/RES/733; Rwanda, UNSC Res 918 (17 May 1994) UN Doc S/RES/918; Sierra Leone, UNSC Res 1132 (8 October 1997) UN Doc S/RES/1132; Al-Qaeda and Taliban, UNSC Res 1267 (15 October 1999) UN Doc S/RES/1267; DRC, UNSC Res 1493 (28 July 2003) UN Doc S/RES/1493; Liberia, UNSC Res 1521 (22 December 2003) UN Doc S/RES/1521; Sudan, UNSC Res 1556 (30 July 2004) UN Doc S/RES/1556; Côte d'Ivoire, UNSC Res 1572 (15 November 2004) UN Doc S/RES/1572; Democratic People's Republic of Korea, UNSC Res 1718 (14 October 2006) UN Doc S/RES/1718; Iran, UNSC Res 1737 (27 December 2006) UN Doc S/RES/1737; Eritrea, UNSC Res 1907 (23 December 2009) UN Doc S/RES/1907.

[520] Southern Rhodesia, UNSC Res 217 (20 Nov 1965) UN Doc S/RES/217, UNSC Res 232 (16 December 1966) UN Doc S/RES/232; Iraq-Kuwait, UNSC Res 661 (6 August 1990) UN Doc S/RES/661; former Yugoslavia, UNSC Res 757 (30 May 1992) UN Doc S/RES/757; Libya, UNSC Res 748 (31 Mar 1992) UN Doc S/RES/748; Bosnia and Herzegovina, UNSC Res 787 (16 November 1992) UN Doc S/RES/787 and UNSC Res 820 (17 April 1993) UN Doc S/RES/820; Haiti, UNSC Res 841 (16 June 1993) UN Doc S/RES/841; Angola, UNSC Res 864 (15 September 1993) UN Doc S/RES/864; Sierra Leone, UNSC Res 1306 (5 July 2000) UN Doc S/RES/1306; Al-Qaeda and Taliban, UNSC Res 1267 (15 October 1999) UN Doc S/RES/1267; Iraq, UNSC Res 1483 (22 May 2003) UN Doc S/RES/1483; DRC, UNSC Res 1493 (28 July 2003) UN Doc S/RES/1493; Liberia, UNSC Res 1521 (22 December 2003) UN

transportation,[521] travel restrictions on certain individuals,[522] and diplomatic sanctions.[523] Among these non-military enforcement measures, this section will discuss those that might have a substantial impact on IHL, namely arms embargoes, economic sanctions, and transport restrictions. As noted earlier, *ad hoc* international criminal tribunals will not be discussed since it goes well beyond the scope of this book and is a subject discussed at length elsewhere.[524]

Doc S/RES/1521; Sudan, UNSC Res 1556 (30 July 2004) UN Doc S/RES/1556; Côte d'Ivoire, UNSC Res 1572 (15 November 2004) UN Doc S/RES/1572; Lebanon-Syria, UNSC Res 1636 (31 October 2005) UN Doc S/RES/1636; Democratic People's Republic of Korea, UNSC Res 1718 (14 October 2006) UN Doc S/RES/1718; Iran, UNSC Res 1737 (27 December 2006) UN Doc S/RES/1737; Eritrea, UNSC Res 1907 (23 December 2009) UN Doc S/RES/1907.

[521] Southern Rhodesia, UNSC Res 217 (20 Nov 1965) UN Doc S/RES/217; Iraq-Kuwait, UNSC Res 661 (6 August 1990) UN Doc S/RES/661 and UNSC Res 665 (25 August 1990) UN Doc S/RES/665; Libya, UNSC Res 748 (31 Mar 1992) UN Doc S/RES/748; former Yugoslavia, UNSC Res 787 (16 November 1992) UN Doc S/RES/787 and UNSC Res 820 (17 April 1993) UN Doc S/RES/820; Haiti, UNSC Res 841 (16 June 1993) UN Doc S/RES/841; Bosnia and Herzegovina, UNSC Res 942 (23 September 1994) UN Doc S/RES/942; Sudan, UNSC Res 1070 (16 August 1996) UN Doc S/RES/1070; Angola, UNSC Res 1127 (28 August 1997) UN Doc S/RES/1127 and UNSC Res 1173 (12 June 1998) UN Doc S/RES/1173; Sierra Leone, UNSC Res 1132 (8 October 1997) UN Doc S/RES/1132 and UNSC Res 1171 (5 June 1998) UN Doc S/RES/1171; Serbia and Montenegro, UNSC Res 1160 (31 March 1998) UN Doc S/RES/1160; Al-Qaeda and Taliban, UNSC Res 1267 (15 October 1999) UN Doc S/RES/1267 and UNSC Res 1333 (19 December 2000) UN Doc S/RES/1333; Liberia, UNSC Res 1343 (7 March 2001) UN Doc S/RES/1343; DRC, UNSC Res 1493 (28 July 2003) UN Doc S/RES/1493 and UNSC Res 1596 (3 May 2005) UN Doc S/RES/1596; Liberia, UNSC Res 1521 (22 December 2003) UN Doc S/RES/1521; Sudan, UNSC Res 1556 (30 July 2004) UN Doc S/RES/1556; Côte d'Ivoire, UNSC Res 1572 (15 November 2004) UN Doc S/RES/1572; Democratic People's Republic of Korea, UNSC Res 1718 (14 October 2006) UN Doc S/RES/1718; Iran, UNSC Res 1737 (27 December 2006) UN Doc S/RES/1737; Eritrea, UNSC Res 1907 (23 December 2009) UN Doc S/RES/1907.

[522] Bosnia and Herzegovina, UNSC Res 942 (23 September 1994) UN Doc S/RES/942; Sudan, UNSC Res 1054 (26 April 1996) UN Doc S/RES/1054; Sierra Leone, UNSC Res 1132 (8 October 1997) UN Doc S/RES/1132 and UNSC Res 1171 (5 June 1998) UN Doc S/RES/1171; Iraq-Kuwait, UNSC Res 1137 (12 November 1997) UN Doc S/RES/1137; Al-Qaeda and Taliban, UNSC Res 1267 (15 October 1999) UN Doc S/RES/1267 and UNSC Res 1333 (19 December 2000) UN Doc S/RES/1333; Liberia, UNSC Res 1343 (7 March 2001) UN Doc S/RES/1343; Liberia, UNSC Res 1521 (22 December 2003) UN Doc S/RES/1521; Côte d'Ivoire, UNSC Res 1572 (15 November 2004) UN Doc S/RES/1572; DRC, UNSC Res 1596 (3 May 2005) UN Doc S/RES/1596, UNSC Res 1649 (21 December 2005) UN Doc S/RES/1649, and UNSC Res 1698 (31 July 2006) UN Doc S/RES/1698; Lebanon-Syria, UNSC Res 1636 (31 October 2005) UN Doc S/RES/1636; Democratic People's Republic of Korea, UNSC Res 1718 (14 October 2006) UN Doc S/RES/1718; Eritrea, UNSC Res 1907 (23 December 2009) UN Doc S/RES/1907.

[523] Former Yugoslavia, UNSC Res 713 (25 September 1991) UN Doc S/RES/713; Libya, UNSC Res 748 (31 Mar 1992) UN Doc S/RES/748 and UNSC Res 883 (11 Nov 1993) UN Doc S/RES/883; Sudan, UNSC Res 1054 (26 April 1996) UN Doc S/RES/1054.

[524] See n 20 above. *Ad hoc* international criminal tribunals were established under Art 41 of the UN Charter. See *Tadic Case* (Jurisdiction, Appeals), para 36.

A. Arms Embargoes and IHL

Arms embargoes have been the most frequent form of sanction imposed under Article 41 of the UN Charter or under Chapter VII. Among the 25 cases of sanctions, 19 have included an arms embargo.[525] It can complement IHL by: 1) imposing the prohibition on acquisition or transfer of weapons beyond what is required by IHL; and 2) preventing further or future violations of IHL by limiting the availability of certain weapons. However, a particular problem arises when an arms embargo indirectly contributes to violations of IHL. These issues will be discussed in turn.

The prohibition on the acquisition and transfer of weapons can be found in IHL treaties themselves, namely in the 1972 Biological Weapons Convention,[526] 1993 Chemical Weapons Convention,[527] 1997 Anti-Personnel Mines Convention,[528] and 2008 Convention on Cluster Munitions,[529] but these only cover certain weapons, namely biological and chemical weapons, anti-personnel mines, and cluster munitions.[530] On the other hand, arms embargoes imposed under Article 41 or Chapter VII have invariably been applied to all weapons as can be seen, for example, from the recent arms embargo on Côte d'Ivoire:

> *The Security Council* . . . *Decides* that all States shall . . . take the necessary measures to prevent the direct or indirect supply, sale or transfer to Côte d'Ivoire, from their territories or by their nationals, or using their flag vessels or aircraft, of arms or any related materiel, in particular military aircraft and equipment, whether or not originating in their territories.[531]

Since such arms embargoes are invariably imposed under Chapter VII, all states are obliged to comply with them, unlike IHL treaties, which require consent to be bound from states for those states to be bound by the treaties. However, since a Chapter VII arms embargo only applies temporarily and in relation to a specific situation, it does not have the permanent character or the categorical nature of the above-mentioned IHL treaties which apply in 'any circumstances' and to any state party. Thus, Chapter VII arms embargoes can complement the prohibition on the acquisition and transfer of certain weapons by categorically prohibiting the movement of any weapons, but in other aspects, namely the duration, it is more limited than certain IHL treaties.

[525] See n 519 above.
[526] Art I of the 1972 Biological Weapons Convention.
[527] Art I(1)(a) of the 1993 Chemical Weapons Convention.
[528] Art 1(1)(b) of the 1997 Convention on Anti-Personnel Mines.
[529] 2008 Convention on Cluster Munitions.
[530] Prohibitions can be further found in disarmament treaties and certain Security Council resolutions. See UN Office for Disarmament Affairs website, www.un.org/disarmament; International Atomic Energy Agency website, www.iaea.org; UNSC Res 1540 (28 April 2004) UN Doc S/RES/1540.
[531] UNSC Res 1572 (15 November 2004) UN Doc S/RES/1572, para 7.

Secondly, Chapter VII arms embargoes can prevent further or future IHL violations, thereby complementing IHL. The link between the availability of weapons and violations of IHL is already widely recognised. The ICRC, based on its long experience in armed conflict situations, noted that the 'availability of weapons, in particular small arms and light weapons . . . facilitates violations of IHL'.[532] A UN expert report leading to the UN Conference on the Illicit Trade in Small Arms and Light Weapons also noted that 'Small arms and light weapons . . . are widely used in conflicts in which violence has been perpetrated in violation of domestic law and the norms of international humanitarian law'.[533] While the whole question on the relationship between arms availability and IHL violations is beyond the scope of this book, these are important indications that Chapter VII arms embargoes could prevent further or future violations of IHL, thereby complementing IHL.

On the other hand, it has been suggested by Judge *ad hoc* Lauterpacht in the *Bosnian Genocide* case that a Chapter VII arms embargo might have indirectly fuelled genocide by obstructing Bosnia-Herzegovina from preventing the ethnic cleansing by the Federal Republic of Yugoslavia, in which case the Security Council could have been in violation of *jus cogens*.[534] With regard to the legal consequences of such a situation, Judge Lauterpacht noted that 'One possibility is that . . . it [resolution 713 imposing arms embargo on the former Yugoslavia] ceased to be valid and binding in its operation against Bosnia-Herzegovina; and that Members of the United Nations then became free to disregard it.'[535] As discussed earlier, it is widely seen that Article 103 of the UN Charter does not enable Chapter VII decisions to prevail over *jus cogens*.[536] More recently, the UN International Law Commission provided as follows in the Draft Articles on the Responsibility of International Organizations:

> An international organization incurs international responsibility if it adopts a decision binding a member State or international organization to commit an act that would be internationally wrongful if committed by the former organization and would circumvent an international obligation of the former organization.[537]

[532] ICRC, 'Unregulated Arms Availability, Small Arms and Light Weapons and the UN Process: Background Paper' (2006), ICRC website, www.icrc.org/eng. See also ICRC, *Arms Availability and the Situation of Civilians in Armed Conflict* (Geneva, International Committee of the Red Cross, 1999).

[533] UNGA, 'Report of the Group of Governmental Experts on Small Arms' (19 August 1999) UN Doc A/54/258, para 14. See also UNSC Res 1919 (29 April 2010) UN Doc S/RES/1919.

[534] *Bosnia Genocide* case (Order of 13 September 1993), Separate Opinion of Judge Lauterpacht, paras 98–104.

[535] *Bosnia Genocide* case (Order of 13 September 1993), Separate Opinion of Judge Lauterpacht, para 103.

[536] See section 4.II.B.

[537] Art 16(1) of the ILC Draft Articles on the Responsibility of International Organizations.

If the approach of Judge Lauterpacht is followed by analogy, an arms embargo might contribute to further IHL violations by obstructing one of the conflicting parties from preventing IHL violations by another conflicting party. If the rules of IHL that were violated were *jus cogens*, the Chapter VII decision imposing such an arms embargo is likely to be void.[538] If the rules of IHL that were violated were not *jus cogens*, the Chapter VII decision imposing such an arms embargo would still entail the responsibility of the UN. In this case, the Security Council may be falling short of complying with Article 24(2) of the UN Charter, which requires it to act in accordance with, among others, Article 1(3) on the international co-operation on humanitarian issues and promotion of the respect for human rights. In such a case, Chapter VII decisions might no longer be valid.[539] If one follows this approach, there are many relevant cases such as Liberia, Angola, Eritrea–Ethiopia, Rwanda, Sierra Leone, DRC, Sudan, and Côte d'Ivoire. In these cases, arms embargoes might have contributed to further IHL violations by obstructing one of the conflicting parties from preventing IHL violations by another conflicting party. Thus, the Security Council might have been violating Article 24(2) and hence Chapter VII decisions might have been invalid.

For example, in the Eritrea–Ethiopia Conflict, did the arms embargo obstruct either Eritrea or Ethiopia from preventing IHL violations by either side and hence did the Security Council fail to comply with Article 24(2) of the UN Charter? Did IHL rules which might be *jus cogens* prevail over the Chapter VII decisions and hence invalidate the latter? Similarly, did the arms embargo on Liberia hamper the Liberian armed forces to effectively prevent IHL violations by armed groups and hence did the Security Council fall short of its obligation under Article 24(2)?

[538] On the question of the extent of IHL rules having *jus cogens* status, see generally *Legality of the Threat or Use of Nuclear Weapons Case* (Advisory Opinion) [1996] ICJ Rep 226, para 83; G Abi-Saab, 'The Specificities of Humanitarian Law' in Swinarski (ed), *Studies and Essays*, 270 *ff*; L Hannikainen, *Peremptory Norms (Jus Cogens) in International Law: Historical Development, Criteria, Present Status* (Helsinki, Lakimiesliiton Kustannus, 1988) 82–111, 139–45, and 596 *ff*; Gowlland-Debbas, 'Security Council Enforcement Action', 93; C Bassiouni, 'International Crimes: *Jus Cogens* and *Obligatio Erga Omnes*' (1996) 59 *Law and Contemporary Problems* 63, 68; E David, *Principes de droit des conflits armés*, 3ème edn (Brussels, Bruylant, 2002) 94 *ff*; R Kolb, *Ius in bello: Le droit international des conflits armés* (Bâle, Helbing et Lichtenhahn, 2003) 223 *ff*; R Nieto-Navia, 'International Peremptory Norms (*Jus Cogens*) and International Humanitarian Law' in L Vohrah et al (eds), *Man's Inhumanity to Man: Essays on International Law in Honour of Antonio Cassese* (The Hague, Kluwer Law International, 2003); A Orakhelashvili, *Peremptory Norms in International Law* (Oxford, Oxford University Press, 2006) 61 *ff*.

[539] For the possible legal consequences of unlawful Chapter VII decisions, see Gill, 'Legal and Some Political Limitations', 106 *ff*; Akande, 'The International Court of Justice', 309 *ff*; Kolb, *Ius contra bellum*, 132. See generally E Lauterpacht, 'The Legal Effects of Illegal Acts of International Organisations' in *Cambridge Essays in International Law: Essays in Honour of Lord McNair* (London, Steven and Sons, 1965); E Osieke, 'The Legal Validity of Ultra Vires Decisions of International Organizations' (1983) 77 *American Journal of International Law* 239 and the works cited in these articles.

A fundamental problem is to identify which side had been made militarily weaker as a result of the arms embargo and was failing to prevent IHL violations by the other side. The various factual and legal problems inherent were acknowledged by Judge Lauterpacht:

> It must be recognized that the chain of hypotheses in the analysis just made involves some debatable links – elements of fact, such as that the arms embargo has led to the imbalance in the possession of arms by the two sides and that that imbalance has contributed in greater or lesser degree to genocidal activity such as ethnic cleansing.[540]

For example, in the case of Rwanda, it is arguable that the arms embargo obstructed the Rwandan Patriotic Front (RPF) from preventing genocide by the government. However, before concluding that a Chapter VII decision imposing an arms embargo was invalid, it should be established whether the RPF was in fact made militarily weaker as a result of the arms embargo and failed to prevent genocide by the government. This would certainly raise controversies on facts.

In practice, the Security Council has occasionally imposed an arms embargo on only one of the conflicting parties.[541] However, it is not clear whether the motive was to enable the other conflicting party to build up its military strength to allow it to prevent IHL violations by its adversary. It rather seemed that the adversary was clearly contributing to the escalation of the armed conflict and hence an arms embargo was specifically imposed upon it.[542] Thus, the nexus between the Security Council's decisions to impose an arms embargo on one of the conflicting parties and the possibility of the other conflicting party to prevent IHL violations more effectively is not clear. However, whatever the motive of the Security Council, if such an arms embargo on one of the conflicting parties limits IHL violations as a result, either because of the arms embargo itself or because the other conflicting party was successful in preventing violations of IHL, it may be the case that the Security Council is not only avoiding the potential violation of *jus cogens* but also complementing the enforcement of IHL.

[540] *Bosnia Genocide* case (Order of 13 September 1993), Separate Opinion of Judge Lauterpacht, para 104.

[541] In five cases, an arms embargo was imposed only on one of the conflicting parties. The arms embargoes against armed groups were on UNITA in Angola, UNSC Res 864 (15 September 1993) UN Doc S/RES/864; armed groups in Sierra Leone, UNSC Res 1132 (8 October 1997) UN Doc S/RES/1132 and UNSC Res 1171 (5 June 1998) UN Doc S/RES/1171; armed groups in the DRC, UNSC Res 1493 (28 July 2003) UN Doc S/RES/1493 and UNSC Res 1596 (3 May 2005) UN Doc S/RES/1596; armed groups in the Sudan, UNSC Res 1556 (30 July 2004) UN Doc S/RES/1556; and the arms embargo on a government was on the Taliban in Afghanistan, UNSC Res 1333 (19 December 2000) UN Doc S/RES/1333.

[542] For example, resolution 864 imposing arms embargo on UNITA recognises that UNITA had contributed to the escalation of the armed conflict: '*The Security Council . . . condemns* UNITA's repeated attempts to seize additional territory and its failure to withdraw its troops from the locations which it has occupied since the resumption of the hostilities.' UNSC Res 864 (15 September 1993) UN Doc S/RES/864, para 8.

In short, an arms embargo can be complementary to IHL but the suggestion that arms embargoes can have the potential to hamper a conflicting party in preventing IHL violations by the other conflicting party is yet to be proved.

B. Economic Sanctions/Restrictions on Certain Means of Transportation and IHL

Some have pointed out that economic sanctions and restrictions on certain means of transportation can hinder the implementation of IHL during an armed conflict, particularly with regard to the provision of humanitarian assistance,[543] but in fact this concern has already been addressed by the Security Council, at least when adopting Chapter VII resolutions imposing economic sanctions and restrictions on transportation.[544] The following section sets out the legal framework of IHL on humanitarian assistance and then discusses whether economic sanctions and restrictions on transportation have hindered the implementation of IHL. The following section only concerns economic sanctions and restrictions on transportation during armed conflict since without an armed conflict, IHL does not apply and thus there will be no potential conflict between Chapter VII sanctions and IHL.

The legal framework of IHL on humanitarian assistance differs between international and non-international armed conflict. In international armed conflict, the obligations of states and the entitlement of humanitarian organisations with regard to humanitarian assistance are extensive, and they are also rules of customary international law. With regard to states' obligations, they can be divided into the obligations of all states and those that are specific to the conflicting parties. The obligations of all states with regard to humanitarian assistance during international armed conflict are to permit free passage of humanitarian assistance,[545] facilitate rapid and unimpeded passage of humanitarian assistance,[546] facilitate humanitarian assistance by the ICRC and other humanitarian organisations,[547] and not to starve out civilians.[548] In occupied territories, the additional

[543] T van Baarda, 'The Involvement of the Security Council in Maintaining International Humanitarian Law' (1994) *Netherlands Human Rights Quarterly* 137.

[544] See generally n 514 above.

[545] Art 23 of the 1949 Fourth Geneva Convention. See also Rule 55 in Henckaerts and Doswald-Beck, *Customary International Humanitarian Law* Vol I, 193.

[546] Art 70 of the 1977 First Additional Protocol. See also Rule 55 in Henckaerts and Doswald-Beck, *Customary International Humanitarian Law* Vol I, 193.

[547] Arts 71 and 81 of the 1977 First Additional Protocol. See also Rule 56 in Henckaerts and Doswald-Beck, *Customary International Humanitarian Law* Vol I, 200.

[548] Art 54 of the 1977 First Additional Protocol. See also Rules 53 and 54 in Henckaerts and Doswald-Beck, *Customary International Humanitarian Law* Vol I, 186 and 189.

obligations for all states are to protect humanitarian assistance,[549] permit the transit and transport of humanitarian assistance,[550] and supply the ICRC and other humanitarian organisations with transport and safe conduct in order for them to provide humanitarian assistance for civilian internees.[551]

On the other hand, the specific obligations imposed on the conflicting parties in relation to humanitarian assistance are to accept the offer of service of the ICRC and other humanitarian organisations,[552] and to facilitate the activities of these organisations.[553] In occupied territories, the additional obligations of occupying powers are to provide humanitarian assistance,[554] not to divert humanitarian assistance,[555] and not to restrict the right of civilian internees to receive humanitarian assistance.[556] The obligations are cumulative and thus if a state is a party to a conflict, it should comply with both the obligations addressed to all states as well as to the conflicting parties specifically. If a state is an occupying power, the obligations addressed to all states, conflicting parties, and occupying powers apply cumulatively.

Besides the states' obligations on humanitarian assistance in international armed conflict, IHL provides a number of entitlements to the ICRC and other humanitarian organisations in relation to humanitarian assistance. First, the ICRC is entitled to a special status,[557] to access all protected persons[558] and to carry out humanitarian activities.[559] In occupied territories specifically, the ICRC is entitled to provide humanitarian assistance[560] and supervise the delivery of humanitarian assistance.[561]

Moreover, other humanitarian organisations are generally entitled to access protected persons[562] and provide humanitarian assistance (including transportation and distribution).[563] In occupied territories, humanitarian

[549] Art 59 of the 1949 Fourth Geneva Convention. See also Rule 32 in Henckaerts and Doswald-Beck, *Customary International Humanitarian Law* Vol I, 109.

[550] Art 61 of the 1949 Fourth Geneva Convention. See also Rule 55 in Henckaerts and Doswald-Beck, *Customary International Humanitarian Law* Vol I, 193.

[551] Art 111 of the 1949 Fourth Geneva Convention. See also Rule 56 in Henckaerts and Doswald-Beck, *Customary International Humanitarian Law* Vol I, 200.

[552] Art 11 of the 1949 Fourth Geneva Convention.

[553] Art 81 of the 1977 First Additional Protocol. See also Rule 56 in Henckaerts and Doswald-Beck, *Customary International Humanitarian Law* Vol I, 200.

[554] Art 55 of the 1949 Fourth Geneva Convention.

[555] Art 60 of the 1949 Fourth Geneva Convention.

[556] Art 109 of the 1949 Fourth Geneva Convention.

[557] Art 142 of the 1949 Fourth Geneva Convention.

[558] Art 143 of the 1949 Fourth Geneva Convention.

[559] Art 81(1) of the 1977 First Additional Protocol.

[560] Art 59 of the 1949 Fourth Geneva Convention.

[561] Art 61 of the 1949 Fourth Geneva Convention.

[562] Art 142 of the 1949 Fourth Geneva Convention.

[563] Art 71 of the 1977 First Additional Protocol.

organisations are generally entitled to provide humanitarian assistance[564] and supervise the delivery of humanitarian assistance.[565]

On the other hand, in non-international armed conflict, the only treaty obligation of states and armed groups is not to starve out civilians,[566] but customary law establishes that the conflicting parties must facilitate rapid and unimpeded passage of humanitarian assistance,[567] ensure the freedom of movement of humanitarian relief personnel,[568] and to respect and protect humanitarian relief personnel and objects used for humanitarian relief operations.[569] In addition, there are only a few entitlements for humanitarian organisations, namely the ICRC and other humanitarian organisations' entitlement to offer its services[570] and provide humanitarian assistance with the consent of the concerned state.[571]

As a matter of law, economic sanctions and restrictions on transportation can be in conflict with these IHL rules during armed conflict, since the former require the UN Member States to prevent the flow of goods and transportation into a particular state but at the same time, the latter aim to ensure the provision of humanitarian assistance to the victims of armed conflict in the same state. However, in practice, this has not happened since, as will be seen below, the relevant Chapter VII resolutions provide safeguards to preserve IHL obligations on humanitarian assistance.

Economic sanctions and restrictions on transportation are two of the most frequent non-military enforcement measures taken under Chapter VII. Among the 25 cases of Chapter VII non-military sanctions, there have been at least 17 cases of economic sanctions and 18 cases of restrictions on transportation.[572] With regard to economic sanctions, not all cases raise the question of whether they conflict with IHL rules relating to humanitarian assistance since 1) economic sanctions can be imposed outside armed conflict situation; and 2) they are not always directed to essential products and commodities required for humanitarian assistance. In practice, among the 17 cases of economic sanctions, only two cases had the potential of hindering the implementation of IHL rules on humanitarian assistance, which were Iraq-Kuwait and the Federal Republic of

564 Art 59 of the 1949 Fourth Geneva Convention.

565 Art 61 of the 1949 Fourth Geneva Convention.

566 Art 14 of the 1977 Second Additional Protocol. See also Rules 53 and 54 in Henckaerts and Doswald-Beck, *Customary International Humanitarian Law* Vol I, 186 and 189.

567 See Rule 55 in Henckaerts and Doswald-Beck, *Customary International Humanitarian Law* Vol I, 193.

568 See Rule 56 in Henckaerts and Doswald-Beck, *Customary International Humanitarian Law* Vol I, 200.

569 See Rules 31 and 32 in Henckaerts and Doswald-Beck, *Customary International Humanitarian Law* Vol I, 105 and 109.

570 Common Art 3 of the 1949 Geneva Conventions.

571 Art 18 of the 1977 Second Additional Protocol.

572 See nn 520 and 521 above respectively. In many cases, a particular resolution contained several types of sanctions.

Yugoslavia. Other cases were either not a situation of armed conflict or only involved measures which did not have the direct potential to hinder the implementation of IHL rules on humanitarian assistance, such as arms embargoes and the freezing of assets of certain persons.

Both the cases of concern, Iraq-Kuwait and the Federal Republic of Yugoslavia, involved situations of international armed conflict in which the Security Council imposed comprehensive economic sanctions, but with provisions to avoid hindering humanitarian assistance. Security Council resolution 661 imposed a comprehensive economic sanction on Iraq and Kuwait under Chapter VII in the following terms:

> *The Security Council* . . . *Decides* that all States shall prevent . . . The sale or supply by their nationals or from their territories or using their flag vessels of any commodities or products . . . to any person or body in Iraq or Kuwait or to any person or body for the purposes of any business carried on in or operated from Iraq or Kuwait.[573]

Resolution 757 imposed comprehensive economic sanctions on the Federal Republic of Yugoslavia:

> *The Security Council* . . . *Decides also* that all States shall prevent . . . The sale or supply by their nationals or from their territories or using their flag vessels or aircraft of any commodities or products . . . to any person or body in the Federal Republic of Yugoslavia (Serbia and Montenegro) or to any person or body for the purposes of any business carried on in or operated from the Federal Republic of Yugoslavia (Serbia and Montenegro).[574]

These provisions appear to hinder the implementation of a number of IHL rules on humanitarian assistance noted above, but there have been at least three types of safeguards to avoid such a consequence: 1) explicit exception to humanitarian assistance; 2) demand to facilitate humanitarian assistance; or 3) recognition of the applicability of IHL.

With regard to the first type of safeguard, resolution 661 on Iraq-Kuwait explicitly provided that the economic sanction did not include 'supplies intended strictly for medical purposes, and, in humanitarian circumstance, foodstuffs'.[575] A similar safeguard was also provided for the Federal Republic of Yugoslavia in several resolutions.[576] Such an exception is built into Chapter VII resolutions imposing economic sanctions and thus leaves the existing IHL rules on humanitarian assistance unaffected.

573 UNSC Res 661 (6 August 1990) UN Doc S/RES/661, para 3(c).
574 UNSC Res 757 (30 May 1992) UN Doc S/RES/757, para 4(c).
575 UNSC Res 661 (6 August 1990) UN Doc S/RES/661, para 3(c).
576 See, eg, UNSC Res 820 (17 April 1993) UN Doc S/RES/820, para 22: '*The Security Council* . . . *Decides* to prohibit the transport of all commodities and products across the land borders or to or from the ports of the Federal Republic of Yugoslavia (Serbia and Montenegro), the only exceptions being: (a) The importation of medical supplies and foodstuffs . . . (b) The importation of other essential humanitarian supplies.' See also UNSC Res 757 (30 May 1992) UN Doc S/RES/757, para 4(c) and UNSC Res 760 (18 June 1992) UN Doc S/RES/760.

With regard to the second type of safeguard on demand to facilitate humanitarian assistance, resolution 666 on Iraq-Kuwait provides as follows:

> *The Security Council . . . Directs* the Committee [Security Council Sanctions Committee] that in formulating its decisions it should bear in mind that foodstuffs should be provided through the United Nations in co-operation with the International Committee of the Red Cross or other appropriate humanitarian agencies and distributed by them or under their supervision.[577]

A similar safeguard was also provided for the Federal Republic of Yugoslavia in resolution 757.[578] These provisions further preserve the existing IHL rules on humanitarian assistance, particularly the entitlements of the ICRC and other humanitarian organisations to provide and supervise the delivery of humanitarian assistance.

With regard to the third type of safeguard on recognition of the applicability of IHL, the Security Council in resolution 670 on Iraq-Kuwait reaffirmed that 'Iraq retains full responsibility in this regard under international humanitarian law including, where applicable, the Geneva Convention relative to the Protection of Civilian Persons in Time of War, of 12 August 1949'.[579] A similar safeguard was also provided for the Federal Republic of Yugoslavia in resolution 771.[580] These provisions confirm that IHL rules on humanitarian assistance are not affected with the imposition of the economic sanctions. Thus, in practice, the potential conflict between Chapter VII decisions imposing economic sanctions and IHL rules on humanitarian assistance has been avoided.

The restrictions on transportation under Chapter VII can also have the potential to hinder the IHL rules on humanitarian assistance. There are at least two types of such restrictions: 1) restrictions on the UN Member States to allow certain transportations affiliated to them to transport certain products and commodities; and 2) prohibition and restrictions on ground, aerial, or maritime transportation per se.

With regard to the first type, the restrictions are almost invariably imposed on the transportation of arms by means of transportation affiliated to the UN Member States. An example is Security Council resolution 1556 on the Sudan in which the Security Council decided that 'all states shall take the necessary measures to prevent the sale or supply

[577] UNSC Res 666 (13 September 1990) UN Doc S/RES/666, para 6.

[578] UNSC Res 757 (30 May 1992) UN Doc S/RES/757, para 17: '*The Security Council . . . Demands* that all parties and others concerned create immediately the necessary conditions for unimpeded delivery of humanitarian supplies to Sarajevo and other destinations in Bosnia and Herzegovina.'

[579] UNSC Res 670 (25 September 1990) UN Doc S/RES/670, para 13.

[580] UNSC Res 771 (13 August 1992) UN Doc S/RES/771, para 1: '*The Security Council . . . Reaffirms* that all parties to the conflict are bound to comply with their obligations under international humanitarian law and in particular the Geneva Conventions of 12 August 1949.'

. . . by their nationals or from their territories or using their flag vessels or aircraft, of arms and related materiel of all types'.[581] Among the 18 cases of restrictions on transportation, 15 cases imposed such a restriction,[582] of which all 15 imposed a restriction on maritime transportation,[583] 12 cases imposed an additional restriction on aerial transportation,[584] and one case on ground transportation.[585]

With regard to the second type, an example is resolution 1127 on Angola:

> *The Security Council . . . Decides* that all States shall take the necessary measures . . . to deny permission to any aircraft to take off from, land in, or overfly their territories if it has taken off from or is destined to land at a place in the territory of Angola.[586]

The difference with the first type is that it imposes a restriction on the means of transportation themselves, whatever is carried within them. Among the 18 cases of restrictions on transportation, 11 cases included this type of restriction,[587] of which seven related to aerial

[581] UNSC Res 1556 (30 July 2004) UN Doc S/RES/1556, para 7.

[582] Southern Rhodesia, UNSC Res 217 (20 Nov 1965) UN Doc S/RES/217; former Yugoslavia, UNSC Res 787 (16 November 1992) UN Doc S/RES/787; Haiti, UNSC Res 841 (16 June 1993) UN Doc S/RES/841; Sierra Leone, UNSC Res 1132 (8 October 1997) UN Doc S/RES/1132; Serbia and Montenegro, UNSC Res 1160 (31 March 1998) UN Doc S/RES/1160; Angola, UNSC Res 1173 (12 June 1998) UN Doc S/RES/1173; Al-Qaeda and Taliban, UNSC Res 1333 (19 December 2000) UN Doc S/RES/1333; Liberia, UNSC Res 1343 (7 March 2001) UN Doc S/RES/1343; DRC, UNSC Res 1493 (28 July 2003) UN Doc S/RES/1493; Liberia, UNSC Res 1521 (22 December 2003) UN Doc S/RES/1521; Sudan, UNSC Res 1556 (30 July 2004) UN Doc S/RES/1556; Côte d'Ivoire, UNSC Res 1572 (15 November 2004) UN Doc S/RES/1572; Democratic People's Republic of Korea, UNSC Res 1718 (14 October 2006) UN Doc S/RES/1718; Iran, UNSC Res 1737 (27 December 2006) UN Doc S/RES/1737; Eritrea, UNSC Res 1907 (23 December 2009) UN Doc S/RES/1907.

[583] See n 582 above.

[584] Haiti, UNSC Res 841 (16 June 1993) UN Doc S/RES/841; Sierra Leone, UNSC Res 1132 (8 October 1997) UN Doc S/RES/1132; Serbia and Montenegro, UNSC Res 1160 (31 March 1998) UN Doc S/RES/1160; Angola, UNSC Res 1173 (12 June 1998) UN Doc S/RES/1173; Al-Qaeda and Taliban, UNSC Res 1333 (19 December 2000) UN Doc S/RES/1333; Liberia, UNSC Res 1343 (7 March 2001) UN Doc S/RES/1343; DRC, UNSC Res 1493 (28 July 2003) UN Doc S/RES/1493; Liberia, UNSC Res 1521 (22 December 2003) UN Doc S/RES/1521; Sudan, UNSC Res 1556 (30 July 2004) UN Doc S/RES/1556; Côte d'Ivoire, UNSC Res 1572 (15 November 2004) UN Doc S/RES/1572; Democratic People's Republic of Korea, UNSC Res 1718 (14 October 2006) UN Doc S/RES/1718; Iran, UNSC Res 1737 (27 December 2006) UN Doc S/RES/1737; Eritrea, UNSC Res 1907 (23 December 2009) UN Doc S/RES/1907.

[585] Haiti, UNSC Res 841 (16 June 1993) UN Doc S/RES/841.

[586] UNSC Res 1127 (28 August 1997) UN Doc S/RES/1127, para 4(d)(i).

[587] Southern Rhodesia, UNSC Res 217 (20 Nov 1965) UN Doc S/RES/217 ; Iraq-Kuwait, UNSC Res 661 (6 August 1990) UN Doc S/RES/661; former Yugoslavia, UNSC Res 787 (16 November 1992) UN Doc S/RES/787 and UNSC Res 820 (17 April 1993) UN Doc S/RES/820; Libya, UNSC Res 748 (31 Mar 1992) UN Doc S/RES/748; Bosnia and Herzegovina, UNSC Res 942 (23 September 1994) UN Doc S/RES/942; Sudan, UNSC Res 1070 (16 August 1996) UN Doc S/RES/1070; Angola, UNSC Res 1127 (28 August 1997) UN Doc S/RES/1127; Al-Qaeda and Taliban, UNSC Res 1267 (15 October 1999) UN Doc S/RES/1267; Liberia, UNSC Res 1343 (7 March 2001) UN Doc S/RES/1343; DRC, UNSC Res 1596 (3 May 2005) UN Doc S/RES/1596.

transportation,[588] five to maritime transportation,[589] and one to ground transportation.[590] Some cases included two or more categories of transportation at the same time.

In either case, the implementation of these restrictions in practice requires the control of any ground, aerial, or maritime transportation, which can hinder the implementation of a number of IHL rules relating to humanitarian assistance set out earlier in this section. However, in practice, most of the restrictions on transportation included one of the three types of safeguard identified earlier. For example, resolution 1127 on Angola included restrictions on aerial transportation as quoted above but this paragraph is followed by a paragraph providing that the restrictions 'shall not apply to cases of medical emergency or to flights of aircraft carrying food, medicine, or supplies for essential humanitarian needs'.[591] Moreover, resolution 1493 on the DRC is an example which included the second type of safeguard, demanding that 'all the parties guarantee the security of the civilian population thereby enabling MONUC and humanitarian organizations to have total, unrestricted and immediate access

[588] Libya, UNSC Res 748 (31 Mar 1992) UN Doc S/RES/748; Bosnia and Herzegovina, UNSC Res 942 (23 September 1994) UN Doc S/RES/942; Sudan, UNSC Res 1070 (16 August 1996) UN Doc S/RES/1070; Angola, UNSC Res 1127 (28 August 1997) UN Doc S/RES/1127; Al-Qaeda and Taliban, UNSC Res 1267 (15 October 1999) UN Doc S/RES/1267; Liberia, UNSC Res 1343 (7 March 2001) UN Doc S/RES/1343; DRC, UNSC Res 1596 (3 May 2005) UN Doc S/RES/1596.

[589] Southern Rhodesia, UNSC Res 217 (20 Nov 1965) UN Doc S/RES/217; Iraq-Kuwait, UNSC Res 661 (6 August 1990) UN Doc S/RES/661; former Yugoslavia, UNSC Res 787 (16 November 1992) UN Doc S/RES/787 and UNSC 820 (17 April 1993) UN Doc S/RES/820; Bosnia and Herzegovina, UNSC Res 942 (23 September 1994) UN Doc S/RES/942.

[590] Former Yugoslavia, UNSC Res 820 (17 April 1993) UN Doc S/RES/820.

[591] UNSC Res 1127 (28 August 1997) UN Doc S/RES/1127, para 5. See further, Iraq-Kuwait, UNSC Res 661 (6 August 1990) UN Doc S/RES/661, paras 3(c) and 4, UNSC Res 670 (25 September 1990) UN Doc S/RES/670, para 3; Libya, UNSC Res 748 (31 Mar 1992) UN Doc S/RES/748, para 4(a); former Yugoslavia, UNSC Res 757 (30 May 1992) UN Doc S/RES/757, paras 4(c), 5, and 7(a), UNSC Res 760 (18 June 1992) UN Doc S/RES/760, and UNSC Res 820 (17 April 1993) UN Doc S/RES/820, paras 12, 22(a), 22(b), and 27; Haiti, UNSC Res 841 (16 June 1993) UN Doc S/RES/841, para 7 and UNSC Res 917 (6 May 1994) UN Doc S/RES/917, paras 2, 7(a) and 7(b); Bosnia-Herzegovina, UNSC Res 942 (23 September 1994) UN Doc S/RES/942, paras 7(ii)(b), 13(b), and 17; Angola, UNSC Res 1127 (28 August 1997) UN Doc S/RES/1127, paras 5 and 6 and UNSC Res 1173 (12 June 1998) UN Doc S/RES/1173, para 13; Sierra Leone, UNSC Res 1132 (8 October 1997) UN Doc S/RES/1132, para 5; Al-Qaeda and Taliban, UNSC Res 1267 (15 October 1999) UN Doc S/RES/1267, paras 4(a) and (b); Eritrea-Ethiopia, UNSC Res 1298 (17 May 2000) UN Doc S/RES/1298, para 7; Liberia 2001, UNSC Res 1343 (7 March 2001) UN Doc S/RES/1343, para 7(b); Liberia 2003, UNSC Res 1521 (22 December 2003) UN Doc S/RES/1521, para 4(c) and UNSC Res 1532 (12 March 2004) UN Doc S/RES/1532, para 2(a); Côte d'Ivoire, UNSC Res 1572 (15 November 2004) UN Doc S/RES/1572, paras 10 and 12(a); Sudan, UNSC Res 1591 (29 March 2005) UN Doc S/RES/1591, para 3(f), (g), and (i); DRC, UNSC Res 1596 (3 May 2005) UN Doc S/RES/1596, para 14; Lebanon-Syria, UNSC Res 1636 (31 October 2005) UN Doc S/RES/1636, Annex, para 2(i); Democratic People's Republic of Korea, UNSC Res 1718 (14 October 2006) UN Doc S/RES/1718, para 10; Iran, UNSC Res 1737 (27 December 2006) UN Doc S/RES/1737, paras 9, 13(a), and 16.

to the population groups in need'.[592] Finally, resolution 1556 on Sudan is an example which included the third type of safeguard which recognised the applicability of international humanitarian law to the conflicting parties, which in effect left the IHL rules on humanitarian assistance intact.[593]These safeguards ensure that the restrictions on transportation do not hinder the implementation of IHL rules on humanitarian assistance. Two cases, Southern Rhodesia and the Sudan in 1996, did not have any of these safeguards but this might not have been an issue since it was doubtful whether they were situations of armed conflict.[594] Thus, in most cases of economic sanctions and restrictions on certain means of transportation under Chapter VII, safeguards are built in to the relevant Security Council resolutions and do not hinder the implementation of IHL rules on humanitarian assistance.

Such inclusion of safeguards avoids the conflict between Chapter VII decisions and IHL. This is in line with Article 24(2) of the UN Charter, which obliges the Security Council to act in accordance with the Purposes and Principles of the UN, which includes, in Article 1(3), the achievement of international co-operation on humanitarian issues and promotion of the respect for human rights.[595]

As can be seen from the above, non-military enforcement actions can complement IHL, particularly through arms embargoes, which can widen the scope of the prohibition on the transfer of weapons in IHL and prevent further violations of IHL by reducing the availability of weapons.

[592] UNSC Res 1493 (28 July 2003) UN Doc S/RES/1493, para 12. See further Somalia, UNSC Res 733 (23 January 1992) UN Doc S/RES/733, para 8; former Yugoslavia, UNSC Res 752 (15 May 1992) UN Doc S/RES/752, para 8; Bosnia-Herzegovina, UNSC Res 787 (16 November 1992) UN Doc S/RES/787, para 18 and UNSC Res 820 (17 April 1993) UN Doc S/RES/820, para 5; Liberia, UNSC Res 813 (26 March 1993) UN Doc S/RES/813, para 15; Angola, UNSC Res 864 (15 September 1993) UN Doc S/RES/864, para 13; Haiti, UNSC Res 940 (31 July 1994) UN Doc S/RES/940, para 15; Sierra Leone, UNSC Res 1132 (8 October 1997) UN Doc S/RES/1132, para 2; Eritrea-Ethiopia, UNSC Res 1298 (17 May 2000) UN Doc S/RES/1298, para 14; Al-Qaeda and Taliban, UNSC Res 1333 (19 December 2000) UN Doc S/RES/1333, paras 11, 12, 13, and 25; DRC, UNSC Res 1493 (28 July 2003) UN Doc S/RES/1493, para 12; UNSC Res 1649 (21 December 2005) UN Doc S/RES/1649, para 8; Sudan, UNSC Res 1590 (24 March 2005) UN Doc S/RES/1590, para 9.

[593] UNSC Res 1556 (30 July 2004) UN Doc S/RES/1556, Preamble. See further Iraq-Kuwait, UNSC Res 666 (13 September 1990) UN Doc S/RES/666, para 6; Bosnia-Herzegovina, UNSC Res 787 (16 November 1992) UN Doc S/RES/787, Preamble; Liberia, UNSC Res 788 (19 November 1992) UN Doc S/RES/788, para 5; Somalia, UNSC Res 794 (3 December 1992) UN Doc S/RES/794, para 4; Angola, UNSC Res 864 (15 September 1993) UN Doc S/RES/864, para 13; Al-Qaeda and Taliban, UNSC Res 1267 (15 October 1999) UN Doc S/RES/1267, Preamble; Eritrea-Ethiopia, UNSC Res 1297 (12 May 2000) UN Doc S/RES/1297, para 8; DRC, UNSC Res 1234 (9 April 1999) UN Doc S/RES/1234, para 6; Côte d'Ivoire, UNSC Res 1464 (4 February 2003) UN Doc S/RES/1464, para 7; Sudan, UNSC Res 1556 (30 July 2004) UN Doc S/RES/1556, Preamble, paras 1, 6, and 14.

[594] For Southern Rhodesia, see UNGA, 'The Question of Southern Rhodesia' (1965) UNYB 117, 117 *ff*. For the Sudan, see UNGA, 'The Sudan' (1996) UNYB 128, 128 *ff*.

[595] See *Namibia* case (Advisory Opinion), para 110; *Tadic Case* (Jurisdiction, Appeals), para 28; *Lockerbie* case (Order of 14 April 1992), Dissenting Opinion of Judge Weeramantry.

The suggestion that arms embargoes can have the potential to hamper a conflicting party from preventing IHL violations by the other conflicting party is yet to be proved. Economic sanctions and restrictions on certain means of transportation have been cited as potential obstacles to implement the IHL rules on humanitarian assistance but in practice, the relevant Security Council resolutions have included safeguards which explicitly recognise an exception for humanitarian assistance, demand the facilitation of humanitarian assistance, or recognise the applicability of IHL.

This section has discussed how military and non-military enforcement measures under Chapter VII can implement and complement IHL as well as how to avoid the conflict between Chapter VII decisions and IHL as envisaged in Article 103 of the UN Charter. The examples in this chapter show that any attempts to put Chapter VII decisions over IHL rarely contribute to the proper application of both Chapter VII and IHL. The failure to prevent the genocide in Srebrenica vividly showed that the confusion of Chapter VII decisions and IHL can have serious consequences on the victims of armed conflict. Thus, every effort should be made to take practical measures to avoid any conflict between Chapter VII decisions and IHL at the time of drafting the relevant Chapter VII resolutions, or to interpret the relevant Chapter VII decisions in a way which would be consistent with IHL.

VI. CONCLUSIONS

The discussions above have demonstrated that the relationship between *jus ad bellum* and *jus in bello* takes a substantially different form when it is discussed in the context of Chapter VII enforcement measures.

As noted at the beginning of this chapter, the nature of the issues relating to the relationship between Chapter VII and IHL is substantially different from the relationship between the law of self-defence and IHL, particularly in three aspects: Chapter VII decisions may override IHL obligations pursuant to Article 103 of the UN Charter, the thresholds of application of Chapter VII are 'threat to the peace, breach of the peace, or act of aggression' and not 'armed attack', and Chapter VII decisions deal not only with international armed conflict, but also with non-international armed conflict and armed conflict of a mixture of different types of armed conflict.

Chapter VII decisions can prevail over IHL obligations pursuant to Article 103 of the UN Charter, which provides that the obligations under the UN Charter prevail over any other international agreement in case of a conflict between the two. In this sense, the concern that *jus ad bellum* can override *jus in bello* is even more pressing than self-defence. However, considering that the Security Council must take into account the Purposes of the UN pursuant to Article 24(2) of the UN Charter, the rules of IHL, which are essentially humanitarian in character, should not be subjected to Security Council decisions. It is recalled here that Article 1(3) provides that one of the UN's purposes is to achieve international co-operation on humanitarian issues and promote the respect for human rights which, in a very general sense, might include the implementation of IHL. It is also worth recalling that only IHL treaties and customary rules can be in conflict with Chapter VII decisions and IHL rules having *jus cogens* status override Chapter VII decisions.

The practice of the Security Council shows that it determined the existence of a 'breach of the peace' and an 'act of aggression' when the situation was an international armed conflict but 'threat to the peace' can indicate various kinds of armed conflict, a mixture of them, or situations short of armed conflict. The Security Council can therefore authorise the use of force in more diverse situations compared to self-defence. This also means that the relationship between *jus ad bellum* and *jus in bello* is more multifaceted. While a use of force in self-defence is normally employed in the context of international armed conflict, a use of force under Chapter VII can be employed in the context of international or non-international armed conflict, or a mixture of both. Therefore, the IHL rules that bind Chapter VII use of force are also different according to the type of armed conflict.

This can be seen as an advantage of the Chapter VII use of force over self-defence since it can intervene in different types of armed conflict and possibly halt and prevent IHL violations. The obvious disadvantage of the Chapter VII use of force is that it requires the concurring votes of the permanent members of the Security Council, which may not always be possible to obtain.

The Security Council has adopted a vast number of resolutions that invoke IHL treaties and certain provisions therein, as well as contain phrases reflecting certain IHL rules. They are important contributions to the development of customary rules of IHL and the practice of IHL treaties. Chapter VII mandates for UN forces can implement and complement IHL to a certain extent and such measures should be encouraged so far as they do not adversely affect the existing IHL obligations or the equal application of IHL. Any attempts to put Chapter VII decisions over IHL rarely contribute to the proper application of both Chapter VII and IHL. The failure to prevent the genocide in Srebrenica vividly showed that the confusions between Chapter VII decisions and IHL can have serious consequences on the victims of armed conflict. Thus, every effort should be made to take practical measures to avoid any conflict between Chapter VII decisions and IHL at the time of drafting the relevant Chapter VII resolutions, or to interpret the relevant Chapter VII decisions in a way which would be consistent with IHL.

Jus ad bellum and *jus in bello* are one set of rules regulating the use of force by UN forces. *Jus ad bellum* itself already imposes substantial limits.

The use of force by UN-commanded forces not authorised to use force is only permitted in self-defence. Chapter VII use of force is first and foremost regulated by Security Council resolutions, which impose limits on the purposes, duration, and geographical extent of the use of force, and authorises the use of force only within the military capabilities and only when the situation requires. The principles of proportionality and necessity can also bind Chapter VII use of force. IHL, however, imposes additional constraints on the conduct of UN forces.

The applicability of IHL to UN forces, both state-led and UN-commanded, is a complex issue and various legal hurdles should be overcome, but either way, the applicability is now widely accepted. International law protecting UN force personnel has never been intended to put UN forces in an advantageous position vis-à-vis other conflicting parties, or to undermine the principle of the equal application of IHL to the conflicting parties.

Non-military enforcement measures, namely economic sanctions and restrictions on certain means of transportation, do not affect IHL rules on humanitarian assistance since the relevant Security Council resolutions provide safeguards so that the application of the relevant IHL rules are not affected.

5

Particular Problems in Non-international Armed Conflict

ALONGSIDE CHAPTER VII of the UN Charter, non-international armed conflict has been left out of the discussion on the relationship between *jus ad bellum* and *jus in bello*. The relationship between Chapter VII of the UN Charter and IHL was discussed in the previous chapter. In this context, non-international armed conflict appeared frequently as a part of the discussion, particularly in relation to how UN forces operating in a non-international armed conflict situation are regulated by Security Council resolutions and the IHL rules applicable in non-international armed conflict. In this sense, the relationship between *jus ad bellum* and *jus in bello* in the context of non-international armed conflict was discussed extensively in the previous chapter. It confirmed that Chapter VII mandates of UN forces are separate from the IHL rules applicable in non-international armed conflict and that these IHL rules are applicable equally between UN forces and armed groups. Moreover, the previous chapter confirmed that Security Council resolutions and the IHL rules applicable in non-international armed conflict impose substantial control over the use of force by UN forces.

This chapter goes one step further and discusses two particular problems related to non-international armed conflict. One is whether all the IHL rules applicable in non-international armed conflict apply equally to the conflicting parties, particularly between a state's armed forces and armed groups. The nature of non-international armed conflict is substantially different from international armed conflict so that the principle of the equal application of IHL faces several challenges. In particular, the inherent imbalance of legal status between a state's armed forces (lawful forces charged to maintain internal security) and armed groups (illegal organisations) created by national law may have an impact on the equal application of IHL to the conflicting parties.

The other problem is about the difficulties in applying *jus ad bellum* and *jus in bello* to non-international armed conflicts in which foreign armed forces or foreign armed groups intervene. Such armed conflicts are not new, but the potential gap that they create, where the applicability of both *jus ad bellum* and *jus in bello* is doubtful or complicated, has not been given the attention that it requires.

I. EQUAL APPLICATION OF *JUS IN BELLO* IN NON-INTERNATIONAL ARMED CONFLICT

Non-international armed conflict is a situation where the equal application principle may have to be interpreted flexibly. In non-international armed conflict, the status of armed groups and a state's armed forces is already unequal under national law where the former are criminal groups who can be prosecuted for their acts[1] and the latter are entitled to enforce national law against the armed groups to restore law and order. The state's right to maintain law and order is recognised in Article 3(1) of the 1977 Second Additional Protocol:

> Nothing in this Protocol shall be invoked for the purpose of affecting the sovereignty of a State or the responsibility of the government, by all legitimate means, to maintain or re-establish law and order in the State or to defend the national unity and territorial integrity of the State.[2]

However, it is equally clear that the unequal legal status under national law does not affect the equal application of IHL. A commentary confirms the point that 'These rules [in the law of non-international armed conflict] grant the same rights and impose the same duties on both the established government and the insurgent party, and all such rights and duties have a purely humanitarian character.'[3] Article 27 of the 1969 Vienna Convention on the Law of Treaties also provides as follows:

> A party may not invoke the provisions of its internal law as justification for its failure to perform a treaty.[4]

Thus, national law cannot be used as a justification to disregard the law of non-international armed conflict. More difficult questions are: 1) whether

[1] See, eg, Art 77 of the Japanese Criminal Code, which provides that those who committed the crime of insurrection shall be punished by death or life imprisonment. Art 412(6) of the French Criminal Code also provides that leading or organising an insurrectional movement is punished by a life sentence.

[2] Protocol Additional to the Geneva Conventions of 12 August 1949, and Relating to the Protection of Victims of Non-International Armed Conflicts (Protocol II) (hereafter 1977 Second Additional Protocol) (adopted 8 June 1977, entered into force 7 December 1978) 1125 UNTS 609. See also Y Sandoz et al (eds), *Commentary on the Additional Protocols of 8 June 1977 to the Geneva Conventions of 12 August 1949* (Geneva, International Committee of the Red Cross, 1987) para 4441.

[3] Sandoz et al (eds), *Commentary*, para 4442. See also J Pictet et al, *Commentary on the Geneva Conventions of 12 August 1949* Vol I (Geneva, International Committee of the Red Cross, 1952) 60–61.

[4] Vienna Convention on the Law of Treaties (adopted 23 May 1969, entered into force 27 January 1980) 1155 UNTS 331.

armed groups are obliged to comply with IHL; 2) whether all the provisions of the law of non-international armed conflict can be applied equally; and 3) whether war crimes committed by armed groups and a state's armed forces can be punished equally.

A. Applicability of IHL to Armed Groups

First, armed groups have the obligation to comply with the IHL rules if they are incorporated into the national law pursuant to the procedure of the respective state. Treaties may become binding on a state by its mere consent to be bound but for other states, the treaties may have to be legislated as laws. Even though armed groups do not have the capacity to conclude treaties under international law, as a matter of law, they have the duty to comply with the treaties to which the territorial state is a party as well as customary international law as formed through state practice and *opinio juris*.[5] At the same time, the government also has to comply with the same obligations. Armed groups and a state's armed forces are also equally bound by IHL if they agree to comply with it by special agreements as envisaged in Article 3(2) common to the 1949 Geneva Conventions.[6] In this sense, the law of non-international armed conflict is equally applicable to armed groups and a state's armed forces.[7]

The law of non-international armed conflict here refers to common Article 3 of the 1949 Geneva Conventions, the 1977 Second Additional Protocol, and customary rules applicable in non-international armed conflict.[8] When one looks closely at the rules therein, most of them are clearly applicable to both parties to a conflict in an equal manner, such as the humane

[5] See ICRC, *Improving Compliance with International Humanitarian Law, ICRC Expert Seminars* (Geneva, International Committee of the Red Cross, 2003) 20.

[6] Geneva Convention for the Amelioration of the Condition of the Wounded and Sick in Armed Forces in the Field, as revised from 1929 (hereafter 1949 First Geneva Convention) (adopted 12 August 1949, entered into force 21 October 1950) 75 UNTS 31; Geneva Convention for the Amelioration of the Condition of Wounded, Sick and Shipwrecked Members of Armed Forces at Sea, as revised from 1929 (hereafter 1949 Second Geneva Convention) (adopted 12 August 1949, entered into force 21 October 1950) 75 UNTS 85; Geneva Convention Relative to the Treatment of Prisoners of War, as revised from 1929 (hereafter 1949 Third Geneva Convention) (adopted 12 August 1949, entered into force 21 October 1950) 75 UNTS 135; Geneva Convention Relative to the Protection of Civilian Persons in Time of War (hereafter 1949 Fourth Geneva Convention) (adopted 12 August 1949, entered into force 21 October 1950) 75 UNTS 287.

[7] Sandoz et al (eds), *Commentary*, para 4444. Cp A Cassese, 'The Status of Rebels under the 1977 Geneva Protocol on Non-International Armed Conflicts' (1981) 30 *International and Comparative Law Quarterly* 416, 420 *ff*. The compliance with the law of non-international armed conflict in practice by the conflicting parties remains a major challenge. See generally ICRC, *Improving Compliance*.

[8] See J-M Henckaerts and L Doswald-Beck, *Customary International Humanitarian Law* Vol I: Rules (Geneva, International Committee of the Red Cross and Cambridge, Cambridge University Press, 2005).

treatment of persons not or no longer taking direct part in hostilities (including persons deprived of their liberty); protection of medical personnel, units, and transports; respect for the distinctive emblem; and protection of civilians and certain objects during the conduct of hostilities. However, the obligation to respect judicial guarantees faces a particular problem in non-international armed conflict, which will be discussed below.

B. Judicial Guarantees Obligations

Article 3(1)(d) common to the 1949 Geneva Conventions prohibits, among others, the following:

> [T]he passing of sentences and the carrying out of executions without previous judgement pronounced by a regularly constituted court, affording all the judicial guarantees which are recognized as indispensable by civilized peoples.

Article 6(2) of the 1977 Second Additional Protocol also provides as follows:

> No sentence shall be passed and no penalty shall be executed on a person found guilty of an offence except pursuant to a conviction pronounced by a court offering the essential guarantees of independence and impartiality.

In the succeeding paragraphs (a) to (f), the specific guarantees are listed, namely the right to be informed of the offences, right to defence, individual penal responsibility, *nullum crimen sine lege*, presumption of innocence, right to be tried in one's presence, right not to be compelled to testify against oneself or confess guilt, and the right to appeal. There is also a paragraph that prohibits the imposition of death penalty on persons under 18 years old at the time of the offence and the execution of pregnant woman or mothers of young children.[9] Many of these IHL rules are also considered as customary rules applicable in non-international armed conflict.[10]

The question here is how the judicial guarantees obligations apply equally to the government and armed groups. If one were to follow strictly the principle of equal application, then does it mean that armed groups can establish their own courts, adopt penal laws, hand down sentences, and execute them, so long as they meet the conditions in the above-mentioned provisions? If, on the other hand, one maintains that only the courts established by the state can lawfully try offences under the penal code of that state, then a question arises whether this would mean unequal application of certain IHL rules. Common Article 3 of the 1949 Geneva Conventions and the 1977 Second Additional Protocol themselves do not provide a definitive indication on these questions. In order

[9] Art 6(4) of the 1977 Second Additional Protocol.

[10] See Rules 100, 101, 102, and 103 in Henckaerts and Doswald-Beck, *Customary International Humanitarian Law* Vol I, 352, 371, 372, and 374.

to understand how the judicial guarantees obligations apply, it is essential to know clearly who the addressees of these provisions are.

If one looks at the details of common Article 3(1)(d) of the 1949 Geneva Conventions and Article 6 of the 1977 Second Additional Protocol, some provisions are related to the functions normally carried out by government agencies while others are carried out by courts. For example, the obligation to inform of the offences in Article 6(2)(a) of the Second Additional Protocol is normally performed by government agencies such as the prosecutors, the police, and the military.

However, the majority of other judicial guarantees obligations are performed by the courts, such as *nullum crimen sine lege* and to conduct a trial in the accused's presence. Does this mean that the courts also become a 'party' to the conflict since most of the judicial guarantees obligations in common Article 3(1)(d) of the 1949 Geneva Conventions and Article 6 of the 1977 Second Additional Protocol are performed by them? The distinction between government agencies (including the military) and courts is important since only the former can be a party to a conflict in a non-international armed conflict. This is clear from a commentary on common Article 3 of the Geneva Conventions and Article 1(1) of the Second Additional Protocol.[11] Courts may form one part of a state known as the judiciary, but in many countries they are not part of the executive branch, which is normally the government. Therefore, the question of the equal application of common Article 3(1)(d) of the Geneva Conventions and Article 6 of the Second Additional Protocol arises not between courts and armed groups, but between government and armed groups.

The question then is how the government can ensure the equal application of the judicial guarantees obligations to the government and armed groups. First, common Article 3(1)(d) of the 1949 Geneva Conventions and Article 6 of the 1977 Second Additional Protocol oblige the government to ensure, for example through legislation in parliament, that courts are constituted in a way that they respect judicial guarantees, particular their independence and impartiality. Once such courts are established, it is up to the courts to respect judicial guarantees in common Article 3(1)(d) of the Geneva Conventions and Article 6 of the Second Additional Protocol. Whenever the government and armed groups find offences related to an armed conflict, either under the existing penal code, other special penal laws, or IHL, they should bring the case to the existing courts. In this sense, common Article 3(1)(d) and Article 6 prevent the government and armed groups from handing down sentence themselves and executing the concerned persons. It is essential to underline here that the government should also bring the members of their own armed forces to the courts and armed groups should bring their own members to the courts if they commit offences.

[11] Pictet et al, *Commentary* Vol I, 51; Sandoz et al (eds), *Commentary*, para 4460.

If one follows the above approach, the question of whether armed groups can establish courts does not arise. The courts are considered as an actor outside the context of a non-international armed conflict between the government and armed groups, and it is assumed that the courts would try any cases related to violations of IHL or national penal law brought by the government and armed groups in an equal manner as an independent and impartial organ.

However, in reality, there may be various obstacles for armed groups in particular to bring cases related to the armed conflict to the existing courts. For example, in some states, the independence and impartiality of courts may be doubtful and hence, many armed groups may feel reluctant to submit any cases related to the conduct of a state's armed forces to the existing courts. Moreover, there may be more practical obstacles such as how to physically bring the concerned members of armed forces to the existing courts. Article 6(2)(e) of the 1977 Second Additional Protocol requires the following:

> [A]nyone charged with an offence shall have the right to be tried in his presence.

If the armed groups control certain parts of the territory and existing courts are located and functioning in that territory, it may be possible for the armed groups to physically bring the members of armed forces to the courts for trial. However, if the armed groups are highly clandestine, the mere act of bringing the members of armed forces to the existing courts would expose themselves and might help the state's armed forces to identify the position of the armed groups. In such circumstances, the armed groups may consider establishing courts, adopt penal laws, hand down sentences, and carry out executions themselves. Whether these are envisaged in common Article 3(1)(d) of the 1949 Geneva Conventions and Article 6 of the Second Additional Protocol is unclear.

The general rule of treaty interpretation in Article 31 of the 1969 Vienna Convention on the Law of Treaties only clarifies to a certain extent whether the two provisions envisage judicial and legislative acts by an armed group. On the question of whether an armed group can establish a court, common Article 3(1)(d) of the 1949 Geneva Conventions provides that a trial should be held by a 'regularly constituted court'. In its ordinary meaning and the preparatory work behind it, the term implies that a court established by an armed group cannot be considered as 'regularly constituted' under the national law.[12] On the other hand, Article 6 of the 1977 Second Additional Protocol reformulated the rule and provides that a trial should be held by a 'court offering the essential guarantees of independence and impartiality'. A commentary implies that this change was to take into account the possibility of an armed group to establish their

[12] Sandoz et al (eds), *Commentary*, para 4600.

own court.[13] Admittedly, Article 6 concentrates more on the character of the court, in other words to be independent and impartial, than how they were established, in other words 'regularly' as required in common Article 3(1)(d) of the Geneva Conventions.

However, the preparatory work of the 1977 Second Additional Protocol does not clarify if an armed group can establish a court. The International Committee of the Red Cross (ICRC) seemed to envisage the possibility of an armed group to establish a court on the basis that Article 1(1) of the Second Additional Protocol requires exercise of control over a part of the territory as to enable the armed group to implement the Protocol.[14] Some states implicitly recognised the possibility of an armed group to establish a court.[15] Other states agreed with the formulation in Article 6 of the Second Additional Protocol by referring to the 1966 International Covenant on Civil and Political Rights (ICCPR) and national law.[16] This could mean that these states only considered existing courts of the state as legitimate courts, since the ICCPR imposes obligations only on states and not to armed groups, and national penal law can only be applied by the existing courts of the state. Without further clarification, Article 6 of the Second Additional Protocol was adopted by consensus. The preparatory work therefore shows that it was only the ICRC which recognised explicitly the possibility of an armed group to establish a court, and states were neither explicitly nor implicitly for or against such possibility.

Article 31(3)(b) of the 1969 Vienna Convention on the Law of Treaties lists the following to be taken into account during the interpretation of a treaty:

> [A]ny subsequent practice in the application of the treaty which establishes the agreement of the parties regarding its interpretation.

In non-international armed conflicts such as in Nepal and the Philippines, armed groups have established their own courts in various ways.[17] For example in Nepal, the Communist Party of Nepal-Maoist (CPN-M), the former armed group in the non-international armed conflict in Nepal, established 'people's courts' that could try crimes such as murder and rape.[18] In this case, only common Article 3(1)(d) of the 1949 Geneva

[13] Sandoz et al (eds), *Commentary*, para 4600.

[14] *Official Records of the Diplomatic Conference on the Reaffirmation and Development of International Humanitarian Law Applicable in Armed Conflicts, Geneva (1974–1977)* (hereafter *Official Records*) (Bern, Federal Political Department, 1978) Vol VIII, CDDH/I/SR.33, para 24.

[15] Pakistan, *Official Records* Vol VIII, CDDH/I/SR.33, para 67; Iraq, *Official Records* Vol VIII, CDDH/I/SR.33, para 69.

[16] Iran, *Official Records* Vol VIII, CDDH/I/SR.33, para 27; Argentina, *Official Records* Vol VIII, CDDH/I/SR.33, para 29; Belgium, *Official Records* Vol VIII, CDDH/I/SR.33, para 41. International Covenants on Civil and Political Rights (adopted 16 December 1966, entered into force 23 March 1976) 999 UNTS 171.

[17] See also J Somer, 'Jungle Justice: Passing Sentence on the Equality of Belligerents in Non-International Armed Conflict' (2007) 867 *International Review of the Red Cross* 655.

[18] OHCHR, 'Human Rights Abuses by the CPN-M: Summary of Concerns' (21 September 2006) 4, nepal.ohchr.org.

Conventions was relevant since Nepal was not a party to the 1977 Second Additional Protocol. However, as discussed earlier, common Article 3(1)(d) of the Geneva Conventions requires a trial to be held by a 'regularly constituted court' which indicates courts of the state. Hence, in the case of Nepal, it would have been difficult to find a legal basis for the establishment of the 'people's courts'.

In the Philippines, the New People's Army (NPA), the military wing of the Communist Party of the Philippines (CPP), has established 'people's courts' that have arguably dealt with cases related to the non-international armed conflict.[19] Moreover, the NPA has its own military tribunal that can try crimes such as murder, rape and arson, according to the Basic Rules of the NPA adopted by the CPP in 1969.[20] In this case, the 1977 Second Additional Protocol applied between the Government of the Philippines and the NPA since the Philippines had acceded to it. As noted earlier, Article 6 of the Second Additional Protocol requires a trial to be held by a 'court offering the essential guarantees of independence and impartiality', which might leave the possibility for an armed group to establish a court so long as it meets the conditions. Hence, it can be argued that Article 6 of the Second Additional Protocol might provide a legal basis for the establishment of the 'people's courts' by the NPA.

These are indications that armed groups can establish courts themselves. However, the practice is far from enough to establish that common Article 3(1)(d) of the 1949 Geneva Conventions and Article 6 of the 1977 Second Additional Protocol permit the establishment of a court by an armed group. In particular, the reactions from governments are rarely heard about courts established by armed groups, which would form an important part of the interpretation of Article 3(1)(d) of the Geneva Conventions and Article 6 of the Second Additional Protocol. The absence of government reaction may be for various reasons, such as the concern that a mere comment on an armed group's court may legitimise the court.

Supposing that an armed group can establish a court itself, either pursuant to Article 3(1)(d) of the 1949 Geneva Conventions or Article 6 of the 1977 Second Additional Protocol, there are various questions as to how judicial guarantees can be respected. For example, will the court of the armed group apply the existing penal code or adopt a new one? If a new penal code is to be adopted, how will it have to be adopted to ensure the legitimacy of the new penal code? By a council of representatives resembling parliament or by the leadership of the armed group as an execu-

[19] UNHRC, 'Report of the Special Rapporteur on Extrajudicial, Summary or Arbitrary Executions, Philip Alston, Addendum: Mission to Philippines' (16 April 2008) UN Doc A/HRC/8/3/Add.2, para 32.

[20] See New People's Army, 'Basic Rules of the New People's Army' (29 March 1969), New People's Army website, www.philippinerevolution.net/npa/tun.shtml.

tive order? These are questions that need to be answered to comply with the principle of *nullum crimen sine lege* as required by Article 6(2)(c) of the Second Additional Protocol. Moreover, practical questions such as the selection of judges who will ensure the independence and impartiality of the court and ensuring access to a defence lawyer will present significant challenges to armed groups. The difficulty in respecting such fundamental judicial guarantees will be more obvious in the case of a non-international armed conflict between two or more armed groups, which is covered by common Article 3 of the Geneva Conventions (if one takes the position that common Article 3 permits an armed group to establish a court).

In order to ensure that the fundamental judicial guarantees are respected by both the government and the armed groups, one option is to conclude a special agreement as envisaged in common Article 3(2) of the 1949 Geneva Conventions which would provide details such as the handover of detainees to the armed forces or the armed group provided that they will be tried for their crimes, respect for fundamental judicial guarantees by both parties, and transmission of judgments and sentences to the other party. The Comprehensive Agreement on Respect for Human Rights and International Humanitarian Law between the Government of the Philippines and the National Democratic Front of the Philippines[21] (which includes the CPP and its military wing, the NPA) could be considered as a special agreement, but it only listed some judicial guarantees without detailing how to ensure respect for them. In the absence of a special agreement or an explicit reference in a special agreement, armed groups will face the problem of whether their courts can be based on common Article 3(1)(d) of the Geneva Conventions or Article 6 of the 1977 Second Additional Protocol. However, regardless of the legal basis, armed groups may proceed to the establishment of courts in any case. In such cases, it is essential for the armed groups to at least respect the fundamental judicial guarantees at pre-trial, trial, and post-trial stages.

Therefore, the equal application of IHL to the conflicting parties faces particular problems in non-international armed conflict, especially with regard to the judicial guarantees obligations. The legal basis for armed groups to establish courts is particularly unclear, but at least the pre-trial, trial, and post-trial judicial guarantees must be respected by the arresting and detaining authorities as well the courts of armed groups and the state in an equal manner.

It is worth mentioning as a final remark that it is not only armed groups that face problems with regard to the respect for judicial guarantees, but also the courts of the state. The inequality between the punishment of the members of a state's armed forces and that of armed groups remains one of the most difficult questions for a better compliance with IHL by

[21] Adopted 16 March 1998, Centre for Humanitarian Dialogue website, www.hdcentre.org.

armed groups.[22] The problem stems from the fact that national law and IHL operate in totally opposite ways. On one hand, national law creates an unequal status between armed groups and a state's armed forces, of which the members of the former are criminals and can be punished by maximum sentence in many countries while the latter can lawfully use force to maintain law and order.[23] On the other hand, under IHL, conduct of hostilities by armed groups and a state's armed forces is equally lawful so long as it does not violate IHL, and because of this underlying assumption, Article 6(5) of the 1977 Second Additional Protocol even provides as follows:

> [T]he authorities in power shall endeavour to grant the broadest possible amnesty to persons who have participated in the armed conflict.[24]

Thus, the court and the government are faced with two opposing legal obligations: under national law they should hand down maximum sentences against members of armed groups while under IHL they should consider granting them amnesty. In addition, the court is asked to try war crimes committed by the members of both armed groups and the state's armed forces equally. Faced with such a situation, the courts may opt to apply the national law and hand down maximum sentences as well as be stricter with the prosecution of war crimes committed by the members of armed groups.[25]

The choice between punishment based on national law or amnesty is a policy question for the government and this book is not the place to discuss this issue further.[26] However, one point is clear: war crimes prosecution is not a policy question; there should be no exception to the prosecution of war crimes whether they were committed by members of armed groups or a state's armed forces.[27]

[22] ICRC, *Improving Compliance*, 22–23.

[23] Art 3(1) of the 1977 Second Additional Protocol. See also F Bugnion, '*Jus ad Bellum, Jus in Bello* and Non-International Armed Conflicts' (2003) 6 *Yearbook of International Humanitarian Law* 167, 168 and 170.

[24] See also Rule 159 in Henckaerts and Doswald-Beck, *Customary International Humanitarian Law* Vol I, 611.

[25] See, eg, Bugnion, '*Jus ad Bellum*', 168; J Pejic, 'Terrorist Acts and Groups: A Role for International Law?' (2004) 75 *British Year Book of International Law* 71, 75–76.

[26] For a recent case on amnesty for members of armed groups, see Chapter 9 of Annex 'A' of the Agreement for a Cease-Fire in the Democratic Republic of Congo (adopted 10 July 1999, entered into force 11 July 1999) 2312 UNTS 255. The Agreement was signed by Angola, DRC, Namibia, Rwanda, Uganda, Zimbabwe, Congolese Rally for Democracy, and Movement for the Liberation of the Congo.

[27] For further discussions, see generally L Zegveld, *Accountability of Armed Opposition Groups in International Law* (Cambridge, Cambridge University Press, 2002); L Olson, 'Provoking the Dragon on the Patio – Matters of Transitional Justice: Penal Repression vs. Amnesty' (2006) 862 *International Review of the Red Cross* 275; A-M La Rosa, 'Armed Groups, Sanctions and the Implementation of International Humanitarian Law' (2008) 870 *International Review of the Red Cross* 327; E Sottas, 'Transitional Justice and Sanctions' (2008) 870 *International Review of the Red Cross* 371.

II. INTERVENTION BY FOREIGN ARMED FORCES OR ARMED GROUPS AND MIXED ARMED CONFLICT

Throughout this book, situations where *jus ad bellum* and *jus in bello* are clearly applicable have been discussed. This section deals with a potential gap where the applicability, as well as the application, of *jus ad bellum* and *jus in bello* is highly controversial. There are at least two such cases: 1) an armed conflict involving intervention by foreign armed forces or armed groups;[28] and 2) an armed conflict consisting of some or all of international, non-international, and internationalised non-international armed conflicts which exist simultaneously but separately. The uncertainty on the applicability and the complexity of the application of *jus ad bellum* and *jus in bello* in these armed conflicts can have serious consequences on the compliance with the two legal regimes. This section discusses the two types of armed conflict in turn, from *jus ad bellum* and *jus in bello* perspectives.

A. Intervention by Foreign Armed Forces or Armed Groups[29]

When examining the relationship between 'armed attack' and 'armed conflict', the controversial nature of an armed conflict involving an

[28] It is often called 'internationalised non-international armed conflict', since normally the conflicting parties are the same as conventional non-international armed conflict (a state's armed forces v armed groups or armed groups v armed groups), but since one of them comes from outside the international border, it 'internationalises' the armed conflict, thereby putting it outside the conventional framework of international armed conflict (state v state) and non-international armed conflict (confined to one state). While most experts consider that 'internationalisation' is brought about by foreign armed forces, an intervention by foreign armed groups can equally 'internationalise' the armed conflict. See generally the works in n 29 below.

[29] For *jus in bello* aspects, see generally R-J Wilhelm, 'Problèmes relatifs à la protection de la personne humaine par le droit international dans les conflits armés ne présentant pas un caractère international' (1972) 137 *Recueil des Cours de l'Académie de Droit International* 309; D Schindler, 'The Different Types of Armed Conflicts According to the Geneva Conventions and Protocols' (1979) 163 *Recueil des Cours de l'Académie de Droit International* 116, 139–44; H-P Gasser, 'Internationalized Non-International Armed Conflicts: Case Studies of Afghanistan, Kampuchea, and Lebanon' (1983–84) 33 *American University Law Review* 145, 157; Institute of International Law, 'L'application du droit international notamment humanitaire, dans les conflits armés auxquels prennent part des entités non-étatiques' (1999) 68-I *Annuaire de l'Institut de Droit International* 251; E David, *Principes de droit des conflits armés*, 3rd edn (Brussels, Bruylant, 2002) 139 *ff*; R Kolb, *Ius in bello: Le droit international des conflits armés* (Bâle, Helbing et Lichtenhahn, 2003) 88 *ff*. For *jus ad bellum* aspects, see nn 43, 44, 70, and 71 below. See also A McDonald, 'Declarations of War and Belligerent Parties: International Law Governing Hostilities between States and Transnational Terrorist Networks' (2007) 54 *Netherlands International Law Review* 279; E Benvenisti, 'Rethinking the Divide between *Jus ad Bellum* and *Jus in Bello* in Warfare against Nonstate Actors' (2009) 34 *Yale Journal of International Law* 541; C Kress, 'Some Reflections on the International Legal Framework Governing Transnational Armed Conflicts' (2010) 15 *Journal of Conflict and Security Law* 245; N Lubell, *Extraterritorial Use of Force against Non-State Actors* (Oxford, Oxford University Press, 2010); L Moir, *Reappraising the Resort to Force* (Oxford, Hart Publishing, 2010) 12 *ff*.

intervention by foreign armed forces or armed groups was briefly pointed out.[30] This section provides a full exposition on this issue from both *jus ad bellum* and *jus in bello* perspectives.

This type of armed conflict is a gap in *jus ad bellum* and *jus in bello* where the applicability of the two is highly controversial and even if they are applicable, the scope of the applicable rules is limited. It follows that the compliance with *jus ad bellum* and *jus in bello* can face serious difficulties. However, it is also the most prevalent form of modern armed conflict which requires urgent solution.

There are two types of such armed conflict: 1) foreign armed forces v state-sponsored armed groups (or a state's armed forces v foreign state-sponsored armed groups); and 2) foreign armed forces v non-state-sponsored armed groups (or a state's armed forces v foreign non-state-sponsored armed groups). Examples of 1) can be seen in the former Yugoslavia in the early 1990s (between Bosnia-Herzegovina and Bosnian Serb forces backed by the Federal Republic of Yugoslavia)[31] and Sierra Leone/Liberia (between Sierra Leone and armed groups of Sierra Leone backed by Liberia).[32] Examples of 2) can be seen in Somalia in the early 1990s (between the Unified Task Force and armed groups),[33] Uganda/Democratic Republic of the Congo (DRC) (between Uganda and armed groups in the DRC),[34] Iraq (between the US and armed groups),[35] the Occupied Palestinian Territories (between Israel and armed groups),[36] and Lebanon (between Israel and armed groups in Lebanon).[37] The distinction is crucial since in the former case, the law of self-defence and the law of international armed conflict are applicable whereas in the latter case, the applicability and the application of the law of self-defence and IHL are still controversial.

The first type has been briefly discussed earlier: if the support of a state to the armed groups reaches a certain level, it will be considered as an armed conflict between two states and thus, a use of force, armed attack,

[30] See section 3.I.A above.

[31] See *Tadic Case* (Judgment, Appeals) ICTY-IT-94-1 (15 July 1999), para 162.

[32] See *Prosecutor v Taylor* (Case Summary Accompanying the Amended Indictment) SCSL-2003-01-I (16 March 2006), para 30.

[33] See UNSC, 'Report of the Commission of Inquiry Established Pursuant to Security Council Resolution 885 (1993) to Investigate Armed Attacks on UNOSOM II Personnel Which Led to Casualties among Them' (1 June 1994) UN Doc S/1994/653, 170 *ff*.

[34] *Armed Activities on the Territory of the Congo* (hereafter *Armed Activities* case) (*Democratic Republic of the Congo v Uganda*) (Merits) [2005] ICJ Rep 116, para 146.

[35] See UNSC, 'Report of the Secretary-General Pursuant to Paragraph 30 of Resolution 1546 (2004)' (5 December 2006) UN Doc S/2006/945, para 55.

[36] *Legal Consequences of the Construction of a Wall in the Occupied Palestinian Territory* (hereafter *Wall* case) (Advisory Opinion) [2004] ICJ Rep 136, para 139.

[37] See UNHRC, 'Report of the Commission of Inquiry on Lebanon Pursuant to Human Rights Council Resolution S-2/1' (23 November 2006) UN Doc A/HRC/3/2, paras 40 *ff*. The Commission's classification of this armed conflict as an international armed conflict is problematic so far as the fighting between Hizbullah and Israel is concerned.

and international armed conflict exist concurrently.[38] On the *jus ad bellum* aspect, particularly with regard to armed attack, this conclusion is supported by a majority of practice. The International Court of Justice (ICJ) authoritatively set the precedent in the *Nicaragua* case:

> An armed attack must be understood as including not merely action by regular armed forces across an international border, but also 'the sending by or on behalf of a State of armed bands, groups, irregulars or mercenaries, which carry out acts of armed force against another State of such gravity as to amount to' . . . an actual armed attack conducted by regular forces, 'or its substantial involvement therein'.[39]

This approach was followed in the *Wall*[40] and *Armed Activities*[41] cases.

State practice such as the US justification for the use of force against Afghanistan in 2001 also supports the ICJ's approach:

> In accordance with Article 51 of the Charter of the United Nations, I wish . . . to report that the United States of America . . . has initiated actions in the exercise of its inherent right of individual and collective self-defence following the armed attacks that were carried out against the United States on 11 September 2001 . . . Since 11 September, my Government has obtained clear and compelling information that the Al-Qaeda organization, which is supported by the Taliban regime in Afghanistan, had a central role in the attacks.[42]

[38] See section 3.I.A.

[39] *Military and Paramilitary Activities in and against Nicaragua* (hereafter *Nicaragua* case) (*Nicaragua v US*) (Merits) [1986] ICJ Rep 14, para 195.

[40] *Wall* case (Advisory Opinion), para 139: 'Article 51 of the Charter thus recognizes the existence of an inherent right of self-defence in the case of armed attack by one State against another State. However, Israel does not claim that the attacks against it are imputable to a foreign State.' Judges Buergenthal and Higgins expressed reservations particularly on the first sentence, but it should be read together with the second sentence which implies that attacks by armed groups should be imputable to a state to constitute an 'armed attack'. Thus, the Court did not rule out the possibility that attacks from armed groups could be an 'armed attack', provided that they are backed by a state. *Wall* case (Advisory Opinion), Declaration of Judge Buergenthal, para 5; Separate Opinion of Judge Higgins, paras 33 and 34.

[41] *Armed Activities* case (Merits), paras 146 and 147: 'The Court has found above that there is no satisfactory proof of the involvement in these attacks, direct or indirect, of the Government of the DRC. The attacks did not emanate from armed bands or irregulars sent by the DRC or on behalf of the DRC, within the sense of Article 3*(g)* of General Assembly resolution 3314 (XXIX) on the definition of aggression . . . even if this series of deplorable attacks could be regarded as cumulative in character, they still remained non-attributable to the DRC . . . the Court finds that the legal and factual circumstances for the exercise of a right of self-defence by Uganda against the DRC were not present.'

[42] See UNSC, 'Letter Dated 7 October 2001 from the Permanent Representative of the United States of America to the United Nations Addressed to the President of the Security Council' (7 October 2001) UN Doc S/2001/946. See also US, Joint Resolution to Authorize the Use of United States Armed Forces against Those Responsible for the Recent Attacks Launched against the United States, Public Law No 107-40, 115 Stat 224 (2001), Section 2(a); UNSC, 'Letter Dated 7 October 2001 from the Chargé d'Affaires a.i. of the Permanent Mission of the United Kingdom of Great Britain and Northern Ireland to the United Nations Addressed to the President of the Security Council' (7 October 2001) UN Doc S/2001/947. See also UNGA, 'Summary Legal Position of the Government of Israel' (24 November 2003) UN Doc A/ES-10/248, Annex I, para 6; Council of the European Union, Independent

Other experts have also taken the position that attacks from armed groups should be imputable to a state to constitute an armed attack. Gilbert Guillaume succinctly summarised the majority opinion:

> [A]ccording to the majority of authors, acts of terrorism reaching the extent and gravity of the events on 11 September 2001 could be described as acts of armed attack. However, for those acts to be considered as acts of armed attack within the meaning of Article 51 of the Charter, such acts, in the view of those same authors, have to be attributed not only to private individuals liable to criminal prosecution, but further to a State which exercises effective control over those individuals.[43]

Many experts concur.[44]

With regard to the *jus in bello* aspect, an armed conflict between foreign armed forces and state-sponsored armed groups will be seen as an international armed conflict to which the law of international armed conflict is fully applicable. This has been recognised by the International Criminal Tribunal for the former Yugoslavia (ICTY) in the *Tadic* case:

> [I]n case of an internal armed conflict breaking out on the territory of a State, it may become international (or, depending upon the circumstances, be international in character alongside an internal armed conflict) if (i) another State

International Fact-Finding Mission on the Conflict in Georgia, 'Report' Vol II (September 2009) 261, Independent International Fact-Finding Mission on the Conflict in Georgia website, www.ceiig.ch.

[43] G Guillaume, 'Terrorism and International Law' (2004) 53 *International and Comparative Law Quarterly* 537, 546.

[44] See *Wall* case (Advisory Opinion), Separate Opinion of Judge Higgins, para 33. See also H Kelsen, *Principles of International Law*, 2nd edn (New York, Holt, Reinhart, and Wilson, 1966) 62–63; I Brownlie, *International Law and the Use of Force by States* (Oxford, Clarendon Press, 1963) 279; J Rowles, 'Military Responses to Terrorism: Substantive and Procedural Constraints in International Law' (1987) 81 *American Society of International Law Proceedings* 307, 314; O Schachter, 'The Lawful Use of Force by a State against Terrorists in Another Country' (1998) 19 *Israel Yearbook on Human Rights* 209, 215–19; A Arend and R Beck, *International Law and the Use of Force* (London, Routledge, 1993) 159; S Alexandrov, *Self-Defense against the Use of Force in International Law* (The Hague, Kluwer Law International, 1996) 183; N Schrijver, 'Responding to International Terrorism: Moving the Frontiers of International Law for "Enduring Freedom"' (2001) 48 *Netherlands International Law Review* 271, 284–85; M Byers, 'Terrorism, the Use of Force and International Law after 11 September' (2002) 51 *International and Comparative Law Quarterly* 400, 412; S Murphy, 'Terrorism and the Concept of "Armed Attack" in Article 51 of the UN Charter' (2002) 43 *Harvard International Law Journal* 41, 50–51; A Randelzhofer, 'Article 51' in B Simma et al (eds), *The Charter of the United Nations: A Commentary*, 2nd edn Vol I (Oxford, Oxford University Press, 2002) 802; R Wolfrum and C Philipp, 'The Status of the Taliban: Their Obligations and Rights under International Law' (2002) 6 *Max Planck Yearbook of United Nations Law* 559, 591; I Brownlie, *Principles of Public International Law*, 6th edn (Oxford, Oxford University Press, 2003) 713; R Kolb, *Ius contra bellum: Le droit international relatif au maintien de la paix* (Bâle, Helbing et Lichtenhahn, 2003) 191; C Gray, C, *International Law and the Use of Force*, 2nd edn (Oxford, Oxford University Press, 2004) 109; S Preiser, '"Operation Enduring Freedom" and the UN Charter: The Terrorist Attacks of 11 September 2001 and the Subsequent Military Response' (2004) 8 *International Peacekeeping* 213, 227–28; H Duffy, *The 'War on Terror' and the Framework of International Law* (Cambridge, Cambridge University Press, 2005) 160–61.

> intervenes in that conflict through its troops, or alternatively if (ii) some of the participants in the internal armed conflict act on behalf of that other State.[45]

On this basis, the ICTY concluded that the armed conflict between Bosnia-Herzegovina on one hand and the Bosnian Serb forces, supported by the Federal Republic of Yugoslavia, on the other, was an international armed conflict.[46] Thus, it is clear that a use of force, armed attack and international armed conflict exist simultaneously when foreign armed forces attack a state-sponsored armed group, or vice versa.

However, the single difficulty common to *jus ad bellum* and *jus in bello* is to determine whether an armed group is acting on behalf of a state, which also determines whether Article 2(4) of the UN Charter,[47] the law of self-defence, and the law of international armed conflict are applicable. Under the law of state responsibility, the responsibility for the conduct of an armed group can be attributed to a state in the following circumstances:

> The conduct of a person or group of persons shall be considered an act of a State under international law if the person or group of persons is in fact acting on the instructions of, or under the direction or control of, that State in carrying out the conduct.[48]

Thus, when an armed group is acting on behalf of another state's armed forces and attacks another state, a use of force, armed attack and international armed conflict exist concurrently. However, different levels of state control over armed groups have been suggested to attribute the acts of armed groups to a state.

In the *Nicaragua* case, the ICJ employed the following standard:

> For this conduct [of the *contras*, armed groups fighting against the Nicaraguan government] to give rise to legal responsibility of the United States, it would in principle have to be proved that that State had effective control of the military or paramilitary operations in the course of which the alleged violations [of human rights and humanitarian law] were committed.[49]

The standard employed here was whether a state had 1) effective control over 2) specific military operations by armed groups which led to violations of international law. The Court eventually concluded that the acts of the *contras* could not be attributed to the US since it failed to meet the

[45] *Tadic Case* (Judgment, Appeals), para 84.
[46] *Tadic Case* (Judgment, Appeals), paras 170–71.
[47] Charter of the United Nations (hereafter UN Charter) (adopted 26 June 1945, entered into force 24 October 1945) 59 Statutes at Large 1031.
[48] Art 8 of the ILC, 'Articles on Responsibility of States for Internationally Wrongful Acts' (hereafter ILC Articles on State Responsibility) (2001) UN Doc A/56/10 Supp 10, paras 76 *ff*. This was invoked in the *Armed Activities* case (Merits), para 160 when the ICJ concluded that one of the armed groups was not acting on behalf of Uganda.
[49] *Nicaragua* case (Merits), para 115.

above requirements.[50] The Court also later clarified the different levels of state support for armed groups in order for the acts of armed groups to constitute a use of force and an armed attack. In the *Nicaragua* case, the Court indicated the dividing line between 'use of force' and 'armed attack' by stating that the training, arming, and logistical support for armed groups attacking another state amount to a 'threat or use of force' but not to an 'armed attack'.[51] This approach was followed in the *Armed Activities*[52] and *Bosnian Genocide* cases.[53]

On the other hand, the ICTY considered that the mere fact of a state's 'overall control' suffices to establish that armed groups are acting on behalf of that state, and that there was no further requirement that specific military operations should be directed by the state. The ICTY noted as follows in the *Tadic* case:

> [F]or the attribution to a State of acts of these groups [organised and hierarchically structured group] it is sufficient to require that the group as a whole be under the overall control of the State . . . If it is under the overall control of a State, it must perforce engage the responsibility of that State for its activities, *whether or not each of them was specifically imposed, requested or directed by the State*.[54]

The ICTY also set out indications of 'overall control' as follows:

> The control required by international law may be deemed to exist when a State (or, in the context of an armed conflict, the Party to the conflict) *has a role in organising, coordinating or planning the military actions* of the military group, in addition to financing, training and equipping or providing operational sup-

[50] *Nicaragua* case (Merits), para 115: 'financing, organizing, training, supplying and equipping of the *contras*, the selection of its military or paramilitary targets, and the planning of the whole of its operations, is still insufficient in itself . . . for the purpose of attributing to the United States the acts committed by the *contras* in the course of their military or paramilitary operations . . . even the general control by the respondent State [US] over a force with a high degree of dependency on it [*contras*], would not in themselves mean, without further evidence, that the United States directed or enforced the perpetration of the acts contrary to human rights and humanitarian law alleged by the applicant State [Nicaragua].'

[51] *Nicaragua* case (Merits), paras 191, 195, and 228.

[52] *Armed Activities* case (Merits), para 160.

[53] *Application of the Convention on the Prevention and Punishment of the Crime of Genocide* (hereafter *Bosnia Genocide* case) (*Bosnia and Herzegovina v Serbia and Montenegro*) (Merits) 2007, para 399. The judgment is currently available at the ICJ website, www.icj-cij.org. See also Council of the European Union, Independent International Fact-Finding Mission on the Conflict in Georgia, 'Report' Vol II (September 2009), 259.

[54] *Tadic Case* (Judgment, Appeals), paras 120 and 122. It is also worth noting that the 'overall control' is strictly a factual matter. An agreement between armed groups and a state's armed forces declaring that they are distinct forces does not have any significance if the two forces are not distinct forces in reality, as the ICTY noted in the same judgment as follows: 'Undue emphasis upon the ostensible structures and over declarations of the belligerents, as opposed to a nuanced analysis of the reality of their relationship, may tacitly suggest to groups who are in *de facto* control of military forces that responsibility of such forces or by a facile declaration that the reconstituted forces are henceforth independent of their erstwhile sponsors.' *Tadic Case* (Judgment, Appeals), para 154.

> port to that group. Acts performed by the group or members thereof may be regarded as acts of *de facto* State organs regardless of any specific instruction by the controlling State concerning the commission of each of those acts.[55]

The contrast with the ICJ in the *Nicaragua* case is that the ICTY considered that any specific instruction for a specific military operation was unnecessary to establish 'overall control' over the armed groups. As noted above, in applying this standard, the ICTY found that the Bosnian Serb forces were acting on behalf of the Federal Republic of Yugoslavia, rendering the armed conflict between the Bosnian Serb forces and Bosnia-Herzegovina an international armed conflict.

However, perhaps the most important contribution of the ICTY was to recognise that the degree of state control over armed groups does not have to be fixed and can vary from one case to another:

> [I]nternational rules do not always require the same degree of control over armed groups or private individuals for the purpose of determining whether an individual not having the status of a State official under internal legislation can be regarded as a *de facto* organ of the State. The extent of the requisite State control varies.[56]

This was confirmed in the ICJ's *Bosnia Genocide* case.[57] Thus, while the practice of the ICJ and ICTY may be at variance, there is no reason why it should not be so, and the establishment of the state control over armed groups can be done on a case-by-case basis.

Once it is established that armed groups are not acting on behalf of a state, the situation is an armed conflict between foreign armed forces and a non-state-sponsored armed group. This type of armed conflict poses various problems since it does not fit in the framework of use of force, armed attack, or international/non-international armed conflict as they are traditionally understood. Three situations can be distinguished: 1) attack by state A against a non-state-sponsored armed group in state B (such as the attacks by Uganda on the armed groups in the DRC); 2) attack by a non-state-sponsored armed group in state A against state B (such as the armed groups in the DRC against Uganda); 3) attack by non-state-sponsored armed group in state A against non-state-sponsored armed group in state B (such as the armed groups in the DRC v armed groups in Uganda).

[55] *Tadic Case* (Judgment, Appeals), para 137. The ICTY eventually considered the following acts by the Federal Republic of Yugoslavia as constituting 'overall control' over the Bosnian Serb forces in Bosnia-Herzegovina: payment of salaries to the members of the Bosnian Serb forces, placing military officers in the hierarchy of the Bosnian Serb forces, direction and supervision of Bosnian Serb forces' military operations by those officers, directly providing combat support to the Bosnian Serb forces, regular communications between the Bosnian Serb forces and the Yugoslav Government. See *Tadic Case* (Judgment, Appeals), paras 151–54.

[56] *Tadic Case* (Judgment, Appeals), para 137.

[57] *Bosnia Genocide* case (Merits), para 405.

Type 1) is an easier case. It can be a use of force and an armed attack since, even though the attack of state A is not directed against the apparatus of state B, the attack by state A on the territory of state B in itself will be considered as a use of force and an armed attack.[58]

Types 2) and 3) are far more difficult cases. First, whether an attack by a non-state-sponsored armed group can be qualified as a use of force is problematic since Article 2(4) of the UN Charter only regulates use of force by a state against another state and not an attack by a non-state actor against a state. One paragraph in the 1970 Friendly Relations Declaration, which elaborates on Article 2(4), provides as follows:

> Every state has the duty to refrain from . . . acquiescing in organized activities within its territory directed towards the commission of such acts [civil strife or terrorist acts].

This, however, only provides that the state's acquiescence to the presence of armed groups on its territory can amount to a threat or use of force and does not, in any way, recognise that an attack by a non-state-sponsored armed group can amount to a use of force. Thus, an attack by a non-state-sponsored armed group against a state cannot be qualified as a 'use of force' under Article 2(4).

Even so, the mere toleration of the presence of armed groups on a state's territory as a use of force is problematic since it is at variance with the understanding of the threshold of 'use of force' in the *Nicaragua* case. The ICJ indicated that there should be a minimum level of state backing for armed groups in order to constitute a use of force. The Court set the bottom line that 'the mere supply of funds to the *contras* [by the US] . . . does not in itself amount to a use of force'. If the mere supply of funds to armed groups does not amount to a use of force, then the mere acquiescence of armed groups on a state's territory will clearly fall short of a use of force. In this sense, both an attack by a non-state-sponsored armed group against a state and tolerating the presence of such an armed group on a state's territory are problematic to be qualified as a 'use of force'.

With regard to armed attack, it is still controversial whether a non-state-sponsored armed group can launch an armed attack against a state within the meaning of Article 51 of the UN Charter and whether a state can exercise the right of self-defence against such an armed group. As discussed

[58] See UNGA, 'Declaration on Principles of International Law concerning Friendly Relations and Co-operation among States in accordance with the Charter of the United Nations' UNGA Res 2625 (XXV) (24 October 1970) (hereafter 1970 Friendly Relations Declaration); Art 3(a) of the UNGA, 'Definition of Aggression' UNGA Res 3314 (XXIX) (14 December 1974) (hereafter 1974 Definition of Aggression); Article 8 *bis* (2)(a) of the 'Amendments to the Rome Statute of the International Criminal Court on the Crime of Aggression' Review Conference of the Rome Statute of the International Criminal Court (Kampala 31 May – 11 June 2010) (11 June 2010) RC/Res.6, Annex I. See also Rome Statute of the International Criminal Court (adopted 17 July 1998, entered into force 1 July 2002) 2187 UNTS 3.

above, in general, an armed group should be linked to a state for its attack to constitute an armed attack. However, there are some who argue that such a link is not necessary. For example, Israel noted as follows with regard to the 'security fence' built in the Occupied Palestinian Territory:

> The fence is a measure wholly consistent with the right of States to self-defence enshrined in Article 51 of the Charter. International law and Security Council resolutions, including resolutions 1368 (2001) and 1373 (2001), have clearly recognized the right of States to use force in self-defence against terrorist attacks, and therefore surely recognize the right to use nonforcible measures to that end.[59]

Here, Israel was referring to the attacks from armed groups in the West Bank which have no link to a state.[60] It relied on Security Council resolutions 1368 and 1373 to draw an analogy with the terrorist attacks by Al-Qaeda, arguably a non-state-sponsored armed group, on the US on 11 September 2001. It is worth noting that the US did not rely on these resolutions to justify its use of force against Al-Qaeda. Instead, it relied on the Taliban government's support for Al-Qaeda, thus confirming the majority view of experts that an armed group should have a link with a state for its attack to qualify as an armed attack.[61]

The ICJ in the *Nicaragua* case also noted that 'acts by armed bands where such acts occur on a significant scale' cannot be included in the concept of armed attack, which implies that an attack by armed groups should be attributable to a state to constitute an armed attack.[62] In the *Wall*[63] and *Armed Activities*[64] cases, the Court did not discuss whether an attack by a non-state-sponsored armed group can qualify as an armed attack. However, since the Court confirmed in the *Bosnian Genocide* case the conclusion in the *Nicaragua* case that state support to an armed group

[59] Israel, UNGA Verbatim Record (20 October 2003) UN Doc A/ES-10/PV.21, 6. The reliance on these resolutions was later rejected by the ICJ. See *Wall* case (Advisory Opinion), para 139. See also UNSC, 'Identical Letters Dated 12 July 2006 from the Permanent Representative of Israel to the United Nations Addressed to the Secretary-General and the President of the Security Council' (12 July 2006) UN Doc A/60/937-S/2006/515 in relation to the 2006 Lebanon Conflict and UNSC, 'Identical Letters Dated 27 December 2008 from the Permanent Representative of Israel to the United Nations Addressed to the Secretary-General and the President of the Security Council' (27 December 2008) UN Doc S/2008/816 in relation to the 2009 Gaza Conflict.

[60] *Wall* case (Advisory Opinion), para 139.

[61] See UNSC, 'Letter Dated 7 October 2001 from the Permanent Representative of the United States of America to the United Nations Addressed to the President of the Security Council' (7 October 2001) UN Doc S/2001/946.

[62] *Nicaragua* case (Merits), para 195.

[63] *Wall* case (Advisory Opinion), para 139.

[64] *Armed Activities* case (Merits), para 147: 'the Court finds that the legal and factual circumstances for the exercise of a right of self-defence by Uganda against the DRC were not present. Accordingly, the Court has no need to respond to the contentions of the Parties as to whether and under what conditions contemporary international law provides for a right of self-defence against large-scale attacks by irregular forces.'

is required for its attack to qualify as an armed attack,[65] it seems unlikely that it will accept an attack by a non-state-sponsored armed group as an armed attack.[66]

However, certain experts have gone so far as to argue that an attack from a non-state-sponsored armed group can constitute an armed attack. For example, Judge Simma noted as follows in the *Armed Activities* case:

> [L]arge-scale attacks by non-State actors can qualify as 'armed attacks' within the meaning of Article 51 . . . if armed attacks are carried out by irregular forces from such territory [where there is almost complete absence of governmental authority] against a neighbouring State, these activities are still armed attacks even if they cannot be attributed to the territorial State.[67]

This view was shared by Judges Buergenthal and Kooijmans.[68] In particular, Judges Simma and Kooijmans suggested two situations where attacks from non-state-sponsored armed groups can be considered as 'armed attacks': 1) when attacks are on a large-scale; and 2) when attacks are from a territory not controlled by the government.[69]

For example, Thomas Franck also notes as follows:

> Article 51, which, in authorizing a victim state to act in self-defence does not limit this 'inherent' right to attacks by another state. Rather, the right is expressly accorded in response to 'an armed attack' and not to any particular kind of attacker.[70]

Other experts take a similar position.[71] Thus, this position has gained certain support but in the light of the majority opinion that attacks from

[65] *Bosnia Genocide* case (Merits), para 399.

[66] See further J Green, *The International Court of Justice and Self-Defence in International Law* (Oxford, Hart Publishing, 2009) 44 *ff*.

[67] *Armed Activities* case (Merits), Separate Opinion of Judge Simma, paras 11–12.

[68] *Wall* case (Advisory Opinion), Declaration of Judge Buergenthal, para 6; *Armed Activities* case (Merits), Separate Opinion of Judge Kooijmans, paras 29–30. Also implied in *Armed Activities* case (Merits), para 147.

[69] See also C Stahn, 'International Law at a Crossroads? The Impact of September 11' (2002) 62 *Zeitschrift für Ausländisches Öffentliches Recht und Völkerrecht* 183, 214–15 and 222–23; Randelzhofer, 'Article 51', 802; Brownlie, *Principles of Public International Law*, 200; Kolb, *Ius contra bellum*, 200–01; Y Dinstein, *War, Aggression and Self-Defence*, 4th edn (Cambridge, Cambridge University Press, 2005) 205.

[70] T Franck, 'Terrorism and the Right of Self-Defense' (2001) 95 *American Journal of International Law* 839, 840.

[71] Brownlie, *Principles of Public International Law*, 375; R Wedgwood, 'Responding to Terrorism: The Strikes against Bin Laden' (1999) 24 *Yale Journal of International Law* 559, 563–64; Dinstein, *War, Aggression and Self-Defence*, 213–15; Kolb, *Ius contra bellum*, 192 and 200–01; A Cassese, 'Article 51' in J-P Cot et al, *La Charter des Nations Unies: Commentaire article par article* (Paris, Economica, 2005) 1333; D Kretzmer, 'Targeted Killing of Suspected Terrorists: Extra-Judicial Executions or Legitimate Means of Defence?' (2005) 16 *European Journal of International Law* 172, 188; I Canor, 'When *Jus ad Bellum* Meets *Jus in Bello*: The Occupier's Right of Self-Defence against Terrorism Stemming from Occupied Territories' (2006) 19 *Leiden Journal of International Law* 129, 134; C Antonopoulous, 'Force by Armed Groups as Armed Attack and the Broadening of Self-Defence' (2008) 55 *Netherlands International Law Review* 159, 171.

armed groups should be linked to a state, the contrary opinion presented above is, to say the least, still controversial.

Obviously, there are difficult questions with this position: 1) the mere tolerance by a state of the presence of an armed group on its territory is unlikely to amount to an armed attack; 2) the victim state thus risks violating Article 2(4) of the UN Charter by attacking the armed group; and 3) a potentially higher threshold for an armed attack is proposed when classifying an attack from a non-state-sponsored armed group as an armed attack.

The first question is particularly controversial.[72] For example, Oscar Schachter notes as follows:

> Obviously, it would go too far to say that the mere presence of terrorists in a State meant that the State was involved in their armed attacks, but when a government provides weapon, technical advice, transportation, aid and encouragement to terrorists on a substantial scale it is not unreasonable to conclude that the armed attack is imputable to that government.[73]

However, others have taken a contrary position. For example, Uganda noted in the *Armed Activities* case that 'armed attacks by armed bands whose existence is tolerated by the territorial sovereign generate legal responsibility and therefore constitute armed attacks for the purpose of Article 51.'[74] Ian Brownlie also notes as follows:

> Another permutation of fact concerns the situation in which a State tolerates the presence of armed bands which launch armed attacks against a neighbouring State. There can be little doubt that action by way of self-defence is justified in such cases but the response must be proportionate.[75]

This approach has also been taken by other experts.[76]

However, the earlier discussion already pointed out that such negligence of a state may not even amount to a use of force. Even the use of force requires a certain level of state involvement, namely training, arming and logistical support for armed groups as established in the *Nicaragua* case.[77]

[72] See Kolb, *Ius contra bellum*, 191.

[73] Schachter, 'The Lawful Use of Force', 218. See also K Trapp, 'Back to Basics: Necessity, Proportionality, and the Right of Self-Defence against Non-State Terrorist Actors' (2007) 56 *International and Comparative Law Quarterly* 141, 155.

[74] *Armed Activities* case (Merits), Oral Statement of Uganda, 18 April 2005, para 80. The oral proceedings can be found at the ICJ website, www.icj-cij.org.

[75] I Brownlie, 'General Course on Public International Law' (1995) 255 *Recueil des Cours de l'Académie de Droit International* 9, 204.

[76] See Kelsen, *Principles of International Law*, 62–63; J Delbrück, 'The Fight against Global Terrorism: Self-Defense or Collective Security as International Police Action? Some Comments on the International Legal Implications of the "War against Terrorism"' (2001) 44 *German Yearbook of International Law* 9, 15; Murphy, 'Terrorism', 50; Kolb, *Ius contra bellum*, 191; E Wilmshurst, 'The Chatham House Principles of International Law on the Use of Force in Self-Defence' (2006) 55 *International and Comparative Law Quarterly* 963, 969.

[77] See the earlier discussions in this section.

Since 'armed attack' is generally a higher threshold than 'use of force', if such negligence of a state does not amount to a use of force, it is unlikely that the negligence amounts to an armed attack. Thus, it can be said that classifying an attack by a non-state-sponsored armed group as an armed attack departs from the accepted standard of 'armed attack'.[78]

The second question is related to the first. The concern that the victim state risks violating Article 2(4) of the UN Charter does not arise if there is consent from the government to combat the armed groups.[79] A more difficult case is when the government refuses to take action to prevent activities of the armed groups as in the case of the Taliban government tolerating Al-Qaeda activities on its territory.[80] In this case, the victim state has to prove the existence of an armed attack in order to attack the armed groups[81] or otherwise it would violate Article 2(4) by attacking the territorial state. It has just been noted above that the mere tolerance of the presence of an armed group may not amount to a use of force by the territorial state and much less to an armed attack. Thus, attacking the territorial state with the aim of attacking a non-state-sponsored armed group may amount to a violation of Article 2(4) or even to an armed attack, which could then render the victim state an aggressor.

Finally, the propositions of Judges Simma and Kooijmans in the *Armed Activities* case[82] would potentially lead to the establishment of a higher and special threshold to classify an attack by a non-state-sponsored armed group as an armed attack. It has already been noted that 'armed attack' requires a

[78] As noted earlier, the ICJ most recently confirmed in the *Bosnian Genocide* case the higher threshold of state involvement as established in the *Nicaragua* case. See n 65 above. This indicates that the claim that the attacks of non-state-sponsored armed groups are 'armed attacks' is, at the least, not widely accepted. Guillaume also expressed reservation on the proposition that self-defence measures can be taken against non-state actors without any link to a state: 'Certain doubts have been expressed, however, as to the validity of this argument [that self-defence measures can be taken against non-state actors without any link to a state]. It has thus been emphasized that it would be dubious to derive an instantaneous custom from one isolated precedent. It has further been observed that this evolution would amount to such a radical change in international law that it would require a clearer practice and a more constant *opinio juris*.' Guillaume, 'Terrorism', 547. See also Schrijver, 'Responding to International Terrorism', 286.

[79] Art 20 of the ILC Articles on State Responsibility: 'Valid consent by a State to the commission of a given act by another State precludes the wrongfulness of that act in relation to the former State to the extent that the act remains within the limits of the consent.'

[80] The Security Council had demanded the Taliban to end its support to terrorists. See UNSC Res 1214 (8 December 1998) UN Doc S/RES/1214, para 13; UNSC Res 1267 (15 October 1999) UN Doc S/RES/1267, paras 1 and 2; UNSC Res 1333 (19 December 2000) UN Doc S/RES/1333, paras 1, 2, and 3.

[81] The ICJ noted as follows in the *Oil Platforms* case: 'the Court has simply to determine whether the United States has demonstrated that it was the victim of an "armed attack" by Iran such as to justify it using armed force in self-defence; and the burden of proof of the facts showing the existence of such an attack rests on the United States.' See *Case concerning Oil Platforms* (*Iran v US*) (Merits) [2003] ICJ Rep 161, para 57. See also A Orakhelashvili, 'Legal Stability and Claims of Change: The International Court's Treatment of *Jus ad Bellum* and *Jus in Bello*' (2006) 75 *Nordic Journal of International Law* 371, 379 *ff*.

[82] See text to n 67 above.

certain intensity, certainly higher than that of a 'use of force'.[83] However, no one has suggested that an armed attack should be on a 'large scale' or from a territory not controlled by a state. If one takes this approach, it would create a higher threshold for an armed attack carried out by a non-state-sponsored armed group which is distinct from the threshold employed for an armed attack launched by a state. This leads to a peculiar situation where an armed attack from a state-sponsored armed group need only be of the same intensity as when a state launches an armed attack whereas the mere lack of state backing for an armed group would require an attack to be on a 'large scale' to constitute an armed attack, with an added criterion of the absence of state control over the concerned territory. As a matter of practical application, it is doubtful whether such a separate higher threshold is desirable since the key question of the link between an armed group and a state is almost always problematic and hence it would be more problematic if there were different thresholds of armed attack depending on the presence of state support to armed groups.

Turning to the IHL aspect, an armed conflict between foreign armed forces and a non-state-sponsored armed group is problematic since it does not fit in the legal framework of IHL. IHL only envisages two types of armed conflict: 1) international armed conflict, which takes place between two or more states;[84] and 2) non-international armed conflict, which takes place, within a territory of one state, between a state's armed forces and an armed group or between two or more armed groups.[85]

Such armed conflict is often called 'internationalised non-international armed conflict'. Hans-Peter Gasser characterises it as follows:

> Internationalized non-international armed conflicts, civil wars characterized by the intervention of armed forces of a foreign power, are events within a country with international elements superimposed. They have special features that distinguish them from armed conflicts between states and from civil wars. Regrettably, the law of war has no special provisions applicable to this type of conflict.[86]

[83] See section 3.I.A.

[84] Common Art 2 of the 1949 Geneva Conventions. See also Art 1(4) of the 1977 First Additional Protocol, which adds armed conflict in the exercise of the right of self-determination as an international armed conflict. Protocol Additional to the Geneva Conventions of 12 August 1949, and Relating to the Protection of Victims of International Armed Conflicts (Protocol I) (hereafter 1977 First Additional Protocol) (adopted 8 June 1977, entered into force 7 December 1978) 1125 UNTS 3.

[85] Common Art 3 of the 1949 Geneva Conventions and Art 1(1) of the 1977 Second Additional Protocol. See generally T Meron, 'Classification of Armed Conflict in the Former Yugoslavia: Nicaragua's Fallout' (1998) 92 *American Journal of International Law* 136; R Bartels, 'Timeline, Borderlines and Conflicts: The Historical Evolution of the Legal Divide between International and Non-International Armed Conflicts' (2009) 873 *International Review of the Red Cross* 35; S Vité, 'Typology of Armed Conflicts in International Humanitarian Law: Legal Concepts and Actual Situations' (2009) 873 *International Review of the Red Cross* 69.

[86] Gasser, 'Internationalized Non-International Armed Conflicts', 157. For general references, see n 29 above.

However, the fact that an armed conflict between foreign armed forces and a non-state-sponsored armed group does not fit into the conventional framework of IHL has not caused some to argue that this is not an 'armed conflict' and that IHL is not applicable.[87] The controversies have rather been related to: 1) the threshold of 'armed conflict'; and 2) which IHL rules are applicable between them.

With regard to the first question, it was mentioned earlier that an armed conflict between foreign armed forces and non-state-sponsored armed groups is not an international armed conflict. It also cannot be a non-international armed conflict envisaged in the 1977 Second Additional Protocol since in Article 1(1), it clearly states that: 1) such armed conflict should take place in the territory of a state party; and 2) between the armed forces of that state party and armed groups. For example, the armed conflict in the DRC between the DRC armed forces and armed groups can be qualified as a non-international armed conflict within the meaning of the Second Additional Protocol. This is because the DRC is a party to the Protocol and the armed conflict meets the other criterion above, that is, it takes place between the state's armed forces (DRC armed forces) and armed groups in the DRC.

However, with regard to the armed conflict in the DRC territory between the Ugandan armed forces and the Allied Democratic Forces (or ADF, one of the armed groups in the eastern DRC), the ICJ recognised that the ADF was not supported by the DRC and thus it implicitly confirmed that the armed conflict was one between foreign armed forces and a non-state-sponsored armed group.[88] Although Uganda is a party to the 1977 Second Additional Protocol, it could not be applied vis-à-vis the ADF since, according to Article 1(1) of the Protocol, the armed conflict should take place within Uganda in order to apply it. Thus, if the armed conflict between Uganda and the ADF had taken place in Uganda, the armed conflict could have been a non-international armed conflict within the meaning of the Second Additional Protocol. However, the armed conflict took place in the DRC and thus the Second Additional Protocol could not be applied between Uganda and the ADF. Thus, the thresholds of 'armed conflict' in common Article 2 of the 1949 Geneva Conventions and Article 1(1) of the 1977 Second Additional Protocol are not applicable to an internationalised non-international armed conflict.

The remaining option is the threshold provided in common Article 3 of the 1949 Geneva Conventions, which merely provides that it applies in 'case of armed conflict not of an international character occurring in the territory of one of the High Contracting Parties'. No other conditions are attached. As will be seen later, the application of common Article 3 no

[87] See, eg, David, *Principes de droit des conflits armés*, 148.
[88] *Armed Activities* case (Merits), para 146.

longer depends on the character of the armed conflict and thus applies in any kind of armed conflict. Therefore, the criteria normally used for the application of common Article 3 may be applicable by analogy to an internationalised non-international armed conflict.

This conclusion can also be applied to an armed conflict between UN forces (both state-led and UN-commanded) and a non-state-sponsored armed group. As discussed earlier, this type of armed conflict is neither an international armed conflict nor a non-international armed conflict, but rather an internationalised non-international armed conflict.[89] The threshold of application of IHL for an armed conflict in which UN forces are involved is common Article 3 of the 1949 Geneva Conventions when they are fighting non-state-sponsored armed groups. The threshold of application in Article 1(1) of the 1977 Second Additional Protocol cannot be applied since the Protocol itself is most likely not applicable between UN forces and non-state-sponsored armed groups.[90] Some have suggested that a higher threshold of application should be adopted when UN-commanded forces are involved[91] out of concern that they might be bound by IHL too often, even when acting in self-defence, and deprived of the protection under the 1994 Convention on the Safety of UN and Associated Personnel (hereafter the 1994 Safety Convention).[92] However, this concern is unfounded since common Article 3, which is practically the only threshold relevant since UN-commanded forces most often fight with non-state-sponsored armed groups, already has a higher threshold than common Article 2 of the 1949 Geneva Conventions.[93] Thus, in most cases, the 1994 Safety Convention remains applicable while the situation is still internal disturbances and tensions,[94] and IHL only becomes applicable when it surpasses this level and reaches the threshold of armed conflict in common Article 3 and when UN forces become a party to the non-international armed conflict.

The UN also concurs that IHL is applicable to UN-commanded forces when they are a party to an armed conflict, as reflected in the UN Secretary-General's Bulletin:

[89] See section 4.IV.C.

[90] See section 5.II.A.

[91] On this topic, see generally R Kolb, *Droit humanitaire et opérations de paix internationals* (Bâle, Helbing et Lichtenhahn, 2002) 32 *ff*; A Faite and J Grenier (eds), *Expert Meeting on Multinational Peace Operations: Applicability of International Humanitarian Law and International Human Rights Law to UN Mandated Forces* (Geneva, International Committee of the Red Cross, 2004) 10; M Zwanenburg, *Accountability of Peace Support Operations* (Leiden, Martinus Nijhoff, 2005) 186 *ff*.

[92] Convention on the Safety of United Nations and Associated Personnel (hereafter 1994 Safety Convention) (adopted 9 December 1994, entered into force 15 January 1999) 2051 UNTS 363. See section 4.IV.D for the discussion on IHL and 1994 Safety Convention.

[93] For the discussion on the threshold of application in common Art 3 of the 1949 Geneva Conventions, see further below in this section.

[94] Note that IHL does not apply to 'internal disturbances and tensions' as provided in Art 1 (2) of the 1977 Second Additional Protocol. See further below in this section for discussions.

> The fundamental principles and rules of international humanitarian law set out in the present bulletin are applicable to United Nations when in situations of armed conflict they are actively engaged therein as combatants, to the extent and for the duration of their engagement.[95]

The saving clause 'to the extent and for the duration of their engagement' takes into account the primary character of UN-commanded forces as an intermediary and not as a party to an armed conflict. In most cases, UN-commanded forces are not deployed to combat, even though they often find themselves in between crossfire. The UN troops are thus considered primarily as civilians and are protected as such by IHL or the 1994 Safety Convention.[96] IHL only becomes applicable once the UN-commanded forces become a party to the armed conflict by crossing the threshold of common Article 3 of the 1949 Geneva Conventions when fighting a non-state-sponsored armed group (and common Article 2 when fighting a state's armed forces). The above saving clause takes into account this peculiar situation that UN-commanded forces operate in where they can be civilians or combatants depending on whether they are a party to an armed conflict or not.

IHL is applicable so long as an armed conflict in the sense of common Article 3 of the 1949 Geneva Conventions continues between the UN-commanded forces and a non-state-sponsored armed group (or common Article 2 for an armed conflict with a state's armed forces). The above saving clause can be interpreted as rendering the scope of the application of IHL slightly narrower by arguing that the UN troops were not bound by IHL because they were not engaged in active combat, despite the fact that an armed conflict can exist and continue even with the absence of active combat. The above saving clause should not be understood as such. Once drawn into continuous fighting, such as when UNOSOM II (Somalia) had been fighting Somali armed groups, UN-commanded forces remain a party to the armed conflict and IHL continues to apply until the situation of armed conflict ceases or recourse to IHL becomes unnecessary.

Establishing the existence of an 'armed conflict' within the meaning of common Article 3 is a difficulty in itself. First, situations of internal disturbances and tensions can be excluded as provided in Article 1(2) of the 1977 Second Additional Protocol. A commentary on this provision briefly defines 'internal disturbances and tensions' as follows:

> [R]iots, such as demonstrations without a concerted plan from the outset; isolated and sporadic acts of violence, as opposed to military operations carried

[95] UN Secretary-General 'Secretary-General's Bulletin: Observance by United Nations Forces of International Humanitarian Law' (6 August 1999) UN Doc ST/SGB/1999/13, Section 1.1.

[96] UN Secretariat, 'Note on the Protection of Peacekeeping Personnel under International Humanitarian Law' (2006) *United Nations Juridical Yearbook* 518, para 8.

> out by armed forces or armed groups; other acts of a similar nature, including, in particular, large scale arrests of people for their activities or opinions.[97]

Thus, common Article 3 will not be applicable in any situation at this level or lower.

The ICTY in the *Tadic* case also noted that an 'armed conflict' should have a certain degree of intensity:[98] 'an armed conflict exists whenever there is a resort to armed force between States or protracted armed violence between governmental authorities and organized armed groups or between such groups within a State.'[99]

The next step is to assess the situation against various criteria. There are certain core criteria, which were also suggested in the Diplomatic Conference of the 1949 Geneva Conventions:

> (1) That the Party in revolt against the *de jure* Government possesses an organized military force, an authority responsible for its acts, acting within a determinate territory and having the means of respecting and ensuring respect for the Convention.
> (2) That the legal Government is obliged to have recourse to the regular military forces against insurgents organized as military and in possession of a part of the national territory.[100]

Thus, it seems possible to use, by analogy, the criteria to qualify common Article 3 type of non-international armed conflict to an internationalised non-international armed conflict.

Even if an internationalised non-international armed conflict can be qualified as an 'armed conflict' within the meaning of IHL, there is still the question of which IHL rules are applicable. Since such armed conflict is neither international nor non-international armed conflict, the law of international and non-international armed conflict does not apply automatically. However, since it can still be qualified as an 'armed conflict', IHL is applicable. There are at least two positions: 1) the law of international armed conflict is fully applicable; and 2) the rules contained in the law of non-international armed conflict are applicable.

The first position has received little support from states in particular. The proposition that the law of international armed conflict should be applicable in any kind of armed conflict has been advanced time and again.[101] Such a view was taken, for example, by the ICRC, which

[97] Sandoz et al (eds), *Commentary*, para 4474.

[98] For the requirement of intensity for international armed conflict, see J de Preux, *Commentary on the Geneva Conventions of 12 August 1949* Vol III (Geneva, International Committee of the Red Cross, 1960) 23.

[99] *Tadic Case* (Jurisdiction, Appeals) ICTY-IT-94-1 (2 October 1995), para 70.

[100] Pictet et al, *Commentary* Vol I, 49.

[101] See, eg, T Meron, 'International Criminalization of Internal Atrocities' (1995) 89 *American Journal of International Law* 554; J Stewart, 'Towards a Single Definition of Armed Conflict in International Humanitarian Law: A Critique of Internationalized Armed Conflict' (2003) 85 *International Review of the Red Cross* 313.

proposed Article 2 of the draft 1949 Geneva Conventions adopted by the 17th International Conference of the Red Cross in Stockholm in 1948:

> In all cases of armed conflict which are not of an international character, especially cases of civil war, colonial conflicts, or wars of religion, which may occur in the territory of one or more of the High Contracting Parties, the implementing of the principles of the present Convention shall be obligatory on each of the adversaries.[102]

From a humanitarian perspective, such a view must be unreservedly embraced. However, such a view should be seen in context since up to now, the distinction between international and non-international armed conflict has been maintained and the applicable rules are distinguished accordingly.

The second position, that the rules contained in the law of non-international armed conflict are applicable, has received wider support and is most sound as a matter of law. These rules consist of three sets: 1) common Article 3 of the 1949 Geneva Conventions; 2) IHL treaties applicable in common Article 3 type of armed conflict or in all circumstances; and 3) customary law of non-international armed conflict.[103] These IHL rules are applicable in both international and non-international armed conflict and thus they are in any case applicable in any kind of armed conflict. The ICJ also noted as follows in the *Nicaragua* case:

> Because the minimum rules applicable to international and to non-international conflicts are identical, there is no need to address the question whether those actions must be looked at in the context of the rules which operate for the one or for the other category of conflict.[104]

The three sets of IHL rules referred to above are minimum rules applicable in internationalised non-international armed conflict. Any other IHL rules can be applicable if the conflicting parties agree to apply them.[105]

First, common Article 3 of the 1949 Geneva Conventions can be seen as applicable in any kind of armed conflict. The ICJ noted as follows in the *Nicaragua* case:

> There is no doubt that, in the event of international armed conflict, these rules [in common Article 3] also constitute a minimum yardstick . . . they are rules which, in the Court's opinion, reflect what the Court in 1949 called 'elementary considerations of humanity'.[106]

[102] See de Preux, *Commentary*, 31. See also Sandoz et al (eds), *Commentary*, para 86.

[103] This conclusion is supported by the Institute of International Law, 'L'application du droit international', 368. See also Kolb, *Ius in bello*, 88–89.

[104] *Nicaragua* case (Merits), para 219.

[105] See common Art 3(2) of the 1949 Geneva Conventions. A commentary on common Art 3 also notes as follows: 'Care has been taken to state, in Article 3, that the applicable provisions represent a compulsory minimum. The words "*as a minimum*" must be understood in that sense. At the same time they are an invitation to exceed that minimum.' See Pictet et al, *Commentary* Vol I, 52.

[106] *Nicaragua* case (Merits), para 218.

The ICTY Appeals Chamber further noted in the *Tadic* case that 'at least with respect to the minimum rules in common Article 3, the character of the conflict is irrelevant'.[107] This was also confirmed in the Trial Chamber earlier[108] and none of the judges on this case objected to this conclusion.

Secondly, IHL treaties which apply in common Article 3 type of armed conflict or in all circumstances are also applicable to any kind of armed conflict. These are the 1954 Cultural Property Convention and its Protocol,[109] 1972 Biological Weapons Convention,[110] 1980 Conventional Weapons Convention and its Protocols I–V,[111]1993 Chemical Weapons Convention,[112] 1997 Convention on Anti-Personnel Mines[113] and 2008 Convention on Cluster Munitions.[114] These are in any case applicable in both international and non-international armed conflict and thus the character of the armed conflict is irrelevant. They apply in any kind of armed conflict so long as the states involved have consented to be bound by them.

Finally, customary rules of non-international armed conflict can in any case be found in customary rules of international armed conflict and thus, it is applicable in any kind of armed conflict. The scope of the customary

[107] *Tadic Case* (Jurisdiction, Appeals), para 102.

[108] *Tadic Case* (Jurisdiction, Trial) ICTY-IT-94-1 (10 August 1995), para 74 and *Tadic Case* (Judgment, Trial) ICTY-94-1-T (7 May 1997), para 607.

[109] Art 19(1) of the Convention for the Protection of Cultural Property in the Event of Armed Conflict (adopted 14 May 1954, entered into force 7 August1956) 249 UNTS 240. See also Art 22(1) of the Second Protocol to the 1954 Convention for the Protection of Cultural Property in the Event of Armed Conflict (adopted 26 March 1999, entered into force 9 March 2004) 2253 UNTS 172.

[110] Art I of the Convention on the Prohibition of the Development, Production and Stockpiling of Bacteriological (Biological) and Toxin Weapons and on their Destruction (adopted 10 April 1972, entered into force 26 March 1975) 1015 UNTS 163.

[111] See Art 1(2) of the Convention on Prohibitions or Restrictions on the Use of Certain Conventional Weapons Which May Be Deemed to be Excessively Injurious or to Have Indiscriminate Effects, Amendment Article 1 (adopted 21 December 2001, entered into force 18 May 2004) 2260 UNTS 82. See also the Convention on Prohibitions and Restrictions on the Use of Certain Conventional Weapons Which May Be Deemed to Be Excessively Injurious or to Have Indiscriminate Effects (adopted 10 October 1980, entered into force 2 December 1983) 1342 UNTS 137; Protocol on Non-Detectable Fragments (Protocol I) (adopted 10 October 1980, entered into force 2 December 1983) 1342 UNTS 168; Protocol on Prohibitions or Restrictions on the Use of Mines, Booby-Traps and Other Devices (Protocol II) (adopted 10 October 1980, entered into force 2 December 1983) 1342 UNTS 168; Protocol on Prohibitions or Restrictions on the Use of Incendiary Weapons (Protocol III) (adopted 10 October 1980, entered into force 2 December 1983) 1342 UNTS 171; Protocol on Blinding Laser Weapons (Protocol IV) (adopted 13 October 1995, entered into force 30 July 1998) 2024 UNTS 167; Amended Protocol II; Protocol on Explosive Remnants of War (Protocol V) (adopted 28 November 2003, entered into force 12 November 2006) 2399 UNTS 100.

[112] Art I(1) of the Convention on the Prohibition of the Development, Production, Stockpiling and Use of Chemical Weapons and on Their Destruction (adopted 3 September 1992, entered into force 29 April 1997) 1974 UNTS 45.

[113] Art 1(1) of the Convention on the Prohibition of the Use, Stockpiling, Production and Transfer of Anti-Personnel Mines and on their Destruction (adopted 18 September 1997, entered into force 1 March 1999) 2056 UNTS 211.

[114] Convention on Cluster Munitions (adopted 30 May 2008, entered into force 1 August 2010) (2009) 48 ILM 354.

rules is not entirely clear and it evolves with the accumulation of new practice, but a useful indication can be found in Jean-Marie Henckaerts and Louise Doswald-Beck's *Customary International Humanitarian Law*.[115] Thus, even if an internationalised non-international armed conflict does not fit in the traditional framework of IHL, there are still applicable IHL rules.

The determination of whether an armed group is acting on behalf of a state or not is crucial since the applicability of *jus ad bellum* and *jus in bello* is clear when it is acting on behalf of a state but unclear when it is not. Even if *jus ad bellum* and *jus in bello* are applicable in both situations, the applicable rules differ greatly from one to the other. This is particularly the case with IHL since if an armed group is acting on behalf of a state and fighting foreign armed forces, the law of international armed conflict is fully applicable and, for example, the members of an armed group may qualify as prisoners of war who are entitled to the full protection of the 1949 Third Geneva Convention. On the other hand, if an armed group is independent from a state and fighting foreign armed forces, the rules contained in the law of non-international armed conflict are applicable. The difference between the scope of protection in the former and the latter case is evident. Moreover, the applicability of *jus ad bellum* and *jus in bello* is certain in the former case while it is highly uncertain in the latter case and thus, ensuring compliance with the law may be more difficult in the latter case. The US's summary rejection of prisoner-of-war status for the members of the Taliban forces and Al-Qaeda in the aftermath of the US attacks on Afghanistan in 2001 is one example of the danger of the complexity of establishing the applicable IHL rules in an armed conflict between foreign armed forces and a non-state-sponsored armed group.[116]

[115] Henckaerts and Doswald-Beck, *Customary International Humanitarian Law* Vol I. See also J-M Henckaerts and L Doswald-Beck (eds), *Customary International Humanitarian Law* Vol II: Practice (Geneva, International Committee of the Red Cross and Cambridge, Cambridge University Press, 2005).

[116] See, eg, US Government, 'White House Press Secretary Announcement of President Bush's Determination Re Legal Status of Taliban and Al Qaeda Detainees' (7 February 2002), US Department of State website, www.state.gov/s/l/38727.htm. For various views on this topic, see *Rasul v Bush*, 542 US 466, Brief *Amicus Curiae* of Law Professors, Former Legal Advisers of the Department of State and Ambassadors, Retired Judge Advocate General and Retired Military Commanders, and Other International Law Specialists in Support of Respondents; G Aldrich, 'The Taliban, Al Qaeda, and the Determination of Illegal Combatants' (2002) 96 *American Journal of International Law* 891; Y Arai-Takahashi, 'Disentangling Legal Quagmires: The Legal Characterisation of the Armed Conflicts in Afghanistan since 6/7 October 2001 and the Question of Prisoner of War Status' (2002) 5 *Yearbook of International Humanitarian Law* 61; R Goldman and B Tittemore, 'Unprivileged Combatants and the Hostilities in Afghanistan: Their Status and Rights under International Humanitarian and Human Rights Law' (December 2002) *American Society of International Law Task Force on Terrorism*, American Society of International Law website, www.asil.org/taskforce/goldman.pdf; F King and O Swaak-Goldman, 'The Applicability of International Humanitarian Law to the "War against Terrorism"' (2002) 15 *Hague Yearbook of International Law* 39; A McDonald, 'Defining the War on Terror and the Status of Detainees: Comments

Despite various problems on the applicability of the law of self-defence and IHL to an internationalised non-international armed conflict, Chapter VII can play an important role in regulating the use of force in such an armed conflict. First, the determination of a situation as a 'threat to the peace' under Article 39 of the UN Charter in particular does not depend on the character of an armed conflict and in practice, internationalised non-international armed conflicts have been determined as a threat to the peace in a number of cases.[117] Once such determination takes place, Chapter VII enables the Security Council to take non-military and military enforcement action, such as by arms embargoes, economic sanctions, peacekeeping operations, or multinational forces commanded by a state. As was discussed earlier,[118] Chapter VII measures can play an important role in complementing IHL and regulating the use of force, particularly in non-international armed conflict and internationalised non-international armed conflict.

In short, an armed conflict between foreign armed forces and a non-state-sponsored armed group in another state's territory is a serious gap where the applicability of *jus ad bellum* and *jus in bello* is often unclear. When an armed group is supported by a state in such an armed conflict, it is relatively clear that its attack amounts to a use of force, armed attack and international armed conflict, but the difficult question is to establish the nexus between the armed group and the state. In the absence of such a

on the Presentation of Judge George Aldrich' (2002) *Humanitäres Völkerrecht* 206; Y Naqvi, 'Doubtful Prisoner-of-War Status' (2002) 847 *International Review of the Red Cross* 571; US Government, 'President Meets with Afghan Interim Authority Chairman' (28 January 2002), White House archive, georgewbush-whitehouse.archives.gov; R Wolfrum and C Philipp, 'The Status of the Taliban'; K Dörmann, 'The Legal Situation of "Unlawful/ Unprivileged Combatants"' (2003) 849 *International Review of the Red Cross* 45; M Sassòli, '"Unlawful Combatants": The Law and Whether It Needs to Be Revised' (2003) *American Society of International Law Proceedings* 196; R Wolfrum, 'The Attack of September 11, 2001, the Wars against the Taliban and Iraq: Is There a Need to Reconsider International Law on the Recourse to Force and the Rules in Armed Conflict?' (2003) 7 *Max Planck Yearbook of United Nations Law* 1, 36; Y Dinstein, *The Conduct of Hostilities under the Law of International Armed Conflict* (Cambridge, Cambridge University Press, 2004) 47; M Sassòli, 'The Status of Persons Held in Guantanamo under International Humanitarian Law' (2004) 2 *Journal of International Criminal Justice* 96; J Yoo, 'The Status of Soldiers and Terrorists under the Geneva Conventions' (2004) 3 *Chinese Journal of International Law* 135; S Borelli, 'Casting Light on the Legal Black Hole: International Law and Detentions Abroad in the "War on Terror"' (2005) 857 *International Review of the Red Cross* 39; Duffy, *The 'War on Terror'*, 379 *ff*; M Sassòli and L Olson, 'The Relationship between International Humanitarian and Human Rights Law Where It Matters: Admissible Killing and Internment of Fighters in Non-International Armed Conflicts' (2008) 871 *International Review of the Red Cross* 599; K Arai, 'The Status and Treatment of Terrorists under the Law of Armed Conflict' (2009) 108-2 *Journal of International Law and Diplomacy* 28; Chatham House and the International Committee of the Red Cross, 'Expert Meeting on Procedural Safeguards for Security Detention in Non-International Armed Conflict' (2009) 876 *International Review of the Red Cross* 859; R Goodman, 'The Detention of Civilians in Armed Conflict' (2009) 103 *American Journal of International Law* 48.

[117] See, eg, UNSC Res 1234 (9 April 1999) UN Doc S/RES/1234 on the situation in the eastern DRC. For further discussion on this topic, see section 4.II.C.

[118] See sections 4.IV and 4.V.

nexus, whether an attack of such an armed group can be a use of force or an armed attack and the character of such armed conflict is unclear. The applicability of IHL seems relatively clearer but there may still be controversies with the threshold of 'armed conflict' and the applicable IHL rules. Such uncertainties in the applicability of *jus ad bellum* and *jus in bello* to an internationalised non-international armed conflict can potentially be a cause of non-compliance with *jus ad bellum* and *jus in bello*. Thus, clarification on the applicability of *jus ad bellum* and *jus in bello* and applicable IHL rules in such an armed conflict is urgently necessary. Chapter VII of the UN Charter, however, can play an important role since its application does not depend on the character of an armed conflict.

B. Mixed Armed Conflict

The previous section discussed one peculiar type of armed conflict, which was non-international armed conflict where foreign armed forces and armed groups intervene. This section will discuss the common problem for *jus ad bellum* and *jus in bello* arising from an armed conflict consisting of some or all of international, non-international, and internationalised non-international armed conflict (mixed armed conflict).

Many recent armed conflicts consist of some or all kinds of armed conflicts, namely international, non-international, and internationalised non-international armed conflict. The *Tadic* case in ICTY was a prime example[119] but it can also be seen in recent armed conflicts in and around, for example, the eastern DRC,[120] Sudan,[121] Iraq,[122] Lebanon,[123] Georgia,[124]

[119] See *Tadic Case* (Jurisdiction, Appeals), para 77.

[120] See generally *Armed Activities* case (Merits) and the oral and written statements during the proceedings. The oral and written statements can be found at the ICJ website, www.icj-cij.org.

[121] See generally UNSC, 'Report of the International Commission of Inquiry on Darfur to the United Nations Secretary-General' (25 January 2005) UN Doc S/2005/60.

[122] See, eg, K Dörmann and L Colassis, 'International Humanitarian Law in the Iraq Conflict' (2004) 47 *German Yearbook of International Law* 293.

[123] See, eg, UNHRC, 'Report of the Commission of Inquiry on Lebanon Pursuant to Human Rights Council Resolution S-2/1' (23 November 2006) UN Doc A/HRC/3/2. The Commission's classification of this armed conflict as an international armed conflict in paragraph 60 is problematic so far as the fighting between Hizbullah and Israel is concerned. Other reports were more cautious in classifying the armed conflict. See, eg, Human Rights Watch, *Why They Died: Civilian Casualties in Lebanon during the 2006 War* (New York, Human Rights Watch, 2007) 31–32; A Zimmermann, 'The Second Lebanon War: *Jus ad Bellum*, *Jus in Bello* and the Issue of Proportionality' (2007) 11 *Max Planck Yearbook of United Nations Law* 99, 126–29; Vité, 'Typology of Armed Conflicts', 91–92.

[124] Council of the European Union, Independent International Fact-Finding Mission on the Conflict in Georgia, 'Report' Vol II (September 2009) 300–01. See also C Henderson and J Green, 'The *Jus ad Bellum* and Entities Short of Statehood in the Report on the Conflict in Georgia' (2010) 59 *International and Comparative Law Quarterly* 129.

and Gaza.[125] The situation in the eastern DRC in particular represents unprecedented complexity of 'mixed' armed conflict in which at least nine states (Angola, Burundi, Chad, DRC, Namibia, Rwanda, Sudan, Uganda, and Zimbabwe), countless armed groups, and UN forces have been involved in international, non-international, and internationalised non-international armed conflict, and in which some parties were fighting each other at one time and forming a coalition at another.[126] This section will use the DRC case as an example to illustrate the highly complex nature of applying *jus ad bellum* and *jus in bello* in a 'mixed' armed conflict.

First, establishing a use of force and an armed attack is problematic since it is extremely difficult to establish whether an armed group was acting on behalf of a state when there are countless armed groups in the same region, which act on behalf of a state at one time but not at another. In the case of the DRC, there were countless armed groups in the eastern DRC which regularly fought with the DRC, Uganda, Rwanda, and Burundi but it was not clear which armed groups were acting on behalf of which states. The ICJ in the *Armed Activities* case concluded that the Mouvement de libération du Congo was not acting on behalf of Uganda[127] and the Allied Democratic Forces were not acting on behalf of the DRC,[128] but it is extremely cumbersome to conduct such a legal assessment for all the other armed groups.

An additional problem is the difficulty of identifying who carried out a use of force or an armed attack, who is taking self-defence measures against whom, and who should be complying with the principles of necessity and proportionality. For example, the ICJ in the *Armed Activities* case recognised that Uganda had carried out a use of force[129] and, implicitly, an armed attack,[130] and that the DRC was entitled to exercise the right of self-defence against Uganda in an international armed conflict which began in 1998.[131] However, the DRC was also engaged in international armed conflicts with Rwanda[132] and Burundi[133] but it was less clear which side

[125] UNHRC, 'Report of the United Nations Fact-Finding Mission on the Gaza Conflict' (25 September 2009) UN Doc A/HRC/12/48, 270–85; Human Rights Watch, *White Flag Deaths: Killings of Palestinian Civilians during Operation Cast Lead* (New York, Human Rights Watch, 2009) 51–55; Human Rights Watch, *I Lost Everything: Israel's Unlawful Destruction of Property during Operation Cast Lead* (New York, Human Rights Watch, 2010) 107–17.

[126] See generally UNGA, 'Democratic Republic of the Congo' (1998) 52 UNYB 79, 79 *ff*; UNGA, 'Democratic Republic of the Congo' (1999) 53 UNYB 81, 81 *ff*. See also 1999 Agreement for a Cease-Fire in the Democratic Republic of Congo; *Armed Activities* case (Merits).

[127] *Armed Activities* case (Merits), para 160.

[128] *Armed Activities* case (Merits), para 146.

[129] *Armed Activities* case (Merits), para 165.

[130] *Armed Activities* case (Merits), para 304.

[131] *Armed Activities* case (Merits), para 304.

[132] See generally n 137 below.

[133] International Crisis Group, 'Scramble for the Congo: Anatomy of an Ugly War' (20 December 2000) ICG Africa Report No 26, 20, International Crisis Group website, www.crisisgroup.org.

was entitled to exercise the right of self-defence. If the DRC had launched 'armed attacks' against Rwanda and Burundi indirectly by supporting armed groups in the eastern DRC, the DRC would have been the aggressor vis-à-vis Rwanda and Burundi despite the fact that it was a victim state vis-à-vis Uganda. On the contrary, if Rwanda and Burundi had launched an armed attack, the DRC would have been the victim state vis-à-vis all three states (Uganda, Rwanda, and Burundi). When there are multiple states exercising the right of self-defence, it also complicates the application of the principles of necessity and proportionality. Using the above case, the DRC would have to comply with the principles of necessity and proportionality when taking self-defence measures against Uganda but if the DRC was an aggressor vis-à-vis Rwanda and Burundi, then Rwanda and Burundi would have to comply with the principles of necessity and proportionality. The assessment of the proportionality and necessity of self-defence should be done separately between different conflicting parties such as between the DRC and Uganda; Rwanda and the DRC; and Burundi and the DRC.

Another example is the fighting between Rwanda and Uganda in the DRC territory.[134] First, it should be established which side, Rwanda or Uganda, had launched a use of force and an armed attack. Clearly, the fact that they were fighting on the DRC territory does not affect the application of *jus ad bellum* since a use of force and an armed attack can be carried out not only against a state's territory but also against, for example, armed forces outside the territory.[135] Secondly, the legal consequences of their presence on the DRC territory should be established. Was the fighting between Rwanda and Uganda on the DRC territory itself a use of force and an armed attack against the DRC? Could the DRC have carried out self-defence measures against the two states even if its territory was not the specific object of attack by Rwanda and Uganda? Or did Rwanda and Uganda have a justification to be present in the DRC territory because the armed groups in the DRC territory had attacked these two states previously? An indication can be found in the *Armed Activities* case in which the ICJ concluded that whatever the motive for the presence in a foreign state's territory, the fact that foreign armed forces were present in the territory itself amounts to a use of force. After citing the relevant paragraphs of the 1970 Friendly Relations Declaration, the ICJ noted as follows:

> The Court considers that the obligations arising under the principles of non-use of force and non-intervention were violated by Uganda even if the objectives of Uganda were not to overthrow President Kabila [of the DRC], and were directed to securing towns and airports for reason of its perceived security needs, and in support of the parallel activity of those engaged in civil war.[136]

[134] See UNSC Res 1304 (16 June 2000) UN Doc S/RES/1304.
[135] See Dinstein, *War, Aggression and Self-Defence*, 199–201.
[136] *Armed Activities* case (Merits), para 163.

It follows that even if the objective of Rwanda and Uganda was not to attack the DRC territory per se, their invasion of and presence in the DRC themselves constituted a use of force and an armed attack and the DRC was entitled to take self-defence measures against Rwanda and Uganda. Even so, the application of the law of self-defence was overly complicated. Suppose that Uganda was entitled to take self-defence measures against Rwanda. Then, Uganda had to observe the principles of necessity and proportionality vis-à-vis Rwanda while when the DRC was attacking Uganda and Rwanda, it was the DRC which had to observe the principles of necessity and proportionality. Clearly, these are difficult questions on both law and fact. It suffices to note that a 'mixed' armed conflict can cause difficulties in identifying who carried out a use of force or an armed attack, who is taking self-defence measures against whom, and who should be complying with the principles of necessity and proportionality.

With regard to IHL, the situation is more complex since the applicable IHL rules differ in international, non-international, and internationalised non-international armed conflict. For example, in the eastern DRC since 1997, a number of international armed conflicts took place between the DRC, Zimbabwe, Namibia on one hand and Burundi, Rwanda, and Uganda on the other.[137] There have also been non-international armed conflicts between the DRC armed forces and non-state-sponsored armed groups in the DRC, as well as among different armed groups.[138]

[137] See the UN Secretary-General's reports on MONUC: UNSC, 'Second Report of the Secretary-General on the United Nations Organization Mission in the Democratic Republic of the Congo' (18 April 2000) UN Doc S/2000/330, para 30 (DRC, Namibia, Zimbabwe v Rwanda, Uganda) and para 35 (DRC v Rwanda, Rwanda-backed armed group); UNSC, 'Third Report of the Secretary-General on the United Nations Organization Mission in the Democratic Republic of the Congo' (12 June 2000) UN Doc S/2000/566, paras 13–16 (Rwanda v Uganda); UNSC, 'Fourth Report of the Secretary-General on the United Nations Organization Mission in the Democratic Republic of the Congo' (21 September 2000) UN Doc S/2000/888, para 23 (DRC v Uganda-backed armed group) and para 26 (DRC v Rwanda, Rwanda-backed armed group); UNSC, 'Fifth Report of the Secretary-General on the United Nations Organization Mission in the Democratic Republic of the Congo' (6 December 2000) UN Doc S/2000/1156, para 26 (DRC v armed group), paras 28 and 29 (DRC v Republic of the Congo), and para 30 (DRC, Namibia, Zimbabwe v Rwanda, Rwanda-backed armed group); UNSC, 'Sixth Report of the Secretary-General on the United Nations Organization Mission in the Democratic Republic of the Congo' (21 February 2001) UN Doc S/2001/128, para 20 (DRC v Rwanda, Rwanda-backed armed groups); UNSC, 'Twenty-First Report of the Secretary-General on the United Nations Organization Mission in the Democratic Republic of the Congo' (13 June 2006) UN Doc S/2006/390, para 31 (DRC v Uganda).

[138] See UN Secretary-General's reports on MONUC: UNSC, 'Second Report of the Secretary-General on the United Nations Organization Mission in the Democratic Republic of the Congo' (18 April 2000) UN Doc S/2000/330, paras 30, 31, and 36 (DRC v armed groups, armed groups v armed groups); UNSC, 'Third Report of the Secretary-General on the United Nations Organization Mission in the Democratic Republic of the Congo' (12 June 2000) UN Doc S/2000/566, paras 22 and 23 (DRC v armed groups) and para 24 (armed groups v armed groups); UNSC, 'Fourth Report of the Secretary-General on the United Nations Organization Mission in the Democratic Republic of the Congo' (21 September 2000) UN Doc S/2000/888, para 22 (DRC v armed group) and para 27 (armed groups v armed groups); UNSC, 'Fifth Report of the Secretary-General on the United Nations Organization Mission

Finally, there have been internationalised non-international armed conflicts between, on one hand, Rwandan/Ugandan/DRC armed forces, and MONUC (UN forces in the DRC), and on the other hand, non-state-sponsored armed groups in and around the eastern DRC.[139] Thus,

in the Democratic Republic of the Congo' (6 December 2000) UN Doc S/2000/1156, para 26 (DRC v armed group) and para 34 (armed groups v armed groups); UNSC, 'Sixth Report of the Secretary-General on the United Nations Organization Mission in the Democratic Republic of the Congo' (21 February 2001) UN Doc S/2001/128, para 24 (DRC v armed group), para 25 (armed groups v armed groups), and para 26 (armed group v armed group); UNSC, 'Seventh Report of the Secretary-General on the United Nations Organization Mission in the Democratic Republic of the Congo' (17 April 2001) UN Doc S/2001/373, para 27 (DRC v armed groups); UNSC, 'Eighth Report of the Secretary-General on the United Nations Organization Mission in the Democratic Republic of the Congo' (8 June 2001) UN Doc S/2001/572, para 19 (DRC v armed groups); UNSC, 'Ninth Report of the Secretary-General on the United Nations Organization Mission in the Democratic Republic of the Congo' (16 October 2001) UN Doc S/2001/970, para 21 (armed groups v armed groups); UNSC, 'Tenth Report of the Secretary-General on the United Nations Organization Mission in the Democratic Republic of the Congo' (15 February 2002) UN Doc S/2002/169, paras 25–27 (armed group v armed group); UNSC, 'Eleventh Report of the Secretary-General on the United Nations Organization Mission in the Democratic Republic of the Congo' (18 October 2002) UN Doc S/2002/1180, paras 15, 17, 20, and 21 (armed group v armed group); UNSC, 'Thirteenth Report of the Secretary-General on the United Nations Organization Mission in the Democratic Republic of the Congo' (21 February 2003) UN Doc S/2003/211, paras 7 and 9 (armed group v armed group); UNSC, 'Second Special Report of the Secretary-General on the United Nations Organization Mission in the Democratic Republic of the Congo' (27 May 2003) UN Doc S/2003/566, paras 8, 16, and 18 (armed group v armed group); UNSC, 'Fourteenth Report of the Secretary-General on the United Nations Organization Mission in the Democratic Republic of the Congo' (17 November 2003) UN Doc S/2003/1098, para 3 (armed group v armed group); UNSC, 'Sixteenth Report of the Secretary-General on the United Nations Organization Mission in the Democratic Republic of the Congo' (31 December 2004) UN Doc S/2004/1034, para 16 (armed groups v armed groups) and para 19 (DRC v armed group); UNSC, 'Seventeenth Report of the Secretary-General on the United Nations Organization Mission in the Democratic Republic of the Congo' (15 March 2005) UN Doc S/2005/167, para 14 (armed groups v armed groups); UNSC, 'Nineteenth Report of the Secretary-General on the United Nations Organization Mission in the Democratic Republic of the Congo' (26 September 2005) UN Doc S/2005/603, para 21 (armed groups v armed groups) and para 25 (DRC v armed groups); UNSC, 'Twentieth Report of the Secretary-General on the United Nations Organization Mission in the Democratic Republic of the Congo' (28 December 2005) UN Doc S/2005/832, paras 23 and 26 (DRC v armed groups); UNSC, 'Report Pursuant to Paragraphs 10 and 14 of Security Council Resolution 1649 (2005)' (22 May 2006) UN Doc S/2006/310, para 29 (DRC v armed groups); UNSC, 'Twenty-First Report of the Secretary-General on the United Nations Organization Mission in the Democratic Republic of the Congo' (13 June 2006) UN Doc S/2006/390, para 33, 36, and 39 (DRC v armed groups).

139 See UN Secretary-General's reports on MONUC: UNSC, 'Second Report of the Secretary-General on the United Nations Organization Mission in the Democratic Republic of the Congo' (18 April 2000) UN Doc S/2000/330, para 30 (armed groups v Rwanda); UNSC, 'Third Report of the Secretary-General on the United Nations Organization Mission in the Democratic Republic of the Congo' (12 June 2000) UN Doc S/2000/566, para 24 (armed groups v Rwanda); UNSC, 'Fifth Report of the Secretary-General on the United Nations Organization Mission in the Democratic Republic of the Congo' (6 December 2000) UN Doc S/2000/1156, para 26 (DRC v armed group) and para 30 (armed groups v Rwanda, Rwanda-backed armed group); UNSC, 'Sixth Report of the Secretary-General on the United Nations Organization Mission in the Democratic Republic of the Congo' (21 February 2001) UN Doc S/2001/128, para 26 (armed group v Uganda); UNSC, 'Seventh Report of the Secretary-General on the United Nations Organization Mission in the Democratic Republic of the

one conflicting party has been involved in different kinds of armed conflict and hence had to comply with different IHL rules according to the adversary.

For example, the DRC armed forces had to apply the law of international armed conflict when fighting armed groups supported by Rwanda and Uganda but had to apply the rules contained in the law of non-international armed conflict when fighting armed groups not supported by any state. Similarly, Rwanda and Uganda had to apply the law of international armed conflict when fighting the DRC armed forces but had to apply the rules contained in the law of non-international armed conflict when fighting non-state-sponsored armed groups in the DRC. The armed groups in and around the DRC had to apply the law of international armed conflict when backed by a state and fighting against a state's armed forces. When the armed groups were not backed by any state, they had to apply the rules contained in the law of non-international armed conflict when fighting against Rwanda, Uganda, DRC, MONUC, and other armed groups. As can be seen, the application of IHL is highly complex in a 'mixed' armed conflict.

On one hand, some suggest that such a 'mixed' armed conflict should be considered as one single international armed conflict and apply the law of international armed conflict.[140] On the other hand, the practice of the ICJ, ICTY and ICRC is to distinguish different types of armed conflicts even if they exist side by side, and apply different IHL rules according to the type of armed conflict. As a matter of law, the latter approach is correct since international armed conflict and non-international armed conflict

Congo' (17 April 2001) UN Doc S/2001/373, para 27 (DRC allied forces v armed groups); UNSC, 'Ninth Report of the Secretary-General on the United Nations Organization Mission in the Democratic Republic of the Congo' (16 October 2001) UN Doc S/2001/970, para 24 (armed groups v Rwanda-backed armed groups); UNSC, 'Eleventh Report of the Secretary-General on the United Nations Organization Mission in the Democratic Republic of the Congo' (18 October 2002) UN Doc S/2002/1180, para 18 (armed group v Rwanda, Rwanda-backed armed group); UNSC, 'Third Special Report of the Secretary-General on the United Nations Organization Mission in the Democratic Republic of the Congo' (16 August 2004) UN Doc S/2004/650, para 45 (armed group v MONUC); UNSC, 'Sixteenth Report of the Secretary-General on the United Nations Organization Mission in the Democratic Republic of the Congo' (31 December 2004) UN Doc S/2004/1034, para 11 (armed group v MONUC); UNSC, 'Seventeenth Report of the Secretary-General on the United Nations Organization Mission in the Democratic Republic of the Congo' (15 March 2005) UN Doc S/2005/167, paras 16 and 19 (MONUC v armed groups); UNSC, 'Eighteenth Report of the Secretary-General on the United Nations Organization Mission in the Democratic Republic of the Congo' (2 August 2005) UN Doc S/2005/506, para 34 (armed group v MONUC); UNSC, 'Twentieth Report of the Secretary-General on the United Nations Organization Mission in the Democratic Republic of the Congo' (28 December 2005) UN Doc S/2005/832, paras 23 and 26 (armed groups v MONUC); 'Report Pursuant to Paragraphs 10 and 14 of Security Council Resolution 1649 (2005)' (22 May 2006) UN Doc S/2006/310, para 29 (armed groups v MONUC); UNSC, 'Twenty-First Report of the Secretary-General on the United Nations Organization Mission in the Democratic Republic of the Congo' (13 June 2006) UN Doc S/2006/390, paras 33, 35, 36, 37, and 39 (armed groups v MONUC).

[140] See n 101 above.

are distinguished in IHL. However, as the DRC case and the *Tadic* case prove, the application of IHL is highly complex when there are several armed conflicts existing at the same time in the same region, which consist of a mixture of international, non-international, and internationalised armed conflict. This will potentially have a negative effect on the compliance with IHL when the conflicting parties have to comply with different IHL rules according to the adversary. At the same time, the former approach, that such a 'mixed' armed conflict should be seen as one single international armed conflict, is not strictly in conformity with IHL since, as noted above, international armed conflict and non-international armed conflict are separated in IHL and different rules are applicable to each of them.

At present, it is inevitable that different types of armed conflict are distinguished even when they are mixed but clearly there needs to be a development in IHL to respond more effectively to such a 'mixed' armed conflict.[141] The development of IHL is a different question which deserves a separate study and thus will not be dealt with further.[142]

Finally, as similar to an armed conflict involving interventions by foreign armed forces or armed groups, Chapter VII of the UN Charter can play an important role in 'mixed' armed conflict as its application does not depend on the character of the armed conflict. Once a situation is determined as either 'threat to the peace, breach of the peace, or act of aggression' under Article 39, Chapter VII enables the Security Council to take non-military and military enforcement actions.[143]

In short, 'mixed' armed conflict is potentially a gap where the application of *jus ad bellum* and *jus in bello* is highly complex and where there could be negative effects on the compliance with these laws. With regard to *jus ad bellum,* it is difficult to establish the existence of a use of force and an armed attack, and to identify who is taking self-defence measures against whom and who should be complying with the principles of necessity and proportionality. With regard to IHL, the application of different sets of IHL rules to different types of armed conflict in a 'mixed' armed conflict is highly complex and can have negative effects on the compliance with IHL. However, as similar to an armed conflict involving foreign intervention, Chapter VII of the UN Charter can complement the law of self-defence and IHL since its application does not depend on the character of an armed conflict.

[141] See Gasser, 'Internationalized Non-International Armed Conflicts', 157; David, *Principes de droit des conflits armés*, 152; Kolb, *Ius in bello*, 92.

[142] See, eg, ICRC, 'Strengthening Legal Protection for Victims of Armed Conflicts' (21 September 2010) Official Statement, ICRC website, www.icrc.org/eng.

[143] See sections 4.IV and 4.V.

III. CONCLUSIONS

The above discussions revealed that interventions of foreign armed forces or armed groups in non-international armed conflict and a mixture of different types of armed conflict render the application of *jus ad bellum* and *jus in bello* extremely complex. The underlying cause is that the determination of who is carrying out an armed attack and who is the victim state, and the classification of an armed conflict, is based on a bilateral relation between two parties. In other words, it is assumed that an armed attack emanates from one armed group or one state against another armed group or a state. Similarly, it is assumed that an armed conflict takes place between two states, a state and an armed group, or two armed groups. If there are multiple armed groups or states involved in an armed conflict, the bilateral relation between the parties will multiply and eventually become a web of bilateral relations, each with different classification under *jus ad bellum* and *jus in bello*.

In terms of *jus in bello*, certain trends can be observed to apply certain fundamental rules of IHL to any type of armed conflict. The ICJ and ICTY have declared that common Article 3 of the 1949 Geneva Conventions applies to any type of armed conflict. The ICRC has also identified customary rules of IHL that apply to both international and non-international armed conflict. It is hoped that more rules of IHL will be identified as customary rules of IHL applicable in both international and non-international armed conflict, and enjoy endorsements from states. Such development will be a positive one particularly for the enhanced regulation of non-international armed conflict and internationalised non-international armed conflict. However, when an international armed conflict exists alongside non-international armed conflict and internationalised non-international armed conflict, the full range of IHL rules applicable in international armed conflict must not be curtailed by simply applying customary rules of IHL to all types of armed conflict. In this sense, so long as the customary rules applicable in both international and non-international armed conflict fall short of those applicable only in international armed conflict, the applicable rules have to be distinguished according to the type of armed conflict to preserve the maximum protection in times of international armed conflict.

In terms of *jus ad bellum*, there seems to be no similar process to address the complexity of a situation where multiple armed groups and states are using force at the same time. Further deliberations are necessary to address this issue.

6

Conclusions

THE TRADITIONAL PRINCIPLES of the separation between *jus ad bellum* and *jus in bello*, equal application of IHL to the conflicting parties, and concurrent application of *jus ad bellum* and *jus in bello* still remain the cornerstone governing the relationship between *jus ad bellum* and *jus in bello*, whether it be in the context of self-defence or Chapter VII use of force, or in the context of international, non-international, or internationalised non-international armed conflict, or a mixture of the three.

In discussing the relationship between *jus ad bellum* and *jus in bello* in different contexts, this book attempted to go beyond a mere doctrinal debate. It extracted specific substantive rules of *jus ad bellum* and *jus in bello* found in treaty and customary international law, and examined the relationship between these substantive rules in the light of the three principles mentioned above. A substantial amount of practice of states, international organisations, international and national courts and tribunals, and opinions of experts were employed as tools to demonstrate the relationship between *jus ad bellum* and *jus in bello* in concrete terms.

This chapter does not offer a summary of the conclusions, which can be found at the end of each chapter and each section therein, but summarises some of the methods used to apply the above principles in specific contexts.

The **separation between *jus ad bellum* and *jus in bello*** has a different meaning in the context of the law of self-defence and Chapter VII of the UN Charter. The separation between the law of self-defence and IHL is universally accepted in all aspects. The thresholds of application are distinct between 'armed attack' and 'armed conflict'; subsequent operation of IHL, which applies equally to the conflicting parties, is unaffected; and the principles of proportionality and necessity in *jus ad bellum* and *jus in bello* are kept separate. Chapter VII is not so straightforward. While the thresholds of application are distinct between Article 39 of the UN Charter and 'armed conflict', the subsequent operation of IHL might be affected by Article 103 of the UN Charter, which leaves room for Chapter VII decisions to prevail over IHL obligations. However, considering that the Security Council must take into account the Purposes of the UN pursuant to Article 24(2) of the UN Charter, including Article 1(3) on achieving international co-operation on humanitarian issues and promoting the respect for human rights, the rules of IHL, which are essentially humanitarian in character, should not be subjected to Security Council decisions. Therefore, it is all the more important, as a practical matter, to avoid conflicts between Chapter VII decisions and IHL obligations at the drafting stage of the resolutions or to interpret the resolutions so that they would be consistent with IHL.

The **equal application of IHL to the conflicting parties** is a principle that is well-established in both self-defence and Chapter VII contexts. As briefly noted above, the equal application of IHL to an aggressor and a victim state in the context of self-defence is universally accepted. The arguments on possible unequal application between the two is now only of a historical interest. The equal application in the context of Chapter VII can be complicated by Article 103 of the UN Charter as noted above, but any speculation of unequal application of IHL under Chapter VII decisions is unfounded in Security Council practice. In addition, nowhere in international law does it put UN forces authorised under Chapter VII in a more advantageous position than other conflicting parties in terms of IHL obligations when they are a party to an armed conflict. This is also accepted by the practice of key actors such as states, the UN, and the International Committee of the Red Cross (ICRC).

Non-international armed conflict is a delicate case where the equal application principle should be seen in a context different from international armed conflict. In particular, the implementation of the judicial guarantees obligations in the law of non-international armed conflict by armed groups pose a number of questions, such as the legal basis to establish their own courts and the human, material, and financial resources to implement the judicial guarantees obligations. Whether an armed group has established its court according to the law of non-international armed conflict and whether they are capable of and are in fact implementing the judicial guarantees obligations need to be examined on a case-by-case basis. Moreover, there is a serious conflict between the national law and IHL since the national law normally requires a heavy punishment of members of armed groups whereas IHL encourages amnesty for them. The solution to this problem largely depends on a wider question of reconciliation and peace process between the conflicting parties.

The **concurrent application of *jus ad bellum* and *jus in bello*** is a principle which has an immense potential to pave the way for a more positive understanding of the relationship between the two, which has been largely overlooked for fear that one might prejudice the separation of the two. Two phases can be distinguished: determination of the concurrent application of *jus ad bellum* and *jus in bello* and the subsequent legal interaction between the substantive rules of the two legal regimes.

The determination of the concurrent application of *jus ad bellum* and *jus in bello* is the prerequisite for subsequent legal interactions between the two, but such determination requires a meticulous analysis of whether the thresholds of application of both *jus ad bellum* and *jus in bello* have been met. Since the adoption of the UN Charter, the thresholds of application for *jus ad bellum* and *jus in bello* have shifted from 'war' to diverse thresholds and hence the distinction and nexus between the respective thresholds have become blurred or complex. The UN Charter established the following thresholds of application of *jus ad bellum*: 'use of force'; 'armed attack' for self-defence; and 'threat to the peace, breach of the peace, or act of aggression' for Chapter VII. Moreover, the 1949 Geneva Conventions and 1977 Additional Protocols created separate thresholds for international and non-international armed conflict. Accordingly, the nexus between the *jus ad bellum* thresholds and IHL thresholds has also become more diverse and when exactly the two legal regimes are concurrently applicable has become a complex question. 'Use of force' and 'armed attack', in most cases, amount to an international armed conflict in the IHL sense. However, the nuances among the three thresholds, particularly with regard to the intensity of force required, are such that there are situations where the three thresholds cannot be met at the same time. Thus, it is best not to expect a quick and simple answer that a 'use of force' and 'armed attack' always amount to an international armed conflict. Each threshold of application should be applied separately and according to the particular requirements therein.

The situation is slightly less complex in Chapter VII context. Practice shows that when the Security Council determined a situation as 'breach of the peace' or 'act of aggression', it always amounted to an international armed conflict. However, 'threat to the peace' can imply international, non-international, or internationalised armed conflict, or a mixture of some or all of them, or even situations short of armed conflict. Thus, it is not recommended to assume that 'threat to the peace' always amount to some kind of an 'armed conflict'. However, the sheer flexibility of the concept of 'threat to the peace' can in fact be an advantage, since it can circumvent all the complexities of determining the type of armed conflict in the IHL sense. A determination of a 'threat to the peace' would enable the Security Council to regulate the use of force, whatever the nature of the armed conflict.

Once the concurrent application of *jus ad bellum* and *jus in bello* is established, examination on the legal interaction between the substantive rules of the two legal regimes is possible. In both self-defence and Chapter VII contexts, if *jus ad bellum* and *jus in bello* are seen as one set of legal regimes governing the use of force, or as dual constraints applicable in every use of force, the combining force can strengthen the regulation of excessive use of force by states acting in self-defence and UN forces in particular.

In the self-defence context, the principle of proportionality in the law of self-defence and the IHL rules on methods / means of warfare and occupation in particular complement each other when regulating the conduct of self-defence. The principle of proportionality can set broader limits on the conduct of self-defence such as appropriate targets and geographical and temporal extent, but IHL regulates more detailed aspects such as which objectives can be attacked, how they can be attacked, what weapons can be used, and how force can be used in a situation of occupation. The same relationship can be found with regard to the principle of necessity in the law of self-defence and IHL, and the prohibition on reprisals in *jus ad bellum* and *jus in bello*.

In the Chapter VII context, the dual constraints of *jus ad bellum* and *jus in bello* on the use of force by UN forces are often overlooked. In practice, *jus ad bellum* already imposes substantial limits on the use of force by UN forces through Security Council resolutions and the principle of self-defence. These apply to three different kinds of use of force: 1) use of force by UN-commanded forces not authorised under Chapter VII is permitted only in self-defence; 2) use of force authorised for UN Member States under Chapter VII is subject to Security Council resolutions; and 3) use of force by Chapter VII UN-commanded forces is subject to both Security Council resolutions and the principle of self-defence. On top of these *jus ad bellum* limits, IHL is applicable to the use of force by state-led UN forces and UN-commanded forces alike. Thus, Security Council resolutions and the principle of self-defence set the broader limits on the use of force by UN forces such as the purpose and temporal and geographical extent, whereas IHL regulates more detailed aspects as noted above in the self-defence context.

However, there are **gaps in the regulation of the use of force by *jus ad bellum* and *jus in bello*.** These are, an armed conflict involving intervention by foreign armed forces or armed groups, and a mixture of international, non-international, and internationalised non-international armed conflict. They pose difficult questions on the applicability as well as the actual application of *jus ad bellum* and *jus in bello*. First, there is a problem with establishing 'use of force' and 'armed attack'. When an armed group is backed by a state and attacking another state, it can amount to a 'use of force' and an 'armed attack' but the establishment of the nexus between the armed group and the state is always problematic. Secondly, when an armed group is acting independently from a state, it is still controversial whether it amounts to a 'use of force' or an 'armed attack' when it is attacking a state. Thirdly, the determination of who launched the 'use of force' or 'armed attack' and who is entitled to exercise the right of self-defence is extremely complicated when there are numerous and diverse types of conflicting parties.

With regard to the IHL aspect, an armed conflict involving foreign intervention by armed forces or armed groups is a so-called 'internationalised non-international armed conflict' to which IHL is applicable. The problem, however, is that there are still debates over the threshold of application and the scope of the applicable IHL rules, since neither the law of international nor non-international armed conflict is automatically applicable. Nevertheless, common Article 3 of the 1949 Geneva Conventions can be the threshold of application by analogy and with regard to the applicable IHL rules, an emerging consensus is to apply the rules contained in the law of non-international armed conflict, which consist of three sets: 1) common Article 3 of the 1949 Geneva Conventions, 2) IHL treaties applicable to common Article 3 type of armed conflict or in all circumstances, and 3) customary law of non-international armed conflict. This position is legally most sound. However, whether this is adequate is a different question.

The other problem is the application of IHL in a 'mixed' armed conflict. The difficulty is that when there are a number of conflicting parties in the same region, each involved in a number of different types of armed conflict, each conflicting party has to apply different sets of IHL rules according to whom they are fighting. Here, the law and reality seem to be quite far apart. As a matter of law, different sets of IHL rules apply according to the nature of the armed conflict, but it does not seem realistic to expect the conflicting parties to switch the applicable IHL rules every time when they fight a different adversary. There are certain trends to identify customary rules of IHL that apply in both international and non-international armed conflict, so that these rules can be applied in any kind of armed conflict. It is hoped that more rules of IHL will be identified as customary rules of IHL applicable in both international and non-international armed conflict, and enjoy endorsements from states.

Thus, a further clarification and consensus are necessary on the application of *jus ad bellum* and *jus in bello* to an armed conflict involving intervention by foreign armed forces or armed groups, and a mixture of international, non-international, and internationalised non-international armed conflict.

In the end, there is no quick solution to solve the problems arising from the relationship between *jus ad bellum* and *jus in bello*. A specific solution is necessary for each particular case of use of force or armed conflict. However, the existing law offers an adequate solution to regulate the relationship between the two legal regimes. In particular, the three principles governing the relationship between *jus ad bellum* and *jus in bello* (the separation between *jus ad bellum* and *jus in bello*, equal application of IHL to the conflicting parties, and concurrent application of *jus ad bellum* and *jus in bello*) provide an adequate legal framework to avoid any conflict between the two, preserve the proper application of the respective legal regime, and ensure the regulation of the excessive use of force.

Bibliography

I. PRIMARY MATERIALS

Advisory Committee of the Harvard Research in International Law, 'Draft Convention on Rights and Duties of States in Case of Aggression' (1939) 33 *American Journal of International Law Supplement* 827.

Chatham House and the International Committee of the Red Cross, 'Expert Meeting on Procedural Safeguards for Security Detention in Non-International Armed Conflict' (2009) 876 *International Review of the Red Cross* 859.

Council of the European Union, Independent International Fact-Finding Mission on the Conflict in Georgia, 'Report' Vols I–III (September 2009).

'Declaration' Conference of High Contracting Parties to the Fourth Geneva Convention (Geneva 5 December 2001) in (2001) 847 *International Review of the Red Cross* 661.

'Destruction of the "Caroline"' (1906) 2 *Digest of International Law* 409.

Doswald-Beck, L (ed), *San Remo Manual on International Law Applicable to Armed Conflicts at Sea* (Cambridge, Cambridge University Press, 1995).

'Draft International Convention on the Condition and Protection of Civilians of Enemy Nationality Who Are on Territory Belonging to or Occupied by a Belligerent', XVth International Conference of the Red Cross (Tokyo 1934).

Fourth Review Conference of the Parties to the Convention on the Prohibition of the Development, Production and Stockpiling of Bacteriological (Biological) and Toxin Weapons and on their Destruction (Geneva 25 November–6 December 1996), 'Final Declaration' (1996) BWC/CONF.IV/9 Part II.

Group of Governmental Experts of the States Parties to the Convention on Prohibitions or Restrictions on the Use of Certain Conventional Weapons Which May Be Deemed to Be Excessively Injurious or to Have Indiscriminate Effects, Eleventh Session (Geneva 2–12 August 2005) 'Explosive Remnants of War and International Humanitarian Law: Submitted by France' (11 August 2005) CCW/GGE/XI/WG.1/WP.17.

—— 'Replies to Document CCW/GGE/X/WG.1/WP.2, Entitled "International Humanitarian Law and ERW, Dated 8 March 2005": Reply from the Argentine Republic' (2 August 2005) CCW/GGE/XI/WG.1/WP.10.

—— 'Responses to Document CCW/GGE/X/WG.1/WP.2, Entitled IHL and ERW, Dated 8 March 2005: Response from Canada' (29 June 2005) CCW/GGE/XI/WG.1/WP.2.

—— 'Responses to Document CCW/GGE/X/WG.1/WP.2, Entitled IHL and ERW, Dated 8 March 2005: Response from New Zealand' (5 August 2005) CCW/GGE/XI/WG.1/WP.16.

—— 'Responses to Document CCW/GGE/X/WG.1/WP.2, Entitled IHL and ERW, Dated 8 March 2005: Response from Norway' (29 July 2005) CCW/GGE/XI/WG.1/WP.5.

Group of Governmental Experts of the States Parties to the Convention on Prohibitions or Restrictions on the Use of Certain Conventional Weapons Which May Be Deemed to Be Excessively Injurious or to Have Indiscriminate Effects, Eleventh Session (Geneva 2-12 August 2005) 'Responses to Document CCW/GGE/X/WG.1/WP.2, Entitled IHL and ERW, Dated 8 March 2005: Response from Switzerland' (3 August 2005) CCW/GGE/XI/WG.1/WP.13.

—— 'Responses to Document CCW/GGE/X/WG.1/WP.2, Entitled IHL and ERW, Dated 8 March 2005: Response from the United Kingdom of Great Britain and Northern Ireland' (24 June 2005) CCW/GGE/XI/WG.1/WP.1.

—— 'Responses to Document CCW/GGE/X/WG.1/WP.2, Entitled IHL and ERW, Dated 8 March 2005: Response from the United States of America' (25 July 2005) CCW/GGE/XI/WG.1/WP.4.

Human Rights Watch, *I Lost Everything: Israel's Unlawful Destruction of Property during Operation Cast Lead* (New York, Human Rights Watch, 2010).

—— *White Flag Deaths: Killings of Palestinian Civilians during Operation Cast Lead* (New York, Human Rights Watch, 2009).

—— *Why They Died: Civilian Casualties in Lebanon during the 2006 War* (New York, Human Rights Watch, 2007).

Institute of International Law, 'L'application du droit international notamment humanitaire, dans les conflits armés auxquels prennent part des entités non-étatiques' (1999) 68-I *Annuaire de l'Institut de Droit International* 251.

—— 'Equality of Application of the Rules of the Law of War to Parties to an Armed Conflict' (1963) 50-II *Annuaire de l'Institut de Droit International* 376.

—— 'The Laws of War on Land, Oxford, 9 September 1880' in D Schindler and J Toman (eds), *The Laws of Armed Conflicts: A Collection of Conventions, Resolutions and Other Documents* (Leiden, Martinus Nijhoff, 2004).

—— 'Manual of the Law of Naval War, Oxford, 9 August 1913' in D Schindler and J Toman (eds), *The Laws of Armed Conflicts: A Collection of Conventions, Resolutions and Other Documents* (Leiden, Martinus Nijhoff, 2004).

—— 'Resolution on the Effects of Armed Conflicts on Treaties' (1986) 61-II *Annuaire de l'Institut de Droit International* 278.

International Committee of the Red Cross, 'L'action du Comité international au Moyen-Orient' (1973) 660 *Revue internationale de la Croix-Rouge* 727.

—— 'Afghanistan: ICRC Calls on All Parties to Conflict to Respect International Humanitarian Law' (2001) 844 *International Review of the Red Cross* 1181.

—— *Arms Availability and the Situation of Civilians in Armed Conflict* (Geneva, International Committee of the Red Cross, 1999).

—— 'Le Comité international et le conflit au Proche-Orient' (1967) 583 *Revue internationale de la Croix-Rouge* 303.

—— 'Conflit au Moyen-Orient' (1991) 787 *Revue internationale de la Croix-Rouge* 23.

—— 'Conflict in Iraq: Memorandum to the Belligerents' (2003) 850 *International Review of the Red Cross* 423.

—— 'Conflit Irak–Iran' (1980) 720 *Revue internationale de la Croix-Rouge* 341.

—— 'Conflit sino-vietnamien' (1979) 716 *Revue internationale de la Croix-Rouge* 98.

—— *Direct Participation in Hostilities under International Humanitarian Law* (Geneva, International Committee of the Red Cross, 2009).

—— 'Existing Principles and Rules of International Humanitarian Law Applicable to Munitions that May Become Explosive Remnants of War' (28 July 2005) CCW/GGE/XI/WG.1/WP.7.
—— *Handbook of the International Red Cross and Red Crescent* (Geneva, International Committee of the Red Cross and International Federation of Red Cross and Red Crescent Societies, 2009).
—— *Improving Compliance with International Humanitarian Law, ICRC Expert Seminars* (Geneva, International Committee of the Red Cross, 2003).
—— 'International Humanitarian Law and the Challenges of Contemporary Armed Conflicts' (2003) Report prepared for the 28th International Conference of the Red Cross and Red Crescent, Geneva, 2–6 December 2003.
—— *International Humanitarian Law: Answers to Your Questions* (Geneva: International Committee of the Red Cross, 2002).
—— 'Interpretive Guidance on the Notion of Direct Participation in Hostilities under International Humanitarian Law' (2008) 872 *International Review of the Red Cross* 991.
—— 'Israel and Lebanon: ICRC Gravely Concerned About the Plight of Civilians Caught Up in Hostilities' (13 July 2006) News Release 06/78.
—— 'Memorandum from the International Committee of the Red Cross to the States Parties to the Geneva Conventions of August 12, 1949 concerning the Conflict between Islamic Republic of Iran and Republic of Iraq' in M Sassòli and A Bouvier (eds), *How Does Law Protect in War?*, 2nd edn, Vol II (Geneva, International Committee of the Red Cross, 2006) 1529.
—— 'Memorandum on the Applicability of International Humanitarian Law' (1991) 280 *International Review of the Red Cross* 24.
—— 'Middle East: Gulf Crisis' (1990) 278 *International Review of the Red Cross* 444.
—— 'Outline of Legal Aspects of the Conflict in the Middle East' (1991) 280 *International Review of the Red Cross* 28.
—— 'Réponse à l'appel du CICR pour le respect des règles humanitaires au Vietnam' (1965) 562 *Revue internationale de la Croix-Rouge* 485 (English translation in (1965) 5 *International Review of the Red Cross* 527).
—— 'Report on the Protection of War Victims' (1993) 296 *International Review of the Red Cross* 391.
—— 'Statement by the International Committee of the Red Cross of 26 April 1999' (1999) 834 *International Review of the Red Cross* 408.
—— 'Strengthening Legal Protection for Victims of Armed Conflicts' (21 September 2010) Official Statement.
—— *Symposium on Humanitarian Action and Peace-keeping Operations* (Geneva, International Committee of the Red Cross, 1994).
—— 'Unregulated Arms Availability, Small Arms and Light Weapons and the UN Process: Background Paper' (2006).
International Criminal Tribunal for the former Yugoslavia, 'Final Report to the Prosecutor by the Committee Established to Review the NATO Bombing Campaign against the Federal Republic of Yugoslavia' (2000) 39 ILM 1257.
International Crisis Group, 'Scramble for the Congo: Anatomy of an Ugly War' (20 December 2000) ICG Africa Report No 26.

International Law Association, 'Committee on the Charter of the United Nations' in International Law Association Report of the Fiftieth Conference (Brussels 1962) (International Law Association, Brussels 1962) 157.

—— 'Report on the Effect of the Briand-Kellogg Pact of Paris on International Law: Articles of Interpretation Proposed by the Committee' in International Law Association Report of the Thirty-Eighth Conference (Budapest 1934) (International Law Association, Budapest 1934) 66.

International Military Tribunal in Nürnberg, *The Trial of German Major War Criminals: Proceedings of the International Military Tribunal Sitting at Nuremberg, Germany* (London, UK Stationery Office, 1948).

Israel Ministry of Foreign Affairs, 'Responding to Hamas Attacks from Gaza – Issues of Proportionality' (29 December 2008).

—— 'Responding to Hizbullah Attacks from Lebanon: Issues of Proportionality' (25 July 2006).

Non-aligned Movement, XII Summit (Durban, 2–3 September 1998), 'Basic Documents of the XII Summit of the Non-Aligned Movement' (1998).

Official Records of the Diplomatic Conference on the Reaffirmation and Development of International Humanitarian Law Applicable in Armed Conflicts, Geneva (1974–1977) (Bern, Federal Political Department, 1978).

Röling, B and Rüter, C (eds), *The Tokyo Judgment* (Amsterdam, APA-University Press Amsterdam BV, 1977).

Schwarzenberger, G, 'Report on Self-Defence under the Charter of the United Nations and the Use of Prohibited Weapons' in International Law Association Report of the Fiftieth Conference (Brussels 1962) (International Law Association, Brussels 1962) 192.

Singh, R and Kilroy, C, 'In the Matter of the Potential Use of Armed Force by the UK against Iraq and in the Matter of Reliance for That Use of Force on United Nations Security Council Resolution 1441' in G Farebrother and N Kollerstrom (eds), *The Case against War: The Essential Legal Inquiries, Opinions and Judgments concerning War in Iraq* (Hailsham, The Legal Inquiry Steering Group, 2003).

United Kingdom Attorney-General, 'Iraq: Resolution 1441' (7 March 2003).

United Nations Commission on Human Rights, 'Guiding Principles on Internal Displacement' (11 February 1998) UN Doc E/CN.4/1998/53/Add.2.

United Nations General Assembly, 'An Agenda for Peace: Preventive Diplomacy, Peacemaking and Peace-keeping' (17 June 1992) UN Doc A/47/277-S/24111.

—— 'Declaration on Principles of International Law concerning Friendly Relations and Co-operation among States in Accordance with the Charter of the United Nations' UNGA Res 2625 (XXV) (24 October 1970).

—— 'Definition of Aggression' UNGA Res 3314 (XXIX) (14 December 1974).

—— 'Guidelines for Military Manuals and Instructions on the Protection of Environment in Times of Armed Conflict' (19 August 1994) UN Doc A/49/323, Annex.

—— 'Model Agreement between the United Nations and Member States Contributing Personnel and Equipment to United Nations Peace-keeping Operations' (23 May 1991) UN Doc A/46/185.

—— 'A More Secure World: Our Shared Responsibility, Report of the High-level Panel on Threats, Challenges and Change' (2 December 2004) UN Doc A/59/565.

——'Report of the Group of Governmental Experts on Small Arms' (19 August 1999) UN Doc A/54/258.
——'Report of the Panel on United Nations Peace Operations' (21 August 2000) UN Doc A/55/305-S/2000/809.
——'Report of the Secretary-General on Financing of the United Nations Protection Force, the United Nations Confidence Restoration Operation in Croatia, the United Nations Preventive Deployment Force and the United Nations Peace Forces Headquarters' (20 September 1996) UN Doc A/51/389.
——'Report of the Secretary-General Pursuant to General Assembly Resolution 53/35: The Fall of Srebrenica' (15 November 1999) UN Doc A/54/549.
——'Request for an Advisory Opinion from the International Court of Justice on the Legality of the Threat or Use of Nuclear Weapons' UNGA Res 49/75K (15 December 1994) UN Doc A/RES/49/75 K.
——'Summary Legal Position of the Government of Israel' (24 November 2003) UN Doc A/ES-10/248.
——'United Nations Decade of International Law: Report of the Secretary-General' (21 September 1999) UN Doc A/54/362.
United Nations Human Rights Council, 'Report of the Commission of Inquiry on Lebanon Pursuant to Human Rights Council Resolution S-2/1' (23 November 2006) UN Doc A/HRC/3/2.
——'Report of the Special Rapporteur on Extrajudicial, Summary or Arbitrary Executions, Philip Alston, Addendum: Mission to Philippines' (16 April 2008) UN Doc A/HRC/8/3/Add.2.
——'Report of the United Nations Fact-Finding Mission on the Gaza Conflict' (25 September 2009) UN Doc A/HRC/12/48.
United Nations International Law Commission, 'Articles on Responsibility of States for Internationally Wrongful Acts' (2001) UN Doc A/56/10 Supplement No 10.
——'Draft Code of Crimes against the Peace and Security of Mankind' (1996) UN Doc A/CN.4/SER.A/1996/Add.1 (Part 2).
——'Fragmentation of International Law: Difficulties Arising from the Diversification and Expansion of International Law, Report of the Study Group of the International Law Commission' (13 April 2006) UN Doc A/CN.4/L.682.
——'Responsibility of International Organizations' (2009) UN Doc A/64/10 Supplement No 10.
——'Second Report on the Law of Treaties, by Sir Humphrey Waldock, Special Rapporteur' (20 March, 10 April, 30 April, and 5 June 1963) UN Doc A/CN.4/156 and Add.1-3.
——*Yearbook of the International Law Commission* (New York, United Nations).
United Nations Office of the High Commissioner for Human Rights, 'Human Rights Abuses by the CPN-M: Summary of Concerns' (21 September 2006).
United Nations Secretariat, 'The Comprehensive Report on Lessons Learned from the United Nations Operation in Somalia (UNOSOM)' (1995).
——'The Effect of Armed Conflict on Treaties: An Examination of Practice and Doctrine (Memorandum by the Secretariat)' (1 February 2005) UN Doc A/CN.4/550.
——*Handbook on United Nations Multidimensional Peacekeeping Operations* (New York, United Nations, 2003).

United Nations Secretariat, 'Interoffice Memorandum to the Chief, Legal Affairs Section, Executive Office, Office of the High Commission for Refugees, regarding the Voluntary Repatriation (Tripartite) Agreement' (2004) *United Nations Juridical Yearbook* 362.
—— 'Interoffice Memorandum to the Director of the Codification Division, Office of Legal Affairs and Secretary of the International Law Commission regarding the Topic Responsibility of International Organizations' (2004) *United Nations Juridical Yearbook* 352.
—— 'Letter to the Representative/President of the Unification and National Security Central Council in the Freedom Centre (Tongil Anbo Joongang Hyeopuih) in Seoul, Republic of Korea, regarding the Eligibility of Prisoners of War for Payments for Their Labour in War Camps during the Korean War' (2004) *United Nations Juridical Yearbook* 363.
—— 'Memorandum to the Senior Political Adviser to the Secretary-General' (1993) *United Nations Juridical Yearbook* 371.
—— 'Memorandum to the Special Adviser to the Secretary-General' (1994) *United Nations Juridical Yearbook* 502.
—— 'Memorandum to the Under-Secretary-General for Peacekeeping Operations' (1993) *United Nations Juridical Yearbook* 447.
—— 'Note on the Protection of Peacekeeping Personnel under International Humanitarian Law' (2006) *United Nations Juridical Yearbook* 518.
—— 'Note to the Assistant Secretary-General for Peacekeeping Operations regarding the United Nations Mission in Kosovo (UNMIK) and the Protection of Cultural Heritage' (2004) *United Nations Juridical Yearbook* 350.
—— 'Note to the Director of the Africa Division, Department of Peacekeeping Operations, United Nations' (2003) *United Nations Juridical Yearbook* 534.
—— 'Note to the Director of Asia and the Pacific Division, Office of the Assistant Secretary-General, Department of Political Affairs, United Nations' (2003) *United Nations Juridical Yearbook* 553.
—— 'Note to the Under-Secretary-General of the Department of Peacekeeping Operations, United Nations' (2003) *United Nations Juridical Yearbook* 538.
—— 'Question of the Possible Accession of Intergovernmental Organizations to the Geneva Conventions for the Protection of War Victims' (1972) *United Nations Juridical Yearbook* 153.
—— *Repertory of Practice of United Nations Organs* (New York, United Nations).
—— *Yearbook of the United Nations* (New York, United Nations).
United Nations Secretary-General, 'Regulations for the United Nations Emergency Force' 271 UNTS 168.
—— 'Regulations for the United Nations Force in Congo' (15 July 1963) UN Doc ST/SGB/ONUC/1.
—— 'Regulations for the United Nations Force in Cyprus' 555 UNTS 132.
—— 'Secretary-General's Bulletin: Observance by United Nations Forces of International Humanitarian Law' (6 August 1999) UN Doc ST/SGB/1999/13.
United Nations Security Council, 'Aide-Mémoire of the Secretary-General concerning Some Questions Relating to the Function and Operation of the United Nations Peace-keeping Force in Cyprus' (11 April 1964) UN Doc S/5653.

——'Eighteenth Report of the Secretary-General on the United Nations Organization Mission in the Democratic Republic of the Congo' (2 August 2005) UN Doc S/2005/506.

——'Eighth Report of the Secretary-General on the United Nations Organization Mission in the Democratic Republic of the Congo' (8 June 2001) UN Doc S/2001/572.

——'Eleventh Report of the Secretary-General on the United Nations Organization Mission in the Democratic Republic of the Congo' (18 October 2002) UN Doc S/2002/1180.

——'Fifth Report of the Secretary-General on the United Nations Mission in Sierra Leone' (31 July 2000) UN Doc S/2000/751.

——'Fifth Report of the Secretary-General on the United Nations Organization Mission in the Democratic Republic of the Congo' (6 December 2000) UN Doc S/2000/1156.

——'Fourteenth Report of the Secretary-General on the United Nations Organization Mission in the Democratic Republic of the Congo' (17 November 2003) UN Doc S/2003/1098.

——'Fourth Report of the Secretary-General on the United Nations Mission in Sierra Leone' (19 May 2000) UN Doc S/2000/455.

——'Fourth Report of the Secretary-General on the United Nations Organization Mission in the Democratic Republic of the Congo' (21 September 2000) UN Doc S/2000/888.

——'Further Report of the Secretary-General on the Implementation of Security Resolution 598 (1987)' (9 December 1991) UN Doc S/23273.

——'Further Report of the Secretary-General Submitted in Pursuance of Paragraphs 18 and 19 of Resolution 794 (1992)' (3 March 1993) UN Doc S/25354.

——'Further Report of the Secretary-General Submitted in Pursuance of Paragraph 18 of Resolution 814 (1993)' (17 August 1993) UN Doc S/26317.

——'Further Report of the Secretary-General Submitted in Pursuance of Paragraph 19 of Resolution 814 (1993) and Paragraph A 5 of Resolution 865 (1993)' (12 November 1993) S/26738.

——'Identical Letters Dated 12 July 2006 from the Permanent Representative of Israel to the United Nations Addressed to the Secretary-General and the President of the Security Council' (12 July 2006) UN Doc A/60/937-S/2006/515.

——'Identical Letters Dated 27 December 2008 from the Permanent Representative of Israel to the United Nations Addressed to the Secretary-General and the President of the Security Council' (27 December 2008) UN Doc S/2008/816.

——'Letter Dated 5 July 1951 from the Representative of the United States of America to the Secretary-General' (6 July 1951) UN Doc S/2232.

——'Letter Dated 17 April 1985 from the Secretary-General Addressed to the President of the Security Council' (24 April 1985) UN Doc S/17127.

——'Letter Dated 29 November 1992 from the Secretary-General Addressed to the President of the Security Council' (30 November 1992) UN Doc S/24868.

——'Letter Dated 19 January 1993 from the Permanent Representative of the United States of America to the United Nations Addressed to the President of the Security Council' (19 January 1993) UN Doc S/25126.

——'Letter Dated 6 February 1994 from the Secretary-General Addressed to the President of the Security Council' (7 February 1994) UN Doc S/1994/131.

United Nations Security Council, 'Letter Dated 18 April 1994 from the Secretary-General Addressed to the President of the Security Council' (19 April 1994) UN Doc S/1994/466.
—— 'Letter Dated 20 August 1998 from the Permanent Representative of the United States of America to the United Nations Addressed to the President of the Security Council' (20 August 1998) UN Doc S/1998/780.
—— 'Letter Dated 7 October 2001 from the Chargé d'Affaires a.i. of the Permanent Mission of the United Kingdom of Great Britain and Northern Ireland to the United Nations Addressed to the President of the Security Council' (7 October 2001) UN Doc S/2001/947.
—— 'Letter Dated 7 October 2001 from the Permanent Representative of the United States of America to the United Nations Addressed to the President of the Security Council' (7 October 2001) UN Doc S/2001/946.
—— 'Letter Dated 20 March 2003 from the Permanent Representative of the United States of America to the United Nations Addressed to the President of the Security Council' (21 March 2003) UN Doc S/2003/351.
—— 'Mission to Inspect Civilian Areas in Iran and Iraq Which Have Been Subject to Military Attack' (20 June 1983) UN Doc S/15834.
—— 'Nineteenth Report of the Secretary-General on the United Nations Organization Mission in the Democratic Republic of the Congo' (26 September 2005) UN Doc S/2005/603.
—— 'Ninth Report of the Secretary-General on the United Nations Organization Mission in the Democratic Republic of the Congo' (16 October 2001) UN Doc S/2001/970.
—— 'Report of the Commission of Inquiry Established Pursuant to Security Council Resolution 885 (1993) to Investigate Armed Attacks on UNOSOM II Personnel Which Led to Casualties among Them' (1 June 1994) UN Doc S/1994/653.
—— 'Report of the Independent Inquiry into the Actions of the United Nations during the 1994 Genocide in Rwanda' (16 December 1999) UN Doc S/1999/1257.
—— 'Report of the International Commission of Inquiry on Darfur to the United Nations Secretary-General' (25 January 2005) UN Doc S/2005/60.
—— 'Report of the Mission Dispatched by the Secretary-General to Investigate Allegations of the Use of Chemical Weapons in the Conflict between the Islamic Republic of Iran and Iraq' (12 March 1986) UN Doc S/17911.
—— 'Report of the Mission Dispatched by the Secretary-General to Investigate Allegations of the Use of Chemical Weapons in the Conflict between the Islamic Republic of Iran and Iraq' (8 May 1987) UN Doc S/18852.
—— 'Report of the Mission Dispatched by the Secretary-General to Investigate Allegations of the Use of Chemical Weapons in the Conflict between the Islamic Republic of Iran and Iraq' (25 April 1988) UN Doc S/19823.
—— 'Report of the Mission Dispatched by the Secretary-General to Investigate Allegations of the Use of Chemical Weapons in the Conflict between the Islamic Republic of Iran and Iraq' (19 August 1988) UN Doc S/20134.
—— 'Report of the Officer-in-Charge of the United Nations Operation in the Congo to the Secretary-General on Developments Relating to the Application of the Security Council Resolutions of 21 February and 24 November 1961' (9 January 1962 – 30 January 1963) UN Doc S/5053 and UN Doc S/5053/Add.1–15.

—— 'Report of the Officer-in-Charge of the United Nations Operation in the Congo to the Secretary-General Relating to the Implementation of Paragraph A-2 of the Security Council Resolution of 21 February 1961' (14 September 1961–22 December 1961) UN Doc S/4940 and UN Doc S/4940/Add.1–19.
—— 'Report of the Secretary-General on the Implementation of Security Council Resolutions 340 (1973)' (27 October 1973) UN Doc S/11052/Rev.1.
—— 'Report of the Secretary-General on the Implementation of Security Council Resolution 425 (1978)' (19 March 1978) UN Doc S/12611.
—— 'Report of the Secretary-General Pursuant to Paragraph 30 of Resolution 1546 (2004)' (5 December 2006) UN Doc S/2006/945.
—— 'Report of the Secretary-General Pursuant to Resolution 844 (1993)' (9 May 1994) UN Doc S/1994/555.
—— 'Report of the Secretary-General Pursuant to Resolution 871 (1993)' (16 March 1994) UN Doc S/1994/300.
—— 'Report of the Secretary-General Pursuant to Resolution 908 (1994)' (17 September 1994) UN Doc S/1994/1067.
—— 'Report of the Secretary-General Pursuant to Resolution 913 (1994)' (19 May 1994) UN Doc S/1994/600.
—— 'Report of the Secretary-General Pursuant to Resolution 947 (1994)' (22 March 1995) UN Doc S/1995/222.
—— 'Report of the Secretary-General Pursuant to Resolution 959 (1994)' (1 December 1994) UN Doc S/1994/1389.
—— 'Report of the Secretary-General Pursuant to Security Council Resolutions 981 (1995), 982 (1995) and 983 (1995)' (23 November 1995) UN Doc S/1995/987.
—— 'Report of the Secretary-General Pursuant to Security Council Resolutions 982 (1995) and 987 (1995)' (30 May 1995) UN Doc S/1995/444.
—— 'Report of the Secretary-General to the Security Council on the Protection of Civilians in Armed Conflict' (8 September 1999) UN Doc S/1999/957.
—— 'Report of the Specialists Appointed by the Secretary-General to Investigate Allegations by the Islamic Republic of Iran concerning the Use of Chemical Weapons' (26 March 1984) UN Doc S/16433.
—— 'Report Pursuant to Paragraphs 10 and 14 of Security Council Resolution 1649 (2005)' (22 May 2006) UN Doc S/2006/310.
—— 'Second Report of the Secretary-General on the United Nations Operation in Côte d'Ivoire' (27 August 2004) S/2004/697.
—— 'Second Report of the Secretary-General on the United Nations Organization Mission in the Democratic Republic of the Congo' (18 April 2000) UN Doc S/2000/330.
—— 'Second Special Report of the Secretary-General on the United Nations Organization Mission in the Democratic Republic of the Congo' (27 May 2003) UN Doc S/2003/566.
—— 'Seventeenth Report of the Secretary-General on the United Nations Organization Mission in the Democratic Republic of the Congo' (15 March 2005) UN Doc S/2005/167.
—— 'Seventh Report of the Secretary-General on the United Nations Organization Mission in the Democratic Republic of the Congo' (17 April 2001) UN Doc S/2001/373.

United Nations Security Council, 'Sixteenth Report of the Secretary-General on the United Nations Organization Mission in the Democratic Republic of the Congo' (31 December 2004) UN Doc S/2004/1034.

—— 'Sixth Report of the Secretary-General on the United Nations Organization Mission in the Democratic Republic of the Congo' (21 February 2001) UN Doc S/2001/128.

—— 'Statement by the President of the Security Council' (27 July 2006) UN Doc S/PRST/2006/34.

—— 'Tenth Report of the Secretary-General on the United Nations Organization Mission in the Democratic Republic of the Congo' (15 February 2002) UN Doc S/2002/169.

—— 'Third Report of the Secretary-General on the United Nations Organization Mission in the Democratic Republic of the Congo' (12 June 2000) UN Doc S/2000/566.

—— 'Third Special Report of the Secretary-General on the United Nations Organization Mission in the Democratic Republic of the Congo' (16 August 2004) UN Doc S/2004/650.

—— 'Thirteenth Report of the Secretary-General on the United Nations Organization Mission in the Democratic Republic of the Congo' (21 February 2003) UN Doc S/2003/211.

—— 'Twentieth Report of the Secretary-General on the United Nations Organization Mission in the Democratic Republic of the Congo' (28 December 2005) UN Doc S/2005/832.

—— 'Twenty-First Report of the Secretary-General on the United Nations Organization Mission in the Democratic Republic of the Congo' (13 June 2006) UN Doc S/2006/390.

United States of America, 'President Meets with Afghan Interim Authority Chairman' (28 January 2002).

—— 'White House Press Secretary Announcement of President Bush's Determination Re Legal Status of Taliban and Al Qaeda Detainees' (7 February 2002).

United States of America, Department of the Army, 'FM 100-23 Peace Operations' (December 1994).

United States of America, Department of Defense, 'Final Report to Congress on the Conduct of Hostilities in the Persian Gulf' (1992).

Wilmshurst, E, 'The Chatham House Principles of International Law on the Use of Force in Self-Defence' (2006) 55 *International and Comparative Law Quarterly* 963.

II. SECONDARY MATERIALS

Abi-Saab, G, 'The Specificities of Humanitarian Law' in C Swinarski (ed), *Studies and Essays on International Humanitarian Law and Red Cross Principles in Honour of Jean Pictet* (The Hague, Martinus Nijhoff, 1984) 265–80.

—— *The United Nations Operation in the Congo 1960–1964* (Oxford, Oxford University Press, 1978).

Aeschlimann, A, 'Overview of Protection Issues in Contexts of Multinational Peace Operations' in A Faite and J Grenier (eds), *Expert Meeting on Multinational*

Peace Operations: Applicability of International Humanitarian Law and International Human Rights Law to UN Mandated Forces (Geneva, International Committee of the Red Cross, 2004) 23–30.

Akande, D, 'The International Court of Justice and the Security Council: Is There Room for Judicial Control of Decisions of the Political Organs of the United Nations?' (1997) 46 *International and Comparative Law Quarterly* 309.

Aldrich, G, 'The Taliban, Al Qaeda, and the Determination of Illegal Combatants' (2002) 96 *American Journal of International Law* 891.

Alexandrov, S, *Self-Defense against the Use of Force in International Law* (The Hague, Kluwer Law International, 1996).

Al-Nauimi, N and Messe, R, *International Legal Issues Arising Under the United Nations Decade of International Law: Proceedings of the Qatar International Law Conference 1994* (The Hague, Martinus Nijhoff, 1995).

Antonopoulous, C, 'Force by Armed Groups as Armed Attack and the Broadening of Self-Defence' (2008) 55 *Netherlands International Law Review* 159.

Arai, K, 'The Status and Treatment of Terrorists under the Law of Armed Conflict' (2009) 108-2 *Journal of International Law and Diplomacy* 28.

Arai-Takahashi, Y, 'Disentangling Legal Quagmires: The Legal Characterisation of the Armed Conflicts in Afghanistan since 6/7 October 2001 and the Question of Prisoner of War Status' (2002) 5 *Yearbook of International Humanitarian Law* 61.

Arend, A and Beck, R, *International Law and the Use of Force* (London, Routledge, 1993).

Arsanjani, M, 'Defending the Blue Helmets: Protection of United Nations Personnel' in L Condorelli et al (eds), *Nations Unies et le droit international humanitaire: Actes du Colloque international à l'occasion du cinquantième anniversaire de l'ONU* (Paris, Éditions Pedone, 1996) 115–47.

Aurescu, B, 'Le conflict libanais de 2006: Une analyse juridique à la lumière de tendances contemporaines en matière de recours à la force' (2006) 52 *Annuaire français de droit international* 137.

Austin, J and Bruch, C (eds), *The Environmental Consequences of War: Legal, Economic, and Scientific Perspectives* (Cambridge, Cambridge University Press, 2000).

van Baarda, T, 'The Involvement of the Security Council in Maintaining International Humanitarian Law' (1994) *Netherlands Human Rights Quarterly* 137.

Barber, R, 'Facilitating Humanitarian Assistance in International Humanitarian and Human Rights Law' (2009) 873 *International Review of the Red Cross* 371.

Barsotti, R, 'Armed Reprisals' in A Cassese (ed), *The Current Legal Regulation of the Use of Force* (Dordrecht, Martinus Nijhoff, 1986) 79–110.

Bartels, R, 'Timeline, Borderlines and Conflicts: The Historical Evolution of the Legal Divide between International and Non-International Armed Conflicts' (2009) 873 *International Review of the Red Cross* 35.

Bassiouni, C, 'International Crimes: *Jus Cogens* and *Obligatio Erga Omnes*' (1996) 59 *Law and Contemporary Problems* 63.

Benvenisti, E, 'Rethinking the Divide between *Jus ad Bellum* and *Jus in Bello* in Warfare against Nonstate Actors' (2009) 34 *Yale Journal of International Law* 541.

Bernhardt, R, 'Article 103' in B Simma et al (eds), *The Charter of the United Nations: A Commentary*, 2nd edn, Vol II (Munich, CH Beck, 2002).

—— (ed), *Encyclopaedia of Public International Law* Vol III (Amsterdam, Elsevier Science BV, 1997).

Blokker, N, 'Is the Authorization Authorized? Powers and Practice of the Security Council to Authorize the Use of Force by "Coalitions of the Able and Willing"' (2000) 1 *European Journal of International Law* 541.

Blokker, N and Schrijver, N (eds), *The Security Council and the Use of Force: Theory and Reality – A Need for Change?* (Leiden, Martinus Nijhoff, 2005).

Bloom, E, 'Protecting Peacekeepers: The Convention on the Safety of United Nations and Associated Personnel' (1995) 89 *American Journal of International Law* 621.

Boisson de Chazournes, L, 'Les résolutions des organs des Nations Unies, et en particulier celles du Conseil de sécurité, en tant que source de droit international humanitaire' in L Condorelli et al (eds), *Nations Unies et le droit international humanitaire: Actes du Colloque international à l'occasion du cinquantième anniversaire de l'ONU* (Paris, Éditions Pedone, 1996) 149–73.

Boisson de Chazournes, L and Condorelli, L, 'Common Article 1 of the Geneva Conventions Revisited: Protecting Collective Interests' (2000) 837 *International Review of the Red Cross* 67.

Boisson de Chazournes, L and Sands, P (eds), *International Law, the International Court of Justice and Nuclear Weapons* (Cambridge, Cambridge University Press, 1999).

Boothby, W, *Weapons and the Law of Armed Conflict* (Oxford, Oxford University Press, 2009).

Borelli, S, 'Casting Light on the Legal Black Hole: International Law and Detentions Abroad in the "War on Terror"' (2005) 857 *International Review of the Red Cross* 39.

Bothe, M, 'Le droit de la guerre et les Nations Unies' (1967) 5 *Études et travaux de l'Institut Universitaire de Hautes Études Internationales* 135.

—— 'Peace-keeping' in B Simma et al (eds), *The Charter of the United Nations: A Commentary*, 2nd edn, Vol I (Oxford, Oxford University Press, 2002) 648–700.

—— 'The Status of Captured Fighters in Non-International Armed Conflict' in C Tomuschat et al (eds), *The Right to Life* (Leiden, Martinus Nijhoff, 2010) 195–214.

—— 'The United Nations Actions for the Respect of International Humanitarian Law and the Coordination of Related International Operations' in L Condorelli et al (eds), *Nations Unies et le droit international humanitaire: Actes du Colloque international à l'occasion du cinquantième anniversaire de l'ONU* (Paris, Éditions Pedone, 1996) 213–47.

Bourloyannis, C, 'The Convention on the Safety of United Nations and Associated Personnel' (1995) 44 *International and Comparative Law Quarterly* 560.

—— 'The Security Council of the United Nations and the Implementation of International Humanitarian Law' (1991–92) 20 *Denver Journal of International Law and Policy* 335.

Bouvier, A, 'Assessing the Relationship between *Jus in Bello* and *Jus ad Bellum*: An "Orthodox View"' (2006) *American Society of International Law Proceedings* 109.

—— 'Convention on the Safety of United Nations and Associated Personnel: Presentation and Analysis' (1995) 309 *International Review of the Red Cross* 638.

van Boven, T, 'Reliance on Norms of Humanitarian Law by United Nations' Organs' in A Delissen and G Tanja (eds), *Humanitarian Law of Armed Conflict: Challenges Ahead, Essays in Honour of Frits Kalshoven* (Dordrecht, Martinus Nijhoff, 1991) 495–513.

Bowett, D, 'Judicial and Political Functions of the Security Council and the International Court of Justice' in H Fox (ed), *The Changing Constitution of the United Nations* (London, British Institute of International and Comparative Law, 1997) 73–88.

—— 'Reprisals Including Recourse to Armed Force' (1972) 66 *American Journal of International Law* 1.

—— *Self-Defence in International Law* (Manchester, Manchester University Press, 1958).

—— *United Nations Forces* (London, Sweet and Maxwell, 1964).

Brand, G, 'The War Crimes Trials and the Laws of War' (1949) 26 *British Year Book of International Law* 414.

Bring, O, 'The Falklands Crisis and International Law' (1982) 51 *Nordic Journal of International Law* 129.

Broms, B, 'The Definition of Aggression' (1977) 154 *Recueil des Cours de l'Académie de Droit International* 297.

Brown, B, 'The Proportionality Principle in the Humanitarian Law of Warfare: Recent Efforts at Codification' (1976–77) 10 *Cornell International Law Journal* 134.

Brownlie, I, 'General Course on Public International Law' (1995) 255 *Recueil des Cours de l'Académie de Droit International* 9.

—— *International Law and the Use of Force by States* (Oxford, Clarendon Press, 1963).

—— *Principles of Public International Law*, 6th edn (Oxford, Oxford University Press, 2003).

—— 'The Use of Force in Self-Defence' (1961) 37 *British Year Book of International Law* 183.

Bugnion, F, 'Guerre juste, guerre d'agression et droit international humanitaire' (2002) 847 *Revue international de la Croix-Rouge* 523.

—— *The International Committee of the Red Cross and the Protection of War Victims* (Geneva, International Committee of the Red Cross, 2003).

—— '*Jus ad Bellum, Jus in Bello* and Non-International Armed Conflicts' (2003) 6 *Yearbook of International Humanitarian Law* 167.

—— 'Just Wars, Wars of Aggression and International Humanitarian Law' (2002) 847 *International Review of the Red Cross* 523.

—— 'Red Cross Law' (1995) 308 *International Review of the Red Cross* 491.

Burns, A and Heathcote, N, *Peace-keeping by U.N. Forces* (London, Pall Mall Press, 1963).

Byers, M, 'Terrorism, the Use of Force and International Law after 11 September' (2002) 51 *International and Comparative Law Quarterly* 400.

Cadoux, C, 'La supériorité du droit des Nations Unies sur le droit des États membres' (1959) 63 *Revue générale de droit international public* 649.

Cannizario, E, 'Contexualizing Proportionality: *Jus ad Bellum* and *Jus in Bello* in the Lebanese War' (2006) 864 *International Review of the Red Cross* 779.

Canor, I, 'When *Jus ad Bellum* Meets *Jus in Bello*: The Occupier's Right of Self-Defence against Terrorism Stemming from Occupied Territories' (2006) 19 *Leiden Journal of International Law* 129.

Carnahan, B, 'Lincoln, Lieber and the Laws of War: The Origins and Limits of the Principle of Military Necessity' (1998) 92 *American Journal of International Law* 213.

Cassese, A, 'Article 51' in J-P Cot et al, *La Charter des Nations Unies: Commentaire article par article* (Paris, Economica, 2005) 1329–61.

Cassese, A, *International Criminal Law*, 2nd edn (Oxford, Oxford University Press, 2008).

—— 'The Status of Rebels under the 1977 Geneva Protocol on Non-International Armed Conflicts' (1981) 30 *International and Comparative Law Quarterly* 416.

—— 'Terrorism Is Also Disrupting Some Crucial Legal Categories of International Law' (2001) 12 *European Journal of International Law* 993.

—— (ed), *The Current Legal Regulation of the Use of Force* (Dordrecht, Martinus Nijhoff, 1986).

—— (ed) *The New Humanitarian Law of Armed Conflict* (Napoli, Editoriale Scientifica, 1979).

Castren, E, *The Present Law of War and Neutrality* (Helsinki, Suomalaisen Tiedeakatemian Toimituksia, 1954).

Combacau, J, 'The Exception of Self-Defence in U.N. Practice' in A Cassese (ed), *The Current Legal Regulation of the Use of Force* (Dordrecht, Martinus Nijhoff, 1986) 9–38.

—— *Le pouvoir de sanction de l'ONU: Étude théorique de la coercion non militaire* (Paris, Éditions Pedone, 1974).

Condorelli, L, 'La compatibilité des sanctions du Conseil de Sécurité avec le droit international humanitaire – Commentaire' in V Gowlland-Debbas (ed), *United Nations Sanctions and International Law* (The Hague, Kluwer Law International, 2001) 233–40.

—— 'Le Droit Humanitaire dans la Crise et la "Guerre" du Golfe' in B Stern (ed), *Les Aspects Juridiques de la Crise et de la Guerre du Golfe: Aspects de Droit International Public et de Droit International Privé* (Paris, Montchresties, 1991) 187–97.

—— et al (eds), *Nations Unies et le droit international humanitaire: Actes du Colloque international à l'occasion du cinquantième anniversaire de l'ONU* (Paris, Éditions Pedone, 1996).

Conforti, B, 'Cours général de droit international public' (1988) 212 *Recueil des Cours de l'Académie de Droit International* 9.

Corten, O, *The Law against War* (Oxford, Hart Publishing, 2010).

Cot, J-P et al, *La Charter des Nations Unies: Commentaire article par article* (Paris, Economica, 2005).

de Courten, J, 'Le Comité international de la Croix-Rouge et l'action des Nations Unies dans les conflits armés' in L Condorelli et al (eds), *Nations Unies et le droit international humanitaire: Actes du Colloque international à l'occasion du cinquantième anniversaire de l'ONU* (Paris, Éditions Pedone, 1996) 339–44.

Craven, M, 'Humanitarianism and the Quest for Smarter Sanctions' (2002) 13 *European Journal of International Law* 43.

Crawford, E, *The Treatment of Combatants and Insurgents under the Law of Armed Conflict* (Oxford, Oxford University Press, 2010).

Crawford, J et al (eds), *The Law of International Responsibility* (Oxford, Oxford University Press, 2010).

—— 'Responsibility of States and Non-State Actors' (2005) 104-2 *Journal of International Law and Diplomacy* 42.

David, E, *Principes de droit des conflits armés*, 3ème edn (Brussels, Bruylant, 2002).

Dekker, I and Post, H (ed), *The Gulf War of 1980–1988* (Dordrecht, Martinus Nijhoff, 1992).

Delbrück, J, 'The Fight against Global Terrorism: Self-Defense or Collective Security as International Police Action? Some Comments on the International Legal Implications of the "War against Terrorism"' (2001) 44 *German Yearbook of International Law* 9.

—— 'Proportionality' in R Bernhardt (ed), *Encyclopaedia of Public International Law* Vol III (Amsterdam, Elsevier Science BV, 1997) 1140–44.

Delissen, A and Tanja, G (eds), *Humanitarian Law of Armed Conflict: Challenges Ahead, Essays in Honour of Frits Kalshoven* (Dordrecht, Martinus Nijhoff, 1991).

Dinstein, Y, *The Conduct of Hostilities under the Law of International Armed Conflict* (Cambridge, Cambridge University Press, 2004).

—— *The Conduct of Hostilities under the Law of International Armed Conflict*, 2nd edn (Cambridge, Cambridge University Press, 2010).

—— *The International Law of Belligerent Occupation* (Cambridge, Cambridge University Press, 2009).

—— *War, Aggression and Self-Defence*, 3rd edn (Cambridge, Cambridge University Press, 2001).

—— *War, Aggression and Self-Defence*, 4th edn (Cambridge, Cambridge University Press, 2005).

—— (ed), *International Law at A Time of Perplexity: Essays in Honour of Shabtai Rosenne* (Dordrecht, Matrinus Nijhoff, 1989).

Dominicé, C, 'L'article 103 de la Charte des Nations Unies et le droit international humanitaire' in L Condorelli et al (eds), *Nations Unies et le droit international humanitaire: Actes du Colloque international à l'occasion du cinquantième anniversaire de l'ONU* (Paris, Éditions Pedone, 1996) 175–92.

Doswald-Beck, L, 'The Legal Validity of Military Intervention by Invitation of the Government' (1985) 56 *British Year Book of International Law* 189.

Draper, G, 'Military Necessity and Humanitarian Imperatives' (1973) 12 *Revue de droit pénal militaire et de droit de la guerre* 129.

Duffy, H, *The 'War on Terror' and the Framework of International Law* (Cambridge, Cambridge University Press, 2005).

Dunbar, N, 'Military Necessity in War Crimes Trials' (1952) 29 *British Year Book of International Law* 442.

Dupuy, P-M, 'The Constitutional Dimension of the Charter of the United Nations Revisited' (1997) 1 *Max Planck Yearbook of United Nations Law* 1.

Dörmann, K, *Elements of War Crimes under the Rome Statute of the International Criminal Court: Sources and Commentary* (Geneva, International Committee of the Red Cross, 2003).

—— 'The Legal Situation of "Unlawful/Unprivileged Combatants"' (2003) 849 *International Review of the Red Cross* 45.

Dörmann, K and Colassis, L, 'International Humanitarian Law in the Iraq Conflict' (2004) 47 *German Yearbook of International Law* 293.

Engdahl, O, 'Compliance with International Humanitarian Law in Multinational Peace Operations' (2009) *Nordic Journal of International Law* 513.

—— 'The Status of Peace Operation Personnel under International Humanitarian Law' (2008) 11 *Yearbook of International Humanitarian Law* 109.

Evans, M (ed), *International Law*, 2nd edn (Oxford, Oxford University Press, 2006).

Faite, A, 'Applicability of the Law of Occupation to United Nations-Mandated Forces' in A Faite and J Grenier (eds), *Expert Meeting on Multinational Peace*

Operations: Applicability of International Humanitarian Law and International Human Rights Law to UN Mandated Forces (Geneva, International Committee of the Red Cross, 2004) 71–78.

Faite, A, 'Multinational Forces Acting Pursuant to a Mandate of the United Nations: Specific Issues on the Applicability of International Humanitarian Law' (2007) 11 *International Peacekeeping (The Yearbook of International Peace Operations)* 143.

Faite, A and Grenier, J (eds), *Expert Meeting on Multinational Peace Operations: Applicability of International Humanitarian Law and International Human Rights Law to UN Mandated Forces* (Geneva, International Committee of the Red Cross, 2004).

Falk, R, 'Kosovo, World Order, and the Future of International Law' (1999) 93 *American Journal of International Law* 847.

Farebrother, G and Kollerstrom, N (eds), *The Case against War: The Essential Legal Inquiries, Opinions and Judgments concerning War in Iraq* (Hailsham, The Legal Inquiry Steering Group, 2003).

Fenrick, W, 'Attacking the Enemy Civilian as a Punishable Offense' (1997) 7 *Duke Journal of Comparative and International Law* 539.

—— 'The Rule of Proportionality and Protocol I in Conventional Warfare' (1982) 98 *Military Law Review* 91.

Fernández-Sánchez, PA (ed), *The New Challenges of Humanitarian Law in Armed Conflicts* (Leiden, Martinus Nijhoff, 2005).

Findlay, T, *The Use of Force in UN Peace Operations* (Oxford, Oxford University Press, 2002).

Fischer, G, 'Le bombardement par Israël d'un réacteur nucléaire irakien' (1981) 27 *Annuaire français de droit international* 147.

Fitzmaurice, G, 'The Juridical Clauses of the Peace Treaties' (1948) 73 *Recueil des Cours de l'Académie de Droit International* 255.

—— *The Law and Procedure of the International Court of Justice* Vol 2 (Cambridge, Grotius Publications, 1986).

Fleck, D, 'International Humanitarian Law after September 11: Challenges and the Need to Respond' (2003) 6 *Yearbook of International Humanitarian Law* 41.

—— (ed), *The Handbook of Humanitarian Law in Armed Conflicts* (Oxford, Oxford University Press, 1995).

—— *The Handbook of the Law of Visiting Forces* (Oxford, Oxford University Press, 2001).

Fox, H (ed), *The Changing Constitution of the United Nations* (London, British Institute of International and Comparative Law, 1997).

Franck, T, *Fairness in International Law and Institutions* (Oxford, Clarendon Press, 1995).

—— 'On Proportionality of Countermeasures in International Law' (2008) 102 *American Journal of International Law* 715.

—— 'Terrorism and the Right of Self-Defense' (2001) 95 *American Journal of International Law* 839.

Frowein, J and Krisch, N, 'Article 39' in B Simma et al (eds), *The Charter of the United Nations: A Commentary*, 2nd edn, Vol I (Oxford, Oxford University Press, 2002) 717–29.

—— 'Article 41' in B Simma et al (eds), *The Charter of the United Nations: A Commentary*, 2nd edn, Vol I (Oxford, Oxford University Press, 2002) 735–49.

Fujita, H, 'Kokusaijindōhō no kinōtenkai: Kokurenhō to no sōgoshintō' in H Fujita et al (eds), *Jinkenhō to jindōhō no shinseiki* (Tokyo, Tōshindō, 2001).

—— (eds), *Jinkenhō to jindōhō no shinseiki* (Tokyo, Tōshindō, 2001).

Gardam, J, *Necessity, Proportionality and the Use of Force* (Cambridge, Cambridge University Press, 2004).

—— 'Proportionality and Force in International Law' (1993) 87 *American Journal of International Law* 391.

Gasser, H-P, 'Collective Economic Sanctions and International Humanitarian Law' (1996) 56 *Zeitschrift für Ausländisches Öffentliches Recht und Völkerrecht (Heidelberg Journal of International Law)* 871.

—— *International Humanitarian Law: An Introduction* (Bern, Haupt, 1993).

—— 'Internationalized Non-International Armed Conflicts: Case Studies of Afghanistan, Kampuchea, and Lebanon' (1983–84) 33 *American University Law Review* 145.

—— 'Notes on the Law on Belligerent Occupation' (2006) 45 *Revue de droit militaire et de droit de la guerre* 229.

—— 'The United Nations and International Humanitarian Law: The International Committee of the Red Cross and the United Nations' Involvement in the Implementation of International Humanitarian Law' in L Condorelli et al (eds), *Nations Unies et le droit international humanitaire: Actes du Colloque international à l'occasion du cinquantième anniversaire de l'ONU* (Paris, Éditions Pedone, 1996) 259–84.

Gazzini, T, *The Changing Rules on the Use of Force in International Law* (Manchester, Manchester University Press, 2005).

—— 'NATO Coercive Military Activities in the Yugoslav Crisis (1992–1999)' (2001) 12 *European Journal of International Law* 391.

Gill, T, 'Legal and Some Political Limitations on the Power of the Security Council to Exercise Its Enforcement Powers under Chapter VII of the Charter' (1995) 26 *Netherlands Yearbook of International Law* 33.

—— 'The Nuclear Weapons Advisory Opinion of the International Court of Justice and the Fundamental Distinction between the *Jus ad Bellum* and *Jus in Bello*' (1999) 12 *Leiden Journal of International Law* (1999) 613.

—— 'The Temporal Dimension of Self-Defense: Anticipation, Pre-emption, Prevention and Immediacy' in M Schmitt and J Pejic (eds), *International Law and Armed Conflict: Exploring the Faultlines* (The Netherlands, Koninklijke Brill BV, 2007) 133–55.

Gill, T, and Fleck, D, *The Handbook of the International Law of Military Operations* (Oxford, Oxford University Press, 2010).

von Glahn, G, *The Occupation of Enemy Territory* (Minneapolis, University of Minnesota Press, 1957).

Goldman, R and Tittemore, B, 'Unprivileged Combatants and the Hostilities in Afghanistan: Their Status and Rights under International Humanitarian and Human Rights Law' (December 2002) *American Society of International Law Task Force on Terrorism*.

Goodman, R, 'The Detention of Civilians in Armed Conflict' (2009) 103 *American Journal of International Law* 48.

Goodwin-Gill, G and Talmon, S (eds) *The Reality of International Law: Essays in Honour of Ian Brownlie* (Oxford, Oxford University Press, 1999).

Gordon, K, *The United Nations in the Congo: A Quest for Peace* (New York, Carnegie Endowment for International Peace, 1962).
Gowlland-Debbas, V, 'Security Council Enforcement Action and Issues of State Responsibility' (1994) 43 *International and Comparative Law Quarterly* 55.
—— (ed), *United Nations Sanctions and International Law* (The Hague, Kluwer Law International, 2001).
Gray, C, 'A Crisis of Legitimacy for the UN Collective Security System?' (2007) 56 *International and Comparative Law Quarterly* 157.
—— 'The Eritrea/Ethiopia Claims Commission Oversteps Its Boundaries: A Partial Award?' (2006) 17 *European Journal of International Law* 699.
—— 'From Unity to Polarization: International Law and the Use of Force against Iraq' (2002) 12 *European Journal of International Law* 1.
—— *International Law and the Use of Force*, 2nd edn (Oxford, Oxford University Press, 2004).
Green, J, 'Fluctuating Evidentiary Standards for Self-Defence in the International Court of Justice' (2009) 58 *International and Comparative Law Quarterly* 163.
—— *The International Court of Justice and Self-Defence in International Law* (Oxford, Hart Publishing, 2009).
—— 'Self-Defence: A State of Mind for States?' (2008) 55 *Netherlands International Law Review* 181.
Green, L, *The Contemporary Law of Armed Conflict*, 2nd edn (Manchester, Manchester University Press, 2000).
Greenwood, C, 'The Concept of War in Modern International Law' (1987) 36 *International and Comparative Law Quarterly* 283.
—— 'Historical Development and Legal Basis' in D Fleck (ed), *The Handbook of Humanitarian Law in Armed Conflicts* (Oxford, Oxford University Press, 1995) 1–43.
—— 'International Humanitarian Law and the *Tadic* Case' (1996) 7 *European Journal of International Law* 265.
—— 'International Humanitarian Law and United Nations Military Operations' (1998) 1 *Yearbook of International Humanitarian Law* 3.
—— 'International Humanitarian Law (Law of War)' in F Kalshoven (ed), *The Centennial of the First International Peace Conference: Reports and Conclusions* (Boston, Kluwer Law International, 2000) 161–260.
—— 'International Law and the United States' Air Operation against Libya' (1986–87) 89 *West Virginia Law Review* 933.
—— 'International Law and the "War against Terrorism"' (2002) 78 *International Affairs* 301.
—— 'New World Order or Old? The Invasion of Kuwait and the Rule of Law' (1992) 55 *Modern Law Review* 153.
—— 'Protection of Peacekeepers: The Legal Regime' (1996–97) 7 *Duke Journal of Comparative and International Law* 203.
—— 'The Relationship between *Jus ad Bellum* and *Jus in Bello*' (1983) 9 *Review of International Studies* 221.
—— 'Scope of Application of Humanitarian Law' in D Fleck (ed), *The Handbook of Humanitarian Law in Armed Conflicts* (Oxford, Oxford University Press, 1995) 39–63.

—— 'Self-Defence and the Conduct of International Armed Conflict' in Y Dinstein (ed), *International Law at a Time of Perplexity: Essays in Honour of Shabtai Rosenne* (Dordrecht, Matrinus Nijhoff, 1989) 237–88.

—— 'Terrorism and Humanitarian Law – The Debate over Additional Protocol I' (1989) 19 *Israel Yearbook on Human Rights* 187.

—— 'Twilight of the Law of Belligerent Reprisals' (1989) 20 *Netherlands Yearbook of International Law* 35.

Guillaume, G, 'Terrorism and International Law' (2004) 53 *International and Comparative Law Quarterly* 537.

de Guttry, A et al (eds), *The 1998–2000 War between Eritrea and Ethiopia: An International Legal Perspective* (The Hague, TMC Asser Press, 2009).

Hampson, F, 'Belligerent Reprisals and the 1977 Protocols to the Geneva Conventions of 1949' (1988) 37 *International and Comparative Law Quarterly* 818.

Hannikainen, L, *Peremptory Norms (Jus Cogens) in International Law: Historical Development, Criteria, Present Status* (Helsinki, Lakimiesliiton Kustannus, 1988).

Harroff-Tavel, M, 'Neutralité et impartialité – De l'importance et de la difficulté, pour le Mouvement international de la Croix-Rouge et du Croissant-Rouge, d'être guidé par ces principes' (1989) 780 *Revue international de la Croix-Rouge* 563.

Hayashi, N, 'Requirements of Military Necessity in International Humanitarian Law and International Criminal Law' (2010) 28 *Boston University International Law Journal* 39.

Hegelsom, G-J van, 'The Law of Armed Conflict and United Nations Peace-keeping and Peace-enforcing Operations' (1993) 6 *Hague Yearbook of International Law* 45.

Henckaerts, J-M, 'Study on Customary International Humanitarian Law: A Contribution to the Understanding and Respect for the Rule of Law in Armed Conflict' (2005) 857 *International Review of the Red Cross* 175.

Henckaerts, J-M and Doswald-Beck, L, *Customary International Humanitarian Law* Vol I: Rules (Geneva, International Committee of the Red Cross and Cambridge, Cambridge University Press, 2005).

—— (eds), *Customary International Humanitarian Law* Vol II: Practice (Geneva, International Committee of the Red Cross and Cambridge, Cambridge University Press, 2005).

Henderson, C and Green, J, 'The *Jus ad Bellum* and Entities Short of Statehood in the Report on the Conflict in Georgia' (2010) 59 *International and Comparative Law Quarterly* 129.

Higgins, R, *The Development of International Law through the Political Organs of the United Nations* (London, Oxford University Press, 1963).

—— *Problems and Process: International Law and How We Use It* (Oxford, Clarendon Press, 1994).

Hladík, J, 'The 1954 Hague Convention for the Protection of Cultural Property in the Event of Armed Conflict and the Notion of Military Necessity' (1999) 835 *International Review of the Red Cross* 621.

Holland, J, 'Military Objective and Collateral Damage: Their Relationship and Dynamics' (2004) 7 *Yearbook of International Humanitarian Law* 35.

Hoskyns, C, *The Congo Since Independence: January 1960 – December 1961* (London, Oxford University Press, 1965).

Ipsen, K, 'International Law Preventing Armed Conflicts and International Law of Armed Conflict – A Combined Functional Approach' in C Swinarski (ed), *Studies and Essays on International Humanitarian Law and Red Cross Principles in Honour of Jean Pictet* (The Hague, Martinus Nijhoff, 1984) 349–58.

Jennings, R, 'The Caroline and McLeod Cases' (1938) 32 *American Journal of International Law* 82.

Jennings, R and Watts, A (eds), *Oppenheim's International Law*, 9th edn, Vol 1: Peace, Introduction and Part 1 (London, Longman, 1992).

Jessup, P, 'Political and Humanitarian Approaches to Limitation of Warfare' (1957) 51 *American Journal of International Law* 757.

Jinks, D, Remarks in 'Self-Defense in an Age of Terrorism' (2003) *American Society of International Law Proceedings* 144.

Kaikobad, K, 'Self-Defence, Enforcement Action and the Gulf Wars, 1980–88 and 1990–91' (1992) 63 *British Year Book of International Law* 299.

Kalshoven, F, *Belligerent Reprisals* (Leiden, Martinus Nijhoff, 2005).

—— 'Belligerent Reprisals Revisited' (1990) 21 *Netherlands Yearbook of International Law* 43.

—— 'Implementing Limitations on the Use of Force: The Doctrine of Proportionality and Necessity, Remarks' (1992) 86 *American Society of International Law Proceedings* 40.

—— 'Prohibitions or Restrictions on the Use of Methods and Means of Warfare' in I Dekker and H Post (ed), *The Gulf War of 1980–1988* (Dordrecht, Martinus Nijhoff, 1992).

—— 'State Responsibility for Warlike Acts of the Armed Forces: From Article 3 of the Hague Convention IV of 1907 to Article 91 of the Additional Protocol I of 1977 and Beyond' (1991) 40 *International and Comparative Law Quarterly* 827.

—— (ed), *The Centennial of the First International Peace Conference: Reports and Conclusions* (Boston, Kluwer Law International, 2000).

Kelsen, H, *The Law of the United Nations: A Critical Analysis of Its Fundamental Problems* (London, Stevens and Sons, 1950).

—— *Principles of International Law*, 2nd edn (New York, Holt, Reinhart, and Wilson, 1966).

King, F and Swaak-Goldman, O, 'The Applicability of International Humanitarian Law to the "War against Terrorism"' (2002) 15 *Hague Yearbook of International Law* 39.

Kolb, R, 'Considération sur l'application du droit international humanitaire par la Commission arbitrale Erythrée/Ethiopie' in B Vukas and T Sosic (eds), *International Law: New Actors, New Concepts, Continuing Dilemmas: Liber Amicorum Bozidar Bakotic* (Leiden, Martinus Nijhoff, 2010) 519–44.

—— 'Does Article 103 of the Charter of the United Nations Apply Only to Decisions or Also to Authorizations Adopted by the Security Council?' (2004) 64 *Zeitschrift für Ausländisches Öffentliches Recht und Völkerrecht (Heidelberg Journal of International Law)* 21.

—— *Droit humanitaire et opérations de paix internationals* (Bâle, Helbing et Lichtenhahn, 2002).

—— *Ius contra bellum: Le droit international relatif au maintien de la paix* (Bâle, Helbing et Lichtenhahn, 2003).

—— *Ius in bello: Le droit international des conflits armés* (Bâle, Helbing et Lichtenhahn, 2003).
—— 'Occupation in Iraq since 2003 and the Powers of the UN Security Council' (2008) 869 *International Review of the Red Cross* 29.
—— 'Origin of the Twin Terms *Jus ad Bellum/Jus in Bello*' (1997) 320 *International Review of the Red Cross* 553.
—— et al, *L'application du droit international humanitaire et des droits de l'homme aux organisations internationales: Forces de paix et administrations civiles transitoires*, (Bruxelles, Bruylant, 2005).
Kooijmans, P, 'Is There a Change in the *Ius ad Bellum* and, if so, What Does It Mean for the *Ius in Bello*?' in L Lijnzaad et al (eds), *Making the Voice of Humanity Heard* (Dordrecht, Martinus Nijhoff, 2004).
Kress, C, 'Some Reflections on the International Legal Framework Governing Transnational Armed Conflicts' (2010) 15 *Journal of Conflict and Security Law* 245.
Kretzmer, D, 'Targeted Killing of Suspected Terrorists: Extra-Judicial Executions or Legitimate Means of Defence?' (2005) 16 *European Journal of International Law* 172.
Kritsiotis, D, 'On the *Jus ad Bellum* and *Jus in Bello* of Operation Enduring Freedom' (2003) *American Society of International Law Proceedings* 35.
Kälin, W, 'Flight in Times of War' (2001) 843 *International Review of the Red Cross* 629.
Lagrange, E, 'Le Conseil de Sécurité des Nations Unies peut-il violer le droit international?' (2004) 37 *Revue belge de droit international* 568.
Lamb, S, 'Legal Limits to United Nations Security Council Powers' in G Goodwin-Gill and S Talmon (eds), *The Reality of International Law: Essays in Honour of Ian Brownlie* (Oxford, Oxford University Press, 1999).
Lauterpacht, E, 'The Legal Effects of Illegal Acts of International Organisations' in *Cambridge Essays in International Law: Essays in Honour of Lord McNair* (London, Steven and Sons, 1965).
Lauterpacht, H, 'The Limits of the Operation of the Laws of War' (1953) 30 *British Year Book of International Law* 206.
—— (ed), Oppenheim, L, *International Law: A Treaties* Vol II: Disputes, War and Neutrality, 7th edn (London, Longmans, Green and Co, 1952).
Lauwaars, R, 'The Interrelationship between United Nations Law and the Law of Other International Organizations' (1983–84) 82 *Michigan Law Review* 1604.
Lavoyer, J-P, 'Guiding Principles on International Displacement: A Few Comments on the Contribution of International Humanitarian Law' (1998) 324 *International Review of the Red Cross* 467.
Lee, R, 'The *Jus ad Bellum* in Outer Space: The Interrelation between Article 103 of the Charter of the United Nations and Article IV of the Outer Space Treaty' (2002) *Proceedings of the Forty-Fifth Colloquium on the Law of Outer Space (Houston 10–19 October 2002)* 139.
Lefever, E, *Crisis in the Congo: A United Nations Force in Action* (Washington DC, The Brookings Institution, 1965).
Liivoja, R, 'The Scope of the Supremacy Clause of the United Nations Charter' (2008) 57 *International and Comparative Law Quarterly* 583.
Lijnzaad, L et al (eds), *Making the Voice of Humanity Heard* (Dordrecht, Martinus Nijhoff, 2004).

Lobel, J and Ratner, M, 'Bypassing the Security Council: Ambiguous Authorizations to Use Force, Cease-Fires and the Iraqi Inspection Regime' (1999) 93 *American Journal of International Law* 124.

Lowe, V, 'Clear and Present Danger: Responses to Terrorism' (2005) 54 *International and Comparative Law Quarterly* 185.

Lubell, N, *Extraterritorial Use of Force against Non-State Actors* (Oxford, Oxford University Press, 2010).

Maresca, L, 'A New Protocol on Explosive Remnants of War: The History and Negotiation of Protocol V to the 1980 Convention on Certain Conventional Weapons' (2004) 856 *International Review of the Red Cross* 815.

Martelli, G, *Experiment in World Government: An Account of the United Nations Operation in the Congo 1960–1964* (London, Johnson Publications, 1966).

Martínez, LMH, 'The Legislative Role of the Security Council in Its Fight Against Terrorism: Legal, Political and Practical Limits' (2008) 57 *International and Comparative Law Quarterly* 333.

Matheson, M, 'The Opinions of the International Court of Justice on the Threat or Use of Nuclear Weapons' (1997) 91 *American Journal of International Law* 417.

McCoubrey, H and White, N, *The Blue Helmets: Legal Regulation of United Nations Military Operations* (Aldershot, Dartmouth, 1996).

McDonald, A, 'Declarations of War and Belligerent Parties: International Law Governing Hostilities between States and Transnational Terrorist Networks' (2007) 54 *Netherlands International Law Review* 279.

—— 'Defining the War on Terror and the Status of Detainees: Comments on the Presentation of Judge George Aldrich' (2002) *Humanitäres Völkerrecht* 206.

McDougal, M and Feliciano, F, *The International Law of War* (New Haven, New Haven Press, 1994).

McMahan, J, 'Morality, Law, and the Relation between *Jus ad Bellum* and *Jus in Bello*' (2006) *American Society of International Law Proceedings* 112.

Mégret, F, '*Jus in Bello* and *Jus ad Bellum*' (2006) *American Society of International Law Proceedings* 109.

Melzer, N, *Targeted Killing in International Law* (Oxford, Oxford University Press, 2008).

—— 'Targeted Killing or Less Harmful Means? Israel's High Court Judgment on Targeted Killing and the Restrictive Function of Military Necessity' (2006) 9 *Yearbook of International Humanitarian Law* 87.

Meng, W, 'War' in R Bernhardt (ed), *Encyclopaedia of Public International Law* Vol IV (Amsterdam, Elsevier Science BV, 2000) 1334–42.

Meron, T, 'Classification of Armed Conflict in the Former Yugoslavia: Nicaragua's Fallout' (1998) 92 *American Journal of International Law* 136.

—— 'International Criminalization of Internal Atrocities' (1995) 89 *American Journal of International Law* 554.

Mertus, J, 'The Danger of Conflating *Jus ad Bellum* and *Jus in Bello*' (2006) *American Society of International Law Proceedings* 114.

Meyrowitz, H, *Le Principe de l'égalité de belligérants devant le droit de la guerre* (Paris, Éditions Pedone, 1970).

Mogami, T, 'Non-State Actors and International Law: A Tentative Theorization on the Conversion of the Principle of the Legal Order' (2009) 108-2 *Journal of International Law and Diplomacy* 1.

Moir, L, *Reappraising the Resort to Force* (Oxford, Hart Publishing, 2010).
Momtaz, D, 'La compatibilité des sanctions du Conseil de Sécurité avec le droit international humanitaire' in V Gowlland-Debbas (ed), *United Nations Sanctions and International Law* (The Hague, Kluwer Law International, 2001) 223–32.
Monaco, R, 'Les conventions entre belligérants' (1949) 75 *Recueil des Cours de l'Académie de Droit International* 18.
Moussa, J, 'Can *Jus ad Bellum* Override *Jus in Bello*? Reaffirming the Separation of the Two Bodies of Law' (2008) 872 *International Review of the Red Cross* 963.
Murphy, S, 'Terrorism and the Concept of "Armed Attack" in Article 51 of the U.N. Charter' (2002) 43 *Harvard International Law Journal* 41.
—— (ed), 'U.S. Nationals Detained as Unlawful Combatants' (2003) 97 *American Journal of International Law* 196.
Naqvi, Y, 'Doubtful Prisoner-of-War Status' (2002) 847 *International Review of the Red Cross* 571.
Nieto-Navia, R, 'International Peremptory Norms (*Jus Cogens*) and International Humanitarian Law' in L Vohrah et al (eds), *Man's Inhumanity to Man: Essays on International Law in Honour of Antonio Cassese* (The Hague, Kluwer Law International, 2003) 595–640.
O'Connell, M, 'Debating the Law of Sanctions' (2002) 13 *European Journal of International Law* 63.
Oeter, S, 'Civil War, Humanitarian Law and the United Nations' (1997) 1 *Max Planck Yearbook of United Nations Law* 195.
Okimoto, K, 'The Protection of Detainees in International Humanitarian Law' in S Perrigo and J Whitman (eds), *The Geneva Conventions under Assault* (London, Pluto Press, 2010) 99–135.
—— 'Violations of International Humanitarian Law by United Nations Forces and Their Legal Consequences' (2003) 6 *Yearbook of International Humanitarian Law* 199.
Olson, L, 'Provoking the Dragon on the Patio – Matters of Transitional Justice: Penal Repression vs. Amnesty' (2006) 862 *International Review of the Red Cross* 275.
Oppenheim, L, *International Law: A Treaties* Vol II: Disputes, War and Neutrality (London, Longmans, Green and Co, 1906).
Orakhelashvili, A, 'The Acts of the Security Council: Meaning and Standards of Review' (2007) 11 *Max Planck Yearbook of United Nations Law* 143.
—— 'Legal Stability and Claims of Change: The International Court's Treatment of *Jus ad Bellum* and *Jus in Bello*' (2006) 75 *Nordic Journal of International Law* 371.
—— 'Overlap and Convergence: The Interaction between *Jus ad Bellum* and *Jus in Bello*' (2007) *Journal of Conflict and Security Law* 157.
—— *Peremptory Norms in International Law* (Oxford, Oxford University Press, 2006).
Osieke, E, 'The Legal Validity of Ultra Vires Decisions of International Organizations' (1983) 77 *American Journal of International Law* 239.
Oswald, B, 'The Creation and Control of Places of Protection during United Nations Peace Operations' (2001) 844 *International Review of the Red Cross* 1013.
Österdahl, I, 'Dangerous Liaison? The Disappearing Dichotomy between *Jus ad Bellum* and *in Bello*' (2009) *Nordic Journal of International Law* 553.
Palwankar, U, 'Applicability of International Humanitarian Law to United Nations Peace-keeping Forces' (1993) 294 *International Review of the Red Cross* 227.

Papastavridis, E, 'Interpretation of Security Council Resolutions under Chapter VII in the Aftermath of the Iraqi Crisis' (2007) 56 *International and Comparative Law Quarterly* 83.

Parker, T, 'Proportionality Principle in the War on Terror' (2002) 15 *Hague Yearbook of International Law* 3.

Pastor-Ridruejo, J, 'On the Relationship between *Ius in Bello* and *Ius ad Bellum*: Can a Notion of International Humanitarian Law Influence in the Determination of the Legality of the Use of Force?' in PA Fernández-Sánchez (ed), *The New Challenges of Humanitarian Law in Armed Conflicts* (Leiden, Martinus Nijhoff, 2005) 3–12.

Peck, J, 'The UN and the Law of War: How Can the World's Peacekeepers Be Held Accountable?' (1995) 21 *Syracuse Journal of International Law and Commerce* 283.

Pejic, J, 'Procedural Principles and Safeguards for Internment/Administrative Detention in Armed Conflict and Other Situations of Violence' (2005) 858 *International Review of the Red Cross* 375.

—— 'Terrorist Acts and Groups: A Role for International Law?' (2004) 75 *British Year Book of International Law* 71.

Perrigo, S and Whitman, J (eds), *The Geneva Conventions under Assault* (London, Pluto Press, 2010).

Pictet, J et al, *Commentary on the Geneva Conventions of 12 August 1949* Vols I and II (Geneva, International Committee of the Red Cross, 1952).

Post, H (ed), *International Economic Law and Armed Conflict* (Dordrecht, Martinus Nijhoff, 1994).

Preiser, S, '"Operation Enduring Freedom" and the UN Charter: The Terrorist Attacks of 11 September 2001 and the Subsequent Military Response' (2004) 8 *International Peacekeeping* 213.

de Preux, J, *Commentary on the Geneva Conventions of 12 August 1949* Vol III (Geneva, International Committee of the Red Cross, 1960).

Randelzhofer, A, 'Article 2(4)' in B Simma et al (eds), *The Charter of the United Nations: A Commentary*, 2nd edn, Vol I (Oxford, Oxford University Press, 2002) 112–36.

—— 'Article 51' in B Simma et al (eds), *The Charter of the United Nations: A Commentary*, 2nd edn, Vol I (Oxford, Oxford University Press, 2002) 788–806.

Reuter, P, *Introduction au droit des traités*, 3ème edn, revue et augmentée par Philippe Cahier (Paris, Presses Universitaires de France, 1995).

Roberts, A, 'The End of Occupation: Iraq 2004' (2005) 54 *International and Comparative Law Quarterly* 27.

—— 'The Equal Application of the Laws of War: A Principle under Pressure' (2008) 872 *International Review of the Red Cross* 931.

—— 'Transformative Military Occupation: Applying the Law of War and Human Rights' (2006) 100 *American Journal of International Law* 580.

Roberts, A and Guelff, R (eds), *Documents on the Laws of War*, 3rd edn (Oxford, Oxford University Press, 2000).

Rona, G, 'Interesting Times for International Humanitarian Law: Challenges from the "War on Terror"' (2003) 27 *Fletcher Forum of World Affairs* 55.

Ronen, Y, 'Israel, Hizbollah, and the Second Lebanon War' (2006) 9 *Yearbook of International Humanitarian Law* (2006) 362.

La Rosa, A-M, 'Armed Groups, Sanctions and the Implementation of International Humanitarian Law' (2008) 870 *International Review of the Red Cross* 327.

Rousseau, C, *Le droit des conflits armés* (Paris, Pedone, 1983).
Rowe, P (ed), *The Gulf War 1990–91 in International and English Law* (London, Routledge, 1993).
Rowles, J, 'Military Responses to Terrorism: Substantive and Procedural Constraints in International Law' (1987) 81 *American Society of International Law Proceedings* 307.
Rueger, C, 'The Law of Military Occupation' (2006) 45 *Revue de droit militaire et de droit de la guerre* 215.
Röling, B, 'The Law of War and the National Jurisdiction since 1945' (1960) 100 *Recueil des Cours de l'Académie de Droit International* 323.
—— 'The 1974 U.N. Definition of Aggression' in A Cassese (ed), *The Current Legal Regulation of the Use of Force* (Dordrecht, Martinus Nijhoff, 1986) 413–21.
Sandoz, Y, 'The Establishment of Safety Zones for Persons Displaced within Their Country of Origin' in N Al-Nauimi and R Messe, *International Legal Issues Arising under the United Nations Decade of International Law: Proceedings of the Qatar International Law Conference 1994* (The Hague, Martinus Nijhoff, 1995) 899–927.
—— 'Rapport général' in L Condorelli et al (eds), *Nations Unies et le droit international humanitaire: Actes du colloque international à l'occasion du cinquantième anniversaire de l'ONU* (Paris, Éditions Pedone, 1996) 56–83.
—— et al, 'Special Issue: The Advisory Opinion on the International Court of Justice on the Legality of Nuclear Weapons and International Humanitarian Law' (1997) 316 *International Review of the Red Cross* 1.
—— et al, (eds), *Commentary on the Additional Protocols of 8 June 1977 to the Geneva Conventions of 12 August 1949* (Geneva, International Committee of the Red Cross, 1987).
Sarooshi, D, *The United Nations and the Development of Collective Security: The Delegation by the UN Security Council of Its Chapter VII Powers* (Oxford, Clarendon Press, 1999).
Sassòli, M, '*Ius ad Bellum* and *Ius in Bello* – The Separation between the Legality of the Use of Force and Humanitarian Rules to Be Respected in Warfare: Crucial or Outdated?' in M Schmitt and J Pejic (eds), *International Law and Armed Conflict: Exploring the Faultlines* (The Netherlands, Koninklijke Brill BV, 2007) 241–64.
—— 'Outline of *de Jure* and *de Facto* Applicability of the Law of Occupation to United Nations-Mandated Forces' in A Faite and J Grenier (eds), *Expert Meeting on Multinational Peace Operations: Applicability of International Humanitarian Law and International Human Rights Law to UN Mandated Forces* (Geneva, International Committee of the Red Cross, 2004) 33–34.
—— 'Sanctions and International Humanitarian Law – Commentary' in V Gowlland-Debbas (ed), *United Nations Sanctions and International Law* (The Hague, Kluwer Law International, 2001) 241–52.
—— 'State Responsibility for Violations of International Humanitarian Law' (2002) 846 *International Review of the Red Cross* 401.
—— 'The Status of Persons Held in Guantanamo under International Humanitarian Law' (2004) 2 *Journal of International Criminal Justice* 96.
—— '"Unlawful Combatants": The Law and Whether It Needs to Be Revised' (2003) *American Society of International Law Proceedings* 196.
Sassòli, M and Bouvier, A (eds), *How Does Law Protect in War?*, 2nd edn, Vol II (Geneva, International Committee of the Red Cross, 2006).

Sassòli, M and Olson, L, 'The Relationship between International Humanitarian and Human Rights Law Where It Matters: Admissible Killing and Internment of Fighters in Non-International Armed Conflicts' (2008) 871 *International Review of the Red Cross* 599.
Scelle, G, 'Quelques réflexions sur l'abolition de la compétence de guerrer' (1954) 25 *Revue générale de droit international public* 5.
Schachter, O, 'General Course in Public International Law' (1982) 178 *Recueil des Cours de l'Académie de Droit International* 1.
—— *International Law in Theory and Practice* (Dordrecht, Martinus Nijhoff, 1991).
—— 'The Lawful Use of Force by a State against Terrorists in Another Country' (1998) 19 *Israel Yearbook on Human Rights* 209.
—— 'United Nations Law in the Gulf Conflict' (1991) 85 *American Journal of International Law* 452.
Scheffer, D, 'Beyond Occupation Law' (2003) 97 *American Journal of International Law* 842.
Schindler, D, 'The Different Types of Armed Conflicts According to the Geneva Conventions and Protocols' (1979) 163 *Recueil des Cours de l'Académie de Droit International* 116.
—— 'State of War, Belligerency, Armed Conflict' in A Cassese (ed), *The New Humanitarian Law of Armed Conflict* (Napoli, Editoriale Scientifica, 1979) 1–20.
—— 'Transformations in the Law of Neutrality since 1945' in A Delissen and G Tanja (eds), *Humanitarian Law of Armed Conflict: Challenges Ahead, Essays in Honour of Frits Kalshoven* (Dordrecht, Martinus Nijhoff, 1991) 367–86.
—— 'United Nations Forces and International Humanitarian Law' in C Swinarski (ed), *Studies and Essays on International Humanitarian Law and Red Cross Principles in Honour of Jean Pictet* (The Hague, Martinus Nijhoff, 1984) 521–30.
Schindler, D and Toman, J (eds), *Droit des conflits armés: Recueil des conventions, resolutions et autres documents* (Genève, Comité international de la Croix-Rouge and Institut Henry-Dunant, 1996).
—— *The Laws of Armed Conflicts: A Collection of Conventions, Resolutions and Other Documents* (Leiden, Martinus Nijhoff, 2004).
Schmitt, M, 'Military Necessity and Humanity in International Humanitarian Law: Preserving the Delicate Balance' (2010) 50 *Virginia Journal of International Law* 795.
—— 'Targeting and Humanitarian Law: Current Issues' (2004) 34 *Israel Yearbook on Human Rights* 59.
Schmitt, M and Pejic, J (eds), *International Law and Armed Conflict: Exploring the Faultlines* (The Netherlands, Koninklijke Brill BV, 2007).
Schrijver, N, 'Responding to International Terrorism: Moving the Frontiers of International Law for "Enduring Freedom"' (2001) 48 *Netherlands International Law Review* 271.
—— 'The Use of Economics Sanctions by the UN Security Council: An International Law Perspective' in H Post (ed), *International Economic Law and Armed Conflict* (Dordrecht, Martinus Nijhoff, 1994) 123–158.
Schwarzenberger, G, 'The Fundamental Principles of International Law' (1955) 87 *Recueil des Cours de l'Académie de Droit International* 195.
—— *International Law as Applied by International Courts and Tribunals* Vol II: The Law of Armed Conflict (London, Stevens and Sons, 1968).

Schwebel, S, 'Aggression, Intervention and Self-Defence in Modern International Law' (1972) 136 *Recueil des Cours de l'Académie de Droit International* 411.

Scobbie, I, 'Words My Mother Never Taught Me: "In Defense of the International Court"' (2005) 99 *American Journal of International Law* 76.

Segall, A, 'Economic Sanctions: Legal and Policy Analysis' (1999) 836 *International Review of the Red Cross* 763.

Seyersted, F, *United Nations Forces in the Law of Peace and War* (Leyden, Sijthoff, 1966).

—— 'United Nations Forces: Some Legal Problems' (1961) 37 *British Year Book of International Law* 351.

Sharma, S, 'Reconsidering the Jus ad Bellum/Jus in Bello Distinction' in C Stahn and J Kleffner, *Jus post Bellum: Towards a Law of Transition from Conflict to Peace* (The Hague, TMC Asser Press, 2008) 9–30.

Shraga, D, 'The United Nations as an Actor Bound by International Humanitarian Law' (1998) 5 *International Peacekeeping* 64.

—— 'UN Peacekeeping Operations: Applicability of International Humanitarian Law and Responsibility for Operation-Related Damage' (2000) 94 *American Journal of International Law* 407.

Sicilianos, L-A, 'Entre multilatéralism et unilatéralism: l'autorisation par le Conseil de sécurité de recourir à la force' (2008) 339 *Recueil des Cours de l'Académie de Droit International* 9.

Siekmann, R, *Basic Documents on United Nations and Related Peace-keeping Forces* (The Hague, TMC Asser Instituut, 1985).

Simma, B et al (eds), *The Charter of the United Nations: A Commentary*, 2nd edn, Vols I and II (Oxford, Oxford University Press, 2002).

Somer, J, 'Jungle Justice: Passing Sentence on the Equality of Belligerents in Non-International Armed Conflict' (2007) 867 *International Review of the Red Cross* 655.

Sottas, E, 'Transitional Justice and Sanctions' (2008) 870 *International Review of the Red Cross* 371.

Stahn, C, 'International Law at a Crossroads? The Impact of September 11' (2002) 62 *Zeitschrift für Ausländisches Öffentliches Recht und Völkerrecht* 183.

Stahn, C and Kleffner, J, *Jus post Bellum: Towards a Law of Transition from Conflict to Peace* (The Hague, TMC Asser Press, 2008).

Starita, M, 'L'occupation de l'Iraq: Le Conseil de Sécurité, le droit de la guerre et le droit des peuples à disposer d'eux-mêmes' (2004) 108 *Revue générale de droit international public* 883.

Stern, B (ed), *Les aspects juridiques de la crise et de la guerre du Golfe: Aspects de droit international public et de droit international privé* (Paris, Montchresties, 1991).

Stewart, J, 'Towards a Single Definition of Armed Conflict in International Humanitarian Law: A Critique of Internationalized Armed Conflict' (2003) 85 *International Review of the Red Cross* 313.

Steyn, J, 'Guantanamo Bay: The Legal Black Hole' (2004) 53 *International and Comparative Law Quarterly* 1.

Suy, E, 'International Humanitarian Law and the Security Council Resolutions on the 1990–1991 Gulf Conflict' in A Delissen and G Tanja (eds), *Humanitarian Law of Armed Conflict: Challenges Ahead, Essays in Honour of Frits Kalshoven* (Dordrecht, Martinus Nijhoff, 1991) 515–26.

Swinarski, C (ed), *Studies and Essays on International Humanitarian Law and Red Cross Principles in Honour of Jean Pictet* (The Hague, Martinus Nijhoff, 1984).
Tanca, A, *Foreign Armed Intervention in Internal Conflict* (Dordrecht, Martinus Nijhoff, 1993).
Thouvenin, J-M, 'Article 103' in J-P Cot et al, *La Charte des Nations Unies: Commentaire article par article* (Paris, Economica, 2005) 2133–47.
Tigroudja, H, 'Le régime d'occupation en Iraq' (2004) 50 *Annuaire français de droit international* 77.
Tomuschat, C et al (eds), *The Right to Life* (Leiden, Martinus Nijhoff, 2010).
Tondel, L (ed), *The Legal Aspects of the United Nations Action in the Congo* (New York, Oceana Publications, 1963).
Toublanc, A, 'L'article 103 et la valeur juridique de la Charte des Nations Unies' (2004) 108 *Revue générale de droit international public* 439.
Trapp, K, 'Back to Basics: Necessity, Proportionality, and the Right of Self-Defence against Non-State Terrorist Actors' (2007) 56 *International and Comparative Law Quarterly* 141.
Turley, S, 'Keeping the Peace: Do the Laws of War Apply?' (1994) 73 *Texas Law Review* 139.
Uhler, O and Coursier, H et al, *Commentary on the Geneva Conventions of 12 August 1949* Vol IV (Geneva, International Committee of the Red Cross, 1958).
Verhoeven, J, 'Les "étirements" de la légitime défense' (2002) 48 *Annuaire français de droit international* 47.
Viotti, A, 'In Search of Symbiosis: The Security Council in the Humanitarian Domain' (2007) 865 *International Review of the Red Cross* 131.
Vité, S, 'Typology of Armed Conflicts in International Humanitarian Law: Legal Concepts and Actual Situations' (2009) 873 *International Review of the Red Cross* 69.
Vohrah, L et al (eds), *Man's Inhumanity to Man: Essays on International Law in Honour of Antonio Cassese* (The Hague, Kluwer Law International, 2003).
Vukas, B and Sosic, T (eds), *International Law: New Actors, New Concepts, Continuing Dilemmas: Liber Amicorum Bozidar Bakotic* (Leiden, Martinus Nijhoff, 2010).
Waldock, H, 'The Regulation of the Use of Force by Individual States in International Law' (1952) 81 *Recueil des Cours de l'Académie de Droit International* 455.
Watkin, K, 'Assessing Proportionality: Moral Complexity and Legal Rules' (2005) 8 *Yearbook of International Humanitarian Law* 3.
Wedgwood, R, 'Responding to Terrorism: The Strikes against Bin Laden' (1999) 24 *Yale Journal of International Law* 559.
Weller, M, *Iraq and the Use of Force in International Law* (Oxford, Oxford University Press, 2010).
—— 'The United Nations and the *Jus ad Bellum*' in P Rowe (ed), *The Gulf War 1990–91 in International and English Law* (London, Routledge, 1993) 29–54.
Westing, A (ed), *Environmental Warfare: Technical, Legal and Policy Appraisal* (London, Taylor and Francis, 1984).
Wetzel, R and Rauschning, D, *The Vienna Convention on the Law of Treaties: Travaux Preparatoires* (Frankfurt am Main, Alfred Metzner Verlag, 1978).
White, N, 'The Legality of Bombing in the Name of Humanity' (2000) 5 *Journal of Conflict and Security Law* 27.
White, N and Abass, A, 'Countermeasures and Sanctions' in M Evans (ed), *International Law*, 2nd edn (Oxford, Oxford University Press, 2006) 531–58.

Wilhelm, R-J, 'Problème relatifs à la protection de la personne humaine par le droit international dans les conflits armés ne présentant pas un caractère international' (1972) 137 *Recueil des Cours de l'Académie de Droit International* 309.

Wilmshurst, E and Breau, S (eds), *Perspectives on the ICRC Study on Customary International Humanitarian Law* (Cambridge, Cambridge University Press, 2007).

Wolfrum, R, 'The Attack of September 11, 2001, the Wars against the Taliban and Iraq: Is There a Need to Reconsider International Law on the Recourse to Force and the Rules in Armed Conflict?' (2003) 7 *Max Planck Yearbook of United Nations Law* 1.

Wolfrum, R and Philipp, C, 'The Status of the Taliban: Their Obligations and Rights under International Law' (2002) 6 *Max Planck Yearbook of United Nations Law* 559.

Wood, M, 'Detention during International Military Operations: Article 103 of the UN Charter and the *Al-Jedda* Case' (2009) 47 *Revue de droit militaire et de droit de la guerre* 139.

—— 'The Interpretation of Security Council Resolutions' (1998) 2 *Max Planck Yearbook of United Nations Law* 73.

—— 'The UN Security Council and International Law, First Lecture: The Legal Framework of the Security Council' (7 November 2006) Sir Hersch Lauterpacht Memorial Lectures.

Wright, Q, 'The Outlawry of War and the Law of War' (1953) 47 *American Journal of International Law* 365.

—— 'The Strengthening of International Law' (1959) 98 *Recueil des Cours de l'Académie de Droit International* 5.

Yoo, J, 'The Status of Soldiers and Terrorists under the Geneva Conventions' (2004) 3 *Chinese Journal of International Law* 135.

Zacklin, R, *The United Nations Secretariat and the Use of Force in a Unipolar World* (Cambridge, Cambridge University Press, 2010).

—— 'The Use of Force in Peacekeeping Operations' in N Blokker and N Schrijver (eds), *The Security Council and the Use of Force: Theory and Reality – A Need for Change?* (Leiden, Martinus Nijhoff, 2005) 91–106.

Zegveld, L, *Accountability of Armed Opposition Groups in International Law* (Cambridge, Cambridge University Press, 2002).

Zemanek, K, 'The Legal Foundations of the International System' (1997) 266 *Recueil des Cours de l'Académie de Droit International* 9.

Zimmermann, A, 'The Second Lebanon War: *Jus ad Bellum, Jus in Bello* and the Issue of Proportionality' (2007) 11 *Max Planck Yearbook of United Nations Law* 99.

Zwanenburg, M, *Accountability of Peace Support Operations* (Leiden, Martinus Nijhoff, 2005).

—— 'Compromise or Commitment: Human Rights and International Humanitarian Law Obligations for UN Peace Forces' (1998) 11 *Leiden Journal of International Law* 229.

—— 'Existentialism in Iraq: Security Council Resolution 1483 and the Law of Occupation' (2004) 856 *International Review of the Red Cross* 745.

—— 'The Law of Occupation Revisited: The Beginning of an Occupation' (2007) 10 *Yearbook of International Humanitarian Law* 75.

—— 'Pieces of the Puzzle: Peace Operations, Occupation and the Use of Force' (2006) 45 *Revue de droit militaire et de droit de la guerre* 239.

Annex 1: United Nations Security Council Resolutions Relevant to IHL

Security Council resolution	Reference to IHL
UNSC Res 85 (31 July 1950) UN Doc S/RES/85	CIHL
UNSC Res 111 (19 January 1956) UN Doc S/RES/111	CIHL
UNSC Res 169 (24 November 1961) UN Doc S/RES/169	CIHL
UNSC Res 188 (9 April 1964) UN Doc S/RES/188	CIHL
UNSC Res 190 (9 June 1964) UN Doc S/RES/190	CIHL
UNSC Res 191 (18 June 1964) UN Doc S/RES/191	CIHL
UNSC Res 237 (14 June 1967) UN Doc S/RES/237	GCIII GCIV CIHL
UNSC Res 242 (22 November 1967) UN Doc S/RES/242	CIHL
UNSC Res 248 (24 March 1968) UN Doc S/RES/248	GCIII GCIV CIHL
UNSC Res 252 (21 May 1968) UN Doc S/RES/252	CIHL
UNSC Res 256 (16 August 1968) UN Doc S/RES/256	CIHL
UNSC Res 264 (20 March 1969) UN Doc S/RES/264	CIHL
UNSC Res 265 (1 April 1969) UN Doc S/RES/265	CIHL
UNSC Res 267 (3 March 1969) UN Doc S/RES/267	CIHL
UNSC Res 268 (3 July 1969) UN Doc S/RES/268	CIHL
UNSC Res 270 (26 August 1969) UN Doc S/RES/270	CIHL
UNSC Res 271 (15 September 1969) UN Doc S/RES/271	GCs CIHL
UNSC Res 273 (9 December 1969) UN Doc S/RES/273	CIHL
UNSC Res 275 (22 December 1969) UN Doc S/RES/275	CIHL
UNSC Res 276 (30 January 1970) UN Doc S/RES/276	CIHL
UNSC Res 280 (19 May 1970) UN Doc S/RES/280	CIHL
UNSC Res 290 (8 December 1970) UN Doc S/RES/290	CIHL

Security Council resolution	Reference to IHL
UNSC Res 294 (15 June 1971) UN Doc S/RES/294	CIHL
UNSC Res 301 (20 October 1971) UN Doc S/RES/301	CIHL
UNSC Res 307 (21 December 1971) UN Doc S/RES/307	GCs CIHL
UNSC Res 310 (4 February 1972) UN Doc S/RES/310	CIHL
UNSC Res 312 (4 February 1972) UN Doc S/RES/312	CIHL
UNSC Res 316 (26 June 1972) UN Doc S/RES/316	CIHL
UNSC Res 326 (2 February 1973) UN Doc S/RES/326	CIHL
UNSC Res 332 (21 April 1973) UN Doc S/RES/332	CIHL
UNSC Res 347 (24 April 1974) UN Doc S/RES/347	CIHL
UNSC Res 361 (30 August 1974) UN Doc S/RES/361	CIHL
UNSC Res 366 (17 December 1974) UN Doc S/RES/366	CIHL
UNSC Res 385 (30 January 1976) UN Doc S/RES/385	CIHL
UNSC Res 387 (31 March 1976) UN Doc S/RES/387*	CIHL
UNSC Res 392 (19 June 1976) UN Doc S/RES/392	CIHL
UNSC Res 393 (30 July 1976) UN Doc S/RES/393	CIHL
UNSC Res 403 (14 January 1977) UN Doc S/RES/403	CIHL
UNSC Res 405 (14 April 1977) UN Doc S/RES/405*	CIHL
UNSC Res 417 (31 October 1977) UN Doc S/RES/417	CIHL
UNSC Res 427 (3 May 1978) UN Doc S/RES/427	CIHL
UNSC Res 428 (6 May 1978) UN Doc S/RES/428	CIHL
UNSC Res 434 (18 September 1978) UN Doc S/RES/434	CIHL
UNSC Res 435 (29 September 1978) UN Doc S/RES/435	CIHL
UNSC Res 436 (6 October 1978) UN Doc S/RES/436	CIHL
UNSC Res 445 (8 March 1979) UN Doc S/RES/445*	CIHL
UNSC Res 446 (22 March 1979) UN Doc S/RES/446	GCIV CIHL
UNSC Res 447 (28 March 1979) UN Doc S/RES/447*	CIHL
UNSC Res 452 (20 July 1979) UN Doc S/RES/452	GCIV CIHL
UNSC Res 454 (2 November 1979) UN Doc S/RES/454*	CIHL
UNSC Res 455 (23 November 1979) UN Doc S/RES/455*	CIHL

Security Council resolution	Reference to IHL
UNSC Res 459 (19 December 1979) UN Doc S/RES/459	CPC CIHL
UNSC Res 463 (2 February 1980) UN Doc S/RES/463	CIHL
UNSC Res 465 (1 March 1980) UN Doc S/RES/465	GCIV CIHL
UNSC Res 466 (11 April 1980) UN Doc S/RES/466*	CIHL
UNSC Res 467 (24 April 1980) UN Doc S/RES/467	CIHL
UNSC Res 468 (8 May 1980) UN Doc S/RES/468	GCs CIHL
UNSC Res 469 (20 May 1980) UN Doc S/RES/469	Arts 1, 49 GCIV CIHL
UNSC Res 471 (5 June 1980) UN Doc S/RES/471	Art 27 GCIV CIHL
UNSC Res 473 (13 June 1980) UN Doc S/RES/473	CIHL
UNSC Res 475 (27 June 1980) UN Doc S/RES/475*	CIHL
UNSC Res 476 (30 June 1980) UN Doc S/RES/476	GCIV CIHL
UNSC Res 478 (20 August 1980) UN Doc S/RES/478	GCIV CIHL
UNSC Res 484 (19 December 1980) UN Doc S/RES/484	GCIV CIHL
UNSC Res 496 (15 December 1981) UN Doc S/RES/496	CIHL
UNSC Res 497 (17 December 1981) UN Doc S/RES/497	GCIV CIHL
UNSC Res 507 (28 May 1982) UN Doc S/RES/507	CIHL
UNSC Res 512 (19 June 1982) UN Doc S/RES/512	GCs 1907 HRs CIHL
UNSC Res 513 (4 July 1982) UN Doc S/RES/513	GCs 1907 HRs CIHL
UNSC Res 514 (12 July 1982) UN Doc S/RES/514	CIHL
UNSC Res 515 (29 July 1982) UN Doc S/RES/515	GCs 1907 HRs CIHL

Security Council resolution	Reference to IHL
UNSC Res 518 (12 August 1982) UN Doc S/RES/518	CIHL
UNSC Res 520 (17 September 1982) UN Doc S/RES/520	CIHL
UNSC Res 521 (19 September 1982) UN Doc S/RES/521	CIHL
UNSC Res 522 (4 October 1982) UN Doc S/RES/522	CIHL
UNSC Res 527 (15 December 1982) UN Doc S/RES/527*	CIHL
UNSC Res 532 (31 May 1983) UN Doc S/RES/532	CIHL
UNSC Res 539 (28 October 1983) UN Doc S/RES/539	CIHL
UNSC Res 540 (31 October 1983) UN Doc S/RES/540	GCs 'IHL' CIHL
UNSC Res 542 (23 November 1983) UN Doc S/RES/542	CIHL
UNSC Res 545 (20 December 1983) UN Doc S/RES/545	CIHL
UNSC Res 546 (6 January 1984) UN Doc S/RES/546*	CIHL
UNSC Res 552 (1 June 1984) UN Doc S/RES/552*	CIHL
UNSC Res 556 (23 October 1984) UN Doc S/RES/556	CIHL
UNSC Res 560 (12 March 1985) UN Doc S/RES/560	CIHL
UNSC Res 564 (31 May 1985) UN Doc S/RES/564	CIHL
UNSC Res 566 (19 June 1985) UN Doc S/RES/566	CIHL
UNSC Res 567 (20 June 1985) UN Doc S/RES/567*	CIHL
UNSC Res 568 (21 June 1985) UN Doc S/RES/568*	CIHL
UNSC Res 569 (26 July 1985) UN Doc S/RES/569	CIHL
UNSC Res 571 (20 September 1985) UN Doc S/RES/571*	CIHL
UNSC Res 572 (30 September 1985) UN Doc S/RES/572*	CIHL
UNSC Res 573 (4 October 1985) UN Doc S/RES/573*	CIHL
UNSC Res 574 (7 October 1985) UN Doc S/RES/574*	CIHL
UNSC Res 577 (6 December 1985) UN Doc S/RES/577*	CIHL
UNSC Res 580 (30 December 1985) UN Doc S/RES/580*	CIHL
UNSC Res 581 (13 February 1986) UN Doc S/RES/581*	CIHL
UNSC Res 582 (24 February 1986) UN Doc S/RES/582	GP 'IHL' CIHL
UNSC Res 587 (23 September 1986) UN Doc S/RES/587	CIHL
UNSC Res 588 (8 October 1986) UN Doc S/RES/588	CIHL

Security Council resolution	Reference to IHL
UNSC Res 592 (8 December 1986) UN Doc S/RES/592	GCs GCIV CIHL
UNSC Res 598 (20 July 1987) UN Doc S/RES/598*	GP GCs GCIII 'IHL' CIHL
UNSC Res 602 (25 November 1987) UN Doc S/RES/602*	CIHL
UNSC Res 605 (22 December 1987) UN Doc S/RES/605	GCIV CIHL
UNSC Res 606 (23 December 1987) UN Doc S/RES/606	CIHL
UNSC Res 607 (5 January 1988) UN Doc S/RES/607	Arts 47, 49 GCIV CIHL
UNSC Res 608 (14 January 1988) UN Doc S/RES/608	CIHL
UNSC Res 611 (25 April 1988) UN Doc S/RES/611*	CIHL
UNSC Res 612 (9 May 1988) UN Doc S/RES/612	GP CIHL
UNSC Res 616 (20 July 1988) UN Doc S/RES/616	CIHL
UNSC Res 620 (26 August 1988) UN Doc S/RES/620	GP CIHL
UNSC Res 636 (6 July 1989) UN Doc S/RES/636	Arts 47, 49 GCIV CIHL
UNSC Res 638 (31 July 1989) UN Doc S/RES/638	CIHL
UNSC Res 641 (30 August 1989) UN Doc S/RES/641	Arts 47, 49 GCIV CIHL
UNSC Res 661 (6 August 1990) UN Doc S/RES/661**	CIHL
UNSC Res 662 (9 August 1990) UN Doc S/RES/662	CIHL
UNSC Res 664 (18 August 1990) UN Doc S/RES/664**	CIHL
UNSC Res 666 (13 September 1990) UN Doc S/RES/666**	GCIV 'IHL' CIHL
UNSC Res 667 (16 September 1990) UN Doc S/RES/667**	CIHL
UNSC Res 670 (25 September 1990) UN Doc S/RES/670**	GCIV CIHL

Security Council resolution	Reference to IHL
UNSC Res 672 (12 October 1990) UN Doc S/RES/672	GCIV CIHL
UNSC Res 674 (29 October 1990) UN Doc S/RES/674**	GCIV CIHL
UNSC Res 677 (28 November 1990) UN Doc S/RES/677**	CIHL
UNSC Res 681 (20 December 1990) UN Doc S/RES/681	Art 1 GCIV CIHL
UNSC Res 686 (2 March 1991) UN Doc S/RES/686**	GCIII CIHL
UNSC Res 687 (3 April 1991) UN Doc S/RES/687**	GP BWC CIHL
UNSC Res 688 (5 April 1991) UN Doc S/RES/688	CIHL
UNSC Res 692 (20 May 1991) UN Doc S/RES/692**	CIHL
UNSC Res 694 (24 May 1991) UN Doc S/RES/694	GCIV CIHL
UNSC Res 706 (15 August 1991) UN Doc S/RES/706**	CIHL
UNSC Res 712 (19 September 1991) UN Doc S/RES/712**	CIHL
UNSC Res 713 (25 September 1991) UN Doc S/RES/713**	CIHL
UNSC Res 724 (15 December 1991) UN Doc S/RES/724**	CIHL
UNSC Res 726 (6 January 1992) UN Doc S/RES/726	GCIV CIHL
UNSC Res 727 (8 January 1992) UN Doc S/RES/727	CIHL
UNSC Res 728 (8 January 1992) UN Doc S/RES/728	CIHL
UNSC Res 733 (23 January 1992) UN Doc S/RES/733**	CIHL
UNSC Res 743 (21 February 1992) UN Doc S/RES/743*	CIHL
UNSC Res 745 (28 February 1992) UN Doc S/RES/745	CIHL
UNSC Res 746 (17 March 1992) UN Doc S/RES/746*	CIHL
UNSC Res 751 (24 April 1992) UN Doc S/RES/751*	CIHL
UNSC Res 752 (15 May 1992) UN Doc S/RES/752	CIHL
UNSC Res 757 (30 May 1992) UN Doc S/RES/757**	CIHL
UNSC Res 758 (8 June 1992) UN Doc S/RES/758	CIHL
UNSC Res 761 (29 June 1992) UN Doc S/RES/761	CIHL
UNSC Res 764 (13 July 1992) UN Doc S/RES/764	GCs 'IHL' CIHL

Security Council resolution	Reference to IHL
UNSC Res 766 (21 July 1992) UN Doc S/RES/766	CIHL
UNSC Res 767 (24 July 1992) UN Doc S/RES/767*	CIHL
UNSC Res 769 (7 August 1992) UN Doc S/RES/769	CIHL
UNSC Res 770 (13 August 1992) UN Doc S/RES/770**	CIHL
UNSC Res 771 (13 August 1992) UN Doc S/RES/771	GCs 'IHL' CIHL
UNSC Res 775 (28 August 1992) UN Doc S/RES/775*	CIHL
UNSC Res 776 (14 September 1992) UN Doc S/RES/776	CIHL
UNSC Res 779 (6 October 1992) UN Doc S/RES/779	CIHL
UNSC Res 780 (6 October 1992) UN Doc S/RES/780	GCs 'IHL' CIHL
UNSC Res 781 (9 October 1992) UN Doc S/RES/781	CIHL
UNSC Res 783 (13 October 1992) UN Doc S/RES/783	CIHL
UNSC Res 786 (10 November 1992) UN Doc S/RES/786	CIHL
UNSC Res 787 (16 November 1992) UN Doc S/RES/787**	GCs 'IHL' CIHL
UNSC Res 788 (19 November 1992) UN Doc S/RES/788*	'IHL' CIHL
UNSC Res 794 (3 December 1992) UN Doc S/RES/794*	'IHL' CIHL
UNSC Res 798 (18 December 1992) UN Doc S/RES/798	CIHL
UNSC Res 799 (18 December 1992) UN Doc S/RES/799	GCIV CIHL
UNSC Res 802 (25 January 1993) UN Doc S/RES/802	CIHL
UNSC Res 804 (29 January 1993) UN Doc S/RES/804	'IHL'
UNSC Res 807 (19 February 1993) UN Doc S/RES/807**	CIHL
UNSC Res 808 (22 February 1993) UN Doc S/RES/808*	GCs 'IHL' CIHL
UNSC Res 810 (8 March 1993) UN Doc S/RES/810	CIHL
UNSC Res 811 (12 March 1993) UN Doc S/RES/811	'IHL' CIHL
UNSC Res 812 (12 March 1993) UN Doc S/RES/812	'IHL' CIHL

Security Council resolution	Reference to IHL
UNSC Res 813 (26 March 1993) UN Doc S/RES/813*	'IHL' CIHL
UNSC Res 814 (26 March 1993) UN Doc S/RES/814**	'IHL' CIHL
UNSC Res 815 (30 March 1993) UN Doc S/RES/815*	GCs 'IHL'
UNSC Res 816 (31 March 1993) UN Doc S/RES/816**	CIHL
UNSC Res 819 (16 April 1993) UN Doc S/RES/819**	'IHL' CIHL
UNSC Res 820 (17 April 1993) UN Doc S/RES/820**	'IHL' CIHL
UNSC Res 822 (30 April 1993) UN Doc S/RES/822	'IHL' CIHL
UNSC Res 823 (30 April 1993) UN Doc S/RES/823	CIHL
UNSC Res 824 (6 May 1993) UN Doc S/RES/824**	CIHL
UNSC Res 826 (20 May 1993) UN Doc S/RES/826	CIHL
UNSC Res 827 (25 May 1993) UN Doc S/RES/827**	'IHL' CIHL
UNSC Res 834 (1 June 1993) UN Doc S/RES/834	'IHL' CIHL
UNSC Res 836 (4 June 1993) UN Doc S/RES/836**	'IHL' CIHL
UNSC Res 837 (6 June 1993) UN Doc S/RES/837**	CIHL
UNSC Res 844 (18 June 1993) UN Doc S/RES/844**	'IHL'
UNSC Res 846 (22 June 1993) UN Doc S/RES/846	'IHL'
UNSC Res 851 (15 July 1993) UN Doc S/RES/851	'IHL' CIHL
UNSC Res 853 (29 July 1993) UN Doc S/RES/853	'IHL' CIHL
UNSC Res 858 (24 August 1993) UN Doc S/RES/858*	CIHL
UNSC Res 859 (24 August 1993) UN Doc S/RES/859**	CIHL
UNSC Res 863 (13 September 1993) UN Doc S/RES/863	CIHL
UNSC Res 864 (15 September 1993) UN Doc S/RES/864	'IHL' CIHL
UNSC Res 865 (22 September 1993) UN Doc S/RES/865	CIHL

Security Council resolution	Reference to IHL
UNSC Res 866 (22 September 1993) UN Doc S/RES/866	'IHL' CIHL
UNSC Res 868 (29 September 1993) UN Doc S/RES/868	CIHL
UNSC Res 872 (5 October 1993) UN Doc S/RES/872	CIHL
UNSC Res 874 (14 October 1993) UN Doc S/RES/874	'IHL' CIHL
UNSC Res 876 (19 October 1993) UN Doc S/RES/876*	'IHL' CIHL
UNSC Res 880 (4 November 1993) UN Doc S/RES/880	CIHL
UNSC Res 881 (4 November 1993) UN Doc S/RES/881*	'IHL'
UNSC Res 882 (5 November 1993) UN Doc S/RES/882	CIHL
UNSC Res 884 (12 November 1993) UN Doc S/RES/884	CIHL
UNSC Res 886 (18 November 1993) UN Doc S/RES/886**	CIHL
UNSC Res 890 (15 December 1993) UN Doc S/RES/890	CIHL
UNSC Res 892 (22 December 1993) UN Doc S/RES/892	CIHL
UNSC Res 896 (31 January 1994) UN Doc S/RES/896	CIHL
UNSC Res 897 (4 February 1994) UN Doc S/RES/897**	CIHL
UNSC Res 898 (23 February 1994) UN Doc S/RES/898	CIHL
UNSC Res 900 (4 March 1994) UN Doc S/RES/900**	CIHL
UNSC Res 903 (16 March 1994) UN Doc S/RES/903	CIHL
UNSC Res 904 (18 March 1994) UN Doc S/RES/904	GCIV CIHL
UNSC Res 906 (25 March 1994) UN Doc S/RES/906	CIHL
UNSC Res 908 (31 March 1994) UN Doc S/RES/908**	CIHL
UNSC Res 911 (21 April 1994) UN Doc S/RES/911	'IHL' CIHL
UNSC Res 912 (21 April 1994) UN Doc S/RES/912	'IHL' CIHL
UNSC Res 913 (22 April 1994) UN Doc S/RES/913**	CIHL
UNSC Res 916 (5 May 1994) UN Doc S/RES/916	CIHL
UNSC Res 918 (17 May 1994) UN Doc S/RES/918*	'IHL' CIHL
UNSC Res 922 (31 May 1994) UN Doc S/RES/922	CIHL
UNSC Res 923 (31 May 1994) UN Doc S/RES/923**	CIHL

Security Council resolution	Reference to IHL
UNSC Res 925 (8 June 1994) UN Doc S/RES/925	CIHL
UNSC Res 929 (22 June 1994) UN Doc S/RES/929**	CIHL
UNSC Res 931 (29 June 1994) UN Doc S/RES/931	CIHL
UNSC Res 932 (30 June 1994) UN Doc S/RES/932	CIHL
UNSC Res 935 (1 July 1994) UN Doc S/RES/935	'IHL' CIHL
UNSC Res 937 (21 July 1994) UN Doc S/RES/937	CIHL
UNSC Res 940 (31 July 1994) UN Doc S/RES/940	CIHL
UNSC Res 941 (23 September 1994) UN Doc S/RES/941**	GCs 'IHL' CIHL
UNSC Res 945 (29 September 1994) UN Doc S/RES/945	CIHL
UNSC Res 946 (30 September 1994) UN Doc S/RES/946	CIHL
UNSC Res 947 (30 September 1994) UN Doc S/RES/947**	CIHL
UNSC Res 950 (21 October 1994) UN Doc S/RES/950	'IHL' CIHL
UNSC Res 952 (27 October 1994) UN Doc S/RES/952	CIHL
UNSC Res 954 (4 November 1994) UN Doc S/RES/954**	CIHL
UNSC Res 955 (8 November 1994) UN Doc S/RES/955**	'IHL' CIHL
UNSC Res 958 (19 November 1994) UN Doc S/RES/958**	CIHL
UNSC Res 959 (19 November 1994) UN Doc S/RES/959	CIHL
UNSC Res 965 (30 November 1994) UN Doc S/RES/965	CIHL
UNSC Res 966 (8 December 1994) UN Doc S/RES/966	CIHL
UNSC Res 968 (16 December 1994) UN Doc S/RES/968	CIHL
UNSC Res 971 (12 January 1995) UN Doc S/RES/971	CIHL
UNSC Res 972 (13 January 1995) UN Doc S/RES/972	'IHL' CIHL
UNSC Res 976 (8 February 1995) UN Doc S/RES/976	CIHL
UNSC Res 978 (27 February 1995) UN Doc S/RES/978	CIHL
UNSC Res 981 (31 March 1995) UN Doc S/RES/981**	CIHL
UNSC Res 982 (31 March 1995) UN Doc S/RES/982**	CIHL
UNSC Res 985 (13 April 1995) UN Doc S/RES/985	'IHL' CIHL

Security Council resolution	Reference to IHL
UNSC Res 987 (19 April 1995) UN Doc S/RES/987**	CIHL
UNSC Res 988 (21 April 1995) UN Doc S/RES/988**	CIHL
UNSC Res 993 (12 May 1995) UN Doc S/RES/993	'IHL' CIHL
UNSC Res 994 (17 May 1995) UN Doc S/RES/994**	CIHL
UNSC Res 997 (9 June 1995) UN Doc S/RES/997	CIHL
UNSC Res 998 (16 June 1995) UN Doc S/RES/998**	CIHL
UNSC Res 999 (16 June 1995) UN Doc S/RES/999	CIHL
UNSC Res 1001 (30 June 1995) UN Doc S/RES/1001	'IHL' CIHL
UNSC Res 1004 (12 July 1995) UN Doc S/RES/1004**	CIHL
UNSC Res 1005 (17 July 1995) UN Doc S/RES/1005**	CIHL
UNSC Res 1008 (7 August 1995) UN Doc S/RES/1008	CIHL
UNSC Res 1009 (10 August 1995) UN Doc S/RES/1009**	'IHL' CIHL
UNSC Res 1010 (10 August 1995) UN Doc S/RES/1010	'IHL' CIHL
UNSC Res 1011 (16 August 1995) UN Doc S/RES/1011	CIHL
UNSC Res 1012 (28 August 1995) UN Doc S/RES/1012	'IHL' CIHL
UNSC Res 1014 (15 September 1995) UN Doc S/RES/1014	'IHL' CIHL
UNSC Res 1016 (21 September 1995) UN Doc S/RES/1016	CIHL
UNSC Res 1019 (9 November 1995) UN Doc S/RES/1019	'IHL' CIHL
UNSC Res 1020 (10 November 1995) UN Doc S/RES/1020	'IHL' CIHL
UNSC Res 1029 (12 December 1995) UN Doc S/RES/1029	CIHL
UNSC Res 1030 (14 December 1995) UN Doc S/RES/1030	CIHL
UNSC Res 1031 (15 December 1995) UN Doc S/RES/1031**	'IHL' CIHL
UNSC Res 1034 (21 December 1995) UN Doc S/RES/1034	'IHL' CIHL
UNSC Res 1036 (12 January 1996) UN Doc S/RES/1036	'IHL' CIHL

Security Council resolution	Reference to IHL
UNSC Res 1037 (15 January 1996) UN Doc S/RES/1037**	CIHL
UNSC Res 1039 (29 January 1996) UN Doc S/RES/1039	CIHL
UNSC Res 1040 (29 January 1996) UN Doc S/RES/1040	CIHL
UNSC Res 1041 (29 January 1996) UN Doc S/RES/1041	'IHL' CIHL
UNSC Res 1045 (8 February 1996) UN Doc S/RES/1045	CIHL
UNSC Res 1049 (5 March 1996) UN Doc S/RES/1049	CIHL
UNSC Res 1050 (8 March 1996) UN Doc S/RES/1050	CIHL
UNSC Res 1052 (18 April 1996) UN Doc S/RES/1052	'IHL' CIHL
UNSC Res 1055 (8 May 1996) UN Doc S/RES/1055	CIHL
UNSC Res 1059 (31 May 1996) UN Doc S/RES/1059	'IHL' CIHL
UNSC Res 1061 (14 June 1996) UN Doc S/RES/1061	CIHL
UNSC Res 1062 (28 June 1996) UN Doc S/RES/1062	CIHL
UNSC Res 1064 (11 July 1996) UN Doc S/RES/1064	CIHL
UNSC Res 1065 (12 July 1996) UN Doc S/RES/1065	CIHL
UNSC Res 1067 (26 July 1996) UN Doc S/RES/1067	CIHL
UNSC Res 1068 (30 July 1996) UN Doc S/RES/1068	CIHL
UNSC Res 1071 (30 August 1996) UN Doc S/RES/1071	'IHL' CIHL
UNSC Res 1072 (30 August 1996) UN Doc S/RES/1072	'IHL' CIHL
UNSC Res 1073 (28 September 1996) UN Doc S/RES/1073	CIHL
UNSC Res 1075 (11 October 1996) UN Doc S/RES/1075	CIHL
UNSC Res 1076 (22 October 1996) UN Doc S/RES/1076	'IHL' CIHL
UNSC Res 1078 (9 November 1996) UN Doc S/RES/1078*	CIHL
UNSC Res 1079 (15 November 1996) UN Doc S/RES/1079**	CIHL
UNSC Res 1080 (15 November 1996) UN Doc S/RES/1080**	'IHL' CIHL
UNSC Res 1083 (27 November 1996) UN Doc S/RES/1083	'IHL' CIHL
UNSC Res 1087 (11 December 1996) UN Doc S/RES/1087	CIHL
UNSC Res 1088 (12 December 1996) UN Doc S/RES/1088**	CIHL

Security Council resolution	Reference to IHL
UNSC Res 1089 (13 December 1996) UN Doc S/RES/1089	CIHL
UNSC Res 1092 (23 December 1996) UN Doc S/RES/1092	CIHL
UNSC Res 1093 (14 January 1997) UN Doc S/RES/1093*	CIHL
UNSC Res 1095 (28 January 1997) UN Doc S/RES/1095	CIHL
UNSC Res 1096 (30 January 1997) UN Doc S/RES/1096	CIHL
UNSC Res 1097 (18 February 1997) UN Doc S/RES/1097	'IHL' CIHL
UNSC Res 1099 (14 March 1997) UN Doc S/RES/1099	CIHL
UNSC Res 1100 (27 March 1997) UN Doc S/RES/1100	CIHL
UNSC Res 1101 (28 March 1997) UN Doc S/RES/1101*	CIHL
UNSC Res 1113 (12 June 1997) UN Doc S/RES/1113	CIHL
UNSC Res 1114 (19 June 1997) UN Doc S/RES/1114	CIHL
UNSC Res 1118 (30 June 1997) UN Doc S/RES/1118	CIHL
UNSC Res 1119 (14 July 1997) UN Doc S/RES/1119*	CIHL
UNSC Res 1120 (14 July 1997) UN Doc S/RES/1120**	CIHL
UNSC Res 1122 (29 July 1997) UN Doc S/RES/1122	CIHL
UNSC Res 1123 (30 July 1997) UN Doc S/RES/1123	CIHL
UNSC Res 1124 (31 July 1997) UN Doc S/RES/1124	CIHL
UNSC Res 1125 (6 August 1997) UN Doc S/RES/1125	CIHL
UNSC Res 1127 (28 August 1997) UN Doc S/RES/1127**	CIHL
UNSC Res 1128 (12 September 1997) UN Doc S/RES/1128	CIHL
UNSC Res 1132 (8 October 1997) UN Doc S/RES/1132**	CIHL
UNSC Res 1136 (6 November 1997) UN Doc S/RES/1136	CIHL
UNSC Res 1138 (14 November 1997) UN Doc S/RES/1138	CIHL
UNSC Res 1145 (19 December 1997) UN Doc S/RES/1145	CIHL
UNSC Res 1149 (27 January 1998) UN Doc S/RES/1149	CIHL
UNSC Res 1150 (30 January 1998) UN Doc S/RES/1150	CIHL
UNSC Res 1151 (30 January 1998) UN Doc S/RES/1151	CIHL
UNSC Res 1152 (5 February 1998) UN Doc S/RES/1152**	CIHL
UNSC Res 1155 (16 March 1998) UN Doc S/RES/1155*	CIHL
UNSC Res 1157 (20 March 1998) UN Doc S/RES/1157	CIHL
UNSC Res 1159 (27 March 1998) UN Doc S/RES/1159**	CIHL
UNSC Res 1161 (9 April 1998) UN Doc S/RES/1161	CIHL

Security Council resolution	Reference to IHL
UNSC Res 1164 (29 April 1998) UN Doc S/RES/1164	CIHL
UNSC Res 1165 (30 April 1998) UN Doc S/RES/1165**	CIHL
UNSC Res 1166 (13 May 1998) UN Doc S/RES/1166**	CIHL
UNSC Res 1170 (28 May 1998) UN Doc S/RES/1170	'IHL'
UNSC Res 1173 (12 June 1998) UN Doc S/RES/1173	CIHL
UNSC Res 1174 (15 June 1998) UN Doc S/RES/1174**	CIHL
UNSC Res 1176 (24 June 1998) UN Doc S/RES/1176**	CIHL
UNSC Res 1180 (29 June 1998) UN Doc S/RES/1180	CIHL
UNSC Res 1181 (13 July 1998) UN Doc S/RES/1181	'IHL' CIHL
UNSC Res 1187 (30 July 1998) UN Doc S/RES/1187	CIHL
UNSC Res 1188 (30 July 1998) UN Doc S/RES/1188	CIHL
UNSC Res 1190 (13 August 1998) UN Doc S/RES/1190	CIHL
UNSC Res 1193 (28 August 1998) UN Doc S/RES/1193	GCs 'IHL' CIHL
UNSC Res 1195 (15 September 1998) UN Doc S/RES/1195	CIHL
UNSC Res 1199 (23 September 1998) UN Doc S/RES/1199**	'IHL' CIHL
UNSC Res 1202 (15 October 1998) UN Doc S/RES/1202	CIHL
UNSC Res 1203 (24 October 1998) UN Doc S/RES/1203**	CIHL
UNSC Res 1206 (12 November 1998) UN Doc S/RES/1206	CIHL
UNSC Res 1207 (17 November 1998) UN Doc S/RES/1207**	CIHL
UNSC Res 1208 (19 November 1998) UN Doc S/RES/1208	'IHL'
UNSC Res 1213 (3 December 1998) UN Doc S/RES/1213	'IHL' CIHL
UNSC Res 1214 (8 December 1998) UN Doc S/RES/1214	'IHL' CIHL
UNSC Res 1216 (21 December 1998) UN Doc S/RES/1216	CIHL
UNSC Res 1225 (28 January 1999) UN Doc S/RES/1225	CIHL
UNSC Res 1227 (10 February 1999) UN Doc S/RES/1227*	'IHL' CIHL
UNSC Res 1229 (26 February 1999) UN Doc S/RES/1229	CIHL
UNSC Res 1231 (11 March 1999) UN Doc S/RES/1231	'IHL' CIHL

Security Council resolution	Reference to IHL
UNSC Res 1233 (6 April 1999) UN Doc S/RES/1233	'IHL' CIHL
UNSC Res 1234 (9 April 1999) UN Doc S/RES/1234*	GCs APs 'IHL' CIHL
UNSC Res 1237 (7 May 1999) UN Doc S/RES/1237	CIHL
UNSC Res 1239 (14 May 1999) UN Doc S/RES/1239	GCs APs 'IHL' CIHL
UNSC Res 1242 (21 May 1999) UN Doc S/RES/1242**	CIHL
UNSC Res 1244 (10 June 1999) UN Doc S/RES/1244**	CIHL
UNSC Res 1246 (11 June 1999) UN Doc S/RES/1246	CIHL
UNSC Res 1251 (29 June 1999) UN Doc S/RES/1251	CIHL
UNSC Res 1252 (15 July 1999) UN Doc S/RES/1252	CIHL
UNSC Res 1254 (30 July 1999) UN Doc S/RES/1254	CIHL
UNSC Res 1258 (6 August 1999) UN Doc S/RES/1258	'IHL' CIHL
UNSC Res 1260 (20 August 1999) UN Doc S/RES/1260	'IHL' CIHL
UNSC Res 1261 (30 August 1999) UN Doc S/RES/1261	GCs APs 'IHL' CIHL
UNSC Res 1264 (15 September 1999) UN Doc S/RES/1264**	'IHL' CIHL
UNSC Res 1265 (17 September 1999) UN Doc S/RES/1265	GCs APs Art 90 API 'IHL' CIHL
UNSC Res 1267 (15 October 1999) UN Doc S/RES/1267**	'IHL'
UNSC Res 1268 (15 October 1999) UN Doc S/RES/1268	CIHL
UNSC Res 1269 (19 October 1999) UN Doc S/RES/1269	'IHL'
UNSC Res 1270 (22 October 1999) UN Doc S/RES/1270**	'IHL' CIHL

Security Council resolution	Reference to IHL
UNSC Res 1272 (25 October 1999) UN Doc S/RES/1272**	'IHL' CIHL
UNSC Res 1274 (12 November 1999) UN Doc S/RES/1274	CIHL
UNSC Res 1279 (30 November 1999) UN Doc S/RES/1279	'IHL'
UNSC Res 1283 (15 December 1999) UN Doc S/RES/1283	CIHL
UNSC Res 1284 (17 December 1999) UN Doc S/RES/1284**	CIHL
UNSC Res 1286 (19 January 2000) UN Doc S/RES/1286	CIHL
UNSC Res 1289 (7 February 2000) UN Doc S/RES/1289**	CIHL
UNSC Res 1291 (24 February 2000) UN Doc S/RES/1291**	CIHL
UNSC Res 1296 (19 April 2000) UN Doc S/RES/1296	CCW PII APMC 'IHL' CIHL
UNSC Res 1297 (12 May 2000) UN Doc S/RES/1297*	'IHL' CIHL
UNSC Res 1298 (17 May 2000) UN Doc S/RES/1298*	CIHL
UNSC Res 1304 (16 June 2000) UN Doc S/RES/1304**	CIHL
UNSC Res 1313 (4 August 2000) UN Doc S/RES/1313	CIHL
UNSC Res 1314 (11 August 2000) UN Doc S/RES/1314	GCs APs 'IHL' CIHL
UNSC Res 1315 (14 August 2000) UN Doc S/RES/1315*	CIHL
UNSC Res 1318 (7 September 2000) UN Doc S/RES/1318	'IHL' CIHL
UNSC Res 1320 (15 September 2000) UN Doc S/RES/1320	'IHL' CIHL
UNSC Res 1322 (7 October 2000) UN Doc S/RES/1322	CIHL
UNSC Res 1325 (31 October 2000) UN Doc S/RES/1325	CIHL
UNSC Res 1327 (13 November 2000) UN Doc S/RES/1327	'IHL'
UNSC Res 1329 (5 December 2000) UN Doc S/RES/1329**	'IHL'
UNSC Res 1332 (14 December 2000) UN Doc S/RES/1332	CIHL
UNSC Res 1333 (19 December 2000) UN Doc S/RES/1333**	'IHL' CIHL
UNSC Res 1344 (15 March 2001) UN Doc S/RES/1344	'IHL'

Security Council resolution	Reference to IHL
UNSC Res 1346 (30 March 2001) UN Doc S/RES/1346	CIHL
UNSC Res 1355 (15 June 2001) UN Doc S/RES/1355**	GCIV 'IHL' CIHL
UNSC Res 1359 (29 June 2001) UN Doc S/RES/1359	'IHL' CIHL
UNSC Res 1366 (30 August 2001) UN Doc S/RES/1366	'IHL'
UNSC Res 1369 (14 September 2001) UN Doc S/RES/1369	'IHL' CIHL
UNSC Res 1370 (18 September 2001) UN Doc S/RES/1370	CIHL
UNSC Res 1378 (14 November 2001) UN Doc S/RES/1378*	'IHL' CIHL
UNSC Res 1379 (20 November 2001) UN Doc S/RES/1379	GCs APs CIHL
UNSC Res 1386 (20 December 2001) UN Doc S/RES/1386**	CIHL
UNSC Res 1389 (16 January 2002) UN Doc S/RES/1389**	CIHL
UNSC Res 1393 (31 January 2002) UN Doc S/RES/1393	CIHL
UNSC Res 1397 (12 March 2002) UN Doc S/RES/1397	'IHL' CIHL
UNSC Res 1398 (15 March 2002) UN Doc S/RES/1398	GCs 'IHL' CIHL
UNSC Res 1400 (28 March 2002) UN Doc S/RES/1400	'IHL' CIHL
UNSC Res 1405 (19 April 2002) UN Doc S/RES/1405	'IHL' CIHL
UNSC Res 1410 (17 May 2002) UN Doc S/RES/1410	CIHL
UNSC Res 1417 (14 June 2002) UN Doc S/RES/1417	CIHL
UNSC Res 1422 (12 July 2002) UN Doc S/RES/1422**	CIHL
UNSC Res 1429 (30 July 2002) UN Doc S/RES/1429	'IHL' CIHL
UNSC Res 1430 (14 August 2002) UN Doc S/RES/1430	GCs 'IHL' CIHL
UNSC Res 1434 (6 September 2002) UN Doc S/RES/1434	GCs CIHL

Security Council resolution	Reference to IHL
UNSC Res 1435 (24 September 2002) UN Doc S/RES/1435	GCIV CIHL
UNSC Res 1445 (4 December 2002) UN Doc S/RES/1445	CIHL
UNSC Res 1456 (20 January 2003) UN Doc S/RES/1456	CIHL
UNSC Res 1457 (24 January 2003) UN Doc S/RES/1457*	CIHL
UNSC Res 1460 (30 January 2003) UN Doc S/RES/1460	GCIV 'IHL' CIHL
UNSC Res 1464 (4 February 2003) UN Doc S/RES/1464*	'IHL'
UNSC Res 1466 (14 March 2003) UN Doc S/RES/1466	'IHL' CIHL
UNSC Res 1467 (18 March 2003) UN Doc S/RES/1467	'IHL'
UNSC Res 1468 (20 March 2003) UN Doc S/RES/1468*	CIHL
UNSC Res 1472 (28 March 2003) UN Doc S/RES/1472**	HRs GCs Art 55 GCIV CIHL
UNSC Res 1478 (6 May 2003) UN Doc S/RES/1478**	CIHL
UNSC Res 1479 (13 May 2003) UN Doc S/RES/1479*	'IHL' CIHL
UNSC Res 1483 (22 May 2003) UN Doc S/RES/1483**	GCs 1907 HRs CIHL
UNSC Res 1484 (30 May 2003) UN Doc S/RES/1484**	'IHL' CIHL
UNSC Res 1487 (12 June 2003) UN Doc S/RES/1487**	CIHL
UNSC Res 1493 (28 July 2003) UN Doc S/RES/1493**	'IHL' CIHL
UNSC Res 1495 (31 July 2003) UN Doc S/RES/1495	'IHL' CIHL
UNSC Res 1496 (31 July 2003) UN Doc S/RES/1496	CIHL
UNSC Res 1497 (1 August 2003) UN Doc S/RES/1497**	CIHL
UNSC Res 1499 (13 August 2003) UN Doc S/RES/1499	CIHL
UNSC Res 1502 (26 August 2003) UN Doc S/RES/1502	GCs HRs 'IHL' CIHL

Security Council resolution	Reference to IHL
UNSC Res 1509 (19 September 2003) UN Doc S/RES/1509**	'IHL' CIHL
UNSC Res 1528 (27 February 2004) UN Doc S/RES/1528**	'IHL' CIHL
UNSC Res 1529 (29 February 2004) UN Doc S/RES/1529**	CIHL
UNSC Res 1533 (12 March 2004) UN Doc S/RES/1533**	CIHL
UNSC Res 1535 (26 March 2004) UN Doc S/RES/1535	'IHL'
UNSC Res 1539 (22 April 2004) UN Doc S/RES/1539	GCs APs CIHL
UNSC Res 1540 (28 April 2004) UN Doc S/RES/1540	BWC CWC
UNSC Res 1542 (30 April 2004) UN Doc S/RES/1542	'IHL' CIHL
UNSC Res 1544 (19 May 2004) UN Doc S/RES/1544	GCIV 'IHL' CIHL
UNSC Res 1545 (21 May 2004) UN Doc S/RES/1545**	'IHL' CIHL
UNSC Res 1546 (8 June 2004) UN Doc S/RES/1546**	'IHL' CIHL
UNSC Res 1547 (11 June 2004) UN Doc S/RES/1547	'IHL'
UNSC Res 1556 (30 July 2004) UN Doc S/RES/1556**	'IHL' CIHL
UNSC Res 1564 (18 September 2004) UN Doc S/RES/1564**	'IHL' CIHL
UNSC Res 1565 (1 October 2004) UN Doc S/RES/1565**	'IHL' CIHL
UNSC Res 1566 (8 October 2004) UN Doc S/RES/1566**	'IHL'
UNSC Res 1572 (15 November 2004) UN Doc S/RES/1572**	'IHL'
UNSC Res 1574 (19 November 2004) UN Doc S/RES/1574*	'IHL' CIHL
UNSC Res 1577 (1 December 2004) UN Doc S/RES/1577**	'IHL' CIHL
UNSC Res 1589 (24 March 2005) UN Doc S/RES/1589	'IHL'
UNSC Res 1590 (24 March 2005) UN Doc S/RES/1590**	'IHL' CIHL

Security Council resolution	Reference to IHL
UNSC Res 1591 (29 March 2005) UN Doc S/RES/1591**	'IHL' CIHL
UNSC Res 1592 (30 March 2005) UN Doc S/RES/1592**	'IHL' CIHL
UNSC Res 1593 (31 March 2005) UN Doc S/RES/1593**	CIHL
UNSC Res 1598 (28 April 2005) UN Doc S/RES/1598	'IHL' CIHL
UNSC Res 1602 (31 May 2005) UN Doc S/RES/1602**	'IHL' CIHL
UNSC Res 1603 (3 June 2005) UN Doc S/RES/1603**	CIHL
UNSC Res 1604 (17 June 2005) UN Doc S/RES/1604	CIHL
UNSC Res 1606 (20 June 2005) UN Doc S/RES/1606	CIHL
UNSC Res 1609 (24 June 2005) UN Doc S/RES/1609**	CIHL
UNSC Res 1610 (30 June 2005) UN Doc S/RES/1610**	CIHL
UNSC Res 1612 (26 July 2005) UN Doc S/RES/1612	GCs APs CIHL
UNSC Res 1614 (29 July 2005) UN Doc S/RES/1614	CIHL
UNSC Res 1615 (29 July 2005) UN Doc S/RES/1615	CIHL
UNSC Res 1621 (6 September 2005) UN Doc S/RES/1621**	'IHL'
UNSC Res 1622 (13 September 2005) UN Doc S/RES/1622	CIHL
UNSC Res 1624 (14 September 2005) UN Doc S/RES/1624	'IHL'
UNSC Res 1633 (21 October 2005) UN Doc S/RES/1633**	'IHL' CIHL
UNSC Res 1635 (28 October 2005) UN Doc S/RES/1635**	'IHL'
UNSC Res 1637 (11 November 2005) UN Doc S/RES/1637**	'IHL'
UNSC Res 1639 (21 November 2005) UN Doc S/RES/1639**	CIHL
UNSC Res 1643 (15 December 2005) UN Doc S/RES/1643**	'IHL' CIHL
UNSC Res 1649 (21 December 2005) UN Doc S/RES/1649**	'IHL' CIHL
UNSC Res 1653 (27 January 2006) UN Doc S/RES/1653	'IHL' CIHL
UNSC Res 1655 (31 January 2006) UN Doc S/RES/1655	CIHL
UNSC Res 1662 (23 March 2006) UN Doc S/RES/1662	'IHL' CIHL

Security Council resolution	Reference to IHL
UNSC Res 1663 (24 March 2006) UN Doc S/RES/1663*	CIHL
UNSC Res 1666 (31 March 2006) UN Doc S/RES/1666	CIHL
UNSC Res 1671 (25 April 2006) UN Doc S/RES/1671**	CIHL
UNSC Res 1674 (28 April 2006) UN Doc S/RES/1674	1899 HRs 1907 HRs GCs APs 'IHL' CIHL
UNSC Res 1687 (15 June 2006) UN Doc S/RES/1687	CIHL
UNSC Res 1690 (20 June 2006) UN Doc S/RES/1690	CIHL
UNSC Res 1698 (31 July 2006) UN Doc S/RES/1698**	CIHL
UNSC Res 1701 (11 August 2006) UN Doc S/RES/1701*	CIHL
UNSC Res 1702 (15 August 2006) UN Doc S/RES/1702**	CIHL
UNSC Res 1704 (25 August 2006) UN Doc S/RES/1704	CIHL
UNSC Res 1706 (31 August 2006) UN Doc S/RES/1706**	CIHL
UNSC Res 1707 (12 September 2006) UN Doc S/RES/1707**	CIHL
UNSC Res 1709 (22 September 2006) UN Doc S/RES/1709*	CIHL
UNSC Res 1710 (29 September 2006) UN Doc S/RES/1710	CIHL
UNSC Res 1711 (29 September 2006) UN Doc S/RES/1711**	'IHL' CIHL
UNSC Res 1713 (29 September 2006) UN Doc S/RES/1713**	CIHL
UNSC Res 1714 (6 October 2006) UN Doc S/RES/1714*	CIHL
UNSC Res 1716 (13 October 2006) UN Doc S/RES/1716	CIHL
UNSC Res 1718 (14 October 2006) UN Doc S/RES/1718**	CIHL
UNSC Res 1721 (1 November 2006) UN Doc S/RES/1721**	'IHL' CIHL
UNSC Res 1722 (21 November 2006) UN Doc S/RES/1722**	CIHL
UNSC Res 1723 (28 November 2006) UN Doc S/RES/1723**	'IHL'
UNSC Res 1725 (6 December 2006) UN Doc S/RES/1725**	CIHL
UNSC Res 1727 (15 December 2006) UN Doc S/RES/1727**	'IHL' CIHL
UNSC Res 1728 (15 December 2006) UN Doc S/RES/1728	CIHL
UNSC Res 1736 (22 December 2006) UN Doc S/RES/1736**	'IHL' CIHL

Security Council resolution	Reference to IHL
UNSC Res 1738 (23 December 2006) UN Doc S/RES/1738	GCs GCIII Art 4 (A) (4) GCIII APs Art 79 API 'IHL' CIHL
UNSC Res 1739 (10 January 2007) UN Doc S/RES/1739**	CIHL
UNSC Res 1740 (23 January 2007) UN Doc S/RES/1740	CIHL
UNSC Res 1741 (30 January 2007) UN Doc S/RES/1741	CIHL
UNSC Res 1743 (15 February 2007) UN Doc S/RES/1743**	CIHL
UNSC Res 1744 (21 February 2007) UN Doc S/RES/1744**	CIHL
UNSC Res 1746 (23 March 2007) UN Doc S/RES/1746**	'IHL' CIHL
UNSC Res 1752 (13 April 2007) UN Doc S/RES/1752	CIHL
UNSC Res 1754 (30 April 2007) UN Doc S/RES/1754	CIHL
UNSC Res 1755 (30 April 2007) UN Doc S/RES/1755*	CIHL
UNSC Res 1756 (15 May 2007) UN Doc S/RES/1756**	'IHL' CIHL
UNSC Res 1758 (15 June 2007) UN Doc S/RES/1758	CIHL
UNSC Res 1762 (29 June 2007) UN Doc S/RES/1762**	GP BWC CWC CIHL
UNSC Res 1765 (16 July 2007) UN Doc S/RES/1765**	'IHL' CIHL
UNSC Res 1769 (31 July 2007) UN Doc S/RES/1769**	'IHL' CIHL
UNSC Res 1770 (10 August 2007) UN Doc S/RES/1770	GCs HRs 'IHL' CIHL
UNSC Res 1771 (10 August 2007) UN Doc S/RES/1771**	CIHL
UNSC Res 1772 (20 August 2007) UN Doc S/RES/1772**	'IHL' CIHL
UNSC Res 1773 (24 August 2007) UN Doc S/RES/1773*	CIHL

Security Council resolution	Reference to IHL
UNSC Res 1776 (19 September 2007) UN Doc S/RES/1776**	'IHL' CIHL
UNSC Res 1778 (25 September 2007) UN Doc S/RES/1778*	'IHL' CIHL
UNSC Res 1779 (28 September 2007) UN Doc S/RES/1779**	CIHL
UNSC Res 1780 (15 October 2007) UN Doc S/RES/1780**	CIHL
UNSC Res 1781 (15 October 2007) UN Doc S/RES/1781	CIHL
UNSC Res 1782 (29 October 2007) UN Doc S/RES/1782**	'IHL' CIHL
UNSC Res 1783 (31 October 2007) UN Doc S/RES/1783	CIHL
UNSC Res 1784 (31 October 2007) UN Doc S/RES/1784*	CIHL
UNSC Res 1785 (21 November 2007) UN Doc S/RES/1785**	CIHL
UNSC Res 1787 (10 December 2007) UN Doc S/RES/1787	'IHL'
UNSC Res 1790 (18 December 2007) UN Doc S/RES/1790**	'IHL' CIHL
UNSC Res 1794 (21 December 2007) UN Doc S/RES/1794**	'IHL' CIHL
UNSC Res 1795 (15 January 2008) UN Doc S/RES/1795**	'IHL' CIHL
UNSC Res 1796 (23 January 2008) UN Doc S/RES/1796	CIHL
UNSC Res 1798 (30 January 2008) UN Doc S/RES/1798	CIHL
UNSC Res 1801 (20 February 2008) UN Doc S/RES/1801**	'IHL' CIHL
UNSC Res 1804 (13 March 2008) UN Doc S/RES/1804	'IHL' CIHL
UNSC Res 1805 (20 March 2008) UN Doc S/RES/1805	'IHL'
UNSC Res 1806 (20 March 2008) UN Doc S/RES/1806	'IHL' CIHL
UNSC Res 1807 (31 March 2008) UN Doc S/RES/1807**	'IHL' CIHL
UNSC Res 1808 (15 April 2008) UN Doc S/RES/1808	CIHL
UNSC Res 1810 (25 April 2008) UN Doc S/RES/1810**	BWC CWC 'IHL'
UNSC Res 1812 (30 April 2008) UN Doc S/RES/1812*	'IHL' CIHL

Security Council resolution	Reference to IHL
UNSC Res 1813 (30 April 2008) UN Doc S/RES/1813	CIHL
UNSC Res 1814 (15 May 2008) UN Doc S/RES/1814**	'IHL' CIHL
UNSC Res 1816 (2 June 2008) UN Doc S/RES/1816**	CIHL
UNSC Res 1820 (19 June 2008) UN Doc S/RES/1820	'IHL' CIHL
UNSC Res 1822 (30 June 2008) UN Doc S/RES/1822**	'IHL'
UNSC Res 1825 (23 July 2008) UN Doc S/RES/1825	CIHL
UNSC Res 1826 (29 July 2008) UN Doc S/RES/1826**	'IHL' CIHL
UNSC Res 1828 (31 July 2008) UN Doc S/RES/1828*	'IHL' CIHL
UNSC Res 1830 (7 August 2008) UN Doc S/RES/1830	GCs HRs 'IHL' CIHL
UNSC Res 1831 (19 August 2008) UN Doc S/RES/1831**	CIHL
UNSC Res 1832 (27 August 2008) UN Doc S/RES/1832*	CIHL
UNSC Res 1833 (22 September 2008) UN Doc S/RES/1833**	'IHL' CIHL
UNSC Res 1834 (24 September 2008) UN Doc S/RES/1834*	'IHL' CIHL
UNSC Res 1838 (7 October 2008) UN Doc S/RES/1838**	CIHL
UNSC Res 1840 (14 October 2008) UN Doc S/RES/1840**	CIHL
UNSC Res 1841 (15 October 2008) UN Doc S/RES/1841**	CIHL
UNSC Res 1842 (29 October 2008) UN Doc S/RES/1842**	'IHL' CIHL
UNSC Res 1843 (20 November 2008) UN Doc S/RES/1843**	'IHL' CIHL
UNSC Res 1845 (20 November 2008) UN Doc S/RES/1845**	CIHL
UNSC Res 1846 (2 December 2008) UN Doc S/RES/1846**	CIHL
UNSC Res 1851 (16 December 2008) UN Doc S/RES/1851**	'IHL' CIHL
UNSC Res 1856 (22 December 2008) UN Doc S/RES/1856**	'IHL' CIHL

Security Council resolution	Reference to IHL
UNSC Res 1857 (22 December 2008) UN Doc S/RES/1857**	'IHL' CIHL
UNSC Res 1860 (8 January 2009) UN Doc S/RES/1860	CIHL
UNSC Res 1861 (14 January 2009) UN Doc S/RES/1861**	'IHL' CIHL
UNSC Res 1863 (16 January 2009) UN Doc S/RES/1863**	'IHL' CIHL
UNSC Res 1864 (23 January 2009) UN Doc S/RES/1864	CIHL
UNSC Res 1865 (27 January 2009) UN Doc S/RES/1865**	'IHL' CIHL
UNSC Res 1866 (13 February 2009) UN Doc S/RES/1866	CIHL
UNSC Res 1868 (23 March 2009) UN Doc S/RES/1868	'IHL' CIHL
UNSC Res 1870 (20 May 2009) UN Doc S/RES/1870*	'IHL' CIHL
UNSC Res 1871 (30 April 2009) UN Doc S/RES/1871	CIHL
UNSC Res 1872 (26 May 2009) UN Doc S/RES/1872**	CIHL
UNSC Res 1879 (23 July 2009) UN Doc S/RES/1879	CIHL
UNSC Res 1880 (30 July 2009) UN Doc S/RES/1880**	'IHL' CIHL
UNSC Res 1881 (6 August 2009) UN Doc S/RES/1881*	'IHL' CIHL
UNSC Res 1882 (4 August 2009) UN Doc S/RES/1882	GCs APs CRC OPI 'IHL' CIHL
UNSC Res 1883 (7 August 2009) UN Doc S/RES/1883	GCs APs 'IHL' CIHL
UNSC Res 1884 (27 August 2009) UN Doc S/RES/1884*	CIHL
UNSC Res 1888 (30 September 2009) UN Doc S/RES/1888	GCs APs CRC CRC OPI 'IHL' CIHL

Security Council resolution	Reference to IHL
UNSC Res 1889 (5 October 2009) UN Doc S/RES/1889	GCs APs 'IHL' CIHL
UNSC Res 1890 (8 October 2009) UN Doc S/RES/1890**	'IHL' CIHL
UNSC Res 1891 (13 October 2009) UN Doc S/RES/1891**	CIHL
UNSC Res 1893 (29 October 2009) UN Doc S/RES/1893**	'IHL' CIHL
UNSC Res 1894 (11 November 2009) UN Doc S/RES/1894	GCs APs API 'IHL' CIHL
UNSC Res 1895 (18 November 2009) UN Doc S/RES/1895**	CIHL
UNSC Res 1896 (7 December 2009) UN Doc S/RES/1896**	'IHL' CIHL
UNSC Res 1897 (30 November 2009) UN Doc S/RES/1897**	CIHL
UNSC Res 1904 (17 December 2009) UN Doc S/RES/1904**	'IHL' CIHL
UNSC Res 1906 (23 December 2009) UN Doc S/RES/1906**	'IHL' CIHL
UNSC Res 1907 (23 December 2009) UN Doc S/RES/1907**	CIHL
UNSC Res 1909 (21 January 2010) UN Doc S/RES/1909	CIHL
UNSC Res 1910 (28 January 2010) UN Doc S/RES/1910**	'IHL' CIHL
UNSC Res 1911 (28 January 2010) UN Doc S/RES/1911**	'IHL' CIHL
UNSC Res 1912 (26 February 2010) UN Doc S/RES/1912	CIHL
UNSC Res 1916 (19 March 2010) UN Doc S/RES/1916**	CIHL
UNSC Res 1917 (22 March 2010) UN Doc S/RES/1917	'IHL' CIHL
UNSC Res 1919 (29 April 2010) UN Doc S/RES/1919*	'IHL' CIHL
UNSC Res 1920 (30 April 2010) UN Doc S/RES/1920	CIHL
UNSC Res 1921 (12 May 2010) UN Doc S/RES/1921	CIHL

Security Council resolution	Reference to IHL
UNSC Res 1923 (25 May 2010) UN Doc S/RES/1923*	'IHL' CIHL
UNSC Res 1925 (28 May 2010) UN Doc S/RES/1925**	'IHL' CIHL
UNSC Res 1933 (30 June 2010) UN Doc S/RES/1933**	'IHL' CIHL
UNSC Res 1935 (30 July 2010) UN Doc S/RES/1935*	'IHL' CIHL
UNSC Res 1936 (5 August 2010) UN Doc S/RES/1936	HRs GCs 'IHL' CIHL
UNSC Res 1937 (30 August 2010) UN Doc S/RES/1937*	CIHL

*	Adopted under Article 39 of the United Nations Charter
**	Adopted under Chapter VII or both Chapter VII and Article 39 of the UN Charter
APs	Additional Protocols to the Geneva Conventions, 1977
API	Protocol Additional to the Geneva Conventions of 12 August 1949, and Relating to the Protection of Victims of International Armed Conflicts (Protocol I), 1977
APMC	Convention on the Prohibition of the Use, Stockpiling, Production and Transfer of Anti-Personnel Mines and on Their Destruction, 1997
BWC	Convention on the Prohibition of the Development, Production and Stockpiling of Bacteriological (Biological) and Toxin Weapons and on Their Destruction, 1972
CCW PII	Convention on Prohibitions and Restrictions on the Use of Certain Conventional Weapons Which May Be Deemed to Be Excessively Injurious or to Have Indiscriminate Effects, Protocol on Prohibitions or Restrictions on the Use of Mines, Booby-Traps and Other Devices (Protocol II), 1980
CIHL	customary international humanitarian law
CPC	Convention for the Protection of Cultural Property in the Event of Armed Conflict, 1954
CRC	Convention on the Rights of the Child, 1989
CRC OPI	Optional Protocol to the Convention on the Rights of the Child on the Involvement of Children in Armed Conflict, 2001
CWC	Convention on the Prohibition of the Development, Production, Stockpiling and Use of Chemical Weapons and on Their Destruction, 1993
GCs	Geneva Conventions, 1949
GCIII	Geneva Convention Relative to the Treatment of Prisoners of War, 1949

GCIV	Geneva Convention Relative to the Protection of Civilian Persons in Time of War, 1949
GP	Protocol for the Prohibition of the Use of Asphyxiating, Poisonous or Other Gases, and of Bacteriological Methods of Warfare, 1925
HRs	Both or either of 1899 HRs and/or 1907 HRs (not specified in the resolution)
1899 HRs	Convention (II) with Respect to the Laws and Customs of War on Land and Its Annex: Regulations concerning the Laws and Customs of War on Land, 1899
1907 HRs	Convention (IV) Respecting the Laws and Customs of War on Land and Its Annex: Regulations concerning the Laws and Customs of War on Land, 1907

Annex 2: United Nations Security Council Resolutions Reflecting Customary Rules of IHL

I. SPECIFICALLY PROTECTED PERSONS

Prohibition on attacks on civilians in general

UNSC Res 169	UNSC Res 256	UNSC Res 265	UNSC Res 268
UNSC Res 270	UNSC Res 273	UNSC Res 275	UNSC Res 280
UNSC Res 290	UNSC Res 294	UNSC Res 316	UNSC Res 326
UNSC Res 332	UNSC Res 347	UNSC Res 393	UNSC Res 403
UNSC Res 405	UNSC Res 427	UNSC Res 428	UNSC Res 434
UNSC Res 445	UNSC Res 447	UNSC Res 454	UNSC Res 459
UNSC Res 466	UNSC Res 467	UNSC Res 507	UNSC Res 512
UNSC Res 513	UNSC Res 514	UNSC Res 515	UNSC Res 520
UNSC Res 521	UNSC Res 522	UNSC Res 527	UNSC Res 540
UNSC Res 542	UNSC Res 545	UNSC Res 546	UNSC Res 564
UNSC Res 572	UNSC Res 577	UNSC Res 587	UNSC Res 588
UNSC Res 598	UNSC Res 602	UNSC Res 611	UNSC Res 616
UNSC Res 713	UNSC Res 727	UNSC Res 733	UNSC Res 743
UNSC Res 745	UNSC Res 746	UNSC Res 751	UNSC Res 752
UNSC Res 757	UNSC Res 758	UNSC Res 761	UNSC Res 766
UNSC Res 767	UNSC Res 769	UNSC Res 770	UNSC Res 771
UNSC Res 775	UNSC Res 783	UNSC Res 787	UNSC Res 788
UNSC Res 794	UNSC Res 802	UNSC Res 804	UNSC Res 810
UNSC Res 811	UNSC Res 813	UNSC Res 814	UNSC Res 819
UNSC Res 820	UNSC Res 823	UNSC Res 824	UNSC Res 826
UNSC Res 834	UNSC Res 836	UNSC Res 837	UNSC Res 851
UNSC Res 853	UNSC Res 858	UNSC Res 859	UNSC Res 864
UNSC Res 865	UNSC Res 866	UNSC Res 868	UNSC Res 872
UNSC Res 880	UNSC Res 884	UNSC Res 890	UNSC Res 892
UNSC Res 897	UNSC Res 904	UNSC Res 906	UNSC Res 911

Prohibition on attacks on civilians in general (*cont.*)

UNSC Res 912	UNSC Res 913	UNSC Res 918	UNSC Res 923
UNSC Res 925	UNSC Res 929	UNSC Res 931	UNSC Res 935
UNSC Res 940	UNSC Res 945	UNSC Res 946	UNSC Res 950
UNSC Res 952	UNSC Res 954	UNSC Res 955	UNSC Res 958
UNSC Res 959	UNSC Res 965	UNSC Res 966	UNSC Res 976
UNSC Res 978	UNSC Res 981	UNSC Res 982	UNSC Res 985
UNSC Res 987	UNSC Res 993	UNSC Res 994	UNSC Res 997
UNSC Res 998	UNSC Res 999	UNSC Res 1001	UNSC Res 1004
UNSC Res 1009	UNSC Res 1010	UNSC Res 1014	UNSC Res 1016
UNSC Res 1019	UNSC Res 1020	UNSC Res 1030	UNSC Res 1031
UNSC Res 1036	UNSC Res 1039	UNSC Res 1040	UNSC Res 1041
UNSC Res 1049	UNSC Res 1052	UNSC Res 1055	UNSC Res 1059
UNSC Res 1064	UNSC Res 1065	UNSC Res 1068	UNSC Res 1071
UNSC Res 1072	UNSC Res 1073	UNSC Res 1075	UNSC Res 1076
UNSC Res 1080	UNSC Res 1083	UNSC Res 1087	UNSC Res 1088
UNSC Res 1089	UNSC Res 1092	UNSC Res 1093	UNSC Res 1095
UNSC Res 1096	UNSC Res 1097	UNSC Res 1099	UNSC Res 1101
UNSC Res 1113	UNSC Res 1114	UNSC Res 1118	UNSC Res 1119
UNSC Res 1122	UNSC Res 1123	UNSC Res 1124	UNSC Res 1125
UNSC Res 1127	UNSC Res 1128	UNSC Res 1136	UNSC Res 1138
UNSC Res 1149	UNSC Res 1150	UNSC Res 1151	UNSC Res 1152
UNSC Res 1155	UNSC Res 1157	UNSC Res 1159	UNSC Res 1161
UNSC Res 1164	UNSC Res 1173	UNSC Res 1174	UNSC Res 1176
UNSC Res 1180	UNSC Res 1181	UNSC Res 1187	UNSC Res 1188
UNSC Res 1190	UNSC Res 1193	UNSC Res 1195	UNSC Res 1199
UNSC Res 1202	UNSC Res 1203	UNSC Res 1206	UNSC Res 1213
UNSC Res 1225	UNSC Res 1227	UNSC Res 1229	UNSC Res 1233
UNSC Res 1234	UNSC Res 1237	UNSC Res 1242	UNSC Res 1246
UNSC Res 1251	UNSC Res 1252	UNSC Res 1254	UNSC Res 1258
UNSC Res 1260	UNSC Res 1261	UNSC Res 1265	UNSC Res 1268
UNSC Res 1270	UNSC Res 1272	UNSC Res 1274	UNSC Res 1286
UNSC Res 1289	UNSC Res 1296	UNSC Res 1297	UNSC Res 1313
UNSC Res 1314	UNSC Res 1333	UNSC Res 1355	UNSC Res 1369
UNSC Res 1370	UNSC Res 1378	UNSC Res 1379	UNSC Res 1389
UNSC Res 1393	UNSC Res 1398	UNSC Res 1400	UNSC Res 1417
UNSC Res 1430	UNSC Res 1434	UNSC Res 1445	UNSC Res 1466
UNSC Res 1468	UNSC Res 1472	UNSC Res 1478	UNSC Res 1479

Prohibition on attacks on civilians in general (*cont.*)

UNSC Res 1484	UNSC Res 1493	UNSC Res 1496	UNSC Res 1502
UNSC Res 1528	UNSC Res 1529	UNSC Res 1539	UNSC Res 1542
UNSC Res 1544	UNSC Res 1545	UNSC Res 1556	UNSC Res 1564
UNSC Res 1565	UNSC Res 1574	UNSC Res 1577	UNSC Res 1590
UNSC Res 1591	UNSC Res 1592	UNSC Res 1602	UNSC Res 1609
UNSC Res 1614	UNSC Res 1615	UNSC Res 1633	UNSC Res 1639
UNSC Res 1643	UNSC Res 1649	UNSC Res 1653	UNSC Res 1655
UNSC Res 1662	UNSC Res 1663	UNSC Res 1666	UNSC Res 1671
UNSC Res 1674	UNSC Res 1687	UNSC Res 1690	UNSC Res 1697
UNSC Res 1698	UNSC Res 1701	UNSC Res 1704	UNSC Res 1706
UNSC Res 1707	UNSC Res 1709	UNSC Res 1710	UNSC Res 1713
UNSC Res 1714	UNSC Res 1716	UNSC Res 1721	UNSC Res 1722
UNSC Res 1727	UNSC Res 1738	UNSC Res 1739	UNSC Res 1740
UNSC Res 1741	UNSC Res 1743	UNSC Res 1744	UNSC Res 1746
UNSC Res 1752	UNSC Res 1755	UNSC Res 1756	UNSC Res 1765
UNSC Res 1769	UNSC Res 1770	UNSC Res 1772	UNSC Res 1773
UNSC Res 1776	UNSC Res 1778	UNSC Res 1779	UNSC Res 1780
UNSC Res 1781	UNSC Res 1782	UNSC Res 1784	UNSC Res 1790
UNSC Res 1794	UNSC Res 1795	UNSC Res 1796	UNSC Res 1798
UNSC Res 1801	UNSC Res 1806	UNSC Res 1807	UNSC Res 1808
UNSC Res 1812	UNSC Res 1813	UNSC Res 1820	UNSC Res 1825
UNSC Res 1826	UNSC Res 1828	UNSC Res 1830	UNSC Res 1831
UNSC Res 1832	UNSC Res 1833	UNSC Res 1834	UNSC Res 1838
UNSC Res 1840	UNSC Res 1841	UNSC Res 1843	UNSC Res 1845
UNSC Res 1856	UNSC Res 1857	UNSC Res 1860	UNSC Res 1861
UNSC Res 1863	UNSC Res 1864	UNSC Res 1865	UNSC Res 1868
UNSC Res 1870	UNSC Res 1872	UNSC Res 1879	UNSC Res 1880
UNSC Res 1881	UNSC Res 1883	UNSC Res 1884	UNSC Res 1888
UNSC Res 1889	UNSC Res 1890	UNSC Res 1891	UNSC Res 1893
UNSC Res 1894	UNSC Res 1895	UNSC Res 1896	UNSC Res 1906
UNSC Res 1907	UNSC Res 1909	UNSC Res 1910	UNSC Res 1911
UNSC Res 1917	UNSC Res 1919	UNSC Res 1921	UNSC Res 1923
UNSC Res 1925	UNSC Res 1933	UNSC Res 1935	UNSC Res 1936

Obligation to protect relief personnel

UNSC Res 564	UNSC Res 733	UNSC Res 746	UNSC Res 751
UNSC Res 757	UNSC Res 758	UNSC Res 761	UNSC Res 767
UNSC Res 770	UNSC Res 775	UNSC Res 787	UNSC Res 794
UNSC Res 813	UNSC Res 814	UNSC Res 819	UNSC Res 820
UNSC Res 823	UNSC Res 824	UNSC Res 834	UNSC Res 836
UNSC Res 851	UNSC Res 859	UNSC Res 864	UNSC Res 866
UNSC Res 868	UNSC Res 897	UNSC Res 911	UNSC Res 913
UNSC Res 918	UNSC Res 923	UNSC Res 925	UNSC Res 929
UNSC Res 940	UNSC Res 945	UNSC Res 946	UNSC Res 950
UNSC Res 952	UNSC Res 954	UNSC Res 965	UNSC Res 966
UNSC Res 976	UNSC Res 982	UNSC Res 985	UNSC Res 987
UNSC Res 993	UNSC Res 997	UNSC Res 998	UNSC Res 999
UNSC Res 1001	UNSC Res 1010	UNSC Res 1030	UNSC Res 1036
UNSC Res 1040	UNSC Res 1041	UNSC Res 1049	UNSC Res 1055
UNSC Res 1059	UNSC Res 1064	UNSC Res 1065	UNSC Res 1071
UNSC Res 1072	UNSC Res 1075	UNSC Res 1080	UNSC Res 1083
UNSC Res 1087	UNSC Res 1088	UNSC Res 1093	UNSC Res 1096
UNSC Res 1099	UNSC Res 1101	UNSC Res 1113	UNSC Res 1114
UNSC Res 1119	UNSC Res 1123	UNSC Res 1124	UNSC Res 1127
UNSC Res 1128	UNSC Res 1138	UNSC Res 1149	UNSC Res 1150
UNSC Res 1157	UNSC Res 1159	UNSC Res 1164	UNSC Res 1173
UNSC Res 1176	UNSC Res 1180	UNSC Res 1187	UNSC Res 1190
UNSC Res 1193	UNSC Res 1195	UNSC Res 1199	UNSC Res 1202
UNSC Res 1203	UNSC Res 1206	UNSC Res 1213	UNSC Res 1225
UNSC Res 1229	UNSC Res 1233	UNSC Res 1234	UNSC Res 1237
UNSC Res 1258	UNSC Res 1260	UNSC Res 1261	UNSC Res 1264
UNSC Res 1265	UNSC Res 1268	UNSC Res 1270	UNSC Res 1272
UNSC Res 1274	UNSC Res 1296	UNSC Res 1314	UNSC Res 1333
UNSC Res 1355	UNSC Res 1369	UNSC Res 1370	UNSC Res 1378
UNSC Res 1379	UNSC Res 1389	UNSC Res 1398	UNSC Res 1417
UNSC Res 1430	UNSC Res 1445	UNSC Res 1466	UNSC Res 1472
UNSC Res 1478	UNSC Res 1479	UNSC Res 1484	UNSC Res 1493
UNSC Res 1502	UNSC Res 1528	UNSC Res 1529	UNSC Res 1542
UNSC Res 1544	UNSC Res 1545	UNSC Res 1556	UNSC Res 1564
UNSC Res 1565	UNSC Res 1590	UNSC Res 1591	UNSC Res 1592
UNSC Res 1574	UNSC Res 1609	UNSC Res 1615	UNSC Res 1633
UNSC Res 1649	UNSC Res 1653	UNSC Res 1666	UNSC Res 1674

Obligation to protect relief personnel *(cont.)*

UNSC Res 1701	UNSC Res 1704	UNSC Res 1706	UNSC Res 1713
UNSC Res 1721	UNSC Res 1739	UNSC Res 1743	UNSC Res 1744
UNSC Res 1755	UNSC Res 1756	UNSC Res 1769	UNSC Res 1770
UNSC Res 1772	UNSC Res 1778	UNSC Res 1779	UNSC Res 1780
UNSC Res 1784	UNSC Res 1794	UNSC Res 1801	UNSC Res 1806
UNSC Res 1812	UNSC Res 1813	UNSC Res 1828	UNSC Res 1830
UNSC Res 1838	UNSC Res 1841	UNSC Res 1843	UNSC Res 1856
UNSC Res 1861	UNSC Res 1868	UNSC Res 1870	UNSC Res 1872
UNSC Res 1881	UNSC Res 1883	UNSC Res 1894	UNSC Res 1906
UNSC Res 1907	UNSC Res 1910	UNSC Res 1917	UNSC Res 1919
UNSC Res 1923	UNSC Res 1925	UNSC Res 1935	UNSC Res 1936

Obligation to protect peacekeeping personnel

UNSC Res 427	UNSC Res 467	UNSC Res 587	UNSC Res 727
UNSC Res 743	UNSC Res 745	UNSC Res 752	UNSC Res 757
UNSC Res 766	UNSC Res 783	UNSC Res 788	UNSC Res 802
UNSC Res 804	UNSC Res 810	UNSC Res 811	UNSC Res 814
UNSC Res 819	UNSC Res 823	UNSC Res 826	UNSC Res 837
UNSC Res 858	UNSC Res 859	UNSC Res 865	UNSC Res 868
UNSC Res 872	UNSC Res 880	UNSC Res 892	UNSC Res 897
UNSC Res 906	UNSC Res 911	UNSC Res 912	UNSC Res 913
UNSC Res 918	UNSC Res 923	UNSC Res 925	UNSC Res 940
UNSC Res 946	UNSC Res 950	UNSC Res 954	UNSC Res 966
UNSC Res 976	UNSC Res 981	UNSC Res 982	UNSC Res 985
UNSC Res 987	UNSC Res 993	UNSC Res 994	UNSC Res 997
UNSC Res 998	UNSC Res 999	UNSC Res 1001	UNSC Res 1004
UNSC Res 1009	UNSC Res 1014	UNSC Res 1016	UNSC Res 1019
UNSC Res 1020	UNSC Res 1030	UNSC Res 1031	UNSC Res 1036
UNSC Res 1039	UNSC Res 1041	UNSC Res 1052	UNSC Res 1055
UNSC Res 1059	UNSC Res 1064	UNSC Res 1065	UNSC Res 1068
UNSC Res 1071	UNSC Res 1080	UNSC Res 1083	UNSC Res 1088
UNSC Res 1089	UNSC Res 1092	UNSC Res 1093	UNSC Res 1095
UNSC Res 1096	UNSC Res 1099	UNSC Res 1101	UNSC Res 1113
UNSC Res 1114	UNSC Res 1118	UNSC Res 1119	UNSC Res 1122
UNSC Res 1123	UNSC Res 1124	UNSC Res 1125	UNSC Res 1127
UNSC Res 1128	UNSC Res 1136	UNSC Res 1138	UNSC Res 1149

Obligation to protect peacekeeping personnel (*cont.*)

UNSC Res 1150	UNSC Res 1151	UNSC Res 1152	UNSC Res 1155
UNSC Res 1157	UNSC Res 1159	UNSC Res 1164	UNSC Res 1173
UNSC Res 1174	UNSC Res 1176	UNSC Res 1180	UNSC Res 1181
UNSC Res 1187	UNSC Res 1188	UNSC Res 1190	UNSC Res 1195
UNSC Res 1202	UNSC Res 1206	UNSC Res 1213	UNSC Res 1225
UNSC Res 1246	UNSC Res 1251	UNSC Res 1252	UNSC Res 1254
UNSC Res 1274	UNSC Res 1289	UNSC Res 1313	UNSC Res 1355
UNSC Res 1389	UNSC Res 1393	UNSC Res 1400	UNSC Res 1417
UNSC Res 1430	UNSC Res 1466	UNSC Res 1484	UNSC Res 1493
UNSC Res 1496	UNSC Res 1502	UNSC Res 1528	UNSC Res 1542
UNSC Res 1545	UNSC Res 1565	UNSC Res 1590	UNSC Res 1592
UNSC Res 1603	UNSC Res 1609	UNSC Res 1614	UNSC Res 1615
UNSC Res 1633	UNSC Res 1639	UNSC Res 1655	UNSC Res 1666
UNSC Res 1671	UNSC Res 1697	UNSC Res 1701	UNSC Res 1704
UNSC Res 1706	UNSC Res 1710	UNSC Res 1716	UNSC Res 1721
UNSC Res 1722	UNSC Res 1727	UNSC Res 1739	UNSC Res 1740
UNSC Res 1741	UNSC Res 1743	UNSC Res 1752	UNSC Res 1755
UNSC Res 1756	UNSC Res 1769	UNSC Res 1772	UNSC Res 1773
UNSC Res 1778	UNSC Res 1780	UNSC Res 1781	UNSC Res 1782
UNSC Res 1794	UNSC Res 1796	UNSC Res 1798	UNSC Res 1801
UNSC Res 1808	UNSC Res 1825	UNSC Res 1828	UNSC Res 1831
UNSC Res 1832	UNSC Res 1840	UNSC Res 1845	UNSC Res 1856
UNSC Res 1861	UNSC Res 1863	UNSC Res 1864	UNSC Res 1872
UNSC Res 1879	UNSC Res 1881	UNSC Res 1884	UNSC Res 1893
UNSC Res 1895	UNSC Res 1906	UNSC Res 1907	UNSC Res 1909
UNSC Res 1910	UNSC Res 1921	UNSC Res 1923	UNSC Res 1925
UNSC Res 1933	UNSC Res 1935	UNSC Res 1937	

Protection of journalists

UNSC Res 1738 UNSC Res 1910

II. SPECIFICALLY PROTECTED OBJECTS

Prohibition on attacks on civilian objects and other protected objects

UNSC Res 256	UNSC Res 265	UNSC Res 268	UNSC Res 270
UNSC Res 275	UNSC Res 280	UNSC Res 290	UNSC Res 326
UNSC Res 393	UNSC Res 403	UNSC Res 405	UNSC Res 428
UNSC Res 447	UNSC Res 454	UNSC Res 466	UNSC Res 507
UNSC Res 514	UNSC Res 522	UNSC Res 527	UNSC Res 540
UNSC Res 545	UNSC Res 546	UNSC Res 552	UNSC Res 564
UNSC Res 572	UNSC Res 577	UNSC Res 582	UNSC Res 588
UNSC Res 598	UNSC Res 602	UNSC Res 713	UNSC Res 851
UNSC Res 853	UNSC Res 897	UNSC Res 931	UNSC Res 1009
UNSC Res 1052	UNSC Res 1067	UNSC Res 1181	UNSC Res 1261
UNSC Res 1265	UNSC Res 1539	UNSC Res 1690	UNSC Res 1701
UNSC Res 1739	UNSC Res 1756	UNSC Res 1769	UNSC Res 1772
UNSC Res 1778	UNSC Res 1830	UNSC Res 1861	UNSC Res 1868
UNSC Res 1882	UNSC Res 1894	UNSC Res 1917	UNSC Res 1923

Obligation to protect medical units

UNSC Res 467	UNSC Res 771	UNSC Res 794	UNSC Res 1882

Obligation to protect medical transports

UNSC Res 771

Obligation to protect relief consignments

UNSC Res 918	UNSC Res 925	UNSC Res 950	UNSC Res 1059
UNSC Res 1071	UNSC Res 1075	UNSC Res 1087	UNSC Res 1083
UNSC Res 1265	UNSC Res 1772	UNSC Res 1870	UNSC Res 1910

Prohibition on attacks on cultural properties

UNSC Res 271	UNSC Res 459	UNSC Res 465	UNSC Res 1265

Obligation to return cultural properties

UNSC Res 686	UNSC Res 687	UNSC Res 1284

Prohibition on attacks on the natural environment

UNSC Res 687

III. TREATMENT OF CIVILIANS AND HORS DE COMBAT

Obligation to undertake the function of occupying power

UNSC Res 836	UNSC Res 837	UNSC Res 1037	UNSC Res 1244
UNSC Res 1264	UNSC Res 1272	UNSC Res 1410	UNSC Res 1484
UNSC Res 1497	UNSC Res 1528	UNSC Res 1529	UNSC Res 1702
UNSC Res 1725	UNSC Res 1739		

Obligations of the occupying power to respect the local law in force

UNSC Res 252	UNSC Res 267	UNSC Res 476	UNSC Res 478
UNSC Res 484	UNSC Res 497	UNSC Res 670	

Protection of civilians in occupied territories

UNSC Res 237	UNSC Res 248	UNSC Res 512	UNSC Res 513
UNSC Res 592	UNSC Res 605	UNSC Res 672	UNSC Res 1397
UNSC Res 1435	UNSC Res 1544		

Humane treatment of detainees

UNSC Res 770	UNSC Res 1010	UNSC Res 1011	UNSC Res 1019

Right of aliens to leave the territory of a party to the conflict

UNSC Res 664	UNSC Res 674

Prohibition on practising apartheid

UNSC Res 392	UNSC Res 473

Prohibition on violence to life

UNSC Res 392	UNSC Res 417	UNSC Res 473	UNSC Res 556
UNSC Res 560	UNSC Res 569	UNSC Res 872	UNSC Res 1019
UNSC Res 1072			

Prohibition on torture and other forms of treatment

UNSC Res 674	UNSC Res 770	UNSC Res 771	UNSC Res 1072

Prohibition on rape and sexual violence

UNSC Res 798	UNSC Res 820	UNSC Res 827	UNSC Res 1019
UNSC Res 1034	UNSC Res 1261	UNSC Res 1325	UNSC Res 1468
UNSC Res 1743	UNSC Res 1769	UNSC Res 1780	UNSC Res 1804
UNSC Res 1807	UNSC Res 1820	UNSC Res 1828	UNSC Res 1840
UNSC Res 1842	UNSC Res 1843	UNSC Res 1856	UNSC Res 1857
UNSC Res 1861	UNSC Res 1865	UNSC Res 1880	UNSC Res 1882
UNSC Res 1888	UNSC Res 1889	UNSC Res 1891	UNSC Res 1896
UNSC Res 1906	UNSC Res 1911	UNSC Res 1923	UNSC Res 1925
UNSC Res 1933	UNSC Res 1935		

Prohibition on slavery and forced labour

UNSC Res 1019	UNSC Res 1034

Prohibition on hostage taking

UNSC Res 638	UNSC Res 664	UNSC Res 674	UNSC Res 686
UNSC Res 706	UNSC Res 1776	UNSC Res 1806	UNSC Res 1807
UNSC Res 1833	UNSC Res 1857	UNSC Res 1868	UNSC Res 1882
UNSC Res 1904	UNSC Res 1917		

Prohibition on the use of human shields

UNSC Res 1776	UNSC Res 1806	UNSC Res 1828	UNSC Res 1833
UNSC Res 1868	UNSC Res 1882	UNSC Res 1890	UNSC Res 1894
UNSC Res 1917			

Prohibition on arbitrary deprivation of liberty

UNSC Res 347 UNSC Res 392 UNSC Res 417 UNSC Res 473
UNSC Res 556 UNSC Res 560 UNSC Res 569 UNSC Res 1019
UNSC Res 1034 UNSC Res 1072

Fair trial guarantees

UNSC Res 1034 UNSC Res 1778 UNSC Res 1923

Obligation not to carry out executions without judgment by a court affording judicial guarantees

UNSC Res 1843 UNSC Res 1856 UNSC Res 1906 UNSC Res 1925

Obligation to respect family life

UNSC Res 1754 UNSC Res 1783 UNSC Res 1813 UNSC Res 1871
UNSC Res 1920

Obligation to evacuate wounded, sick, and shipwrecked

UNSC Res 436

Obligation to return deceased combatants

UNSC Res 686

Obligation to search for missing persons

UNSC Res 1283 UNSC Res 1359 UNSC Res 1429 UNSC Res 1687
UNSC Res 1728 UNSC Res 1758

International co-operation to account for missing persons

UNSC Res 1019 UNSC Res 1034

Obligation to accept ICRC visits to detainees

UNSC Res 770 UNSC Res 968 UNSC Res 1009 UNSC Res 1010
UNSC Res 1019

Access of certain organisations to detainees

UNSC Res 1868	UNSC Res 1917

Obligation to release detainees

UNSC Res 463	UNSC Res 473	UNSC Res 727	UNSC Res 998
UNSC Res 1004	UNSC Res 1008	UNSC Res 1010	UNSC Res 1045
UNSC Res 1369			

Obligation to release prisoners of war

UNSC Res 686	UNSC Res 968	UNSC Res 1369	UNSC Res 1466

Obligation for the prompt release and repatriation of prisoners of war

UNSC Res 582	UNSC Res 1430	UNSC Res 1434

Obligation to release of detained civilians in occupied territories

UNSC Res 686	UNSC Res 1004	UNSC Res 1430	UNSC Res 1434

Obligation for a safe return of released detainees

UNSC Res 776

Prohibition of forced movement of civilians

UNSC Res 752	UNSC Res 771	UNSC Res 779	UNSC Res 799
UNSC Res 808	UNSC Res 814	UNSC Res 819	UNSC Res 820
UNSC Res 822	UNSC Res 878	UNSC Res 896	UNSC Res 918
UNSC Res 941	UNSC Res 1009	UNSC Res 1019	UNSC Res 1034
UNSC Res 1150	UNSC Res 1187	UNSC Res 1261	UNSC Res 1539
UNSC Res 1574	UNSC Res 1615	UNSC Res 1674	UNSC Res 1807
UNSC Res 1857	UNSC Res 1896		

Prohibition on deportations of civilians in occupied territories

UNSC Res 468	UNSC Res 469	UNSC Res 484	UNSC Res 607
UNSC Res 608	UNSC Res 636	UNSC Res 641	UNSC Res 681
UNSC Res 694	UNSC Res 726	UNSC Res 799	

Prohibition to transfer own population to occupied territories

UNSC Res 446	UNSC Res 452	UNSC Res 465	UNSC Res 476
UNSC Res 674	UNSC Res 677	UNSC Res 752	

Obligation to ensure adequate conditions for displaced persons

UNSC Res 361	UNSC Res 688	UNSC Res 752	UNSC Res 918
UNSC Res 925	UNSC Res 1004	UNSC Res 1010	UNSC Res 1019
UNSC Res 1034	UNSC Res 1040	UNSC Res 1078	UNSC Res 1097

Right of displaced persons to return

UNSC Res 237	UNSC Res 307	UNSC Res 361	UNSC Res 726
UNSC Res 745	UNSC Res 779	UNSC Res 820	UNSC Res 859
UNSC Res 872	UNSC Res 874	UNSC Res 876	UNSC Res 882
UNSC Res 892	UNSC Res 896	UNSC Res 906	UNSC Res 898
UNSC Res 937	UNSC Res 941	UNSC Res 947	UNSC Res 971
UNSC Res 993	UNSC Res 999	UNSC Res 1009	UNSC Res 1019
UNSC Res 1029	UNSC Res 1036	UNSC Res 1037	UNSC Res 1078
UNSC Res 1079	UNSC Res 1096	UNSC Res 1120	UNSC Res 1124
UNSC Res 1145	UNSC Res 1150	UNSC Res 1187	UNSC Res 1199
UNSC Res 1203	UNSC Res 1225	UNSC Res 1239	UNSC Res 1244
UNSC Res 1264	UNSC Res 1272	UNSC Res 1544	UNSC Res 1615
UNSC Res 1674	UNSC Res 1701	UNSC Res 1716	UNSC Res 1752
UNSC Res 1756	UNSC Res 1765	UNSC Res 1770	UNSC Res 1778
UNSC Res 1781	UNSC Res 1785	UNSC Res 1795	UNSC Res 1806
UNSC Res 1808	UNSC Res 1826	UNSC Res 1828	UNSC Res 1830
UNSC Res 1856	UNSC Res 1865	UNSC Res 1866	UNSC Res 1868
UNSC Res 1870	UNSC Res 1880	UNSC Res 1881	UNSC Res 1883
UNSC Res 1906	UNSC Res 1917	UNSC Res 1923	UNSC Res 1925
UNSC Res 1933	UNSC Res 1936		

Special protection of elderly persons

UNSC Res 819	UNSC Res 1755

Special protection of women

UNSC Res 798	UNSC Res 819	UNSC Res 1076	UNSC Res 1193
UNSC Res 1231	UNSC Res 1261	UNSC Res 1296	UNSC Res 1314
UNSC Res 1325	UNSC Res 1333	UNSC Res 1379	UNSC Res 1674
UNSC Res 1743	UNSC Res 1745	UNSC Res 1755	UNSC Res 1780
UNSC Res 1807	UNSC Res 1820	UNSC Res 1826	UNSC Res 1857
UNSC Res 1868	UNSC Res 1880	UNSC Res 1881	UNSC Res 1883
UNSC Res 1888	UNSC Res 1889	UNSC Res 1906	UNSC Res 1910
UNSC Res 1923	UNSC Res 1933	UNSC Res 1935	UNSC Res 1936

Special protection of children

UNSC Res 819	UNSC Res 1181	UNSC Res 1261	UNSC Res 1265
UNSC Res 1296	UNSC Res 1314	UNSC Res 1379	UNSC Res 1460
UNSC Res 1468	UNSC Res 1539	UNSC Res 1612	UNSC Res 1674
UNSC Res 1743	UNSC Res 1745	UNSC Res 1755	UNSC Res 1780
UNSC Res 1807	UNSC Res 1826	UNSC Res 1840	UNSC Res 1865
UNSC Res 1868	UNSC Res 1880	UNSC Res 1881	UNSC Res 1882
UNSC Res 1883	UNSC Res 1888	UNSC Res 1889	UNSC Res 1894
UNSC Res 1906	UNSC Res 1910	UNSC Res 1917	UNSC Res 1933
UNSC Res 1935	UNSC Res 1936		

Prohibition on recruitment of child soldiers

UNSC Res 1071	UNSC Res 1083	UNSC Res 1231	UNSC Res 1261
UNSC Res 1314	UNSC Res 1460	UNSC Res 1468	UNSC Res 1479
UNSC Res 1493	UNSC Res 1539	UNSC Res 1612	UNSC Res 1674
UNSC Res 1698	UNSC Res 1771	UNSC Res 1778	UNSC Res 1794
UNSC Res 1804	UNSC Res 1806	UNSC Res 1807	UNSC Res 1834
UNSC Res 1843	UNSC Res 1856	UNSC Res 1857	UNSC Res 1861
UNSC Res 1868	UNSC Res 1891	UNSC Res 1896	UNSC Res 1906
UNSC Res 1917	UNSC Res 1923	UNSC Res 1925	UNSC Res 1935

Prohibition on participation of child soldiers in hostilities

UNSC Res 1071	UNSC Res 1083	UNSC Res 1261	UNSC Res 1771
UNSC Res 1807	UNSC Res 1917	UNSC Res 1935	

IV. METHODS OF WARFARE

Prohibition on indiscriminate attacks

UNSC Res 1199	UNSC Res 1772	UNSC Res 1801	UNSC Res 1813
UNSC Res 1863	UNSC Res 1882	UNSC Res 1891	UNSC Res 1894

Principle of proportionality

UNSC Res 1092	UNSC Res 1160	UNSC Res 1199	UNSC Res 1322
UNSC Res 1776	UNSC Res 1806	UNSC Res 1863	UNSC Res 1882
UNSC Res 1894			

Precautions in attacks

UNSC Res 1776	UNSC Res 1868	UNSC Res 1917

Precautions against the effects of attacks

UNSC Res 807

Prohibition on the destruction of public and private properties

UNSC Res 465	UNSC Res 670	UNSC Res 1019	UNSC Res 1397
UNSC Res 1435	UNSC Res 1544		

Prohibition on pillage

UNSC Res 912	UNSC Res 1019	UNSC Res 1034

Prohibition on starvation of civilians

UNSC Res 518	UNSC Res 1009	UNSC Res 1296	UNSC Res 1539
UNSC Res 1674			

Obligation to facilitate humanitarian assistance

UNSC Res 85	UNSC Res 307	UNSC Res 361	UNSC Res 512
UNSC Res 513	UNSC Res 515	UNSC Res 564	UNSC Res 577
UNSC Res 666	UNSC Res 674	UNSC Res 686	UNSC Res 687
UNSC Res 688	UNSC Res 706	UNSC Res 712	UNSC Res 724
UNSC Res 733	UNSC Res 746	UNSC Res 751	UNSC Res 752
UNSC Res 757	UNSC Res 758	UNSC Res 761	UNSC Res 764
UNSC Res 767	UNSC Res 770	UNSC Res 771	UNSC Res 775
UNSC Res 787	UNSC Res 788	UNSC Res 794	UNSC Res 807
UNSC Res 811	UNSC Res 812	UNSC Res 813	UNSC Res 819
UNSC Res 820	UNSC Res 822	UNSC Res 824	UNSC Res 834
UNSC Res 836	UNSC Res 851	UNSC Res 853	UNSC Res 859
UNSC Res 863	UNSC Res 864	UNSC Res 866	UNSC Res 872
UNSC Res 874	UNSC Res 876	UNSC Res 882	UNSC Res 892
UNSC Res 897	UNSC Res 898	UNSC Res 900	UNSC Res 908
UNSC Res 911	UNSC Res 912	UNSC Res 918	UNSC Res 925
UNSC Res 931	UNSC Res 932	UNSC Res 941	UNSC Res 945
UNSC Res 950	UNSC Res 952	UNSC Res 966	UNSC Res 972
UNSC Res 976	UNSC Res 981	UNSC Res 982	UNSC Res 985
UNSC Res 988	UNSC Res 994	UNSC Res 997	UNSC Res 998
UNSC Res 999	UNSC Res 1001	UNSC Res 1004	UNSC Res 1008
UNSC Res 1009	UNSC Res 1014	UNSC Res 1019	UNSC Res 1029
UNSC Res 1029	UNSC Res 1041	UNSC Res 1045	UNSC Res 1059
UNSC Res 1071	UNSC Res 1072	UNSC Res 1076	UNSC Res 1078
UNSC Res 1083	UNSC Res 1097	UNSC Res 1100	UNSC Res 1101
UNSC Res 1114	UNSC Res 1132	UNSC Res 1181	UNSC Res 1187
UNSC Res 1193	UNSC Res 1199	UNSC Res 1213	UNSC Res 1216
UNSC Res 1229	UNSC Res 1231	UNSC Res 1233	UNSC Res 1234
UNSC Res 1237	UNSC Res 1239	UNSC Res 1244	UNSC Res 1258
UNSC Res 1261	UNSC Res 1264	UNSC Res 1265	UNSC Res 1270
UNSC Res 1272	UNSC Res 1286	UNSC Res 1289	UNSC Res 1291
UNSC Res 1296	UNSC Res 1298	UNSC Res 1314	UNSC Res 1333
UNSC Res 1346	UNSC Res 1355	UNSC Res 1370	UNSC Res 1378
UNSC Res 1379	UNSC Res 1389	UNSC Res 1393	UNSC Res 1398
UNSC Res 1468	UNSC Res 1478	UNSC Res 1479	UNSC Res 1483
UNSC Res 1493	UNSC Res 1497	UNSC Res 1502	UNSC Res 1528
UNSC Res 1529	UNSC Res 1539	UNSC Res 1542	UNSC Res 1544
UNSC Res 1556	UNSC Res 1564	UNSC Res 1574	UNSC Res 1590

Obligation to facilitate humanitarian assistance (*cont.*)

UNSC Res 1609	UNSC Res 1622	UNSC Res 1674	UNSC Res 1706
UNSC Res 1713	UNSC Res 1721	UNSC Res 1739	UNSC Res 1744
UNSC Res 1756	UNSC Res 1769	UNSC Res 1770	UNSC Res 1772
UNSC Res 1778	UNSC Res 1779	UNSC Res 1784	UNSC Res 1794
UNSC Res 1801	UNSC Res 1806	UNSC Res 1812	UNSC Res 1813
UNSC Res 1816	UNSC Res 1830	UNSC Res 1838	UNSC Res 1843
UNSC Res 1846	UNSC Res 1851	UNSC Res 1857	UNSC Res 1860
UNSC Res 1861	UNSC Res 1863	UNSC Res 1866	UNSC Res 1866
UNSC Res 1870	UNSC Res 1872	UNSC Res 1881	UNSC Res 1882
UNSC Res 1883	UNSC Res 1889	UNSC Res 1894	UNSC Res 1897
UNSC Res 1906	UNSC Res 1910	UNSC Res 1916	UNSC Res 1917
UNSC Res 1919	UNSC Res 1923	UNSC Res 1925	UNSC Res 1935
UNSC Res 1936			

Obligation to facilitate the work of the ICRC

UNSC Res 436	UNSC Res 512	UNSC Res 515	UNSC Res 564
UNSC Res 582	UNSC Res 666	UNSC Res 724	UNSC Res 770
UNSC Res 771	UNSC Res 776	UNSC Res 814	UNSC Res 968
UNSC Res 978	UNSC Res 988	UNSC Res 1009	UNSC Res 1010
UNSC Res 1019	UNSC Res 1034	UNSC Res 1089	UNSC Res 1284
UNSC Res 1320	UNSC Res 1369	UNSC Res 1405	UNSC Res 1429
UNSC Res 1466	UNSC Res 1472	UNSC Res 1495	UNSC Res 1598

Prohibition on the misuse of UN emblem

UNSC Res 1769	UNSC Res 1779	UNSC Res 1841

V. MEANS OF WARFARE

Prohibition on the use of biological weapons

UNSC Res 1762

Prohibition on the use of chemical weapons

UNSC Res 687	UNSC Res 1762

Obligation to destroy chemical weapons

UNSC Res 687	UNSC Res 1762

Obligation to declare locations of chemical weapons

UNSC Res 687

Obligation to co-operate to ensure compliance with chemical weapons convention

UNSC Res 1762	UNSC Res 1810

Obligation to co-operate to ensure compliance with biological weapons convention

UNSC Res 1810

Obligation to clear booby-trapped areas

UNSC Res 1062

Prohibition on the use of mines

UNSC Res 294	UNSC Res 945	UNSC Res 965	UNSC Res 1005
UNSC Res 1008	UNSC Res 1065	UNSC Res 1076	UNSC Res 1089
UNSC Res 1096	UNSC Res 1124	UNSC Res 1127	UNSC Res 1150
UNSC Res 1190	UNSC Res 1213	UNSC Res 1225	UNSC Res 1868
UNSC Res 1882	UNSC Res 1917		

Obligation to clear mines

UNSC Res 728	UNSC Res 814	UNSC Res 866	UNSC Res 872
UNSC Res 886	UNSC Res 1005	UNSC Res 1055	UNSC Res 1062
UNSC Res 1064	UNSC Res 1075	UNSC Res 1087	UNSC Res 1093
UNSC Res 1119	UNSC Res 1233	UNSC Res 1251	UNSC Res 1687
UNSC Res 1706	UNSC Res 1756	UNSC Res 1917	

Obligation to destroy stockpiled mines

UNSC Res 1055 UNSC Res 1064 UNSC Res 1075 UNSC Res 1087

Obligation to mark mined areas

UNSC Res 766 UNSC Res 783

International co-operation for mine clearance

UNSC Res 1004

Obligation to clear explosive remnants of war

UNSC Res 1773 UNSC Res 1868 UNSC Res 1917

Prohibition to use cluster munitions

UNSC Res 1882

VI. IMPLEMENTATION OF INTERNATIONAL HUMANITARIAN LAW

Prohibition on reprisals

UNSC Res 1378

Prohibition on reprisals against civilian objects

UNSC Res 1738

State responsibility for violations of IHL

UNSC Res 290	UNSC Res 387	UNSC Res 405	UNSC Res 455
UNSC Res 471	UNSC Res 475	UNSC Res 527	UNSC Res 545
UNSC Res 546	UNSC Res 567	UNSC Res 571	UNSC Res 572
UNSC Res 573	UNSC Res 577	UNSC Res 580	UNSC Res 674
UNSC Res 686	UNSC Res 687	UNSC Res 692	UNSC Res 827
UNSC Res 1304	UNSC Res 1756	UNSC Res 1894	

Individual criminal responsibility for grave breaches and other violations of IHL

UNSC Res 670	UNSC Res 674	UNSC Res 764	UNSC Res 771
UNSC Res 780	UNSC Res 794	UNSC Res 808	UNSC Res 814
UNSC Res 820	UNSC Res 827	UNSC Res 859	UNSC Res 913
UNSC Res 925	UNSC Res 935	UNSC Res 941	UNSC Res 955
UNSC Res 978	UNSC Res 1009	UNSC Res 1012	UNSC Res 1034
UNSC Res 1072	UNSC Res 1087	UNSC Res 1193	UNSC Res 1214
UNSC Res 1264	UNSC Res 1272	UNSC Res 1315	UNSC Res 1355
UNSC Res 1653	UNSC Res 1711		

Command responsibility

UNSC Res 670	UNSC Res 771	UNSC Res 780	UNSC Res 764
UNSC Res 794	UNSC Res 808	UNSC Res 820	UNSC Res 1193
UNSC Res 1493	UNSC Res 1820	UNSC Res 1865	UNSC Res 1880
UNSC Res 1888			

Serious IHL violations as war crimes

UNSC Res 955

Obligation to investigate and prosecute war crimes

UNSC Res 1193	UNSC Res 1199	UNSC Res 1234	UNSC Res 1291
UNSC Res 1304	UNSC Res 1355	UNSC Res 1464	UNSC Res 1468
UNSC Res 1479	UNSC Res 1483	UNSC Res 1484	UNSC Res 1493
UNSC Res 1509	UNSC Res 1528	UNSC Res 1556	UNSC Res 1565
UNSC Res 1574	UNSC Res 1577	UNSC Res 1602	UNSC Res 1606
UNSC Res 1612	UNSC Res 1633	UNSC Res 1635	UNSC Res 1649
UNSC Res 1653	UNSC Res 1711	UNSC Res 1736	UNSC Res 1738
UNSC Res 1756	UNSC Res 1794	UNSC Res 1804	UNSC Res 1813
UNSC Res 1820	UNSC Res 1833	UNSC Res 1856	UNSC Res 1865
UNSC Res 1868	UNSC Res 1880	UNSC Res 1882	UNSC Res 1888
UNSC Res 1890	UNSC Res 1894	UNSC Res 1896	UNSC Res 1911
UNSC Res 1912	UNSC Res 1917	UNSC Res 1925	UNSC Res 1933
UNSC Res 1935			

*** In three cases, the prosecution of UN peacekeepers by the International Criminal Court was blocked:**

UNSC Res 1422	UNSC Res 1487	UNSC Res 1497

Granting of amnesty

UNSC Res 190	UNSC Res 191	UNSC Res 473	UNSC Res 581
UNSC Res 1055	UNSC Res 1064	UNSC Res 1120	UNSC Res 1315
UNSC Res 1820			

International co-operation for war crimes prosecution

UNSC Res 978	UNSC Res 1207	UNSC Res 1610	UNSC Res 1638
UNSC Res 1785	UNSC Res 1804	UNSC Res 1895	UNSC Res 1906
UNSC Res 1925			

Index

Introductory Note

References such as '178–79' indicate (not necessarily continuous) discussion of a topic across a range of pages. Wherever possible in the case of topics with many references, these have either been divided into sub-topics or only the most significant discussions of the topic are listed. Because the entire work is about 'jus ad bellum' and 'jus in bello', the use of these terms (and certain others which occur constantly throughout the book) as an entry point has been minimised. Information will be found under the corresponding detailed topics.

www.ingramcontent.com/pod-product-compliance
Ingram Content Group UK Ltd.
Pitfield, Milton Keynes, MK11 3LW, UK
UKHW020229290926
15470UKWH00002B/442

9 781849 460552